Pacifism

IN EUROPE TO 1914

A HISTORY OF PACIFISM

by Peter Brock

I. PACIFISM IN EUROPE TO 1914
(Princeton University Press, 1972)

II. PACIFISM IN THE UNITED STATES:
FROM THE COLONIAL ERA TO THE FIRST WORLD WAR
(Princeton University Press, 1968)

III. TWENTIETH-CENTURY PACIFISM
(Van Nostrand Reinhold, 1970)

Pacifism

IN EUROPE TO 1914

by PETER BROCK

PRINCETON UNIVERSITY PRESS

PRINCETON, NEW JERSEY

1972

AGAIN TO C.

Contents

Preface

THE present volume completes my history of pacifist thought and practice. The preparation of this history has occupied a considerable portion of any time free from teaching duties during the last decade. But the idea of composing a study of this kind originally occurred to me much earlier when I was a conscientious objector in Great Britain in World War II, though circumstances prevented its realization for many years. The rest of my history of pacifism is to be found in two companion volumes: *Pacifism in the United States: From the Colonial Era to the First World War* (Princeton, N.J.: Princeton University Press, 1968) and *Twentieth-Century Pacifism* (New York: Van Nostrand Reinhold Company, 1970). Each of the three books forms an independent entity, each being constructed on its own different pattern and at its own depth. J. L. Talmon has written of "the immemorial tensions of the historian—the desire to be exhaustive, which has to be disciplined by the necessity to be selective; the anxiety to go back to the original sources, which has to be moderated by the inevitability of relying on secondary works." I have endeavored everywhere to go more deeply into primary sources where the existing secondary works are either scanty or unreliable. In addition, I have depicted the twentieth century with a more sweeping brush than earlier centuries and have painted the American scene with greater intensity than the European.

In 1962, on a glorious late autumn afternoon, I visited the small Shaker community at Sabbathday Lake, Maine, and was shown around the buildings under the firm guidance of Sister Mildred. When in the course of the conversation I told her that I was planning to write a book discussing, among other things, the peace activities of groups like the Shakers, she thought for a moment and then said to me sternly, using the traditional terminology of her sect: "Well then—do it *decent!*" I have tried to follow her advice and do the whole work decent but I am aware of at least some of its many shortcomings. On several points, however, I would like, if possible, to forestall criticism. I have not attempted to write a general history of the peace movement in the sense of all efforts aimed at achieving international peace and organization: this is a noble theme but one which far transcends the more modest limits of my study. Nor have I tried to give a historical analysis of the theory and practice of nonviolence, though its development is closely related to the history of pacifism. Again, the history of conscientious objection to war figures prominently in the pages of all three volumes, yet that topic by no means exhausts their contents. My main concern has been to explore the ideas and activities of individuals and of groups of people who, even if sometimes only implicitly, have rejected participation in all forms of war. But, as with any other subject of investigation, here too it is not always easy to define with complete precision the area within which such a study should be pursued.

Much of the basic research for the present volume was carried out in London and Amsterdam. I would like to express my gratitude to Edward Milligan of the Library of the Society of Friends, in London, and to Mrs. Y. de Swart-Pot of the Bibliotheek der Vereenigde Doopsgezinde Gemeente and Dr. S. L. Verheus of the Universiteitsbibliotheek, in Amsterdam, for their unfailing readiness to help me in my work. I am also happy to acknowledge the kind assistance I received from staff while working in the British Museum and in the Universitätsbibliothek in Heidelberg as well as from my own University Library in Toronto, especially from the Interlibrary Loan Service. My friend Sol E. Yoder brought my attention to several items in Dutch and another Mennonite friend, Nelson P. Springer, Curator of the Mennonite Historical Library at Goshen College, Goshen, Indiana, supplied me with photocopies of materials not easily available elsewhere: my thanks go to them for this. The task of preparing my manuscript for publication has been carried out most ably by Mrs. Arthur Sherwood, of Princeton University Press. Finally, I am much indebted to the Canada Council which awarded me a Leave Fellowship for a year's research in Europe in 1968-1969 and to the University of Toronto, and in particular to its Centre for Russian and East European Studies, which have provided funds for typing and for travel in connection with research on this continent.

Toronto, Ontario, September 1971   PETER BROCK

Pacifism

IN EUROPE TO 1914

Introduction

ANTIMILITARISM IN THE EARLY
CHRISTIAN CHURCH

Homo sapiens, the species to which we belong, has existed on this earth for tens of thousands of years. Yet, just as man himself is a comparative newcomer in global history, not to speak of the history of the universe, so civilization and written record are very late developments indeed in human history. And, although at times a longing for international peace and human brotherhood appeared in the thought patterns of some early civilizations, and war was denounced and passive forms of resistance practised occasionally, pacifism in the strict sense of an unconditional renunciation of war by the individual is, so far as we can tell, a little less than two thousand years old.

The first clearcut renunciation of this kind appears among the early Christians (who of course formed a part of the religious milieu of the Near East as it existed at the outset of the Roman Empire). "It is," writes Henry J. Cadbury, "historically speaking, original with Christianity." "For the Christian, antimilitarism . . . is a well-defined opposition to war as a system and to participation in war in any form." Even the peace-loving Jewish Essenes, with whom the Qumran community was probably associated, were not entirely weaponless. There is no known instance of conscientious objection to participation in war or of the advocacy of such objection before the Christian era, and until roughly the last one hundred and fifty years pacifism in the West was confined to those who stood inside the Christian tradition. It is not found, at least in explicit form, in any non-Christian Asian or African civilization until very recent times, or in the early and indigenous American civilizations, or in primitive cultures (although, it is true, the idea of nonviolence does occur in the traditions of peoples as distant from each other as the Chinese, Indians, Jews, and North American Indians). Thus some prior discussion, however brief, of the antimilitarism of early Christianity is clearly essential to an understanding of European pacifism as it developed from the Middle Ages onward.

The teaching of Jesus, in the form it has come down to us, does not deal specifically with war, just as it omits, for example, to give any detailed instruction concerning the institution of slavery. "War," writes Walther Bienert, "does not stand in the centre of the New Testament

3

message." No pronouncement is to be found in the Gospels concerning the rightness or wrongness of military service. Yet Christians for almost two millennia have sought confirmation in the books of the New Testament for either a pacifist or an antipacifist stand, for war has been too ever-present a social reality for Christians to have been able to escape making a judgment. That since the fourth century pacifists have formed a very small minority of the total number of Christians is incontrovertible. However, I will argue that until early in that century the official stand of the church—and presumably the majority of believers—opposed Christian participation in war or the shedding of human blood. That these early generations of Jesus' followers supported antimilitarism may in itself be taken as circumstantial evidence for the pacifism of the Gospel era.

C. J. Cadoux, the most thorough among the students of the early Christian attitude to war, has described as "cumulative" the evidence for the view that Jesus himself regarded war as not permissible either for himself or for his adherents. Jesus' pacifism depends on the spirit of his teaching and actions; it flows from the higher righteousness with which he fulfilled the Law and the Prophets of the old dispensation; it forms an ethic of conciliation in place of retaliation and preaches, instead of revenge, an outflowing love even to enemies and evildoers.

Central to Jesus' pacifism are of course the nonresistant injunctions of the Sermon on the Mount (Matt. 5:38-48). Even the spirit, not to speak of the letter, of these passages would appear to exclude a Christian's participation in war. At least there is nothing to show that he meant the application of such teaching to be limited only to certain areas of conduct. Again, in the Beatitudes Jesus says (Matt. 5:5, 9): "Blessed are the meek: for they shall inherit the earth," and "Blessed are the peacemakers: for they shall be called the children of God." Could this blessing be bestowed on a soldier without destroying the whole meaning of Jesus' words? "The Christian theologian who attempts to justify a war and who denies that pacifism is the Christian program in a given situation must never forget for a moment that both the word 'pacifism' and the ideal it stands for are to be derived from this saying of Jesus' (*beati pacifici!*)": thus Hans Windisch, himself a nonpacifist theologian, in his study of *The Meaning of the Sermon on the Mount* (Philadelphia, 1951; originally published in German in 1937).

Perhaps the most cogent argument in favor of a pacifist exegesis lies in Jesus' stubborn refusal to countenance military force either to achieve Jewish national aims or to bring in his own kingdom. The militantly nationalist Zealots, exponents of a "warlike Messianism," were

4

a party of influence among contemporary Jews; Jesus obviously differed from them concerning the violent means to overthrow Roman rule, which they urged on their fellow countrymen. His deft reply concerning the tribute money ("Render therefore unto Caesar the things which are Caesar's; and unto God the things that are God's" [Matt. 22: 21]) is one example of this attitude, just as the story of his rejection of Satan's offer to bring in an earthly kingdom witnesses to his opposition to establishing his own power on earth by violence. Throughout the Gospels are scattered a number of sayings attributed to Jesus which, especially when taken collectively, demonstrate his belief in the power of love and his repudiation of the way of the sword. The virtues which he extolled were the direct opposite of those esteemed by militant Jewish patriots: patience, humility, love of peace. Indeed, the path of suffering which he urged his disciples to follow seems to exclude the possibility of their ever using injurious force. "All they that take the sword shall perish with the sword," he told Peter (Matt. 26:52). And to Pontius Pilate he declared: "My kingdom is not of this world: if my kingdom were of this world, then would my servants fight" (John 18: 36). Finally, Jesus' nonviolent ethic and his rejection of all physical force were exemplified in his suffering execution by the Roman authorities on a cross outside Jerusalem.

True, certain passages in the Gospels and certain incidents in Jesus' career might appear to cast in doubt a consistently pacifist witness even when we disregard, as being clearly incapable of literal interpretation, the fairly frequent parabolic use of military terms in the Gospels and in the other books of the New Testament. There is, for instance, the admittedly "most puzzling" passage in Luke (22:36-38) where, if —as indeed is extremely doubtful—Christ intended his words to be understood literally, he appears to have approved his disciples' purchase of a sword for self-defense. Or take the story of the expulsion of the traders from the Temple. Yet "a scourge of small cords" (John 2: 15), the instrument Jesus employed on this occasion, was surely of purely symbolic significance rather than an aggressive weapon. It was Jesus' moral authority that brought success. And in regard to his encounter with the centurion at Capernaum, an incident which has often been cited in support of the antipacifist case, it may be said in the first place that although Jesus did not condemn the man's profession, the praise he bestowed was for his faith and not his soldiering. Second, and even more illuminating, is the fact that the centurion was connected with an alien army of occupation. Moreover, since troops also fulfilled police functions, and Jesus recognized—at least passively—the place of civil government in human affairs, it is possible that he re-

5

frained from comment on the centurion's calling from a desire not to attack what seemed to him a legitimate aspect of army duties.

This is no place to enter into a detailed analysis of all the New Testament passages which bear to a greater or less degree on questions of peace and war (nor, I should add, do I possess the competence to do so). Agreement has been fairly general in recent times among New Testament scholars and among theologians that Jesus preached an ethic of nonviolence. However, among those acknowledging that it was a thoroughgoing pacifist ethic there exist sharp differences of opinion whether its precepts were meant for application at all times and in all circumstances. Even Christian pacifists down the centuries have held conflicting views concerning the nature and limitations of nonviolence.

The nonpacifist interpretation has relied on one or more of five major, and partly overlapping, arguments to support its case for the justifiability of Christian participation in war, despite the condemnation of violence and the nonresistant injunctions contained in the Gospels. In the first place, it is said, these are counsels of perfection, which sinful man cannot hope to follow in their fullness—or at least only a dedicated minority (e.g., monks) will be found capable of pursuing a vocational pacifism. Second, such precepts, it is said, refer to an inner state of mind rather than to outward action. The Christian warrior is not a contradiction in terms, for he may preserve love toward his enemy even while engaged in the act of killing him. Nonresistance, third, may be regarded as a purely personal ethic, which does not find application in the political arena or, more particularly, in the relations between states. Righteousness, it has been argued, is a component of the New Testament ethic of equal importance to love. War, although indeed never a thoroughly Christian means, may still be the only alternative open to men of good-will if righteousness is to prevail in an evil world. And the decision whether a given war is really one on behalf of righteousness may be left to the rulers, on whom the guilt of a faulty judgment will rest. Fourth, some theologians have maintained that Jesus' nonviolent precepts were intended merely as *ad hoc* advice, for application only in the circumstances in which they were promulgated, and not necessarily as general precepts with a wider application. Finally, there is the view that Jesus' pacifism and nonviolence formed *solely* an interim-ethic, which may be explained by "the eschatological hope" of a speedy second coming, an expectation that slowly waned among his followers in the course of the succeeding centuries. Cadoux has described this concept of an interim-ethic as "the last fortress of militarism on Christian soil."

Let us now turn to examine the character and extent of the anti-militarism manifested by the early church.

The era of the early church may be broadly defined as the period from the death of Jesus in 29 A.D. until the year 313, when Emperor Constantine the Great declared his conversion to the Christian faith. This is a stretch of historical time roughly the same as that which in English history divides the "Glorious" Revolution of 1688 from the present day. However, chronological treatment of the early church's attitude to war does not seem appropriate here; indeed, chronological sequence is not always easy to ascertain in regard to early Christian literature. But a thematic approach, such as I attempt, leads only too easily to obliteration of the transformations which institutions, including churches, undergo in the course of time: in other words, to a static picture rather than a dynamic vision of events. That the early church covered a span of almost three centuries must be kept in mind in reading what is said below, first concerning the pacifist elements present in that period of church history and then concerning the seeds of a more militaristic stance contained already in that same epoch.

Among early Christian writers we may find a multitude of passages condemning war in general terms and emphasizing its incompatibility with the Christian way of life. Sometimes war is depicted as the work of demons. Killing in war is branded as murder; the sword is accursed. Warfare is regarded as fit only for non-Christians, for the "gentiles." The satanic character of the Roman Empire is deduced, *inter alia*, from the fact that preparation for war and engagement in battle are among its most important functions. The church fathers condemned the pomp and glory of soldiery, and the work of war they castigated as an iniquity, "madness," a product of the lusts of the flesh. "For how can he be just, who injures, hates, despoils, kills?" wrote Lactantius at the beginning of the fourth century of the warrior. Indeed the early Christians saw homicide as the essential characteristic of the soldier. Thus it was that the magistrate's office came to seem polluted as a result of its connection with war.

These writers also stress the peaceful character of Christianity. Of course, peace appears as a concept wider than a mere absence of war, but a critique of war was subsumed within it. "Nothing is better than peace, by which all war . . . is abolished," wrote Ignatius (d. ca. 107). Christians were adjured to walk in the ways of peace. Many writers stress that the followers of Christ had beaten their swords into plough-shares and their spears into pruning-hooks and had abandoned alto-gether the instruments of war. They had exchanged the old law of re-

7

taliation, as Christ had told them to do, for the new law of peace. Universal peace would ensue as a result of God's grace when man accepted the teachings of the new dispensation introduced by Christ. Origen in the first half of the third century even went so far as to argue that God had brought the Empire with its Pax Romana into existence in order to facilitate the spread of the Christian doctrine of peace, which in earlier periods of internecine warfare might have been suppressed. If, for instance, the ancient Jews, he writes, had been forbidden by God to become soldiers (as he implies Christians had been), they would have been utterly annihilated by their enemies.

In particular, the church fathers in many of their writings stressed that love of enemies and the doing of good even to evildoers formed an essential element in Jesus' message to the world. Returning good for evil was Christ's way; avenging a wrong was the pagan path. "Christians," according to Clemens of Alexandria, around 200 A.D., "are not allowed to correct by violence sinful wrongdoings." Jesus, writes Arnobius the elder about a century later, taught that it was "better to endure a wrong than to inflict [it], to shed one's [blood] rather than stain one's hands and conscience with the blood of another." Gentleness and nonresistance and innocent suffering were Christ's methods of overcoming evil: this theme occurs constantly throughout the period of the early church. Take, for instance, Athenagoras in the second half of the second century: "We have learnt," he writes, "not only not to strike back and not to go to law with those who plunder and rob us, but with some, if they buffet us on the side of the head, to offer the other side of the head to them for a blow, and with others, if they take away our tunic, to give them also our cloak." Even as late as the last half of the third century, the Sermon on the Mount was still being given a rigorous interpretation: any idea of its constituting merely an interim-ethic does not seem to have existed then. In addition, no exception to the nonresistant imperative is yet made in regard to a supposed obligation to defend others. The presumption appears to be that nonresistance is incumbent on a Christian not only in respect to the defense of his own person but in relation to his duties towards his fellow men.

We have seen that many of the fathers of the early church looked with considerable disapproval at the military profession, despite the fact that in the Roman Empire soldiers were called upon to act as policemen as well as warriors. But there were other reasons, apart from the question of war, why we might expect to meet with frequent indictments of soldiering in the writings of the early church fathers. In the first place, soldiers were usually mercenaries and were often drawn from the roughest elements of the community. Their conduct would frequently be offensive to Christian morality. (The same factor, for instance, accounts in large part for the latent antimilitarism long displayed by the educated classes of China, where it was unsupported by any pacifism on principle.) Secondly, Roman soldiers acted as the instruments of the persecution suffered by Christians until the very end of our period. True, this persecution was not continuous and universal but rather "sporadic and erratic," yet, when applied, it was extremely harsh and unpleasant. Thus soldiering and persecution became associated in the minds of the Christians.

To what extent, then, did the aversion to war and to army life, which was an undoubted feature of Christian thought in these centuries, remain a somewhat amorphous opposition stemming in part from non-pacifist roots and, even when based on pacifist principle, constitute a merely generalized sentiment? And to what extent did the Christians of that time go further and refuse military service? And what was the character of their conscientious objection?

We must begin our discussion of these questions by calling attention to the comparatively minor role which the problem of military service occupied in the life and thought of the early church. For most of the period it was not a pressing issue for the Christian community. The imperial armies were usually raised on a voluntary basis and only rarely was conscription employed. Groups from which at first the church drew some of its chief support—e.g., Jews or women or slaves —were not under any circumstances eligible to undertake military duties. True, fairly late on, the question of voluntary enlistment does occur (see below), but the adverse opinion of military life held by most church leaders was likely, in many instances, to act as an effective deterrent here. There were cases too, of course, of the conversion of serving soldiers to Christianity; once again, however, the general Christian environment long remained unfavorable for widespread missionary activity within the ranks of the army.

"The application of Jesus' teaching to the question of military service was in a way unmistakable," writes the pacifist scholar Cadoux. Yet, he goes on, although conscientious objection appears to be its logical outcome, "at any time after the inception of Christianity, the existence of Christian soldiers was at least a possibility." If the first properly authenticated instances of Christians serving in the Roman army date from shortly after 170, during the reign of Emperor Marcus Aurelius (161-180), the first positive evidence that Christians also refused on grounds of conscience to undertake military service comes from the same decade. In his *True Discourse* (*Sermo verus*) written ca. 178, the pagan polemicist Celsus accused Christians of a disinclination to fight in the imperial armies and of thus helping to expose the Empire to barbarian attack. It is perhaps not a mere coincidence that evidence for the two contrary positions derives from roughly the same time; it probably indicates that the question of military service had in this period become a matter of lively concern to at least some sections of the Christian community. Where no Christians served and no Christians were required to serve, there was little likelihood that the problem of military service would come up for discussion. As Bernhard Schöpf remarks, the chief impulse leading the church fathers to deal with the problem of soldiering is usually a practical one: the conversion of Roman legionaries, for example, or young Christians enlisting in the army. Apart from several doubtful cases, and so far as the evidence goes, the fact that Christians appear to have held altogether aloof from the army for well over a century after Jesus' death, is circumstantial evidence in favor of an antimilitarist stand on the part of the church as a whole, especially when this fact is seen within the framework of the antimilitarist thought pattern of the early church fathers. Therefore, when Christian soldiers first appeared, they—and not the objectors to war and military service—represented the minority view within the church.

Among the church fathers, pacifism, which during the first and second centuries A.D. had been formulated only in fairly general terms, found most explicit expression in the works of Tertullian in the first half of the third century and in those of the greatest intellect in the early church before Augustine, Origen, who was active during roughly the same period.

Let us look briefly at what these two writers have to say about military service.

Tertullian's pacifism emerges both in his *Concerning Idolatry* (*De idololatria*) (ca. 198-202), composed when he was still an orthodox Catholic in his theology, and in his *Concerning the Soldier's Garland* (*De corona militis*) (211), written after he had embraced the Montanist heresy. His antimilitarist stand cannot, therefore, be explained away, as some writers have tried to do, as the outcome of heretical leanings, since this stand remained constant despite his theological waverings. In his *De idololatria*—which incidentally provides the first evidence of the presence within the army of Christians already baptized before their enlistment, as distinct, that is, from converted soldiers—Tertullian raises the question whether a Christian might serve in the lower ranks of the army where neither the obligation to sacrifice to the emperor and the gods nor the duty as a magistrate of

10

imposing death sentences or cruel judicial tortures existed. By his negative answer Tertullian registers his opposition to military service not merely because it involved a danger of idolatry but because of the wrongfulness of the sword in the hands of a Christian. For a Christian to kill in battle was always a sin. He asks: "Shall the son of peace, for whom it will be unfitting even to go to law, be engaged in a battle?" But even peacetime service was wrong. "How will [a Christian] make war—nay, how will he serve as a soldier in [time of] peace without the sword, which the Lord has taken away?" The old law allowing the use of the sword has, he points out, been supplanted by the new law which removes the need for its use. "Christ in disarming Peter ungirt every soldier." A Christian convert within the ranks had only two legitimate alternatives: either to resign, if this were possible, or to suffer martyrdom as a result of refusal to obey when, as would inevitably happen, the command came to perform some action contrary to his Christian conscience.

Origen's defense of the pacifist position was written nearly a half century after Tertullian's. It is embedded mainly in Book VIII (sections 73-75) of a larger work which Origen composed in 248 in answer to the pagan philosopher Celsus' earlier critique of Christianity (*Contra Celsum*). In reply to Celsus' argument that the adoption of Christianity, with its antimilitarism and opposition to the magistracy, would mean the submergence of the Roman Empire by the barbarians, Origen explains that Christians were in fact fighting for the emperor more efficaciously by means of their prayers and their godly lives than his soldiers were doing through arms. We Christians, Origen writes, compose "a special army of piety through our intercessions to God" (from Henry Chadwick's translation, published by the Cambridge University Press in 1953). This is their service to the state. And he goes on to point out that even among pagans certain priests and temple-keepers refrained from shedding human blood so as to remain undefiled, and that they had been exempted by the state from any obligation to do military service. Surely it is equally, if not more, reasonable for Christians to render service in the same manner as these pagan priests did, he states. Christians truly are citizens of another city, the city of God and not the earthly one. They are not shirkers when they refuse to become soldiers or take on civil office, for their primary duty is toward "the church of God."

"We [Christians] do not become fellow-soldiers with him [i.e., the emperor], even if he presses for this": these words of Origen form a striking confirmation of the views of such modern scholars as Cadoux who maintains that the antimilitarist fathers, with their support of con-

11

scientious objection, were not simply individual dissenters. Despite the fact "that no general or authoritative ruling on the point had yet been given—circumstances not having called for it," they expressed the consensus of opinion within the church.

Several further comments on Origen's views on war need to be made. In the first place, he clearly allowed for a conditional justification of war and the state on a sub-Christian level. He gave qualified approval to Caesar's righteous rule and to those who fought to defend it; it seems, however, anachronistic to say, as the Polish scholar Leszek Winowski has done, that Origen believed in the existence of just wars in which Christians were forbidden to join *manu militari* only. With Origen conscientious withdrawal from military service was surely something more basic, for his view was that, while Christians might pray for the prosperity and success of such undertakings, they might never themselves participate in any way in military activities or in government without compromising their religion. Secondly, we may note that some scholars have argued that Origen's pacifism was the outcome of his eschatology: believing in the imminent end of the world, he saw no need for Christians to fight. But whatever validity this opinion may have in respect to some earlier Christian writers, the eschatological view had subsided in the second century and it is not applicable in Origen's case. "He contemplated an indefinite prolongation of human history under the divine control" (Cadoux). Again, in regard to the argument that Origen opposed military service because of the idolatry involved, it must be said that, as with Tertullian, it is the association of military service with bloodshed rather than idolatry that is the target of his attacks.

Finally, we should note that the positive case against war is stressed by Origen. He states his belief that God's protection of those who follow his commands may act as a viable alternative to military security, even though Christians must be ready on occasion to face death rather than abandon the peaceable example of their Saviour. True, Origen's pacifism was in a sense vocational, in that it applied only to those who accepted Christianity. But, within a somewhat narrow framework, it offers an outgoing approach in presenting the church's task as a moral agency leavening the life of the Empire and thus creating the conditions for peace and the conversion of the barbarians. The incompatibility of war and military service—and indeed many other aspects of the contemporary machinery of state—with agape as presented in the New Testament was what Origen and the early Christian antimilitarists urged. Their opposition was not the result, at least primarily, of the taint of idolatry or of aversion to Rome as a persecuting power or of eschatology. Their pacifism was not legalistic, though legalistic arguments were sometimes used, nor—except in the case of a quite unrepresentative figure like Marcion in the middle of the second century, who rejected carnal warfare along with marriage as examples of the evil of the corporeal world—was it based on a "gnostic repugnance" to physical bloodshed, though they indeed regarded homicide as a deadly sin. But, as Bainton has written, "the primary ground of their aversion [to military service and war] was the conviction of its incompatibility with love. . . . Concretely, the early church saw an incompatibility between love and killing." In other words, early Christian pacifism was "redemptive" in its rejection of war rather than representative of a merely defensive stance. "Le motif de respect de la vie," as Hornus has well said, is the central core of its teaching.

Tertullian states that in his day many soldiers left the army after being converted to Christianity, feeling that further service was incompatible with their new-found religion. How many did this, or who exactly they were, is not known. A patron saint of conscientious objectors does not occur until the appearance of St. Maximilianus near the very end of the third century. Maximilianus was a boy from Numidia who in 295, at the age of twenty-one, had been called up for military service. His father had been a soldier in the Roman army; the son, as the child of a veteran, was therefore liable for military service. After receiving the summons Maximilianus told Dion, the proconsul of Africa, that as a Christian he could not obey, for his service was to Christ. The boy, supported by his father who was sympathetic though not entirely in agreement with his son's stand, stubbornly persisted in his refusal, saying: "I cannot serve as a soldier; I cannot do evil; I am a Christian." Then Dion cited the example of contemporary Christians serving under the four co-rulers of the Empire, asking Maximilianus, "What evil do they do who serve?" "Thou knowest what they do," Maximilianus replied. He was then led away for execution. There is no evidence of heretical Montanist influence on Maximilianus' antimilitarism, nor is there any mention in the saint's *Acta* of pagan sacrifice as a factor in his objection to military service. Pacifism *stricto sensu* appears as the sole motivation.

It is true, however, that in the second half of the third and the beginning of the fourth centuries idolatry did become an important issue. Regulations obliging officers to make the customary sacrifices (these were never required of ordinary soldiers) were now being enforced with greater regularity; earlier they had largely lapsed. And cases now occur of martyrdom for refusal to sacrifice. But some of these martyred Christian officers, we should note, suffered death not merely for opposing sacrifices but also because they had come to feel the military profession to be in itself incompatible with genuine Christianity. For instance, Marcellus the centurion, although his main objection was to offering pagan sacrifices, in 298 stated: "I threw down [my arms]; for it was not seemly that a Christian man, who renders military service to the Lord Christ, should render it [also] by [inflicting] earthly injuries." Again, we find Tarakhos of Cicilia in the first decade of the fourth century telling his judge that he had given up soldiering "because I am Christian." "I have now chosen to be a civilian," he explained. And two praetorian soldiers who were martyred ca. 303 had left military service, according to the inscription on a tombstone later erected for them, not merely because they had come to disapprove of "the general's impious camp," but on account of their own "bloodstained weapons." Indeed, if Cadoux's judgment is correct on this point, so many were the cases of Christians' refusing military service around this time that it became one of the factors in the big persecution of Christians which began in 303.

Not only do the blood of its martyrs and the verdict of the church fathers bear witness to the pacifist stand of the early church. We also find traces of antimilitarism in the fragments of ecclesiastical legislation that have come down to us from this period. A difficulty here lies in the fact that the early church legislation has survived only in versions dating not earlier than the middle of the fourth century, that is, after the official church had abandoned its pacifist stand and when record of earlier pacifism could have been largely removed. Only one such document, the "Testament of Our Lord Jesus Christ," still retains a stringent position toward soldiering. The "Testament," writes Cadoux, "arose among the conservative Christians of Syria or southeastern Asia Minor"; it clearly contains material dating back several centuries. If soldiers or magistrates desire baptism, runs one of its articles: "Let them cease from military service or from the [post of] authority, and if not let them not be received." And here is another article of the same tenor: "Let a catechumen or a believer of the people, if he desire to be a soldier, either cease from his intention, or if not let him be rejected. For he hath despised God by his thought, and leaving the things of the Spirit, he hath perfected himself in the flesh, and hath treated the faith with contempt." Other legislative collections of the same period which often exist in several versions, such as the "Egyptian Church Order" or the "Hippolytean Canons," although they accept soldiers conditionally for baptism, frame these conditions in such a way that makes it clear that they are surviving remnants of a much more thoroughgoing condemnation of the military profession.

For example, soldiers are adjured not to be too forward in killing; otherwise they cannot receive baptism. Or they are required to cleanse themselves by penance from the sin of bloodshed before being admitted to "the mysteries." Christians, it is said, may become soldiers—but only if they have been compelled to act in this capacity. Although what Harnack once defined as a "compromise-ethic" is clearly uppermost in these documents, their strong reservations concerning war and soldiering point to their derivation from earlier church canons no longer extant, in which the ban on participation in military service would have been as explicitly framed as in the works of the church fathers we have discussed above.

Yet it is clear, too, that even before Constantine's conversion to Christianity, indeed at least since the reign of Marcus Aurelius, there were Christian soldiers in the Roman armies despite the church's disapproval of war, as there were already Christian magistrates despite the church's hostility to the state. And these servants of the emperor sometimes fulfilled their duties with the tacit consent of their church authorities; for though the records are no longer extant, we know that whereas probably official rebuke was on occasion administered to Christian soldiers, certainly some remained in these callings without disciplinary action against them from the ecclesiastical leaders. Further discussion of this question is necessary in order to elucidate the precise position of pacifism within the context of early Christian thought and practice.

The "soldier-question," we have seen, begins roughly with Marcus Aurelius' time. Before then, as Harnack remarks, "the baptized Christian would never be a soldier." "Apart from Cornelius and the one or two soldiers who may have been baptized with him by Peter at Caesarea . . . and the gaoler baptized by Paul at Philippi . . . , we have no direct or reliable evidence for the existence of a single Christian soldier until after 170 A.D." (Cadoux). There is no evidence, either, of Christian participation in any Jewish nationalist revolts, although Christianity was at first a predominantly Jewish sect. Yet, it must be acknowledged, there were certain elements within the framework of early Christian ideology which might provide support for war in certain circumstances.

Indeed, just as massive evidence can be adduced from the writings of the church fathers in condemnation of war in general terms, so a certain degree of acceptance of war in abstract terms may also be found in these same writings alongside, and sometimes even embedded within, their pacifistic sentiments. We may divide this early Christian "militarism" under three broad headings: the use of military

15

metaphors, parables, and illustrations; approval of the Old Testament warfare waged by the Hebrews; visions of apocalyptic struggles to come.

Military metaphor is present in all early Christian literature from St. Paul onward; it is used, too, even by explicitly pacifist polemicists like Tertullian or Origen. Essentially it represents an attempt to present the Christian message in a form that would appeal to the martial Romans, for whom the suffering cross was at first an alien symbol more appropriate for Jews and orientals than for the citizens of a military empire. The Christians' struggle against evil and sin is depicted as a war. Christians are *milites Christi* fighting under a rigorous discipline, though engaged, it is true, in a spiritual fight. Nevertheless, praise for prowess in this type of warfare might easily induce admiration, too, for worldly soldiering.

Since, with very few exceptions, for Christians up into the eighteenth century the whole body of scripture—the Old as well as the New Testament—was the result of divine inspiration, pacifist Christianity until comparatively recent times has always had to grapple with the question of Old Testament warfare. In the pages of the Old Testament such military figures as Gideon, Samson, Joshua, David, or the Maccabees are portrayed as heroes who, so long as they listened to God's commandments, were blessed with success. In the era of the early church, and for long thereafter, there was no thought of a progressive revelation of God in history. But though at first the discrepancy between the spirit of the two Testaments seemingly did not cause much trouble, the concept of a higher righteousness introduced by Jesus soon began to take shape. Certainly such Old Testament institutions as prostitution, concubinage, and polygamy were never approved by the early Christian church. And in regard to war, whereas it was thought that God had of old approved the Jewish military cause and Jewish military leaders were indeed regarded with admiration, the church fathers still considered that under the new dispensation waging war was no longer permissible in a follower of Jesus. The view promoted by Marcion and the dualistic Marcionites, that the wars and bloody punishments of the Old Testament emanated from an inferior Hebrew god and had never had the approval of the benevolent supreme Deity associated with Jesus, remained a heresy and unacceptable to the great majority of early Christians. But a writer like Origen, for instance, did go far toward allegorizing the wars of the Old Testament. These he regarded primarily as "types" of the spiritual, non-carnal battles which Christians must wage against the forces of Satan;

16

though at the same time he did not attempt to deny that the Jewish wars had actually taken place and with God's consent.

Thus, acceptance of a conditional validity for the wars of the Old Testament was not incompatible with a thoroughgoing pacifism. But we do know that by Tertullian's day, around 200, some Christians were already arguing in favor of military service on the grounds that God had thrown the blanket of his approval over the war service of the ancient Hebrews.

Early Christianity inherited something of the spirit of Jewish apocalypticism. For Jesus himself wars and turmoil in the future were part of God's plan for the world; they would intervene before the millennium was reached and the reign of peace began. For the early church the strange prophecies of the book of Revelation provided further confirmation for the belief that Jesus would one day return to earth, whereupon his enemies would be destroyed after a victorious conflict. The pre-Constantinian church tended to spiritualize such conflict in a manner somewhat similar to Origen's treatment of Old Testament warfare. The fathers saw the approaching war against darkness as a spiritual struggle in which only spiritual, and not carnal, weapons would be used; some of them, however, believed that destructive war would be waged, but by God's angels rather than by men. These rather misty concepts may not always have been easy for simple believers to grasp. As Cadoux admits, "this belief in a warrior-Christ who would conquer his enemies, played a certain part in preventing a unanimous and uncompromising rejection of warfare as a permissible element in Christian life."

In addition, contemporary wars such as, for example, the Jewish war of 67-71 were usually regarded by the church as God's way of punishing man for his sins. Here was a taste of God's judgment against the wicked. Of course, this did not mean either that the early church fathers believed that Christians would be right in acting as the instruments of God's wrath or that the agencies he actually chose, e.g., the Roman legionaries, were themselves sinless. Moreover, God also punished man's sins by means of such natural catastrophes as plague, famine, fire, and earthquake, none of which could be said to be good in themselves. Yet the belief that wars were to be an inevitable accompaniment of man's life on earth even though Christians were not supposed to take part in them, and that warfare in the present was in however qualified a sense part of God's scheme for the world, eventually made it easier for members of the church to accommodate themselves to the possibility of participating in military service.

War is a function of the state (though, we might add, not its inevitable concomitant). The early Christian attitude to the state implied, writes Cadoux, "a quasi-recognition" of war. True, some Christians regarded the state as a diabolic agency, not least because of its practice of religious persecution, and, furthermore, there was a strong feeling that the magistrate's office was incompatible with the Christian life. Yet, following the injunctions given by St. Paul (especially in Romans 13:1-6) early Christians recognized righteous rulers, even though they were not themselves Christians, as "God's ministers" who would act as "a terror . . . to the evil." They would bear "not the sword in vain" if they maintained law and order throughout their dominions. Church teaching, therefore, insisted not only on passive obedience, the payment of taxes and the observance of laws that did not impugn on conscience; it recognized, too, that the state possessed a place within the divine order. The fact that early Christian writers made no distinction between policemen and soldiers—understandably, since both functions were usually united in one person who wielded the military sword as well as the sword of justice—led easily to a more positive attitude toward participation in military service once a more favorable view of civil government grew up within the church.

"It is a good thing when evildoers are punished. Who but an evildoer will deny this?" wrote the staunchly pacifist Tertullian. Other Christian writers in this period praise the Roman armies for their military prowess and write disparagingly of rulers who are unwarlike. They sometimes deplore decline in military valor or in the number of new recruits to the Roman army. They speak of the army's usefulness to society and they are prepared, as we have seen in the case of Origen in his *Contra Celsum*, to recommend that their co-believers pray for state and emperor, and even for the success of Roman arms. All this, of course, presumed that army and state were only relatively justified: God could use them for his purposes even when these institutions were in the hands of evil men. They belonged to a sub-Christian level of behavior. This alone explains, for example, why such writers can speak of rulers "justly" carrying out the death sentence and, in almost the same breath, of the illegitimacy of a Christian's shedding human blood under any conditions whatsoever, or how they can allude to the legionaries' "righteously" performing their service and at the same time deny that a true Christian may serve in the imperial army. This seeming contradiction was resolved by the juxtaposition of two different, indeed mutually conflicting, standards of right conduct. Yet it remains true that the early church was never entirely able to resolve the dilemma of why, if Jesus' way were that of nonviolence and love, God

18

should employ the sword in war and domestic administration to carry out his purposes when these methods were so entirely opposed to Jesus' teaching and example. The temptation to prove that in fact the two methods were not really so incompatible as they might appear at first sight is certainly comprehensible. In later centuries, from the time of Constantine on, almost the whole corpus of orthodox Christian thought on the subject of war was to become a variation on this theme.

Even in the early church the Christian soldier might look back to examples of Christian knighthood: "The penitent soldiers baptized by John the Baptist, the centurion of Capernaum, who built the Jews a synagogue and at whose faith Jesus marvelled, the centurion at the cross who explained at the death of Jesus: 'Truly this man was a son of God,' Cornelius, the centurion of Caesarea, and the 'pious soldier' who waited on him, Sergius Paulus, the proconsul of Cyprus . . . the various military officials who had charge of Paul." But if such instances should not be taken as necessarily proving the acceptability of military service at the very beginning of the church's existence, they do at least show another side of the early Christian estimate of the military career. The early Christians thus showed awareness not only of the seamy side of camp life, its immorality and blood-stained weapons, but also of warriors who had received their message readily and shown kindness and a winning faith. Moreover, in the New Testament no record occurs of any requirement that soldier converts renounce their profession and, although once again this is no definitive proof of the acceptability of military service (especially in view of other evidence to the contrary), the omission might understandably give rise later to the supposition that it did constitute proof of this kind.

We do not in fact know for how long a period before Marcus Aurelius' reign conversions had been taking place in the army. We may presume, however, that they had been proceeding for some years. The Christian soldiers revealed as having served in the Twelfth or "Thundering Legion" around 174 were recruited mainly in Asia Minor on the borders of the Empire. From this region, too, came Abgar IX, King of Edessa, who in 202 declared himself a Christian and made Christianity the official religion of his realm. Clearly in this area, where the population was predominantly Armenian or Syriac, pacifism and the Christian faith by this date were not necessarily associated. As Bainton remarks: "Pacifism best flourished within the interior of the *Pax Romana* [especially in the Hellenistic East] and was less prevalent in the frontier districts menaced by the barbarians. . . . The Constantinian revolution was thus anticipated on the eastern fringe of the Empire by fully a century." At the same time, however, we must also

point out that this part of the Empire was the scene of ascetic monasticism's earliest growth, and monasticism involved a renunciation of
military service even after the abandonment of pacifism by the church
as a whole. The Mesopotamian ascetic Tatian, in the second century,
was expressing the views of this trend within the church when he said:
"I do not want to be a king: I do not want to be rich: *I decline military
command*: I hate fornication" (my italics).

Tertullian around the turn of the second century was, we have seen,
clearly aware of Christians serving in the army, both soldier converts
and Christian recruits. Although he was not averse himself to expressing pride in their numbers when arguing against pagan accusations of
Christian disloyalty to the state, he was vehement in his disapproval
of military service while addressing his fellow-Christians. The evidence indicates a steady increase in the numbers of Christians in the
imperial army during the third century; some of them suffered death
in the sporadic persecutions of this period. We do know of martyred
conscientious objectors but we do not hear of any specific instances of
Christian soldiers being required by their ecclesiastical authorities to
resign from the army (that is, apart from general church regulations
against soldiering and bloodshed). However, as we have already
noted, it is not improbable that record of disfellowshipping or other
disciplinary action has disappeared along with so many other documents of this era. Thus there might seem to be some validity, at least
for this later period, in a judgment like that of Schöpf, who writes:
"One can even say that an official [church] teaching [on war] did not
exist at all during the first three centuries. One opinion stands over
against the other": on the one hand the antimilitarists like Origen, Tertullian, and Lactantius, on the other the Christian soldiers and the
Christian magistrates and provincial governors appearing toward the
end of the third century, and the writers like Julius Africanus, Tertullian's contemporary and an authority on military science.

But such a view, which sees the early church officially divided on the
question of participation in war and extending indulgence indiffer-
ently toward both the pro-war and the antimilitarist standpoints, is
not, in my opinion, acceptable. That by the third century soldiering
was tolerated within the Christian community is an undoubted fact;
that it represented a majority position, however, is extremely doubtful,
unless at the very end of the period. And even if it did do so, the *official* church teaching would still appear to have come down clearly and
continuously on the side of antimilitarism right down to Constantine's
time. (An analogy could be drawn here with the Society of Friends in
present-day America, where the consensus of opinion within the

Society accepts pacifism as the collective Quaker stand even though only a minority of individual members have adopted the pacifist position for themselves.)

We should note, too, that "no Christian author of our period undertook to show that Christians might be soldiers"; Julius Africanus, with his interest in military affairs, was quite exceptional in early Christian literature. Schöpf was not able to discover a single instance, either, of pre-Constantinian approval by the church of the infliction of death in self-defense, whatever the provocation, or of the imposition of capital punishment, however deserved, by a Christian. Thus, even if individual members failed to live up to this pattern of perfection, and even though toward the end the nonpacifist position was obviously gaining ground within the Christian community and Christian soldiering was silently tolerated in many areas, as for example in Spain, North Africa, or the eastern borderlands, the literal interpretation of the Sermon on the Mount remained the church's teaching down to the beginning of the fourth century.

Let us take, for example, the figure of Lactantius, who was active toward the end of the third century and in the early decades of the fourth. Lactantius became tutor to Constantine's son, Crispus, and was close, therefore, to court circles; he was a man of moderate views untainted with heresy, no extremist but a theologian within the main stream of the church's tradition. Yet even at this late date he emerges as an uncompromising apologist for pacifism.

> When God prohibits killing [he wrote], he not only forbids us to commit brigandage, which is not allowed even by the public laws; but he warns [us] that not even those things which are regarded as legal among men are to be done. And so it will not be lawful for a just man to serve as a soldier—for justice itself is his military service—nor to accuse anyone of a capital offence, because it makes no difference whether thou kill with a sword or with a word, since killing itself is forbidden. And so, in this commandment of God, no exception at all ought to be made [to the rule] that it is always wrong to kill a man, whom God has wished to be [regarded as] a sacrosanct creature.

A more unconditional expression of the sanctity of human life could scarcely be found in all the annals of pacifism than this statement of Lactantius.

With Constantine's acceptance of Christianity, as Harnack remarks, "the *milites Christi* placed themselves at the service of the emperor." Already in 303 we find Julius, a veteran of twenty-seven years' service who was to suffer execution in that year as a Christian, declaring proudly before his judges: "I fought as well as any." Clearly the tide was turning against the pacifist view. At the battle of Milvian Bridge in 312 the many Christian soldiers in Constantine's army inscribed the sign of the cross on their shields and had it woven on the standards they carried into battle. Even those who thereafter remained non-resistant Christians could scarcely fail to rejoice at the victory of the head of the Empire who had chosen Jesus of Nazareth for his god. Constantine soon came to be regarded by the whole church as the champion of Christianity. A Christian emperor was a guarantee that persecution would not recur, even if in later times some were to see in the alliance now inaugurated between church and state a "fall of Christianity." At any rate, "official Christianity was now committed to the sanction of war" and those who disagreed were eventually silenced.

In 314, two years after Constantine's victory over his rivals, a church synod was held in Arles. One of its canons runs as follows: "De his qui arma projiciunt in pace, placuit abstineri eos a communione." The Latin is somewhat ambiguous. Cadoux translates it: "Concerning those who lay down their arms in time of peace, let them be excluded from communion," i.e., suffer excommunication. The synod, therefore, still recognized conscientious objection as a legitimate position in time of war though it disapproved of it in peacetime. This appears a reasonable interpretation. Even Tertullian, a century earlier, had distinguished between army service in peacetime, when homicide was not involved, and fighting in war, which inevitably entailed the shedding of human blood. In other words, *if* army duties could be performed without sin, then a Christian might well stay in military service so long as this condition still held. Some branches of the Roman army were engaged in purely administrative or police duties, and we know of Christians who were serving in this way before 312, perhaps because the risk of bloodshed was not great. "The distinction of police service," writes Bainton, "makes sense of the baffling canon . . . [of the synod of Arles]. The meaning then is that the Christian is not to lay down his arms in time of peace, when he may be called upon only for police duty, but he is still at liberty to withdraw in case of war." On the other hand, Winowski, for instance, considers that the canon in question forbade Christians to desert in peacetime as well as in war, although he admits that the actual wording gives the impression that desertion was reprehensible only in the former case. At any rate, whatever the correct interpretation may be, it is evident that official church sanction had now been bestowed on military service, though possibly only in time of peace.

The view put forward here by Cadoux and Bainton appears to find confirmation in a cause célèbre that occurred twenty-two years after the synod of Arles. In 336 a young Christian legionary—the future St. Martin of Tours—threw down his arms on the eve of battle and refused further service, declaring: "I am a soldier of Christ; I cannot fight (Christi ego miles sum: pugnare mihi non licet)," words that echo those of St. Maximilianus earlier. Martin, likewise the son of a veteran and therefore destined from birth for a military career, had continued to serve in the army for two years after his conversion to Christianity. Scholars like Winowski and Schöpf have seen in Martin's gesture simply a desire to dedicate the rest of his life to God's service. "I have fought for you," he told the emperor, "allow me now to become a soldier for God (militavi tibi: patere ut nunc militem Deo)." This would imply a purely vocational position and not any basic disagreement with the idea of Christians' participating in warfare (such as St. Maximilianus obviously felt). Yet this interpretation does not explain why Martin chose the very eve of battle to take such a stand, surely the most inappropriate hour for an action of this kind. Only a feeling on Martin's part that bloodshed was unchristian, even if a Christian soldier might remain in his calling so long as it did not involve homicide, can make his decision at that moment an intelligible one. Moreover, accused of cowardice, Martin avowed his readiness to go unarmed into battle in front of the army, which surely makes sense only if the early Christian *horror sanguinis* were involved.

The waning antimilitarism of the fourth century produced further examples of conscientious objection from within the circle of St. Martin of Tours' friends. For instance, St. Victricius, later bishop of Rouen, followed St. Martin's example, stating as one of his reasons that he had cast away "the weapons of blood (*arma sanguinis*)." In the second half of the century, St. Basil the Great laid down that Christians who had shed blood should not present themselves for communion for the space of three years thereafter. As late as ca. 400 we find St. Paulinus of Nola writing to persuade a fellow-Christian to leave the army. Further examples from the fourth century might be cited as evidence of a continuing uneasiness on the part of some church leaders concerning Christian participation in war. But these must be placed alongside even more abundant instances of official Christian support for war. "It is not lawful to kill," writes Athanasius, "but to destroy opponents in war is lawful and worthy of praise." Or take this sentence from the writings of St. Ambrose of Milan, who still believed that Christians should practise nonresistance—even unto death—in their private relations: "The bravery, which guards the fatherland in war from the barbarians or defends the weak at home or one's allies from robbers, is full of justice." In 438 non-Christians were forbidden to serve at all in the imperial armies; the legions henceforward were to be filled exclusively from the ranks of the Christians. And pacifism, before its submergence in the avalanche of the barbarian invasions, finally became a subterranean element within the church. Hornus has well summarized the process which led up to this state of affairs. "Il y a donc eu," he writes, "un glissement progressif dans l'attitude de l'Eglise. Elle a successivement pardonné au soldat répentant, toléré le soldat non violent, pardonné au soldat homicide, et enfin demandé au fidèle de cacher ses sentiments les plus profonds."

Early in the fifth century St. Augustine of Hippo evolved the theory of the "just war" which, along with the concept of the crusade or holy war, was to become the chief contribution of medieval Christianity to the philosophy of peace and war. Only a vocational quasi-pacifism lingered on for many centuries in the custom, not always in fact observed, that the clergy, and especially members of the monastic orders, should be exempt from participation in war, in part because of the taint of blood which such service involved (also illustrated, rather curiously, in the practice among fighting clerics of sometimes using a club instead of a sword when they participated in battle!).

"The barbarians militarized Christianity," writes Bainton; the medieval epoch was one of "pacifism in recession." When pacifism emerges again as a minor current within the framework of Western Christendom, it is not in the orthodox Roman church that it is found, but among obscure sects which had crystallized in the course of the Middle Ages.

ONE. *Medieval Sectarian Pacifism: The Czech Brethren*

THE establishment of Christianity as the official religion of the Roman Empire, which took place under Constantine the Great, had signified the fall of early Christian antimilitarism. The soldier of Christ replaced the Christian martyr as the symbol of the faith. A small residue of pacifistic sentiment survived the barbarization of the West, to revive after the successive waves of invaders began to subside. In the tenth century the church, mindful again of its role as a peacemaker, turned to the task of ameliorating the ravages of almost incessant war which had been the fate of Western Europe for many centuries. It attempted now to institute a "peace of God," which would serve to protect at least certain categories of persons regarded as in some way sacred (e.g., clerics, widows, virgins, pilgrims) and to exclude certain places (e.g., churches or monasteries) or times (e.g., Sundays or holy days) from being profaned by warlike activities. In the next century, the church extended its peacemaking role by establishing the "truce of God," whereby the carrying on of war was to be limited only to certain periods of the year. Those who contravened these edicts were subject to excommunication.

Monasticism was in large part "a religious protest against, and retreat from, the prevailing militarism and barbarity of the feudal age" (John T. McNeill). It offered to medieval man, at any rate, an outlet for vocational pacifism; in the thirteenth century, for instance, Franciscan Tertiaries were strictly forbidden to bear arms. Even the idea of "chivalry," though associated with soldiering, may be seen as an attempt to shield the innocent and the weak (e.g., women) from the worst evils of war. From the High Middle Ages onward the Catholic church continued its efforts to limit the incidence of warfare, to devise a "law of nations" that could regulate interstate affairs without recourse to bloodshed, and to provide a shelter for those who felt called to a peaceful way of life. Yet Roman Catholicism repudiated pacifism on principle as a perfectionist counsel. The idea that was rejected by the medieval church was often accepted by the medieval sectary. Among the Cathars and the Waldenses, the Lollards and the Czech Brethren, pre-Constantinian antimilitarism was renewed, so that beginning from the eleventh century we may once more, though at first only gropingly, take up the story of pacifist development.

25

If the Waldensian appears as the typical Gospel-centered, medieval sectary, the dualistic—and only externally Christian—Cathar was in fact the first to reintroduce pacifism in the medieval world. The origins of the sect can be traced back to the prophet Mani, who lived in third-century (A.D.) Mesopotamia. From there Manichaeism first spread across the frontiers into the Eastern Roman Empire where it absorbed many of the pacifistic Marcionites and then, some centuries later, into the Balkan States set up by the newly arrived Slavs, where its adherents called themselves Bogomils, the loved ones of God. By this time the religion had acquired a Christian coloring, though retaining its dualistic rejection of the world and of matter as Satan's realm and its exaltation of the realm of the spirit. The full vigor of the asceticism such otherworldliness brought with it applied however only to the celibate "perfect" and not to the ordinary "believers." Abstinence from meat-eating and from alcoholic beverages were among the requirements demanded of the sect's adherents. They were admonished, too, to suffer wrong peacefully and to avoid the shedding of blood. Originally the objection to killing seems to have been connected with a belief in reincarnation. Embodiment of a spirit in a human being or in certain animals was regarded as providing a means of expiating past sins; therefore, to kill signified to ruin, by cutting short, the penitential process.

It is by no means clear how far the Bogomils went in the practice of nonviolence. It appears improbable that they rejected participation in warfare; at any rate, pacifism was certainly not a tenet of belief of the Bosnian nobles who became Bogomils in the later Middle Ages and converted to Islam after the Turkish conquest.

When the dualistic heresy penetrated from the Balkans into northern Italy early in the eleventh century and from there rapidly spread westward and northward, its devotees became known as Cathars (in the southern French province of Languedoc, however, they were called Albigenses). Ruthlessly persecuted by church and state and regarded as outcasts by the rest of society—and drawn, moreover, from the humbler sections of the community—the Cathars elevated the principle of nonviolence, which had been implicit in the teachings of their forerunners, into an absolute injunction against the taking of human life. "This Church refrains from killing, nor does it consent that others may kill," since killing was forbidden by Christ and his disciples: the words are taken from a doctrinal exposition in Provençal recently identified as being of specifically Cathar provenance and dating from the mid-thirteenth century. The Cathars naturally rejected war, along with participation in government and courts of law, as a transgression of their religious ethic. Among the "errors" of the Cathars, according to the findings of an inquisitorial court, were the following: "Item, they say that it is not lawful for anyone to defend himself if the attacker can be injured thereby. Item, they say that no earthly authority can use the carnal sword for the punishment of malefactors." The execution of evildoers or the killing of an assailant in self-defense or in battle was murder, for it was God's prerogative alone to give or to take life.

In the first half of the thirteenth century, under the inspiration of Pope Innocent III, a prolonged and bloody crusade was waged against the Albigenses. The latter, it is true, took the decision to offer armed resistance; as in the case of Bosnia earlier, the sect had gained powerful adherents among the local nobility. Yet, according to Arno Borst, though the rank-and-file "believers" fought, the "perfect," so far as we know, maintained their nonviolent stance, at least to the point of abstaining from actual bloodshed.

Mention has been made of the fiercely repressive measures taken by the medieval church, and backed by the secular authorities, against Cathars and Albigenses. The same severity was employed in rooting out the other major medieval heresy—the Waldensian. Moreover, it was not only the bodies of the heretics that suffered under persecution; their spiritual culture was suppressed too. Before the fifteenth century at least, we are dependent for our knowledge of these two sects almost exclusively upon the accounts left by their opponents, with all the possibilities of omission and distortion to which ignorance or prejudice on the part of the official church could give rise. Often it is difficult to determine exactly what group is under discussion. In addition, as S. Harrison Thomson has remarked: "The Waldenses and Cathari were, because of their admittedly wide dispersion, extremely subject to local influence and heretical vagaries." Complete uniformity of belief was impossible under the conditions of secrecy and decentralization which provided the framework of their church life. Yet it is interesting to find certain tenets of belief recurring repeatedly in the reports of the investigating authorities.

"The hallmark of the Waldensians . . . was that they were *ydiote et illiterati*—simple and unlettered," writes Gordon Leff in his two-volume history of *Heresy in the Later Middle Ages* (Manchester, 1967). Unlike the Cathars, they derived their inspiration from a literal Christian discipleship centered on the Sermon on the Mount. Its injunctions they considered to be not mere counsels without binding force on Christians, as the church taught, but precepts which were obligatory on all professing to be followers of Christ. This stand had caused the sect's founder, Pierre Valdes, a prosperous merchant of

27

Lyons who around the year 1170 sold his goods and distributed them among the poor in obedience to Christ's commandments and with a desire to reinstate apostolic poverty, eventually to separate from the church; it soon brought down on him and his "Poor Men of Lyons" the accusation of heresy. Early in the thirteenth century a split occurred between the French branch, which attempted to conform outwardly to the official church, and the more radical north Italian branch, which broke completely with the ecclesiastical system. The Waldenses soon came under the influence of the earlier Cathar heresy; in the course of time a partial fusion of their beliefs took place. That Waldensian opposition to human bloodshed, as well as to oaths, derived from Cathar teaching and was not present at the outset is the opinion of some recent scholars (e.g., K.-V. Selge who describes Cathar doctrine as the "historic catalyst" of Waldensian pacifism). Yet the Waldenses' intense New Testament faith, if not responsible for the genesis of their pacifism, must surely have contributed to its steady maintenance for some three centuries. By the end of the twelfth century, at any rate, "refusal of oath and death penalty—and also of course of military service, which fell under the same prohibition of homicide—is unanimously attested for the whole Waldensian community (*das gesamte Waldensertum*)."

In one of the few major pieces of Waldensian literature to have survived the ravages of the Holy Inquisition—"La noble leçon (La nobla leiçon)," a long poem written in the fifteenth century in the Piedmont dialect used by the local Waldensian community—patient and even joyful suffering of persecution and wrong is presented as the Christian way of facing evil. Retribution, however deserved, proceeds from Satan. And indeed Waldenses saw suffering as the mark of the true church: they themselves remained a persecuted remnant in the midst of a world dominated by the allied forces of a wealthy and arrogant ecclesiastical body and a merely externally Christian state. Their alliance (according to the curious Waldensian variation on the legend of the Donation of Constantine) had originally been concluded between the Emperor Constantine the Great and his contemporary Pope Sylvester I and had signified thenceforward the corruption of primitive Christianity. In the Waldensian view the secular power, with its enforcement of the death penalty and its use of scarcely less harsh punishments to establish order in a lawless age, remained a pagan institution even though supported by official Christianity. Thus a Waldensian from Vienne in southern France confessed in 1319 "that the authorities, whether lay or ecclesiastical, through the exercise of temporal jurisdiction involving the killing of malefactors subject to them are commiting a sin"; his wife, who like her husband belonged to the category of the "perfect," declared "that no man ought to be killed, not excluding malefactors." Such views recur constantly in the reports on the hearings of persons arrested on suspicion of being Waldenses. Their justification is usually derived from the teachings of the New Testament where love, not human slaughter, is enjoined.

Thus the whole state apparatus stood condemned in the eyes of the Waldenses for its association with legal homicide and with war, whether among Christians or against the "Saracens." Yet in a late fifteenth-century declaration made by a Waldensian group in Saxony, the nonresistant injunctions of the Sermon on the Mount are described as indeed "Christ's precepts, but lesser ones." As shown by J. Th. Müller (from whose article "Über eine Inquisition gegen die Waldenser in der Gegend von Altenburg und Zwickau," *Zeitschrift für Brüderge-schichte* [Herrnhut, 1908], II, these words are quoted), by this date the Waldensian testimony against war was beginning to fade.

Despite the Waldenses' loose organization and the antisacerdotal character of their beliefs, their leaders' strong missionary impulse spread the new faith throughout most parts of Western Christendom. Whereas at first it had found adherents mainly among the lower ranks of the urban population of southern France and Lombardy, its message later also proved attractive to the German-speaking peasants of Central Europe. Though everywhere it remained the creed of a small minority, its vigor and its wide geographical spread were enough to frighten the church authorities into carrying out periodical investigations into the activities of the sect. Refusal under any circumstances to approve the taking of human life was one of the signs which indicated to the inquisitors that they had uncovered a Waldensian group.

One country where there appear to be no clear traces of Waldensian influence was England. The English kingdom was, however, the home of the intellectual "arch-heretic" of the later Middle Ages, John Wyclif. After his death in 1384 the movement was driven underground by the authorities, though small conventicles of Lollards, as his followers were known, survived until the coming of the Reformation in the second quarter of the sixteenth century. Wyclif himself, though he denounced war as unchristian, explicitly allowed Christian rulers to wage a just war and their subjects to participate in a conflict of this kind. Yet his followers, evidently influenced by their master's ardent Biblicism, went further than he was prepared to go. Wyclif's successor in the leadership, and like him an Oxford-trained theologian, Nicholas of Hereford (who, however, was to recant in the early 1390's), wrote: "Jesus Christ, duke of our battle, taught us [the] law of patience, and not to fight bodily." And in a petition presented to the House of Commons in 1395—"the first pacifist petition ever laid before" that house, Geoffrey Nuttall has remarked—the Lollards asserted in the tenth article "that manslaughter by battle or . . . law . . . without special revelation is express contrarious to the New Testament, the which is a law of grace and full of mercy." Their conclusion they held to be proven "by example of Christ preaching here in earth, the which most taught for to love and to have mercy on his enemies, and not for to slay them." Fighting entailed a lack of charity, and those lacking charity would be consigned to hell. "But the law of mercy, that is the New Testament, forbad all manslaughter: *in evangelio dictum est antiquis, Non occides.*" The authors of the petition condemned knights who slew their fellow men in pursuit of renown. This was behavior befitting heathens, "for by meakness and sufferance our belief was multiplied, and fighters and manslayers Jesus Christ hateth and menaceth. *Qui gladio percutit, gladio peribit.*" It is clear, however, that not all Lollards remained loyal to the nonresistant position; many were involved, along with a leading knightly adherent, Sir John Oldcastle, in the abortive uprising in 1414 provoked by the increasing severity of the government's measures to suppress heresy.

Wyclif's writings, both philosophical and theological, exercised an immense influence, alongside that of the native religious reform movement, on developments in the kingdom of Bohemia at the beginning of the fifteenth century. These were soon to issue in the first successful breakaway from the Roman allegiance carried out by a west European country. The Hussite revolution in Bohemia has been termed by the Czech historian, Amedeo Molnár, the "First Reformation." The movement is important in the history of pacifism because it witnessed the emergence into the open of the pacifist tendencies nurtured for several centuries in secret by illegal heretical groups which had imbibed Waldensian principles. Jan Hus, it is true, shared Wyclif's conditional acceptance of war. But the Hussite left wing drew a considerable part of its inspiration at the beginning from Waldensian sources. Whereas in the course of the fifteenth century the Waldenses were to be finally rooted out in almost all areas apart from certain remote Alpine valleys (where, however, at the end of the century they abandoned their pacifism in the face of attempts at forcible suppression), Hussitism became the established religion of the kingdom of Bohemia and survived intact into the Reformation era.

We do not know exactly when the first Waldensian missionaries arrived in Bohemia. But there is evidence of the sect's activities in the southern part of the kingdom adjacent to the Austrian frontier from the second half of the thirteenth century; it spread to Bohemia in its radical variant originally derived from north Italy. The first converts, naturally, were found among the German-speaking colonists of the area. It seems most likely, as many writers have claimed, that Czechs were won over, too, in the course of time, though a leading authority, F. M. Bartoš, maintains that in pre-Hussite Bohemia German Waldenses did not succeed in proselytizing among their Czech fellow peasants.

Despite sporadic attempts to eradicate it, Waldensianism persisted in Bohemia, and even grew in strength and influence. "Its appeal, as well as its strength," writes S. Harrison Thomson, "lay among the common people." Two facts are worth noting at this point. First, the sect had its center in an area where later the most radical element in the Hussite movement—the Taborites—was also to be centered. There was clearly a genetic connection between the earlier and the later currents of religiopolitical radicalism. Secondly, the Waldenses, even though most of them were country folk and their Christianity a simple discipleship, exercised through the purity of their moral impulse a considerable influence on the thinking of the radically minded theologians in Hussite Prague. A good example of such influence is the case of Master Nicholas of Dresden, a German-born convert to Hussitism who was executed as a heretic on a visit to his native land in 1417. Not long before his death he spoke out against all taking of human life (as well as against oaths) in a thoroughly Waldensian spirit. Evildoers should not be resisted, he said, for Christ had forbidden this, recommending instead that we pray for enemies and those who illtreat us. "Any writing of the doctors [of the church] that seems to legitimize killing on the basis of the common evangelical law is either contrary to Scripture or points back to the righteousness of 'them of old time,'" i.e., of the Old Testament, which Christ had put aside in favor of a higher righteousness.

After Hus's execution as a heretic by the Council of Constance in 1415, support for his idea of church reform, buttressed by an upsurge of national consciousness among the Czech-speaking inhabitants of Bohemia and Moravia, grew until the movement embraced a wide cross-section of the population of the two lands. From its adoption of the practice of communion in two kinds, *sub utraque specie*, it became known as the Utraquist movement. Whereas, once the reform impulse had died down, the practice of utraquism alone differentiated the Hussite right wing from the orthodox Catholic church, its left wing, which was centered in the newly founded town of Tábor in south Bohemia, aimed at a complete reshaping of the religious and politicosocial order of the country. The radicals found their support among the peasant masses of this area, which was also, as we have seen, the home of Bohemian Waldensianism and the area, too, where Hus in the period of his exile from Prague around 1412-1413 had preached in the open air to vast numbers of hearers.

In the years 1418 and 1419 the movement reached boiling point. Peasant enthusiasts and radical clergy awaited the second coming of Christ and the establishment of the Kingdom of God on earth. At first, however, the expectation was that the extirpation of the ungodly would be carried out by God alone without the intervention of human hands. Rejection of violence, including the death penalty and war, and the patient suffering of wrong even unto death, were tenets of this "primitive Taboritism" (to use the phrase coined by Josef Pekař), thus reflecting the strong influence exercised by Waldensian pacifism on Bohemian religious radicals at this time. Even the Prague preacher, Jan Želivský, who was soon to become an apostle of violent revolution in the name of Christ, declared to his listeners: "Thou shalt not kill." Whether such utterances were intended as a rejection of violence of every kind, as Nicholas of Dresden had advocated, or expressed merely a generalized disapproval of its use except in the direst emergency, is unclear. An anonymous critic of the radicals was to write: "Now they walk hypocritically with staffs, but when they increase in numbers they will wage great war." And, in fact, when over the winter of 1419-1420 the threat of an invading army of Catholic crusaders bent on rooting out the Hussite heresy loomed increasingly larger, the Taborites abandoned their nonresistant position and began to arm. The godly, they now said, must help bring in the Kingdom by destroying God's enemies; Christ's second advent was at hand and his people must take possession of their inheritance by force. "Brethren," proclaimed the Taborite priest, Václav Koranda the elder, "it is time to lay aside pilgrims' staffs and to take up arms, for the enemy grows in numbers and goats are bearing down on the flourishing vineyard of the Lord."

A brief period of communistic living was succeeded by the reintroduction of the feudal order. Yet the Taborites' religious radicalism continued unabated for several decades. In the 1420's, after the defeat of successive crusading armies, the Taborites, in alliance with the more moderate Hussites of Prague, moved over onto the offensive. The humble disciples of the peaceful sectaries were now transformed into the armed "Warriors of God," whose name became a terror to the rest of Western Christendom. The Taborites' great military leader, Jan Žižka

32

(until his death in 1424), and their fighting priests became famous throughout Europe as exemplars of Hussite militancy.

In mid-1420, when Prague was menaced by the crusading army of the Emperor Sigismund, who also claimed the Bohemian throne in succession to his recently deceased brother, Václav IV, crowds of Taborite supporters had streamed up from the south to bring succor to the beleaguered capital. Among them was a young man named Petr Chelčický, who was destined to become one of the most eloquent and thoroughgoing exponents of nonresistance before Tolstoy in the nineteenth century. Chelčický shared much of the Taborites' theology; he had enthusiastically embraced their social radicalism; and he believed in their initial renunciation of the sword as unchristian. Whether now his faith in nonviolence was temporarily shaken by the invasion of his country (as the American historian of the Hussite revolution, Howard Kaminsky, has suggested as a possibility), or whether he came merely from curiosity or from a desire to accompany his fellow believers in their trek, is difficult to determine in view of the silence of the sources concerning the motives for his action at this point. At any rate, if indeed he entertained momentary doubts as to the Christian's obligation of employing nonresistance under all circumstances, he soon recovered his faith in nonviolence.

Concerning the facts of Chelčický's life we know almost nothing. He was probably born in the 1380's in the south Bohemian village of Chelčice. Various theories have been propounded in regard to his social origin, the most likely being that put forward by F. M. Bartoš, who identifies Chelčický with a well-to-do squire Petr Záhorka. If this hypothesis is correct, then Chelčický was not a peasant by birth, as has often been supposed, but a farmer who chose this calling in preference to a knightly career because it appeared to him to be closest to the simple life of apostolic Christianity. In an agrarian environment Chelčický sought, as Tolstoy was to attempt to do half a millennium later, the milieu best suited to the pursuit of nonviolence.

Early in his career Chelčický must have come under Waldensian influence; we have learned above of their congregations in the area of his birth. Though he received no university training and succeeded in acquiring no more than a smattering of Latin, a lack that excluded him from direct acquaintance with the learning of his age, he was well read in the Bible, by now available in Czech translation, and in the theological literature circulated in the Czech language. After the relief of Prague he returned to south Bohemia where he remained, so far as we know, for the rest of his life. Over the years his close ties with the

Taborites relaxed, and among the main reasons for the cooling of relations was his strong disagreement with his former companions' present reliance on the sword to defend and extend their faith. However, he continued to enjoy friendly relations not only with leading Taborites like the theologian Mikuláš Biskupec of Pelhřím but also with moderate Hussites, including their Archbishop-elect Jan Rokycana. The three decades following 1420 are filled with intensive literary activity on Chelčický's part; his masterpiece *The Net of Faith* (*Síť víry*), dealing in great detail with the relationship between church and socio-political life and elaborating a version of Christian anarchism which rejected the existing feudal order as a pagan institution, is a product of the early 1440's. By now he had gathered round him a small group of followers, many of whom after his death at some unknown date in the late 1450's eventually merged with the Unity of Czech Brethren (Unitas Fratrum, Bohemian Brethren), for their master's writings provided one of the main inspirations behind the work of the Unity's founders.

While in Prague in 1420 Chelčický had sought out on two occasions the learned theologian Jakoubek of Stříbro, universally regarded as Hus's successor in the leadership of the Utraquist movement, in order to discuss with him the burning question whether a Christian was ever justified in resorting to force. Could personal participation in war, asked Chelčický, ever be compatible with a genuine Christian discipleship? Jakoubek, we know, followed Wyclif in his view that the properly constituted secular authorities had the right—indeed the obligation—to defend the faith by force of arms even though, again like Wyclif, he considered peaceableness a mark of the true Christian and though he was opposed to the militant adventism of his Taborite allies. At the outset of their discussion Chelčický asked Jakoubek what sanction he could cite to back his view that it was permissible under certain circumstances for a Christian to engage in warfare. Jakoubek was forced to admit that he had only the injunctions of "the saints of old" for his opinion and that he could not quote any New Testament source in its favor. Describing their second interview which took place in the autumn of the same year, Chelčický wrote:

> After many people had been killed on both sides, Jakoubek excused those who had done the killing, saying that [he] could not tax their consciences with such things, since otherwise the whole knightly estate would stand condemned. . . . How [Jakoubek] would have launched out against anyone who dared to eat pork on a Friday, and yet now he cannot make the shedding of men's

blood a matter of conscience, this man whose own conscience has been filched from him by those saints of old!

Here indeed we see the uncompromising restitutionist doctrine of Chelčický displayed in its full vigor.

In his writings he was to call for a return to primitive Christianity. All things necessary to salvation, he claimed, are contained in the books of the New Testament, and at the core of its teaching is Christ's "Law of Love." We must, therefore, reject later doctors of the church if they attempt to justify behavior inconsistent with this law. Chelčický was ready to criticize even his revered master, Jan Hus, because he taught that to take life was not a sin in every instance: according to Chelčický, Hus and other church leaders who did not share the former's belief in nonresistance had all drunk of the cup "the whore [of Babylon] had proffered," for it was impossible, in Chelčický's view, to kill and still retain love in one's heart.

Chelčický accepted the legend current among the Waldenses that their founder, Pierre Valdes, had lived at the time of Constantine the Great. When Valdes's friend, Pope Sylvester, accepted the emperor into the church and inaugurated the long alliance between state and church, Valdes and a few companions who remained faithful to the principles of apostolic Christianity fled into the forests to avoid contamination with an institution become corrupt through power. Poison had been injected into God's church: henceforward Antichrist ruled in the counsels of official Christianity. A gaping hole had been rent in the net of the true Christian faith.

Government for Chelčický was pagan, for it was impossible to exercise it without contravening the law of love. True, the state was necessary, as St. Paul had shown, to maintain good order among non-Christians. But power should be wielded by those who did not recognize Christ as their lawgiver. In this world the church's lot was inevitably that of a small, persecuted minority. The idea of progress, of man's perfectibility, of society's improvement, all these were concepts totally alien to Chelčický's thinking. Over against the Christian community, arranging its internal affairs according to the precepts set forth by its master and totally nonresistant *vis-à-vis* the outside world, Chelčický placed society, superficially Christian but in fact essentially pagan in its mores and ethos. "These two divisions, the temporal order of force and Christ's way of love, are far removed from each other," he wrote. "For the fullness of authority lies in the accumulation of wealth and vast gatherings of armed men, castles, and walled towns, while the fullness and completion of faith lies in God's wisdom and the strength of the Holy Spirit." Thus Chelčický directs some of his most passionate invective, some of his most biting criticism, against the existing social structure which combined the extremes of feudal affluence with oppression of a serf peasantry. The wealth of the upper class was accumulated as a result of the unceasing labors of the poor. Even seemingly innocuous aspects of the contemporary civilization—trade and commerce, the culture of cities, university learning—stand condemned in Chelčický's eyes. His ideal was the simple countryman, with sufficient letters to understand the Scriptures and a calling which permitted neither the amassing of wealth nor the extravagances of power. (Some Czech Marxists, however, have like Radim Foustka in his *Petra Chelčického názory na stát a právo* [Prague, 1955] branded Chelčický's views on state and society as "typically petit-bourgeois.")

Violence, in Chelčický's view, was inseparably connected with the institution of government; political "power," he explained in his tract *On the Triple Division of Society* (*O trojím lidu*) composed in the mid-1420's, "breeds fear, for power makes it possible for cruelty to rule, threaten, abuse, . . . imprison, beat and kill." "There can be no power without cruelty. If power forgives, it prepares its own destruction, because none will fear it when they see that it uses love and not the force before which one trembles." Therefore, government could never be christianized. True, Christians must observe its commands— but only insofar as conscience allowed. This qualification set the limits to Christian obedience. A Christian state was a contradiction in terms.

> For God did not, through His apostles, ordain a king for the Holy Church, to bear her tribulations on his sword, to fight for her against her enemies, and through force to make that Church serve Him. Nor did He give her judges or magistrates, so that the Holy Church might come before them and litigate over the goods of this world. Nor did He give her bailiffs and hangmen, so that some members of the Holy Church could hang others, or torture others on the rack, for the sake of material things—this is for the pagans and for this world.

This passage comes from one of Chelčický's earliest tracts ("On the Holy Church"). Though by the 1430's his protest had become rather more subdued, his principled rejection of the state remained unchanged. Within their community the Christians' method was that of arbitration and of restitution for damage done, of punishment by exhortation and rebuke alone. The penitent transgressor ought to be forgiven; he who persevered in wrongdoing must be expelled from the

36

company of the godly. But "no harm should be done him, such as killing him in his sins." By casting him out the Christian community would preserve its purity without resort to unlawful means of dealing with evil.

In his dialogue with his erstwhile friends, the Taborite theologians, Chelčický warned that they were in fact donning the devil's armor in attempting to resist evil by means of carnal weapons. God's truth could never be defended in this way, for the hatred engendered in battle would burn love from their hearts. The only fighting permitted the follower of Christ was in the spiritual struggle against Satan and all his works; for this reason Chelčický gave his first tract, written in the late summer of 1420 to counteract Taborite chiliasm which had reached its peak around this time, the significant title *On Spiritual Warfare* (*O boji duchovním*). Of the Taborite leaders, he wrote there, "The Devil came to them clothed . . . in the prophets and the Old Testament, and from these they sought to confect an imminent Day of Judgment, saying that they were angels who had to eliminate all scandals from Christ's Kingdom, and that they were to judge the world. And so they committed many killings and impoverished many people." The days of wrath, which the chiliasts predicted for February 1420, had already passed; yet, Chelčický lamented, they continued to rely on military might, despite the fact that Christ had replaced the old law by a new and higher one.

War, in Chelčický's view, originated with Antichrist, the Beast who had taken possession of the souls of the rulers of church and state ("benighted Christians" is how Chelčický described the latter). "God cannot say: 'Thou shalt not kill,' since the Beast commands men to kill, hang, burn, execute, destroy villages and homes," he writes ironically. True, the Old Testament did permit the Jews to fight their enemies; also, warfare was natural among pagans ignorant of the Christian way of life while physical force was the mainstay of earthly kingdoms which would otherwise disintegrate due to the evil propensities of unredeemed man. But Christ forbade his disciples to take human life under any circumstances; this was proved by the example of the master himself, of his apostles, and of the early church. Henceforward all men were brothers. No ecclesiastical authority, however exalted, could set aside the law of Christ, the obligation to test every action by its consonance with love. "If," wrote Chelčický, "[St. Peter] himself should suddenly appear from Heaven and begin to advocate the sword and to gather together an army in order to defend the truth and establish God's order by worldly might, even then I would not believe him." Chelčický was filled with disgust at the willingness of Taborite priests to administer the sacraments to soldiers who had taken part in battle: "murderers and robbers," in Chelčický's eyes. He poured scorn on the blind and the false followers of Christ who had perverted their master's teachings. He denounced with biting sarcasm the absurdity of prayers offered for victory. Such prayers were, in fact, "a terrible blasphemy." For him the commandment "Thou shalt not kill" admitted of no exceptions, for only God had the power to take, as well as to create, life.

Nonresistance to evil, combined with outgoing creative love, was Chelčický's answer to violence. If the body perished as a result of this stance, nevertheless the soul would live eternally, whereas warriors—even warriors of God—would be consigned to everlasting damnation. In an eloquent passage in his treatise "On the Triple Division of Society" (reminiscent of the dying words of the seventeenth-century English Quaker, James Naylor), he wrote:

> When we are established under mercy and without complaints, we have in ourselves and in our hearts the foundation of the higher justice that has love for all. When that love prevails, it wishes good to all from its heart, and it not only wishes but does good to all, as it is able according to its strength, goods, and understanding. Nor does it wish, ask for, or do evil to anybody; nor does it deprive, hinder, or torture anyone, or harm anyone, but rather consoles and helps everyone according to its power and the other's need. Even more, that love suffers the injustice done by others, and in return loves, prays for, and benefits those who scorn or harm it.

Chelčický appears as the protagonist of Christian pacifism for the first time, so far as we know, in 1420. The next sixteen years were filled with war and violence until a precarious peace was reestablished in 1436 as a result of the compromise reached between Sigismund and the moderate Hussites—at the expense of the Taborites, whose leaders had perished at the disastrous battle of Lipany two years earlier. The material destruction of this period and the accompanying moral deterioration only confirmed Chelčický in his critique of war. He saw the common people as the chief sufferers. What the one side did not take from them, the other side seized and carried off. Thus, interspersed with his condemnation of war on Christian principles come fierce denunciations of the horrors and havoc of war which read almost as if they came from the pen of a modern antimilitarist.

During the long years of war peasants and artisans, especially, were subject to conscription—against their will—into one or other of the opposing armies. Chelčický complains bitterly of such practices. "In time of war," he writes, "you make warriors of tanners and shoemakers and weavers, of anyone able to wield a club. . . . For neither the king nor the princes nor the nobles nor the lesser gentry do the fighting themselves, but compel the peasants to do it for them." "The people are herded together like sheep and driven to the slaughter" at the behest of the authorities, clerical as well as lay and in defiance of the gospel injunction against fighting. Thus Christian is pitted against Christian and brother against brother. Alas, the people had "neither sufficient understanding, nor sufficient charity, to realize that they should choose death at the hands of their lord rather than commit such evil acts." They failed to realize that princes and prelates must be disobeyed when their command conflicted with the precepts of the higher justice of Christ. Since participation in war was incompatible with these precepts, Christians should refuse military service; if all who owned the name did this, "whom," Chelčický asked, "would rulers find to accompany them to the wars?" Although persecution from the side of the "paganized rulers" would certainly be the lot of those who adopted this course, nevertheless Christians must be prepared to suffer for their faith and face even death rather than act in opposition to God's commandment.

Chelčický's unyielding nonviolence stemmed from the Gospel imperative and the teachings of the Waldensian sectaries. His philosophy was already formed before the outbreak of hostilities in 1420. During the 1420's, when the Hussites of left and right expected a glorious conclusion to their struggle for God's truth, Chelčický stood practically alone in his pacifist witness. However, from the 1430's on, when the proud Hussite slogan "The Truth shall prevail" began to wear thin and war-weariness and disillusionment with ideology spread among all classes, Chelčický's ideas appeared in a new light. There was an increasing number now who came to share, at least to some extent, his belief in nonresistance as an essential mark of the Christian brotherhood. True, it was in the lower strata of society—small craftsmen, artisans, and peasants, including the dispersed remnant of the Taborite community—that such views found readiest acceptance. Yet we find in the mid-1450's a figure of national importance like Archbishop-elect Rokycana preaching against war and an acquisitive society and praising Chelčický for his denunciation of these evils. Even though some of Rokycana's audience read considerably more into his words than he had intended, his sermons provided indeed the initial impulse which led to the foundation of a new focus of religiosocial radicalism —the Unity of Brethren.

The Unity came into being in the course of the decade between 1457 and 1467. By the latter date Chelčický was dead and his brethren without a leader. Chelčický's work was now taken up by a young man named Řehoř, who was Rokycana's nephew and a member of the minor gentry though he had adopted the trade of tailoring as a means of gaining a livelihood. Brother Řehoř, as he became known in the new community, was energetic, an able organizer, and endowed with charismatic gifts. He had little formal education and no originality of thought but he was an able exponent of the ideas of others. Indeed the Unity, at least in regard to its view of the relationship of religion to society, adopted almost *in toto* the ideology elaborated by Chelčický in his writings. Thus Chelčický became in fact "the spiritual father" of the Unity of Czech Brethren during the first phase of its existence.

The Unity, like Chelčický, sought Christian perfection in the simple way of life of the countryman or humble artisan. Like him, it regarded with suspicion the activities of the merchant and the scholar and condemned the class structure of society which elevated the warrior class into a privileged group fattening on the laboring peasantry. It accepted Chelčický's view of the state which he regarded as opposed, along with war and the taking of oaths, to the Christian discipleship elaborated in the pages of the New Testament. Such discipleship the Unity, like its master, regarded as a code of moral law superseding the Mosaic. On the principle of an eye for an eye and a tooth for a tooth the Mosaic law had permitted physical warfare, the execution of sinners, and other bloody punishments. Instead, Christ had ordered the carnal sword back into its scabbard and commanded his followers to disobey their rulers if these required them to fight. For the Christian there were no just wars, no excuses for ever taking the life of a fellow man. Rather than kill even the cruel Turk in self-defense or in defense of the faith he must be ready to stand defenseless and suffer what might come. As Řehoř told the vice-chamberlain of the kingdom of Bohemia in 1461, his brethren strove "to live according to the Scriptures alone, following the example of Christ and his holy apostles in quietness, humility and patience, loving one's enemies and doing good to them . . . and praying for them." They were aware that they would always remain a small minority in a world plunged in unbelief and sin; they formed a society of poor men and women of humble origin leading a frugal and toilsome existence. They saw themselves as pilgrims on earth, a people apart, separated from the affairs of this world and content to await peaceably its inevitable, and probably imminent, end.

A report composed in 1480 by a panel of Catholic priests, which investigated four leading Brethren who were on a visit abroad, confirms this picture of a community attempting to conform exactly to the pattern of primitive Christianity. "In their church, so they assert, they admit no tribunal involving blood, saying that this would be against the Gospel." Disputes and misdoings among members were settled by arbitration with the help of the elders. "If one of their own is erring and incorrigible, they exclude him from their congregation after having anathematized and excommunicated him. If, however, he acknowledges his fault and seeks atonement, they accept him back again into the church."

Following Chelčický the Brethren saw the essence of government in "fear, cruelty, beating, fighting, killing, reviling, violence, imprisonment, cutting off of limbs, murder, and other physical torments." And war, too, was an inevitable concomitant of the exercise of governmental authority. There are indications in contemporary Unity literature that in the late 1460's, when Bohemia under its Hussite king, George (Jiří) of Poděbrady, again came under attack from crusading forces bent on overthrowing the Czech heresy and the militia was called up to repel the invaders, Brethren—both in the towns and in the countryside—were conscripted for military service. Some went into hiding, probably retiring into the forests and mountains; some stood their ground and undoubtedly suffered severe penalties; others may have conformed with an uneasy conscience to the demands of the state or succeeded in extricating themselves in one way or another. There seem, too, to have been a few Brethren who now abandoned their belief in nonresistance in face of the external threat to extirpate Hussitism.

It is from this period that the Brethren's only attempt to deal systematically with the question of the state and war dates. The "Tract on the Civil Power or the Power of the Sword" (*Psaní o moci světské neb o moci mečové*), though issued anonymously, was almost certainly from the pen of Brother Řehoř. The work is for the most part a literal transcription of Chelčický's treatise "On the Triple Division of Society," with some additional materials relating mainly to the implementation of pacifist principles in the existing situation of war. The author's immediate object in compiling the tract was to present a reasoned apologia for his brethren's refusal to participate in the defense of country and religion against the foreign invaders. Like Chelčický, he protests vehemently against the enrollment of "poor people, workers, and tenants," which he regards as an innovation unknown in former times, when ploughmen and craftsmen were not snatched away from their labors to serve in the wars. Fighting, in his view, was the business of the knightly estate, which received temporal power and the dues and services of the common people in exchange, or of mercenaries, who obtained money for their hire. But in Bohemia today, the author complains, "whoever is at all capable of bearing arms is reckoned among the warrior class."

The Brethren had shocked the moderate Hussites, who had come into their own again with the election of George of Poděbrady to the throne in 1458, when in 1467 they broke with official Utraquism and instituted a separate priesthood. Under King George the Unity was subjected to several periods of sharp persecution, even though it continued to regard itself as part of the Hussite succession. However, under the weak rule of George's successor, the Polish-born Vladislav II (1471-1516), the Brethren enjoyed long spells of freedom from outside interference so that, under the aegis of friendly nobles ready to grant these industrious and frugal subjects protection against attempts to intervene on the part of the central government, the Unity grew in numbers and influence. Before his death in 1474, Brother Řehoř had succeeded in organizing a network of small but flourishing congregations throughout large areas of Bohemia and Moravia and in giving the sect an efficient administration.

Řehoř's successor as leader was the simple, saintly, but somewhat ineffective Matěj, who had been chosen in 1467 to be the Unity's first bishop. It was under Matěj's stewardship that the Brethren (to quote the East German historian, Erhard Peschke) evolved "from sect to church"; emerged, that is, from the sectarian otherworldliness of the period of the "Old Brethren" onto the path which ultimately led them during the sixteenth century to full participation in the political and cultural life of their country. The catalyst which brought about this development is to be sought in the schism of the 1490's between the protagonists of the sociopolitical rigorism, which had prevailed until then, and those Brethren wishing to widen the horizons of their coreligionists.

During the 1470's and the 1480's freedom from persecution had resulted in a rapid expansion of the membership of the Unity (by the end of the century it numbered well over 10,000 adherents). Its outreach now extended to classes of the community affected little, if at all, by its teachings hitherto. The typical Brother was still for the most part an obscure peasant sectary living in rustic seclusion from the affairs of this world. Yet the importance in its counsels of the urban, of the educated, and even of the noble member was increasing. This was a development which, though a sign of health and vitality, at the same time brought with it the seeds of disunity.

The roots of the schism in the 1490's should be traced back to

42

changes which had taken place during the two previous decades in the character of its membership, and in particular in the character of those elements within the Unity which set the tone for the whole body. The revolution in its sociopolitical ideology, accomplished by the end of the century, reflected the underlying shift from a predominantly rural and self-educated leadership to one controlled by the younger generation of university-educated Brethren working in association with a handful of noble recruits to the Unity. Until the 1490's the latter elements had been sparsely represented. This is understandable in a body which angrily rejected learning as, at best, indifferent to salvation and which required all to follow "the narrow path," even if, in the case of the landed nobility, it entailed the renunciation of their property, on account of the obligations incumbent upon estate-owners of exercising patrimonial jurisdiction and of providing for military service. We know of several members of the nobility who joined the Unity before 1490; they had either given up their property altogether and earned a living by the labor of their hands or brains, or at least renounced the power of the sword while retaining a part of their inherited wealth. This last solution, however, was possible only in exceptional circumstances.

The Unity at this time needed, we have seen, noble protectors to shield it against the state, should this be inclined once again to unleash persecution against the Brethren, as indeed happened early in the next century. There was no certainty that the protection of a Utraquist or a Catholic lord would not cease, as a result either of a change of mind on his part or of the death of the owner. Thus, only the existence of a Brethren nobility could provide security against such uncertainties.

It would be unjust to imply that calculations of this sort were the sole, or even the main, reason for the eventual relaxation in the traditional Unity ban on admitting the sword-wielding nobility into membership. Yet that they played a role in the changes about to be described cannot be doubted. In the same way, we should not attribute to the educated "modernizers" (who were to provide the driving force behind the movement within the Unity to bring its ethical code into closer conformity with that of the society environing it) a conscious insincerity, on their first joining the Unity, in accepting those obligations of Unity membership which separated the sect from the society of its time. But the educational background of these young scholars, with their close ties with university and city life, a milieu very different from that of the unlettered country Brethren of Řehoř's day, made conflict at some future date almost inevitable. A broader outlook, a desire, free though it might be of personal ambition, to see the Unity extend its influence and to make a more effective impact on the affairs of the land than had been possible hitherto, an easily acquired ascendancy in the counsels of the sect as a result of superior education and professional theological training: all these things provided ample reason for an eventual clash between the views of the younger leaders and the outlook of the Old Brethren.

Among this second generation of Brethren one man stands out as endowed with special gifts and intellectual attainments: Brother Lukáš, born shortly before 1460, bachelor of arts of the University of Prague in 1481, and a member of the Unity since soon after that date. Though in the days of his conversion a keen devotee of Chelčický and his works, Lukáš developed before long into an unbending opponent of the heritage of Chelčický within the Unity. It was he who was now to be chiefly responsible for persuading it to turn its back on its inheritance by making peace with that world which the sage of Chelčice had angrily rejected.

The immediate origins of the crisis which tore the Unity apart in the 1490's (a crisis, however, whose beginnings reach back earlier) related not so much to military service as to the problem of officeholding. For in respect to demands for service in the town militia or in the feudal levy, to which in an emergency all able-bodied males were liable, substitutes could usually be bought, a practice that was approved by the Unity leadership (grouped in an executive committee known as the Narrow Council) as a way out of a difficult situation. But Brethren, especially in the towns, could not, if called upon, so easily opt out of the obligation to fill offices such as alderman or judge. This had happened in 1490 to the Brethren in Litomyšl, who thereupon appealed to Bishop Matěj and the Narrow Council for advice concerning the proper response to demands of this kind. The Council's answer was both confused and evasive. In effect it permitted Brethren to accept office, but only if there was absolutely no other way of escape. It may indeed have represented an attempt to reach consensus between the opinions of the older generation wedded to the narrow path to salvation as set forth by Chelčický and Brother Řehoř, which regarded the state as essentially unclean, and the party represented by the generation of Brother Lukáš. Matěj was obviously finding it difficult to defend the narrow path against their attacks.

The root of the trouble lay in the growth in the town congregations of a new type of Unity member. The townsman, even if only a humble journeyman, was not content with the meager subsistence of a peasant. He was more ambitious; his horizons were wider; moreover, his environment pressed in upon him with a greater insistency. There was indeed a certain logical consistency in the advice which Matěj and his colleagues now gave to the brethren: if you cannot wriggle out of such things as office or oath or mustering with weapons, then move back again into the countryside. Yet this step really provided no lasting solution, even if the Brethren in the towns could have been prevailed upon to take it, for villagers too were liable for minor office and might be conscripted to bear arms in an emergency.

Thus, the practical interest of the urban Brethren in arriving at a *modus vivendi* with the surrounding world coincided with the theoretical reservations entertained by the young and learned theologians of the Unity, who emerged as spokesmen for all who desired a relaxation of the earlier rigorism. So we find now the "learned" Jan Klenovský declaring: "If we forbid the Brethren to take part in the administration of justice, we shall be placing an unbearable yoke upon [their] necks, which even our fathers were unable to bear."

The ferment continued. Later in the same year a general assembly of "all the priests, deacons, assessors, and assistants" of the Unity was held at Brandýs nad Orlicí. The assembled Brethren accepted a resolution which, although in theory it paid lip-service to the principles of the Old Brethren, in practice went far in the direction of relaxing their stringency. Certainly, the resolution declared, magistracy and swearing of official oaths and serving in the wars were in themselves highly dangerous for the God-fearing man. Countless were the temptations they offered to the unwary.

> If [nevertheless] a Brother should be forced by the civil authority, against his conscience, to accept any of these things, being unable to escape either through humble pleading or in any other way, he should according to [our] counsel submit to the authorities in whatever is not against God. . . . For in such matters as these, although it is difficult to preserve a good conscience and shun evil, it is not impossible. . . . We cannot give uniform instruction and teaching how one should conduct oneself [in such cases], on account of the divergence of cause, place, time, and persons.

If the local teachers could not resolve dubious cases, then, the resolution concluded, the matter should be referred to Bishop Matěj for decision.

The Brandýs resolution aroused strong resentment among the rigorists, who—correctly—saw in it a conscious attempt to water down the purity of the old doctrine. It is from this time that we must date the beginnings of an opposition group within the Unity. However, the Minor Party (as it became known after it had become apparent that its members represented a minority opinion within the sect) remained silent at the beginning, unwilling perhaps to appear to be the first to break the unanimity and concord seemingly achieved at the Brandýs assembly. This tactic proved a mistake in the long run, since it gave the Minor Party's opponents (who eventually emerged as the Major Party of the Unity) an opportunity to brand it as a disrupter of the sect's discipline and as a rebellious element *vis-à-vis* the properly constituted leadership when it finally emerged in open opposition. One may doubt, however, if a tactical error of this kind, which undoubtedly lost the Minor Party some support, was responsible for its ultimate defeat in the coming ideological struggle.

The Minor Party was led by two country Brethren, Jakub the Miller and a tradesman named Amos. Its supporters were drawn mainly from the village congregations, or from the older generation who clung to the tenets made familiar by the teachings of the fathers of the Unity, or from the poorest members in the towns. These were all men who retained something of the uncompromising thirst for righteousness unsullied by contact with the world which had characterized the Brethren's way of life during the first few decades of the Unity's existence. Jakub and Amos also had allies within the Narrow Council; Bishop Matěj himself sympathized to a large extent with their position, although eventually, after much heart-searching and no little prevarication, he chose the side of the Major Party. Geographically, the Minor Party's following was scattered throughout the congregations. But the rigorists were especially strong in south Bohemia, the country of the Waldenses and of Chelčický and the Taborites, whose inhabitants, therefore, were familiar with the traditions of the radical wing of Hussitism. Both Jakub and Amos themselves came from this area, which remained their stronghold throughout.

During the first half of the 1490's the struggle for ascendancy between the two parties swayed backward and forward. First the rigorists, supported at this point by Bishop Matěj, succeeded in ousting the antirigorists from the Narrow Council and replacing them by "the good old Brethren," who thereupon proceeded to re-enact the earlier unconditional ban on participation in administration and war. However, throughout the three years during which the Old Brethren were able to maintain their renewed control over the Unity the Narrow Council found itself continually subjected to requests from the town congregations for advice. These wanted to know, above all, how to react to the frequent official attempts to press their members into office. Fines, imprisonment, and even torture were the lot of those who resisted. The situation became so acute that finally Matěj, under mounting pressure from the antirigorists, agreed to summon another general assembly of the Unity, which was held at Rýchnov in May 1494. And now at Rýchnov the Old Brethren were, in their turn, ousted and the edict passed at Brandýs four years earlier was reenacted. Shortly afterwards the leaders of the Major Party, henceforward in firm control of the Narrow Council, succeeded in removing the vacillating Matěj from all but a merely formal headship of the Unity, which he retained until his death in 1500.

The fury of Jakub and Amos at this reversal of fortune knew no bounds. Jakub wrote:

> Now the Brethren say: Let us, therefore, open the gates of the fold in order to gather in more sheep. And when they have opened up the fold, the sheep that are already there run out and the wolves tear them to pieces. . . . The gates are God's commandments and the prohibition of Christ the strait path and the narrow doorway. And whoever broadens these . . . saying that a Brother may become an alderman and a judge, and take oaths, and exercise the bloody rights of the sword, is like unto a rogue and a thief who comes not in by the door.

The two men began to campaign actively against the new leadership, rejecting scornfully the latter's contention that it was ready to tolerate within the Unity the rigorist viewpoint alongside its own relaxed sociopolitical ethic—provided the Minor Party granted its opponents a similar freedom. But such latitudinarianism was anathema to Jakub and Amos; therefore, despite a number of attempts at reconciliation, the split between the parties became permanent. Disciplinary action was eventually taken against the leaders of the Minor Party, who continued nonetheless to defend their own orthodoxy and the right of their group to be considered the true Unity. The schism was complete by the beginning of the new century.

In 1494 another gathering had been held at Rýchnov toward the end of the year. At this second meeting, to which only the leading pastors were invited, a momentous decision was taken. The writings of Chelčický as well as of Řehoř were declared as no longer enjoying authority within the Unity, for these authors, it was stated, took up an "immoderately lofty" position toward the world.

Henceforward, according to a contemporary statement by Brother Lukáš, who was soon to emerge as the most capable and most thoroughgoing among the leaders of the Major Party, "the civil power with its laws and punishments can be allowed in our Unity and in the holy church. A lord owning estates, castles, fortresses, and towns may be accepted into our Unity without having to relinquish the sword, and may become a Brother while he continues to order punishments and executions." And indeed we hear now of Unity congregations engaging actively in law enforcement as well as participating in armed conflicts between rival agencies of the law (to the scandal of those Brethren who still clung to the old ways).

It was possible, Lukáš argued, to hang or maim a man and still retain love for him in one's heart. The Minor Party were wrong, therefore, in identifying the wielding of civil power, of temporal authority, with unconditional acceptance of worldly values. Yet in the course of the first quarter of the sixteenth century, the Unity which Lukáš was to direct until his death in 1528 became something very different from the otherworldly and separated sect of the previous half-century, although it might still retain much of its puritan ethos and even of its suspicion of the political realm. This transformation was a matter of internal restructuring, already accomplished before first Lutheranism and then Calvinism made their impact on the theology of the Brethren. The new sociopolitical ideology came into effect gradually, cautiously, piecemeal, hedged at first with innumerable reservations which slowly, however, fell into desuetude. Lukáš and his nearest associates like Brother Vavřinec Krasonický, who was also a university graduate, were the moving spirits behind the promulgation from 1497 onward of a long series of decrees either by the Narrow Council or at general assemblies of the church, by means of which the new approach to society was codified. The legalism with which the rigorist ethic had been enforced under the Old Brethren was continued and adapted to the broader outlook of the new Unity. As Lukáš wrote in 1523, the Brethren now possessed "full instructions for all classes and ranks, for all trades and professions and all walks of life . . . and each, according to his ability, should order his life by them."

The obligation of charity continued to be incumbent on the rich: but henceforward there was an increasing proportion of well-to-do members within the church and the renunciation of landed property which entailed exercising jurisdiction over the tenantry was no longer a requirement of membership. A Puritan morality still prevailed, yet distinctions in rank were permissible, as was the outward display associated with noble status. The life of the husbandman remained the Brethren's ideal: increasingly, however, prosperous townsmen, scholars, and gentlemen came to prevail in the counsels of the Unity, even though they were adjured always to remember the spiritual equality of all in the eyes of God. Thus the holding of fellow creatures in a condition of serfdom was no longer regarded as a sin, provided man's basic equality was recognized, and provided, too, that the lord's subjects were not overburdened with services and dues and were humanely treated in other respects. Pastors were still required, as at the beginning, to earn a living by the labor of their hands; this rule, however, eventually became a formality and, instead, a learned clergy became the pattern, adding luster to the Unity's name by its varied contribution to Czech culture and culminating in the work of Comenius in the seventeenth century. If, like Luther, the Brethren retained, at any rate for a time, a belief in nonresistance insofar as personal relations were concerned and, like the Catholic church, regarded the path of nonviolence as at least a counsel of perfection (but with no greater validity than a mere counsel possessed), they also saw no inconsistency either in resorting to courts of law, or in participation in the magistracy and other organs of law enforcement, or in bearing arms at the behest of duly constituted authorities. True, their leaders continued to apprise the Brethren of the dangers that lurked in such activities and to warn them against voluntarily entering upon them if necessity or their station in life did not require it. They must ever seek righteousness as the goal of their endeavors; they must exercise mercy and shun all unnecessary cruelty and, where the execution of the law was concerned, must attempt to match the punishment with the gravity of the crime. But henceforward neither litigation, nor the taking of judicial oaths, nor the infliction of the death penalty or of mutilation, nor service in war or with weapons for the maintenance of civil order were to be considered as wrong in themselves.

The Unity's revised position in respect to military service was crystallized in a decree issued early in the sixteenth century. It did not mark an unconditional break with pacifism even if its effect was to put an end to the incidence of conscientious objection among members of the Major Party of the Unity. The decree begins by advising Brethren to avoid military service wherever possible, suggesting such means of escape as the hiring of a substitute. Voluntary enrollment was strictly forbidden, even in a just war where a country was the victim of an unprovoked attack and therefore might be considered as fighting in self-defense. (The decree, however, assumes that the motive of any Brethren who volunteered must lie in desire either for gain or for glory; the obligation of personal nonresistance was then still regarded as incumbent on them in the case of a direct assault, even by an enemy.) Yet if no escape from service in the army appeared possible—apart, that is, from suffering the penalties of refusal, an alternative that, significantly, the decree does not even consider—conscripted Brethren should seek assignment to noncombatant duties "wherever it would be suitable for them, by the wagons or in other services, or at home where they might stand guard in the castle or carry out other duties." If, however, they failed to persuade the military authorities to allow them tasks of this kind and they were compelled to take an active part in the fighting, then, the decree instructed, they should at least "avoid pushing themselves forward as well as the acquisition of glory through bravery, since excessive bravery as well as cruelty and looting and booty and avaricious desires and other unrighteousness must be shunned. They should not proceed willingly to [battle] but only under compulsion with the wish to be free. . . . They were to beseech God to deliver them from evil, for in war many evils come to pass."

The new Unity still regarded war as intrinsically sinful; it was "contrary to the natural, Jewish, and Christian laws." But in answer to the question, who must bear the guilt for killing in war, an advice—undated, but issued not long after the schism took place—put this guilt squarely on the shoulders of the ruler who had started the war. "Whoever starts a war and compels the people to it, is primarily responsible for whatever evil may result . . . , and not the subject people, who merely obey." Less moral harm flowed from war waged "against the infidel Turks" than from war between Christian states. Of all types of war the worst was civil war, waged "against men of the same language." (We may recall here that in Bohemia after Hus's death internecine warfare had been endemic up into the early years of the then reigning monarch Vladislav.) Thus, under the Unity's new dispensation, wherever the fault might lie between the rulers engaged in a war, the ordinary conscripted Brother might rest assured that he was acting in conformity with his religious profession if, after having made every effort to escape service, he were forced to take part even in actual combat. Little, if any, blame attached to "those who being under compulsion cannot escape, yet have no thought of murder . . . nor of any unrighteousness."

At first, at any rate, the new Unity displayed some of its earlier social radicalism in the way it urged rulers to spare the common people the burden of military conscription and recruit soldiers solely from mercenaries (a profession of course still strictly forbidden for a Unity member). In 1502, at a time when there was growing danger of a Turkish invasion and the country was being put into a state of military preparedness, a leading protagonist of the Major Party, Brother Tůma Přeloučský, denounced the authorities for imposing military conscription on the people instead of recruiting soldiers on a voluntary basis as was customary; he urged, too, that the upper classes should shoulder the financial burden of defense themselves and not attempt to extract the necessary funds from the poor by means of special war taxation. Yet we should note that Brother Tůma was not arguing from a pacifist position; he acknowledged (in his *Spis o původu Jednoty bratrské a o chudých lidech*) that if ever a war were justified it was the present one against the Turks.

We should now take a brief look at the basic arguments with which the transition from uncompromising rejection of the state and of war to their cautious approval were justified. It is chiefly on the writings of Lukáš and Krasonický, both those published in their lifetime and their tracts which remained in manuscript, that we must draw for a reasoned apologia of the new position.

In essence, the whole dispute revolved around the question whether indeed Christ had replaced the Old Testament—the Law and the Prophets—by a higher righteousness. Chelčický's contention and that of the Old Brethren and the Minor Party was that he had. As one of the latter, Matouš the Weaver, told Krasonický: "What have we to do with the Jews? We have the New, not the Old Testament." Krasonický, on the other hand, argued that while Christ in the Sermon on the Mount had indeed taught a moral code superior to that of the contemporary scribes and pharisees, it was their corruption of the older teaching which he attacked and not the original law. In one of his polemical treatises against the Minor Party, Krasonický wrote:

> Therefore . . . He is not the creator of new commandments, but refers back to the old . . . in their purity . . . Christ never said or intended that another Christian righteousness be contained in these injunctions [of the Sermon on the Mount]. . . . He never meant that Christian righteousness should be higher than the Jewish in these moral commandments, which are ever pure in themselves, for the will of God is eternal . . . Christ never created any new commandments beside or above the old.

Christ, Krasonický added, came to fulfil and not to destroy the Law and the Prophets, even though he tempered these with mercy and love.

The Major Party considered the early Brethren's *Weltanschauung* to be perfectionism (a perfectionism in fact unwarranted by Scripture). For in this world even the community of believers would never succeed in maintaining the high standards of ethical conduct Řehoř and his associates had demanded. Instead, thought Krasonický, the Brethren would be doing satisfactorily "if they continue not to give way to open wickedness . . . without repentance." On the other hand the Minor Party, we have seen, were far from distressed at the thought that observance of the "higher righteousness" would limit the Unity in numbers and influence; for them, it was this very rejection by the world that marked the chosen few as the true church.

The Major Party dismissed as false logic their opponents' contention that although the sword was essential to curb the wickedness of the ungodly, a follower of Christ was forbidden to wield it. Lukáš branded the rigorist position as an evasion of responsibility. Why, he asked of the Minor Party, did they accept the benefits of civil society in a Christian commonwealth instead of settling among pagans whom alone they considered to be justified in carrying the magistrate's sword. In his view condemnation of a Christian magistracy was hypocrisy. He wrote:

> Since evil and unrighteousness must, according to the scriptures, inevitably go on increasing in Christendom until the end of the world, God has raised some men above others . . . in order to put down evil. The reason for His doing this has not grown less. He has not . . . abolished power by the Law of Love, so that it should not be exercised over evildoers and the turbulent; nor has He now made it a sin and unrighteous because of the promulgation of this Law.

True, the state should never intervene in religious affairs (the separation of church and state was to remain a firm principle among the Brethren); civil authority must be duly constituted and it could indeed be passively resisted should its actions contravene divine law; governors ought to seek their subjects' welfare, acting in a fatherly capacity toward them. But the magistracy was not basically an unchristian institution, even if the sword belonged among the essentials of office. It was only the misuse of the magistrate's office, which Christ had condemned.

To love one's enemies, Lukáš agreed, was truly the obligation of a Christian. On the other hand, "those who take the part of wrongdoers," he wrote scornfully in reference to Chelčický, Řehoř, and the Minor Party, "urging that these should be loved, do not show love for peaceable folk or for widows and orphans." It was one thing to love our personal enemies and to forgive those who do evil against us; it was quite a different matter, and in no way contrary to the Law of Love, when in the course of their official duties men set in authority protected the innocent by punishing criminals, even with death, or by driving out invaders by force. Forgiveness of injuries, in fact, was possible—indeed, mandatory—in the case of the individual Christian. But justice, tempered of course with mercy where extenuating circumstances existed, and not forgiveness, of evildoing was the conduct befitting the Christian magistrate. "To kill and destroy" those who acted contrary to God's righteousness was not inconsistent, Lukáš argued, with Christian love, provided the power of the sword were exercised "justly and without hatred."

It was Lukáš who attempted a new exegesis of the Fifth Commandment. He had heard the words "Thou shalt not kill" continually in the mouths of the spokesmen of the opposing party, who considered them to constitute an absolute prohibition of all forms of homicide. Lukáš, on the other hand, understood that commandment as being directed simply against any "who spilt human blood without proper authority and contrary to God's law and justice," and not against the magistrate who ordered the execution of a malefactor, or against a soldier fighting in a just war, or against a person attacked who should kill his assailant in self-defense. Christ had not attempted to obliterate the distinction between "murder" and "legitimate killing."

The injunction "Resist not evil" in the Sermon on the Mount seems to have presented no more difficulty to Lukáš than the words of the decalogue had done. He saw it simply as an attempt on Christ's part to counteract overemphasis by the Jews on retribution for wrong committed. The words meant no more than that his followers should not "resist evil from anger, from an inordinate desire for revenge . . . , without judgment by those placed in authority and without pity or mercy." He denied that they constituted an attack on the civil power among Christians provided that it acted "not from [a desire for] vengeance, but in order to bring about peace or due reformation" of the wrongdoer.

In fact, the Major Party argued, the individual Christian, although obligated to act nonviolently where recourse could be had to the protection of the law, might carry some sort of weapon for use in self-defense in circumstances where the law was unable to provide protection for person or for property (a position which appears to be a watering down of the personal nonresistance still mandatory for the Brethren in the period immediately following the schism of the 1490's). If such were the case, Lukáš wrote, then "I cannot properly regard it as wrong to go about with daggers," though characteristically he adds the proviso that nothing be done to lead persons of a fiery disposition into the commission of bloodthirsty deeds. "There is need of moderation in this matter."

Under Lukáš's tutelage Chelčický was now replaced in the affections of the Brethren by the military hero Žižka. "No one," wrote Lukáš, "should conduct himself according to [Chelčický's] writings, for he . . .

53

was not under the rule of salvation." Lukáš's victory over his adversaries within the Unity represented a defeat of the ideals for which Chelčický had stood. With the slow withering away of the Minor Party Chelčický's works gradually fell into oblivion, and even the memory of the pacifism of the early Unity grew dim and eventually faded away altogether.

The fate of the Minor Party after it separated from the majority requires only brief treatment here. Whereas Jakub the Miller soon abandoned his colleague Amos to return for a time to the main branch of the Unity, Amos persevered to the end. The exact date of his death in the early 1520's is not known. By this time the Amosites, as Minor Party supporters were often called, had dwindled into a small and insignificant group; no Unity pastor, indeed no Brethren of education, had joined it. In Prague the sect underwent a brief revival in the mid-1520's as a result of the energy of Amos's successor, Jan Kalenec, a cutler by trade and a convert to the Minor Party from official Utraquism. However, within several years of their leader's expulsion from the capital at the end of 1524 the Prague congregation was suppressed. Kalenec seemingly made his way from Prague to Moravia: at least, we find him settled at Letovice in that province some fifteen years later with a small circle of adherents gathered around him. The group used the Unity name, claiming succession through the Amosites. Kalenec, like Amos before him, carried on a fierce paper war with the apologists of the Major Party. Both men ardently espoused the social radicalism and the pacifism and antistate position of the Old Brethren (to which Kalenec in his Moravian period added antitrinitarian views). But their writings display no new theoretical insights.

We may note here the Minor Party's practice of carrying a wooden staff in place of the customary weapon, remarked on in a tract against Kalenec composed by Brother Lukáš in 1523: "I greatly disapprove," wrote the leader of the Major Party, "of these vain pharisees wandering around with staffs, who display their righteousness, angrily and poisonously condemning other people and upsetting men's minds." It is just possible (although we possess no positive evidence for this) that it was from the Minor Party of the Czech Brethren that the Hutterites, communistic Anabaptist *émigrés* from German-speaking lands who were settled from the late 1520's in Moravia, derived this symbolic expression of their pacifist way of life. And it was from the Hutterites, as we shall see, that the Polish Antitrinitarian, Piotr of Goniądz (Gonesius), in 1555 brought the custom back to his future coreligionists in Poland.

The last remnant of the Minor Party, Kalenec's group at Letovice, disappeared at some unknown date before mid-century. Long before, contact had been severed with the Unity proper; Kalenec seems to have exercised no attractive influence on its members, despite the fact that his views reflected those of the founding fathers of the Unity. He and his group were indeed in touch with their neighbors, the Moravian Anabaptists, who were split into several competing factions, of which the Hutterites were numerically the strongest and intellectually the most significant; yet apart from the doubtful instance cited above of the carrying of wooden staffs it was rather the German sectaries who influenced Kalenec than the other way around. Kalenec eventually adopted adult baptism as well as community of goods within his congregation: nonresistance and rejection of the state, on the other hand, were tenets already held by many of the Anabaptist exiles before they left their native land and are not likely, therefore, to have been derived from the Czech Minor Party.

Kalenec's Brethren, however, did succeed in finding a convert for their sociopolitical ideology in the founder of an indigenous Moravian sect, a small nobleman named Jan Dubčanský. His followers, all Czechs, were usually known as Habrovany Brethren: from its beginnings in 1528 the sect remained confined to the area around his estates at Habrovany and Lilcč. Dubčanský, an amateur theologian reared in the Utraquist church, had derived his theology from the Swiss reformer Zwingli, whose sacramentarianism was somewhat alien to the main Hussite tradition. Contacts with Kalenec as well as independent study of the writings of Chelčický and the early Unity led the Habrovany Brethren to adopt nonresistance and to reject the state as unchristian, at least in theory. For there is some unclarity concerning the exact views of Dubčanský and his associates on the subject, and even more concerning their practical implementation. Whereas in statements issuing from the group we find acceptance of the Minor Party's interpretation of the "higher righteousness" as involving a ban on killing, violence against a fellow human being, and the taking of oath or office, Dubčanský himself did not renounce his estates or even the patrimonial jurisdiction associated with landownership, and the sect's opponents even accused its members of warlike activities and of an ambivalent attitude toward office and litigation. We do not know to what extent accusations of this sort tallied with reality or whether they did not stem from malice or gossip. One of the difficulties here lies in the fact that the group issued no systematic exposition of its doctrines. We may conclude perhaps that among both the leaders and the rank-and-file members there existed differing opinions concerning the binding character of the rigorist ethical theory.

The Habrovany Brethren declined rapidly after the death of their founder and patron Dubčanský in 1543; indeed, the sect began to disintegrate when in 1538 Dubčanský was arrested and held in prison for some years on account of his theological radicalism. The last trace of its continued existence occurs in 1558. With the expiry of both the Minor Party and the Habrovany Brethren, pacifism ceases to be represented among the Czech-speaking population of Bohemia and Moravia (it was not represented at all in the Polish branch of the Unity whose origins went back to the year 1547). During the first half of the sixteenth century the major Unity approximated its views on society to those held by the rest of the community, whether Protestant or Catholic. "Prosperous capitalists, . . . skilled tradesmen, . . . decorous burgomasters and jurors, . . . capable generals and statesmen"—these, as Anton Gindely pointed out in his classic history of the Czech Brethren, were the kind of people who increasingly gave tone and character to the new Unity, along with the highly educated pastorate which guided its spiritual life.

In regard to participation in war, as in other areas of social behavior, the restrictions and reservations which the Unity leaders had imposed even after their rejection of the old rigorism eventually fell away. By the 1530's it is clear that Brethren were entering military service. Although it is not certain whether at this date voluntary acceptance of the military life was approved, yet this too was to come in the course of time. Lukáš's successor as head of the Unity, Jan Roh, in 1530 published a volume written specially for Brethren serving in the wars against the Turks. To respond to a call to such service, Roh writes, was a thing to be commended in a Christian, for the Turks were a cruel and bloodthirsty people, more like wild beasts than men, whom it was right to drive out by force if they attacked Christendom. On the whole, war does not figure as a primary concern of the Unity during this period. In 1559, however, a conference of elders dealt briefly with the issue along with a number of other subjects considered of equal or greater importance. The Brethren were simply told: "If they are called up for the militia, they should conduct themselves in all things obediently, submissively, and humbly . . . so that they be not reckoned as traitors or as Anabaptists who say: 'I don't know; let this Turk come if he must, etc.'" If the last section of this passage conceals (as the wording might imply) the existence among Unity members of those who sympathized with the Anabaptist nonresistance which had once, some six decades earlier, been officially professed by the Unity as a whole, there is no confirmatory evidence elsewhere in the sources.

The Brethren were to occupy a leading position in the political struggle for religious freedom in Bohemia in the later decades of the sixteenth, and in the early decades of the seventeenth, centuries. We find them taking up arms against the Habsburg monarch in 1620, and for their participation in the war against Ferdinand II Unity nobles suffered on the scaffold after the defeat of the Bohemian Protestant cause at the battle of the White Mountain. When during the subsequent decade Protestantism was suppressed along with the autonomous status of the Bohemian kingdom, the Czech Brethren suffered the same fate as their fellow Protestants. Unity members either went into exile or were forcibly converted to Catholicism. Although a "hidden seed" of Protestant faith remained buried in the soil of these lands and early in the eighteenth century German-speaking Brethren of the Unity's Moravian branch crossed the frontier into Saxony where they were instrumental with Count von Zinzendorf in founding the Moravian Church, the free exercise of a non-Catholic form of worship was not again permitted in the Czech lands until the enlightened absolutist Joseph II's patent of toleration in 1781.

The central issue in the controversies which raged between the Major and Minor Parties in the Unity around the turn of the fifteenth century had been not pacifism as such, but the wider problem of the sword-bearing magistracy. Even the question of the oath loomed larger than that of war. Yet each of these separate components formed an integral part of a tightly fitting whole: a philosophy of nonretaliation based on total rejection of a social order which was founded, in the view of the Old Brethren and their forerunners, on violence and oppression. If one element of this complex were removed, the whole ethos tended to disintegrate rapidly. The intellectual system was too rigid to allow of adaptation when new circumstances arose. Thus a social ethic framed to fit a rural sect whose typical member was a semi-literate villager with horizons extending not much further than the district boundaries proved inapplicable when Brethren came to settle in increasing numbers in the towns and when the educated and the well-born elements began to demand a greater say in the affairs of the Unity. The country Brethren of the first phase of Unity history before 1490 had been more willing to suffer the disadvantages of separation from the world than were their successors, because separation made sense to them; for the urban Brethren and the learned young theologians who formed the core of the Major Party at its inception in the 1490's, the sect's social ethos appeared antiquated. Moreover, the penalties which resulted now from its observance were considerably greater than hitherto. In the refurbishing of the Unity's sociopolitical ethics carried out by Lukáš and the other leaders of the Major Party, pacifism was discarded along with other elements of the old ideology which were hostile to state and society. The simple and literalist leaders of the Minor Party, however, did not possess sufficient flexibility to evolve a new rationale for nonviolence that would possess meaning for the rising generation. Therefore their following dwindled and finally disappeared.

TWO. *The Early Anabaptists*

SWITZERLAND was the birthplace of Anabaptism. The movement arose in the early 1520's in the German-speaking city of Zürich as an extension of the Reformation introduced there by the city's leading preacher Ulrich Zwingli. Obvious parallels between the Anabaptists and the Unity of Czech Brethren in regard to both theology and *Weltanschauung* have given rise to theories concerning a genetic influence of the Czech Brethren on the Anabaptists. This hypothesis was put forward, for instance, in the late nineteenth century by the German scholar Ludwig Keller. Yet despite its seeming plausibility, no substantial evidence has so far been adduced in its support. It would seem more reasonable, therefore, to seek the genesis of Anabaptist nonresistance (*Wehrlosigkeit*), of the Anabaptist doctrine of the sword, in insights gained through immediate contact with the New Testament sources as well as in the direct influence of the early Anabaptists' intellectual, spiritual, and social environment. And the same holds for the whole theological and sociopolitical outlook of these Swiss Brethren from whom later Anabaptists, as well as the Mennonites, have derived their spiritual heritage.

The Protestant Reformation began in Zürich in 1519 and its goal had been virtually achieved by early 1524. Among Zwingli's most enthusiastic associates in the early work of reform was a group of young men of education headed by a local patrician's son, Conrad Grebel. Eventually, however, Grebel and his friends became disillusioned with Zwingli when they realized that he was not prepared to go as far as they were in restoring primitive Christianity. What Zwingli sought was church reform, with the *jus reformandi* in the hands of a godly magistracy. What Grebel's group desired was a complete restitution of the apostolic church. The views of Zwingli and Grebel began to diverge during the months following the Disputation of October 1523. Grebel then hoped, vainly as it proved, that the Zürich city council might be so reconstructed as to approve a really radical change in the city's ecclesiastical order, whereas Zwingli adopted a more accommodating attitude toward the city fathers' tardiness in promoting the work of reform. From coolness relations between the two groups finally developed into fierce hostility, and an open break took place in the autumn of 1524. With their institution of adult, i.e., believer's, baptism beginning in January 1525, the Swiss Brethren separated from their fellow Protestants. Although they repudiated the designation Anabaptist (*Wiedertaüfer*, rebaptizer), for they denied the validity of infant baptism altogether, this was the name that soon became affixed to their movement.

Nonresistance had preceded adult baptism as an element in the Grebel circle's restitutionism. The first clear statement of nonresistance occurs in a letter written by Grebel in the name of his group to Thomas Müntzer, the German revolutionary leader (who should not be considered an Anabaptist any more than should other contemporary religious radicals like Carlstadt or the Zwickau prophets, despite eminent opinion to the contrary). The letter is dated 5 September 1524 and the relevant portions, which I quote from G. H. Williams's revision of Walter Rauschenbusch's translation done in 1905, run as follows:

> The gospel and its adherents are not to be protected by the sword, nor are they thus to protect themselves, which as we learn . . . is thy opinion and practice. [Grebel was of course mistaken on this point.] True Christian believers are sheep among wolves, sheep for the slaughter; they must be baptized in anguish and affliction, tribulation, persecution, suffering, and death; they must be tried with fire, and must reach the fatherland of eternal rest, not by killing their bodily, but by mortifying their spiritual, enemies. Neither do they use worldly sword or war, since all killing has ceased with them—unless, indeed, we would still be of the old law. And even there [i.e., in Old Testament times], so far as we recall, war was a misfortune after they had once reconquered the promised land.

A few days later Grebel, having meanwhile been told that his belief in Müntzer's nonviolence was mistaken, penned another letter asking if it were indeed true that the letter defended war and other practices not to be found "in express words" of Scripture. And he admonished Müntzer "by the common salvation of us all" to "cease from all notions of thy own now and hereafter," trusting instead in Christ and his holy word to strengthen him in his sufferings if he should fall into the hands of his enemies, and not at all in the protection of the sword.

Thus, in his letter Grebel formulates nonresistance in terms not only of nonretaliation in regard to religious persecution or social oppression (a view, incidentally, shared by Luther and many of the other magisterial reformers), but of refusal to participate in the sword-bearing magistracy and war, which was then a novel concept among Protestant reformers. Whence did Grebel and his friends derive such ideas, which were to become typical of what some scholars have called "evangelical" Anabaptism?

Biblical humanism appears as an important agent in the formation of early Anabaptist nonresistance. Though they approach their subject from very different viewpoints, Grebel's biographer, the Mennonite Harold S. Bender, and James M. Stayer, author of a recent monographic study on early Anabaptism's doctrine of the sword, agree that Erasmian pacificism probably exercised a strong influence on Grebel and his circle, the members of which were all enthusiasts for humanistic learning. Zwingli himself, despite his end on the battlefield at Cappel in 1531, had expressed antiwar views early in his career; his antimilitarism reflected humanist dislike of war as well as patriotic revulsion against the current use of Swiss mercenaries by foreign states. It was probably as much from their still greatly admired leader as from the writings of Erasmus and other antiwar humanists that the young radicals in Zwingli's entourage derived their first lessons on the unchristian character of warfare.

In August 1520 we find Grebel, then in his early twenties, writing to the eminent Swiss humanist scholar, Vadian: "I have read . . . [Oswald] Myconius' dialogue—'Philirenus'—against waging war, which is worthy of publication on account of its truth." Two years later another of Grebel's circle, the bookseller Andreas Castelberger, gave a course of lectures to Zürich townsmen, in which he discussed what he considered the most important topics raised by a study of the Bible. Of his views on war a contemporary reported:

> Andreas said much about war; how the divine teaching is so strong against it and how it is sin; and he expressed the idea that the soldier who had plenty at home in his fatherly inheritance and goods and yet went to war, and received money and pay to kill innocent persons and to take their possessions from people who had never done him any harm, such a soldier was before Almighty God, and according to the content of Gospel teaching, a murderer and not better than one who would murder and steal on account of his poverty, regardless of the fact that this might not be so according to human law, and might not be counted so bad.

Although Castelberger calls war in general "sin," his remarks are directed against the immorality of mercenary soldiering rather than against the inadmissibility of carnal warfare in any form (that is, presuming we have a complete and accurate record of what Castelberger did in fact say on this point). Between the humanitarian antimilitarism of the Erasmians, which Zwingli had shared with his more radical followers, and the Bible-centered nonresistance which eventually emerged among the latter, there is an essential difference. The one emphasized the cruelty and absurdity of war and looked forward to peace on earth through the awakening of good-will among Christian men; the other expected to endure suffering and scorn from a nominally Christian world on account of unwillingness to resist evil by violent means.

Stayer, among others, has explained the transition by reference to "disillusioment" engendered in Grebel and his friends by their realization, after the Disputation of October 1523, that restitutionism could not be effected by means of "a truly Christian council," as they had at first hoped. This marked the beginnings of their pacifist absolutism. "Grebel's religious wisdom lay in his pessimism," writes Stayer, for he saw that the "Anabaptist vision" would not prevail against the church-state establishment and that it could preserve its purity only among a small persecuted remnant separated from a corrupt world. It was a conclusion in which he and his associates were confirmed as they went back and sought guidance in the New Testament. This interpretation is certainly plausible, though it remains a conjecture and, in view of the lack of more definitive evidence, would seem to need some qualification before being acceptable as at least a working hypothesis.

There can be no doubt concerning the New Testament inspiration of the whole ideology of the Swiss Brethren, including their views on war and the magistracy. That in the early 1520's they entertained hopes of establishing a "church of the restitution" (to use Franklin H. Littell's definition) through a decision of a converted city council is also indicated by the sources. Yet it is far from clear that these hopes presupposed approval of a sword-bearing magistracy after a church restitution had taken place. There is little, if anything, to indicate that, as some writers have implied, if Grebel's aspirations in 1523 had been fulfilled, Zürich would have become, as it were, a premature Anabaptist Münster, thereby making his earlier pacifistic views into a "proto-revolutionary" pacifism akin to that of the chiliastic Taborite preachers of Bohemia in 1419. What does seem likely is that the shattering of vague dreams of making Zürich a holy—and peaceable—city by the conversion of its people and rulers to the primitive faith led Grebel and his friends to re-examine and to reformulate in more exact terms the principles on which they had based their faith hitherto. What emerged from this fresh return to the New Testament sources was the doctrine of nonresistance as first enunciated in Grebel's letter to Müntzer.

Nonresistance for the Swiss Brethren (with a few exceptions to be discussed below) was an integral part of a composite whole. It cannot be understood in isolation from the other major elements which made up their total *Weltanschauung*. Before moving on to discuss the development of Anabaptist nonresistance among both the German-speaking Swiss (Swiss Anabaptism did not spread to either the country's French- or Italian-speakers) and the closely connected southern Germans during the decade following 1525, we must first survey briefly the "Anabaptist vision" which upheld these men and women in face of a hostile state, society, and church.

At the center of this vision stands the principle of *sola scriptura*. Every act, every institution, derived its validity solely from its consonance with the scriptural teachings. This belief the Anabaptists held with even greater intensity and with a more insistent rigorism than did the magisterial reformers. Like the other reformers the Anabaptist brethren foresaw no possibility of ambiguity in interpreting scripture: it would always speak to the Christian believer plainly and meaningfully. Only what passed the scriptural test received their approval. They were Biblical literalists, yet not unconditionally so. For like the Czech Brethren before them they recognized a distinction between the Old and the New Testaments, giving priority to the latter as the purest expression of God's word. The Old Testament constituted a mere foreshadowing of the New Testament introduced by Christ's covenant with those who chose to follow him. "In Anabaptist writings *Testament*, covenant, and law are synonymous terms," writes Clarence Bauman. Henceforward, therefore, God's word, as it was reflected in Christ's new dispensation of love which had replaced the Mosaic commandments, must be as a law to men who wished to attain eternal salvation; this divine code, and not man-made rules, provided the touchstone by which human actions should be judged. But it was a law which sought to love and convert the evildoer and the enemy and not to punish him, which maintained good order by the ban and not the scaffold, and which called its subjects to suffer rather than to avenge and kill. This law, as a leading Anabaptist (Pilgram Marbeck) put it, was "not a carnal law of ruling, or worldly, earthly judicial procedures as that of yesterday, but . . . a law or commandment of the Spirit—love and patience—which God yesterday promised and today for the first time wrote in [our] hearts." It was exemplified not only in the Sermon on the Mount but in the whole Gospel.

The contrast, which the Anabaptists asserted between the perfection of Christ's revelation in the New Testament and the imperfect revelation the books of the Old Testament embodied, remained a constant source of disagreement between the Anabaptists and the magisterial reformers; the two views are reflected in the series of formal disputations which took place between the two parties at intervals throughout the sixteenth century, and the matter formed one of the chief points at issue at these gatherings. The two sides differed, too, in regard to other aspects of the Anabaptist vision. Rejecting the Lutheran concept of justification by faith as well as the predestinarianism developed a little later by Calvin, the Anabaptists placed a simple discipleship as the quintessential element of Christian practice. Christians, in their view, must be *Nachfolger Christi* if they were to remain worthy of their calling. This concept perhaps resembles the Catholic doctrine of justification by works, if we divest the latter of its ecclesiastical encumbrances. Two characteristics distinguish the disciple of Christ: first, love which manifests itself in meekness and humility, patience and peace, mercy and compassion; and a willingness to bear the Master's cross in suffering and even martyrdom. Love and suffering form the two great themes of Anabaptist hymnology; they are both reflected in Anabaptist literature.

Discipleship, although it sprang from the conscience of each individual, was for the Anabaptists essentially a social product. It could not be divorced from the holy community (*Gemeinde*), the brotherhood of those who sought to obey Christ's law of love and share the sufferings of their fellow members as their own. Entry into the brotherhood was by baptism on confession of faith. There could be no birthright members, for discipleship was the result solely of mature choice. Within the brotherhood only the ban and never the sword (the two instruments were mutually exclusive, in the Anabaptist's view) might be used against those who had transgressed the law of Christ; its use was conditioned by desire not to punish the erring brother but to lead him back into the ways of righteousness. "While God instituted the sword in the Old Testament that is altered since Christ gave us the ban and instituted it for that purpose," one of the Swiss Brethren declared at a disputation held in Bern in 1531. Anabaptists often supported their position in regard to the sword by referring to the parable of the wheat and the tares. The exercise of wrath remained God's prerogative; He had called men to follow the path of peace.

Bauman has called attention to the ethical dualism contained in the Anabaptist concept of community. The holy brotherhood is placed in contrast to the world of pagans and paganized Christians. "Brotherhood" and "world" form two physically contiguous yet morally exclusive realms. The brotherhood must withdraw from the world, at least in spirit, and live separated from it through exact obedience to the higher righteousness of Christ and nonconformity to the norms of secular society. The ethical dualism of the Anabaptists to some extent paralleled, though it was by no means identical with, the ethical dualism of the medieval Catholic church which posited a higher monastic ideal over against that of lay society. But whereas with Catholicism both levels of moral conduct enjoyed the church's approval, Anabaptism refused to acknowledge a double standard in the case of those who professed to be Christians, allowing conditional justification of a lower righteousness only in the case of non-Christians or those whose Christianity, in their view, was no more than nominal. For true Christians the Law of Love was absolute; it permitted neither utilitarian considerations nor regard for consequences to modify the full stringency of its demands.

Indeed, willingness to bear the cross, to suffer persecution for righteousness' sake, was the hallmark of the holy community, as it was of individual disciples of Christ. Suffering and persecution would be its inevitable fate until the end of time, for Anabaptists held out no hope of redeeming the world as a whole apart from a handful of individuals within it. False Christians were unprepared to endure suffering, and it was suffering which since apostolic times had distinguished the true from the false church. The theologian Ethelbert Stauffer has spoken of an Anabaptist "theology of martyrdom," shared not merely by the nonresistant majority but by nonpacifist Anabaptists like Hubmaier. Whereas it seems not entirely appropriate to use the term "theology" in reference to the extremely practical Anabaptist religious ethic, Stauffer was right in pointing to the important role which the idea of suffering played in the Anabaptist vision. It was readiness to suffer, even unto death, which called for "defenselessness (*Wehrlosigkeit*)" in face of the persecutors and provided the justification for the nonresistant stance. A church whose Christ-given task it was to endure persecution rather than resist evil could not wield the magistrate's sword or don the soldier's dress: "For the weapons of our warfare are not carnal" (II Cor. 10:4). The true church would conquer through love and nonresistant suffering.

Beginning in 1525 a long series of mandates was directed by the authorities against the Anabaptists in all the lands to which their faith had spread. Over two hundred such decrees are recorded down to the end of the eighteenth century. In 1529 the Emperor Charles V had persuaded the Diet of Speyer to re-enact the ancient Roman imperial edict against the heretical Donatists, which made death the penalty for rebaptism. Although the question not so much of baptism as of "two mutually exclusive concepts of the church"—the territorial church and the free church—was at stake in the case of the Anabaptists, baptism, as F. H. Littell has pointed out, "became important because it was the most obvious dividing line between the two systems, and because it afforded the authorities an excuse for suppressing the radicals by force." For several centuries, though with decreasing vigor, this persecution was carried on by Catholics and Protestants alike ("für Calvin und seine Freunde war die Ketzerverbrennung gut protestantisch," Bauman has aptly remarked). The extensive sixteenth-century Anabaptist martyrology was to become part of the "mythology" of their Mennonite descendants.

The clash with the state revolved at first around the question of adult baptism. Most of the prisoners and the martyrs suffered on account of their obstinate adherence to antipedobaptism, to their custom of believer's rather than infant baptism. But there were other areas of conflict, though they were secondary to the major issue: refusal to take a judicial oath, for instance, or a conscientious objection to bearing arms in the defense of township or country.

Anabaptists, like Roman Catholics and magisterial reformers, did not usually distinguish between war and the coercion used by the magistrate in the exercise of civil government. They saw "no essential difference in kind between the police and the military" (Guy F. Herschberger). Both activities were subsumed under the heading of the "sword"; they were regarded as merely different aspects of the same *jus gladii*. Both were condemned by evangelical Anabaptists as worldly functions expressly forbidden to the disciple of Christ; each constituted a dereliction of the Law of Love. Anabaptists, therefore, were mainly interested in enunciating a general doctrine of the sword and only very incidentally concerned with evolving a critique of war and an apologia for conscientious objection to military service. A discussion of Anabaptist pacifism, therefore, must consider this within the context of their total nonresistant outlook.

The Anabaptist objection to magistracy was summed up eloquently by a south German brother who told his inquisitors: "The world regime is after the flesh, but the Christian regime is according to the spirit. . . . The world citizenship is in this world, but the Christian's citizenship is in heaven. Their warfare and armaments are fleshly and according to the flesh, but the Christian's arms and warfare are spiritual against the sovereignty of the devil. The worldly are equipped with armor, according to the flesh, but the Christian's arms are the armor of God, that is truth, righteousness, peace, faith, sanctity, and . . . the word of God." Thus, we can see, this stand was fundamentally apolitical. It totally rejected the state ethic in the name of a higher system of values. Thereby Anabaptism condemned itself forever to the political wilderness, a renunciation its followers made with joy, seeing in it a liberation from the order of wrath into the order of grace promised by God to his children who should walk according to his commandments. Even if magistracy were to be conducted without the use of war or the death penalty or other forms of punishment, an unbridgeable gap would still exist between the secular world and the holy community, because the one disregarded the Master's call while the other heard it and abandoned all to follow him.

Yet the early Anabaptists' otherworldliness is accompanied by an eager expectation of the imminent coming of the Kingdom. "The Reformers," writes John H. Yoder, "were no freer from the apocalyptic feelings of their time than were the Anabaptists, but only with the Anabaptists did eschatology take on present historical relevance." Zürich Anabaptists were to denounce Zwingli as "the dragon of the Apocalypse" and to shout "Woe! Woe!" along the streets of that city (just as in the next decade Dutch Anabaptists were to walk the streets of Amsterdam naked for a sign, as were some Quakers to do in England a century and a quarter later). The Swiss Brethren believed in the imminent end of the world as intensely as other more militant chiliasts have done at various points in Christian history; but these *Stillen* preserved their nonviolence intact when others abandoned it in favor of revolutionary violence to bring in Christ's kingdom on earth.

Nonresistance, then, from the beginning represented the norm among the Swiss and south German Anabaptists. In Switzerland, persecution soon removed the educated humanist and burgher leaders from the scene either by execution or by exile. The faith, however, had been quickly carried from Zürich to other Swiss cities in the German-speaking area and to most of the towns of south Germany and Austria, mainly by artisans and craftsmen, for it was they who possessed the greatest opportunity of movement. (Nowhere, however, did the movement gain any considerable following among the landed nobility.) As a result of these efforts the Anabaptist movement came to possess a certain cohesion from Strasbourg in the west through Switzerland, southern Germany, and Austria to Moravia in the east. Finally, as the Anabaptists in the area were driven out of one town after another, both Catholic and Protestant, and forced to take refuge in the countryside, where from the beginning there had been congregations of believers too, Anabaptism became almost exclusively a peasant faith. In Catholic states it was eventually suppressed altogether.

In Switzerland the rebaptized at once became known, too, for their

67

faith in nonviolence. A contemporary chronicler from St. Gallen, Johannes Kessler, wrote of them in his *Sabbata* (edited by Emil Egli and Rudolf Schoch, St. Gallen, 1902): "They do not carry any weapon, neither a sword nor a dagger, only a pointless bread knife, saying that these are wolf's clothing which the sheep should not wear." According to the humanist Vadian, who was Grebel's brother-in-law and therefore in a good position to report on the practices of the new sect, its members declared that "no Christian might wage war or carry or use any weapon either in his own defense or that of his nearest ones." This occurs in the entry for the year 1525 in his *Chronik der Aebte des Klosters St. Gallen* (ed. Ernst Götzinger, pt. II, St. Gallen, 1877). In the Zürich city records for this date we find statements by Anabaptists denying the possibility of a Christian magistrate: a Christian, one Anabaptist is reported as saying in the autumn of 1525, can be neither a judge nor a councillor. In the middle of the same year at Waldshut, a town about twenty-five miles north of Zürich just across the Swiss border in present-day Baden, we learn of the first Anabaptist conscientious objectors, Jakob Gross, a furrier by trade, and Ulrich Teck. Gross refused to carry weapons in defense of his city, then threatened by attack, when he was called upon to do so by the authorities—even though power, as we shall see below, was temporarily in the hands of a group of Anabaptists led by the nonpacifist Hubmaier, who had baptized the two men. Gross was thereupon expelled. Though unwilling actually to bear arms, he had declared his readiness to do noncombatant service in exchange for exemption from having to fight in person. He was prepared, he stated, to do sentry duty and to work at digging trenches or building ramparts as well as to pay a war tax or fine. His accommodating spirit, which failed to find acceptance with the authorities, did not reflect the rather more uncompromising position of most Anabaptist or Mennonite objectors later. Next year, at Strasbourg, Gross went even further, and expressed his readiness not merely "to stand watch [and] guard," but "to wear armor [and] to hold a pike in his hands" as well, so long as he did not actually have to kill, for that was against "God's command."

Gross, who eventually, in 1531, recanted his Anabaptism after several years of hectic missionary activity, had been in touch at the beginning with Grebel and his Zürich circle. The leading Zürich radicals were united on the question of nonresistance; Zwingli testified to this in a series of utterances from December 1524 on, attacking his erstwhile adherents for their present repudiation of the magistracy and all its works as unchristian. It was due largely to their influence that nonresistance became an integral part of the credo of the Swiss Brethren.

Shortly before his execution at the beginning of January 1527, we find Felix Mantz, who stood second only to Grebel in the radical leadership, stating as his firm conviction: "No Christian smites with the sword nor resists evil," for the sword-bearing magistracy possesses no scriptural authority. In the next month came what Stayer has rightly called "the first authoritative statement" of the doctrine of nonresistance: the Schleitheim Confession of 24 February 1527. It was drawn up by a gathering of leading Anabaptists held at Schleitheim in the Swiss canton of Schaffhausen, and the south German Anabaptist missionary Michael Sattler was almost certainly responsible for composing it. Throughout, the Confession expresses the Anabaptist concept of discipleship as the core of Christian faith and practice, the sixth of its seven articles dealing with the sword-bearing magistracy. This is granted a conditional place in the divine order, but the exercise of its powers is regarded as "outside the perfection of Christ" and therefore forbidden to any who strove to be his disciples. War is not considered explicitly but its condemnation, along with that of the other functions of "the sword," is obviously taken for granted by the author.

The article became a basic text for all subsequent generations of Anabaptist and Mennonite nonresistants. It is, therefore, worth quoting here in full:

> We are agreed as follows concerning the sword: The sword is ordained of God outside the perfection of Christ. It punishes and puts to death the wicked, and guards and protects the good. In the Law the sword was ordained for the punishment of the wicked and for their death, and the same [sword] is [now] ordained to be used by the worldly magistrates.
>
> In the perfection of Christ, however, only the ban is used for a warning and for the excommunication of the one who has sinned, without putting the flesh to death—simply the warning and the command to sin no more.
>
> Now it will be asked by many who do not recognize [this as] the will of Christ for us, whether a Christian may or should employ the sword against the wicked for the defense and protection of the good, or for the sake of love.
>
> Our reply is unanimously as follows: Christ teaches and commands us to learn of Him, for He is meek and lowly in heart and so shall we find rest to our souls. Also Christ says to the heathenish woman who was taken in adultery, not that one should stone her according to the law of His Father (and yet He says, As the Fa-

ther has commanded me, thus I do), but in mercy and forgiveness and warning, to sin no more. Such [an attitude] we also ought to take completely according to the rule of the ban.

Secondly, it will be asked concerning the sword, whether a Christian shall pass sentence in worldly disputes and strife such as unbelievers have with one another. This is our united answer: Christ did not wish to decide or pass judgment between brother and brother in the case of the inheritance, but refused to do so. Therefore we should do likewise.

Thirdly, it will be asked concerning the sword, Shall one be a magistrate if one should be chosen as such? The answer is as follows: They wished to make Christ king, but He fled and did not view it as the arrangement of His Father. Thus shall we do as He did, and follow Him, and so shall we not walk in darkness. For He Himself says, He who wishes to come after me, let him deny himself and take up his cross and follow me. Also, He Himself forbids the [employment of] the force of the sword saying, The worldly princes lord it over them, etc., but not so shall it be with you. Further, Paul says, Whom God did foreknow He also did predestinate to be conformed to the image of His Son, etc. Also Peter says, Christ has suffered (not ruled) and left us an example, that ye should follow His steps.

Finally it will be observed that it is not appropriate for a Christian to serve as a magistrate because of these points: The government magistracy is according to the flesh, but the Christians' is according to the Spirit; their houses and dwelling remain in this world, but the Christians' are in heaven; their citizenship is in this world, but the Christians' citizenship is in heaven; the weapons of their conflict and war are carnal and against the flesh only, but the Christians' weapons are spiritual, against the fortification of the devil. The worldlings are armed with steel and iron, but the Christians are armed with the armor of God, with truth, righteousness, peace, faith, salvation and the Word of God. In brief, as in the mind of Christ toward us, so shall the mind of the members of the body of Christ be through Him in all things, that there may be no schism in the body through which it would be destroyed. For every kingdom divided against itself will be destroyed. Now since Christ is as it is written of Him, His members must also be the same, that His body may remain complete and united to its own advancement and upbuilding. [Translation from John

70

Christian Wenger, *Glimpses of Mennonite History and Doctrine*
(Scottdale, Pa.), 1959 edn.]

The Schleitheim Confession represents a landmark in the history of
Anabaptist nonresistance. On the one hand, it provided a model on
which the sect could pattern its conduct henceforward: thus it helped
to give a firm foundation to what had hitherto been a somewhat
inchoate doctrine despite the efforts of the Zürich radicals to give sta-
bility to the nonresistant ideal, and subject to a certain degree of
variation from area to area. On the other hand, the Confession tended
to formalize nonresistance, linking it inextricably with a position of
separation from society and creating a syndrome out of Anabaptist
nonresistance and nonconformity to the world; thus it also helped to
make nonresistance, in the course of time, a dogma rather than a living
faith.

In the Swiss lands, the Schleitheim model is reproduced in the practice of Anabaptist congregations. Hans Marquardt, for instance, who
acted as minister to the brethren at St. Gallen, in a sermon in 1528
unequivocally stated the sect's opposition to participation in war. The
believer, although he must obey the powers that be in all matters not
conflicting with his duty to God, should not hesitate to refuse compliance if required "to use violence, or go to war, or use the sword"; he
must do this even if he should thereby be reduced to penury as a result
of the government's confiscating his goods. As Marquardt reminded
his listeners, "the fact that under the Old Covenant God permitted His
people the use of the sword does not bind us, for the old law has been
replaced by the new commandment of Christ that we should love our
enemies." We are not surprised, therefore, when we learn that the St.
Gallen executioner, Master Conrad, after being converted by Marquardt to Anabaptism in the early 1530's, resigned his office at once,
saying that he no longer felt able to take human life.

Nonresistance appears now, at least in the main congregations, as an
essential feature of Anabaptist practice; the mounting persecution to
which the sectaries were everywhere subject may have made them
more inclined to accept the renunciation of the world which nonresistance entailed. At any rate, it had become a distinguishing mark of the
Brethren. We find town authorities, like those of Bern and Zürich,
recommending, as a sure method of discovering if a suspect belonged
to the Brethren, the ascertainment of whether he carried a weapon. If
he did, then he was not an Anabaptist. Often the Brethren, whether in
prison or at large, themselves volunteered the information that they
were not prepared to bear arms and serve in war. In the armed con-

flict between the Protestant and Catholic Swiss cantons in 1529 and again in 1531, Anabaptists appear as conscientious objectors. In 1530 a Basel brother, Hans Hersberger, declared his unwillingness to employ "weapons or armament even against the Turks." "In Basel," writes Stayer of this period, "one Anabaptist feigned sickness, while three others were openly disobedient. In Soluthurn complaints were addressed to several bailiffs about Anabaptists who refused both to fight and to pay for substitutes." In the Swiss cantons, with their citizen armies, militia service presented a problem for early Anabaptists. Bullinger, who succeeded Zwingli as Zürich's spiritual leader, writing in 1531—the year of Zwingli's death—accused Anabaptists of, among a number of other serious faults, subverting government through preaching of nonresistance; this, he lamented, meant depriving the state of their aid just at the moment when it was most needed, i.e., in time of war.

Beginning in 1531 at Bern, a long series of colloquies were held at intervals between Anabaptists, first the Swiss and then in the second half of the century the German and Dutch, and representatives of the established Protestant churches. In each instance the Anabaptists defended nonresistance as a fixed tenet of the brotherhood. At the *Gespräch* held at Zofingen in 1532, for instance, the Anabaptist delegates argued that one who killed, either in war or in execution of the death penalty, failed to display spiritual love and, therefore, ought to be excluded from the congregation until he repented. For if an unbeliever were killed in his sins a soul, instead of being saved, would be consigned to everlasting damnation. It is not clear, however, exactly to what extent the ban was used at that time in regard to those who did not remain nonresistant.

Though the earliest of these colloquies were held on Swiss soil and Zürich was the cradle of Anabaptism, the movement, as we have seen, had soon spread to the towns and countryside of large parts of southern and central Germany: Alsace, Baden, Württemberg, Bavaria, the Tirol, Austria, and Moravia all had their Anabaptist congregations by the end of the 1520's, and the message was being taken northward, too, to the Palatinate, Hesse, Thuringia, and Saxony, though these areas remained for the time being on the periphery of the movement. Sattler, the presumed author of the Schleitheim Confession and one of the most energetic and dedicated propagators of the Anabaptist faith, came from Baden. To men like Sattler political frontiers meant nothing, and no language barriers existed here to hinder swift communication. The Anabaptists failed to make conversions, however, among their French, Italian, or Czech speaking neighbors; the movement continued to be confined to speakers of the German (and later Dutch and English) languages.

In May 1527, shortly before his execution at Rottenburg on the Neckar, Sattler spoke to his judges of his belief in nonresistance. Christians should practice it not merely among themselves, but even against enemies of Christendom like the Turks, who were at that date advancing northward and threatening the Habsburg dominions. He stated:

> If the Turks should come, we ought not to resist them. For it is written [Matt. 5:21]: Thou shalt not kill. We must not defend ourselves against the Turks and others of our persecutors, but are to beseech God with earnest to repel and resist them. But that I said that, if warring *were* right, I would rather take the field against so-called Christians who persecute, capture and kill pious Christians than against the Turks was for the following reason. The Turk is a true Turk, knows nothing of the Christian faith, and is a Turk after the flesh. But you who would be Christians and who make your boast of Christ persecute the pious witnesses of Christ and are Turks after the spirit!

The duty of Christians not to resist the Turkish advance was voiced by a number of other south German Anabaptists around this time; sentiments which, of course, brought charges of danger to the state and friendliness to the enemy from the movement's opponents and persecutors. In the Tirol and elsewhere, Anabaptists began to carry a staff in place of the customary side-weapon, so as to make their nonresistant stance clear to all; it is probably from them that the Moravian Anabaptists derived this practice rather than from the Minor Party of the Czech Brethren (see Chapter 1). In many areas, whenever polemical fury or collective fear subsided enough for clear thought on the subject to become possible, people recognized the essentially nonviolent character of the Anabaptist outlook on the world. Court records and the utterances of individuals who had had contact with the sect bear witness to this. "The Anabaptists carry no arms; they desire to do no wrong either to friend or foe." But their very defenselessness gave cause to impose penalties upon them. The town council of Ulm, for instance, in 1531 sentenced the tailor Leonhard Seidler to banishment for refusing to give an assurance that he would fight in defense of the city if it were attacked.

South German Anabaptism led a semi-underground existence; whereas in some places, e.g., Strasbourg, it was granted a measure of practical toleration, elsewhere its followers were subjected to savage persecution. On the whole, it was easier to escape the eye of the authorities in the countryside than in the cities, but this was not always the case. Conversion was usually achieved by the preaching and example of the missionaries who spread over the land; discipline within a congregation, once it had been formed, was upheld through the teaching of the elders and the combined efforts of fellow believers. The early Anabaptists were mostly simple folk; yet in the towns most of them were at least literate, and a few belonged to the intelligentsia. Whereas the spoken word remained the most important factor in extending and deepening the faith, the written word also counted for something.

One early Anabaptist tract on the Christian attitude to the state has survived the endeavors of the movement's enemies, then and over the subsequent centuries, to remove so far as possible all traces of the abominated sect. It cannot be dated exactly, but it belongs within the first decade of Anabaptism. Since the doctrine it expounds is roughly that of the Schleitheim Confession, it was probably produced subsequently, although this is merely a supposition since the Confession's stand on war and the magistracy represents a codification of existing opinion within the brotherhood rather than innovation. The treatise is entitled the *Uncovering of the Babylonian Whore* (*Aufdeckung der babylonischen Hurn*) and contains twenty-seven pages. Neither the date nor the author's name nor the place of publication is given—obviously as a precaution against the possibility of retaliatory measures on the part of the authorities against printer or author. However, the writer, though anonymous, is clearly an Anabaptist.

The disclosure of infamy promised in the title refers to the sinful character of the temporal state, which the author identifies with the legendary whore of Babylon. "I confront all who want to join the kingdom of Christ with worldly powers with the judgment . . . of Christ." And he continues: "He who seeks Christ other than under the cross in patience will not find him. . . . I do not wish to confront [any person] . . . with anybody but the crucified, patient and loving Christ. The true Christians will let themselves be dominated, ruled, and overcome in patience and love even unto the end of the world." Although the Mosaic Law permitted the use of the sword, and even now "pagans" and "wicked" Christians allow it among themselves—in both instances with God's approval—Christ's disciples, while they should obey the magistracy, follow a quite different ethic, which takes away need of the sword. "Let us not worry about the magistracy; we will find rulers in abundance," concludes the author. Of the short tract Stayer has written: "The *Aufdeckung* is the product of a keen intellect well aware of the issues which nonresistance raises."

Neither the *Aufdeckung* nor another roughly contemporaneous product of an Anabaptist pen—*The View of the Sword with the Varying Power of the Three Principalities of the World, the Jews and the Christians with Other Related Matters* (*Das Urteil von dem Schwert mit underschidlichem Gewalt dreier Fürstenthum der Welt, Juden und Christen mit anderen anliegenden Sachen*)—dealt specifically with war, yet once again the question of war is clearly included within the broader discussion of the sword-bearing magistracy. We know the name of the author of this second treatise, Clemens Adler, and its date of composition (it was finished on 12 April 1529), and the place where it was written, Austerlitz (Slavkov) in Moravia. It was apparently never printed, but the manuscript has survived in an early eighteenth-century copy discovered two decades ago in a Mennonite farmhouse in the canton of Bern. Like the *Aufdeckung*, Adler's tract defends a rigorous nonresistance; it emphasizes the contrast between the kingdoms of this world, even though their rulers may claim to be Christians, and the congregation of the faithful. "If the world lifts up its sword against them, yet they take no sword against it nor against anyone, for they have made their swords into ploughshares and their spears into pruning hooks." For a Christian, only spiritual weapons are permissible for maintaining discipline within the community: first, brotherly admonishment and, if this fails, then disfellowshipping of stubborn offenders. "Not that one is to kill them, for excommunication is not killing, burning nor drowning, like the world does, as does also the law of Moses." To place a sword in the hands of a Christian is to mix what should never come together. Sword-bearing Christians, Adler exclaims, "are neither heathen, Jews, nor Christians. They do not know themselves what they are, for they mix and patch the one to the other, namely the sword of the world, of Moses, and of Christ together. That fits well together, cabbage, peas, and turnips, that this should all be one thing! O blindness, blindness!"

The author of the *Aufdeckung* and Clemens Adler were both consistent nonresistants. Nevertheless, there did exist among early Anabaptists—both before and after Schleitheim—other doctrines of the sword, which permitted its exercise by members of the holy community. Hans J. Hillerbrand has designated the nonpacifists as a "minority within the minority" which Anabaptists as a whole constituted in contemporary Swiss and south German Protestantism; other writers, like Stayer, for instance, are inclined to assign to these nonpacifists a more significant role within the movement and to view its early years as a gradual, and somewhat irregular, development toward a nonresistant orthodoxy. Even before the Münster incident of 1535 some of the Anabaptists' contemporaries seem to have feared that their non-resistance was merely a cover for subversive designs (even the conscientious objection of the peaceable, of course, was sometimes regarded as undermining the loyalty of subjects) and they linked them with Christian revolutionaries like Thomas Müntzer, despite the fact that most Anabaptists repudiated all such connections. These suspicions were voiced not only by Luther, who made no distinction between peaceable and nonpacifist Anabaptists and considered the former's nonresistance to be little better than hypocrisy, but also by Zwingli, who charged the Swiss Brethren with the intention of discarding their practice of nonviolence as soon as they were strong enough to have some chance of overthrowing the government. Whereas Luther never had close contacts with Anabaptists and may therefore be forgiven his ignorance of their principles, the same excuse cannot be pleaded on behalf of the Zürich reformer, from whose closest followers the original Anabaptists had come. We must now take a look at the character and probable extent of the nonpacifist "opposition" among early Anabaptists, which magisterial reformers like Luther and Zwingli (and even Bucer in Strasbourg, who opposed the death penalty for members of the sect) mistook for the Anabaptist majority.

Among the nonpacifists we may distinguish between those Anabaptists who supported what was in fact roughly the position of the magisterial reformers on war and government and those who tended to favor some form of revolutionary apocalypticism. In each case nonresistance was repudiated and either the sword-bearing magistracy in the present or chiliastic violence in the imminent future was given approval.

A note of caution, however, is necessary at this point. At hearings and trials of Anabaptists the accused, when asked whether in their opinion the Christian might occupy a magistrate's office, sometimes replied with a conditional affirmative, whereas a simple denial might be expected if the accused were in fact a genuine nonresistant. Yet we must remember the circumstances in which such evidence was extracted: simple and sometimes unlettered men and women against often learned and always hostile examiners eager to twist every word of the accused into an indictment against them; the threat and sometimes the reality of torture; and, in the background in most instances, the shadow of the gallows or some other instrument of execution. Moreover, our main sources of information concerning such examinations, the *Täuferakten*, although generally reliable, were compiled by the Anabaptists' enemies; the possibility of misrepresentation of the

76

Anabaptist view, though not necessarily conscious, can rarely be discounted.

Thus when after his arrest in Strasbourg at the end of 1526, Jakob Gross, being pressed to say if a believer might wield the sword, replied that God alone could judge as to this, it scarcely appears likely that the recent Waldshut conscientious objector to military service had renounced his nonresistant views. He was merely being as circumspect in the face of grave danger as his conscience permitted. Again, throughout this early phase of Anabaptism, in Switzerland and southern Germany some Anabaptists under examination expressed the view that a Christian might indeed be a magistrate provided that he was not required to take human life or contravene the other requirements of the Law of Love. Or the examined person might reply that in his view a Christian could take office but was not likely to remain in it for long. They mostly stressed loyalty to their prince and readiness to obey the law insofar as their consciences allowed; they echoed the conditional justification of magistracy as ordained by God, which was a basic tenet of Anabaptist nonresistance. One Plathans in Hesse, when examined as to his readiness to bear arms for his country against its enemies, says: "A Christian prince will neither fight nor murder." Yet this implied recognition that a Christian might be a ruler if he renounced the *jus gladii*—or should we say, this implied recognition that a Christian might not be a ruler since he could not renounce the *jus gladii*?—was accompanied by Plathans's flatly refusing his assent to military service: "This he will not do: defend or resist." Certainly the heroic way was the one followed by Michael Sattler, who did not hesitate to state the full Anabaptist doctrine of the sword and to do so plainly and without any prevarication or conditions; for this he was prepared to pay with the loss of his life. But there were others who, though not willing to compromise on what they considered the essentials of their faith, desired to save their lives, if possible, by conceding to their persecutors what they considered to be matters of secondary importance, where compromise was possible. To call such people "undogmatic" nonresistants, as Stayer does, seems to exaggerate the difference in the nature of their witness and that of other nonresistants. The distinction lay most often not in doctrine or dogma but in human character.

After this brief digression we must return to our discussion of the "resistant" trend in early Anabaptism. On the whole, this trend showed itself strongest either in peripheral areas, where severe persecution made congregational life and discipline difficult and where distance from the centers of the Anabaptist brotherhood easily led to a watering-down of its doctrine, including the tenet of nonresistance, or in places where a powerful leader appeared teaching views opposed to the nonresistant norm, as happened in the case of Hubmaier at Waldshut and Moravian Nikolsburg (Mikulov).

However, even among the Swiss Brethren whose devotion to nonresistance soon became a marked characteristic of the sect, some variation of view existed at the very beginning. Grebel's total rejection of the sword-bearing magistracy and of war was not shared, at least to the same degree, by quite all his coreligionists. Whereas most converts came from the artisanry and peasantry and therefore were not likely to face personally the problem of election to office, some magistrates joined the brotherhood during the first few years of its existence; yet they do not appear to have resigned. In most instances the office held was a minor one where the infliction of death or serious bodily punishment was not involved. But we do hear of one Hans Hottinger, guard at the gate of the city of Zürich, remaining in this occupation after his baptism early in 1525. It is not known if he continued as guard for long after that date. The effect of the Schleitheim Confession, with its total repudiation of the "world" as the domain of Satan, put an end to any limited approval of office. True, as late as 1532, an Anabaptist of St. Gallen told its burgomaster, the humanist Vadian: "It would be harsh to say that you, my lords, were not Christians. I do not want to say or think such a thing." Yet this too sounds like just another attempt to soften the full asperity of the sect's opposition to the *jus gladii* by limiting its practical implications to a purely personal witness, and thereby to ward off the anger of the authorities if they were denied the title of good Christians.

One of Grebel's closest associates, the ebullient Georg Blaurock, was a church disturber—but so was the founder of Quakerism, George Fox. On this score, doubts cast on his adherence to nonresistance are not very convincing. More compelling evidence exists, though it is still merely circumstantial rather than direct, concerning the militancy of two other members of Grebel's circle, Hans Brötli and Heinrich Aberli, both of whom had appended their signatures to Grebel's letter to Müntzer in 1524 enunciating for the first time the doctrine of nonresistance. Brötli, who in 1525 missionized among the peasants of Hallau, near Schaffhausen, who were then in a state of incipient rebellion, is not known to have chided them for their bellicose spirit or to have withheld baptism until converts agreed to renounce the use of arms. And it was their armed stance which in fact protected Brötli from seizure by the authorities; although, it must be added, there is no evidence, either, that he actively supported this stance. (A similar case to Brötli's is that of Johannes Krüsi, who went as missionary to the peasants of Tablet near St. Gallen, where he, too, baptized among rebellious rustics whose arms protected him from arrest—without protest, seemingly, from the Anabaptist preacher.)

Silence again provides the main evidence for a "resistant" stance in the case of Aberli. In October 1524 volunteers from Zürich, who had gone to the defense of Protestant Waldshut, appealed to Aberli back in Zürich to "send . . . about forty or fifty honest well-armed Christian fellows" to reinforce the town's defense against the threatened attack from its Austrian overlord. "It is not known," writes Stayer, "how Aberli responded to this letter or whether at any time he was himself a member of the Zürich garrison at Waldshut." It is impossible, therefore, to say with any certainty whether he agreed with the pro-war stand of the writer of the letter. Yet there is evidence of Aberli's friendship with Waldshut's minister Balthasar Hubmaier, who continued to uphold the *jus gladii* after his conversion from Lutheranism to Anabaptism in April 1525, and this fact speaks in favor of Aberli's having shared the latter's viewpoint on the sword.

Concerning Hubmaier's defense of war and the sword no uncertainty exists. He stated his views in print and without equivocation. For Hubmaier, as for Luther, the church remained an inclusive church coterminous with the state; the idea of separation between state and church, which is central to the mainstream of Anabaptism, was foreign to Hubmaier. When the Waldshut town council soon followed their minister into the Anabaptist fold, Anabaptism became the established religion of this semi-autonomous city state. Hubmaier's doctrine of the sword, it has been pointed out, coincides almost exactly with Luther's, and the town's resistance to its Habsburg overlord, which continued after the reception of Anabaptism as the official religion, enjoyed Hubmaier's full approval. In his view, it was not rebellion or, still less, social revolution; instead, he and his fellow townsmen viewed their resistance as an exemplification of both the traditional *Widerstands-recht* sanctified by feudal custom as protection against injustice and of the defense of true religion, conducted in proper fashion by the duly constituted civil authority. Contacts between Waldshut and the peasant revolutionaries of Germany—1525 was the year of the famous Peasants' War—represented a purely strategic alliance; both parties had roughly the same enemies, though their ultimate aims differed widely.

Even in Waldshut Hubmaier's defense of war and the magistracy met with opposition from some members of his Anabaptist community; the unanimity he had hoped to achieve on this question eluded him.

Indeed we read of opponents among the baptized already accusing him of being "drunk with blood (*Blutsäufer*)," and at least two of his converts, we have seen, conscientiously objected to serving the city with arms. The experiment of an Anabaptist-controlled city state did not last long; the town fell to its enemies at the end of the year and Hubmaier was forced to flee, finally making his way to Nikolsburg in south Moravia, where he arrived in July 1526. Hubmaier's message found a ready welcome there among the German-speaking Protestant townspeople, and its feudal overlord, Leonhard von Liechtenstein, was favorably inclined too. He soon accepted baptism at Hubmaier's hands. There was no question of course of his being required on conversion to renounce his noble status or the exercise of the sword, since the type of Anabaptism officially received in Nikolsburg was Hubmaier's version. He had written exactly a year earlier, while still in Waldshut: "We confess publicly that there should be a government which carries the Sword. . . . The more Christian the government is, the more it, like Solomon, asks God for wisdom to rule." But once again, in Nikolsburg Hubmaier had to face opposition from his own congregation, a minority of whom adhered to the doctrine of nonresistance: according to his own words, they contradicted him "publicly in church on this subject" and revived the recent charge that he had made himself "a man of blood" on account of his positive support of the sword-bearing magistracy. The nonresistants were drawn chiefly, though not exclusively, from Anabaptist immigrants who streamed to Nikolsburg from lands like the Tirol where there was sharp persecution. These newcomers had in many cases already been confirmed in their views on the sword before leaving their homeland. Converts from among the local people, however, mostly followed Hubmaier.

The political situation at that time was critical. A Turkish advance into Habsburg territory was threatening, and Moravia's Habsburg ruler, Ferdinand I (brother of the Emperor Charles V), was engaged, along with the landowning nobility, in organizing defensive measures. Thus, to the authorities Anabaptist nonresistance appeared as a potential menace to the security of the state; after all, many Anabaptists had stated their intention of submitting passively to the Turks, should they come. Both Lord Leonhard von Liechtenstein and Hubmaier himself were alarmed at the possible consequences for their community if nonresistant ideas gained ascendancy among them. Above all, they feared government reprisals if nonresistance took root. Hubmaier, therefore, seized his pen and wrote a short treatise *On the Sword* (*Von dem Schwert*) refuting the nonresistant position and elaborating his own views on the Christian character of the magistracy. He dedicated the booklet, which appeared in June 1527, to a high Moravian official, Lord Arkleb of Boskovice, a relation by marriage of Hubmaier's protector. It bore this subtitle: "A Christian Exposition of the Scriptures, earnestly announced by Certain Brothers as against Magistracy (that is, that Christians should not sit in judgment, nor bear the Sword)."

Hubmaier, before he joined the Reformation, had been a university professor of theology. He was both well-read in the Scriptures and well-schooled in the learning of his age. His style of writing was forceful and clear. On this occasion his method of treatment consisted in first choosing fifteen passages from the New Testament, which had been used by his nonresistant opponents as proof texts in support of their viewpoint, and then analyzing them in detail so as to determine their exact meaning. In each case Hubmaier was able to show, at least to his own satisfaction, that the nonresistants misinterpreted their text. Since government remained essential in this fallen world, a Christian magistracy, Hubmaier argued, was obviously more beneficial and more concerned to fulfil God's will than a government of unbelievers. In his view, the achievement of justice, not the exercise of wrath against the disorderly, was the primary aim of government. It possessed a moral purpose, therefore, and not purely a repressive function. "What he [the magistrate] does with the sword he does not perform out of hatred and envy, but according to the command of God." True, he may have to take human life in the course of his duties but this is in line with God's purpose: the command "Thou shalt not kill" was not absolute. Those who considered the work of the magistracy to be unchristian showed themselves at the same time as rebels against God's authority. "Accordingly," wrote Hubmaier addressing his nonresistant coreligionists, "I counsel you with true love, brothers, turn back, take heed to yourselves. You have stumbled badly, and under the cloak of spirituality and humility have devised much mischief against God and brotherly love." He taunted them with inconsistent practice: while they denounced the office of the sword as pagan, they still paid taxes to the state, knowing that these were going to "help and preserve" the sword. Hubmaier, we may note, failed to appreciate the basic point in Anabaptist nonresistance: that government and the sword, while indispensable in the world as presently constituted, are incompatible with true Christian discipleship. Nevertheless, like Luther but even more insistently and with greater vigor, Hubmaier supported nonresistance in personal relations. In an account of his faith addressed to King Ferdinand I (*Ein Rechenschaft des Glaubens*, dated 3 January 1528) he wrote: "A Christian does not fight, strike out, and kill unless he is in the government and that is his duty, or unless he does so at the command of the regular government. But, otherwise, before a Christian draws the sword he gives away coat and cloak, offers the cheek, indeed body and life—that is how peaceful Christian demeanor is." At this point at any rate Hubmaier shows himself a proponent of the Anabaptist "theology of suffering."

The *Rechenschaft* was written in prison after Hubmaier had been arrested during a visit to Vienna in July of the previous year. In March 1528 he was burned at the stake. In the same month, back in Nikolsburg, the slowly developing schism was complete between those Anabaptists who followed Hubmaier in approving the sword (known as *Schwertler*) and those led by a member of his congregation, Jakob Widemann "the one-eyed," who allowed only spiritual weapons (known as *Stäbler* from the staffs they bore as symbols of nonviolence). The *Stäbler* then left Nikolsburg, though the exact reasons for their departure at that particular moment remain unclear. "The points of tension lay not only in the theological and ethical spheres but also in the sociological contrasts" between the immigrants and the local people (J. K. Zeman). Stayer supposes that the *Stäbler* went voluntarily because they already had another possible place of refuge in mind and did not wish to remain longer than was absolutely necessary alongside their *Schwertler* brethren. On the other hand a Mennonite writer, Heinold Fast, thinks the cause of their exodus stemmed from attempts on the part of Leonhard von Liechtenstein to make them participate in armed defense to ward off a threatened incursion from the side of the hostile authorities against Nikolsburg. At any rate, the refugees, after vainly seeking some place of safety, were allowed to settle at Austerlitz on the estates of the Kounic family. During its wanderings the group had adopted a communal way of living, at first probably as a response to the exigencies of the situation in which it found itself, though communitarianism soon became a matter of faith and the communal principle became part of the creed of the Hutterite brotherhood which eventually emerged from the *Stäbler* party. But this story must be postponed until a later chapter. The subsequent history of the *Schwertler* party is shrouded in obscurity; it appears to have disintegrated in the early 1530's, perhaps even before the death of Leonhard von Liechtenstein around the middle of that decade.

Shortly before Hubmaier's arrest, in May 1527, Nikolsburg had been the scene of a debate in which not only the leading local Anabaptists, including Hubmaier himself, but also a visitor, Hans Hut, took part. Exactly what transpired at its sessions is still disputed by historians, because of defects in the sources available. Hut is a somewhat controversial figure in the history of early Anabaptism. A former follower of the revolutionary Müntzer, Hut was attracted to Anabaptism after the collapse of Müntzer's cause and underwent baptism in May 1526. The ceremony was performed by Hans Denck, rightly considered the most eminent example of mystical, "contemplative" Anabaptism. We know that Denck, unlike most of the unaffiliated "spiritualists" of the Radical Reformation (e.g., Caspar von Schwenckfeld or Sebastian Franck), was a convinced nonresistant and an opponent of the sword (though Stayer attempts to make an "undogmatic" nonresistant out of him, in fact the grounds of his rejection of the sword-bearing magistracy appear to differ little from Grebel's). Yet it is by no means clear if Hut, who soon began to exert considerable influence on the Anabaptist movement in southern and central Germany, himself believed in nonresistance. The center of Hut's message, which he preached with fervor throughout the south German lands, was an eschatological doctrine which saw the day of judgment as imminent and the malaise of the times, including the persecution of true Christians like the Anabaptists, as proof of the approaching end of the present world. Christ's return on earth would be accompanied by destruction of the ungodly rulers, and this act would serve as a prelude to the resurrection of the dead, the last judgment, and the establishment of Christ's kingdom. Though for the present the faithful must remain peaceable, obeying the authorities in all things lawful to them, the moment of revenge for persecution and wrong was not far off. According to Hut: "A Christian can indeed have a sword, as long as he allows it to remain in the sheath until the Lord tells him to draw it. [That time would come] after they had been dispersed and tested. Finally, the Lord would reassemble them all and come to them with his future [kingdom]. At that time the saints would punish the others, the sinners who had not repented. Then the priests who had preached falsely would have to give an account of their teaching and the powerful of their government."

Some of his followers misinterpreted Hut and believed that he was preaching a gospel of immediate insurrection. This he was not doing, for the sword, he said, must remain in its sheath until after Christ's second coming. Yet their mistake was understandable; even a careful observer like Sebastian Franck, who was on the whole sympathetic to the Anabaptist position, considered Hut to be an advocate of violence. There was undoubtedly a strong element of barely suppressed violence in utterances like that of Hut's close associate Georg Nespitzer, who declared to his followers early in 1528: "Keep order and definitely in about eight or fourteen days [the Lord will come]; then carry out the command of the Lord and spare no one." But against such declarations we may place others which show that Hut's disciples included those peaceably disposed, the *Stillen*, who professed a genuine faith in nonviolence, at least until the sounding of the last trump and Christ's coming "in the clouds" to judge the quick and the dead. "There is some evidence," writes Stayer, "that Hut [himself] taught nonparticipation in warfare [to his Anabaptist congregation] at Königsberg in Franconia." "Whoever has two coats," declared a follower, one Beutelhans, "should sell one and buy a sword. Nevertheless, as a Christian, he should not defend himself with it." Another of Hut's congregation stated: "If the Turk were to invade the country the baptized should help no one, but simply trust God." These *Stillen* may have constituted a minority, and even with them nonresistance probably represented merely a kind of interim-ethic. But we must note that, in fact, no revolutionary outbreak on the part even of the violently disposed among his followers resulted from Hut's preaching. Moreover, many whom he had converted to Anabaptism finally ended as unequivocal adherents of nonresistance of the Schleitheim variety or as members of the Moravian Hutterite communities, whose devotion to nonviolence was, if possible, even more uncompromising. Thus what with Hut probably began as an interim-ethic grew after his death (he died in prison in December 1527) in the minds of a section of his followers into a principled belief in nonresistance.

At the Nikolsburg *Gespräch* Hut, according to the Hutterite "Great Chronicle," defended the nonresistant position during the course of discussion. He had opposed the magistrate's sword in the hands of Christians as well as participation in war either in person or by paying war taxes, and thereby found himself in trouble with Lord Leonhard von Liechtenstein for voicing such seditious views—and at such a dangerous moment. The chronicle, however, was composed forty years after the event described and the reliability of its account has been contested. Despite a wealth of other sources, writes the foremost authority on the Hutterites, Robert Friedmann, the problem "still remains confusing." Friedmann, tentatively agreeing with Stayer that in fact Hut did not support nonresistance on this occasion, adds that the account in the "Great Chronicle" represents merely "a belated glorification of Hut along with Hutterite nonresistant ideals." The most likely explanation of Hut's clash with Lord Leonhard, who afterward detained the visitor in his castle for a while to show his displeasure, seems to be his defense not of nonresistance but of chiliasm, to which Lord Leonhard and his protégé Hubmaier were as much opposed as they were to pacifism.

At any rate Hut, after his arrest a few months later in Augsburg, told his examiners that he had never supported nonresistance nor denied the Christian character of magistracy. Whereas Hillerbrand supposes that Hut had changed his mind in the intervening months, and Herbert Klassen believes that he spoke in this way in order to avoid the charge of sedition which an open avowal of nonresistance might have incurred, Stayer argues in favor of a consistently "resistant" stand on Hut's part: that neither at Nikolsburg in May nor at Augsburg in September did he support the Schleitheim view that the true believer must always keep the sword in its scabbard. Probably Hut was not greatly concerned to formulate a detailed and completely watertight doctrine of the sword: the end of the present world was at hand and thereafter nonresistance would become irrelevant, for the extirpation of the wicked must ensue before a new order, Christ's kingdom, could be inaugurated. Such a *Weltanschauung* was far removed from that of the Swiss Brethren and those who accepted the Schleitheim Confession, with their emphasis on love and nonretaliation.

After Hut's death the yeast of his doctrine continued to ferment within south German Anabaptism. Yet there was certainly a feeling in most congregations that noncombatancy was the proper stance for a member of the brotherhood, and this feeling grew stronger with the years. Vengeance for wrong suffered must be left entirely to God. In 1529 Wolfgang Brandhuber, for instance, who acted as Anabaptist minister at Linz in Upper Austria, warned his congregation against the false brethren "who want to preserve the sword from the Mosaic Law . . . and wish to allow a Christian to judge over life and death." But at first the ban does not seem to have been regularly applied against those who could not, or did not wish to, accept nonresistance. "A person may take it or leave it, according to whether he is strong or weak in the faith," as Hans Nadler said in 1529. Nadler, one of Hut's followers, had come to accept nonresistance for himself but, as we see, did not wish to impose it on others as a condition of membership. And if even the Swiss Brethren were willing to pay war taxes, it is no wonder that Anabaptists in the scattered and sometimes weak congregations farther north were prepared on occasion to make far-going compromises in regard to the sword; at other times they seemed uncertain concerning the proper attitude to be taken up towards the demands of the state.

In the Esslingen congregation in Württemberg, for instance, which had felt the impact of Hut's teachings, a variety of positions can be found, and Esslingen at that date appears to have been a fairly typical example of a south German congregation. Some members there refused to carry weapons or "to stand guard on the wall," and expressed their conviction, as Hans Feigenbutz put it in 1527, that "if the city were in distress no resistance was to be offered." In 1531 Michael Eck was told by some of the brethren: "If the government ordered him to go to war against the enemy, be it Jew, Turk, heathen, or something else, he should not do it, for Christ said, when someone strikes you on one cheek you shall offer him the other." Others, however, carried sidearms and were prepared to use them either in self-defense or at the command of the magistrates in defense of the town. Stephan Böhmerle, who in October 1528 became Esslingen's first Anabaptist martyr, was ready to do guard duty with an axe but at the same time was not willing to use it to kill since, as he stated, a Christian was obliged to do good even to his enemies. Pressed under examination to say what he would do "if the city were besieged and he were on the wall," he admitted that he was not sure "what he would do, whether he would defend himself or not." There were Anabaptists elsewhere, too, who expressed the same bewilderment when the claims of the civic authorities and of religious conscience clashed. In 1528 at Strasbourg Michel Ecker confessed: "If he were in a city invaded by an enemy army he would present himself in arms. Indeed he would go ahead to the enemy and plead for the city. He would kill no one, however, rather let himself be killed." (This appears to be one of the first suggestions made for attempting passive resistance to enemy attack.) In the mid-1530's we find one Ulrich Gässli distinguishing between police action on the one hand and soldiering on the other (a viewpoint which was rather unusual in Anabaptism). "He could not accept," he said, "that the government should be obeyed when it orders war on an outside enemy. However, in the city he approved of and was willing to help in the defense and protection of widows and orphans." We hear in Ulm of an Anabaptist weapon-smith; it is possible that he did not consider this profession incompatible with nonresistance since it did not involve direct participation in killing. And in Hesse the *Täuferakten* show considerable confusion in the minds of Anabaptists under examination concerning the sword. There were some who were ready to grant the Christian character of the magistracy while asserting at the same time the Christian's obligation to remain completely nonviolent.

Cases of explicit violence can be found in the Anabaptist movement even before Münster. Stayer remarks: "This violent fringe—it was no more than a fringe—was most obvious in the Saxon and Thuringian regions where Müntzer's combination of religion and social demagoguery was still remembered." Often, however, allegedly Anabaptist conspiracies turn out to have been inventions concocted by their enemies, the joint products of feverish and excited imagination on the part of the authorities and of confessions extracted by torture from the accused. Where such enterprises seem fairly well authenticated, they were led by men who were only peripherally connected with the Anabaptist movement. One of the leaders of the Erfurt conspiracy of late 1527, Volkmar Fischer, appears to have learnt of nonresistance only after his flight to Basel! Again, in the case of the two violent outbreaks which occurred in 1532-1533 in the ecclesiastical statelet of Fulda at the instigation of "Anabaptist" groups, these groups were unconnected in any direct way with the Anabaptist mainstream, or indeed with any other Anabaptist congregations, sharing with them only the practice of adult baptism. Even though Melchior Rink, whose preaching and teaching was an important influence during the early 1530's in shaping central German Anabaptism, remains—like Hut, whose chiliastic visions Rink to some extent shared—a somewhat "enigmatic figure" (he had fought with Müntzer at Frankenhausen before his conversion to Anabaptism), and even though Rink himself seems to have allowed the possibility of a Christian magistracy, his followers in many instances showed themselves consistent nonresistants.

Concerning the Swiss and south German Anabaptists' doctrine of the sword during the first decade of the movement's existence, the most we can say, therefore, in regard to elements of violence is that in the northernmost areas, like Thuringia, where the social motif in Anabaptism was especially strong and the idea of nonresistance to some extent an importation from outside rather than an indigenous growth, there was much less uniformity of creed and conduct than elsewhere. Here nonresistance might fairly easily be discarded if the eschatological situation appeared to warrant the adoption of violent means. Pointing to "the peaceful character of the movement" as a whole, Stayer goes on: "Only on the religious frontier in central Germany did the nonresistant consensus disappear." Outside this area, "occasionally," it is true, "an eccentric religious demagogue would stray from the path [of nonresistance] . . . more frequently a dullard would fail to grasp the common teaching." The absence as yet of a strictly enforced congregational discipline in the matter permitted some variations still in belief and behavior.

Thus, by the early 1530's nonresistance was firmly embedded in Anabaptist ideology. It had been generated within the closed circle of intellectuals and well-to-do bourgeoisie who gathered in Zürich around the young humanist scholar, Conrad Grebel (his early death in 1526 deprived the Swiss Brethren of their most capable leader). The sixth article of the Schleitheim Confession of 1527 gave "credal formulation" to the hitherto somewhat nebulous doctrine. Henceforward, war and governmental office remained unacceptable to all who looked to this Confession for the tenets of their faith. Gradually the nonresistant formula became required doctrine throughout the congregations of south Germany as well as in Switzerland, where it had taken root earlier, and in some parts of central Germany. Variations in its interpretation and application continued to be permissible, however; the occasional deviant who stated his basic disagreement with the principle of nonresistance still escaped official church censure. For the day when the conscientious objector to nonresistance would be subject to disfellowshipping, along with members who violated this regulation on less conscientious grounds, had not yet arrived. But in the early 1530's Hubmaier's *Schwertler*, with their conventional doctrine of the sword, were fast disappearing, and the followers of the chiliastic Hut were turning more and more toward nonresistance. Only at the extreme north of this Anabaptist territory were there groups, isolated from the main body of Anabaptism and often sharing with the latter little more than the name, which were largely unaffected by the nonresistant doctrine and nursed wild schemes for destroying political oppression and religious persecution by violent revolution. However, in this same period, in the northwest of Germany and spreading over into the Netherlands, there arose a new type of Anabaptism—apocalyptic, nurturing a scarcely repressed social violence— which in the middle of the decade was to emerge into the open in the city of Münster. The beginnings of this trend are associated with the name of Melchior Hofmann. The later—and notorious—Munsterites grew out of the Melchiorites who followed Hofmann. We must turn our attention, therefore, to the consequences for Anabaptist nonresistance of the new twist given to the movement by its extension into northern Germany and the Netherlands.

THREE. *The Later Anabaptists*
(FROM MÜNSTER TO MENNO)

At the beginning of the 1530's Anabaptism appeared for the first time in northwest Germany and in the Netherlands. It was carried from the south, not in the form of the evangelical faith of the Swiss Brethren but as a chiliastic, millenarian belief more akin to the creed of Hans Hut than to Conrad Grebel's. Its apostles taught adult baptism but they also preached the fast-approaching destruction of the world and the annihilation of the wicked, especially those in high places. Eventually, in the north, the movement erupted into violence and its holy city, Münster, became a symbol for centuries to come of religious fanaticism and Anabaptist proclivity to the use of the sword.

That the Munsterites were not pacifists scarcely needs mentioning. However, concerning the doctrine of the sword professed in the period before Münster by the Anabaptists of Westphalia, East Friesland, and the Netherlands there exist considerable differences of view among modern scholars. Roughly three positions may be distinguished. First there are those who regard Anabaptism in this area as having been essentially nonresistant from the very beginning; this view is held by such American Mennonite historians as H. S. Bender or Cornelius Krahn, who speaks of it as "a peace-loving pacifist" movement. A second group of writers agree that this movement was indeed peace-loving (*vreedzaam*), but in their opinion it was not absolutely pacifist, not completely nonviolent in the sense that the Schleitheim Confession, for instance, interpreted the concept of nonresistance. The most eloquent exponent of this thesis was the late W. J. Kühler. Both these viewpoints, however, regard the Munsterites as a temporary aberration in the history of northern Anabaptism; as Kühler writes, "the peaceable . . . exist before Münster, during Münster, after Münster." They represented no single class within the community but were drawn from the well-to-do as well as from the poor. A third standpoint is one elaborated in most detail by Dutch historians like Karel Vos. Such writers consider nonresistance to have been virtually unknown among Netherlands and north German Anabaptists until many years after the Münster episode. True, its apostles did not always urge their followers to immediate violence but the movement was essentially revolutionary and an expression of the pent-up antagonism nurtured by the lower orders against the oppression of

89

their social superiors. From vague popular protest it eventually billowed out into a wave of politically revolutionary violence. To argue that here Anabaptism possessed a peaceful character appeared to Vos "a sign of ignorance or dishonesty"; even the martyrs of the faith at this time were, in his view, not nonresistants but revolutionaries. With the loving discipleship of the Swiss Brethren this militant creed had little in common apart from the external practice of adult baptism.

Recent research has shown that in the Netherlands Anabaptism, though indeed imported from without, found a ready hearing among indigenous reformers belonging to the Sacramentarian movement of the 1520's, a movement deeply rooted in the late medieval piety of Netherlands Catholicism. These men were Biblical humanists who had been influenced by Zwingli's denial of a real presence of Christ in the communion elements; they were critical, too, of other aspects of contemporary church practice. They seem to have been, like Erasmus and other contemporary Christian humanists, opponents of war. In 1523, for example, when a debate on various articles of religion was held in one of the main churches of Groningen, war was among the subjects disputed. "I question whether any war is permissible to a Christian, who is commanded by Christ even to love his enemies" (translation in Henry Elias Dosker, *The Dutch Anabaptists*, Philadelphia, 1921): the thesis, of course, was being posed merely as an academic exercise. But that the subject should be discussed at all was probably due to the doubts concerning war raised by groups like the Sacramentarians. At any rate, when Anabaptism reached the Netherlands at the beginning of the 1530's, many Sacramentarians joined the new movement.

The man mainly responsible for bringing the Anabaptist message to the north was, however, a German, not a Dutchman: Melchoir Hofmann, a furrier from Swabia. Hofmann, a questing spirit with a genuinely religious impulse, but a man easily carried away by fantastic visions and messianic dreams, had been a Lutheran for a time before he accepted Anabaptism during a short sojourn in Strasbourg. In that city he had not been closely connected with the main Anabaptist congregation, which followed the Schleitheim Confession as its rule; instead, he associated with a peripheral group gathered around Lienhard and Ursula Jost, a married couple who claimed prophetic powers. Forced to leave Strasbourg, Hofmann settled in Emden in the county of East Friesland where, finding a ready response among those discontented with the existing Protestant establishment, he set up an Anabaptist congregation; it was an energetic convert, Jan Volkertsz Trypmaker, a Dutchman from Hoorn, who then carried Anabaptism for the first time to the Netherlands. Dutch Anabaptism, therefore, begins only with Trypmaker's arrival in Amsterdam toward the end of 1530. Amsterdam became the country's first Anabaptist congregation, but the faith soon spread throughout most of the Dutch- and Flemish-speaking provinces of the Netherlands and even into the French-speaking areas of the south. Hofmann also visited the Netherlands, though only briefly, and he was active, too, as a preacher in northwest Germany and the Rhineland until in 1533 during another visit to Strasbourg he was arrested and kept in confinement there until his death ten years later.

Clarence Bauman has well characterized Hofmann as a typical "chiliastischer Charismatiker." Indeed his charismatic personality served to reinforce the chiliastic message which he preached to all who would listen and to make him undisputed leader of the movement in the areas which formed his mission field. His converts called themselves "Covenanters" (*Bondgenooten* in Dutch; *Bundesgenossen* in German), for, according to Hofmann, those who accepted baptism at his hands or at the hands of his disciples had thereby concluded a covenant with God. If they abided by their baptismal undertaking, God would save them at the day of wrath which was now at hand. But all who remained outside the covenant would be consigned to everlasting damnation—including fellow Anabaptists of other shades of belief (a degree of intolerance hitherto foreign to the movement, even in the case of Hans Hut).

Stayer has stressed "the gap between Melchiorite and non-Melchiorite Anabaptism." Its eschatological vision and its sublimated vengefulness are certainly alien to evangelical Anabaptism of the Schleitheim variety. Concerning the Melchiorite doctrine of the sword, as we have seen, there is some difference of opinion among scholars. No evidence exists to show that he advocated violence himself; the faithful, he believed, must remain quiet and leave vengeance to the coming of the Lord. Elijah, whom Hofmann finally came to believe he incarnated, and his followers had but to wait patiently, and pray. The destruction of the wicked would happen, as it were, *ex opere operato*. Hofmann, moreover, in his commentary on Paul's epistle to the Romans, which he published in 1533, supported a position on the magistracy which was not far removed—according to the letter at least, if not the spirit—from that of the Schleitheim Confession. At one point he writes: "Although the true Christians can wield no other sword than the sword of the spirit, still it does not follow from this that the sword should be taken away, too, from the rulers who stand outside [i.e., the true Christian community]. The sword, the punishment of evildoers, is a great and necessary thing. For that reason the lover

91

of truth, also, even though he does not need the sword and the magistracy for himself, shall not hinder the maintenance of the government; instead he should promote it so that the magisterial office should not disappear." Yet Hofmann's exposition was not without ambiguity, for in the same work he appears unwilling to accept the uncompromising rejection of a Christian magistracy enunciated by the Anabaptist mainstream. In his comments on Romans 13:4, he writes: "That some people do not want to accept the magistrates as Christians in performing their legitimate duties is a great blindness—since they do not distinguish the offices. . . . For, although the priests and Israelites wielded no other Sword in the New Testament than that of the spirit, . . . killing according to God's command through the Sword is not put aside but is God's good pleasure, as is also the spiritual killing through the spiritual Sword." (This translation is quoted from Stayer's dissertation.) Thus, Hofmann's nonresistance may have been indeed only an interim-ethic as Hans Hut's probably was. Hofmann's treatise *On the Sword* (*Von dem Swert*) is no longer extant; in the absence of more conclusive evidence, the most we can say at present is that Hofmann's teaching, though containing potentially violent elements, was nevertheless intended to be essentially peaceable.

The question whether a Christian might exercise the office of the sword appeared, in all likelihood, of little importance either to Hofmann himself or to his disciples. For one thing, most of these were drawn from the poor and lowly, whose situation in society often precluded them from being called to office. In this case the problem of magistracy remained a merely theoretical one. (There is some evidence, however, of Dutch Anabaptists' holding minor offices at this period; at the same time we hear, too, of four weapon-smiths being members of the Amsterdam congregation.) Moreover, with the end of the world near, the kingdoms of this world dimmed in significance before the stupendous events about to take place. If Christ at some point thereafter should call his faithful to arms, then there could be no doubt as to their duty to obey; even the nonresistant Anabaptists agreed that God had approved warfare under the old dispensation, and when a third order came in to inaugurate Christ's kingdom on earth, the carnal sword might again become a legitimate weapon in the hands of His covenanters. Meanwhile the faithful must remain quiet.

The situation in the early 1530's, especially in the northern Netherlands, was explosive however. In the towns of the Netherlands unemployment existed, caused by the economic fluctuations of the now expanding capitalist order; in the countryside similar trends were at work, and the small independent peasant often faced expropriation or reduction to the status of a mere tenant. Mendicancy was rife; the authorities complained of wandering men and idlers who menaced the security of the country. The Dutch seaboard provinces at this date were locked, too, in a struggle with the Hanseatic city of Lübeck; trade with the Baltic declined temporarily, prices rose, and the shipping industry and the fisheries suffered severely as a result of this dislocation of the economy. Conditions generally were unsettled. It was chiefly among the economically hard-hit and the socially dissatisfied that Anabaptism in the northwest made its earliest converts. "Les pauvres, les ouvriers, les matelots s'attachèrent passionément à une doctrine qui leur annonçait le renversement de l'ordre établi, l'arrivée prochaine du règne des justes, la disparition des rois, des princes, des magistrats, la victoire enfin de l'esprit sur la chair dans un monde nouveau, éblouissant, surnatural": in these words Henri Pirenne describes the genesis of Netherlands Anabaptism in the third volume of his classic *Histoire de Belgique* (vol. III, Brussels, 1907, p. 112). Though it should not be overlooked that early Anabaptist congregations included persons of affluence, and occasionally even of influence, and that they were by no means exclusively proletarian or peasant conventicles, contemporary evidence nevertheless indicates that the new sect's appeal was primarily to the oppressed, to the underdog. The twentieth-century *Doopsgezinden* historian Vos was certainly exaggerating when he described early Netherlands Anabaptists as the "swill of the slums." Nonetheless it was the victim of social injustice rather than the noble, the burgher, or the prosperous farmer who heard the message and believed. An official report, dated July 1534, describes the Anabaptists of the northern Netherlands as in general "gens non letterez, povres, mécaniques." The typical Anabaptist of this period was most likely to be an artisan or an apprentice, a dock laborer, a sailor, or perhaps a peasant. Among the elders some lower clergy could be found; Menno Simons, for instance, had been a country priest before he joined the Anabaptists.

Even if we assume therefore (what in fact is not proven) that Hofmann himself was an adherent of thoroughgoing nonresistance, in theory as well as in practice, it is extremely unlikely that his followers were, for their leader made little attempt to inculcate such a doctrine among the Covenanters beyond a general charge to stay peaceable during the short while remaining before Christ came in his glory, to judge and to punish. What stood out in Hofmann's message was not nonviolence but the chiliastic vision.

Anabaptism, although its progress was at first slow in the German northwest, made rapid strides in the Dutch and Flemish Netherlands.

Here the sect very soon became numerically the strongest branch of the Protestant Reformation, and remained so until it was displaced by Calvinism three to four decades later. The first few years constitute an especially obscure period in the history of northern Anabaptism. The congregation in Amsterdam, we know, formed its center; from there emissaries went out into the towns and countryside of the Netherlands and across the border into Germany. In Hofmann's absence a leading role was played by a flamboyant young man, Jan Matthijsz, a baker from Haarlem whom Hofmann had baptized and who, like his mentor, soon came to regard himself as a prophet sent to proclaim the approaching end of the world; in Matthijsz's case, Enoch was the personage whom the prophet chose to represent. For the time being Matthijsz called for the quiet endurance of wrong. Obbe Philips in his "Confession" has left the following account of the doctrine as preached by two of Matthijsz's closest associates, when in late 1533 they visited Leeuwarden and there baptized both Obbe and his brother Dirk, who were both to play important parts in the post-Münster period of northern Anabaptist history: "They proposed and proclaimed to us peace and patience. . . . They also comforted us and said we need have no fear as we had long had because of the great tyranny, since no Christian blood would be shed on earth, but in a short time God would rid the earth of all shedders of blood and all tyrants and the godless . . . [They] told us that no more blood would be shed on earth." Although Obbe Philips's efforts in his "Confession" to dissociate himself from the eschatological violence embedded in the peaceable gospel of Matthijsz's deputies may be suspect as a *post factum* justification for his own conduct at this time, his words probably represent accurately the current views of leading northern Anabaptists.

The "apostles" who converted the Philips brothers were responsible for a bizarre episode a few months later when, in March 1534, they went through the streets of Amsterdam brandishing swords and crying: "The new city [i.e., Amsterdam's west side] is given to the children of God," and "Repent ye, repent ye and do penance," and "Woe, woe to all the godless." No more than the actions of the seven "naked walkers" of February 1535, who also paraded the Amsterdam streets, were such manifestations of extreme religious enthusiasm a sign of open revolutionary violence. They do show, nevertheless, that the movement was entering a dangerous stage in its development, when the Melchiorites might feel themselves led to hasten the fulfilment of the divine wrath, to take up the sword and use it against the godless who stood outside the holy covenant.

At first, the Melchiorites had regarded Strasbourg as the New

94

Jerusalem, whose liberation would usher in the millennium. A little later it was Amsterdam, not Strasbourg, that appeared to many of them to have been chosen by God for this exalted role; there the Covenanters would come into their own after the divine—and miraculous—intervention had delivered the city into their hands. In the end it was Münster, capital of the autonomous Westphalian bishopric of that name, where the New Jerusalem was in fact proclaimed. And its establishment was not to be the result of divine intervention but of human hands. Between February 1532 and January 1534 Münster had moved over from a Lutheran-oriented reformation to a Melchiorite Anabaptist revolution, albeit at first a peaceful one. At the beginning the leading figure in the changes was a former priest turned Lutheran, Bernhard Rothmann, who accepted baptism, however, only in January 1534. Though Rothmann continued to provide intellectual ballast for the Anabaptist revolutionary party, the direction of affairs soon fell into more vigorous, though unscrupulous, hands. Netherlanders had originally spread the Melchiorite message in Westphalia, and it was they who soon secured control of the movement in Münster as it passed over from the waiting stage to actual violence. Control was exercised first by Jan Matthijsz of Haarlem, who arrived there early in February 1534 but was killed in battle a couple of months later, and then by another and even more exotic young Dutchman, Jan Bockelszoon of Leiden, whom Jan Matthijsz had baptized in the previous November and thereupon dispatched to preach his gospel.

During January the Anabaptists, though in control of the city, did not yet resort to violence. Indeed they seem to have believed, as Hofmann had taught, that nonviolence was expected of them by the Lord. As Rothmann himself testified later: "Around the time we were baptized we all laid down our weapons and prepared ourselves as a sacrifice. It was our opinion that it would not be proper to resist the godless except in accepting suffering, and death itself, with patience." But patience eventually gave out. Already the godless were threatening counter-action; the Catholic bishop of Münster, Franz von Waldeck, was gathering an army to recover his city and seeking allies among the princes of the Empire to aid him in this task. Everywhere the faithful Covenanters were undergoing cruel persecution. Was not the time of meek waiting, of mildness, of suffering the blows of the persecutors now over? Should not the faithful themselves take the initiative and strike at the godless, now that the holy city was established and the hour of deliverance come at last? Was it not, in fact, their duty to act, so that Christ could descend in his glory to an already cleansed earth? Should not the faithful take up the sword at last and forward the divine plan by their own efforts? Thus the Anabaptists reasoned now that the period of peaceableness was passed. And by the time Jan Matthijsz arrived in Münster, the decision to resort to arms in defense of the New Jerusalem had already been reached: Matthijsz, although he had adopted a peaceable stance hitherto, approved the new policy. The first armed clash between Munsterites and their external enemies occurred during the second week of February, and the policy of revolutionary "terror" against the internal enemy soon followed. As the bishop's army encircled the city and the siege of Münster began in earnest, and as Jan of Leiden's hold on his followers—a reflection of the charismatic powers of this complex figure, half prophet, half charlatan—grew stronger with the mounting pressure from without, the measures taken by the regime of the Anabaptist "saints" became more extreme. The kingship of John of Leiden, the sentences of banishment and execution against opponents (including those within the Anabaptist brotherhood), war communism, and polygamy—these things were to make "Münster" synonymous, in the minds of most contemporaries and for centuries to come, with antinomianism and moral nihilism. The episode cast a shadow over the whole Anabaptist movement and seemed to confirm the opinion of those who had maintained from the beginning that Anabaptist nonresistance was a mere cloak for violent revolution.

The Munsterites, however, were ready to defend their switch from nonviolence to violent action, to any who would listen. Essentially their case rested on the argument that differing ethical stances were appropriate at different epochs in the working out of God's plan for the world (a view which the evangelical Anabaptists in fact accepted in principle when they distinguished between the Old Testament dispensation which permitted the sword and the New dispensation introduced by Christ, which forbade its use by the faithful). In his *Eyne Restitution*, published in 1534, Rothmann, who was responsible for much of the propaganda material put out by the Munsterites, observed: "We must pay close attention to the time so that we do not undertake something too early or too late." And in the same work he wrote, obviously with an eye to his fellow Anabaptists who still clung to a peaceable apocalypticism: "Someone might think . . . it is the Christian's role to suffer, whereas we have used violence. Here let the good-hearted be instructed. First there has been a time of the cross and of Babylon's captivity in which the measure of the godless must be filled. There is also a time of deliverance in which the godless shall be repaid with the same measure, indeed with doubled measure. . . . We say [Christ] will yet be king and have all his enemies killed before his eyes—and this will happen here on earth." As Stayer has rightly pointed out, "Rothmann's entire theory of history and *Obrigkeit* could have stayed in the realm of violent fantasy and been *de facto* peaceful —with one alteration. If it had counseled the faithful to wait for the return of Christ before using the double-edged Sword or establishing the transformed *Obrigkeit*, its violence would have been pushed off into a supernatural future."

Violent fantasy, however *de facto* peaceful, is not quite the same thing of course as nonviolence *stricto sensu*. We must try to determine whether a truly nonviolent, as well as a *de facto* "peaceable," trend continued to exist within Melchiorite Anabaptism during the mid-thirties, at the time of the Münster episode. Although the extant evidence is fragmentary, it soon becomes clear that in the northwest the Munsterites' appeal to the sword did not by any means win unanimous approval among Anabaptists there. Even in Münster itself there was opposition to the use of violence among the faithful. At the beginning, not all who made their way to the holy city realized the ideological transformation that had been accomplished until after they arrived; most assented and girded on the sword, but there were some, too, who then withdrew from the city, disapproving the new doctrine. At Wessel in Westphalia, just across the Dutch border, an Anabaptist stocking-maker is reported as having said: "The king [i.e., Jan of Leiden] and people of Münster were wrong to harm anyone. Love permits no vengeance." Taken at its face value, a remark of this kind would appear to indicate adherence to complete nonresistance. Yet an examination of the Netherlands congregations at this time shows the need for caution in this respect, for, as in the case of Hofmann himself, it usually remains uncertain whether his followers were accepting nonviolence on principle or merely as an interim-ethic to be discarded after Christ's return to earth ushered in the work of wrath, or perhaps as a merely personal stance permitting, at least in theory, the use of the sword by a Christian magistracy.

In the important Amsterdam congregation, for instance, while Munsterite persuasions to support the work of revolution found scant support, nonresistance was evidently far from being a requirement of membership. The influential elder, Jacob van Campen, may with justification be claimed as one of the *stillen*; he rebuffed the overtures of the emissaries from Münster (though without completely dissociating himself from the possibility of violence of the kind employed by the Munsterites). Yet, on the other hand, he supported the right of personal self-defense and did not oppose the purchase of weapons by the faithful for use in some dire emergency or at God's special command.

And though the deacon Jan Pauw, a figure of equal importance among Amsterdam Anabaptists, believed in personal nonresistance—as the very "resistant" Anabaptist Balthasar Hubmaier had done too, we may note—he seems to have shared the apocalyptic and scarcely nonviolent expectations of other Melchiorite enthusiasts. At the end of December 1534 he testified in the course of examination by the authorities in Amsterdam: "This town would be given over by God for the need of those who were in the Covenant." Stayer aptly describes Pauw as "a true Melchiorite of the original strain," who continued to expect Christ's earthly reign to be inaugurated solely as the result of an act of divine intervention. But whether Pauw can rightly be called a "supporter of nonresistance" (W. J. Kühler) cannot be decided with any certainty from the incomplete evidence available. In the case of another contemporary leader of Dutch Anabaptism, the colorful David Joris, who opposed the Munsterites vigorously, telling them that he "could not approve of striking with the Sword [since] . . . the Lord did not so conduct himself and it was not taught by the Apostles but rather to bear the cross and endure all injustice," we know from other statements of his made shortly afterward that in fact he did not share the evangelical Anabaptists' view of the magistracy as being "outside the perfection of Christ."

The Netherlands remained quiet in 1534-1535, except for a few minor and unsuccessful outbreaks of violence, e.g., at Oldeklooster near Bolsward (Friesland) in March 1535 and in Amsterdam in the following May. Where there was no influential leader to counter the influence of Munsterite emissaries, the Anabaptist rank and file usually became disorientated. Most of them were simple folk without much book-learning; they had long been used to trusting to ecclesiastical leadership under the old church. Moreover, they had only recently attached themselves to the Anabaptist movement since it was a new phenomenon in these parts; its principles and practices were not yet deeply ingrained in their way of life. Even though Melchioritism had hitherto possessed a peaceable character, its fiery prophecies and prognostications of impending doom must have accustomed its followers to the idea of destruction and a cataclysmic transformation of the existing order. In addition, those who belonged to the socially downtrodden and the economically oppressed easily came to merge their grievances with their religious longings and expectations.

In March 1534, for instance, in north Holland some three thousand Anabaptists—men, women, and children—took ship (twenty-seven vessels were needed to transport them) across the Zuider Zee in an attempt to make their way to Münster. They had been incited to this action by emissaries sent from the city, who had also told them to buy arms. When the authorities in Overijssel, on the other side of the water, intervened, seizing the ships and detaining all who did not succeed in escaping, they found on board, according to the official report, "about 1500 spears, many guns, battleswords, halberds and all kinds of arms, with four standards and four drums." Yet the company, on being stopped, made no attempt to put up any resistance, passively allowing themselves to be arrested. The authorities described them as for the most part "harmless people." Though they were prepared blindly to obey the orders of their spiritual leaders even when, as now, these orders had reversed completely the sect's nonviolent stand and though, if they had succeeded in reaching Münster, they might well have then joined enthusiastically in the bloody work, their behavior at this point surely indicates that these people still remained *stillen* in spirit. Moreover, Kühler has shown that many of them were well-to-do people who before leaving home had sold houses, land, and jewels to pay the expenses of the journey to the New Jerusalem; they had not been recruited exclusively from economically discontented, proletarian elements.

No figures are available concerning the respective strengths of the *vreedzamen* and of the convinced Munsterites; therefore a definitive verdict is impossible between the conflicting views of those who, like Kühler and van der Zijpp, believe the overwhelming majority of Netherlands Anabaptists remained at least peaceably inclined, if not unconditionally nonresistant, and those who, like Vos and Mellink, consider support for Münster to have been practically unanimous. It is even more difficult to ascertain whether among the peaceable Melchiorites there were some who took a stand against all violence on principle. It seems, however, that throughout the Münster period both the revolutionaries and their opponents still considered themselves as members of a single brotherhood. They were all Covenanters even if their views on the way to the Kingdom of Christ differed. The peaceable might denounce the Munsterites as "false brethren" but they remained brethren none the less. The movement was still one.

Münster finally fell to its enemies in June 1535. The episode, despite its violence, certainly belongs within the framework of Anabaptist history. The leaders of revolutionary Anabaptism, as well as their more humble supporters, all took their origin in the Melchiorite branch. Although defeat discredited the Munsterites and eventually gave renewed strength to those Anabaptists who had opposed them, its immediate outcome was to spread confusion throughout the ranks of Netherlands and north German Anabaptism. The Münster authorities took a cruel revenge on all on whom they could lay their hands. Little distinction was made, either here or in many other areas, between those who had participated in the violence and those who stood aside from it. Persecution against the sect was stepped up everywhere, and the *stillen* suffered alongside their "resistant" brethren.

At this point we must turn aside for a moment to consider the condition of Anabaptist nonresistance during this period in the areas to the south, where Melchioritism had made little or no impact. In Switzerland by this time the nonresistant position had found final acceptance as a tenet of the faith: Melchiorite influences or echoes of Münster militancy are absent in this area. At the disputation of Bern in 1538 (as at Zofingen six years earlier) the Swiss Anabaptists stated their belief in nonresistance without any equivocation. As they told their Protestant opponents in the debate:

> We grant that in the non-Christian world government authorities have a legitimate place, to keep order, to punish the evil, and to protect the good. But we as Christians live according to the Gospel and our only authority and lord is Jesus Christ. Christians consequently do not use the sword, which is worldly, but they use the Christian ban. There is a great difference between Christians and the world, the former living by the standards of the Sermon on the Mount and the latter being perverted and governed by Satan. The world uses the sword; Christians use only spiritual weapons.

At Strasbourg in Alsace it was the same story. Here in June 1534, at the height of the Münster outbreak, as Jan of Leiden's messengers travelled up and down the Netherlands and northern Germany visiting Anabaptist groups in an effort to obtain money and recruits for the beleaguered city, we find a leading member of the Strasbourg congregation, the Tirolean Leupold Scharnschlager, expounding unqualified nonresistance to the city council as his people's faith. He condemned Zwingli for taking up the sword in defense of religion, and he contrasted "worldly power" wielding "the physical sword" with "Christian power." This, he said, has its own "peculiar nature, rule and characteristic and belongs to a special people, which will endure to eternity." Throughout southern Germany during the 1530's—and indeed for the remainder of the century, as shown in recent studies like those of Hans J. Hillerbrand or Elsa Bernhofer-Pippert—Anabaptists were nonresistant "almost without exception (*fast ausnahmlos*)." They objected on principle to performing military service. Although they were sometimes ready to contribute in money or in kind to warlike purposes if the state demanded it of them, there were some, too, who took up a more uncompromising stand. For instance, in Thuringia in 1538 a brother refused to go on earning his living as a gunmaker since, as he declared, "it was sinful." In 1535 a Saxon Anabaptist, one Georg Köhler, arguing that killing was "forbidden in the Ten Commandments" as well as by Christ, explained that his coreligionists carried "no big weapon unless it be sometimes a broad-axe for labor or a staff" (quoted from Eduard Jacobs, "Die Wiedertäufer am Harz," *Zeitschrift des Harz-Vereins für Geschichte und Altertumskunde* [Wernigerode], xxxii [1899]). And this was an area where a decade earlier Thomas Müntzer had been active! Usually, when pressed for an opinion by the authorities, south German Anabaptists were willing to allow that the state had a (conditional) right to wage war in defense of its borders and to suppress crime by the sword. Yet for Christians, they insisted, the only law was that contained in the Sermon on the Mount.

Occasional deviants from nonresistance were still to be found in central Germany at the time of Münster and for several decades to come. But their doctrine of the sword resembled the conventional one held by Hubmaier and was not the result of Melchiorite or Munsterite influence. Indeed a man like Georg Schnabel in western Hesse, even though he held that Christians could serve in office and fight at the command of the magistrate in just wars or in protection of the helpless, such as widows and orphans, was at pains to dissociate the Anabaptist faith from the legacy of Münster. Moreover, he considered that Christians should refuse service in wars of aggression and conquest (thus appearing as a forerunner of the "selective objector" of the twentieth century).

In fact, during the war emergency that prevailed in central Germany in the mid-1530's as a consequence of the Münster uprising and the unrest this caused throughout the neighboring German states, there were princes who were even somewhat perturbed by the fact that Anabaptist principles precluded bearing arms or resisting invasion. At Marburg, for instance, the capital of Landgrave Philip of Hesse, the pastor tried to persuade a local Anabaptist that Christ's injunction to love one's enemies was not intended to prevent the *Obrigkeit* from taking human life if this were unavoidable in the fulfilment of its duties. However, he had been unsuccessful, the pastor reported to his master. The man "could give me no other answer than 'Thou shall not kill'; thus he remained obdurate in his error." Other officials in Hesse experienced the same failure in their encounters with Anabaptists. Finally, in 1538, the Landgrave persuaded Bucer to visit his principality for the purpose of disputing with the stubborn sectaries and persuading them of their mistaken views in regard to nonresistance as well as to other points where they differed from the magisterial Reformers. Bucer carried out his mission with considerable success, and there were a number of recantations. After Bucer had returned to Strasbourg a former Anabaptist, one Hermann Bastian, convinced now that a Christian could show "true love to him who was killed, in regular punishment of the magistracy," was set the task of continuing the work of conversion among the "erring sheep" who remained in the Anabaptist fold. Nevertheless Anabaptism was not rooted out of Hesse. Landgrave Philip, a man of tolerant views if not of impeccable morals, distinguished among Anabaptists between the evangelicals, men of peaceful principles who erred, it is true, in doctrine but were otherwise model subjects, and the violent wing whose adherents needed to be ruthlessly suppressed.

The foremost protagonist of Swiss and south German Anabaptism from the early 1530's to his death in 1556—and after Michael Sattler's execution the most formative influence on the movement—was the Tirolean Pilgram Marbeck, a mining engineer and a man of considerable education and ability. Marbeck was a convinced nonresistant; the few passages in his works cited to support the view that he took a positive attitude to the magistrate's office are not very convincing, especially in view of a large number of other passages showing the opposite. When, for instance, in 1531 Marbeck was banished from Strasbourg, the municipal council brought up against him his rejection of the citizen's obligation to defend his city, which Marbeck had called an unchristian act. Marbeck in his writings insisted that true Christians did not belong to any earthly kingdom but were subjects of Christ alone. Under the Old Covenant God permitted magistracy and the sword.

> Today [there is] another king, another kingdom, another priesthood, another law, which is not a carnal law of ruling, or worldly, earthly judicial procedures as that of yesterday, but a spiritual one, and a law or commandment of the Spirit—love and patience, which God "yesterday" promised and "today" for the first time wrote in [our] hearts . . . Christ commanded His priests who were appointed today [in the New Covenant] . . . that they should love all people, not merely their friends or dear ones, but also their enemies, and not resist evil, . . . also that [they] should not use carnal weapons . . . against their enemies. All bodily, worldly, carnal, earthly fighting, conflicts and wars are annulled and abolished among them through such law. . . . Which law of love, Christ

. . . then, as the present High Priest, Himself observed and thereby gave His followers a pattern to follow after. In contrast, the worldly government is not one which shows mercy, but is a revenger.

Later, in his *Judicium* Caspar Schwenckfeld, the radical spiritualist reformer who, though not unsympathetic to the Anabaptists, disapproved of their negative attitude to the magistracy, cited the case of the centurion Cornelius to justify the soldier's profession and the acceptance of office among Christians (a frequent argument in the anti-nonresistant repertoire). Marbeck had replied: "Who knows how long the Holy Spirit and his conscience allowed Cornelius to remain in his captaincy after he had become a Christian" (from the *Verantwortung* of 1544, published by Johann Loserth in *Quellen und Forschungen zur Geschichte der oberdeutschen Taufgesinnten im 16. Jahrhundert*, Vienna and Leipzig, 1929).

In his *Verantwortung* Marbeck was speaking in the name of the Anabaptists of southern Germany. Despite the congregational organization of the sect, in this area as in Switzerland, Anabaptism, we have seen, presented by now a fairly well-defined unity of doctrine and outlook. Nonresistance was generally accepted as an integral part of the faith, and only a few scattered individuals continued to have reservations concerning a total rejection of the sword. In northern Germany and the Netherlands, on the other hand, the Münster episode had left an aftermath of confusion and conflict. More than a decade elapsed before unity was restored once more among the Anabaptists of these lands.

Here Münster proved a turning point; eventually, violent Anabaptism disappeared and the peaceable trend gained an unchallenged ascendancy throughout the whole movement. But immediately after the fall of Münster three main parties contended within the hitherto nominally united movement.

First there were the peaceable who had viewed with mounting indignation the deeds done at Münster in the name of Anabaptism. At the outset there was as yet no formal break, but from early 1535 onwards the Philips brothers in the northern Netherlands began to rally all those who opposed the use of violence to bring in the Kingdom. In his "Confession" Obbe Philips wrote later of this incipient schism: "Still we poor people could not yet open our eyes, for it all happened so crudely that we were not able to put our hands on the lies and obscurities. But God knows that Dirk [Philips] and I could never find it in our hearts that such onslaughts were right; we taught firmly against this, but it did us no good, for most of the folks were inclined to this." It was in fact not until disaster had overtaken the Munsterites that the Philipses were able to make any great headway. Many of their nearest associates had become enthusiasts for the avenging sword and some of them, like Hans Scheerder for instance, continued now to advocate violence. The original Melchiorites, including Obbe Philips himself, had eagerly expected the end of the world, though they and their master saw no need for the sword to bring this about. The failure of Hofmann's prophecies spread disillusionment among his followers who had remained faithful to his instructions to remain nonviolent. Thus, from peaceable waiting for a speedy second coming of the Lord, his followers, under Obbe Philips's guidance, began to develop the idea of patient suffering until in the Lord's good time the day of judgment should come.

Second, the Munsterites after their kingdom's fall still went on nursing their eschatological hopes. Not the hopes themselves were false, they argued, it was the time-table for their realization that had been wrong. They agreed, therefore, on the need for temporarily putting the sword on one side and awaiting a divine call before girding it on again to do battle for the Kingdom of God on earth. Third, a new trend now appeared in northern Anabaptism: certain extremist elements among the Munsterites led by Jan van Batenburg, a man of aristocratic origin who suffered execution in 1538, broke with the main body and continued to practice a policy of revolutionary terror. The era of God's mercy was ended, said Jan van Batenburg. Unbelievers must be put to the sword and their property destroyed, and the same treatment should be meted out to those faithful who had lapsed from righteousness. The Batenburgers proceeded to put their beliefs into practice, robbing churches and houses and killing selected victims, including members of other Anabaptist groups.

In the summer of 1536, a few months after the fall of Münster, David Joris, in an attempt to restore the movement's shattered unity, had called a conference at Bocholt in Westphalia. Both Batenburgers and Obbenites stayed away. Those who attended were drawn mainly from the "orthodox" Munsterites and various shades of the more peaceable Melchiorites. Little was, in fact, achieved at Bocholt. Within a decade or so (the sources are very meager concerning these developments) the Munsterites had disintegrated: it is hard to maintain mass enthusiasm for long if the promised dénouement is postponed indefinitely. The Batenburgers also dwindled and disappeared; the sect's activities degenerated into banditry and murder, and toward the end criminal elements rather than pious fanatics gave the tone to the group. The future lay with Obbe Philips's party, for Christian patience and the expectation of suffering in this world now appeared a more effective stance for the faithful than chiliasm, even in the peaceable form preached by Melchior Hofmann. But it was not to be Obbe himself who would eventually reunite northern Anabaptism on the basis of nonresistance. By 1540 Obbe had left the movement; his place as leader was taken by a former Catholic country parson from Friesland, Menno Simons, who had first openly espoused Anabaptism only in January 1536. Thus the Obbenites became transformed into Mennonites.

Recently a manuscript confession of faith issued by the German Anabaptist congregation at Kempen on the Lower Rhine in 1545 was uncovered (it has been published by J.F.G. Goeters: "Das älteste rhenische Täuferbekenntnis," in Cornelius J. Dyck, ed., *A Legacy of Faith: A Sixtieth Tribute to Cornelius Krahn* [Newton, Kansas], 1962). In its sections on the magistracy and arms-bearing it expounds the doctrine of the sword entirely in the spirit of the Schleitheim Confession; indeed, it foreshadows the doctrine of the sword exemplified in the later writings of the Dutch and German Mennonites. While the *Obrigkeit* was ordained by God to keep the public peace and was entitled to obedience, Christians were permitted to wield no other weapon than the sword of God's word. Their model must remain Christ's cross and sufferings. The whole tone of these paragraphs is entirely non-resistant.

It would seem, therefore, that the wave of Munsterite violence within the northern Anabaptist movement must already have subsided by the early 1540's if, in an area like the lower German Rhineland where Munsterite influence had been strong, nonresistance was already accepted as official church doctrine. There is, it is true, some doubt as to the extent south German nonresistance was known among northern Anabaptists during the 1530's. But something more than a vague knowledge of it must have penetrated this area at least by the end of that decade. Whether the Kempen Anabaptists derived their nonresistance primarily from Menno and his followers just across the border, or whether it came chiefly from influences from the south where nonresistance, as we have seen, had long been a characteristic of normative Anabaptism, we cannot say with any certainty. Eventually, however, northern and southern Anabaptism merged to create a single, loosely organized, yet interconnected movement: the Mennonite brotherhood.

Menno was already forty when he finally joined the Anabaptists after a long period of hesitation. Convinced of the correctness of adult

105

baptism and disillusioned with many doctrines and practices of the Catholic church, he had allowed his ingrained caution and a certain lack of civic courage, which characterized him throughout his life, to keep him back from the final break. When violence broke out in Münster his formal rejection of Catholicism was still to come. But he reacted strongly against the new trend and wrote a pamphlet entitled "The Blasphemy of Jan of Leiden," denouncing the use of the sword to institute Christ's kingdom. "How can Christians fight with the implements of war?" he demanded. They should leave the punishment of the wicked to Christ's verdict on the Day of Judgment when he would divide the sheep from the goats, the wheat from the tares. "These words are as clear as the sun, yet some do not understand them. . . . Christ has not taken His kingdom with the sword, but He entered it though much suffering. Yet they think to take it by the sword! Oh, blindness of man!"

From the outset of his career among the Anabaptists, therefore, Menno stood squarely on the side of the "peaceable." Attempts (e.g., by Vos) to prove that at the beginning he entertained some sympathy with the Munsterites, either because he addressed them in 1539 as "dear brethren" who had strayed "a little" from the path of righteousness or because through Obbe Philips he had derived his baptism from Jan Matthijsz of Haarlem and Melchior Hofmann, are unconvincing. His overtures to the rank-and-file Munsterites are quite understandable, since the peaceable had not yet given up hope of winning them away from their leaders' delusive trust in violence, and give no evidence of desire on Menno's part to excuse the conduct of the Munsterite leaders; and the genealogy of Menno's baptism shows merely a genetic connection with pre-Munsterite Anabaptism in its Melchiorite variant. True, Vos was justified in detecting a bias among previous *Doopsgezinden* historians who had tended to obscure their church's Melchiorite origin. But as van der Zijpp has remarked, "Menno and Münster may both take their beginning from Melchior Hofmann, but the two are not of one spirit."

The existence of "a certain continuity" between the Melchiorite and Mennonite stages in Netherlands Anabaptism, both as to the leadership and the ideology of the movement (e.g., its eschatological hopes) certainly poses problems in regard to the character of Menno's nonresistance. Dutch *Doopsgezinden* historians like Dyserinck or Kühler, for instance, have argued that Menno was never an uncompromising nonresistant in the style of the Swiss Brethren. While he rejected the use of force to effect political or social change or to impose religious uniformity or to resist religious persecution, he approved a Christian magistracy and its employment of the sword in war and policing as well as the right of personal self-defense. According to this view, unconditional nonresistance was adopted as a tenet of the faith only sometime after Menno's death in 1561.

In fact, nonresistance does not figure among Menno's chief concerns during the twenty-eight years of his itinerant ministry, which took him to most areas in the northern Netherlands and northern Germany where there were Anabaptist congregations. In his numerous writings he does not explicitly articulate the concept of nonresistance, at least to the extent that the Swiss and south German brethren do; it is never put forward as an essential qualification for membership of the sect. On the other hand, the gospel of love, the principle of nonretaliation, and the creative power of suffering—all the elements of "the theology of martyrdom"—are strongly emphasized. His religion is centered on the New Testament; the Anabaptist congregation is seen as a community of disciples modelling themselves exactly on the apostolic pattern. We cannot, therefore, presume from Menno's failure to formulate precisely a belief in nonviolence and a principled opposition to military service, or to incorporate these doctrines creedally, that he was not a thoroughgoing nonresistant. For Menno was not a man of great intellectual stature; he was but a weak theologian. His chief concern was pastoral, and his object, usually, to serve the immediate needs of his people.

Menno, it is clear, distinguished a "Jewish doctrine of the sword," which was different from that taught by Christ under the New Covenant. "To aid with the sword," he wrote early in the 1540's "is forbidden to all true Christians. In the New Testament all true believers should suffer patiently and not fight and do battle with swords and muskets." In one of his most popular works first published in 1539-1540, *Dat Fundament des Christelycken Leers* (*The Foundation of Christian Doctrine*) or *Fundamentboek*, he elaborated this theme in some detail.

> Our weapons are not weapons with which cities and countries may be destroyed, walls and gates broken down, and human blood shed in torrents like water. But they are weapons with which the spiritual kingdom of the devil is destroyed and the wicked principle in man's soul is broken down. . . . We have and know no other weapons besides this, the Lord knows, even if we should be torn into a thousand pieces. . . . Christ is our fortress; patience our weapon of defense; the Word of God our sword; and our victory a courageous, firm, unfeigned faith in Jesus Christ.

And iron and metal spears and swords we leave to those who, alas, regard human blood and swine's blood alike.

Here and elsewhere Menno contrasted the realms of Christ and of Satan. "The Scriptures," he wrote in "A Humble and Christian Apology and Reply . . . concerning False Accusations" (1552), "teach that there are two opposing princes and two opposing kingdoms: the one is the prince of peace; the other the prince of strife. Each of these princes has his particular kingdom and as the prince is so is also the kingdom." And "the children of peace" (to cite now from a work written in the late 1530's) are those "who have beaten their spears into pruning hooks, and know war no more." "Their citizenship is in heaven"; and, though they pay taxes to Caesar as their Lord demanded of them, they remain separate from the kingdoms of this world. In the *Fundamentboek*, after stressing that obedience to, and respect for, the magistracy "in so far as they are not contrary to the Word of God" was an essential part of Christian discipleship, Menno went on: "But the civil sword we leave to those to whom it is committed." The only instruments of discipline which a Christian could employ were brotherly admonition and, in the last resort, the ban. In face of the Beatitudes and the rest of the Sermon on the Mount, "tell me," he asks in his "Humble and Christian Apology" quoted above, "how can a Christian defend scripturally retaliation, rebellion, *war*, striking, slaying, torturing, stealing, robbing and plundering and burning cities, and conquering countries?" (my italics). To do so was quite impossible for disciples of Christ: "They are the children of peace; their hearts overflow with peace; their mouths speak peace, and they walk in the way of peace; they are full of peace. They seek, desire, and know nothing but peace; and are prepared to forsake country, goods, life, and all for the sake of peace."

The general tenor of Menno's pronouncements (here I have merely culled a few out of a large number of passages written in a similar spirit) appears to speak decisively in favor of an unconditionally, an absolutely pacifist, stance on Menno's part, at least in the years following his conversion, if not earlier still. Moreover, in Menno's view religious persecution and war merged (as the nineteenth-century scholar Wilhelm Mannhardt pointed out). The same state both persecuted and waged war: Menno's condemnation of the one included condemnation of the other activity in many cases. In addition, his uncompromising rejection of the oath, a feature of sectarian pacifism, might be taken as *a priori* proof, in view of his generalized condemnation of coercion and war, of his complete pacifism. Yet, in regard to nonresist-

108

ance, the sword-bearing magistracy and personal self-defense, there are passages in his works which should prompt caution on the subject before any final judgment is reached.

Despite his many admonitions to maintain strict nonconformity to the world, Menno seems eventually to have contemplated the possibility of a Christian magistracy. At first, however, his attitude toward office holding seems to have been more hostile; it mellowed only with the passing of the years and the waning of his earlier eschatological expectations. It is true that in 1544, in the "Brief and Clear Confession" which Menno presented to the Polish reformer Jan Łaski in Latin, there is already a reference which has been interpreted by some writers to imply Menno's approval of Christian participation in the sword-bearing aspects of magistracy. He wrote: "We are taught and warned [in the Scriptures] not to take up the literal sword, nor ever to give our consent thereto (excepting the ordinary sword of the magistrate when it must be used [*excepto ordinario potestatis gladio, in debitum usum verso*]), but to take up the two-edged, powerful, sharp sword of the Spirit, . . . namely, the Word of God." Certainly the wording of this passage is not crystal clear. Desire on Menno's part to dissociate himself and his coreligionists from the Munsterites' rebellion against lawful authority, as well as Menno's well-known timidity which he might well feel in view of his formidable opponent Łaski, may have led him to go further in this instance in justifying magistracy than his true opinions at that date warranted. Even so, the words, taken literally, need not imply more than the traditional respect shown by evangelical Anabaptists for the office of the sword "outside the perfection of Christ."

In the early 1550's, however, we can indeed detect a somewhat more positive attitude to magistracy on Menno's part. There is evidence that he now felt, if he had not done so before, that holding office did not debar a man from belonging to an Anabaptist congregation, though it was probably the lower levels of the governmental hierarchy that alone were in question. In 1554, for instance, he wrote: "I should not wish to force a Christian to lay down his office; I would leave him to his own conscience and the authority of the Holy Spirit." This, it is true, is a little ambiguous. Menno probably meant to imply that a decision whether to hold office or not could be left to the individual conscience: the problem was a personal one and not a matter for communal decision. Yet it is also possible that Menno presumed that conscience and the Holy Spirit would eventually lead a Christian to resign (just as, in the same spirit, the Quaker George Fox was to tell young William Penn to wear his sword as long as he could).

109

Two years later, however, in 1556, Menno, in his "Epistle" to the Zwinglian theologian Martin Micron, spoke plainly of "a true Christian ruler." In this case he still lays down certain conditions which would remove the power of the sword from a Christian magistracy. Capital punishment was wrong, he wrote, because it might lead to the death of an impenitent wrongdoer whose soul would then be eternally lost. On the other hand, if the man truly repented and became a "Christian," then "for such an one to be hanged on the gallows, put on the wheel, placed on the stake, or in any manner be hurt in body or goods by another Christian, who is of one heart, spirit and soul with him, would look somewhat strange and unbecoming in the light of the compassionate, merciful, kind nature . . . of Christ, the meek Lamb." Menno praised the heathen Lacedaemonians who sentenced criminals not to death but to hard labor, thus showing themselves more generous than so-called Christians. For Christian magistrates "to fight and retaliate . . . and destroy their enemies," as did "Moses and the patriarchs," made a mockery of "the holy Gospel," which taught mercy and love. "That the office of the magistrate is of God and His ordinance I freely grant," Menno went on. "But him who is a Christian and wants to be one and then does not follow his Prince, Head and Leader Christ, but covers and clothes his unrighteousness . . . with the name of magistrate, I hate. For he who is a Christian must follow the Spirit, Word and example of Christ, no matter whether he be emperor, king, or whatever he be."

This may just possibly have been Menno's way of saying that in reality the duties of a Christian and a magistrate were totally incompatible since the practice of nonresistance was the Christian's obligation and the wielding of the sword the magistrate's. It seems more likely, however, that by that date, at least, he foresaw the possibility, as the British Quakers did later, of squaring pacifism and politics, at least within certain limits. W. E. Keeney, in his study of Dutch Anabaptist thought and practice, has suggested that this more positive attitude to magistracy on Menno's part may have resulted from his contacts with Bartholomäus von Ahlefeldt, a petty German ruler on whose lands Menno found a refuge from 1554 until his death in 1561. For whatever reason, then, Menno's final stand on the magistracy represented a less negative one than that adopted by the Swiss Brethren and south German Anabaptists, who followed the Schleitheim Confession.

If Menno's approval of magistracy as expressed in his writings still seems to have implied disapproval of its coercive aspects, there is other evidence indicating that during his lifetime the religious community which he led was not yet wedded indissolubly to nonresistance, at least as this was understood in southern Anabaptism. The main stumbling block for those who have contested this has lain in the resolutions of the conference of elders held at Wismar in Mecklenburg in 1554. This conference was attended by the foremost personalities in northern Anabaptism, including Menno himself, Dirk Philips, who was in charge of the Danzig congregation and whose views on the sword coincided more or less with Menno's, and Dirk's later rival for the leadership Leenaert Bouwens. The eighth of the conference's nine resolutions dealt with self-defense and military service. Leonard Verduin has translated the Dutch original as follows: "In the eighth place, touching weapons, the elders are unable to consider it impure when a believer travelling on the roads, according to the conditions of the land, carries an honest staff or a rapier on his shoulder, according to the custom and the manner of the land. But to carry weapons of defense, and to present them according to the command of the magistracy, this the elders do not consider permissible—unless it be in case of *soldiers on guard*" [my italics]. The words italicized appear in variant readings in two different manuscripts: "die *weerlijcke* knechten" and "die *onweerlijcke* knechten." As Samuel Cramer, the co-editor of *Bibliotheca Reformatoria Neerlandica* where the resolutions are printed in volume VII, pp. 51-53, has remarked: "The one [reading] is as unclear as the other." It is possible that the original text has not been transmitted to us in accurate form, since the earliest version extant dates from 1576, thirty-two years later.

In any case, the resolution marks a departure from unconditional nonresistance. Whether the brethren, while journeying, were not permitted actually to use these lethal weapons, or whether it was envisaged merely that they would be carried in order to frighten away robbers and highwaymen, as the pacifist Socinus would recommend to the Polish Brethren later in the century (see next chapter), is not clear. A literal interpretation would allow their full use; however, in the context of contemporary Anabaptist thought, and in view of the evident reluctance with which the concession was granted, a more likely presumption is that the elders hoped that their previous teaching concerning the duties of true Christians would restrain their brethren from wounding or killing, if attacked.

The sentence dealing with military service is the most obscure of all. The best approach seems to be to accept the reading *weerlijcke*, as Verduin does, and to interpret the passage as an injunction to refuse military service except in the watch, when arms might be carried; though, for the reasons given just above, it may have been intended that they should not actually be used. Doornkaat Koolman thinks the *weerlijcke knechten* referred to may have been serving soldiers who had joined the brotherhood and for whom an exception was now being made in regard to the usual requirement imposed on members not to serve with arms. But this seems not very plausible, especially in view of the first part of the resolution. Vos read the passage to mean that the elders were approving professional soldiering among the brethren while disapproving their exercising in arms as volunteers (this is surely a very forced interpretation). For him, it all signified that non-resistance had not yet found general acceptance as a tenet of northern Anabaptism. Van der Zijpp and Krahn (in his biography of Menno), on the other hand, favor the reading *onweerlijcke*, in the sense of "unarmed" soldiers and not "non-defensive" soldiers, which it could also mean. They suppose that some form of noncombatant alternative service—watching but without arms—was being proposed as the proper course for the brethren; though what the latter were to do if the authorities were unwilling to offer it, is not explained in the resolution.

Whereas van der Zijpp regards both this passage and the rest of the eighth resolution as expressing a temporary decline in the purity of the brotherhood's nonresistant principles, Krahn (in his recent study of Dutch Anabaptism) speaks of "the developing principle of nonresistance" and Kühler of a compromise between opposing views reached here largely as a result of Menno's conciliatory spirit. These last two viewpoints together appear to me to be fairly convincing. Although by mid-century nonresistance was rapidly gaining ground within the brotherhood of northern Anabaptists, it does not yet appear to have gained their universal assent. At any rate, adherence to it had not probably yet become an essential qualification for membership. We do not know whether the carrying of weapons and mustering with the watch were already being practiced by some of the brethren before the Wismar meeting but were only now officially, though grudgingly, approved, or (though this is less likely) whether such things had not in fact been done before but might be done henceforward without fear of incurring disciplinary action. Whatever the true explanation of this obscure phase in the brotherhood's history, it is clear that nonresistance was by this time a problem of some importance in northern Anabaptism.

Even in the leadership there were evidently some who, whether for tactical reasons or from conviction, were reluctant to confront members with a choice of either totally abandoning the sword, including the magistrate's sword, or leaving the brotherhood. Menno himself was a nonresistant (at least if my reasoning above is correct), but he was unwilling to renounce altogether the eventuality of a Christian magistracy which would dispense with the harsher aspects of the office of the sword. Moreover, Menno was a man who sought to reconcile (his critics have called this timidity, accusing him of sometimes displaying a lack of courage), and he dreaded the consequences of too sharp a stand on the issue. He may have been swayed at Wismar, as he was to be at other times, by the opinion of some of his fellow elders. He certainly feared the implications for the brotherhood of any suspicion of opposition to established authority or of disaffection to the magistracy. Therefore, he must have reasoned, let each man follow his conscience and the Gospel truth would prevail in the end. Among the northern Anabaptists who looked to Menno for leadership, nonresistance was becoming a way of life: we have only to read the statements of early Anabaptist martyrs, like Adriaen Cornelisz who was executed at Leiden in 1552, to realize that the same spirit as suffused the Schleitheim Confession was at work now among the Anabaptists of the north. The Confession itself had appeared in Dutch in 1560. But among Anabaptists in this section of the Anabaptist movement nonresistance had not yet been elevated into a dogma.

FOUR. *The Polish Antitrinitarians*

ANABAPTISM was long regarded as a phenomenon virtually confined within the ancient historical boundaries of the Holy Roman Empire. Apart from a few scattered individuals elsewhere, its adherents, it was thought, were almost all either Germans or Swiss, Dutch or Flemings. In Western scholarship, a new dimension to the history of Anabaptism has been added within recent years by the revelation of a strong Anabaptist trend during the early phases of the Polish Antitrinitarian movement which broke away from the Calvinist church in the course of the third quarter of the sixteenth century to form a separate Minor Church. George H. Williams, one of those to whom we are most indebted for bringing knowledge of Polish Antitrinitarianism to the Anglo-American scholarly world, has written: "Polish-speaking Anabaptism emergent within the context of the Minor Church of Poland and Lithuania was, both by analogy and by genetic succession, a regional variant of the same Radical Reformation which swept Central Europe in the sixteenth century." "Antitrinitarian Anabaptism was, then, the result of the direct penetration of Poland and Lithuania by the same forces which, and occasionally the same personalities who, were carrying the immensely popular reform movement throughout the whole of Central Europe." The federated Polish-Lithuanian state should, therefore, be included in any survey of Anabaptist development; for the theme of pacifism the Polish Antitrinitarians are especially important since war and the exercise of the magistrate's sword were among the topics most keenly debated in their congregations.

The full impact of the Protestant Reformation was felt later in Poland and the other countries of Eastern Europe than in the central and western areas of the continent, even if first Lutheranism and then Calvinism had fairly soon spread among the nobility and townsfolk of the Polish-Lithuanian state. This delayed action may account for the fact that we do not find much trace of Anabaptist views among the Polish-speaking population until the mid-1550's; though Dutch Anabaptists had been emigrating to Danzig since the early 1530's, they settled in a German-speaking area of the Polish kingdom, and their influence outside it appears to have been slight.

In the same decade in which the Dutch Anabaptists began to arrive we find an early Polish Protestant writer, Biernat of Lublin, arguing

114

after the fashion of the evangelical Anabaptists against the infliction of the death penalty, "for no one has given [a judge] this power." Only God, he said, never man, might take human life, since only God possessed the power to create life; legal punishments should never exceed a fifteen-year term of imprisonment. But the earliest Anabaptists to come to Poland from the Netherlands must have been Melchiorites or even Munsterites: Biernat's rejection of legal homicide probably did not derive from them. And anyhow Biernat, if we may believe his adversary Jan of Pilzno, to whom we owe the preservation of these fragments from his no longer extant treatise, did not deny the right of personal self-defense, as did most proponents of evangelical Anabaptism. In sixteenth-century Poland there were stout opponents of the custom of war among the country's outstanding humanists, for example the Protestant Andrzej Frycz-Modrzewski. But they were by no means complete pacifists, as a perusal of the latter's chapter on war (Book III) in the famous *De Republica emendenda* which first appeared in 1551 clearly shows.

The first advocate of Antitrinitarian views in Poland appears to have been Piotr Giezek of Goniądz (Gonesius), who imbibed them during several years of study and teaching at the University of Padua. There his master Matteo Grimaldi had introduced him to the works of Servetus, whose execution at Calvin's instigation in Geneva took place in 1553. On his journey home from Italy Gonesius passed through Moravia, where he visited the Hutterite brethren and became an enthusiast not only for adult baptism but for the nonresistant principles and practice of the Moravian communitarians. Therefore, when in January 1556, not long after his arrival in Poland, he made an appearance at the synod held by the Polish Calvinist church at Secemin, he wore merely "a wooden sword, according to the antimilitary custom of the Moravian Brethren," as he explained. However, while he criticized the concept of the Trinity in the declaration which he presented to that assembly he did not mention his pacifist views. But these must have been plain from his symbolic adoption of a staff in place of the customary weapon (the symbol, as we have seen, may just possibly have been borrowed by the Hutterites from the Minor Party of the Unity of Czech Brethren).

Later Gonesius elaborated his nonresistant and antistate views in a tract composed in the first half of the 1560's and entitled *De primatu ecclesiae christianae*. The work is no longer extant, but the tenor of its arguments is known from other writers. "To put a believer in office is nothing else than to bring him into the world and commend him to the world," Gonesius had stated; the true Christian, in his view, had no business to become involved in the affairs of a paganized world. Not only was the *jus gladii* unchristian; it was wrong for a "pious man to have an estate such that he may support a war." Moreover, personal self-defense was inadmissible too; it was "not right to wear or carry any kind of weapon, even on a journey, or to defend oneself against robbers."

Gonesius' opinions created consternation among the Calvinists from the very first. The ancient antitrinitarian heresy of the Arians and the modern deviations of the Anabaptists were no less detestable to the orthodox Reformed than to their Catholic opponents. In another synod held at Włodzisław in 1558 the Calvinists explicitly condemned non-resistance and upheld the legitimacy of the magistrates' office. "We are bound," they said, "to defend ourselves from the superstition of the Anabaptists, who will not drive off a biting dog." Kot describes Gonesius as "a lucid thinker, dry, logical," a man of erudition, by training a dialectician. Therefore, despite the efforts of the Calvinist leaders, his arguments brought conviction to many who heard or read him. Those who accepted antitrinitarian Anabaptism were a minority within the church but some of the most talented and respected members became adherents of the new trend. The split in organization between the two wings of the Reformed, which began to appear in 1562-1563, was realized in 1565 when a separate Minor Church was formed. Antitrinitarianism had now taken institutional form.

In the sixteenth century Poland was rapidly evolving into a *Ständestaat* in which the monarch was little more than a crowned president and the landowning nobility enjoyed far reaching autonomy on their estates, holding in their grasp the power taken from the central government. This trend was accelerated after the extinction of the Jagiellonian dynasty in 1572 and the institution of an elective monarchy. The "noble republic" succeeded in reducing the peasantry to a condition of ever more abject serfdom and in excluding the burghers from effective participation in running the state. These developments constitute the darker side of its history. Yet noble predominance, if it sought to whittle away the freedom of the non-noble majority of the kingdom's inhabitants, led also to the creation of strong guarantees against encroachments on the political and religious liberties of the privileged class. Thus, in Poland—almost uniquely in sixteenth-century Europe— radical religious opinion enjoyed wide freedom of growth, especially where such opinion was supported by influential members of the nobility, as had happened, too, in Hussite Bohemia. Antitrinitarianism found proselytes among the landowning class, a phenomenon not found in the case of the contemporary Swiss, German, or Dutch Anabaptists or earlier with the fifteenth-century Czech Brethren. The reasons for its attractiveness to a class (even though, of course, to a comparatively small minority of that class), which we would not normally expect to be drawn to theological and sociopolitical radicalism, are not easy to find. The high intellectual quality of the Minor Church, which could develop its cultural potentialities without hindrance, has been suggested as one cause of its expansion among the Polish nobility; the democratic character of its congregations, as compared with the major Reformed denomination where the influence of the magnates was considerable, has also been seen (e.g., by Wacław Urban) as an important factor in winning the allegiance of the gentry, who were often discontented with the magnates' drive towards ascendancy in the state. In the early days the urban component played an important role in the Minor Church, especially in the town congregations, and pastors of plebeian origin provided much of the spiritual and intellectual leadership of the church. It was these elements, along with individual converts from the nobility, which succeeded in imposing both Anabaptism and pacifism on the early Antitrinitarian church.

An Antitrinitarian chronicler, Andrzej Lubieniecki, in his *Polonoeutychia*, written early in the next century, reports of the situation during these early years: "There were those who incited godly and honest men to relinquish their offices, put away their arms, refuse litigation regardless of the wrong sustained, and who forbade the repeating of an oath. Many decent men left their offices and sold their estates or scattered their possessions." In his antipacifist polemic of 1583 Budny asserts that, early on, the Polish congregations promulgated a "canon" excluding from the sacraments members who declined to renounce the power of the sword, "however piously they might live." The regulation was not accepted by the congregations in the Grand Duchy of Lithuania (united since 1569 by an organic union with the Polish kingdom) and there were individuals, too, in the Polish half of the state, like Mikołaj Sienicki, marshal of the Polish diet in 1566, or the minister from Podlasie Marcin Krowicki, who strongly disagreed with the nonresistant position. It is not clear, therefore, for how long or to what extent or in exactly which congregations disciplinary measures of this kind were enforced.

Social radicalism within the Minor Church reached its climax in 1569, the year in which the Union of Lublin was concluded between Poland and Lithuania. During the sessions of the Lublin diet there were alarmed reports that "Anabaptists" were preaching to the people, that "disregard of the magistrate was being openly taught and that Christians might recognize only one king, crowned with thorns." At

117

the diet itself a strange sight could be seen, which attracted the attention even of Cardinal Hosius—the figure of "a certain important noble . . . in a mean grey garment, without sword, without wallet, without attendant, rebaptized just a few days before." This was Jan Niemojewski, a prominent landowner from the province of Kujawy who, along with several others of the same persuasion, had recently sold his estates and given the proceeds to the poor in the belief that it was wrong for him "to live on such estates which were given [to his ancestors] for shedding blood." Such was the agitation produced among the deputies by the activities of the "Anabaptists" that only the opposition of the Catholic bishops, who welcomed the appearance of dissension in the Protestant camp, prevented the enactment of repressive measures against the sect.

At that time, too, the radicals instituted an income-pooling community at Raków on the estate of a sympathetic landowner, Jakub Sienieński, who held the office of Castellan of Żarnów. It was designed by its founders to be "a sort of New Jerusalem or Zion," a kind of non-violent Münster. From the various congregations came penitent noblemen, Anabaptist-inclined ministers, pious artisans, and even a few peasants, as well as a number of foreigners whose religious enthusiasm had brought them to distant Poland to participate in the venture. All who joined the community were accounted equal. At first an air of expectancy reigned, for the end of the world was deemed imminent and Raków was seen as a pattern of Christ's kingdom which was soon to be inaugurated. A mood of weariness ensued, however, when these hopes proved false, and eventually endless discussion and fruitless disputes concerning doctrine and practice produced more frustration than light among the communitarians. An attempt to reach union with the Moravian Hutterites broke down in mutual recriminations as to the cause of the failure of negotiations. Kot has shown that both "the social structure" of the two parties and their "political situation" made close or lasting affiliation between them virtually impossible. The Moravians, an alien and outcast minority existing only on sufferance, were drawn mainly from simple craftsmen and peasants; the Poles, representing a cross-section of society, with gentry and educated ministers setting the tone, constituted a community whose renunciation of property and power was a voluntary act by no means cutting the innumerable ties with the environing state and society. After several years of confusion and uncertainty order was restored at Raków. This was due largely to the efforts of the Cracow apothecary Szymon Ronemberg, a social radical but a gifted mediator who disliked extremes. Community of goods was abandoned: instead of a model for the expected kingdom of Christ, Raków now became the intellectual and cultural center of Polish Antitrinitarianism until in the second quarter of the seventeenth century the advancing tide of religious intolerance finally overwhelmed it.

Even after this fermentation had died down the social radicals maintained their ascendancy in many important congregations of the Minor Church. Niemojewski had settled in Lublin and together with Marcin Czechowic, one of the most talented exponents of the Anabaptist position among the pastorate, he became the main spokesman of the Antitrinitarians in that area. Cracow, another center of the movement, was controlled by plebeian elements led by such capable personalities as Ronemberg and Georg Schomann. On the Polish side, those of a contrary mind remained silent, at least for the time being. On the other hand, in the Lithuanian Grand Duchy events had taken a different turn. For one thing, in Lithuania the influence of the magnates within the Antitrinitarian church was much greater than in Poland: in particular, the wealthy landowner Jan Kiszka, closely related to the Radziwiłł clan and no friend to political extremism although he eventually underwent immersion, was a powerful force in favor of social conservatism in the mainly rural congregations of the more economically backward Lithuania. These eastern territories, moreover, were wilder than the Polish kingdom and remained more exposed to the incessant border warfare waged against Muscovites and Cossacks, Tatars and Turks. Pacifism and the renunciation of the protection of the state, therefore, appeared less attractive here to religious radicals.

During the interregnum of 1572-1573, which ensued on the death of the last Jagiellonian, King Zygmunt August, Poland too was put on a war footing, in view of the dangers which might threaten the country in the absence of a ruler. Members of the nobility (*szlachta*) were liable in such emergencies as this for armed service in the general levy (though the obligation did not extend beyond defense of the frontiers of the kingdom). How should noble members of the Minor Church react in a situation of this kind? Torn between their duty to a state in which they enjoyed extensive political and religious freedom (the Confederation of Warsaw of 1573 guaranteed full religious liberty) as well as their respect for ancestral traditions and what they were now taught were the obligations of the true faith, some may have hesitated. Yet many stood loyal to the precepts of their church. Under its influence, "many of the gentry," we read, "even of famous families, refused to bear arms, lest they act contrary to the Gospel and the teaching of Christ; but for such there was of old an ancient penalty provided by the law, and that the most severe."

119

Some church members, however, started openly to question the validity of the pacifist position. Debates on the issue were held first in Cracow and then at Raków. The antipacifists began to mobilize their forces. A tract putting forward their viewpoint was composed in Polish; however, it is no longer extant. To strengthen their hands at the forthcoming Raków conference Jacob Palaeologus, an Antitrinitarian exile from Greece then resident in Cracow, took up his pen. His "De bello sententia" was completed by August 1572. While the treatise instilled new courage into the social conservatives of the Minor Church, the views expressed in it scandalized the radicals not only on account of their content but even more on account of the tone adopted by the author in setting them out.

For Palaeologus was not content merely to state a reasoned argument in favor of defensive wars and the admissibility of Christian support of and participation in such wars (as well as in the magistracy whose duty it was to wage them), and to urge that Christ had not in fact replaced the Mosaic Law, which therefore still remained valid for the church. He went further, equating refusal to fight with cowardice and abandonment of the public good. Pacifism he branded as treason. "It is lawful," he concluded, "for a Christian to bear arms and to defend the boundaries of his country in order to save his own and to exterminate the enemy; whoever acts otherwise and refuses to take up arms in such case, is both wicked and unworthy of the name of Christian." Although Palaeologus was ready to grant that the avenging of personal injuries must be replaced by due process of law and that peace was preferable to war, he argued: "God himself has so ordained that it is better to suffer war than to betray one's native land and lose civil freedom; . . . it is more honorable to die for a just cause than to be born merely to increase the population." He went on to accuse his nonresistant brethren of willingness to enjoy the advantages of peacetime citizenship without a corresponding readiness to shoulder the burden of defense if the security of the state were threatened by an external enemy. Such a stand he called shameful. If, he taunted them, they took "Resist not evil" literally (as he considered pacifists did), then even to cry out when attacked was a form of resistance and should not be permitted.

Among innumerable jibes directed against the nonresistants, Palaeologus charged them with inconsistency in respect to their behavior toward military demands. His remarks here help us to answer a puzzling question: how is it that, if the law made no provision for conscientious objection, and severe penalties attached to the refusal of military service (even in the last resort the penalty of death), we have no record of Antitrinitarians being punished at this juncture for their stand against war. Palaeologus indicates two ways in which objectors were able to fulfil the demands of the state in conformity with the dictates of their consciences. He tells us that they were willing either to buy a substitute to go in their stead or even, if this did not prove feasible, themselves to perform guard duty provided they could do so without carrying arms. He also informs us that the radicals did not object to paying war taxes. If these devices satisfied the nonresistant Antitrinitarians (at least for the time being), they did not satisfy Palaeologus, for he brands such conduct as in effect contributing to the killing, even though indirectly.

Palaeologus' attack on the nonresistant position called for a prompt reply. Indeed, his accusations of lack of patriotism, even of treason, could prove highly dangerous to the pacifist majority in the Polish Minor Church in view of the war emergency prevailing during the period of the interregnum. They entrusted their answer to one of their ablest supporters, the Cracow minister Grzegorz Paweł of Brzeziny. There could not have been a greater contrast in character than that between Palaeologus and Paweł. The Greek's intellect was cold but logical, his arguments often highly personal yet well constructed and urged with clarity and precision. True, he lacked understanding of his opponents' position, heaping scorn, ridicule, and insult upon them; his objections to it, however, were sustained by a clear analysis and were not simply the outcome of indignation. The Pole's work, on the other hand, was suffused with emotion; it belongs primarily to the literature of protest. Konrad Górski in his biography of Paweł (Cracow, 1929) has described his temperament as "typically sanguine." Paweł "either loves or hates; whether it is the one or the other, it is done with his whole spirit, with all the drive of his restless nature. He cannot reason quietly in matters of theology, because his fanatical devotion to the new . . . idea excites him. A fanatic in regard to the faith, he burns with hatred toward those who think differently." While these qualities represent the reverse side of his character, Górski notes also his enthusiasm for the cause he has espoused and his unrelenting energy. Primarily a polemicist, Paweł, like so many of his contemporaries, was not always careful in his choice of verbal weapons; the violence of his arguments, even when employed in defense of pacifism, is striking.

Paweł's reply to Palaeologus did not take long to prepare. It appeared in late 1572 under the title "Adversus Iacobi Palaeologi de bello sententiam, Gregorii Pauli Bresinensis responsio." Issued in the name not only of its author but of the whole Raków community too (this gives it a semiofficial character), the treatise is the first surviving work which presents in any detail the pacifist, antistate position of the Antitrinitarian radicals. Kot describes its contents as "a kind of speech, saturated with emotion and producing its effect by its feeling."

At the outset Paweł accuses Palaeologus of giving an entirely erroneous presentation of Christ's character and teachings. The master was full of gentleness and love; he was longsuffering, humble, merciful. He preached nonresistance, forbidding his followers to go to law or to enter administration. He told them, instead, to turn the other cheek, to love and pray for their enemies. "This love of enemies [Christ] calls perfection and he demands it from his own, since God is shown to be perfect by the fact of his perfectly loving not only the good but likewise the bad." If all this were so, then how, asked Paweł, could Christians now hate and torture and kill at the behest of the state as Palaeologus demanded that they should do? Could they ever consent to commit acts directly contrary to their teacher's words? Paweł vehemently denied that Christ had not abrogated the Mosaic Law and accused his opponent of confusing the New Testament with the Old; the Old frequently ran contrary to the meaning of the Christian dispensation. He wrote: "Christians were commanded to obey the government and fear it, but not to exercise it nor to obey its orders when it condemns a man to death or beheads criminals. [Office] is unworthy of a Christian, who is bound to be merciful and to forgive unto seventy times seven, while the government can not be merciful nor forgive any man, even once, but must punish him according to his deed, else it injures the other party and does not fulfil its obligations." Christians, in his view, must remain a separated people, admitting only Christ as their king, though passively obedient to the rulers of this world in all things lawful. To Palaeologus' accusations of disloyalty Paweł returned countercharges: those who urged Christians to participate in the work of government were the real traitors and deserters—in respect to Christ's kingdom. "If those reproaches [of Palaeologus] are just, then they fall on you, O Christ, who abandoned your own and cruelly betrayed them, who yourself put on no armor in defense of your country, nor commanded your own to do it. . . . Let our opponents heap such reproaches on Christianity and prove to all that they are defenders of Antichrist, or rather of paganism."

Kot has noted a certain—unwonted—caution in Paweł's reply to Palaeologus. For one thing, he does not deal directly with conscientious objection to participation in war, which is the main target of Palaeologus' attacks. Kot, therefore, surmises that Paweł wished thereby to avoid arousing further ill-feeling by voicing seemingly unpatriotic views at so critical a juncture in the state's affairs. In particular, this motive would explain his omission of any direct discussion of the question whether a Christian community might ever engage in a just war of defense and his concentration, instead, on the broader issue of the admissibility of Christian participation in the state as such, which was by no means the central one in Palaeologus' discussion. Since Anabaptist nonresistance had always envisaged a conditional justification of government, i.e., for the unregenerate, whether Christians in name or outside the faith altogether, Paweł was thus able to give his arguments a less obviously subversive coloring than he could have done if he had tackled the question of war directly.

Kot's thesis is certainly plausible. Considerations of this kind may very well have been present in the minds of Paweł and his Racovian sponsors. Yet it is also, I think, possible that their chief motive for broadening the discussion may simply have been a feeling that the basic point at issue was itself wider than mere pacifism. Only by showing the inner consistency of the nonresistant vision, as applied to state and society in its entirety, could they have hoped to successfully refute Palaeologus' arguments.

Little Poland (*Małopolska*) was the stronghold of Antitrinitarian radicalism. But even here Palaeologus' opinions evoked some support. In October 1573 the aged Krowicki, then near death, addressed a letter to the Racovians, criticizing them for the rigor with which they sought to anathematize all who disagreed with their rejection of the state. He viewed with alarm the possibility that the governance of this world might fall entirely into the hands of men excluded from salvation. God, he thought, would indeed be cruel if this were his real intention. "Much was ordained at Raków that came to nothing, bringing infamy to God, laughter to men, and offence to the Church of God." Among its causes of offense, in his view, was its continuing negative attitude to the *jus gladii*.

If the Racovians thought that Paweł's answer would satisfy Palaeologus, they were mistaken. Within a few months of its appearance the Greek had begun on a new work, which he completed early in 1574: "Ad scriptum fratrum Racoviensium de bello et iudiciis forensibus, Iacobi Palaeologi responsio." "In acuteness of argument," writes Kot, "in skill in drawing conclusions, in political thinking, Palaeologus' reply surpasses Gregory's [i.e., Paweł's] pamphlet, but Palaeologus offends by his haughty treatment of his opponent and by an unjustified readiness to impute to him wrong intentions." "It is hard to resist the impression," Kot concludes, "that [Paweł's work] is closer to the spirit of the Gospel and the teachings of Christ than the arguments of the Greek." Dubbing Paweł's stand as absurd, and even insane, Palaeologus accuses him of quoting isolated passages from the New Testament and then twisting their meaning by treating them out of context. This time centering his discussion, as Paweł had done, on the issue of the Christian attitude to the state in general rather than on war alone, Palaeologus sought to prove that the nonresistant injunctions of the Sermon on the Mount and similar texts applied only to individuals in their private capacity and not to their dealings as officials of the state. Thus a ruler who in the exercise of the *jus gladii* ordered the execution of a condemned criminal was not committing murder but fulfilling his duty as a Christian toward God and his fellow men, since Christ, in Palaeologus' opinion, had never advised his disciples to "flee from the world"; instead, they were told to live uprightly within it. Self-defense was permissible if life and property could not be protected adequately by the magistracy. And to ensure such protection the magistracy was fully entitled to impose flogging, torture, and other harsh penalties, including deprivation of limbs and of life itself where these were appropriate, and still retain his claim to the Christian name.

Indeed, if Palaeologus' denunciations of the rigorists as cowards and traitors caused grave offense, the rigorists' denial of their opponents' right to be considered Christians, had in its turn created a keen sense of grievance. As one of the leading antirigorists, Stanisław Budzyński, wrote ironically at this time, the Racovians "saw an iron sabre on someone and forthwith condemned him and sent him to hell."

It was indeed difficult for these men, even if they were members of the same church and as such all subject to bitter attacks from the other Christian denominations within the country, to tolerate each other and to suffer differing opinions on these matters within their religious community: it was especially difficult for the radicals to do so (as it had been for the Minor Party of the Czech Brethren before them), because the concept of a nonresistant fellowship appeared to them to constitute an essential element in Christian discipleship, as it did, too, for most of the other Anabaptists of central Europe. To accept without protest a less perfect pattern of behavior among the brethren seemed like readiness to betray the mission of the church committed to it by Christ himself and an infringement of that law of love which, they believed, he had placed at the center of his message for mankind.

Therefore, the reaction of the Racovian party to Palaeologus now was one of anger mixed with contempt. When Budzyński, to whom Palaeologus had lent a copy of his "Responsio," in turn showed the manuscript to leading Racovians even the circumspect Schomann, who disliked all controversy, was upset. Some of them told Budzyński that they considered it a waste of their time to have to read such a piece, others "were so disdainful that they did not even glance at it, saying that they did not want to occupy themselves with vain philosophy and so on." To make matters worse, Budzyński then proceeded to circulate Palaeologus' treatise among members of the Minor Church who were likely to be sympathetic to the latter's viewpoint: "ministers and other pious men," as Budzyński put it, "whose eyes and minds are not so blinded by the Racovian interpretation." Attempts on the part of the radicals to stop the circulation of the tract (they considered its tone needlessly abusive and its tenor highly inflammatory) were not successful. Budzyński around this time was particularly active in trying to create within the congregations of Little Poland an effective counterweight to the radical majority; unfortunately his correspondence with Paweł *super quaestione de magistratu et usu armorum* is no longer extant.

Once more the necessity arose of presenting a reply to Palaeologus' onslaught that would at the same time put an end to Budzyński's influence among the brethren. The man chosen for this task was not Grzegorz Paweł, who had now withdrawn from the fray, but Marcin Czechowic, minister of the staunchly radical Lublin congregation, who had already been asked by the church synod the previous year to draw up a catechism incorporating the radical viewpoint. When it appeared —as *Rozmowy Chrystyjańskie* (Christian Colloquies), published in Cracow in 1575—colloquy XII "on the Christian life" was devoted to the problem of nonresistance. The work was composed in the form of a dialogue between "Pupil," who in this chapter was made to voice the objections to radicalism nurtured in the brotherhood by many of the gentry as well as by a handful of the intellectual leaders, and "Teacher," who expressed the Racovian viewpoint. Unlike Paweł, Czechowic, perhaps because the political situation had eased recently, made no attempt to avoid controversial questions like war. "The work is brilliantly written, lively, and full of temperament," comments Kot. "His dialogue is by no means dull." On the other hand, Czechowic has a tendency to approach each problem in a somewhat roundabout manner.

Three topics dealt with are of interest to us here: self-defense, the *jus gladii*, and war. Pupil starts off by asserting the right of resistance to attacks on one's person and property. "As long as there were any law," he states, "then I should act according to the law; but if the law were difficult of access, or did not exist, then only should I use force: that is, he who is the stronger is the better. I am not a dumb stick or a Stoic, hence I should resort to the sword." Such a stance, he considered, was not only reasonable but a natural right of man. To this

Teacher replies that only means consistent with love are permissible for Christ's followers. Therefore, if self-defense involves "striking, bloodshed, wrath, and carnal revenge," it is ruled out. If spiritual weapons fail to protect either ourselves or our nearest and dearest, "then nothing is to be done except to bear it humbly and thankfully to accept it from the Lord as a divine punishment." In true Anabaptist spirit Czechowic points to the Cross as the quintessence of Christian discipleship. "Without the Cross it is difficult to imitate Christ," he remarks.

Concerning the office of the sword Czechowic repeats the familiar radical arguments with their conditional approval of magistracy "for the defense of the good and for the punishment of the wicked," if undertaken by non-Christians, and with their absolute prohibition at the same time of any participation in the work of government on the part of genuine Christians. Teacher explains to his hitherto somewhat incredulous Pupil:

> A congregation of faithful and sincere disciples of Christ has no need of a magistrate or civil officer with sword, prison, fire, hangman, halter, gallows, which this earthly officer cannot be without, for God giveth not the sword into his hands in vain. Thus it is in the world, not in the Church, that there is need of a magistracy, which would, however, not only be for the alarm and punishment of the wicked—for these do nothing good, save as a result of force and fear—but also for the comfort and defense of the good, who do everything good out of love.

On the question of war Czechowic writes quite openly. He makes no attempt to gloss over the problem by reference to the more general issue of the magistracy. Pupil introduces the discussion by asking how a Christian ought to react if ordered by the ruler to participate in war. Even the papists, Teacher pointed out, agree that a priest shall not fight. In fact, no "regenerate Christian" should do so either; "no one may kill another without God's permission" (a viewpoint, incidentally, which allowed for a conditional justification of warfare in Old Testament times, while disallowing it under Christ's new dispensation). True, God would use the strife among this world's governors for his own good purposes, making kingdoms now to rise and now to fall according to his appointed plan. But the Christian's warfare is spiritual. "Christian warfare has nothing in common with the warlike exploits of this world which godless men carry on among themselves." Its weapons are purely spiritual ones and no lives are lost in its waging.

Pupil, however, partly convinced yet obviously not entirely satisfied with the abstract plane to which his Teacher has removed the argument, persists in pursuing the practical problems involved in the Christian attitude to war. If his king became involved in war and commanded him to join the battle, might he not obey, Pupil asks. "If I . . . should yet strike no one when others struck, and moreover even bore no arms, should I then be doing wrong?" Certainly, Teacher answers, for you would be collaborating thereby in the work of unbelievers. Such a course of action would be hypocrisy. Moreover, while there must always be wars and bloodshed in an evil world, this did not mean that "the lambs of God's church have to go to war." "It is the authorities of this world who must punish the wicked and shed blood willy-nilly, but not the disciples of Christ." To this argument Pupil interjects perplexedly: "Yet as to making war, how can [rulers] defend both their dominions and their subjects, if you and I and many others who sincerely adhere to Christ will no longer either fight or [even] go to war?" If a state only had money, Teacher answers, it would have no difficulty in finding soldiers ready to fight for it; but if God wished to humble a people, neither military strength nor money would avail to stave off defeat. Christians, of course, along with their unregenerate fellow citizens must pay their taxes to the state. Here (though the point is not made explicitly by Czechowic) a way of escape obviously opened up for those who conscientiously objected to military service and, though prepared to pay a commutation fee in exchange for not being required to bear arms, were yet unwilling to muster, even without weapons (as some Antitrinitarian objectors at that time were probably ready to do).

Czechowic included in his *Colloquies* a long appendix entitled *de vita et moribus Christianorum primitivae ecclesiae,* in which he cited the opinions of a number of early church fathers who supported antimilitarism and opposed officeholding (Origen, Tertullian, Lactantius, etc.). He did this, it seems, in order to rebut the critics who argued that nonresistance was simply a newfangled notion, a product of Anabaptist enthusiasm, and a doctrine not to be found in apostolic Christianity. Czechowic's erudition and his philosophical approach, contrasting with the emotional outpourings of Grzegorz Paweł, reflected the Erasmian inspiration of his thinking on war. "Czechowic's pacifism," writes G. H. Williams, "is prudential and humanitarian." The suggestion that it does not reflect "the *via crucis* of Germanic Anabaptism" (Williams) appears to me unjustified. Czechowic's renunciation of war, even if expressed in humanist terms, derives from as strict a concept of Christian discipleship as that of other Polish Antitrinitarian radicals and their German Anabaptist predecessors.

Neither the efforts of Paweł and Czechowic to achieve unity on the basis of a nonresistant church discipline, nor the counter-efforts of their nonpacifist opponents like Palaeologus and Budzyński to persuade the brethren of the impracticability and even futility of the radical standpoint, were successful. Reason and fury, eloquence and invective, learning and emotion, were expended in profusion on each side, to no effect. The debate on magistracy and war continued inside the Minor Church with unabated vigor. Tempers often ran high and rancor frequently replaced fraternal love in the hearts of the contestants. Although the division between social radicals and social conservatives was not an exactly geographical one, on the whole the congregations of the Polish kingdom continued to be socially radical and those in the Lithuanian Grand Duchy continued to be socially conservative. At a synod held at Łosk in 1578, for instance, a prominent Byelorussian nobleman from the Grand Duchy, Prince Vasil' Tsyapinski (Ciapiński), supported by several among his compatriots, spoke up in favor of admitting the *jus gladii* within the Christian fellowship. "The office of the sword is not contrary to the teaching of the gospel, nor is the retention of noble property, nor serving in war, nor recourse to the law, etc. The Polish brethren argued against this, until, the evening coming on, they grew quiet."

The same conflict of opinion appeared yet again in another synod later in the same year. And in 1580 the leader of the Lithuanian "conservatives," Szymon Budny, a Pole by origin and a man of radical theological views, took a step which exacerbated the mounting ill-feeling between the two groups still further: in that year he had the whole series of polemical exchanges between Palaeologus and Paweł published in book form at his own printing press at Łosk (in Lithuania) under the resounding title *Defensio verae sententiae de magistratu politico in ecclesiis christianis retinendo*. . . . The money for this costly venture was provided by Budny's wealthy supporter Kiszka. Hitherto, the treatises of the two writers had remained in manuscript; though of course known to some outside Antitrinitarian circles, they had circulated mainly among church members. Now Palaeologus' vitriolic attacks on the pacifism and antistate views of the Polish Minor Church were open for all to read. Even the mild Ronemberg was shocked by Budny's action in making public so bitter an exchange. He and other members of the Racovian party sharply reproved Budny for his conduct, charging him with attempting to discredit the Polish branch of the church in the eyes of the authorities—with acting, that is, in a way which might well result in the direst consequences for that body.

With the possibility of consequences such as these in mind, the

Racovians hastened to put out a rebuttal which would serve to allay any apprehensions that might have been aroused in the government by publication of the book. After Paweł, whom they had approached first, expressed his unwillingness—on grounds of bad health—to undertake the task of composing such a work, it was assigned to a refugee Italian scholar, Fausto Sozzini (or Faustus Socinus as he is usually known) who had recently arrived in Poland. Socinus was not actually a member of the Minor Church (he objected on principle to immersion) and he was never accepted into formal membership in it. Soon, however, his outstanding intellectual powers—and perhaps, too, an ability to mediate between conflicting opinions—gave him an undisputed preeminence in the counsels of the church. During the span of twenty-four years between his settling in Poland in 1580 and his death in 1604 he succeeded in welding together this diverse band of tritheists, ditheists, and unitheists into a compact denomination with a cohesive theology which, while still Christ-centered, acknowledged the oneness of the Godhead and the essential humanity of Jesus Christ. Under Socinus' guidance Raków, hitherto known chiefly as a center of the sociopolitical religious left, and then mainly within the confines of the Polish commonwealth, grew into an internationally renowned seat of radical Protestant learning, a kind of Antitrinitarian Geneva.

Thus, the leaders of the Racovian party, when they now called on Socinus' aid in refuting the arguments of their adversaries, showed a sure sense of the potentialities of the man they had chosen. At this time Socinus shared in full the position of the Racovians even though he differed from them on the subject of adult baptism. Yet as Kot has pointed out, the spirit in which he approached sociopolitical problems differed fundamentally from that of Paweł or Czechowic or other Polish Antitrinitarians of their generation. Whereas the latter emphasized the obligation to stand unyieldingly on Gospel principles even if this meant defying the powers that be, Socinus stressed the need to go the second mile in obedience to the state, before its authority be challenged by appeal to that of a higher righteousness transcending all earthly governments. Perhaps the Poles' stance stemmed in part from a certain sturdy independence generated among the Polish noble class whose members felt themselves to be the equals of elected kings. The *szlachta* had never hesitated to speak truth, as they saw it, to power. Such modes of thought, however, probably appeared alien to the Italian, whose origins lay in the land of the Renaissance despots and whose defiance of the Catholic church was unsupported among his countrymen by any powerful body of opinion such as existed in Poland among both nobility and bourgeoisie.

Socinus' *Responsio* to Palaeologus appeared in Cracow in 1581. A work over 370 pages, it is carefully argued, entering in great detail into the subject of the Christian relationship to state and society. At the outset the author explains the reasons that have prompted him to take up his pen in defense of his colleagues. Not merely had Palaeologus given a false picture of their position; he had also brought the whole Antitrinitarian movement under suspicion of treason in the eyes of the king and his advisers. Socinus' avowed intention, therefore, was to show that in fact the Polish Minor Church, while it stood inexorably opposed to the shedding of human blood as a clear transgression of Christ's commandment, was not hostile in principle to the idea of the state. Warfare and killing would never take place if before engaging in them men waited until Christ had ordered them to do so. The Minor Church forbade its members to hold office or serve as soldiers because these activities involved disobedience to their master, Christ. This was not desertion, as Palaeologus asserted, but loyalty to the highest authority a Christian could have. Since Christ's kingdom was not of this world, his followers, Socinus points out, should not be concerned with the defense of the temporal state's frontiers; they were merely sojourners in the land. Provided they remained quiet and peaceable (which they were bound to do from the very nature of their faith), it was entirely erroneous—indeed deliberately misleading—to accuse them, as Palaeologus had done, of cowardice because they refused to participate in military preparedness. The Racovians, according to Socinus, did not argue that it was always wrong to wage war. Such action might be right or it might be wrong, according to the circumstances. What they did maintain was that it was impermissible for true Christians to engage in war (or in any branch of the magistracy where bloodshed was involved).

Although the tone of Socinus' exposition of the bases of Christian nonresistance might be more conciliatory than his predecessors', the core remained essentially the same. It is in his discussion of the practical implications of a nonresistant witness that we note a fundamental difference in approach, even if Socinus has not yet diverged from "orthodox" Racovianism to the extent that he was to do two decades later.

In regard to the practical implications of nonresistance, the Racovians could have had no reservations as to the way in which Socinus treated the question of guard duty (readiness to perform this, we have seen, had been one of the alleged inconsistencies with which Palaeologus charged his opponents). Such duties, wrote Socinus, were clearly impossible for a Christian: they could not be discharged without readiness to kill an enemy if one approached, and a Christian must permit himself to be killed rather than retaliate. Socinus' advice concerning the payment of war taxes, though more conciliatory than his position in the case of guard duty, also coincides probably with the practice of the rigorists. While feeling that it would be wrong to hire a man directly to take one's place in the fighting, he saw nothing inconsistent in paying a tax which the state intended for warlike purposes. Palaeologus had argued that this was tantamount to approval of war; Socinus disagreed (as most Anabaptists and Mennonites did), contending that a government had the right to dispose of monies it raised in the manner it deemed most expedient and that such matters were of no concern to the taxpayer. The Racovians could scarcely have objected when their advocate stated that a wild animal might be resisted if it attempted to attack. Yet one wonders how the stricter members of the church, men like Paweł, Czechowic, or Niemojewski, reacted to certain others of Socinus' propositions (we have no record, it must be added, of any open disagreement). For Socinus, even at this date, wore his nonresistance with a difference. He saw no point, for instance, in placing an absolute ban on recourse to courts of law. A Christian, he thought, might seek redress in this way provided that he did not demand punishment for any injury incurred and provided, too, that it did not seem likely that the court would impose a penalty as a result of the complaint. Socinus even envisaged the possibility of a Christian's going to the wars if he would otherwise have to face execution for refusing to do so, provided only that he stated to the authorities his unyielding determination never to kill under any circumstances. Having made this declaration, he might even carry arms. This was something that Czechowic, for instance, had been unwilling to concede. Again, Socinus saw nothing sinful in frightening away an assailant who threatened one's womenfolk, by shouting or strong language, provided one did not actually strike him or do him any injury.

Despite Socinus' obvious efforts to make the nonresistance of the Antitrinitarians more palatable to the outside world, his book met with a hostile reception in some quarters. The Magyar Antitrinitarians in Transylvania, for instance, stoutly rejected the theses propounded by Socinus; the church here seems never to have shared the pacifist and antistate position of the Polish Brethren (although Antal Pirnát in his *Die Ideologie der siebenbürger Antitrinitarier in den 1570er Jahren* [Budapest, 1961] has reported echoes of such opinions around 1575 among certain Magyar Antitrinitarian preachers who in rejecting human bloodshed as unchristian may have been reflecting the influence of Polish radicals like Grzegorz Paweł). At home, we find a Catholic

131

priest, Jeremi Powodowski, writing to King Stefan (Batory) to complain of this pernicious and subversive tract recently put out by a foreigner and of its probable bad effect on the security of the realm. As a result of Powodowski's attack, Socinus thought it wisest to leave Cracow for the country estate of a friendly nobleman belonging to the Antitrinitarian church; from his rural retreat he sent a letter to the king denying that his book contained anything directed against the royal government as such. All that he had attempted to do, he wrote somewhat ingenuously, was to discuss the moral obligations of individual Christians.

Socinus' treatise had been framed as a refutation of Palaeologus' arguments. Soon after its appearance, however, the Greek had been removed from the scene by his arrest while visiting Moravia (he was burnt by the Inquisition in Rome in 1585). His role as expositor of the anti-nonresistant case now passed to Szymon Budny. In 1582 heated discussions between the Racovians and the "Lithuanians" had taken place on the question of the magistracy. It appears, though no direct evidence can be cited, that the arguments of the former made a considerable impression on Jan Kiszka, Budny's patron, and to some extent shook his faith in the correctness of the antiradical position which predominated, we have seen, in the Lithuanian congregations. It may, therefore, have been partly the intention of countering a growing influence of the Racovians on the powerful Kiszka (an influence, however, which did not ultimately prove strong enough to persuade the magnate to abandon "the sword") that prompted Budny to take up his pen in defense of Christian magistracy when Palaeologus was no longer able to fulfil this task. Moreover, at one point in the debate it seems that the Racovians contemplated severing relations altogether with those, like Budny and the majority of the Lithuanian brethren, who defended the exercise of the *jus gladii* among the faithful and stressed the obligation of obedience whether from serfs to their landlords or of subjects to their rulers. This would provide one further reason for Budny's appearance in print at this juncture.

His treatise, which he wrote in Polish, evidently wishing thereby to reach a wider audience than he would have done if he had followed Socinus in using Latin, was printed at Łosk in 1583 under the title *Concerning the Sword-Bearing Magistracy* (*O urzędzie miecza używającym*). It is a lengthy work divided into two main parts. The first part reprints *in extenso* passages from the writings of his opponents, especially Czechowic, whom Budny seems to have considered particularly worthy of attention, probably because the Pole's work enjoyed an extensive circulation within the brotherhood. The second part comprises Budny's own counterarguments in favor of permitting Christians to participate in war and the magistracy. Each argument is put forward in the form of a syllogism with numerous supporting proofs drawn largely from the Old Testament. Budny also included a number of supplementary documents which provide us today with valuable information on the development of the controversy concerning "the office of the sword" unobtainable in any other surviving source. The work is erudite, well structured, and written with verve and a polemical sharpness that sometimes borders on the abusive. In a study on Budny Konrad Górski (in his *Studia nad dziejami polskiej literatury antytrynitarskiej XVI w.*, Cracow, 1949) has called him "a typical *esprit fort* not drawing back before the most extreme consequences of his conclusions once he had reached them." Budny's book on the sword-bearing magistracy constitutes perhaps the most powerful indictment of nonresistance produced in the age of Reformation.

The essence of Budny's position lay in his contention that, government having been ordained by God (as was of course conditionally agreed to by the rigorists), the duty of the Christian in a Christian state was to carry out loyally the obligations of a citizen. Thus military service, for instance, should be performed "faithfully and without making complaint." The social functions associated with ownership of land were perfectly compatible with church membership even though they entailed keeping a fellow Christian in a servile status. Christians might indeed be kings, and kings and the servants of kings might have to punish wrongdoers with death. Christians, too, had every right to seek the punishment of a criminal; indeed, they had an obligation to do so, since otherwise law and order would disappear from society. In short, the church should accept as one of its own every sincere believer, "be he king, emperor, prince or duke, hetman, palatine, count, starost, lieutenant, burgomaster, bailiff—or even a soldier."

Budny, as Brother Lukáš and the Major Party in the Unity of Czech Brethren had done earlier in their polemics with the nonresistant Minor Party, claimed to be asking only the right to dissent. Like the Czechs, he accused the opposing party of attempting to institute a new dogmatism in place of the Roman tyranny by enforcing their sociopolitical views on their brethren who disagreed. The ex-nobleman Jan Niemojewski immediately protested against Budny's assertion. His associates, he wrote, had merely enjoined that brethren follow Christ's precepts and thus avoid "quarrels, going to law, wars, and murdering one another." They had but striven to heal the lamentable division stemming from the corruption of Christianity, which separated the church into a laity, to whom use of the sword was permitted, and a clergy bidden to employ only spiritual weapons. Moreover, Niemojewski went on, far from enforcing rigid uniformity on these issues as Budny asserted they had done, they had recognized, though regretfully, that for the present such injunctions must necessarily remain for many members merely counsels of perfection. "We do not forcibly press or constrain anyone to such perfection. There are among us many of those who, not having yet attained Christian patience, go to law for redress of their injuries. Finally, we still suffer among us even such as hold offices, and though we do not seek to win their favor, nor approve these things in them, yet we expect that they will do what they ought to do, not to please us but for God and Christ and their Christian duty."

In this passage Niemojewski does not specifically mention the bearing of arms among the reprehensible social activities which the Minor Church was forced to tolerate in view of the human weakness of some of its members. Socinus, however, had recently approved *faute de mieux* the performance of military duties, if lethal weapons, though carried, were not actually employed. Other sources indicate that even at an earlier date Antitrinitarian gentry were to be found serving as soldiers and taking pride in the military prowess of their country. Despite the categorical tone of the official pronouncements against the taking of human life, such cases appear by no means isolated, even in the Polish branch of the Minor Church.

Ostensibly Niemojewski's tract was a reply to "the calumnies" of Kacper Wilkowski, a former member of his own congregation in Lublin who, having turned Catholic, published late in 1583 a fiery denunciation of his former brethren under the title *Reasons for My Conversion to the Universal Faith from the Sects of the Anabaptists* (*Przyczyny nawrócenia do wiary powszechnej od sekt nowokrzczeńców*). In fact Niemojewski was directing his main fire against his fellow Antitrinitarian Budny, from whom Wilkowski had quoted copiously in order to prove that the Antitrinitarians, because of their views on society, civil government, and war, were subversive of good order and promoters of anarchy, kindred spirits indeed of the monstrous Munsterites. For Niemojewski, it was Budny who presented the greater menace to the purity of his church's faith in nonresistance, for here in his writings was a rich mine of arguments handy for use in the future by all who wished to set the authorities against the Minor Church. The same sense of grievance that Niemojewski felt was expressed, too, by his colleague in the Lublin congregation, Czechowic, who wrote to Budny: "There are those who would wish to drag the office of the sword into their Church, apparently calling themselves also our brethren; but we are resisting them, wishing always to show that we are gladly content with the magistracy given of God to us together with the others. God is witness of this: we are not setting up another [magistracy] for ourselves, for that under which we live is good for us."

By this date, almost three decades had elapsed since Piotr of Goniądz first began to spread both pacifist and antitrinitarian opinions among the Polish and Lithuanian Calvinists. During the intervening period those who seceded to form the Minor Church had carried on, we have seen, a prolonged debate concerning the proper application of Christian principles to society. War and the *jus gladii* were the central themes under discussion. Beginning in the mid-1580's these topics retreated into the background of the Minor Church's intellectual interests—to emerge again at the end of the century. This time, however, they no longer constituted an issue debated in print before a comparatively wide audience. They now formed the subject of private colloquy carried on at church conferences or in even more restricted circles. And as the new century proceeded and social conservatism replaced social radicalism as the practice if not quite as the official doctrine of the church, interest in sociopolitical ideology faded, apart from an occasional upsurge of controversy on the subject between individual Antitrinitarians.

With Palaeologus removed from the scene and with Budny's expulsion from the Minor Church in 1584 (the cause of which, however, was not his defense of a Christian magistracy but his propagation of nonadorantism, regarded as tantamount to Judaism), the antirigorists had lost their most able and aggressive champions. Yet the removal of effective intellectual opposition to the nonresistants eventually proved injurious to the healthy development of their ideas. It meant the absence of stimulation; it resulted in the end in a cessation of ideological growth. As Kot aptly comments: "Victorious, no longer having any opponent, and not attacked by any, the teaching of the [Minor] Church [on nonresistance] unexpectedly began to be weakened and transformed."

One of the reasons for this decline, after the seeming triumph of social rigorism over its adversaries, was the removal by death of the most energetic, ardent, and gifted nonresistants of the first, the Anabaptist, phase in the Minor Church's history. Although Czechowic survived until 1613, Schomann and Grzegorz Paweł died in 1591 and Niemojewski in 1598. This left only Socinus. And Socinus, with his subtlety of intellect and relentless rationalism, was the man who was able to construct a *modus vivendi* between the official sectarian ideology, which rejected participation in political and social life as sinful, and a church membership that increasingly thirsted to play a role as citizens in the life of the fatherland.

Thus we reach the deeper causes of the ideological transformation which set in toward the end of the sixteenth century. These must be sought in shifts in numbers and in influence within the congregations between the various social groups. Unfortunately the sources for this period explored hitherto shed little light on the problem; until further research has been done on the social composition of Antitrinitarian congregations at this time, supposition more often than concrete facts must predominate in our discussion. During the "Anabaptist" period in the history of the Minor Church, intellectual ascendancy in the Polish branch was held by ministers of bourgeois origin or by men like Niemojewski, who had renounced their noble status in deference to the ideals they voluntarily adopted. By the end of the century this ascendancy had largely passed either to religious leaders of foreign origin like Socinus, who were not attached emotionally, as the older generation of ministers of indigenous plebeian background had been, to the sociopolitical ideology and the theological system of Polish "Anabaptism," or to a new generation of Antitrinitarian gentry whose church membership came as a birthright rather than as a consequence of personal conversion as had been the case with their fathers. In the important Lublin congregation we see this process at work when after the death of the revered Niemojewski in 1598 his plebeian colleague Czechowic was relieved of his position as minister, which he had held for several decades. These developments, though they do not seem to have altered the numerical predominance in many congregations of the plebeian class—artisans and craftsmen—gave the upper hand in administering the affairs of the church to the *szlachta* members and their allies. Only where these elements were absent, as for instance in the German-speaking bourgeois congregations in Danzig and its environs, did sporadic opposition occur to the trend towards social conservatism.

"The demand for revision came from the nobility," writes Kot. He goes on to quote the following passage from the Antitrinitarian chronicler Matthäus Radecke: "In the years 1595, 1596, and 1597, someone explained to the brethren, especially to the nobility, that they could with clear conscience possess the estates, rights, and privileges of nobles, *and bear arms*, whereupon the aspect of the Church completely changed, especially among the nobility" (my italics). In 1596 we find a prominent Antitrinitarian gentleman, Stanisław Lubieniecki, writing as follows in response to a Calvinist minister who accused his coreligionists of rejecting magistracy as unchristian: "We receive into the Church of God, in which we are, any man who is in office and regard him as a brother, unless in his office there is involved some injustice or contradiction of the gospel." This full and confident assertion of the Christian character of the magistracy is far removed from the earlier and extremely grudging concession that was granted in this respect solely on account of human imperfectibility. As yet, of course, the party of the social radicals had not been completely routed, as is shown by the almost annual recurrence between 1595 and 1605 of war, self-defense, and the magistracy as topics of discussion at church synods; Niemojewski had led the party with vigor and skill until his death in 1598. But in that very year a synod of the church approved the carrying of arms "to frighten away enemies and to ward off their blows." That a resolution of this kind could gain the assent of a majority was indeed indicative of a very different atmosphere from that which had prevailed only a decade or two earlier.

Socinus' coreligionists attributed to him the chief responsibility for effecting their denomination's transition from a sectarian position toward state and society to one of accommodation to their demands and of conformity to their ethos. All the evidence confirms the correctness of this attribution. From Socinus' correspondence during the second half of the 1590's we find that in private he had already reached the conclusions on these subjects which, as we shall see, during the first few years of the new century he would succeed in making the official teaching of the Minor Church. He now gave approval in general terms to the acceptance of office, even the highest, and to the existing system of law, including the imposition—"where appropriate"—of such sentences as that of flogging, provided only that the death penalty or mutilation were not used even for the gravest offense (from letter of 1599). But Socinus continued to have difficulties when grappling with the question of war. "Christians are forbidden to wage war against their fellow men," he wrote to an Antitrinitarian minister in 1599, for we should fight against evil only with spiritual weapons, as Christ— and St. Paul after him—had taught. Yet four years earlier, in correspondence with members of the Antitrinitarian gentry and at a time when preparations were under way for an expedition to repel a threatened Tatar attack, Socinus had gone a long way further in justifying *szlachta* participation in military service. It would not in any sense be wrong, he then wrote, for a Christian to bear arms if called upon, when "in no manner was it possible to escape" direct service by paying for a substitute to go in his place, and when the only alternative for a gentleman placed in such a situation was the loss of all his property (and thereby, presumably, of his status as a nobleman). However, after he had become a soldier the Christian must in all circumstances abstain from the shedding of blood or the infliction of wounds on an enemy. "But on this matter I would prefer to be instructed rather than myself to instruct another."

These opinions, it is true, did not constitute a complete reversal of Socinus' stand at the time of his arrival in Poland in 1580. Some element of compromise had existed then, too, in the manner in which he expounded the traditional nonresistant ethos of Polish antitrinitarian Anabaptism. But the area of compromise had meanwhile been greatly extended so that, as finally crystallized in the years immediately preceding Socinus' death in 1604, this ethos, while retaining the same external shape, was in spirit changed beyond recognition from that of the Polish Brethren of the "Anabaptist" period. In his later years Socinus, himself a scion of an Italian patrician family whose Polish marriage allied him with the Morsztyns, an Antitrinitarian family of well-to-do gentry, seems to have assimilated very closely in thought and feelings to the Polish Antitrinitarian *szlachta* in whose midst he now passed his life. He became sensitive to their aspirations and in particular he became increasingly sympathetic to the impatience of the younger generation of Antitrinitarian gentry with the strict ethical code which debarred them from participating, as they thought was both their due and their duty, in the life of the Polish political community. At the same time, he never quite abandoned his initial reservations concerning the moral viability of a Christian magistracy and continued to be reluctant to give a blanket approval to exercise of the *jus gladii* and to the soldier's profession.

Socinus' final position is best studied in connection with the series of lectures which he gave at Raków in 1601 and 1602 to a select circle of listeners. In these lectures he upheld the validity of the traditional standpoint on sociopolitical questions, yet in each case he added a number of qualifications and provisos which in effect nullified the force of the original stand. The Antitrinitarian *szlachta* welcomed the opportunity these seemed to offer for untrammelled exercise of activities hitherto engaged in *sub rosa*; for it became comparatively easy to ignore altogether the subtle distinctions which Socinus had drawn between a full recognition of political power, including *inter alia* the right to wage war, and the slightly more reserved attitude which he urged as incumbent on his brethren.

In 1601 legislation and litigation, self-defense and war were among the chief topics Socinus dealt with at Raków. In 1602, among a number of other subjects he covered capital punishment, judicial oaths, usury, property, luxury, and ecclesiastical discipline. "In a lecture given in a closed circle, and not intended for print, he could express his views more freely" than in open discussion. His audience was drawn from the intellectual elite of the Minor Church. Among the names of those who are known to have attended, only Czechowic was an uncompromising supporter of the old rigorism: we do not know what his comments were during the discussions which followed Socinus' exposition of his theme.

By his arguments Socinus sought to justify government office and the legal system, provided that these did not require any act *explicitly* contrary to the profession of a Christian. Despite his continued assertions in the old style that Christians had "no sure fatherland (*Respublica*)," the effect of his discourses was to inculcate the exact opposite: that in fact the brethren formed part of the body politic and might participate in all aspects of its life that did not conflict with their duty as Christians. Our main concern in this place is with the three topics in his discussion most nearly affecting the pacifist witness of the Antitrinitarians: capital punishment, self-defense, and war.

Socinus remains an uncompromising opponent of the death penalty. Although he saw nothing incorrect in a believer's acting as judge and in this capacity inflicting punishment on those who broke the law of the land, yet in a Christian country wrongdoers should be punished in some other fashion than by death. He could see no good reason for capital punishment on grounds either of utility or of morality. To take life destroyed the possibility of reformation: the culprit would be prevented from ever repenting and thereby entering into the church of Christ. Thus, such a penalty was opposed to Christian love and charity. Instead, argued Socinus, let the judge impose certain forms of torture, which would act as a better deterrent to crime, since their unpleasantness could be envisaged more graphically than the state of death (a line of reasoning, incidentally, that we can scarcely imagine in the mouth of spokesmen of the first generation of Antitrinitarians like Grzegorz Paweł, Niemojewski, or Czechowic).

Concerning self-defense Socinus was able to carry his exegesis a stage further toward the full integration of church practice with the behavior of the environing community. Self-defense, he said, was admissible, provided it did not result either in the death or in the mutilation of the assailant. Indeed, the believer might carry weapons so long as he entertained no thought of using them to kill or to wound; to wear them in church, however, was "not done (*indecorum*)." If, nevertheless, in the act of defending himself against an unprovoked assault he should unintentionally kill or maim the attacker, this would be ac-

139

counted a venial sin. Moreover, Socinus went on to explain, it was less sinful to kill Turks or bandits than fellow Christians. Of course in every case a believer ought to prefer his own death to homicide even in self-defense. But there was nothing wrong in shooting a musket into the air or brandishing a sword, these arms being carried without intent to kill; such action might serve to frighten away the assailant. "It is wrong to kill, that is, it is wrong to be in a state of mind where I would prefer to kill another rather than that others should kill me," thus Socinus sums up his position.

In Socinus' discussion of war we meet the same spirit of compromise, the same verbal retention of the earlier rigorist view concerning the inadmissibility of bloodshed under all circumstances together with additional qualifications which virtually destroy its force, as we have seen in his exposition of the Christian attitude to personal self-defense. Whereas antipacifist Antitrinitarians like Palaeologus or Budny had drawn upon the Old Testament for justification of the right of war, Socinus continued to stand squarely on the basis of the New Testament and to deny that the Jewish dispensation could override Christ's injunction of nonresistance. This applied to any who believed in him, "whether . . . magistrate or private citizen." All his followers were commanded to refrain from homicide. "There is no argument in the New Testament which would make us infringe this precept."

Once again, however, Socinus, when he moved from the plane of abstract morality to practical conduct, went very far toward providing not at all a justification for conscientious objection to military service but an apologia for the nobility's participation in war. True, he went over the old rigmarole, explaining how desirable it was for none to go to the wars where so many evils lurked for unwary believers, how the payment of commutation money to obtain exemption from compulsory service was preferable to personal participation, and how Christians really possessed on this earth no country of their own which needed defending. After Socinus had rehearsed these preliminaries, he proceeded to his main problem: how ought Antitrinitarian nobles to react to a call to the colors when enemy attack threatened their country?

Although Christ had commanded his followers to stand aside from battle, for they might not shed the blood of their fellow men, he had never, in Socinus' view, expressly condemned the waging of war. Socinus did not work out in any detail the distinction between aggressive and defensive wars or the nature of the just war; but his underlying assumption in discussing the participation of believers in war (like that of the Antitrinitarian antipacifists of Lithuania before him) was that in the given instance the state was waging a war of defense against unprovoked attack. Under these conditions a Polish gentleman, even though a believer, might muster if the authorities called upon him to do so, for the only alternative was total disgrace. "Everyone knows," Socinus said, "that if a Polish nobleman, after what is popularly known as the general levy [the Polish phrase *pospolite ruszenie* is inserted at this point in the Latin text] has been called out, refuses to go to war, he will be liable to penalties of a nature which could easily be the cause of his own and his family's downfall." His property would be confiscated and he might well be forced to act dishonorably in order to support his dependents. Thus, the resulting sin would be more grave than that accruing from merely attending muster without any intention of killing and, if possible, without actually carrying weapons. Even a minister who was a nobleman might attend muster, Socinus thought, if he had first made every effort to steer clear of this obligation; or he might equally well deliver equipage for use in an impending war if, instead, this were what was required of him.

If a believer were involved in battle or in the defense of a town or fortress, he should exert himself to his utmost to escape being caught in a situation in which he would have to kill. In any case he must eschew any thought of killing if he were to remain worthy of the Christian name. However, should he nevertheless be forced to kill, this undeniably must be accounted a sin—but not so serious a sin as, for instance, adultery. Socinus, indeed, considered infliction of the death penalty a more serious backsliding in a believer than the commission of homicide during battle, for in war the soldier's primary aim was not to kill but to defend himself and his country.

At one point in his exposition Socinus remarks that if his brethren ever became a numerous group within the Polish Commonwealth he would expect them to adopt a more radically pacifist stand than could be demanded of them in existing circumstances. He did not elaborate, however, on this statement. Socinus' pacifism was more rational than heroic. A Marxist historian (Józef Walczewski) has connected Socinus' retraction in 1601-1602 of his earlier, more militant pacifism with his desire so to reframe his church's teachings on the subject as to remove those elements which conflicted with "the class structure of society." Walczewski's approach seems to me valid here. Socinus, in developing a rational critique of war which at the same time assessed positively the humanitarian and utilitarian aspects of the state, sought to soften the sectarian contours of the Anabaptist rejection of society which the first generation of Polish Antitrinitarians had regarded as essential to their rejection of war. He also strove so to adapt the Minor Church's rigorous nonresistance, while still leaving intact the objection to homicide, as to make it possible for the gentry among the Church's members, now an increasingly influential component, to fulfil their citizen duties in war as in peacetime without overstepping the limits of the Church's code of correct conduct. Yet the results of his teaching in this respect were rather different from what Socinus probably expected. It opened up the way to full and uninhibited participation on the part of the Antitrinitarian *szlachta* in the military as well as the civil activities of the Commonwealth. True, there were some, like the Dutchman Dominicus Sapma, who criticized Socinus for not coming out unambiguously in favor of the sword. Calling Socinus' final position a "restricted" one, Sapma wrote sarcastically: "He allows Christians to hold the office of magistrate—on condition, however, of not using the sword, not condemning to death, not mutilating human members, and not performing other important acts of office, or, in plain terms, on condition of not discharging the office." Yet in Poland rank-and-file Antitrinitarians, ignoring the subtle reservations which irked the learned Sapma, interpreted Socinus' message as an invitation wholly to abandon a sectarian sociopolitical ethos.

In some respects we may see in Socinus' viewpoint as expressed in the Raków lectures a foreshadowing of the Quakers' position on the magistracy as it crystallized during the second half of the same century. Both accepted the Christian character of the magistracy, while rejecting its traditional sword. Both regarded the blood shed in war as the result of deviation from the duties of a Christian. Both repudiated the Anabaptists' idea of complete nonconformity to the world while retaining a stricter than worldly code of social behavior. Yet their purposes were very different. Whereas Socinus sought to justify the almost unconditional integration of his coreligionists into the state and military system, the early Quaker pacifists aimed at drawing a clearcut line between the realms of Caesar and Christ. Thus, they still succeeded in making a radical peace testimony and the practice of conscientious objection an integral part of the discipline of their Society of Friends: on the other hand, Socinus' teaching on magistracy and war led to the final disintegration of the pacifist practice of the Polish Antitrinitarians.

It was not until 1618, fourteen years after Socinus' death, when a volume of his selected correspondence was published at the Raków press, that this teaching appeared in print; from many passages in his letters the tenor of his most recent thinking on sociopolitical problems became clear to all who read. Even before this date, however, those who were closest to him and had been present at the Raków lectures must have helped inform fellow members of their revered leader's views. Moreover, several treatises from other pens expounding *inter alia* Socinus' position on the magistracy and war were published during this period.

In 1604, for instance, a work came off the Raków press by Christoff Ostorodt, the German-born minister of the Antitrinitarian congregation at Śmigiel in the Poznań area. It was written in the German language and entitled *Instruction on the Most Important Doctrines of the Christian Religion* (*Unterrichtung von den vornehmsten Hauptpuncten der christlichen Religion*). Like Socinus, Ostorodt saw nothing wrong in believers' accepting office. Effective government, he believed, was possible without the shedding of blood. Not the death penalty, but prison and forced labor, torture and the lash were the best deterrents of crime (clearly an echo of Socinus' argument at Raków a couple of years earlier). Killing in self-defense was also a sin. Yet, Ostorodt went on, "we do not forbid the carrying of a weapon on journeys to frighten off murderers and for protection against dogs and wild beasts; for it is not the carrying of weapons that is forbidden, but killing with them, and one must avoid superstition and prejudice in everything, since they greatly injure religion and the true fear of God." After pointing out that whereas most Christians believed that war was sometimes justifiable it had been condemned as unchristian by men like the humanists Erasmus and Vivès, even though they were Roman Catholics, Ostorodt has this to say: "There are . . . thousands of those who regard it as inconsistent with Christianity; though they are for the most part simple and uneducated people, hence they are laughed at and are regarded as odd by the theologians. . . . We agree with those who condemn war, though we well know that this gives offence to many who, only because of this one view, irresponsibly reject our whole confession, believing that this view of ours upsets order from top to bottom and causes general confusion." He has to admit, however, that the question of war is not a clear case of right on one side and wrong on the other. For this reason his church did not repudiate members who, like the prophets of Old Testament times, held that there were occasions when war could not be avoided. In his own view, a state was best defended by friendly agreements with neighboring powers; if invaded nevertheless, a Christian country should not resist by arms, trusting instead to God for its defense.

From the Racovian Catechism, first published in Polish in 1605 and in Latin in 1609 (with the well-known dedication to James I of England) and subsequently reprinted many times, contemporaries—both Antitrinitarians and those outside the church—could also discover the revisionist position which under Socinus' guidance the Minor Church

143

had reached in sociopolitical matters. (Socinus himself, before his death, had helped to draft the contents of the Catechism.) The Catechism saw nothing wrong in a Christian's accepting office, provided that in fulfilling his duties he acted with mercy and did not infringe any of Christ's injunctions. While it did not explicitly sanction participation in war even in a noncombatant capacity, in fact the vague wording of the Catechism when dealing with the magistrate's office opened the door even wider for the entry of the soldier into the brotherhood.

The Socinian view of the magistracy was again expounded in the course of a lengthy treatise by another Antitrinitarian immigrant from Germany, Valentin Smalcius (Schmaltz), which appeared—also at Raków—in 1614 under the title *Refutatio thesium D. Wolfgangi Frantzii*. Wolfgang Franz was a Wittenberg theologian who had sharply attacked both Roman Catholics and Antitrinitarians. The latter's official nonresistance he considered an invitation to chaos. Smalcius, though by now thoroughly assimilated to his Polish environment, came from a German Lutheran background; this fact may have made him particularly sensitive to Franz's onslaughts. Smalcius' *Refutatio* included ten pages "de rebus civilibus." We need not linger over what he included there: his exposition followed the lines laid down by Socinus. He approved magistracy as well as harsh punishments, provided that the life of the wrongdoer were spared. A Christian country must avoid war under all circumstances: better to practice complete nonresistance than to admit the permissibility of battle, though a state should seek to ward off the possibility of attack both by timely concessions and by means of alliances.

One point raised in the course of these polemical exchanges which continued until 1621, though a minor one, is of interest here since it illustrates the manner in which Socinian pacifism, while fairly uncompromising in theory, opened the door to a relaxation in practice. This was the question of the manufacture of the instruments of war. Smalcius, on the whole, disapproves of such activity. It would ordinarily be wrong for a believer to enter upon a profession of this kind. Yet if he had absolutely no other means of earning a livelihood and he and his family faced starvation were he to refuse, then such employment was permissible. For it was not the instruments that were harmful *per se* (like the knives which the Anabaptists were prepared to make, they might even be of benefit to man, depending on the circumstances); the harm lay in the use to which they were put when they were employed to kill other men. Besides, Smalcius adds, one could never be quite sure in advance if one's handiwork really would result in a man's death.

In the preceding paragraphs we have been considering theory alone. The practical behavior of the Antitrinitarian *szlachta* in the course of the first half of the seventeenth century blended more and more with that of the contemporary Polish nobility of Catholic or Protestant persuasion. During the later decades of the Catholic Vasa king, Zygmunt III, Antitrinitarians took a prominent part in the wars against Muscovites and Tatars. They displayed their patriotism in moments of crisis in the state's affairs. During the Russo-Polish War of 1632-1634, for instance, when a Russian army besieged Smolensk, Antitrinitarian noblemen by their bravery and zeal for the national cause gained the notice and favor of the new king, Władysław IV. Among the younger generation professional soldiers were now to be found in increasing numbers, though this was still frowned on by the church. Moreover, the Minor Church's growing reputation for intellectual and cultural vitality attracted recruits from the educated classes: these new members did not usually share the church's traditional pacifism even in the adulterated form presented by Socinus. Normally even members who became professional soldiers were no longer admonished, let alone disfellowshipped, by their congregations.

As early as 1604-1605, synods held at Raków during these years passed resolutions which permitted resistance, provided that it did not result in serious injury or death to an attacker. Should resistance prove impossible without killing or maiming, then the brethren should emigrate from the danger zone. The whole question had arisen in connection with the frequent Tatar raids on frontier areas like Podolia, where there were Antitrinitarian congregations. What should the brethren do in trying circumstances like these? The answer reflected the advice proffered by Socinus himself just prior to his death. We do know that the synods' decisions met with opposition from the rigorists, who still formed a not uninfluential body of opinion within the church. Some members, previously somewhat hesitant, appear to have entertained second thoughts on the subject and to have had their existing proclivity toward nonresistance strengthened. Ostorodt, for example, after his transference from Śmigiel to Busków near Danzig came out in favor of the exclusion from the church of those who contravened the church's official teaching concerning war and the magistracy. It seems that in his case the influence of the Anabaptist-Mennonite congregations in the northwest corner of Poland (his remarks cited earlier obviously reflect a close knowledge of this denomination) was

145

responsible for his turn toward radicalism. At any rate the Antitrinitarian leadership in Raków expressed its strong disapproval of Ostorodt when he carried his threats of excommunication into practice.

These were decades of transition. On the one hand, the old sociopolitical rigorism inherited from the "Anabaptist" period, though ebbing, still showed considerable vigor, while the new permissiveness made possible through Socinus' casuistical skill, though soon to gain an almost unchallenged ascendancy, had not yet succeeded in eliminating all dissentient voices. On the other hand, patriotism rather than pacifism seemed to many Antitrinitarians the only way to dampen the mounting fires of religious fanaticism that were sweeping the country and threatening the very existence of their church. Kot writes:

> We have unfortunately no sources which would make it possible to look into the inner life of the Polish Brethren and explain this important evolution in greater detail. It must undoubtedly have been preceded by many passionate discussions. Undoubtedly it was influenced by political considerations—the consciousness of the complete consolidation of society behind the banner of intolerance which, at first breaking out sporadically, threatened to root out everything that passed for heretical. Foreseeing a difficult period, the Polish Brethren endeavored to get rid of provocative points in their doctrine which gave grounds for accusing them of lack of patriotism and of disloyalty to the government of the King.

The exigencies of practical politics, then, formed a major reason impelling the Socinians (this appellation, however, was current abroad rather than in Poland itself) to jettison nonresistance. Class sympathies and predilections, as we have seen, already predisposed the powerful gentry element to do this. The publication in 1625 of the Dutch jurist Hugo Grotius' *De jure belli ac pacis* strengthened the position of the antirigorist majority in the Minor Church, for it pleaded for the establishment of the rule of law among the nations while at the same time arguing the case for defensive war and the state's duty to inflict capital punishment as well as for the right of personal self-defense. Of course Grotius' strictures on nonresistance were directed primarily against Dutch Mennonites rather than Polish Socinians. But his arguments drawn both from the New Testament and the law of nature proved extremely useful in controversy with the nonresistant remnant within the Antitrinitarian community; whereas his internationalism appealed, too, to the humanitarian sentiments of the Socinian antirigorist intellectuals, who looked forward to harmony on earth as ardently

146

as their rigorist opponents, despairing of ever attaining concord in a naughty world, sought eternal peace only beyond the grave.

At first, however, official Antitrinitarianism reacted somewhat negatively to Grotius. In 1627, as if in answer to the Dutchman, a second edition of Socinus' *Responsio* to Palaeologus appeared in Raków. At the same time, the church leadership wrote direct to Grotius, informing him of their desire to enter into discussion with him as to "whether it would not be possible to avoid the death penalty and as to what are the just causes of war."

A decade later, in 1636, Raków sponsored the publication of a treatise by Jonasz Szlichtyng, a prominent minister. His *Quaestiones duae . . . contra Balthasarem Meisnerum* was written to refute an attack made on Socinus by yet another Wittenberg theologian. In it the author devotes considerable space to the problem of capital punishment and of bloodshed in general. His position in these matters is decidedly ambiguous: while stressing the misery and horror of war, he carefully avoids the question of what a believer should do if required to undertake active military service, and he does not deal at all with personal self-defense. He agrees that the state has the right to wage war in a just cause and on an important issue as well as to impose sentence of death. Yet he regards voluntary participation on the part of the individual Christian in these activities as incompatible with his religious profession. And he implies, without ever making it quite explicit, that nonresistance remains the correct stance.

More typical, at this time, of the state of mind not only of the Antitrinitarian gentry but also of the Socinian intellectuals who guided the church's affairs was the opinion voiced by Martin Ruar, a minister of German origin, who wrote in 1627: "I recognize that a Christian may hold office, inflict corporal punishments and even the death penalty upon criminals, and also repel invaders by armed force and defend his innocence by war if it cannot otherwise be made safe. Arguments in support I shall not cite, since I am content with those brought forward by Grotius. . . ." Poland's battles in the east against Tatars and Turks appeared to Ruar to be just wars waged in self-defense to meet the attacks of an aggressive foe. Kot considers that Grotius' book influenced many of the Socinian noblemen who, as we have seen, participated with such enthusiasm in the war against Moscow in 1632-1634. (Among them was young Samuel Przypkowski, a member of one of the leading familes of the Antitrinitarian gentry and soon to come forward as an able protagonist of the antipacifist position.)

Grotius gave considerable intellectual ballast to the antipacifist camp which, though by this time clearly in the ascendant as regards numbers and rank, still had the weight of tradition against it. Another Dutchman, Daniël de Breen (Brenius), was partly responsible for a last upsurge of the old, socially radical spirit in the Polish Antitrinitarian movement. Brenius was associated with the Rijnsburg Collegiants; his pacifism will be discussed in the next chapter dealing with Mennonites in the northern Netherlands. Although Brenius did not publish his conclusions on the proper Christian attitude to war and the state until the 1640's, his work had already circulated in manuscript for some years before publication. His contacts with the Polish Socinians date back as far as 1627, if not earlier, so that his influence on the Polish Brethren was felt contemporaneously with that of Grotius, though of course in an opposite direction.

Brenius' ideas were not particularly original. Their essence lay in his assumption that an irremovable barrier existed between Christ's kingdom and the world and that citizens of the former could play no part whatsoever in the government of the latter: a thesis that was indeed at the core of all Anabaptist nonresistance. A doctrine of the two kingdoms, such as Brenius taught, had been present in the writings of Polish Antitrinitarians like Paweł or Czechowic or even the early Socinus. Yet its restatement half a century later by Brenius made a considerable impact in some sections of the Polish Antitrinitarian movement. Such ideas, though widely held at the beginning of its history, were being forgotten as the Socinians accommodated themselves more and more to the world which surrounded them. Therefore the boldness and self-confidence with which Brenius set forth his views strengthened those elements in the Minor Church which craved for an unequivocal testimony in favor of nonresistance—especially after such wholesale backsliding on the part of the noble brethren and with the growing tendency in the church leadership either altogether to ignore, or progressively to whittle away, what remained of nonresistance. It is significant, however, that Brenius found an echo not so much among the Polish Antitrinitarian *szlachta*, who almost uniformly rejected his views, but among the German-speaking congregations, consisting either of *Eingeboren* or newcomers who had fled the harsher religious climate of their fatherland.

Typical of the latter was the Austrian baron, Johann Ludwig von Wolzogen, who settled in Danzig where he became a mainstay of the local Antitrinitarian group. Wolzogen was an amateur but learned theologian, a mathematician of note as well as a philosopher. He knew Brenius personally and translated his *Concerning the Character of Christ's Kingdom* (*Van de hoedanigheid des rijks Christi*) into German. Under Brenius' influence Wolzogen composed a work of his own

148

devoted largely to the problem of church-state relations: "De natura & qualitate Regni Christi ac religionis Christianae," which, though undated and unpublished during the author's lifetime, must have been written sometime during the 1640's.

Government and lordship over fellow men could have no place in Christ's kingdom, Wolzogen states categorically. Christians, here on earth a small band and a select one, should stand aside, regarding the maintenance of order simply as a playing-out of God's judgment which punished evildoers through the instrumentality of pseudo-Christians. Wars, too, were the result of God's verdict against the wickedness of men and their rulers. No believer might fight for country or for faith; he should resort to flight or exile rather than succumb to pressures to bear arms. Yet even the baron made one concession to the spirit of a corrupt age. To demand of the nobility that they abandon their noble rank and the symbols of their exalted social status—titles, fine clothing, and grand houses—before acceptance into the church would, he admitted, be asking too much. True, they should not display pride or undue ostentation; they must steer clear of civil office or any activity which would require them to spill human blood. Yet Wolzogen did not find it possible to deny them the privilege, if they wished it, of wearing a sword after the fashion then followed universally by persons of rank, provided the weapon were never used for inflicting an injury. Thus even Wolzogen, despite the generally uncompromising nature of his pacifist witness, bears the imprint of Socinus' adaptation of the Antitrinitarian peace testimony to the needs of the Antitrinitarian *szlachta*.

The degree of accommodation which Wolzogen was prepared to admit fell far short of what Socinus had allowed. It was even less acceptable to the Socinian nobles of the mid-seventeenth century or to the leadership of the church which they to a large extent controlled. Wolzogen's sectarian spirit aroused the wrath of a leading minister, Szlichtyng, who despite his German-sounding name came from a Polish *szlachta* family. We have seen him in the 1630's defending opinions on war and the state akin to those of Socinus, though even more ambiguous in their practical implications. Subsequently, Szlichtyng threw aside his former reservations and came out squarely in favor of the magistrate's sword. If God had ordained the sword for man's good, he saw no reason now why believers should not exercise it. Moreover, they would use it with greater moderation and humanity than would unbelievers: their participation in government would guarantee that power was employed for righteous ends. "In my view," he wrote, "the Christian religion may include kings and emperors, for it brings to all classes and callings God's grace, which inclines all men to a godly and sober life and kings to a benevolent exercise of their power." To exclude believers from power, therefore, was an absurdity, since thereby righteousness among men would decrease.

Wolzogen's condemnation of a Christian magistracy and of the *jus gladii* in all its aspects provoked Szlichtyng to reply. His "Quaestiones de magistratu, bello, defensione privata" is no longer extant, and the same is true of the "Annotationes oppositae memoratis J. L. Wolzogenii Annotationibus," which he wrote in answer to the baron's "Annotationes ad Quaestiones Jonae Schlichtingii." Wolzogen's work, however, has survived, as has his final riposte against Szlichtyng, "Responsio ad . . . Annotationes in Annotationes." With this the polemic between the two men concluded. The controversy cannot be dated exactly, but it seems to have begun sometime before 1648, the year which ushered in Poland's time of troubles, and it ended around 1650. Though Szlichtyng's tracts are lost, his arguments can be reconstructed from the lengthy citations from them in Wolzogen.

"The discussion on self-defense," writes Kot, to whose book I am indebted for my knowledge of these controversies as of so much else in respect to the Polish Antitrinitarians, "produced no unexpected arguments." Yet the glosses given by the two writers on familiar doctrines sometimes throw an interesting light on the state of opinion within the Socinian community in Poland around mid-century.

Szlichtyng, while granting that nonresistance might well seem attractive to groups like the Anabaptists or Mennonites whose members were drawn almost exclusively from the lower orders, rejected it as unbecoming in a believer from the upper ranks of society. He reminded Wolzogen, who had urged flight from the enemy rather than resort to armed defense, that at that very time marauding bands of Tatars and Cossacks were slaughtering peaceful inhabitants in the southeast parts of the Polish Commonwealth, including numbers of their coreligionists who lived in those areas. In fact, so swift had been the raids that they had had no chance to save their lives by flight. And, besides, to flee from the enemy was disgraceful conduct, especially scandalous in a member of the *szlachta*, whose social position required service as a soldier in defense of his native land. Szlichtyng did not deny that a man could help defend his country by undertaking various auxiliary duties of a noncombatant character, such as supplying food for the army. He seemed even to imply that it was preferable for a Christian, whenever possible, to avoid duties which necessitated shedding blood (other relics of the Socinian exegesis were his disapproval of professional soldiering and his stress on the need for those who at the command of the magistrate bore arms in a just cause to remain free of any deliberate intention to kill). Yet, at the same time, he felt strongly that church members who were ready to fight for their country were not apostates; in undergoing military training they were only fulfilling their civic obligations and were in no manner acting contrary to their Christian faith. In the same way, in wielding the sword of justice, and by restraining and punishing wrongdoers, Christians in authority carried out the will of God, for the sword of justice was an essential part of his plan for mankind.

If we can easily detect the mind of Grotius behind the arguments employed by Szlichtyng, we plainly see Brenius' influence at work in his opponent's reasoning. Wolzogen denied at the outset any possibility of dual citizenship: the two realms—the kingdom of Christ and the terrestrial sphere—required mutually contradictory things of their subjects. Loyalty to the one ruled out anything more than a passive obedience to the other. The baron deplored the growing tendency among his brethren in Poland to approximate their political ethic to the world's; officially to admit rulers into the church would produce a most unfortunate effect, especially on the younger generation already only too prone to ignore the traditional stand of their church and enter into the service of the state.

That his antistate rigorism would keep the church small did not worry Wolzogen in the very least (as it had not alarmed Czech Brethren and Swiss Brethren and German and Dutch Anabaptists before him). Readiness to suffer patiently was essential in members of a martyr church, and this was a quality which numbers could not produce. A Christian must be ready to die rather than kill, for homicide was impossible with love in the heart.

The special problem of war occupied much of Wolzogen's attention. He accused Szlichtyng of inconsistency for opposing soldiering as a profession while at the same time urging noble youths, including the scions of Antitrinitarian families, to train for defense of the Commonwealth. Since full-time service in the armed forces was the best preparation for war, why—he enquired derisively—did Szlichtyng believe that one should wait to be conscripted before joining up? He disagreed, too, with the conclusions drawn by Szlichtyng from the experience of Antitrinitarians in the war-torn frontier zones, for he considered it to be tempting God's patience for a community which desired to live nonresistantly to settle within range of barbarian raiders. He could see no good reason why they could not remove to the center of the country. There, more time would be gained for buying off the invaders with a monetary payment. Moreover, in contrast to the country's sparsely inhabited eastern territories, in central Poland there were nonbelievers in plenty ready to take defensive measures which would protect that area from actual invasion. In the last resort, if his coreligionists were really in earnest in their nonresistance they would leave Poland for a more secure land rather than take up arms.

Wolzogen was a foreigner in Poland. The above arguments (as Kot has emphasized) reflect his nonattachment, a state of detachment which Polish-born members of his church, like Szlichtyng, found more difficult to attain. The threads which bound them to the political community bound them also to observance of that community's ethos. Whereas Wolzogen, like the Old Brethren in the Czech lands in the fifteenth century, felt free to advocate flight from danger or voluntary exile (what Gandhi in our times has described succinctly by the term *hijrat*), the indigenous Polish element among the Socinians felt obliged to choose between sociopolitical conformity or open defiance of the political and military establishment. In fact, they had already opted for the former at least fifty years earlier.

Nonetheless, even at mid-seventeenth century church leaders, as we have seen, were reluctant to abandon certain areas of dissent in this field. Wolzogen had no difficulty in pointing out the absurdities to which this led in Szlichtyng's case. How could Szlichtyng honestly maintain, he asks, that one could prepare for war without any intention of killing? For one thing, a soldier must take life when ordered to do so; if he refused he broke military law, and breaking a law of this kind exposed a gentleman to the very punishment and disgrace which Szlichtyng strove to avoid at all costs. Second, killing was a basic function of all armies. Therefore, Wolzogen thought it only right to exclude from communion those church members who obeyed the call to join the colors, even though they had not actually spilled blood. (From his account it is clear, however, that this practice was no longer in force anywhere in the congregations of his day.) He contested the presupposition accepted in his church from Socinus' time that a war could be just, could be essentially defensive. He disagreed in particular when Socinus urged compromise if war resistance threatened the conscientious objector with social disgrace and material ruin. A believer, in Wolzogen's view, should without hesitation refuse to comply with the law if this entailed disobedience to his religious duty. If it were a sin to take human life (as Wolzogen of course believed it was), then the Christian nobleman must reject an order to join the army even though this brought shame to his family and the loss of his temporal goods.

The émigré baron, like the Anabaptist generation of Polish Brethren, viewed the life of a believer on this earth as an exile from his heavenly fatherland. The state in which he happened to reside during his life was in no sense his true country. Let those who considered it as their country defend it. There would always be a sufficient number of such pseudo-Christians to guarantee its security (a familiar argument, we have seen, in the nonresistant repertoire). Wolzogen thought that Szlichtyng and his like placed undue weight upon the benefits their church derived from the protection of its nobles, and he pointed to those religious groups, including the nonresistant Hutterites and Mennonites, who had survived successfully without any nobility of their own. Therefore, concluded Wolzogen: "Our ancestors would have helped our churches and the truth of God in Poland much better had they either resigned the privilege of nobility or made some other arrangement with the Commonwealth by which they might have retained their nobility and freed themselves from the burden of war as well as from swearing by the Trinity and the crucifix."

Although Wolzogen's arguments were aimed directly at Szlichtyng he may also have had in mind a still more formidable opponent among his coreligionists, Samuel Przypkowski, who around 1650 had prepared two treatises defending the pro-state and pro-war position. The nonresistant doctrines, which his brethren adopted at the beginning, he had described in his biography of Socinus published in 1631 as mere "fancies, with which the ardor of first enthusiasm had unreasonably inoculated them." Actually, Przypkowski went much further than Socinus and rejected the reservations concerning the magistrate's office and the right of war which the latter had still insisted on in his Raków lectures. But it was primarily against Brenius, rather than against the moderate pacifism of Socinus, that Przypkowski aimed his arguments. "The sectarian views of Brenius," writes Kot, "must have spread devastation among the thoughtful if, independently of Szlichtyng, the most highly talented writer of the Polish Brethren, Samuel Przypkowski, undertook to confute them." This he did first in his "Animadversiones in libellum cui titulus De qualitate regni domini nostri Jesu Christi . . ." and later, and less directly, in another tract entitled "De jure Christiani magistratus & privatorum in belli pacisque negotiis." Neither work was published during the author's lifetime, though they circulated in manuscript both in Poland and in Holland. Przypkowski considered that their publication could needlessly multiply tensions within the church at a time when it was subject to bitter attack from outside, and so provide ammunition for its numerous enemies bent on its destruction. Apart from Grotius, Palaeologus and especially Budny were the writers on whom Przypkowski drew most. The force of his logic and his clear and persuasive style appealed to many of his coreligionists, who felt the call of country especially keenly at a time when Poland was threatened successively by Cossack, Muscovite, and Swedish invasions. For Przypkowski, while convinced that the church as such should not exercise temporal authority, found no reason to believe that Christ had intended his followers to refrain from affairs of state, since civil government was essential to the continued existence of human society. And among the legitimate functions of government was the use of the sword, whether in punishing evildoers or in wars of defense. Thus Christians, who as individuals were indeed obligated to love their enemies, must fulfil their civic duties even if these required the use of the sword.

Przypkowski's stand provoked the ire not only of extreme nonresistants of the Wolzogen variety, but also of Antitrinitarians who still adhered to the Socinian position on magistracy and war—who, that is to say, regarded their personal objection to taking human life to be compatible with far-going participation in the life of the state. Among Socinians of this way of thinking a young minister of German origin, Joachim Stegmann, felt prompted to reply to Przypkowski. Stegmann held, with Socinus, that a believer should never take part in war, at least to the point of killing, nor participate in the higher ranks of the administration, since in the course of their duties such officials might be obliged to impose the death penalty. He regretted, therefore, that at so critical a juncture Przypkowski (whom nevertheless he regarded with great respect) "had opened the window" to all wishing to break loose from the Church's teaching on this vital subject.

In a reply entitled "Apologia prolixior tractatus de jure Christiani magistratus" (from which we derive our knowledge of Stegmann's treatise dating from the mid-1650's and now lost), Przypkowski repeated his arguments in favor of a Christian magistracy. He inquired of Stegmann whether, if one were ready to pay his way out from military service as the Socinian pacifists advocated doing, he was not contributing to the bloodshed as substantially as by direct participation in the ranks of the army. In Przypkowski's opinion a man who was ready to surrender his freedom rather than fight deserved to lose his liberty. "Suppose," he wrote, that in battle a Polish nobleman, following the advice given by Socinus and his school for use in such emergencies, "took to flight in good faith, in consequence of a patience which shrank from slaying his enemies; who will say that from his action the glory of God or the edification of men resulted? Only God knows whether in his soul there lay any noble thought, but the public shame involved all in a common disgrace." Certainly peace was a desirable goal but nonresistance, far from decreasing the amount of violence in the world, actually increased its prevalence by opening up the way to the rule of lawless men.

Another leading Socinian who demurred at some of Przypkowski's conclusions was Stegmann's father-in-law, Martin Ruar, a minister of the older generation. Ruar, as we have seen, was not a pacifist, not even in the Socinian sense that Stegmann was. But he disapproved strongly of the way in which young Antitrinitarian noblemen in increasing numbers, under the influence of writers like Przypkowski, chose the career of a professional soldier. In 1656 he wrote: "I cannot condemn a man who under the compulsion of danger to himself or his family takes up arms for necessary defense. But voluntary military service, undertaken for pleasure or for glory or gain, I regard as totally opposed to the rule of life that the Saviour and his apostles prescribed for us." He asked how such service could fail to conflict with Christian love, for those whom the professional injured and despoiled and killed during its course had done him no harm. And if even in a defensive war some wrong must inevitably occur to the innocent, what excuse could one possibly make before God if he shed innocent blood without the plea of self-defense?

During the seventeenth century Catholic fanaticism grew. In the early decades, indeed until near mid-century, Poland still remained a haven for religious dissenters. But the position of the Socinians became increasingly insecure. Their congregations were subjected to mob violence and their meeting houses destroyed. In 1638 the authorities closed the press and academy at Raków. Voices were raised in government circles and in the diet, demanding the expulsion of the hated "Arians." The Antitrinitarians, while accommodating their sociopolitical ethic in practice to that of the Polish environment, had, under Socinus' influence, become theologically more radical; they stood now for the application of reason to religion, including the interpretation of the Scriptures. Such opinions brought down on them the full force of the Counter Reformation, which was felt, too, of course by the other Protestant churches in Poland. The vaunted patriotism of the Antitrinitarian nobility failed to wash away the stain left by their profession of Socinian heresy. Finally, in 1658 came the decree of exile passed by the diet against all who should continue to adhere to the Antitrinitarian church. They were given three years in which to choose between conformity to Roman Catholicism and emigration. A few brethren bowed to fate and accepted forced conversion; this occurred especially in cases where only one married partner was a Socinian. Among the exiles some opted for the tolerant Dutch Republic (i.e.

155

"Holland"); some chose to remain not far from their native land, settling in Protestant districts of Silesia or in Brandenburg or Prussia; others left for distant Transylvania where, alone in Europe at that time, there was another organized Antitrinitarian church. In Poland the Antitrinitarian movement ceased to exist.

"Even in their exile, discussions about war and the magistrate did not quiet down." There were those, like the great Ruthenian magnate Yuriy Nemyrych (who, however, eventually turned Eastern Orthodox) or the Silesian-born minister Jeremias Felbinger, who felt that their church's official pacifist stance, for all its moderation, had contributed substantially to the downfall. Others argued the exact opposite, seeing in the watered-down theory and in the acceptance by many Antitrinitarians of both office and military service an apostasy which had brought down divine displeasure on the church. Holland became the center of such debates among the exiles. Holland was the land of Grotius and the country which would soon embark on a long and arduous struggle against the expansionist designs of Louis XIV. Its intellectual atmosphere, therefore, might appear propitious to those exiles, like Przypkowski, who supported participation in government and defensive wars. But Holland was also the home of the nonresistant Mennonites and Collegiants. Contact with these groups served also to reinvigorate the Antitrinitarians' pacifist testimony, which had progressively wilted in the hostile environment of their native Poland.

Tazbir speaks of "a rebirth of sectarian tendencies in the Arian diaspora" of the 1670's and 1680's. A new edition, for instance, of the Raków Catechism published in Amsterdam in 1680 contained a commentary written by Benedykt Wiszowaty, a minister of the younger generation, in which he pointed to the fact that the early church had for three centuries held aloof from civil government and urged that this example be followed by contemporary Christians. He cited rigorist writers like Piotr of Goniądz, Paweł, Czechowic, and Wolzogen in support of this position. Wiszowaty's stand, we may note, contradicted the wording of the text of the Catechism, where approval was given both to civil government as essential to restrain evildoers and to believers participating in its activities so long as these did nothing "against the laws and precepts of Christ."

The chief protagonist in exile of the rigorist position was a German-speaking oculist from Danzig, Daniel Zwicker, who had joined the Antitrinitarian congregation there. Around the middle of the century he came out as a supporter of communitarianism, as a result of the contacts he had established with the Hutterites in Moravia. Both before and after becoming an émigré (in 1656 he suffered expulsion from

Danzig) Zwicker wrote extensively on this subject as well as on war and the magistracy. On the latter topics he clashed with Przypkowski, whose "Vindiciae tractatus de magistratu contra objectiones Danielis Zwickeri" forms the only surviving fragment of a lengthy controversy between the two men. Zwicker, despite his antagonist's superior powers as a polemicist, finally conceded only one point to him: he granted that the full nonresistant position and a total rejection of the magistracy should be considered essential only for those Christians who strove for perfection in this life.

In exile, Zwicker wrote an exposition of his pacifist views in answer to an anonymous opponent who had assembled thirteen conclusions in favor of permitting "magistracy, the power of the sword, death penalties, and wars" in the Christian community. Christ and his apostles as well as "the Christians of the first centuries" had denied these things to "true Christians." His tract was published anonymously in Amsterdam in 1666 in Latin, under the title *Ecclesia antiqua inermis* . . . In the Dutch translation (which is the version I consulted), published later at an unspecified date as *De Weerloose oude kercke, na soo veel slechter eeuwen eyndelyck wederom met recht bevestight* . . . (*The Old Defenceless Church finally after So Many Corrupt Centuries again Fortified with Right*), the text runs to sixty-four pages.

Zwicker's writings resemble those of Grzegorz Paweł earlier, in the way emotion rather than reason, protest rather than calm persuasion, play the major roles. The thought of a Christian's filling the part of an executioner or fighting as a soldier fills him with a sense of outrage. Imagine, he cries out, Christ while on earth acting as a hangman or commanding an army—and, if this indeed seems impossible, then why should we approve the commission by later generations of his followers of deeds which he would have recoiled from doing himself? To Zwicker war appeared an even greater crime than the state's execution of a criminal. For whereas the criminal was usually guilty of misdoing (though Zwicker points out that some suffered death at the hands of the law who, like thieves for instance, deserved a less harsh punishment), "many innocent men" inevitably died as a result of warfare. Above all else, therefore, must Christians refuse military service, should the magistrate command it; it was useless to plead that in war guilt for shedding innocent blood rested on the heads of the rulers. One could with as much justice argue, Zwicker wrote, that "at the command of the magistrate" one might "persecute and kill" his fellow believers for holding to "the true faith." True, Christ taught us to respect and obey the powers that be, to pay them "tolls and taxes." "But that a Christian man may be a magistrate, or follow the latter in waging war and exercising open wrath" was impossible for Zwicker to conceive of. The marks of a Christian believer, as exemplified in the life of Christ himself, were "humility, love, patience, mercy, peace, gentleness." On the other hand, the traits needed in a magistrate or warrior consisted in the exact opposite.

Outside Holland the rigorist position does not appear to have found much support among the Polish exiles. Those who settled in the lands under Hohenzollern rule, for instance, are found in office and even in military service. Ironically, the last surviving Polish-speaking Socinian was a general, Karol Sierakowski, who died in 1824.

In the Polish congregation which the émigrés to Transylvania established at Kolozsvár (Cluj) in 1660, a brief church discipline (*Observanda fratribus polonis unitariis in Transylvaniam receptis*) was drawn up, forbidding members to accept public office and also requiring them to obtain exemption from every kind of military service even at the expense of having to renounce their noble rank or status as citizens. Such activities, it was stated, presented grave dangers to a Christian's conscience. Whereas Kot in his account of Socinianism's sociopolitical ideology implied that this rule was connected in some way with the then still officially upheld pacifism of the Polish Brethren, more recently Tazbir has contested this view, first in his biography of Stanisław Lubieniecki (Warsaw, 1961), who was responsible for drafting these regulations, and then in his study of the Polish Antitrinitarian community in Transylvania (*Bracia polscy w Siedmiogrodzie 1660-1784*, Warsaw, 1964). Tazbir points out that Lubieniecki and his whole family, far from having any sympathy with pacifism, belonged to the extreme socially conservative wing of Polish Antitrinitarianism; that among leading members of the congregation which commissioned him to prepare the discipline were others of the same persuasion, like Samuel Przypkowski; and that such rigorism in fact had long fallen into desuetude in Poland, at least among the Antitrinitarian *szlachta* (while it had never apparently been practiced by the indigenous Transylvanian congregations). Therefore, Tazbir argues, we must not interpret these regulations as a revival among the exiles of the Polish Brethren's old nonresistant testimony. We must see in them, instead, an attempt to prevent denationalization of the little group of Polish émigrés and thereby to hold up the process of assimilation into the Magyar Unitarian community, which in the opinion of the newcomers stood on a lower ethical level than did the church of their Polish brethren. The requirement of withdrawal from any part in the state, including participation in army life, represented but one among several methods employed to preserve the exiles' national identity. Their condemnation of office and war, moreover, did not extend to their Magyar coreligionists, who continued to exercise the *jus gladii* and to perform military service without any censure from the Poles. There is also no evidence, according to Tazbir, to show how far, if at all, these restrictions were applied within the Polish congregation itself (we may add there is likewise no evidence, either, that they were not applied).

Tazbir's arguments are certainly persuasive. He is probably right. Yet I cannot restrain some lingering doubts. For it does seem possible (though once again this remains merely a hypothesis) that the regulations represented a principled objection to office and war, that at least some of the Kolozsvár exiles were genuine nonresistants who upheld a conscientious objection to magistracy and war in the old Anabaptist spirit. Writers like Urban and Tazbir have shown that in general the Antitrinitarian exiles came preponderantly from the artisan class, for whom it was comparatively easy to take their skills abroad, and not, as Kot had previously supposed, from the *szlachta* and the intellectuals. The plebeian element was numerically strongest in the Kolozsvár congregation, too. Since it was this element which had been most sympathetic to social radicalism until overwhelmed by the rising influence of the Antitrinitarian *szlachta*, it appears to me possible that, once released from the weight of *szlachta* control by the catastrophe which put an end to the church's existence at home, the dormant social radicalism of these plebeians asserted itself once again and led to a return to older ideological positions. Lubieniecki and Przypkowski and others like them may have acquiesced in this development because they saw in it a means to maintain the group's separate religious and ethnic identity in an alien environment (an aim which they supported for the reasons given just above).

A curious aspect of the Polish Socinians' attitude to war outlined in the foregoing pages is the official pacifism the church maintained, even in exile and until its final disappearance through the death of members and the submergence of their descendants in some other Protestant denomination. Beginning early in the seventeenth century, this official stance conflicted, as we have seen, with the opinions and practice of a growing number of members until eventually, despite short-lived upsurges of pacifist sentiment, conscientious objection to the *jus gladii* and to war (even in the moderate Socinian variant which had been adopted by the church, let alone full-blown Anabaptist nonresistance) was professed by only a very small minority. This phenomenon was remarked on by the early French encyclopedist Pierre Bayle, who met Socinian émigrés in Holland during his own exile there. (A parallel

may be found today in the United States in certain midwestern and
far western Quaker meetings which still adhere collectively to the traditional peace testimony of the Society of Friends, yet at the same time
produce an overwhelming majority of nonpacifist members). Unlike
the Czech Brethren at the end of the fifteenth century, who quickly
repudiated altogether their fathers' antistate and antiwar position, the
seventeenth-century Polish Brethren reached a compromise which
permitted both views to coexist within the Antitrinitarian church—or
rather, which permitted the church to pay lipservice to the old sociopolitical ideals while giving free rein to the political and military interests of the increasingly influential gentry. If the Czech Brother Lukáš
had shown himself the more forceful proponent of change, the Polish
Brethren's mentor Faustus Socinus proved that his was the superior
gift for effecting a thoroughgoing revision of doctrine while still preserving the outward framework of the old ideology.

The key to the Minor Church's transition "from radicalism to humanitarianism" seems to lie, as Kot has indicated, in its social stratification. Its social radicalism was rooted not, as with the old Czech Brethren or with the German Anabaptists and early Dutch Mennonites, in
the aspirations of submerged groups of the community. With the Polish Brethren this radicalism was primarily a religio-moral impulse. "It
was motivated not by economic misery nor by the social wrongs of the
lower classes but by absorption in the command to love one's neighbor." To renounce one's political privileges and lands and the right to
employ serf labor, and to live instead by the sweat of one's brow as a
humble artisan, as Jan Niemojewski chose to do; to refuse to serve in
the general levy when the Commonwealth was threatened with attack
or to defend oneself and one's family from the depredations of bloodthirsty Tatars, as some of the early Polish Brethren chose to do: these
were "heroic acts." Without such acts there was in fact no chance in
that period of maintaining a position of complete withdrawal from political life. Long-term withdrawal, though by no means easy, was not
impossible for a group drawn largely from the lower orders of society:
craftsmen, day laborers or peasants. But the gentry, who gave not only
direction but protection to the Minor Church and came to constitute,
too, a not insignificant proportion of its membership, remained en-
meshed in the existing political and social system of a Commonwealth
from which they had gratefully received the gifts of political liberty
and religious toleration. Voluntarily to renounce the polity which had
given them such gifts was to ask too much of the Antitrinitarian
szlachta once the first great wave of enthusiasm had subsided and a

new generation, whose membership of the church was based on birth-right, had grown to maturity.

However, the pacifism and social radicalism of the Polish Antitrini-tarians did not disappear without an echo, as seemed to happen in the case of the Czech Brethren. After being exiled, they continued to circulate these ideas in their new Dutch homeland. In the nine weighty volumes, for instance, which the Polish exiles printed in Amsterdam in 1656 as the *Bibliotheca Fratrum Polonorum*, trea-tises of the radicals found a place beside those of their antagonists. Some of these works were translated into Dutch and printed separately. Along with the practical activities of radical exiles like Zwicker, they exercised considerable influence in developing pacifist thinking in Collegiant congregations and among the liberal wing of the Mennonite community, either directly or by stimulating general dis-cussion on war and the social order (just as, we should add, Socinian-ism had been making a steady impact on the general development of Dutch and English religious thought). But before taking this theme any further we must return to the story of Dutch Mennonitism.

In the chapter discussing Anabaptists and Antitrinitarians in his book, *L'essor de la philosophie politique au XVIe siècle* (2nd edn., Paris, 1952), Pierre Mesnard writes concerning such compromises as Socinus devised: "La masse des fidèles y trouvant avantage, retournera aux tribunaux et aux fonctions non militaires, puis la reste suivra et le système entier sera légitimé." Like the Polish Antitrinitarians yielding progressively "aux exigences du siècle," the Mennonites in the Nether-lands, too, ultimately abandoned their "absenteeism" from the state and set aside their rigorist ethic to meet the demands of society.

161

FIVE. *The Dutch Mennonites*

I. THE SIXTEENTH CENTURY

THE creation of a congregation of Christians "without spot or wrinkle (*zonder vlek of rimpel*)": this was the goal of Menno and his followers. Yet the struggle to achieve Christian perfection here on earth led not to peace and harmony but to strife and division. Within Menno's own lifetime the Anabaptist community, which he had so carefully put together after it had been fragmented as a result of Münster, was rent by a major schism. In 1557 a section of the brotherhood, disagreeing with the increasingly rigid application of the ban, broke away; they became known as Waterlanders, from the "waterland" area in north Holland where they were most strongly represented at the beginning. Ten years later, in 1567, a second schism ensued between "Frisians" and "Flemings." By the end of the century there were as many as twenty separate Mennonite sects in the Netherlands, though only a half dozen of them had a following of any size. And many of these schisms spread to the closely allied Anabaptist groups of northern Germany, some of which were recruited from emigrants from the Netherlands.

Every division led not merely to mutual recrimination, unseemly in a community dedicated to the pursuit of peace and Christian love, but to the banning of the other party and sometimes even to the avoidance on each side of all contact with the banned group. Thus, while each little sect lived righteously within its small enclosure, the high walls, which it had erected not merely to shut out the carnal world but to prevent contamination with coreligionists of differing opinions as to the right road to salvation, proved a stultifying influence on the development of Mennonite religious life.

The Waterlanders were the most tolerant of the various Mennonite groups; writers like Kühler have viewed them as proto-liberal Christians who continued to respect individual conscience at a time when their stricter brethren had begun to elevate the congregation to the position of an idol, and who strove not so much to reproduce an exact model of the apostolic church, but rather to realize an "ecumenical and undogmatic piety" in the spirit of the earlier Netherlands tradition. Although it is doubtful if Menno himself may be regarded (as Kühler regarded him) as an exponent of this kind of undogmatic

162

Christianity, the Waterlanders certainly succeeded in freeing themselves to some extent from the narrow sectarianism which enveloped the Dutch Mennonite community in the second half of the sixteenth century.

The Waterland group was the first officially to sanction the holding of office by its members (although, it is true, the Wismar conference of 1554 had permitted believers to have recourse to courts under certain conditions and there was some ambiguity, as we have seen, concerning the extent of Menno's rejection of the magistracy as an unchristian institution). But, at the same time, the Waterlanders insisted that those positions which required exercise of the sword were unsuitable for members and must be refused. In 1581, for instance, a Waterlander conference in Amsterdam decreed that members who accepted office should on no account collaborate in imposing sentences of death. But from the later sixteenth century we find Waterlanders, who lived mainly in the countryside, serving on village councils and in such government posts as inspectors of the market or trustees of a polder. In the stricter groups acceptance of office automatically brought the disfellowshipping of the member concerned.

The Waterlanders not only prohibited the office of the sword (while approving participation in the noncoercive functions of government), they also forbade their members to participate in military service. At a conference held at Emden in East Friesland in 1568—this was the time of Alva's rule in the Netherlands and the rigorous suppression of religious dissent—a resolution was passed to this effect. Members seeking to acquire citizenship in a town or admission to a gild were told that they should not allow themselves to be enrolled on the list of those liable for the city watch. If they took part in drilling they were to confess their fault before the congregation, express contriteness, and "ask the forgiveness of God and the church" before being reinstated in full membership. The usual penalty which came to be imposed for such transgressions, both by the Waterlanders and their more rigorist brethren, was the so-called *kleine ban*, according to which the guilty person was excluded from the communion service until penitence was shown.

We do not hear much concerning Mennonite conscientious objectors until after the outbreak of the war of independence against Spain in 1572. There are several explanations which may account for this. *Doopsgezinden* historians like Dyserinck or Kühler, who do not think that Menno and his associates espoused unconditional nonresistance, remain sceptical, too, concerning the spread of nonresistant sentiment in the brotherhood in the decades immediately following Menno's

163

death in 1561. They regard it as likely that there were nonpacifists, especially among the Waterlanders, alongside some who had now come to accept the pacifist position of southern Anabaptism.

Complete certainty in the matter is scarcely possible in view of the paucity of the sources; we must not forget that in the Netherlands the Mennonite brotherhood remained an outlawed group right up to the outbreak of war with Spain, and in northern Germany it was, at best, barely tolerated. The strength of the nonresistant position within the brotherhood as a whole, which is revealed during the early years of the war, would argue in favor of its having made headway already over the decades preceding the war. True, we do not know how long the Wismar resolutions were in force among Menno's followers, or indeed exactly what their authors intended to recommend in regard to the question of military service (see chapter 3). Yet if even the tolerant Waterlanders in 1568 prohibited attendance at the watch, we may presume that at this date the strict brethren enforced this position with even greater vehemence. Therefore, instead of explaining the comparative silence of the sources by the continued weakness of the nonresistant principle within the brotherhood, it would seem more plausible to look elsewhere for a cause. And indeed this is not hard to find. At a time when armies were drawn chiefly from mercenaries, obscure sectaries like the Mennonites were unlikely to become involved in activities of this kind unless some special emergency arose. Unlike among the Polish Antitrinitarians, nobles were not represented at all among Netherlands Mennonites. These were chiefly to be found in the poorer sections of the population: the typical Mennonite of this time was a peasant or an artisan. Only as the legal restrictions against Anabaptists' acquiring rights as citizens in the towns began to be lifted, and as urban Mennonites (as Netherlands Anabaptists were now calling themselves) gained in affluence and passed such property tests as there might be for citizenship, did the question of watching and military exercising become acute. Certainly military service for long remained a more pressing problem for Mennonites who resided in the towns than for those who lived in the countryside, where preparations for local defense were not organized to the same degree. In these circumstances, it becomes comprehensible that a serious collision on this issue between Mennonite conscience and the requirements of the state was postponed for many years.

Whatever may have been the precise position in earlier decades, it seems clear that by 1572 the Mennonite brotherhood in the Netherlands, of whatever shading of belief, was opposed to its members' undertaking military service. Exercise of the sword threatened a fellow human being with the loss of eternal salvation; Christ with his gospel of love, they concluded, had called his followers to redeem souls and not to destroy them. Therefore, the believer should not use arms either in self-defense or, at the command of the authorities, for law enforcement or in war. Although the sword remained outside the perfection of Christ, and his disciples were obliged to stay separated from the world, Dutch Mennonites recognized, as the Swiss Brethren and south German Anabaptists had done, that the powers that be were fulfilling a God-given mission in maintaining domestic order and defending the people from enemies from outside. This attitude explains a well-known incident in Mennonite history, which took place at the outset of the War of Independence in the summer of 1572.

In May two leading Mennonites approached William of Orange, who was hard-pressed at that date for funds to carry on the war against the Spaniards, to inquire in what ways their people could help the country in its hour of need. They agreed to raise a sum of money by voluntary subscription and at once set to work to find these funds. In surprisingly quick time a contribution of 1060 guilders was gathered and presented personally to the prince in July. The collection was a joint effort embracing not only the less secluded Waterlanders but strict Frisians as well. When the money was handed over, the Mennonite delegates explained that it was a free gift and not a loan, the givers desiring only that the prince would grant them his friendship "if God would confer upon him the government of the Netherlands." The prince gave them a receipt on which it was stated that the money was being given "for the advancement of the common cause."

John Horsch, the American Mennonite historian, is certainly wrong in concluding that this last phrase was intended by the Prince as "an intimation that [the gift] was not to be used for the purposes of war." There is, instead, every reason to believe that he welcomed it just because it provided a much-needed addition to the insurgents' scanty war treasury. On the other hand, *Doopsgezinden* historians like Kühler and Wessel have equally misunderstood the significance of this gesture when, in their anxiety to prove that the early Dutch Mennonites were not fully nonresistant, they have read into it approval of defensive war. In fact, the givers did not merely register a vocational pacifism, a personal objection to being involved in worldly affairs like war. They were expressing a clear principle: that whereas within the Christian fellowship the sword was never permitted, outside it the *jus gladii* had been instituted by God to fulfil his purposes in the world. Nonetheless, the incident does show that even at this early date patriotic sentiment had made some headway among the otherworldly

Mennonites: we cannot easily imagine Melchior Hofmann or Menno or Dirk Philips undertaking a task of this kind. In some sections of the brotherhood it may have met with disapproval (although there is no concrete evidence of this). But where it did find support, there the chiliastic expectations of earlier days must have died down at last: the task of true believers was still to follow quietly the precepts of the Master and live apart from the world, but the world, they now knew, would remain with them until the end of time.

"For the first years [of war], the period of the famous sieges of Alkmaar, Haarlem, and Leiden, we know virtually nothing about the attitude of the Mennonites," writes van der Zijpp. Only one case of conscientious objection is reported in this period. A Waterlander from Monnikendam, Jan Smit, in the course of the siege of Haarlem was ordered by the Spanish army authorities to act as a rower. He refused to comply, telling them that to do so was against his conscience, "since he had no enemies." He was thereupon arrested, tortured, and finally executed as an unrepentant heretic. Whereas Smit's refusal to do non-combatant duties had first revealed his "Anabaptist" sympathies, his punishment resulted from his membership of a forbidden sect and not from his refusal to obey a military order.

Verheyden in his study of Anabaptism in Flanders mentions several cases of conscientious objection in the southern Netherlands, which remained under Spanish rule; they occurred in towns like Bruges or Ghent where there were Anabaptist congregations and where service in the civic guard was compulsory. "They [i.e., Mennonites] . . . succeeded for a considerable time in avoiding this difficulty by hiring non-Mennonite civilians to take their places in the guard." By the end of the century persecution by the Spanish-dominated authorities, and emigration to the north of those who remained loyal to Mennonitism, had virtually put an end to the sect's activities in this area. Thus our discussion below will be confined to the northern Netherlands that comprised the independent United Provinces.

In the United Provinces the Mennonites gradually achieved a measure of toleration, which they had not known before. Friendly contact continued between them and the country's leader, William of Orange, a man of liberal religious views, and after the latter's death by assassination in 1584 his successor, Maurice of Nassau, remained well disposed towards them. Thus, from being a persecuted sect the fate of whose members, when uncovered, was likely to be imprisonment and perhaps death, Mennonitism was transformed into a denomination which, if not on an equality with the Calvinist establishment, certainly enjoyed wide freedom. Once its members were willing to dismantle the partitions which originally the outside world had erected to enclose them and which they themselves had joyfully accepted at first as protection against contamination by the world, they could have access to prosperity and the fruits of success in business and in most other pursuits engaged in by citizens of a modern state.

Mennonite objections to fighting were soon recognized by the insurgent authorities. After all, at the outset the sect had shown its willingness to assist the anti-Spanish forces by its money gift of 1572, and William of Orange did not forget this. There was no point in forcing a confrontation in these circumstances: this was the sensible conclusion which was reached, probably through William of Orange's influence. In 1575 his representative in North Holland exempted Mennonites from the obligation, now incumbent on all other male citizens of the province, of having to watch with weapons: the first piece of legislation providing for conscientious objection to military service. Instead, they were to help dig ditches and build ramparts. "And if there be any Mennonites there," ran the decree, "they are obliged to come with a sharp spade and a basket and likewise to take their turn in watching." True, the stricter sort of pacifist might find little satisfaction in such a narrowly conceived exemption and consider the noncombatant duties required to be little, if any, improvement on conscription for combatant military service. But it seems to have satisfied the consciences of the Mennonites of that time, who saw it as a welcome opportunity to demonstrate their willingness to go the second mile.

The measure, however, did not find approval with patriots less liberally minded than the Prince. In particular, the Calvinist clergy deprecated this kind of concession to a group whose religious opinions they abominated. Largely at the instigation of local preachers, the town council of Middelburg in the province of Zeeland insisted in late 1576 on Mennonites' participating fully in defense preparations (as well as taking a judicial oath) if they wished to continue to have the right of carrying on trade in the town. An order from the Prince of Orange issued in January 1577 urging the council to respect the Mennonites' conscientious scruples failed to have much effect. The regulation in regard to the watch was still to be enforced, "without any distinction of religion." Since the Mennonites adamantly refused to muster with arms, the town authorities proceeded to close their shops. Finally, after Mennonites had appealed once again to the Prince for help, the latter wrote to the council of Middelburg in July 1578 commanding it to cease pestering its Mennonite citizens. A compromise was then reached whereby the Mennonites promised, in lieu of watching with

167

weapons, to pay a special tax or to undertake noncombtant duties of the kind laid down in the North Holland regulation of 1575: building ramparts and defensive walls or taking measures against the spread of fires. For this, the council agreed to grant exemption "from actually resisting the Spaniards or other enemies with weapons." Trouble broke out again two years later when the council reverted to its old position and refused to acknowledge conscience as a reason for not carrying arms at the watch. Once more the prince had to intervene, and in 1581 another agreement was worked out, by which a head-tax was to be imposed on each Mennonite objector. Finally, in 1588 this was altered by mutual consent of town council and Mennonite congregation, and an overall tax charged yearly to the congregation as a whole was imposed on each individual objector in place of a fine. The arrangement was incorporated in a contract drawn up between the two parties, the elders of the congregation being required to stand security for its fulfilment. In that year there were eighty-five members who were liable for service in the watch; the amount to be paid for exemption was set at "two hundred Flemish pounds," a very considerable sum for those days. As the size of the congregation diminished in the following two centuries, this amount was progressively lowered; it must have become apparent, too, that the assessment had been too high. At any rate, the agreement, with only minor modifications, lasted as long as the Dutch Mennonites retained their nonresistant principles. There was no more trouble on this account at Middelburg.

Gradually other places where there were Mennonite communities adopted either the same system that had been worked out at Middelburg or some variation of it. It was copied exactly, for instance, in 1589 by neighboring Vlissingen, which, like Middelburg, was situated on the island of Walcheren. The province of Friesland freed its Mennonites from militia duty in 1580 in exchange for a head-tax. In the same year its capital, Leeuwarden, exempted them from bearing arms for the city on the condition that they pay higher town rates than citizens who mustered, and in 1591 it altered this condition to payment of a special tax, the proceeds of which were to go toward purchasing military equipment and gunpowder. Deventer in the province of Overijssel had at first told Mennonites that if they were not prepared to serve with arms in the watch they would have to leave the city on the second refusal (the first refusal of service being punished with a fine). However, from the beginning of the 1580's the Mennonites found a way around this regulation by hiring substitutes to watch—with arms—in their place. Some of their fellow citizens were displeased at what they considered an evasion of duty on the Mennonites' part; perhaps they also feared the competition of these thrifty people and looked forward to ridding the town of their presence. But apparently they did not get their way, for the Mennonites remained—and continued to maintain their noncombatant stand, though in the next century difficulties in regard to this occur once more. At Alkmaar in North Holland it was reported in 1591 that the head-tax from local Mennonite objectors amounted to a sum sufficient to buy five sets of armor and 132 pikes. In 1593 Prince Maurice of Orange confirmed the general privilege of exemption from bearing arms granted to the Mennonites by his predecessor, William. Although, as we shall see, in the seventeenth and even in the eighteenth centuries Mennonites were to continue to have sporadic encounters with the authorities on this account, they would be of minor significance. The important thing was that the principle of exemption was now taken for granted by the highest authorities in the land.

"The head-tax [or other form of exemption money] was universally spent for military purposes," writes van der Zijpp in his study of the Dutch Mennonites' attitude to military service, "yet I have nowhere found that the tax was ever refused on this account." Objections were sometimes raised concerning the size of the amounts demanded but they were not objections to the principle of paying. Hiring a substitute as a *pis aller* where the authorities refused to allow purchase of exemption by means of a tax, though unusual, did happen sometimes; it seems to have passed without comment from the church leaders, who made no move to institute disciplinary action. Like the voluntary money offering in 1572, payment of a head-tax or finding a replacement in military service appeared to Mennonites of that time as innocent gestures of good-will toward the powers that be. They caused no offense to conscience, and they permitted the pursuit of godliness undisturbed by rude interruptions from outside. Admittedly, this attitude indicated that the era of the martyrs was passing. However, that such concessions to the state on the Mennonites' part amounted in practice to their contributing to war almost as effectually as their participation personally in combat would have done, probably did not occur to them. At the colloquy of Emden in 1578 the church leaders had explicitly approved money contributions in lieu of military service and, in time of peace, even the hiring of a substitute for the watch. "This does not burden our conscience," they said. Mennonites did not possess that passion for political liberty which British and American Quaker pacifists were later to display when they rejected all alternatives if they considered their conduct right, and they lacked the sensitivity of the contemporary Hutterites who refused to pay taxes furthering the prosecution of war. But according to their own lights the early Dutch Mennonites bore a loyal witness to their faith in nonresistance.

The nonresistant stance is exemplified in the arguments put forward by the Mennonite representatives at the colloquies of Emden (1578) and Leeuwarden (1596). "The oldest extant [Dutch] Anabaptist-Mennonite confession of faith," which was drawn up by the Waterlanders in 1577, breathes the same spirit. This spirit, too, suffuses many of the utterances of the later sixteenth-century martyrs for the faith. In 1569—to cite just one example here—Hendrick Alewijnsz, a Mennonite preacher from the isle of Walcheren, wrote as follows while in prison awaiting execution as a heretic:

> It is needful to distinguish between the New and the Old Covenant. Under the Old Covenant Israel engaged in war, revenge was taken on enemies, there was fighting and taking human life; and under the old law this was done by the will, command, permission and also help of God. But now, in the dispensation of the Gospel under the New Covenant, these things cannot be permitted, they are plainly forbidden by the word and example of Christ. . . . These things, I say, are plainly and clearly prohibited, not by man but by God Himself. . . . In short, the Christian must not fight at all; and yet he must fight, but not with weapons of iron, steel, stone, wood, or other carnal weapons, but with spiritual weapons which are mighty before God. . . . Therefore we may not engage in war.

On the whole, Dutch Mennonites during the period covered by the War of Independence (1572-1609) did not write much about nonresistance. The only piece devoted exclusively to the subject appeared in print at the very end of the century, in 1597 (though an earlier edition, no longer extant, may have been published around 1580). The thin pamphlet of sixty-four pages is without place of publication and bears only the initials I.P., which probably hid the identity of Jacob Pietersz van der Meulen, an elder of the "Old Frisian" congregation at Haarlem. It is entitled *Verantwoordinge eender requeste* (*Justification and Request*), "in which," in the words of the subtitle, "is considered whether war may now be allowed to the disciples of Christ according to either the law [or] the Gospel." The work had been prompted by an attack on Mennonite nonresistance made by certain Calvinist preachers of the Walcheren town of Middelburg who accused the sect of inconsistency, alleging that their members were prepared to manufacture and sell instruments of war. Whether such an accusation was based on fact (as Kühler believes) or constituted a libel is difficult to ascertain; all we have to go on is charge and counter-charge. It is possible that some Mennonites interpreting their noncombatancy narrowly felt obligated merely to refrain personally from shedding human blood. If this were the case, the author I.P. breathes no word of disapproval. He is certainly at pains to uphold strict nonconformity to the world. "Here the true congregation of Jesus Christ has no secure refuge; here on earth it is scattered among diverse kingdoms, it is a community and kingdom or gathering in the faith, which is defended with the armor of God alone." He censures the Calvinists for their attempt to compare the country's present struggle with the wars of the Israelites; these had been waged with God's express approval, whereas Christians had been forbidden to use the carnal sword or to resist evil by violent means. The typically Mennonite emphasis on the Gospel as law appears in I.P.'s arguments. Nonresistance is seen as a direction of the New Covenant rather than as an outgrowth of individual conscience.

One of the most cogent statements of nonresistance in the sixteenth century came not from a Dutch Mennonite but from an English Anabaptist. Anabaptism had led a semi-underground existence in England since the early 1530's. In some senses it may be considered a part of the Netherlands movement. Its original impulse came from the Netherlands, and it went successively through Melchiorite, Munsterite, and "Mennonite" phases (though the Mennonite name does not seem to have been adopted). The small English Anabaptist community was recruited in part from Netherlanders—refugees from religious persecution, traders, and immigrant artisans—though native Englishmen joined the movement, too. Its center was in London and the East Anglian towns, which enjoyed close commercial relations with the Low Countries. Perhaps because the sources for the history of the whole movement are extremely scanty, we do not hear of any English Anabaptists refusing military service during the sixteenth century. That by the 1550's, if not earlier, they had become nonresistant seems to be implied, however, by a sentence in article thirty-seven of the Anglican church's Thirty-nine Articles of 1563, which was obviously directed against "Anabaptist" views: "It is lawful for Christian men, at the commandment of the magistrate, to wear weapons and serve in the wars."

A half-century ago Albert Peel discovered a manuscript dated 1575 and containing the text of a controversial exchange of opinion between a Puritan citizen of London and a native-born "Anabaptist," one "S.B.," a carpenter by trade. (Peel published the document as "A Conscientious Objector of 1575," *Transactions of the Baptist Historical Society* [London], vii, no. 1/2 [1920], pp. 71-128.) The paper debate had been generated by the arrest earlier that year of some thirty Anabaptists (or rather, Mennonites), of whom two were eventually burnt at Smithfield. Thanking God that he had always earned an honest living by carpentering and "never ate one piece of bread nor drank one drop of drink by fighting, warring and contending," the Anabaptist S.B. declared of himself: "I cannot frame my style with such excellence of speech [as his opponent], nor in enticing words of man's wisdom, for I have not been at university to study Aristotle's divinity. Also I pray you to bear with me, that I am not more expert in alleging the scriptures, for that I have small time or none, to follow my book, for that my poor estate will not suffer me, for that my charge is great, which compelleth me more painfully to follow the world; for that I would fain eat mine own bread, and not hinder any man, but truly give unto every man his own."

Despite his convoluted style, however, S.B. succeeded in going straight to the core of the argument for Anabaptist-Mennonite non-resistance: the idea of suffering and martyrdom.

> But this suffering is so hard to the flesh that it can not embrace it, but it must have delay by fleshly glossing, persuading we may live with the Gentiles of this world, and receive glory, honour, riches, and magnificence, purchase, build, and whatsoever, and yet be the true servants of God, and have joy in the world to come, where[as] the true servants of Christ must wander to and fro, having no certain city nor dwelling, they must sell their possessions and not purchase, they must suffer rebukes and blows, they must be hated of all people. Though foxes have holes, and the birds nests, the poor Christian may have no place safely to put his head in. They must be like Israelites, to stand with their staves in their hands, and with their loins girt, to flee at all seasons, they must be brought before kings and rulers and be whipped, scourged, imprisoned, and be condemned to shameful death, whereas with the people of this world, all is otherwise.

A Christian, then, might flee from persecution but never strike a blow in his own or others' defense. For "Christ is the true expounder of the law, and saith, resist not, and gave us example to follow his steps." A Christian should "lose both coat and cloak, rather than . . . resist." Certainly he might expostulate with, and rebuke, an assailant saying "unto him these words or such like, 'Friend, if I have done you any injury, I will make you recompense; if I have not, why strike you me?'" But his weapons must be spiritual ones alone.

S. B., while asserting his loyalty to Queen Elizabeth and his belief that magistracy was ordained by God and stressing that rulers had nothing to fear "if all men were of my mind," denied categorically that a true Christian could ever bear arms either for self-protection or at the command of the magistrate. "I thought it not lawful for me to revenge . . . wrongs done unto me by extremity of law," he writes, "nor to requite any blows given me with the like, concluding thereby that I need wear no weapon." He was not impressed by his opponent's citing the wars waged in Old Testament times with God's approval by Hebrew prophets, patriarchs, and kings. For, "now we are not under the law but under grace, by the Gospel, and our state is altered, and we are delivered from the rigour of the law and the ceremonies thereof by the blood of Christ." The Gospels had forbidden violence and they had forbidden revenge, too. "How can a man be a soldier but he must needs do violence; leave off from violence and leave off from being a soldier." "I am persuaded," S.B. went on, "never since the time of Christ that none hath revenged himself by weapon but he had a revenging mind."

English Anabaptism in the 1580's began to merge with the wider Separatist movement that had grown up to the left of the Anglican establishment. Anabaptists, however, were perhaps not the only group in Elizabethan England professing a conscientious objection to war. The small pantheistic sect of Familists, or Family of Love, founded by the Westphalian-born Hendrik Niclaes around 1540, which had its center in England—as well as adherents in the Netherlands and northern Germany—had been influenced by continental Anabaptism; it probably included nonresistance among its tenets (though its exact stand is not completely clear). The Familists were instructed by Niclaes to cease from "striving, fighting, persecuting, lying, war or battle, destroying, spoiling, oppressing, killing, murdering," since these were contrary to the "holy spirit of love" which taught noninjury to fellow men, and his followers were reported to carry staves in place of weapons. The Familists survived in England until near the end of the seventeenth century.

During the first half of that century there eventually emerged out of the Separatist movement the two main branches of early English nonconformity: Congregationalism and Baptism. The Congregationalists were not pacifists, but the Baptists had links at the beginning with the Dutch Mennonites (although some modern Baptist historians have repudiated this connection). There were English Separatist refugees in the northern Netherlands from 1581 on. And in 1615 one of their congregations fused with the Mennonite "Waterlanders" of Amsterdam. Its leader, John Smyth, a few years before his death in 1612, had accepted nonresistance along with adult baptism. On the other hand, other "Baptist-minded" English Separatists who had found refuge in the United Provinces rejected pacifism. When times were easier in England for opponents of the established church and most of the refugees went back home, some of those returning, however, may already have imbibed Mennonite views on war and magistracy during their stay abroad. At any rate, antimilitarist sentiments crop up occasionally among the antipredestinarian General Baptists; even though back in Holland their founder, Thomas Helwys, had quarrelled with Smyth over the issue of nonresistance, *inter alia*. The English-speaking Mennonite congregation in Amsterdam continued to meet for worship until about 1640.

II. The Seventeenth Century

Whereas in the sixteenth century Mennonite writing on nonresistance was extremely meager, the seventeenth century saw a spate of words poured out on the subject (Dyserinck). Yet this period witnessed the beginnings of a decline in the intensity with which the Dutch Mennonites held to the nonresistant principle, a decline that ended with its total abandonment at the end of the eighteenth century. If we survey seventeenth-century Mennonite literature on nonresistance there is little, it is true, to indicate any falling off in enthusiasm (even if there is little, either, to show much creative thinking on this issue). We must look elsewhere, then, for the causes of this gradual transformation of opinion within the brotherhood.

In the sixteenth century Menno and his associates, and their successors, had all lived on the periphery of respectable society. Driven into exile or hounded to death by church and state, or living in concealment to escape this fate, they felt few ties with the society in which they lived. The state was the enemy—of themselves and of the true religion they believed they alone represented. Therefore, even after they had ceased to expect the immediate second coming of Christ and had accommodated themselves to the thought of its postponement for an indefinite period of time they continued to keep aloof from the world and to live a separated existence sufficient unto themselves, in so far as this was possible. They were mostly humble people; they were content to live in obscurity, anxious only for an opportunity to be able to pattern their behavior on that of Christ's disciples without incurring penalties from the state. When the state ceased to persecute them, as happened after the United Provinces had broken with Spain,

and became willing to grant them a tolerable amount of religious freedom, including the right (within certain limits) to dissent from their
fellow citizens concerning such matters as the judicial oath or military
service, the Mennonites did not at once dismantle the psychological
barriers which divided them from the rest of the community. They
went on considering themselves a people apart; they went on striving
for their ideal of a congregation without spot or wrinkle, as in the days
of the martyrs.

But there were no longer any martyrs: there were no longer even
any exiles. True, the average Dutch Mennonite was still a person of
humble rank: craftsman, artisan, or smallholder. Yet there were other
elements in the brotherhood now, which had not been represented in
the sixteenth century—or had been only in very small numbers. The
rich man who became an Anabaptist had risked losing his life—and
his property. There were some who took these risks, feeling it worth-
while to lose all in this world to gain a heavenly inheritance. But understandably they were few. After the coming of toleration the risks
disappeared. At worst, there was the stigma of belonging to a somewhat peculiar people, peculiar at least in the eyes of many of their
fellow citizens. But even this peculiarity, as Quakers and other British
dissenters were to discover later, might eventually prove of material
advantage, for it channelled the energies released by religious asceticism into such outlets as trade and industry.

Thus, in the seventeenth century we find in Amsterdam and other
major cities prosperous Mennonite merchants and tradesmen who participated in the financial, commercial, and industrial enterprises of the
Netherlands' golden age. In the countryside their coreligionists also
became well-to-do in many cases: the Mennonite farmer, though living
frugally, could not usually be considered among the downtrodden of
the earth. The Mennonite patrician families were distinguished, indeed, by a certain modesty in their style of living; yet, as with the
Quaker "grandees" of Philadelphia in the next century, affluence could
not be entirely concealed by the soberness with which quality found
outward expression. In addition to their increasing participation in the
country's material well-being the upper strata of seventeenth-century
Mennonitism partook, too, in the cultural upsurge which marked the
United Provinces in that era. There were Mennonite poets and paint-
ers, scholars and scientists, as there were also Mennonite patrons of
art, literature, and learning. Although the old hostility to secular culture typical of the first generations of Anabaptism-Mennonitism continued among the country congregations and the stricter sub-sects, in

the urban congregations and among the more liberal sections—the Waterlanders and then the "Lamists"—Mennonites became fully integrated with the main intellectual currents of the age.

An influential part of the membership had now come to have a stake in the material and cultural capital of Netherlands society. It was not so easy for them to withstand such secular influences as patriotism or to maintain the simple Gospel-oriented faith of their forefathers. A birthright in Mennonitism could give its sons legal exemption from military duties; it could not give them that devotion to a nonresistant way of life which had originally won this privilege after the endurance of much hardship.

These changes in the social composition of the brotherhood effected a change in its official stance toward state and society only slowly. The seventeenth- and eighteenth-century confessions of faith issued in the name of the various divisions within Dutch Mennonitism, from the Waterlanders, Hans de Ries and Lubbert Gerritsz's *Korte belijdenis des geloofs* (*Short Confession of the Faith*) (1618), through the Dordrecht Confession of Faith drawn up by the Fleming Adraien Cornelisz in 1632 and still officially recognized by most North American Mennonites today, right up to Cornelis Ris's popular *De geloofsleere der waare Mennoniten of Doopsgezinden* (*The Exposition of the Faith of the True Mennonites or Baptists*) (1766), all stood squarely in favor of nonresistance and against bearing arms and participation in the sword-bearing aspects of magistracy. The same position was set forth in a number of catechetic and expository writings issued in the course of the seventeenth century. We need not pause long over these works, since it was only very rarely that they contained a new approach to the problems of war and violence. Their object, in so far as they dealt with these topics, was to strengthen the brethren in their adherence to the good old way (there was indeed increasing reason to believe that some brethren were weakening in their devotion to nonresistance), and not to examine fresh paths to a warless world or the methods of extending the sect's peace testimony outside the ranks of the brotherhood.

Several new approaches, however, do appear in seventeenth-century *Doopsgezinden* peace literature. First, writers attempted to buttress their case by reference to earlier protest against war; they sometimes displayed considerable erudition in doing so. We see this, for instance, in the case of the Old Frisian elder, Pieter Jansz Twisck, a self-educated man who had accumulated quite a store of learning by his own efforts. It comes out in particular in his *Oorloghs-Vertooninghe: ofte teghen die krijch en voor de vrede . . .* (*War's Exposure, or Against*

War and for Peace) (Hoorn, 1631), where, after surveying the writings of "philosophers, poets, ancient and modern teachers" from Antiquity to the Renaissance, he concludes: "War among Christians is no war but much rather murder." He regarded the strivings for peace in Old Testament times and among pagan philosophers as a prefiguration of "the Peaceful Kingdom of Christ" (the title of a short tract by Twisck extant only in a German version), whose laws bound his faithful followers, the "regenerated and born anew," i.e., the Mennonites. Again, in this seventeenth-century literature there is more emphasis on the horrors of war than with earlier Mennonite authors who emphasized, rather, the need to obey Christ's injunction not to resist evil. There is evidence that Renaissance antiwar writings, e.g., the works of Erasmus as well as of Socinus, had been studied with approval, for much more is now made of the humanistic case against war. The *Doopsgezinden* minister at De Rijp, Engel Arendszoon van Dooregeest, wrote in 1693, for instance: "What is war but a sea of misery, a wilderness with horrors of every description? . . . Who was ever able to reconcile war with the principles of righteousness and equity?" Similar utterances might be culled from other Mennonite writers from Twisck onwards.

Third, Mennonite nonresistants found themselves obliged, especially after the publication of Grotius' *De jure belli ac pacis*, to deal with the problems of defensive war and of war as an instrument of justice. In 1641 Grotius himself enquired of a Mennonite friend: "Pray consider whether the Polish king is bound to submit to the Tatars murdering great numbers of children, . . . and whether he must consent to permit outrages worse than death against women, when he can prevent this by repelling the robbers' violence by the royal power?" These were issues with which early Mennonite nonresistants had felt little concern. They were but transients in this world; their country was not a terrestrial kingdom but a heavenly realm. They held, moreover, that injustice and oppression were the inevitable lot of the godly in this life. But with the sect's gradual acculturation to Dutch society, and with the absorption by the brotherhood of patriotic sentiments, new aspects of the peace problem began to interest Mennonite writers. They took pains to show that hope for the achievement of justice through war was illusory. Did not the innocent in war suffer along with the guilty? Were not war's inevitable concomitants—pillage, rapine, and destruction—incompatible with the ends of justice? Could one in fact discover in history a single instance of a truly just war, one that not merely began but also ended as a just war? Jan Dionys Verburg, a "Waterlander" from Rotterdam, wrote:

177

Christians are forbidden to engage in war, whether it be called defensive or offensive war, that is to say, whether the purpose is to ward off bodily violence or to inflict it on others. The difference which is often made between offensive and defensive, that is, between attacking and resisting attack, is nothing more than an excuse which serves to becloud the issue. The fact is that a defensive war differs from an offensive one only in this respect that the former is waged against an enemy who first attacks us and the latter against one whom we attack first. Nevertheless all that is found possible to do in the way of destruction, murder, and devastation is carried out in the one case as well as in the other. And men fail in their Christian duty toward their enemies even if they defend the walls of a city without undertaking an attacking sally and committing one of the abominations named.

All this sounds very modern: indeed Verburg's comments are reminiscent of the twentieth-century pacifist critique of war. We find little trace in them of that conditional justification of the sword, including the right of war, that was basic in the evangelical Anabaptism of the sixteenth century.

Yet the simple nonresistance of the early days continued to be typical of large numbers of *Doopsgezinden* throughout the seventeenth century. Brethren were expected to display it in their daily lives. We hear of ordinary artisans and peasants behaving toward robbers and marauders as they believed Christ in the Sermon on the Mount commanded them to do. And when they failed to live up to the standards of their community they were publicly rebuked, as happened in 1613, for instance, in the case of an Amsterdam "Waterlander" who physically resisted "two thieves who had come into his room to steal." Later, we are told, he confessed publicly his sorrow at his unchristian conduct "and asked God and the brethren to forgive him." The essence of Mennonite nonresistance has rarely been so well expressed as in the lines by Joost van den Vondel, Holland's greatest poet, written in 1639 (i.e., after the poet's conversion from Mennonitism to Roman Catholicism):

d'Oprechtste Godsdienst leert geen menschen te verkorten,
Aen middelen noch eer, veel min hun bloed te storten,
Die leert ons d'Overheid, alwaer 't een dwingeland,
Te dienen, in al 't geen zich tegens God niet kant.

(The most genuine piety teaches that no man be deprived/ either of his property or his honor; much less should his blood be shed./

It teaches us that the magistracy, although a realm of coercion,/
be served, in everything that does not run contrary to God.)

While the stricter branches of the sect usually disfellowshipped
those who became connected with even the lower magistracy, the
Waterlanders continued, though still rather reluctantly, to allow their
members to hold office if this were not associated with the shedding of
blood (*het bloet-oft halsrecht*, as a *Kerckelijcke Handelinge* of 1647
expressed it). At De Rijpp, in the center of the Waterland district of
North Holland, a report written in 1628 states that almost the entire
town council was made up of Mennonites, and the same situation occurred in other small communities in parts of the country where Mennonites of the Waterland variety were strongly represented.

If Mennonite disapproval of the magistracy had become less rigid
in some sections of the brotherhood, rejection of war remained a fixed
tenet of the whole sect throughout the seventeenth century. The issue
presented itself, as before, as a practical problem where some personal
decision was needed by members. This happened first in regard to military service; usually demands for such service were connected either
with the watch or local town militia or with some special war emergency when all able-bodied males were required to participate in the
country's defense. In the second place there now existed a new area
where nonresistance stood under test—the sea; by the seventeenth
century many Mennonites earned their living from the sea, either as
humble sailors in the merchant navy or as entrepreneurs in various
mercantile activities. The whaling and herring fisheries were largely
in Mennonite hands; Mennonite merchants were prominent, too, in
Holland's trade with the Baltic and Russia. In an age when pirates
roamed the oceans, even times of peace presented problems for a people who professed nonresistance, and in wartime these difficulties were
multiplied many times.

Let us turn first to the way Mennonites reacted to the demands of
the authorities, whether local administration or central government,
for participation in military affairs.

The first seven decades of the seventeenth century saw little change
in the pattern established during the War of Independence against
Spain. From the truce of 1609, which gave the United Provinces *de
facto* independence (*de jure* recognition of this fact did not come until
1648), until the attempted invasion of the country by Louis XIV's
armies in 1672, the existence of the Dutch state was never seriously
threatened even though the country was sporadically involved in war
during this period. There existed, therefore, no special reason for a

change either in the way the state dealt with its Mennonite objectors or, on the other hand, in the way the Mennonite brotherhood reacted to the customary requirements of the state in the matter of military service.

In many towns a *modus vivendi* had been worked out in regard to this issue: by a money payment the *bona fide* Mennonite could usually purchase his release from guard duty. His congregation normally provided the conscientious objector with a certificate confirming his membership; thereafter, his problems were at an end once he had handed the fine over to the authorities. (We learn, for instance, that the well-known painter Salomon van Ruisdael, who was a Mennonite, secured exemption in this way.) Sometimes collective exemption was given to all Mennonite men of military age on payment by their community of a lump sum annually for this purpose. A slight feeling of unease may occasionally be detected on the Mennonites' part, since the money paid usually went for direct military ends. Or perhaps it was that their opponents took the opportunity to charge them with inconsistency on this account. At any rate, a Mennonite leader from time to time took pains to refute this charge. Claes Claesz, for instance, who was active as an elder of the Flemish congregation at Blokzijl (Overijssel) during the first half of the seventeenth century, defended his people's custom of making such payments even when the administration bought replacements with the money. Such a transaction was equivalent to paying a tax, and paying taxes regardless of the ends to which they were put had been enjoined by Christ as Caesar's just due. On the other hand, in Claesz's view, it would be wrong to hire a man directly to take one's place in service. In this case one would bear the sin of blood shed by this replacement. It is clear that Mennonites in this century, too, did resort occasionally to the direct hiring of a substitute if no other means of exemption existed. At the beginning of the century we hear of the Waterlander congregation at Haarlem purchasing the freedom from army service of a young soldier who had been converted to the faith and had applied for baptism: the man, Jan Willemsz, eventually became Waterlander minister at De Rijpp, holding this position for forty years. There is no incidence among Dutch Mennonites of absolutist objection such as British Quakers professed; indeed, such a stand, we have seen, was entirely alien to the mentality of either the *Doopsgezinden* or their German brethren.

Occasionally conflicts still arose with the municipal authorities, whereas Mennonites who lived in the countryside were less liable to demands for watching. Take the case of Aardenburg, a small town in Zeeland, where a Mennonite congregation had been formed in 1614.

At first Mennonites did not encounter difficulties in regard to the watch. In 1628 the governor of Sluis confirmed their exemption "provided they put forward good, sufficient persons . . . to do their watch in their place, as is done in other places of these united lands." But nine years later they ran into trouble. In May 1637, for the first time the town council ordered them to join the watch in person; they were now required "to buy and furnish themselves with the proper weapons, so as thus to muster and march along with other citizens." Seven Mennonites were fined for not obeying the order; one of the seven had his property distrained because he had been unable to pay the fine. Finally, after protracted negotiations between the town council and the local congregation and after the intervention of the States General on the Mennonites' behalf, a contract was drawn up between the two parties. By this, the town council agreed to exempt all Mennonites under its jurisdiction from the obligation of watching, mustering and keeping arms, provided the congregation kept its side of the bargain. And on their side the Mennonites agreed either to supply substitutes for their conscientious objectors—"head for head"—whenever the town watch was called out for duty or to pay annually a lump sum of a reasonable size, so as to provide the council with funds with which it could do this itself. The agreement lasted for twenty years, but then trouble broke out again. These fresh difficulties had several causes: the appointment of a new and aggressive major of the watch; an increase in the local crime rate which called for a more efficient police system (the watch was both police and militia); a feeling on the council's part that the Mennonites had become dilatory in fulfilling their obligations. They were charged with giving unsuitable, sometimes even disabled, men to serve in their stead or with being as much as two years in arrears with promised payments of substitute money. Distress was now made on the goods of the delinquents and the impounded property sold off at auction. In 1661, however, town and congregation once more reached a *modus vivendi* and the tension relaxed.

During the second Anglo-Dutch naval war of 1665-1667 two innovations occur in the pattern of conscientious objection. At Kampen, a town in Overijssel where Mennonites had previously been able to buy their way out of bearing arms and watching, the council required them to perform noncombatant duties now that their fellow citizens were being ordered to be ready in arms to repel attack by the enemy. This is the first occasion, to my knowledge, when Dutch Mennonite objectors were required to do alternative service without being given any option (though the principle is implicit perhaps in the regulation of 1575). The form chosen by the authorities was the auxiliary fire service. In October 1665 Mennonites of military age received an order to man the fire engines and help extinguish fires where these occurred. Certainly this was largely a humanitarian service, yet it could present difficulties to a sensitive conscience (as British conscientious objectors, for instance, were to discover in World War II) if the threatened object were a military target. But, so far as we know, such a dilemma rarely, if ever, presented itself to the conscience of a seventeenth-century Mennonite.

At the same time as Mennonite objectors at Kampen were doing alternative service instead of being able to pay the customary fine, the Frisians were adapting the concept of the individual fine to wartime conditions by means of the large-scale "free-will" offering. In 1665 they raised the considerable sum of 500,000 guilders and presented it to the government in the name of their whole community—with the understanding that it would be used to cover the cost of outfitting warships. Certainly patriotic ardor contributed to the making of this gesture. But the primary objective appears to have been to persuade the state to continue to respect their scruples concerning military service, even though a war was in progress. Next year they had their reward: their menfolk were exempted from military duties.

Both the auxiliary fire service and the large free-will offering were to be employed again later in the century as means of accommodating both the demands of the state and the claims of religious conscience. Perhaps the Mennonite "gift" to William of Orange in 1572 should be regarded as a prototype of the "free-will" offering although its ultimate purpose was broader—to incline the prince to a general tolerance of the hitherto persecuted sect—and was not centered primarily on the issue of military service.

The spring of 1672 saw the invasion of Dutch soil by the armies of Louis XIV. The country faced its greatest crisis since the early days of the War of Independence against Spain. Conquest by the "Sun King" threatened to make the United Provinces a satellite of France; the success of the French forces might even lead to the extinction of Dutch independence and the loss of religious freedom. Both patriotic sentiment and religious loyalty impelled the Mennonites to look favorably on their country's cause. They would not fight; this went against their deepest convictions. Yet they wished to show that they were still good citizens, good Dutchmen, good Protestants, even if their ancestral tradition and their peculiar conception of the duties of a Christian prevented their actually bearing arms.

Money payments in lieu of exemption, noncombatant alternative service—these were in line with the traditional Mennonite peace testimony. Certainly, they would not have satisfied a seventeenth- or eighteenth-century Quaker, or at least a strict one. But such forms of witness were consistent with Anabaptist-Mennonite discipleship as it had been practiced since the days of the Swiss Brethren. Nonetheless, writes van der Zijpp of the Mennonites' conduct in the crisis years of 1672-1673, "what happened then seems to indicate that the old principle had become fossilized, an inheritance from the past rather than a force in the present." This verdict is confirmed by an examination of the ways in which the sect reacted to the military situation at this time.

At Kampen, Groningen, and Deventer, for instance, Mennonites manned the fire engines. In time of siege, while the rest of the male citizenry resisted the enemy, the Mennonite firemen roamed the streets and put out the fire-bombs thrown over the walls by the enemy. During Aardenburg's siege those Mennonites who were liable attended the watch, though, it is true, without weapons. They won the admiration of their old enemies, the Reformed clergy, one of whom wrote: "In the attack they did everything which their creed allowed." From a popular song of the period we learn that this included bringing provisions— "butter, bread, cheese, wine, and beer, and all necessary victuals, brandy, and tobacco" (we may presume a little poetic license here)— to their fellow citizens who were manning the walls. The composer of the song praises the enthusiasm with which the Mennonites carried out these duties. At Blokzijl they even acted as spies, gathering information in the enemy camp, to which as traders they had access. Men from the large Mennonite community in Amsterdam were largely responsible for constructing the defensive line of trenches and ramparts that was hastily erected to stem the French advance northward. (A precedent for this existed, for Amsterdam Mennonites had performed this kind of service in 1650.) They worked now, we are told, in two shifts: one before and one after noon. In exchange for this service, the city authorities saw to it that young Mennonite men were left alone by the military if these attempted to force them to muster with the watch.

Above all, at this time the Mennonite congregations distinguished themselves by donating huge sums to the state for the prosecution of the war. All sections of the brotherhood contributed—the stricter sects along with the more liberal Waterlanders—and the contributions flowed in from all parts of the country. Naturally, amounts varied according to the size and wealth of a given congregation, the rich Mennonite patricians of Amsterdam and the other major cities being able to provide more than could the modest farmers of the *platte land*. Yet most congregations gave enthusiastically according to their means. The government accepted the money thankfully and spent it at once on armaments.

Mennonites also provided comforts for the troops who, during the winter of 1772-1773, suffered severe hardship from lack of warm clothing: shoes and stockings, underclothing, bedding and bed linen, wigs, etc., were supplied by Mennonite congregations. In January 1673 the Estates of North Holland and West Friesland wrote to the Amsterdam city council as well as to rural communities, suggesting that "the Mennonites, who on account of conscience cannot easily be persuaded to participate in any military action or engagement, should be encouraged to contribute wigs, stockings, shoes and the like necessities." H. W. Meihuizen (in his biography of *Galenus Abrahamsz 1622-1706*, Haarlem, 1954) has printed from the archives the reply made by the liberal Lamist congregation in Amsterdam to the government request. This reply is worth quoting in part, since it throws an interesting light on the state of opinion within an important congregation. "We owe a big debt of gratitude to the supreme authority of this land for all the courtesy and freedom [*discretie*] which we have enjoyed hitherto under its rule," said the church leaders. In such circumstances, to grant the aid requested was not in any way to act "contrary to the confession of our faith."

The Estates indeed recognized the significance of the Mennonites' aid. In a missive dated 10 May 1673, this body recorded its opinion that such aid "would be more serviceable to the state than if they were to come forward and take up arms for the defense of the land alongside other good patriots." Indeed, the Mennonites now were generally recognized as being "good patriots (*goede vaderlanders*)," even though they still refused to defend their fatherland with the sword. In this same May, the Stadholder William III of Orange gave an official stamp to this opinion when he decreed, "Every inhabitant of this land is obliged to render military service, except the Mennonites who are excused from this on account of conscience and, instead, should be admonished and encouraged to do works of charity." Thus the somewhat qualified recognition granted to Mennonite conscientious objectors by the Stadholder's predecessor William the Silent early in the War of Independence was confirmed once again, and in more generous terms.

Were all Mennonites without exception content to render the kind of services discussed above? The answer is in the negative, for opposition was met with from certain of the strictest groups, especially the so-called *harde Vriezen*, who objected to those forms of alternative

184

service most closely connected with the war. In February 1672 a number of them had refused to muster "with a sharp spade and a basket," when ordered to do so. Digging trenches and ditches for military defense, they stated, was bound up with the waging of war and therefore absolutely incompatible with their belief in nonresistance. A few years later, some of these rigorously nonresistant Mennonites emigrated to Polish Prussia (Pomerania), where they could enjoy even greater freedom from military obligation than in the Netherlands.

The war against France lasted, on and off, until the Utrecht peace settlement of 1713-1714. During this time and thereafter, the arrangement reached between the Mennonites and the Dutch state at the beginning of the contest remained in force. Mennonite objectors were no longer legally obliged to pay a fine or hire a substitute when their fellow citizens were called out for the watch or other military duties. But it was understood that if they did not make a monetary contribution they would perform some humanitarian or auxiliary war service. Manning and maintenance of the town fire-engine was a popular choice, and it continued in places like Deventer throughout the eighteenth century. When at Amsterdam in the 1680's some citizens called for the reimposition of a regular monthly tax on Mennonite objectors in exchange for the privilege of exemption, the Lords Regent refused to allow it, referring the townsmen to William III of Orange's decree of May 1673. On the whole, though, the Mennonites willingly recognized the obligation incumbent upon them, since they were conscientiously unable to bear arms themselves, to render nonmilitary alternative service to their country, especially in time of war. As the learned Flemish minister Adriaan van Eeghem wrote in his *Catechism* of 1687 in answer to the question, "how must a Christian conduct himself in time of war": "He must not only be loyal to his government, pay tribute, pray for the country's welfare, but he is likewise obligated to give all bodily help to the province or the town except to kill the enemy."

The degree of allegiance given to their peace testimony by seventeenth-century Dutch Mennonites eludes statistical expression. Both contemporaries and later historians have spoken of a weakening of the hold of nonresistance on the brotherhood, at least in its more liberal branches and among the city congregations. They are undoubtedly correct for, even though this view cannot be backed by precise figures, developments in the eighteenth century clearly indicate that many members, even earlier, must have been but lukewarm at best on the peace issue. Dyserinck's verdict—"nonresistance is more taught on paper than applied in practice (*de weerlosheid méér in geschrift is geleerd, dan met de daad in toepassing gebracht*)"—is not quite fair

185

in regard to the seventeenth century. But enthusiasm for nonresistance was certainly cooling, even if open abandonment of a nonresistant stance by undertaking military service continued to be fairly rare. When it occurred, it was still usually dealt with firmly. But by the end of the century we may observe a relaxation of the congregational discipline in the liberal branches of the church: Waterlanders and Lamists. Galenus Abrahamsz de Haan, the outstanding leader of the Lamist congregation of Amsterdam in the latter part of the seventeenth century, while personally upholding the nonresistant position, declared himself in favor of respecting the consciences of "weak Mennonites" who felt unable to fulfil its requirements, and he was ready to admit those who bore arms to the communion. Waterlanders in Rotterdam and other places at the end of the century took the same attitude. This group had long held that the congregation of God was scattered throughout the world and not to be found in one church alone, as the stricter Mennonite sub-sects held. Such a view made it difficult to regard nonresistance as an essential qualification for membership, at least if the logical conclusions were thought through.

Yet throughout most of the period under consideration in this section, and in all branches of the brotherhood, disownment remained the lot of any who actually bore arms, the rule being relaxed, as we have seen, only among some liberal congregations towards the end of the seventeenth century. A writer whose knowledge of the sources of *Doopsgezinden* history has rarely, if ever, been excelled (van der Zijpp) has written: "Throughout the whole seventeenth century—after 1672 too—steps were taken to stem the decline [in nonresistance] that seemed irresistible: in almost every congregational archive we still find documents which prove this, as well as how deep-rooted is the endeavor to remain true to the old principle." Decade after decade the story is the same, variegated only in time of war when instances of backsliding increase. Sometimes the delinquent attempts by some excuse to justify his departure from the by now time-honored stance of conscientious objection. One man pleads "the bad times," another that "necessity" drove him to take up arms, a third promises to stop serving as soon as he can. The records speak of "fear of fines or weakness of belief" as motives for failure to live up to the standards required of members. And indeed those dealt with on account of bearing arms had often offended also on other scores: whether of a moral nature, like drunkenness, or in regard to delinquencies connected with war, such as allowing a vessel which one owned to be armed. There were those, too, who were defiant and did not express regret at their conduct.

186

The pattern followed by each congregation in all such cases was roughly the same. First came a friendly visitation of elders with brotherly admonition. If the guilty party did not show a penitent spirit for having transgressed "the law of Christ," he was excluded from the communion table. If this, too, failed to move the brother to repentance, then the ban was eventually applied, with his consequent exclusion from the church.

In addition to the question of military service on land, seventeenth-century Mennonite congregations were also faced with a second, and related, issue: what to do with members who owned, either in part or in whole, ships which sailed armed, or who served as captain or crew in vessels of this type.

The official attitude in all branches was one of stern disapproval of such practices. At the beginning of the century, a consensus of opinion within the brotherhood led to the withdrawal from participation in the Dutch East India Company of wealthy Mennonite patricians like Pieter Lijntgens, who had more than 100,000 guilders invested in it. The Company had been founded in 1602; it soon became clear that its activities formed part of the country's imperialist expansion and that it often became involved in paramilitary operations. Therefore, the Mennonites sold their shares (at a profit), though it remains uncertain whether all of them did so from a personal conviction of the impropriety of their previous conduct, or whether some were not impelled to this mainly by pressure from their church. Vos's supposition, which he fails to support by any concrete evidence, that Lijntgens and his fellow Mennonite investors sold out because they feared that the Company would now use its armaments for aggressive rather than defensive purposes, appears implausible. At any rate, the dominant feeling in the brotherhood at this period was clearly opposed to any compromise on this issue, whatever may have been the opinion of certain individual members concerned in such ventures.

At a conference in 1619 the Waterlanders, who were usually more lenient than the others in permitting variations from the accepted norm, decreed that any shipowners who allowed their vessels to travel armed or under armed protection (most merchantmen travelled under convoy if there was danger, as there usually was even in peacetime, from pirates or privateers) were to be excluded from the communion, and the same fate would be shared by members who served on such ships. Reinstatement in full membership could be obtained only if the guilty party promised either to remove the guns or to remove himself from such service, as the case might be. Both those who invested in

187

armed mercantile ventures, unless it were impossible for some reason to withdraw (a significant reservation), and those who went in armed ships as passengers were to suffer similar penalties. Since this regulation had to be repeated in 1631 and again in 1647, we may presume that delinquency on this score continued among members connected with the sea. Similar regulations were issued from time to time by the other branches of the brotherhood. The Frisians of North Holland, for instance, in 1639 severely reprimanded members who gained a livelihood on, or profit from, armed merchantmen. Those Mennonite merchants who conveyed their wares in such vessels were reminded that they did "quite a hundred times more damage to their fellow men" than these goods were worth: in case of armed action, sinners would be cut off and their eternal souls endangered. The advice of 1639 continued to be read in the yearly meetings of the Frisians until 1727, the brethren being at the same time admonished to a strict observance of its precepts.

To what extent regulations of this sort were enforced in practice is difficult to say. It was not always easy (as Quakers who encountered similar problems were later to discover in respect to their seafaring congregations) to become fully informed concerning the delinquencies of members on this account. We can hazard the opinion that until near the end of the seventeenth century, even among the less strict groups, those who engaged in such reprehensible conduct at least risked the possibility of disciplinary action's being taken against them by their congregation and that this continued to be the case in the stricter branches throughout most of the next century. At the end of the seventeenth century, however, a relaxation of the discipline can be observed in some quarters. In 1696, for instance, the Frisians of North Holland, while feeling that such conduct should in no way be condoned, at their annual meeting left the matter up to the individual congregation with the foreseeable result that, as was reported four years later, many congregations had in fact failed to take measures against their members who entertained no conscientious scruples at being involved in the arming of vessels.

This position was recognized—and deplored—by those who cleaved to the old ways and regarded nonresistance as a vital element in the witness of the *Doopsgezinden*. Such a one was the Waterlander preacher and physician Klaas Toornburg, who at Alkmaar in 1688 published a defense on Gospel grounds of the old Mennonite positions on nonresistance and refusal of the judicial oath (*Schriftuurlijcke verhandelingh tegens het eed-zweeren, en voor de wraak en weerloos lydsaemheyt en volmaeckte liefde, die de Christenen moeten oeffenen, aen en omtrent de boose en vyanden*). In his preface Toornburg notes the decline of nonresistance among his coreligionists. We do not find him disapproving in any way such alternatives to direct military service as had been sanctioned by Mennonite tradition: fines or fire service or free-will offerings. But he saw much to cause alarm in respect to the general behavior and outlook of the *Doopsgezinden*. Many of them used the law courts and resisted evildoers. They exercised revenge against those who wronged them, instead of showing patience and suffering long. Moreover, he goes on, they did not scruple to travel on armed vessels or to own them. Indeed, Mennonite shipowners had been known to petition the authorities to provide armed convoys for their vessels bound for the ocean fisheries or some other destination. "All these [are] things which go against the character and nature of Christ's teaching and kingdom as well as our confession [of faith]." To those who argued that self-defense was a natural right (and this argument, we know, was finding increasing acceptance among the liberal *Doopsgezinden*), Toornburg answered: "The life of a Christian is not grounded on the law of nature . . . but on the teaching and the example of Jesus Christ, our Lord." If we seek to follow in the footsteps of "that nonresistant and nonavenging Lamb" we must renounce all connection with the instruments of war.

We may mention one last area where a clash could occur between the Mennonites' nonresistant principles and the ethos of the society which surrounded them: armament manufacture. Opponents of the Mennonites sometimes accused them of inconsistency in this regard, alleging that they had members who engaged in the production of various kinds of weapons. Of course, in peacetime guns might well be used for nonmilitary purposes: this fact could provide an excuse for earning a living from the trade, though perhaps rather a specious one.

Early in the seventeenth century a curious episode had taken place, indicating that the brotherhood may have been less sensitive to the implications for its peace testimony of arms manufacturing than we might have supposed. In 1612 a member of the Waterlander congregation in Amsterdam, one Jan Cornelissen, is known to have engaged in the manufacture of gunpowder. His occupation, seemingly, did not bring him into conflict with his congregation until two years later he decided to remove to the East Indies "to manufacture gunpowder there" (as the report on his case stated). Only then did the deacons remonstrate with him, pointing out the danger to his soul involved in such an undertaking. To this Cornelissen replied that it was then too late for him to change his plans since he was already under contract to go, whereupon he departed for his destination. Kühler has suggested an explanation for the ambiguous role played by the Amsterdam congregation in this affair. It may lie, he thinks, in the fact that after the truce of 1609 when the country was no longer at war, gunpowder-making, though obviously still an undesirable occupation for a Mennonite, could have appeared less reprehensible than in wartime; the powder would be destined mainly for nonmilitary uses. On the other hand, overseas, where a state of endemic though unofficial warfare continued after the conclusion of a truce at home, gunpowder manufacture was still carried on almost exclusively for war. But Kühler has to admit: "If my explanation is correct, still the attitude of the brothers remains nevertheless half-hearted."

The Mennonites were not the only pacifist group in the seventeenth-century Netherlands. From the second half of the 1650's we find a few Dutch Quakers; they will be dealt with briefly in a subsequent chapter. There was also another and more numerous group of *Reformateurs*—the Collegiants, whose origins date back to *ca.* 1620. At that time at Rijnsburg near Leiden a group of seekers, becoming dissatisfied with the established Reformed religion, had begun to meet privately for prayer and Bible-reading and for religious discussion. They possessed no priests; all participants, women as well as men, had an equal right to speak when the spirit moved them. These people felt that the churches had failed to meet the requirements of apostolic Christianity which they regarded as their model. They did not attempt, however, to set up a new church or to establish a separate pastorate; instead, they sought to act as a yeast within the existing Protestant dominations. And they did in fact succeed in attracting Reformed, Remonstrants, and Mennonites as well as many persons not affiliated to any church. Gradually their meetings for worship, or *collegia* as they called them, began to follow a fairly regular pattern. But they remained a lay fellowship, not attempting to possess their own church buildings and continuing to meet as before in the homes of members or sympathizers. The Collegiants practiced adult baptism by immersion on confession of faith. But this rite was never considered essential for membership of a *collegium*. The Collegiants had close relations with the more liberal Mennonite groups, especially the Waterlanders and later the Lamists, and there was some overlapping of membership, especially in urban areas. Mennonite influence on the Collegiants was always strong; they were also influenced at first by the ideas of Reformation spiritualists like Jacob Boehme and later by the rationalist current represented by Socinus and the Polish Antitrinitarians. Rijnsburg remained the center of the Collegiant movement, but influential groups arose in cities like Amsterdam and Rotterdam.

Nonresistance, from fairly early on, was among the beliefs held by most Collegiants, though it never became essential for membership in the community. A leading Amsterdam Collegiant, Daniël de Breen (Brenius), in his book *Van de hoedanigheid des rijks Christi (Concerning the Character of Christ's Kingdom)*, which he published in Amsterdam in both Dutch and Latin versions in 1640, had contrasted, in a thoroughly Mennonite spirit, the two realms: on the one hand Christ's kingdom, whose subjects must practice patience and peace, and on the other the kingdoms of this world, whose citizens were committed to use the sword. The disciples of Christ, regulating their lives by the precepts of the New Testament, rejected war and self-defense, law courts and government, rendering a merely passive obedience to the powers that be. To Brenius, Christ's kingdom was essentially a kingdom of peace: it was governed by the Law of Love. It did not depend on Christ's corporeal presence on earth: enough, if his spirit dwelt among men. It should foreshadow the conditions which would eventually ensue after his second coming. "Then shall the church live in the deepest peace, free from all fear, from danger, oppression and persecution. . . . Peoples, who before were like wolves and lions, shall behave toward each other peacefully and as friends." Yet Brenius was unwilling to categorically deny the name of Christian to one whose conscience permitted him to exercise authority or even to fight. Such a man was certainly "a weak Christian," for Brenius was a firm believer in the nonresistant idea, but he urged the exercise of Christian charity in cases like this.

Brenius' works were popular reading among many Dutch Mennonites as well as among his fellow Collegiants, and we have seen in a previous chapter that his vision of a peaceable kingdom exercised considerable influence on contemporary Antitrinitarian pacifists in Poland like Baron von Wolzogen. When on their expulsion from Poland in 1661 many Antitrinitarians found a refuge in the United Provinces, the Socinian influence on the Mennonites and allied groups, which had already been felt since the beginning of the century, greatly increased. The pacifist radicals among the Antitrinitarians, like Daniel Zwicker or von Wolzogen himself, gravitated especially toward the Collegiants and those Mennonite congregations associated with them. Whereas, earlier, Collegiant pacifism derived its prime inspiration from Mennonite sources, now it was these newcomers from Poland who reactivated Collegiant interest in the subject of nonresistance (they also stimulated renewed interest in pacifism among their liberal Mennonite friends both through personal contact and through such publications as the vast *Bibliotheca Fratrum Polonorum*; see chapter 4).

At the end of 1671 the question was debated among the Amsterdam Collegiants whether one should pay taxes to the magistracy for the prosecution of war. That the problem was posed at all indicates that at this date some radical Collegiants had begun to question the moderate Mennonite position on this issue and to conclude that giving for war purposes was tantamount to supporting war. However, the majority of those present at the debate, including Zwicker, the Antitrinitarian *émigré* from Poland who had been invited to act as chairman, agreed that such taxes might be paid in good conscience by those who opposed personal participation in war. Since taxes, they argued, might be paid to the state in peacetime, even though these were known to go toward the upkeep of such unchristian institutions as prisons and courts of law, then they might also be contributed in wartime. If we condemned the latter, then we should refrain from paying the former; and this last course was contrary to the New Testament model. In fact, when war with France broke out in the following February, the Collegiants followed in the footsteps of the Mennonites and paid a monetary contribution in exchange for exemption, sympathetic Mennonite ministers being ready to attest the conscientiousness of their belief in nonresistance if this were required by the authorities. Only a few Quakers associated with the Collegiants took a more radical stand as conscientious objectors and refused, as their English brethren were doing, to pay a fine or perform alternative service when called up for military duties.

Some Collegiants carried the theory of nonresistance to the point of vegetarianism, whereas neither Mennonites nor Quakers extended nonviolence to the animal kingdom. We hear of one Barent Joosten Stol who stated his belief that man should not take the life of even a flea. Others questioned whether a Christian might lock his doors at night or build a fence around his homestead, if he really took nonresistance seriously. The Collegiants, C. B. Hylkema has noted, did not often use the commandment "Thou shalt not kill" as a proof-text, referring instead to the words and spirit of the New Testament for confirmation of nonresistance.

By the 1670's nonresistance was so far accepted among the Collegiants that soldiers as well as magistrates whose duties involved shedding blood were excluded from communion. The ban, however, did not extend to the magistracy *per se*: even an ardent nonresistant like Zwicker, we learn, inclined to the view that a Christian might take office at the lowest level of the administrative hierarchy. At least, there was less risk there of contamination with bloodshed than in the higher ranks of government. In 1682, however, Frans Kuijper, nephew of

Brenius (who had died in 1664) and a leading Collegiant, together with a number of his associates attempted to persuade the *collegia* to go further and declare in favor of admitting to communion only those who actually subscribed to nonresistance, since, as they said, "a Christian was not permitted to wage war or impose the death penalty." There was considerable opposition to the proposal on the grounds that each individual should decide as his conscience directed him. If mutual tolerance ceased, the *collegia* would transform themselves into a closed sect. Discussion continued sporadically for nearly two decades, until in 1700 a decision was reached to leave the matter to the individual conscience of each member.

On the question of personal self-defense there were varying opinions, too, among the Collegiants, even among those who supported nonresistance in principle. Von Wolzogen, as we have seen, was prepared to make concessions to his fellow nobles' concern for social status by sanctioning their carrying arms, provided that they did not use them. His Dutch translator, Pieter Langedult, a Mennonite minister and at the same time an enthusiastic Collegiant, went even further (though no further than the pacifistic Socinus had gone in his Raków lectures) and argued that a Christian while on a journey might carry a sword, not merely as a symbol of his rank but in order to frighten off marauders and suchlike. He compared this to a houseowner's keeping watchdogs which, though they would not hurt, would serve to deter thieves. Or at any rate, Langedult adds, if they hurt intruders it would not be the houseowner's fault, since he had not intended to harm them. In the same way, if a little nonresistant flourishing of the sword should by chance cause injury to an attacker, the traveler ought not to be held responsible. In this case, Langedult went on, the wounded man might be compared to "a careless person [who] injures himself on a sharp spike which I have put on my house, fence or elsewhere." The same spirit of compromise was shown by Langedult in regard to manufacturing weapons and armaments. "I do not see that a Christian is forbidden to make and then to sell weapons," he writes. Everything depended on the use made of them later: in themselves, they were "neither good nor bad" (an opinion held by Wolzogen too). If someone should argue that the manufacturer of lethal weapons gave occasion for evildoers to misuse them, one might answer, Langedult thought, that "to give someone occasion to do evil is not at all the same as doing evil oneself."

These opinions were voiced by Langedult in a fourteen-page preface to a work by Wolzogen which had appeared in Dutch in 1676 as *De werelose Christen, verbeeldende de nature en hoedanigheyt van*

193

het Rycke Christi (The Defenseless Christian exemplifying the Nature and Character of Christ's Kingdom). A more consistent exposition of defenseless Christianity than Langedult provided (Wolzogen's text, it should be said, was more thoroughgoing in regard to nonresistance than his translator's preface) was given two years later by another Dutch Collegiant, Joan Hartigveldt (Jan Hartichfeld) of the Rotterdam *collegium*, in his *De recht weerlooze Christen* (The Truly Defenseless Christian). This was published in Amsterdam by Frans Kuijper in 1678 shortly after the author's death. The volume bore the subtitle: "Or Defense of the Feelings of the Early Christians and Martyred Anabaptists in Respect to Magistracy, War and Violent Resistance." The author was a man of considerable erudition who in his earlier years had studied law and then been a diplomat before joining the Collegiants around mid-century. Thereafter, he lived as a gentleman-farmer, dividing his time between writing and the cultivation of his small estate. In his book Hartigveldt displayed considerable knowledge of the Greek and Latin classics in their original tongues as well as of the Bible and the writings of the early church fathers. His *Truly Defenseless Christian* far excels any work produced by the Dutch Mennonites on nonresistance and represents one of the most eloquent expositions of pacifism ever penned.

Hartigveldt accepted the Anabaptist-Mennonite position on the magistracy. He rejected government not only because most of its functions were incompatible with Christian discipleship, but also because rulership was contrary to the profession of a Christian whose Master had told his followers to serve each other and not to lord it over one another (this argument had been stressed but little by Anabaptists or Mennonites). "From this, then, it appears that in Christ's kingdom the estate of the worldly princes, kings, and great ones has no place, nor have any magistrates who exercise corporeal, coercive power not only over the goods but also over the lives of their subjects." No true Christian was permitted to exercise this kind of authority; though Hartigveldt was prepared, rather hesitantly, to consider the possibility of a Christian's entering minor office without necessarily losing hope of eternal salvation. Where the line should be drawn on the ladder of office between what was permissible and what impermissible, he admitted, was impossible for man to judge. Such questions must be left to the decision of the Almighty.

When we carefully examine Christ's words and deeds, writes Hartigveldt, we find this view of government fully confirmed. Among themselves his disciples were told to live "without coercive authority . . . so that I cannot conceive how a Christian of goodwill can have the very least doubt concerning all this." The laws of Christ's kingdom, of the New Covenant (*Nieuwe Verbond*) with which he replaced the Mosaic code, called for nonresistance to evil and for repaying bad deeds with good. "Had Christ wished that his people should repay evil-doers with bodily penalties, then he would necessarily have set down, clearly and distinctly, appropriate rules or laws according to which every misdeed should be punished." Instead of this, he preached for-giveness of sinners once they had shown penitence: such forgiveness would be rendered impossible by imposition of the death penalty or by harsh bodily punishments such as those the magistracy imposed upon wrongdoers.

Naturally war was forbidden the truly defenseless Christian. "A Christian can kill no one." Against Langedult, Hartigveldt argued that it was as impossible for such a person to make the weapons of war as to exercise in them or actually to use them to kill fellow human beings. Against Wolzogen, he asserted the unseemliness of an armed Chris-tian, even when his weapons were worn merely for show. Such be-havior Hartigveldt went so far as to call "abominable (*verfoeilijk*)," little less detestable indeed than the actual use of such weapons. One might as well argue, wrote Hartigveldt, that in a country like Brazil, where the natives went naked, Christians might follow their example because that was the custom of the land.

Hartigveldt devotes some attention to the problem of the allegedly just war, i.e., one in which the enemy attacks first and our side fights back. The only difference, he concludes, between "offensive" and "de-fensive" war lay in its cause: the manner of waging war was exactly the same in the one instance as in the other, and both involved activ-ities entirely incompatible with right Christian conduct. The innocent perished at the sword of the defenders, and death and destruction re-sulted impartially from the activities of all warring parties. Moreover, if the attacked found themselves in a position where they must take the offensive or perish, they would not hesitate to move into the offensive. "Thus," Hartigveldt concludes, "this distinction [between defensive and offensive war] is only another name for one and the same thing." The original cause of war became irrelevant, for war inevitably degen-erated into murder whatever the motives with which it was entered upon.

Hartigveldt was well acquainted with the history of the pre-Con-stantinian church, and he quotes extensively from the writings of anti-militarist church fathers like Origen, Tertullian, etc., to show that they excluded the office of the sword from the Christian community. True, he admits, there were Christians serving in the Roman army in this period, but they were few in number and might have been performing merely nonmilitary duties there. He pointed, too, to the survival of pacifism in after ages right down to the Mennonites of his own day.

Was a Christian, then, never justified in using coercion? Sometimes he was, Hartigveldt replied. Force might be used in regard to animals, and it might be applied, too, in respect to children, for their own good. In both instances this was allowed "because it is impossible for them to understand Christ's laws." But it did not hold in the case of grown men and women, for adult evildoers could be brought, by loving care and understanding, to a knowledge of Christ and his Gospel teachings.

Six years after the posthumous publication of Hartigveldt's tract, another Collegiant came forward to defend nonresistance in print. Johannes Breedenburg, however, devotes only part of his *Verhandeling, van de oorsprong van de kennisse Gods, en van desselfs dienst* (*Discourse on the Origin of a Knowledge of God and on His Service*) (Amsterdam, 1684) to this issue. He emphasizes the old Anabaptist theology of martyrdom even more perhaps than Hartigveldt, who also stresses that Christians should trust solely in divine protection and prefer patient suffering to violent resistance. Repay hatred with love. Better to be killed than to kill: better even to allow one's wife and children to be killed, if that were God's will, than to kill in their defense. A Christian should shun courts of law altogether, whether as plaintiff, defendant, or witness, since by this total noninvolvement with the office of wrath he would avoid all complicity in the infliction of punishment. It was indeed permissible, Breedenburg conceded, to admonish a robber or a cheat in a loving spirit. But only in the case of drunkards or lunatics, who were not in control of their actions, should one exercise even noninjurious coercion. Such persons might be restrained—but only for their own benefit, and never as a punishment or in order primarily to protect oneself or others.

The seventeenth-century Collegiants, though they were on the whole more tolerant in their attitude toward members who did not share the full nonresistant position than were the stricter Mennonite sects, nevertheless held a corporate testimony in favor of nonresistance. At least, they had come to do so in the second half of the century (the sources on this subject are rather exiguous for the first half, and it is not completely clear when nonresistance came to be almost universally accepted in the *collegia*). An illustration of the strength of this testimony occurred in 1675 when a member of the *collegium* in Amsterdam, after visiting villages around the Zuider Zee, reported to the meeting that he had found there many orphans from Collegiant families, neglected and often indeed running quite wild. The reason for this situation was that the parents, while alive, had not wished that after their death their children should be consigned to orphanages run by the Reformed church, for there they would have been reared in an atmosphere hostile to the very idea of nonresistance. But Collegiants in this area were poor; their religious communities could not afford to care for such children properly. The Amsterdam *collegium*, therefore, decided to set up its own orphanage in that city to house these children (it became known as the *Oranje-Appel*), broadening it three years later, in 1678, to include any needy orphans who could not be located elsewhere.

III. THE EIGHTEENTH CENTURY

The Collegiants continued their activities, though on a diminishing scale, until the end of the eighteenth century. The same period saw a steady decline in the size of the Mennonite or *Doopsgezinden* (the name increasingly preferred) brotherhood. Whereas around the middle of the seventeenth century there were some 120,000 Mennonites and at the outset of the next century they numbered around 200,000, by 1820 this figure had sunk to 30,000. Thereafter it slowly rose, but only from World War I on did a real revival of the church take place.

The causes of decline are not hard to seek. In the first place the constant schisms brought the brotherhood into disrepute with many who might otherwise have been attracted to it, causing embarrassment at the same time to its more sensitive spirits who regretted such dissension in a people devoted to the pursuit of harmony. For instance, a Mennonite pamphleteer writing in 1648 referred his brethren to the European statesmen then engaged in making peace between the nations at the end of the Thirty Years' War, for an example of what they themselves should be doing. "The raw soldiers are laying down swords at the command of their princes and kings," he wrote. "If we *Doopsgezinden* wish to be disciples of Christ, then should we not let the sword of discord drop from out our hands, according to the word of our prince and king, Jesus?" And indeed, by that date the shattered brotherhood had already begun to reunite, though extremely slowly and with many disappointments on the way, until finally by the early nineteenth century almost the whole body came together. Yet growing unity did not stem the decline in numbers which became catastrophic just in the period after unity had been regained and the sectarian barriers between the congregation and the world were being finally dismantled, threatening thereby the continued existence of the church.

A second and more basic reason for the declining membership lies in the decrease in inner dynamism which the brotherhood experienced as it sought to accommodate itself to the society which surrounded it. Certainly, the *Doopsgezinden* had contributed much to the culture of the Netherlands in the seventeenth century and still continued to do so in the eighteenth century. But with the broadening of horizons and the discarding of a narrow sectarian outlook, though these seemed like gains, something irreplaceable, something vital to the health of the denomination, was lost. Or, at least, the *Doopsgezinden* failed to find a new center for their faith or to renew the church on a changed foundation. There was not so very much now to distinguish a Mennonite (he very probably would have disliked this designation) from a Remonstrant, or even from a liberal member of the Reformed church, now that old-time theology was steadily retreating before the advance of rational religion. Like those contemporary Quaker grandee families in Philadelphia who moved over from the Society of Friends to the Anglican church, patrician families in the Netherlands, too, frequently changed from Mennonitism to the Reformed. Indeed there came to be little reason, beyond family tradition, to remain with the *Doopsgezinden* rather than join the established church.

By the eighteenth century the average *Doopsgezinden* was no longer (in the eyes of the world) a rather suspicious character, perhaps even a dangerous fanatic, as in the sixteenth century; he was usually not even a starry-eyed idealist as many had still been in the seventeenth century. Instead, we find him a solid, respectable citizen. He was not always wealthy, but the wealthy members increasingly gave the tone to the congregation, and this was especially so in the more important and influential congregations. True, even in cosmopolitan Amsterdam old-time Mennonite sectaries nursed their apartness in their Noah's arks (the name of one such rigorist congregation). And in remote country districts like Friesland, for example, there were still in the eighteenth century many congregations which strove to exemplify the earlier pattern and live without spot or wrinkle. Here nonconformity to the world, avoidance, and the ban were practiced as of old. But their day was passing. In the nineteenth century the last of their kind disappeared and left no successors. Now *Doopsgezinden* farmers too, like their bourgeois brethren, were conformed to society. Henceforward only a certain severity in their style of life usually distinguished members of this church from other Protestants.

Nonresistance and conscientious objection were among the most obvious characteristics distinguishing the Mennonite from his non-Mennonite neighbor. They were signs that he belonged to a peculiar people, however much he might try to demonstrate his unity with the rest of the population, whether by giving money in times of national emergency or by undertaking noncombatant duties as an alternative to military service. Yet, as the hitherto separated sect fused with society, a stand against war appeared anachronistic to those *Doopsgezinden* for whom nonresistance constituted but an inherited belief lacking the support of interior conviction. As the ban was given up and church discipline relaxed, there was nothing to prevent younger men from openly deviating from their church's traditional stand in regard to such matters as office-holding or military service. For long, the rigorists resisted pressure to jettison the Mennonite peace testimony along with other traditional tenets which appeared to many now to be outmoded. Finally, the resistance collapsed: this happened when it became obvious that there were really very few rigorists left. But, as we shall see, outside events also contributed significantly to this dénouement.

In the early 1740's a German Lutheran pastor, Simeon Friderich Rues, visited the Mennonite communities in the Netherlands, reporting his observations—many of them extremely pertinent—in a volume entitled *Sincere Information on the Present State of the Mennonites . . . in the United Netherlands (Aufrichtige Nachrichten von dem gegenwartigen Zustande der Mennoniten oder Taufgesinnten wie auch der Collegianten oder Reisburger, beyderseits ansehnlicher kirchlicher Gesellschaften in den vereinigten Niderlanden*, 1743; expanded Dutch translation, Amsterdam, 1745). He noted the existence of two conflicting views within the brotherhood on such matters as self-defense, war, and military service; indeed, we may add, the distinction between the "fine [or strict] Mennonites (*fijne Mennisten*)," who continued to observe the traditional prohibition of warlike activities, and the "coarse Mennonites (*groove Mennisten*)," who accepted bearing arms as a civic duty compatible with their religious allegiance, had long been apparent both to the Dutch *Doopsgezinden* themselves and to outsiders. Of the rigorists Rues writes (I use John Horsch's translation):

> They believe that the government is ordained of God, and therefore render willing obedience to its law and commands. They teach that taxes and duties must be paid without murmuring and without asking for what purpose they are to be used. They are thankful to God for the blessing of being permitted to live a quiet and peaceable life under the protection of the government. They believe, however, that in the church of Christ there is no room for government as such, and if all people were true Christians . . . there would be no need for cruel governments. But since this has

199

never been realized and it cannot be hoped that it will be realized, God has instituted the office of the government. He did this in order that the world may not be made a den of thieves. . . . Nevertheless they readily admit that they do not think it right that Christians should hold governmental offices. They say . . . that the duties of a magistrate and of a Christian do not agree, for the worldly governments must exercise vengeance, force and violence, but this is forbidden the believer under the New Testament dispensation. . . . They are very strict as concerns the exercise of force and the use of weapons. While many other Mennonites are far more lenient on this point, the members of this group of churches still purport to be nonresistant Christians. They believe that a Christian may not even use force against such resistance as is contrary to the law, but that he must forfeit his property, liberty, and life to his enemies when he is attacked. Therefore none of their members is allowed to have any weapons. The merchants among their number are not permitted to send freight on armed ships. Hence they confine their business mostly to points on the North Sea and the Baltic, instead of risking the sending of freight to places where, in the absence of provisions for defence, there is danger of falling prey to piracy.

Sentiments of this kind were reflected in the religious literature of the denomination. Exhortatory writings, catechisms, confessions of faith, expositions of doctrine, etc., put out by all branches—including those which took a less rigid line unofficially—almost always contained passages on nonresistance and its place among the essentials of Christianity. All this is familiar stuff. Its prevailing spirit was that of the early sixteenth-century Schleitheim Confession. Only occasionally was a new approach introduced: for instance, we find Kornelius van Huyzen, preacher in the Mennonite congregation at Emden just across the border, defending nonresistance not only from the Bible but also on the grounds that war was irrational. Violent resistance was natural in animals, wrote van Huyzen (in his *Historische verhandeling van de opkomst en voortgang, mitsgaders de God-geleertheyd der Doopsgezinde Christenen* [1712]; I have used the 1734 edition published in Hoorn). But nature had not armed human beings with tooth, claw, and fang to use against attack. Instead, it had given them speech and reason, which were not to be found among the animals. And reason taught men to love their neighbors and not to war against them. But such arguments remained uncommon in the Mennonite antiwar repertoire.

Throughout the eighteenth century in many congregations, and probably in almost all the congregations belonging to the stricter rural subjects, the discipline continued in application against members who infringed the prohibition against bearing arms. (When in 1722 the Mennonites at Brielle in South Holland voted to join the Remonstrant church, they made a special point of getting a guarantee from it that their conscientious objection to bearing arms would be respected.) Action was still taken from time to time, too, against those who served in, or owned, ships which were armed. Van de Zijpp in his brief historical survey of the Dutch Mennonite peace testimony has recorded a number of such cases stretching right down to the end of the century. The rather conservative Zonists reaffirmed their belief in nonresistance and conscientious objection as late as 1789 (though, significantly, without explicitly mentioning the possibility of disciplinary action against deviants from this position).

We hear, too, of congregations splitting on the issue of nonresistance. This happened, for instance, in 1709 within the seafaring congregation at Den Hoorn on the island of Texel. There some members, led by the preacher, objected to disfellowshipping a fellow member who, as pilot, had guided a man-of-war through the dangerous waters surrounding the West Frisian islands. The man excused himself on the plea that he had had no intention of himself manning a gun. The majority of the congregation, however, upheld his expulsion, and the minority left. It should be noted, though, that not all the Mennonite congregations on the island took so stringent a line. Elsewhere, when divisions arose later on this issue, they were usually resolved, finally, by allowing members freedom to decide, according to conscience, whether to serve with arms or not, while at the same time, of course, leaving the official position of the church on nonresistance unchanged. Yet such an arrangement left many dissatisfied, for they feared that eventually the government would abolish the *Doopsgezinden's* legal exemption from military duties if too many members, however conscientious according to their own lights, failed to live up to their church's nonresistant principles.

We can watch the conflict of opinion within one congregation in the diary of the Alkmaar deacon, Cornelis Bruinvis (printed in *Doopsgezinde Bijdragen* [1880]: "Uit de aanteekeningen van een Alkmaarschen diaken, 1778-1809"). The Alkmaar congregation belonged to the Frisian branch, but not to its rigorist wing. By the 1780's its council contained both traditionalists who remained staunchly nonresistant and members who had abandoned pacifism or who at least disagreed with disciplinary measures being taken against those who had done so. In October 1786 the latter succeeded in pushing a resolution through the church council declaring: "Whenever members of the congregation entertained no objection to exercising with weapons, one could not conscientiously disfellowship (*ontbroederen*) them; but . . . we should give them the communion, testifying however that it did not meet with our approval that any should lightly undertake [such action]." The resolution, however, aroused immediate opposition. Many members felt "that this wide approval of arms bearing in our church was a means whereby not only would our teaching become degenerate but, above all, all our holy endeavours would be destroyed and the door opened wide to an all too great toleration." Eventually, in the following January, a general meeting of the congregation overruled the church council's decision, decreeing that "henceforward as hitherto" the bearing of arms be forbidden members. And any of their more liberal Waterlander neighbors who did not observe strict nonresistance would be required to take communion in their own congregation; henceforward, their presence among the Frisians would not be welcome.

At the same time as this clash of views was taking place at Alkmaar, a similar situation arose in another town congregation, that of the united Flemish-Waterlanders at Rotterdam. In 1786 a member on becoming an officer in a "Patriot" company (see below) had been told by the church council that he must either resign or face expulsion if he persisted in bearing arms. The man finally agreed to the former alternative—but the incident revealed that a sizable minority within the council, including one of the ministers, was opposed to disciplinary action of the kind proposed by the majority.

As late as 1796, only three years before the general acceptance of military service by the *Doopsgezinden*, we find the congregation at Giethoorn in Overijssel, a conservative group, entering into sharp controversy with the Mennonites in neighboring Zuidveen, who continued to admit a member to the communion after he had joined the militia. Giethoorn delegated two of its people to visit the brethren at Zuidveen and to enquire whether they did not consider soldiering incompatible with the *Doopsgezinden* confession of faith. The Zuidveeners replied in the affirmative but added that while they did not approve such conduct they were unwilling to set up a Popish tyranny over conscience. They felt that each individual member must be responsible to God for his actions: it was not the congregation's business, they implied, to enforce conformity against the dictates of conscience. Returning home the delegates from Giethoorn reflected sadly how patriotic emotion had gripped the Zuidveeners: the Giethoorn congregation decided to break off contacts with them shortly afterward.

Patriotic feelings had indeed taken hold of the *Doopsgezinden* in the course of the seventeenth century, first naturally in respect to the urban and the more liberal congregations and then to some extent also in respect to the country congregations which still clung to other-worldly patterns of behavior in most other ways; these feelings continued to expand in the course of the eighteenth century. At the beginning of that century, for instance, in a united address to the Bern government drawn up in 1710 in connection with that government's persecution of Mennonites under its jurisdiction, the *Doopsgezinden*, had spoken warmly of their own devotion to their beloved fatherland (*het lieve vaderland*), which had given them freedom to worship as they wished and which protected their right to enjoy liberty of conscience. "Certainly, where one lot of Christians, according to the dictates of their conscience, defend the beloved fatherland with carnal weapons, while another [the Mennonites] resort to spiritual and glowing prayer, there shall the dear fatherland be defended on all sides." The same concept reappears again from time to time even in the writings of the traditionalists. This division of the community into Mennonites praying for their country and non-Mennonites fighting for their country is indeed remote from the old view of the congregation of the faithful, separated from the state and all its ways and regarding patriotism as a snare of the devil.

Mennonite archives, of course, tend to bring into prominence cases where disciplinary action was recorded as being taken against a deviant from the official teaching of the brotherhood. When a man bore arms or served on an armed ship and got away with it, no mention of this would usually appear in the congregation's records. Again, since Mennonites were now legally exempt from military service, many undoubtedly took advantage of this exemption, even though they did not always share the pacifist convictions that were presupposed to exist throughout the brotherhood when the government originally granted the collective exemption. Nevertheless sufficient evidence does exist to show that in the eighteenth century a steady decline took place among the *Doopsgezinden* in their adherence to their historic peace testimony: a process which proceeded most rapidly in the urban congregations. It was observed by outsiders, lamented by the traditionalists inside the sect, and from time to time set down in its official records. Spreading lukewarmness toward nonresistance was of course matched by increasing tepidity in regard to other tenets of the traditional faith:

refusal to swear oaths, rejection of office and courts of law, peculiar dress and speech, the ban, as well as peculiarities of worship like the practice of foot-washing. A rationalist theology replaced the New Testament-oriented discipleship of earlier centuries. And eventually meekness (*lijdzaamheid*) replaced nonresistance (*weerloosheid*) as the cental doctrine of the denomination. But theoretical justification of changes already wrought within the practice of the brotherhood came only in the nineteenth century.

By the middle of the previous century, however, observers had already noted that the then still fashionable side-arms were being worn by some Mennonite "gentlemen." In 1752 the church council at Nijmegen had to take steps to prevent members from attending church services in military uniforms. It instructed the deacons to remonstrate with such persons and to explain that such behavior on the part of a Mennonite was "unseemly, scandalous, and offensive." Yet, significantly, in this congregation disciplinary action does not seem to have been taken against members who bore arms.

For long, the ministry provided the backbone of the opposition to any relaxation in regard to nonresistance. But during the first half of the eighteenth century ministers were to be found who were no longer pacifists; usually, however, they still kept their views to themselves at this time. Such a one was Johannes Stinstra, who was minister of the congregation at Harlingen. Stinstra was a man of deep learning as well as of somewhat unorthodox theological views: his enemies accused him of Socinianism. In 1751 he helped to draw up a catechism for the youth, which was published in the name of the whole congregation in 1751 (*Vraagen over den godsdienst, tot onderwijs der jeugd geschikt door de leeraaren der christelijke Doopsgezinde gemeente te Harlingen*). The library of the Amsterdam Mennonite church possesses a copy of this catechism with extensive handwritten notes by Stinstra. To the question (779) "Is the death penalty permitted?" he answered in the affirmative. It *was* necessary, though it should be applied "sparingly." Concerning war, he noted down his approval of "defensive war" when "no comon judge" existed to arbitrate a dispute. "Unjustified wars [are those] (1) for one people's advantage, (2) to satisfy its glory." And he also condemned the "common way of waging war" as "the greatest injustice." Stinstra also dealt with the question of personal participation in military service. In a "just" war a man might certainly take part "either in person or with his goods. In extremity, one can buy oneself out." In regard to "unjust wars," one should protest if one were able to do so. Taxes, though, should still be paid even for such a war. "If pressed [to serve in an unjust war], one could do so. Otherwise it was preferable to stand clear or to move."

As the century wore on, the nonpacifists in the brotherhood grew bolder. The nonresistants, however much they might try to stem the tide, appeared more and more to be protagonists of a losing cause. When, in the 1780's, republican opponents of the House of Orange formed the radical wing of a "Patriotic" party which had been organized to bring about changes in the constitution, Mennonites joined them in large numbers: pastors, elders, and deacons along with lay members. Members of the brotherhood were now to be found among that section of the population which was particularly attracted to democratic political slogans. The Patriots were by no means proletarians; they were drawn mainly, though not exclusively, from the bourgeois "third estate" which in France would provide the motive force for change during the early years of the Revolution. Mennonite ministers, especially in areas like North Holland or Friesland, were prominent in the Patriot leadership. In the 1780's many of them participated actively in the revolutionary committees which proceeded to throw the old Orangist magistrates out of office. Mennonites helped, too, with the Patriot press. Above all, they were active in the numerous volunteer companies (*exercitie-genootschappen*), which sprang up all over the country in the 1780's in support of the Patriot cause. Admittedly there were some Mennonites who sympathized with the House of Orange, and many more who held to the old nonresistant principles. Yet the wave of enthusiasm for the Patriot cause, which swept the *Doopsgezinden* brotherhood carrying both old and young along with it, witnessed to the far-going decay of the Mennonite peace witness. A figure like François Adriaan van der Kemp, Mennonite minister at Leiden from 1779 until 1787, when he was forced to leave for the United States on account of his political activities, would have been inconceivable even half a century earlier. Commander of the local unit of Patriot volunteers, van der Kemp was accustomed each Sunday, after completing divine service, to change rapidly from his pastor's garb into his captain's uniform and then proceed to the exercising of his men in the art of arms. True, he met with criticism for such activities—a "degenerate son" of "the great master . . . Menno Simons" was how a contemporary Mennonite pamphleteer described him—but he was by no means an isolated phenomenon in the *Doopsgezinden* brotherhood of his time.

The Patriot cause was defeated in 1787, two years before the outbreak of the French Revolution. In 1795 the Patriots returned to power

—behind the bayonets of the French republic's armies. The Batavian Republic was proclaimed: the House of Orange fled. *Egalité* was the battle-cry of the new establishment; it was echoed, too, by many Dutch Mennonites who longed to see the remaining barriers removed between their church and the community. In the new constitution of 1796 the legislators put all religious confessions on an equality before the law. Voices were raised demanding the abolition of the Mennonites' privileged position in regard to military service. Now that all citizens enjoyed equal rights, it was argued, they should share the same obligations. Even to the Mennonites themselves, especially to those who had discarded nonresistance, their military exemption appeared to be an anomaly. Most of them felt its disappearance would constitute no hardship. They had to wait three years, however, before the final step was taken. Then, on 4 May 1799, the legislature decreed that henceforward no exemption to service in "the armed Batavian civil guard" would be permitted on grounds of religious conscience. All ablebodied male citizens had the obligation to help defend "the freedom and independence" of their country from which they derived so many advantages. However, it still remained possible for one on whom the ballot fell to escape personal service by means of a substitute (a way out common to the laws of most countries at that date).

A collective protest was drawn up by the Mennonite congregations of Amsterdam, and similar documents were drafted in other places too. But an attempt to organize joint action on behalf of the whole brotherhood fell through from lack of support. "This," writes van der Zijpp, "indicates indeed that the indignation over the wrong done was not so very great: protest was made more from tradition than from the dictates of conscience. . . . With few exceptions the spirit of the times had won." Patriotism and the values of material prosperity, as well as liberal religion and liberal politics, had replaced evangelical simplicity and otherworldliness, and rejection of the state and of war, in the minds of most *Doopsgezinden*. Even where outward respect was paid to the ethics of Menno's time it proved only too often a cold homage, a bowing of the mind but not the heart to the standards of a past age.

IV. The Nineteenth Century

When the Dutch Mennonites' legal military exemption disappeared in 1799, their conscientious objection went too. This is surprising, indeed disquieting, when we consider that until that date the brotherhood in all its branches had held to nonresistance as one of its most distinctive tenets and that it had officially urged members to take the conscientious objector stand in regard to all demands from the state to bear arms. Not long before, church members, as we have seen, were still being disciplined and even disfellowshipped for infringing the discipline on this score. Yet now all this was gone, almost as if it had never been. Van der Zijpp writes of the period following 1799: "I have uncovered no cases of conscientious objection, though there are some where men hid or got out of service in some way, perhaps by moving. But the real principle [of nonresistance] was dead."

Though essentially correct, van der Zijpp's verdict is formulated perhaps a little too strongly. There is evidence that nonresistance, albeit in diluted form, persisted into the nineteenth century. Hiring of substitutes was resorted to by Mennonites who possessed the means to do this. True, the practice had been frowned on in the old days. For instance, in a catechism published by the Frisians in 1747, "hiring other persons to serve as our substitutes" was roundly condemned. "By no means" should such a practice be condoned. But times had changed, and no other way was now open to one who still entertained old-fashioned scruples on the subject. No one seems to have considered going to jail as an alternative: a reflection, probably, of the low priority given to nonresistance in their scale of values, rather than of any lack of civic courage on the Mennonites' part.

Napoleon's brother, Louis Bonaparte, after he was made King of Holland in 1806, showed his good-will toward the Mennonite communities of his new kingdom by renewing their old legal exemption from bearing arms. But the privilege was lost again when in 1810 the northern Netherlands was incorporated directly into the French Empire. Hundreds of young *Doopsgezinden* were forced into the *grande armée*: some succeeded in evading their call-up, but many perished in Russia and on the other battlefields where the imperial troops fought with those of the anti-Napoleonic allies.

The church council of the United Amsterdam congregation had protested vigorously against members having to serve outside the country —but their protests were ignored by the authorities. These were under overwhelming pressure from France to gather up as many recruits as could possibly be obtained. In the autumn of 1811 the Amsterdam congregation, which administered the orphanage known as the "Oranje-Appel" jointly with a board of governors, was faced with a specially cruel dilemma. The orphanage contained forty-three children, of whom seventeen were of *Doopsgezinden* parentage; now the Mayor of Amsterdam demanded of the governors that all orphans over fourteen years old should be dispatched to Versailles for consignment to military service with the French army. Despite the expostulations of the governors, the Mayor remained adamant; he probably had no choice in view of French control of the country. The governors of the orphanage, acting in agreement with the council of the Amsterdam Mennonite church, finally acquiesced: the first batch of orphans was dispatched immediately afterward. The incident forms a melancholy epilogue to the story of an institution originally founded to care for the children of nonresistants.

Dutch independence was restored in 1814. In respect to military service the position of the Mennonites returned to the *status quo ante* 1806. By now there was little interest in nonresistance, except in certain old-fashioned country congregations, though elsewhere, too, some Mennonites, when called up, continued to resort to the purchase of a substitute. From early in the century we find attempts being made by *Doopsgezinden* scholars to deny that their founder, Menno Simons, had ever advocated absolute pacifism. We may note, though, that Dutch Mennonites did not abandon nonresistance because they had become convinced that the doctrine was a later accretion unknown to the founding fathers of their church. Their scholars reached this conclusion only after the church had already rejected its nonresistant heritage. One of the first to analyze Menno's writings systematically, with a view to discovering if the traditional picture of Menno as an unconditional nonresistant was not in fact mistaken, was the Amsterdam preacher Jan ter Borg. He did so in a lecture delivered in 1818 (and published under the title "Heeft Menno Simons eene volstreekt algemeene weerloosheid gepredikt?" in the *Vaderlandsche Letteroefeningen*, vol. LIX [1819]). Ter Borg concluded, not surprisingly, that Menno had rejected the sword only in matters of religion or for the purpose of political or social revolution (nineteenth-century *Doopsgezinden* remained extremely sensitive to the charge that they owed their origin to "Munsterish" revolutionaries); he could find no trace in Menno of opposition to the sword either for self-defense or in the hands of a duly constituted magistracy.

In 1830, when Belgium broke away from the northern kingdom and the latter attempted to quell the uprising by armed force, Mennonite young men volunteered for service. Indeed, at the *Doopsgezinden* theological seminary in Amsterdam, a wave of patriotic enthusiasm swept the student body. Even though the idea of professional soldiering, of voluntary military service, long continued to be regarded with disapproval by many in the brotherhood even after it had discarded its pacifism, a majority of the seminary's governors now supported the volunteers, feeling that, in a national emergency like the existing one, it would be wrong for Mennonites to hold back, if they wished to go, while others were giving their lives for their country.

Reservations concerning military service persisted until around mid-century, chiefly in a few remote rural congregations which attempted to preserve the old patterns of religious and social behavior. In 1825 the "Old Flemish" at Haarlem had reprinted the mid-eighteenth-century catechism of Pieter Boudewijns, which stated the traditional nonresistant position plainly and unequivocally and called for conscientious objection to military service as the only stand consistent with true Christian discipleship; it was used by several rural conservative groups.

The last to maintain a collective testimony against participation in military service was the small Old Flemish congregation in the Friesland village of Balk. In 1853-1854 the majority of its members, led by its preachers R. J. Smits and R. J. Symensma, emigrated to the United States, settling in Indiana near Goshen where Mennonites were already numerous. Those who remained no longer adhered to nonresistance; the pastor who took over the congregation in 1854 was a learned theologian, D. S. Gorter, who had fought as a volunteer in the war of 1830.

Until the emigration, however, the Balk Mennonites had retained many old forms of belief along with their objections to military service: a lay ministry, extreme simplicity of ritual, dress, and style of living, and even avoidance and the ban. If ballotted, the young men of the congregation regularly paid over to the authorities a sum sufficient to cover the cost of hiring a substitute. The elders justified this by a species of moral sophistry whereby they convinced themselves that the procedure was not tantamount to direct purchase of a man to fight in one's stead, for (so they said) the government retained responsibility for what was done with this money. When a member of the strictly pacifist communitarian settlement at Mijdrecht (see Appendix) who had served as a conscientious objector in the war of 1830 heard of this practice, he was shocked. "What!" he exclaimed, "you buy someone to commit a sin; you are worse than they who themselves commit the sin." That the Balk Mennonites were not happy about the situation appears from the fact that they several times petitioned the government to grant them a more satisfactory form of exemption. "We do not find liberty to do through others what we believe to be sin for ourselves," their leaders stated at the time of their departure. The authorities' refusal to listen to their request, together with the congregation's memories of the war of 1830, when the church treasury had become severely strained on account of the sums expended on buying conscripts out of service (as well as economic motivations for emigration, for the congregation was poor), finally convinced the Balk Mennonites that they could expect no improvement of their situation at home and that no alternative remained except to leave their native land for the New World. By that date they had become entirely isolated within the *Doopsgezinden* fellowship: all other branches had conformed to the new situation.

Accounts of the Balk Mennonites' emigration almost invariably refer to those who left as unconditional nonresistants. Only Vos in his brief survey of the history of the *Doopsgezinden* peace witness asserts that their objection was not to war *per se* but to wars of aggression. A reading of a short pamphlet written by the man who was shortly to become the new minister at Balk, D. S. Gorter, which was published at nearby Sneek in 1853, the year of the emigration, tends to confirm Vos's view. The pamphlet is entitled *Christian Meekness glorified in the Departure of the Old Mennonites of Balk, who removed to North America for the Sake of Freedom from Military Conscription* (*De christelyke lijdzaamheid, aangeprezen bij het vertrek der oud-Doopsgezinden van Balk, die om vrijheid van krijgsdienst naar Nord-Amerika verhuisden*). It reports conversations on the subject of war and military service, which had taken place between Gorter and the preachers, Smits and Symensma, shortly before the group's departure. The writer's tone is friendly, he praises the two preachers and their flock for their devotion to principle, calling them "my friends" and expressing his hope that they would find in their adopted country the freedom to live peaceably which they had not found at home. At the same time, Gorter makes no bones about his own conviction as to the necessity of the office of the sword even among Christians.

According to Gorter, Smits and Symensma were themselves not really so very far from his own position. They had confided in him their belief that participation in a truly defensive war was not incompatible with Christianity: all they opposed in principle were wars of aggression, such as the recent struggle between the northern Netherlands and Belgium. In practice, however, they considered almost every conflict to have been aggressive in character. "The sword . . . was usually misused as a weapon of injustice." This was the lesson of history. Therefore, they went on: "We cannot square it with our consciences to deliver ourselves and our sons over to blind obedience to a government which we cannot trust to order only what is good and right. If we did so, we should consider ourselves to be equally guilty of its unrighteousness." Thus, whereas Gorter believed that *since in* principle Christians were not forbidden by their master to bear arms, they should obey the command of the magistrate and help defend their country (otherwise national defense would be rendered impossible), Smits and Symensma felt that, *although* Christians were not forbidden arms-bearing in principle, they were obliged to refuse military service unless—and until—the improbable happened and an indubitably defensive war occurred.

It is very unlikely that Gorter consciously falsified the two preachers' arguments. He may have misunderstood their meaning, of course. By approving the sword in theory, but only if it were always to act righteously, they could have wished to imply, as we have seen sixteenth-century Anabaptists sometimes did in approving a loving use of the sword, that in fact war and a sword-bearing magistracy were essentially unchristian institutions. Yet in this case, too, it is probable that a rebuttal would have been made by Smits and Symensma when Gorter's pamphlet came to their attention (as it surely must have done). But no such rebuttal was made, so far as I know. The problem is a difficult one to resolve. I would suggest as the most likely solution that Gorter did in fact accurately record the view of Smits and Symensma on the subject of war. Their congregation, on the other hand, probably cleaved to the earlier and more unconditional nonresistance which had prevailed in the *Doopsgezinden* brotherhood until the end of the previous century. On the practical issue of conscientious objection, preachers and congregation, however, remained united: they were united, too, in their resolve to seek freedom from military service across the ocean.

The final stage in the history of the old *Doopsgezinden* witness for nonresistance came in 1898. In that year the Dutch parliament replaced selective service by universal military training, thereby doing away with the possibility of opting out by purchase of a substitute. Most of the brotherhood were indifferent, having long ago abandoned any interest in nonresistance. Outside parliament a few isolated Mennonite voices were raised in protest (e.g., the pastor Tjepke Kielstra), and in the parliamentary First Chamber several Mennonite deputies, including Enno ten Cate Fennema, spoke against the bill in debate and voted against it at the conclusion.

That at that date there were still a few Mennonites who held scruples concerning military service and chose to pay a substitute rather than bear arms personally, appears certain, although there is no means of knowing the number of such persons, or to what extent they were motivated by a conscientious objection or merely by the lingering antimilitarist sentiment within the brotherhood (or even by entirely unconscientious reasons). However, if we exclude several objectors of Mennonite background who as Tolstoyans or as libertarian socialists refused service, after 1898 there were no recorded instances (so far as I can discover) of Mennonite conscientious objectors until a young *Doopsgezinden*, Jan Glijsteen, was jailed for refusal to serve during the First World War. And even Glijsteen, although a practicing member of the church, was influenced strongly by Tolstoyan and anarchist ideas. A modest revival of pacifism within the Dutch Mennonite brotherhood dates only from the period after 1918. It took place then under strong influence from American Mennonites as well as from British Quakers. And the nonresistants, though fairly numerous among *Doopsgezinden* clergy, have remained hitherto a small minority within the membership at large.

By the twentieth century the Dutch Mennonites had become a middle-class church. For the most part, even when of humble station they were respectable citizens, theologically tending to modernism but politically rather conservative, and staunch upholders of the Protestant establishment. There were now Mennonite army and navy officers, Mennonite magistrates and burgomasters, and Mennonite bankers and statesmen, including a minister of the navy and several governors of the Dutch East Indies. Little remained that could bring to mind the days when Mennonites, in the Netherlands as elsewhere, regarded the state as a pagan institution and excluded from their fellowship any who took office or bore arms.

SIX. *The German Mennonites*

(TO THE AGE OF THE DEMOCRATIC REVOLUTION)

AFTER the Anabaptists had merged in the course of the sixteenth century into a loosely organized religious community usually adopting the name of the Dutchman Menno Simons to denote their fellowship, German-speaking Mennonites were to be found in many lands of central and eastern Europe: Switzerland and Alsace-Lorraine; southwest, west-central and north-west Germany; Moravia and Slovakia—if we include the Hutterites here—as well as Polish Pomerania (Prussia), and eventually Russia and Austrian Galicia too. By mid-seventeenth century, however, Mennonitism had been suppressed in the Catholic states of the Empire, and in some of the Protestant ones as well. Where they enjoyed toleration, Mennonites no longer proselytized as the Anabaptists had done. Instead, they lived as closed communities restricting as far as possible their contacts with the world whose rulers, in turn, were happy that these sectaries no longer attempted to win adherents among their subjects. In fact, they ordinarily gave toleration only in exchange for a renunciation on the Mennonites' part of the right to make converts to their religion. Emigration became the standard technique employed by Mennonites (whole settlements, sometimes, as well as individual families) to counter political or economic pressure and religious persecution. Thus, toward the end of the seventeenth century German-speaking Mennonites began to cross the Atlantic, settling first in Quaker Pennsylvania but spreading to other parts of the American continent later.

The division we have made here between Dutch and German Mennonites is somewhat artificial, for until the nineteenth century the Mennonites of northern Germany and of Polish Pomerania, with their offshoots in the Tsarist empire, were in closer communion with the Dutch *Doopsgezinden* than with their coreligionists in the south—not to speak of the Moravian Hutterite Brethren. For northern Mennonitism, Amsterdam for long formed a center of its culture and of its religious communion. East Friesland and the lower German Rhineland formed an integral part, as it were, of the Dutch brotherhood, and even Mennonite communities farther afield like Lübeck or Danzig had been founded by Dutch-speaking Anabaptists. Danzig Mennonites, for

213

instance, retained the Dutch language into the nineteenth century. These facts should be borne in mind while reading the account given below of the peace testimony of German-speaking Mennonites.

In 1591, at a gathering in Cologne, the Dutch and the High German Mennonites had agreed to certain principles of faith and practice, including nonresistance. Not only should Christians, they said, refrain from retaliating "with external weapons"; "one should not repay abuse with abuse," either. But long before the conclusion of the "Concept of Cologne" German-speaking Mennonites from the North and Baltic Seas to the Alps had established nonresistance as an essential element of their belief. In the south, nonresistance predominated from the start; in central and northern Germany it had reasserted itself after the excitement of Münster had died down. Refusal to bear arms or participate in office came to be generally recognized as a characteristic of the sect. Deviants from this position became increasingly rare as the sixteenth century proceeded. Whenever the leaders appeared in public to defend their principles, they reasserted their faith in nonresistance. This happened, for instance, at the *Religionsgespräche* held at Frankenthal in the Palatinate in the summer of 1571, and again at Emden in 1578. They demanded from their opponents evidence out of the New Testament, for "without proof from Christ and the apostles" they refused to agree to the proposition "that a Christian could be a magistrate and punish wrongdoers with the sword" or go to war, however much these practices might be justified on the basis of the Mosaic code. The same spirit is implicit in the hymnbook of the Swiss and south German brethren, the *Ausbund*, compiled between 1564 and 1583. The need for nonresistant suffering and the redemptive quality of martyrdom are among the main themes of the collection.

The brotherhood consisted now of peasants and artisans; even the ministers were humble people, laymen with no pretensions to book-learning. Only gradually did a well-to-do element reappear in the towns, and a ministry which, though still lay, was competent to expound the doctrines of the faith outside the closed circle of their congregations. But when German Mennonite congregations in the seventeenth century once again began to produce considered expositions of their faith, without exception these confessions and catechisms and similar writings all declared explicitly in favor of nonresistance. They were to add little if anything, however, to what had already been said many times on the subject, reiterating, in the words of the Emden Mennonites in their confession of faith issued in 1713: "We believe that it is our duty to abstain from military service."

It is impossible to say exactly when conscientious objection became obligatory among German Anabaptists, a fixed pattern of behavior enforced by the congregational discipline. Its incidence, as we have seen, dates back to 1525—that is, to the very beginning of the movement's history. But the record is very fragmentary; the *Täuferakten* published so far do not go beyond 1535. Moreover, in the sixteenth century it was comparatively simple for those faced with a demand from the authorities to bear arms (usually in the town guard or watch) to escape service, either by removing elsewhere or by payment of a sum of money which was frequently used to hire a substitute in place of the objector. Rural congregations were not too much troubled by demands of this kind. But by the third quarter of the sixteenth century, and in most areas much earlier, all Mennonites (as Anabaptists were now calling themselves) had become potential conscientious objectors, even if for the reasons just cited actual cases of objection may still have been fairly few in number.

In the seventeenth and eighteenth centuries, when congregational discipline had crystallized and action was taken against those who transgressed its requirements, we still find only infrequent instances of a confrontation with the authorities on the issue of military service. In many areas local rulers in the course of time gave their Mennonites a *privilegium*—an official guarantee of protection against expulsion and of the right to worship as they chose—in exchange for a usually considerable monetary contribution to the state treasury. Mennonites were by no means the only religious group which enjoyed such privileges; Jews, too, in many areas paid such protection money (*Schutzgeld*), as did several other Christian sects. Protection might include exemption from military service; more often, this question was treated separately and an additional contribution was required for exemption. In the case of the Jews a desire for separateness, and not religious pacifism, provided the motive for seeking military exemption, while rulers were more interested in tapping an additional source of revenue than in providing relief for the tender consciences of their sectarians.

Sometimes exemption was placed on an individual basis, each Mennonite objector being required to pay a fine or hire a substitute directly. Only very occasionally was the Dutch model copied and some kind of alternative service demanded in lieu of bearing arms. Although the city of Elbing granted Mennonites full citizenship as early as 1585 and several other places followed suit in the course of the next two centuries, in most areas this was not so. Even in the tolerant and liberal Netherlands Mennonites, as we have seen, did not acquire civic equality until 1796. Elsewhere, the usual pattern for them was the same as for the Jews and Karaites: they lived as a semi-autonomous community, foreigners, as it were, in the land of their birth, without citizen's rights though enjoying the protection of the prince or other authority. For Mennonites desiring to live nonconformed to the norms of the surrounding world, this situation proved not unsatisfactory. Their religion forbade them to fight or to seek office. They were free to worship as they chose and to pursue their daily tasks in peace and quiet (unless the arrangement broke down or protection was withdrawn, which occurred only occasionally or to a limited degree). This, they felt, was as much as they had a right to expect in a world governed by sin.

In this chapter we shall survey the peace witness of German-speaking Mennonites until around the end of the eighteenth century: first in Switzerland, Alsace and Lorraine, south, central and north-west Germany, and Galicia, and then in Polish (later Prussian) Pomerania and surrounding areas, together with the offshoot in Russia at the conclusion of our period. Next, something will be said concerning the communitarian Hutterites from their emergence in Moravia around 1530 to their migration to Russia in 1770. Finally, we shall deal briefly with certain pietistic groups or individual Pietists whose pacifism was influenced to a greater or less extent by the Mennonites.

With few exceptions, the Anabaptists of Switzerland had been nonresistant from their institution in 1525. Throughout the period of the Münster troubles they had remained peaceable. In 1561 Heinrich Bullinger, Zwingli's successor in Zürich, had testified to their unconditional nonviolence. "They believe," he wrote, "that Christians should stand ready to suffer (rather than strike back). Christians do not resist violence and do not have recourse to law. . . . Christians do not kill. . . . They do not defend themselves, therefore they do not go to war and are not obedient to the government on this point." They rejected the sword because—and here Bullinger quoted their own words—"this . . . is clearly founded on the New Testament scriptures."

Yet the Swiss authorities took ruthless measures to stamp out the sect. They succeeded in doing so in towns like Zürich, Bern, or Basel, though it continued to live a semi-legal existence among the peasantry whose religious behavior was not usually under so strict a surveillance. By the early eighteenth century Mennonites (as we may now perhaps call them) were to be found only in the country districts of Bern and Basel. Many chose to emigrate either into neighboring Alsace or to the Palatinate or the Netherlands, or across the Atlantic to North America. This emigration, we may add, stemmed at least in part from economic motives (the Swiss mountaineers were a poor, if hardy, people) as well as from reasons of conscience. But fines and imprisonment, torture and the galleys, and the occasional death sentence had done their work. The vigor with which the cantonal authorities pursued these seemingly harmless sectaries is at first sight surprising when compared with the treatment afforded them by other Protestant princely rulers who showed a wider tolerance of, a more generous attitude to, religious dissidence than the democratic Switzers. Yet, although on the whole the freedom-loving Netherlands during the seventeenth and eighteenth centuries gave a fine example of an open society, we shall see in a later chapter that the coming of democracy did not necessarily mean an extended tolerance for dissident social behavior: a conclusion borne out in the wider context of the twentieth-century world. The Swiss cantons feared the consequences of allowing their Anabaptist Mennonites freedom to live according to their own ethical code. They believed it could undermine civil order and destroy the cohesion of their communities, should Anabaptist beliefs spread. They were unwilling to resolve the problem by granting the sect a collective *privilegium*, as some German princes were doing, and thus allowing it to exist as a privileged but separated community, for this was contrary to their egalitarian way of life.

Among the main charges leveled against the Swiss Brethren in justification of the harsh measures used was their steadfast refusal to bear arms. The authorities regarded this as a serious failure in citizens whose duty it was to defend their native canton against attack.

The Thirty Years' War was a particularly difficult period for the Swiss Brethren in this respect, since the general insecurity of the times caused the authorities to take extraordinary measures to guard the frontiers of their cantons. When, for instance, in 1635 in the canton of Zürich a citizen on appointment to the post of military ensign refused to serve on grounds of conscience and was soon after received into the local Anabaptist congregation, the authorities became alarmed. The man lived in a frontier area, and they feared that if others followed his example the security of the canton would be undermined. A wave of persecution, therefore, was unleashed against the Brethren. In 1639, in the canton of Bern, when general mobilization was proclaimed and able-bodied male citizens were ordered to serve in the civil guard, "the Anabaptists," it was officially reported, "collectively refuse to do this, and so they cannot be tolerated." In 1641 in Schleitheim all Mennonite objectors were rounded up and forcibly settled in the cantonal capital where they could be under close surveillance. Further examples could be cited of hardship suffered by Swiss Mennonites during this period on account of their conscientious objection to war.

Sometimes the authorities exploited the Brethren's known objections to bearing arms in an attempt to uncover persons with Anabaptist sympathies. At Emmental (canton of Bern), in 1667 and again in 1671 the town council, according to an ancient custom, made it obligatory for its male citizens to carry side-arms "in the churches, at the market, and on the streets" on pain of imprisonment. In this way, it was hoped, it would be easy to recognize an "Anabaptist." Bern canton indeed was one of the most unbending in its treatment of Mennonites; perhaps, however, this was only because its borders contained the largest Mennonite settlement, for the other cantons had shown that they, too, were sternly set against any relaxation in the severity with which the Brethren were treated. A final wave of persecution took place in Bern in the first decade of the eighteenth century. It culminated in 1711. In February of that year, however, the cantonal government, slightly relenting, issued an *Amnestie-Plakat* permitting the Brethren "free departure from our lands as well as the complete withdrawal of their goods" and the remission of any penalties incurred for previous offenses against the law. The authorities once again gave the failure of the Brethren to fulfil their civic duties as justification for this measure, which in fact amounted to the expulsion of the Mennonites from the land. Not only had the latter adopted a hostile attitude toward the *Obrigkeit*; they had also stubbornly refused either to swear an oath of allegiance, which was required of all citizens, or "to take up arms in case of emergency to defend and protect the dear fatherland." Those who left found a refuge in the Netherlands, whose States General, prompted by the influential Mennonite community in that country, had already intervened on behalf of the Swiss Brethren.

The emigration of 1711, though it depleted the ranks of Swiss Mennonitism still further, did not mean the end of the Anabaptist movement in Switzerland. Some members remained in the canton of Bern; there were also Mennonites in the prince-bishopric of Basel, who moved from Bern around this time hoping to find a more hospitable climate there than in their native canton. Although the bishop's subjects became indignant at the newcomers' unwillingness to share the burden of military defense with them and succeeded in 1730 in pressuring their ruler into issuing an edict of expulsion against the Brethren, the bishop was loath to lose such hardworking, frugal, and peaceable subjects and did his best to retain some of them in his domain. Meanwhile, the position of the Brethren remaining in Bern canton began to ease. True, in 1737 the government proposed to send objectors to service in the militia to work in the silver mines instead, and as late as 1780 it threatened to exile all Mennonites on account of their pacifism. But in neither case were the suggestions implemented. In 1745 the government had ordered Mennonite objectors to pay a fine of twenty to thirty thalers for exemption, and it was this pattern which remained in effect into the nineteenth century.

A solution of this kind, as we know, was satisfactory to the Mennonite conscience. Those Bernese Anabaptists who sought refuge across the frontier in Alsace and Lorraine or in the tiny principality of Montbéliard belonging to the rulers of Württemberg, likewise paid fines in lieu of direct military service. In Alsace, which Louis XIV had attached to France, the settlers were required to contribute annually the sum of forty-six French *livres* per person liable for militia duties. In 1696 the Amish, who had broken away three years earlier from the main body of Swiss Brethren under Jakob Amman, a supporter of the strict application of "avoidance (*Meidung*)" to excommunicated members, were included in this arrangement only after attempts had been made in vain to force them to bear arms. But these privileges aroused the envy of neighbors, whose complaints finally led Louis XIV in 1712 to issue an order of expulsion. Although many Mennonites and Amish emigrated as a result, some stayed and were tolerated on account of the economic advantage obtained by their rulers from their settlements. Among those who remained were families who retained their Bernese citizenship. The Bern government was willing to issue them certificates of citizenship, which automatically gave exemption from military service in their adopted country; in exchange for these certificates, however, Bern required the payment of a special military tax. Again, the Mennonites do not appear to have entertained any scruples concerning payment: the practice continued into the twentieth century, apparently without protest from the church leaders.

The Anabaptists of south Germany, like their Swiss brethren with whom they shared a common set of beliefs, had clung to nonresistance despite attempts to make them bear arms. Participation in war, they declared repeatedly, was a sin, even when against the Turks. In 1568, at a conference they held at Strasbourg attended by church leaders, the question of the watch, which at this date presented a problem even for rural communities, came up for discussion. It was decreed that a brother, if called upon for this service, must either find a substitute or, if this were impossible, appear at the appointed place without a weapon. They were also ready to pay war taxes.

From the mid-seventeenth century the main area of settlement of the south German Mennonite brotherhood which had emerged out of sixteenth-century Anabaptism lay in the Palatinate. The original small community there was reinforced, after the fearsome devastation of the

Thirty Years' War and the later destruction wrought by Louis XIV's armies in the 1670's and 1680's, by Mennonite and Amish immigrants from Switzerland and Alsace as well as by Hutterites from Moravia.

In the several statelets into which the Palatinate fragmented, the fining of Mennonite objectors to watching and to mustering with the local militia soon became standard practice. The sum—often it was the parents of potential militiamen who paid—was usually small, at least at first, but it had a tendency to rise. For instance, in the Electorate, after the government had reaffirmed the existence of Mennonite scruples concerning militia service in its *privilegium* (Concession) of 1664 without specifically giving exemption, "a special annual tax was imposed toward the cost of maintaining the militia, at first three gulden per family, later six and finally twelve gulden. The Mennonites protested this tax, at times on the grounds of poverty, at other times on grounds of conscience [*gewissenshalber*] since they did not want to contribute toward war in any respect." The last consideration was indeed unusual: Mennonites, as we have seen, usually felt no compunction in paying for exemption, reasoning that responsibility for use of the funds handed over lay exclusively with Caesar. They did have qualms, of course, over hiring a substitute but were forced to do it on occasion. Duke Christian IV of Zweibrücken (in the Palatinate), having granted his Mennonites civil equality in 1759, proceeded the next year to demand of all Mennonites of military age, who had been collectively exempted until then by a lump sum contributed by their community, that they find substitutes to take their place during the six years they were liable for service in the ducal militia. The annual cost of a substitute amounted at that time to twelve gulden, and the law allowed every citizen the option of serving by substitute, even if he had no conscientious objection to personal service. Though the Mennonites were not happy about this requirement, they submitted. In the next century the extension of civil rights to the Mennonites of Europe was to create even more acute dilemmas of conscience, for, along with the granting of equality in rights came the demand to abolish old privileges and to enforce equality of obligation on groups like the Mennonites who had been given till then a special position before the law. Apart from the case of Zweibrücken, however, the old method of exemption by payment of a fine continued in force here throughout the eighteenth century, although in some parts of the Palatinate it fell into desuetude around mid-century.

When we move north of the Palatinate, we shift into an area which had once been the center of Melchiorite and, subsequently, Munsterite influence: Westphalia, the lower German Rhineland, East Friesland,

and Schleswig-Holstein. This was an area, too, where the Anabaptist communities remained in close contact with their brethren in the Netherlands; indeed, in some places their founding members had actually come as refugees from the Netherlands. It was in northern and north-west Germany that Menno and many of his closest associates like Dirk Philips were active for many years in spreading and consolidating the faith at a time when their native Netherlands proved unsafe for them. As a result, here too, as in the case of the Dutch Anabaptists, the peaceable, Mennonite stand in the movement finally won the field against the violent trends that had prevailed earlier. Mennonite nonresistance, almost certainly, was accepted by the third quarter of the sixteenth century throughout northern Germany.

The pattern of the Mennonites' conscientious objection in this area mirrors for the most part that of the southern brethren. The earliest phase was usually marked by tacit allowance of such Mennonite peculiarities as their refusal of personal military service. In this period, though, the sect was barely tolerated, living continuously with the possibility of expulsion and permitted to remain only because of its obscurity or its members' economic usefulness to the rulers. Throughout the sixteenth, and well into the seventeenth, centuries Mennonites were suspected of nurturing subversive and violent designs under cover of a meek exterior. Their defenselessness, it was widely thought, concealed their intent to set up a New Jerusalem once again by means of bloody revolution. Eventually, however, old prejudices gave way before the steady impact of reality. It was seen that Mennonites were indeed a harmless people, as they had always said they were, and that the security of the state would in no wise be endangered if they were indulged in the free exercise of conscience even where this ran counter to the demands normally made by the state on its citizens. Henceforward, only occasional outbursts of fanaticism or envy marred the toleration which the Mennonites enjoyed in the lands where they had settled.

In Westphalia and the lower German Rhineland military exemption was obtained by payment of a fee. At Rheydt, a small town in the duchy of Jülich, this privilege led to tragedy in 1694. The Mennonites' success as merchants and weavers had aroused the jealousy of their fellow townsmen, who were Calvinists, and resentment on this score was augmented by the Mennonites' exemption from guard-duty at the local castle (on payment of a fine which did not cause them much hardship): this meant an extra turn of duty to be performed by non-Mennonites. Smoldering anger found outlet finally in a scheme for revenge: on trumped-up charges of arson, the whole Mennonite community was rounded up and, after severe ill-treatment and the confiscation of their goods and chattels, they were expelled from the town.

The incident remains an exception: usually the local prince protected his Mennonites from popular resentment of this kind. In the county of East Friesland, for example, Count Rudolf Christian had issued a *privilegium* for the Mennonites in 1626. It contained no specific mention of exemption from military duties but this was granted by his successor, Enno Ludwig, in 1658 and confirmed in 1738 by Count Carl Edzard. No monetary equivalent was required in lieu of bearing arms in person. When the county came into the possession of Frederick II of Prussia in 1745, Frederick likewise confirmed the Mennonites' military exemption according to the terms laid down in 1658. The only trouble experienced at any time by the Mennonites of this area in connection with military service related to the feudal obligation of providing one or two armed men attaching to certain pieces of land which had come into Mennonite possession. In this case they were required to pay commutation money, although in 1690 the Mennonite community had attempted unsuccessfully to persuade the count that the charter of 1658 freed them also from this obligation.

From the beginning of the seventeenth century Hamburg, along with neighboring Altona, formed one of the most important Mennonite centers in the north. The congregation was actually situated not in the Hanseatic city but in Altona, which belonged to Schleswig-Holstein, a dependency of the Danish crown since 1640. Here the Mennonites' freedom of worship had been guaranteed by law, the first *privilegium* to this effect being issued in 1601. This *liberum exercitium religionis* was presumed to include freedom from military service—on payment, of course, of the customary fine. When in 1686 the city of Hamburg came under siege by King Christian V of Denmark, Mennonites who lived within its walls were required to stand watch for fire-bombs and help to extinguish those which fell inside its precincts. This practice was obviously borrowed from the example of the Netherlands: it was an emergency measure which does not appear to have been repeated. During the war between Denmark and Sweden in 1712-1713 we find Mennonites lamenting the high contributions which they were required to make to the royal treasury. The Hamburg-Altona congregation cleaved strictly to nonresistance, disfellowshipping any who strayed from its principles (as indeed did all other German congregations up into the nineteenth century). A seafaring community like the Mennonite communities of Holland, it experienced difficulty at times in dealing with members who served as crew in armed vessels or who owned ships carrying guns for protection: "shippers and whalers were required to sell their boats rather than arm them in warlike times." Toward the end of the eighteenth century, when Dutch Mennonites became increasingly lax in regard to nonresistance, the congregation at Hamburg-Altona which, in common with the whole north German movement, still looked to the Netherlands as the center of Mennonitism, opposed this trend. In 1787, alarmed by the bellicose behavior of *Doopsgezinden* patriots like van der Kemp, it took the step of addressing a letter of warning to the Dutch Zonists against participation in military activities. The letter referred to the sound nonresistant teaching of their forefathers and deplored any deviations from it now.

Altona was not the only Mennonite settlement of importance in the Schleswig-Holstein area. At Friedrichstadt and at Glückstadt on the Elbe small communities came into existence too. Mennonites in Friedrichstadt, which had been founded in 1619 by Dutch Remonstrants, as well as in adjacent districts received a *privilegium* in 1623. In addition to freedom of worship and exemption from public office and judicial oaths, the charter granted members of the sect the right to make "a suitable monetary payment (*eine ziemliche Darlage*)" in lieu of bearing arms in the watch and for defense, "because," as the document states, "they had a conscientious scruple concerning the use of resistance and weapons (*weil sie sich darüber ein Gewissen machten, Wehr und Waffen zu gebrauchen*)." A similar document was issued in 1631 on behalf of the congregation at Glückstadt, a town which had been founded by King Christian IV of Denmark in 1616 as a commercial rival to nearby Hamburg. Members were exempted from military service on condition they paid "a fitting annual contribution when the need requires such." The tax was to be graduated according to the means of each member liable.

Austrian Galicia formed the site of the last collective settlement of Mennonites to be made in Central Europe, the settlers coming from various parts of western Germany. The move was sponsored by Emperor Joseph II who, though by no means a German chauvinist in the modern meaning of the term, looked with favor on the arrival of stout German *Bauern* in his new dominion only recently seized from Poland. Moreover, he was sufficiently enlightened to wish to safeguard their pacifist scruples, yet enough of a despot to do this by means of an autocratic grant of privilege. The newcomers settled around Lwów (Lviv), the first party coming in 1784. Eventually some eighty families containing about four hundred persons made their home in this area. In 1789 the provincial administration issued a *privilegium* which, *inter alia*, guaranteed the Mennonite settlers, as well as their descendants who remained members of the sect, freedom from military service on payment of the modest sum of one gulden per family. To this guarantee, however, there was added a significant rider: Mennonites were forbidden to proselytize or to accept new members from other churches. Austria was still a staunchly Catholic country, despite the enlightened views of its ruler: religious toleration had been imposed from above and did not yet have deep roots in the community as a whole.

The most cohesive and numerically the largest single Mennonite community was the "West Prussian," i.e., it consisted of Mennonites who settled in "Royal Prussia," which belonged until 1772 to the Polish crown, and in adjacent Polish territory. These settlements were almost entirely of Dutch and Flemish origin and stretched from Danzig (Gdańsk) and the swampy Vistula delta in the north, southward along both banks of the Vistula as far as Thorn (Toruń)—and, in the later eighteenth century even up as far as Modlin near Warsaw. The Prussian Mennonites were predominantly rural people and long retained their rural otherworldliness: the only cities where Mennonites settled were Danzig and Elbing (Elbląg). And in Danzig they were at first admitted only to the suburb of Schottland owned by the bishop of Kujawy, since the Lutheran city fathers had feared the presence in their midst of persons they considered to be dangerous sectaries.

Anabaptists had begun to arrive from the Netherlands in the early 1530's. "Whether they were . . . of the revolutionary type or the evangelical type is difficult to determine. The actual designation 'Mennonite' first appears in 1572" (G. H. Williams). As in the case of Netherlands Anabaptism, the first four decades of the movement form an obscure chapter in its history. Records are almost nonexistent; unsolved problems are numerous. All we can say with any degree of certainty is that by the end of this period at any rate—and probably long before—the Prussian Mennonites had become firmly nonresistant. During Menno's lifetime these Anabaptist communities had become part of the religious movement which looked to him for leadership and, after his death, adopted his name. For roughly a decade before his death in 1668, Menno's close associate Dirk Philips led the church at Danzig. In this period, and indeed for over two centuries to come, the Prussian Mennonites remained closely linked with the Mennonites of their Dutch homeland. Their catechisms and confessions, in which they set forth their beliefs and standards of behavior in respect to nonresistance as well as to the other aspects of the faith, reflected the Dutch model.

In the cities of Danzig and Elbing, both of which enjoyed under

Polish rule a considerable measure of autonomy (especially Danzig), the Mennonites' military obligation came to be regulated by decrees issued by their respective town councils. In the rural communities this was governed either by general privileges granted by the Polish king or by the practice of royal or seigniorial officials. For the earliest period, however, when the sources are silent on the subject, we can only assume, in the absence of any documentary evidence to the contrary, that the Mennonites' scruples in regard to bearing arms were respected.

The city of Danzig provides the first concrete evidence of Mennonite conscientious objection. (At least I have not found reference to it at an earlier date.) In July 1571, when the Polish government organized defensive measures to repel a threatened Danish attack on the neighboring Kashub town of Puck, and sought to obtain reinforcements from Danzig for this purpose, the city council reported: "A number of the suburban inhabitants who declared themselves Anabaptists refused to take part in the expedition to Puck, declaring that they were Christians and not warlike people and did not possess arms, since it had been written that if slapped on one cheek, one should offer the other." It appears that the "Anabaptists" did not incur any penalty for this refusal; probably they secured exemption by means of a monetary payment, though this is not mentioned in the source (as given by Stanisław Kot).

H. G. Mannhardt, in his history of the Danzig congregation, writes: "The refusal to bear arms in Polish times did not cause any particular hardships for the Mennonites in Danzig." By the beginning of the seventeenth century, at any rate, the payment of a fine had become the recognized method of exempting Mennonites from the armed watch or other military duties. We find this stated explicitly in a decree of the city council dated 3 April 1613. The money was to be paid monthly, "and from it soldiers can be hired." Nine years later the decree was revised somewhat. If Mennonites were unwilling either to attend musters in person or to send a suitable substitute ("which, however, such persons have scruples against doing"), they should pay on the occasion of each mustering one gulden if they were well-to-do, half a gulden if they belonged to the less affluent. On receiving each Mennonite's fine, the commander of the watch should put "an able man" in his place. In time of war Mennonite objectors were to pay, monthly, a sum sufficient to maintain a properly equipped substitute. However, in 1656 during Poland's time of troubles known in Polish historiography as the "Flood," when enemy armies overwhelmed the country from all sides, Mennonites were required to support two substitutes instead of one, and this practice continued even after the war was over. Therefore, in 1688 the congregation submitted a petition to the town council referring to the decree of 1624 and requesting that its provisions be observed now that the special war emergency of mid-century had long since passed. But the council proved unwilling to do this. In 1733, on the outbreak of the so-called War of Polish Succession, a revised "watch-ordinance" was drawn up by the city council. "The Mennonites should each supply two doughty (*wehrhafte*) men, who are neither citizens nor inhabitants (as these are liable to be called up in any case)." The following year, while the city was under siege, Mennonites were also required to undertake first-aid and fire-extinguishing duties, "since," as a report stated, "they perform no military service"; they were to earn the praise of the authorities for the efficiency with which they carried out these functions. In 1749 King August III ordered Danzig Mennonites to pay a yearly sum as "protection money (*Schirmgeld*)"; the imposition formed part of the king's scheme of extracting more revenue from the city than he had been receiving hitherto. Although this collective tax was not imposed, even in part, in exchange for military exemption (as writers like Wilhelm Mannhardt have stated), peacetime exemption seems to have resulted from it in practice, nevertheless.

In January 1772, on the eve of the first partition of Poland, which was to leave the city of Danzig, as it were, a Polish island surrounded by Prussian territory, Hans van Steen, a leading Danzig minister, wrote to a friend in Utrecht: "In peacetime we are free from bearing arms, but in wartime and when the burghers must man the walls, our friends [i.e., the Mennonites] must pay for a replacement to the captain of the watch."

Elbing eventually proved more liberal than Danzig in its treatment of its Mennonites. But at the beginning, after they commenced to settle there from around 1550 onward, Elbing had made repeated attempts to expel them. The edicts of banishment, however, were never fully carried out, and from the mid-1580's some Mennonites, even, began to acquire burgher status (this was not granted in Danzig until 1800). The rest were silently tolerated. In 1615 King Zygmunt III (Vasa) issued a decree which, though it did not explicitly mention the Elbing Mennonites' military exemption, referred to their being freed from "all civic burdens," which we may presume included *inter alia* such things as bearing arms or judicial oath-taking. For such toleration, of course, a price had had to be paid: in this case it took the form of an all-inclusive *Schutzgeld* imposed as a collective obligation of the whole congregation. In Lutheran Elbing, restrictions on Mennonite proselytization were not upheld. When in 1700 a former Lutheran who had converted to Mennonitism was cited before the town council for a breach of the law, the magistrates dismissed the case. "The Mennonites," they ruled, "have freedom of religion and ours is not the established one (*Mennonitae habent tolerantiam religionis et nostra non est predominans*)." By implication, therefore, not merely birthright Mennonites but also those who joined from another faith might enjoy the right to military exemption in the city militia.

In the eighteenth century, after the city was pledged to Prussia and came under its administration, the position remained unchanged; Polish law continued in force. But Prussian recruiting officers were soon busy in the area, and occasionally the Mennonites had trouble with them. The practice began under the rule of the military-minded Frederick William I who, however, upon receiving a petition from the Mennonite congregation agreed to release Mennonites whom his officers had seized. Under his son the recruiters were equally busy; in 1746 young Mennonites were once more threatened with enrolment in the Prussian army. Again the congregation decided to appeal to the monarch directly. Designating themselves as "all most truly obedient Mennonites from the Elbing area (*sämmtliche treugehorsamsten Mennoniten aus dem Elbinger Territorio*)," they pointed out to Frederick II that since the time their forefathers had left the Netherlands two centuries earlier to settle in the Polish Commonwealth, they had enjoyed full freedom of religion, including liberty to conduct themselves as "weaponless and nonresistant Christians." And they followed up this petition by another, arranging that a deputation should hand it personally to the king in Potsdam. "We cannot express in words," they said, "into what anxiety we are thrown by this order, for according to the principles of our religion we are not permitted to carry weapons and serve in war. Our sons and servants would thus much rather go into another land than allow their conscience to be shackled." The intervention met with success, the king ordering his recruiting agents to leave the Mennonites in peace. "I will have these people fully protected in their privileges, and especially in their freedom of religion," he wrote.

Protection of the Mennonites and the granting of privileges like military exemption did not ordinarily proceed from any special sympathy toward the sect on the part of their rulers, whether these were the king, a local noble landowner, or a city council. They were not usually due, either, to an abstract belief in religious toleration. Such a belief may indeed have played a role in the case of a monarch like Frederick II: religious toleration still meant something, too, to many Polish *szlachta* despite the rising intolerance of the seventeenth and eighteenth centuries, which found vent in increased ill-treatment of the country's religious "dissidents" and a gradual circumscribing of the freedom they had enjoyed hitherto. But it could scarcely have been present, for instance, in the case of such protectors of the Mennonites as the Roman Catholic bishops of Kujawy or the Vasa kings of Poland. What these sought from toleration of the Mennonites was economic advantage. For the sake of these advantages they were prepared to resist demands from religious bigots to harry, or even expel the Mennonites altogether. And material profit certainly accrued to the areas where the Mennonites settled. The draining of the marshy lands (*Werdern*) at the mouth and along the lower reaches of the Vistula was largely the work of Mennonite hands. Elsewhere, their high standards of farming and their thrift and diligence served as a model of how the soil should be cultivated. Mennonites displayed the same virtues as they did in farming when they earned a livelihood by trade, commerce, or artisanry. Knowing that these people would seek a home elsewhere if they were deprived of their freedom to worship in their own way or were forced to serve with weapons against their best convictions, the authorities were readily convinced of the desirability of acceding to the Mennonites' wishes and granting them the guarantees they sought, or at least of silently assenting to their special status in certain respects. After all, the *ancien régime* in Eastern Europe was built upon privilege of one sort or another. There was really nothing unusual in those which were now given to the Mennonites. It had long ago become clear that these sectaries were in no way subversive, and their almost excessively high moral standards gave assurance that their opinions would not easily spread beyond the confines of the existing congregations. Besides, their principle of nonconformity to the world provided additional security against the extension of the sect and, at least in Polish-speaking rural districts, continued use of a Germanic language erected an effective natural barrier against proselytization of non-Mennonites (which in any case was forbidden by law).

These considerations were exemplified most clearly, perhaps, in the treatment of the rural Mennonite congregations situated between the Vistula and the Nogat rivers (the so-called Marienburg *Werdern*). Here the Mennonites never received from the Polish authorities an explicit guarantee of exemption from military service. Wilhelm Mannhardt speaks of "silent toleration" of their pacifist scruples as well as of their other peculiarities of behavior. There seems to have existed a kind of unwritten agreement in the matter between the Mennonites and the authorities. It was generally understood that such privileges were embodied in the rental contracts (*Pachtverträge*) which the original Mennonite settlers had received, even though freedom from having soldiers quartered on their homesteads was the only military exemption actually mentioned. In wartime they undoubtedly submitted without grumbling to the special imposts levied by the Estates of Royal Prussia for the carrying on of war.

On at least five occasions during the seventeenth century Polish monarchs issued charters confirming the Mennonites' "ancient immunities, liberties, and customs": in 1642 Władysław IV (Vasa); in 1650 and again in 1660 his brother Jan Kazimierz; in 1694 Jan III (Sobieski); and in 1697 the Saxon August II upon his succession to the Polish throne. Sometimes such confirmation was sought by the Mennonites themselves, if they feared encroachment by subordinate officials on their freedom or sensed a mounting popular demand to curtail their liberties or suppress them altogether. The granting in 1642 of the first in this series of charters was apparently eased by the presentation of a gift of money to the king. The series continued in the eighteenth century: further solemn confirmations of Mennonite privileges occurred in 1732 at the end of August II's reign and in 1736 under his son August III, and finally in 1764 at the outset of the reign of the last Polish king, Stanisław August (Poniatowski). In none of these documents was exemption from military service specifically mentioned: in all of them we may assume that its inclusion was understood by both parties. As W. Mannhardt has pointed out, there are no known cases of Mennonites in this area being forced to do military service (apart from a few instances of kidnapping of young men by Prussian recruiters in the eighteenth century). Hans van Steen, from whom I have quoted above, testified in 1768 to the advantageous situation of the Mennonites of the Marienburg district in regard to military service in comparison with that of his own Danzig congregation.

Farther south, the Vistula Mennonites around Świecie, Chełmno, and Grudziądz, who lived either on the estates of the bishop of Kujawy or on those owned by Polish lay nobles, enjoyed similar protection from their lords. It was only in 1750 that King August III officially extended the privileges of the Marienburg Mennonites to these communities and indeed all others within his province of Royal Prussia.

In 1772 almost all the Mennonites of Poland fell within the area seized by Frederick II of Prussia; only those in Danzig and the small communities farthest up the Vistula remained for the time being under Polish rule. Since the 1530's there had also been Anabaptists of Netherlands origin in East Prussia, which had been ruled by the Hohenzollerns since the last Grand Master of the Teutonic Order, Albrecht of

Hohenzollern, converted it into a secular state in 1525. Repeated attempts were made to have these sectaries expelled; yet despite the backing of the Lutheran clergy such efforts proved abortive, for some few always succeeded in remaining. Exactly how they solved the question of military service is not clear; presumably, if they were called upon they were able to buy themselves out as their brethren did in other lands.

In 1710 Frederick I invited the persecuted Bernese Mennonites to settle within his kingdom, offering them complete religious freedom, including freedom from military service, as an inducement. We have seen that in 1711 these Switzers chose Holland as their first place of refuge, but some went on from there to Pennsylvania and a few elected to go to East Prussia. Other Mennonite settlers were enticed later from Polish Prussia by the lure of rental contracts and general conditions of settlement as attractive as those the Swiss had received. There was much empty land in the area around Tilsit, and it was thither that the king directed the newcomers. In 1713 an "Accord" was drawn up, guaranteeing the Mennonites the free exercise of their religion as well as "freedom from enrolment and quartering, both in regard to themselves and to their children and servants, none of whom could be forced to military service."

The Tilsit settlement, however, did not last long. Frederick I had died in 1713 and his successor, Frederick William I, whose overriding passion was his army, although he did not at first abrogate his father's arrangement with the Mennonites, was not favorably disposed towards a group who refused to become soldiers. "I want to have nothing to do with the vermin," he exclaimed. It might be fine for a landowner to have such people on his estates, "but a King in Prussia must . . . have . . . a great, strong, and formidable army." For such purposes Mennonites were useless. "*Ergo* they shall not be tolerated in my lands." In the autumn of 1723 his recruiting officers, apparently on their own initiative, seized upon a number of able-bodied Mennonites and hauled them off to make soldiers of them, brutally ill-treating them in the effort to force their acquiescence; the king expressed no disapproval when the affair came to his notice early in the following year. Moreover, although he ordered the men to be released after their congregation had cited the military exemption granted them in 1713, he now decided to take action against the whole Mennonite community in the Tilsit area. They were evicted from their farms and all six hundred "souls" were forced to migrate elsewhere, despite the remonstrations of the local authorities who testified to the excellence of Mennonite husbandry and despite efforts by the Mennonites themselves to placate the monarch by offering to pay a yearly sum of money into the *Rekrutenkasse* in lieu of doing military service in person. This proposal in fact might have proved acceptable in the end, but it turned out that the Tilsit community did not possess sufficient resources to provide the amount demanded. "I will not have a crowd of rogues (*Schelm-Nation*), who won't be soldiers," was the king's final comment on the affair.

Some of those expelled returned, however, not long afterward, settling at Dannenberg. But in 1732 Frederick William II issued yet another edict expelling all Mennonites from East Prussia, though his officials prevailed upon him to make an exception in the case of the prosperous Königsberg congregation, which had been established in 1722. Thus it appears that the king knew very well how to curb his dislike of Mennonite pacifists when his economic interests—or should we say the economic interests of the state?—were at stake. At Crefeld, a Hohenzollern possession in the Rhineland, for instance, he gave the Mennonites "a *privilegium* permitting the practice of nonresistance for a fee, and in 1738 he even paid them a rather cordial visit." Royal patronage should be ascribed in this case to the fact that Crefeld Mennonites formed the mainstay of the rising silk industry in that city. His severity toward the Mennonites around Tilsit and at Dannenberg might well have been prompted by his nervousness at finding this frontier district settled with "defenseless" nonresistants. Although the Poles and Lithuanians just across the border did not constitute a great menace to the military might of Prussia, the king could still have felt this to be a sensitive spot in his defenses.

In 1740 the death of King Frederick William II brought his son Frederick II to the throne. Frederick II, though certainly bent on the aggrandizement of the Prussian state, was less crudely militaristic than his father. And the need to find suitable colonists for the extensive unpopulated areas of his eastern kingdom continued to be pressing. In the year of his succession he issued a decree inviting the Mennonites to come once more and settle in his East Prussian lands. Although not mentioned explicitly, freedom from enrolment as soldiers in the state militia system, which had been revised in 1726, formed one of the attractions offered. Prussian agents publicized the invitation in the Hague, hoping to arouse interest among the *Doopsgezinden*. Before Frederick II acquired the extensive Mennonite communities of former Royal Prussia (henceforward we may refer to this area as *Westpreussen*, West Prussia) as a result of the Polish partition of 1772, he had shown, therefore, that he supported continuance of the privileged situation of the Mennonites. Yet after 1772 he was to introduce certain innovations in respect to military service, which marked a deterioration of the West Prussian Mennonites' position.

On taking over the former Polish territories in October 1772, the king confirmed the Mennonites' privileges in general terms. "Concerning the military enrolment of themselves and their children" he declared, they might rest assured that their freedom would be respected —but at the same time they would now be required to make an annual monetary contribution to the state in exchange for the privilege. This indeed represented something new for the Mennonites of the Vistula area for, as shown above, they had previously received their military exemption without paying the usual price (presumably their economic contribution was considered by their royal and noble protectors to be a sufficient reward). No wonder, then, that the congregations remained apprehensive as to their future, suspecting that the new administration was in fact planning to conscript their young men: these anxieties were increased by an official survey of the newly gained lands and their population. They felt that only a solemn and unambiguous declaration by the new ruler of their freedom from military service (*Wehrfreiheit*), along with a confirmation of their other liberties, could put their minds finally at rest. The government in reply told them that this could readily be granted provided that it did not entail any diminution of the military strength of the land. For the Prussian state, the issue was complicated by the fact that its system of military obligation depended on ownership of land. Unless some satisfactory alternative were devised, land held by Mennonites would signify just such a decrease in its military potential. Their community numbered over 12,000 at that date. This consideration lay behind a decree of 1774 which henceforward made it impossible for Mennonites to acquire new holdings without special permission from the government, unless they were prepared to establish "a family capable of doing military service (*eine dienstfähige Familie*)" on each of them.

However, in June of this same year the government came up with a solution of the general problem which they hoped would satisfy both the Mennonites and the demands of military efficiency. In exchange for a collective guarantee of military exemption for themselves and their descendants, the Mennonites of West and East Prussia would be required to contribute the substantial sum of 5,000 thalers annually (raised to 5,600 in 1794 after the incorporation of Danzig, with its Mennonite community, into Prussia). The money would go toward the upkeep of the military school at Culm (Chełmno). The guarantee, however, did not include any who joined the sect subsequently to the promulgation of the measure. The Mennonites accepted this proposal willingly and at once set about collecting the first sum which was already due, dividing up the amount to be contributed according to the size and wealth of each congregation. The money having been gathered, two members were deputed to take it to the president of the Marienwerder treasury board, who greeted them upon arrival with the following words: "That's good children, now you'll want to get an assurance from the king." "Yes," they replied, "that is our most ardent wish." And indeed, though only after long bureaucratic delays, a solemn *Gnadenprivilegium* was issued to them in March 1780. Among its provisions was a guarantee of exemption from military service for the community "forever," provided only that its members remained loyal subjects of the Prussian king.

The West Prussian Mennonites welcomed the *Gnadenprivilegium*: it at last put to rest their fears that their military exemption might be annulled. Yet their troubles were not ended. Now, however, it was the land question rather than the question of military service which aroused anxiety in their minds, although the two problems were not unrelated. Under Frederick II Mennonites usually succeeded without too much difficulty in obtaining a permit to purchase non-Mennonite land. But a change came under his successor, Frederick William II (1786-1797), despite the fact that the new king, while still crown prince, had shown his friendly sentiments toward the Mennonites. Prussian officials had become increasingly nervous at the impact on military preparedness of an extension of Mennonite settlement; therefore they urged the new monarch to take effective measures to curb the acquisition by Mennonites of fresh land. And in fact, in edicts of April 1787 and July 1789, Frederick William II, while confirming his uncle's *Gnadenprivilegium*, at the same time reiterated his intention of restricting land purchases by members of the sect since these led to a decline in the manpower available to the army. In addition, the edict of 1789 pointed out that military exemption covered only descendants of the 1772 Mennonite community in the male line and from non-mixed marriages. True, conversion to Mennonitism was not forbidden *per se* as it had been in Polish times when the only course open to a potential convert was to leave the country, join Mennonites abroad, and then return to his homeland as a Mennonite immigrant. Prussia by this date enjoyed far-going religious toleration. But Mennonite converts could escape call-up now only by paying a substitute: an option, as we know, that was usually open in those days to any who wished to avail themselves of it.

The land question indeed was of vital importance to the West Prussian Mennonites on account of their high birthrate. Mennonite farmers sought to buy new holdings in order to set up younger sons on their own. Land hunger, therefore, and not primarily religious persecution or discrimination on account of their nonresistance, explains the large-scale emigration to Russia of Mennonites from this area, which, beginning in 1788, reached a climax in the early decades of the next century. "The Mennonites who remained behind in Prussia," writes William I. Schreiber in his booklet on *The Fate of the Prussian Mennonites* (Göttingen, 1955), "seem, generally speaking, to have been prosperous farmers and townspeople." The emigrants settled in Ukraine, in the sparsely populated lands of so-called "New Russia," where the Tsarina Catherine II since 1763 had promised perpetual exemption from military service, along with other privileges, to any suitable colonists willing to come. Military exemption for "all time" was guaranteed to the Mennonite settlers, too, prior to their departure from West Prussia, and this was confirmed again by a general *privilegium* granted by Tsar Paul in 1800.

The fate of these "Russian" Mennonites will be dealt with in a subsequent chapter. In their new land the immigrants from West Prussia found already settled another, and much smaller, group which derived, as they did themselves, from sixteenth-century Anabaptism. These were the Hutterites. We must return, therefore, to the early 1530's and discuss the character of their nonresistant witness during the subsequent two and a half centuries.

In chapter 2 we learned of the schism which took place in Moravian Anabaptism in 1527-1528 between the "swordsmen (*Schwertler*)" and the nonresistant "staffmen (*Stäbler*)." Whereas the non-pacifists dwindled away within a decade, the nonresistants survived the internal controversies and exterior pressures of this period. In 1533 the majority of them reorganized on a firm communitarian basis under the leadership of an émigré from the Tirol, Jakob Hutter, a simple hatter by trade. Expelled from Moravia in 1535 on account of the Münster troubles, the Hutterite Brethren, as they now called themselves, were permitted to return shortly afterward, the Moravian nobility who had harbored them being unwilling to lose permanently such model tenants as the Hutterites proved to be. In 1536, however, the Brethren lost their leader Hutter, who was arrested and executed while visiting his native Tirol. J. K. Zeman, in a recent study entitled *The Anabaptists and the Czech Brethren in Moravia 1526-1628* (The Hague, 1969), has stressed the diversity of Moravian Anabaptism right up to the final expulsion in the 1620's, and he has identified as many as ten separate groups. "Moravian Anabaptism," he writes, "remained pluralistic from the beginning until the end." After the *Schwertler* had disappeared,

234

all these sub-sects adopted nonresistance, although there was divergence in respect to the strictness with which the principle of nonresistance was applied. The Pilgramites (i.e., followers of Pilgram Marbeck; see chapter 3) allowed members to hold minor office; other groups disfellowshipped all who accepted an administrative post even if it were not connected with the sword. The Hutterites formed the "most numerous section" in the movement; they also constituted its most rigorously nonresistant branch. Whereas the noncommunitarian Anabaptists lived mainly in German-speaking areas, the Hutterites founded their communities (*Brüderhöfe*) almost exclusively in Czech districts, which effectively isolated them from their environment.

The second half of the sixteenth century marked a golden age in the history of the Hutterite Brethren. Secure in the protection of powerful Moravian magnates and bound together by a strong sense of community, they prospered economically. They did not cease to be essentially a body of farmers and artisans. Yet their educational level—and even their cultural achievement—was no mean one, especially if we compare it with the level reached by the indigenous rural population. At its height the fellowship numbered between 20,000 and 30,000 members, scattered among some 100 *Brüderhöfe*. From 1546 on, a few communities came into existence in northern Hungary (i.e., Slovakia). Indeed, at this period the Hutterite brotherhood did not yet constitute the closed sect it was eventually to become, but was filled with missionary zeal to carry its message to other parts of central Europe. If "the whole world were like us," Jakob Hutter had said, "then would all war and injustice come to an end."

What distinguished the Hutterites from other Anabaptists was of course their religious communism, the belief that holding all things common was no mere counsel of perfection but an essential article of the Christian faith. Those who failed to do this acted falsely; true Christians should not hold fellowship with them. For the rest, Hutterites modelled their faith very largely on the pattern of evangelical Anabaptism, from which indeed they had derived their origin. They practiced adult baptism on confession of faith. They rejected oaths, courts of law, and the magistracy, while recognizing the office of the sword as an institution ordained by God which, although outside the perfection of Christ, remained essential, because of man's sinful nature, for the continued existence of the world. But between the "world" and the "kingdom of God" an unbridgeable gulf yawned. Hutterites shared, too, the evangelical Anabaptists' belief in the redemptive value of suffering, regarding suffering as the inevitable lot of true Christians on earth. Like their master, they must be "as a lamb

235

led to the slaughtering-block" (in the words of the Hutterite leader Peter Walbot, written *ca.* 1577). Instead of seeking revenge for injuries done them, Christians must ever exemplify outgoing love.

Hutterites liked to think of themselves as "soldiers of Christ" who had discarded "all outer and iron weapons" and armed themselves only "with spiritual ones." In their own community as with the Mennonites, the spiritual sword alone—that is, the ban—could be used to enforce discipline; in the face of attack from without, they were protected solely by the armor of truth. As Hutter wrote in 1535 before going into exile:

> Ere we would knowingly do injustice to anybody for a penny's worth, we would rather suffer to be deprived of a hundred florins, and to be wronged. And ere we would strike our worst enemy with our hand, let alone with pike, sword, or halberd, as the world does, we would rather die and have our lives taken from us. Moreover, we do not possess material arms, neither pike nor gun, as anybody may well see and which is known everywhere. *In summa*, our message, our speaking, our life and conduct, is this, that one ought to live in peace and unity in God's truth and righteousness, as true Christian disciples of Christ.

Naturally, since all occasion for wrath was taken away by Christ's gospel, and love had replaced the doctrine of "an eye for an eye and a tooth for a tooth," Hutterites condemned participation in war, and they refused military service.

In fact, their witness for peace was more radical than that of the Anabaptist-Mennonite mainstream. Hutterites consistently refused to pay war taxes or to perform any kind of labor they believed to be connected with the prosecution of war. We find, for instance, a Hutterite missionary who worked in the Palatinate and lower German Rhineland during the mid-1550's pointing to his brethren's unwillingness to contribute what he called *Blutgeld*, i.e., war taxation, as one of the chief characteristics distinguishing them from the evangelical Anabaptists who derived directly from the Swiss Brethren.

At the beginning, however, not all the nonresistant *Stäbler* who had settled on the Kounic estates at Austerlitz in 1528 under the leadership of Jakob Widemann "the one-eyed" had objected to such levies. Although on their first coming Widemann had told the owners that they considered payment of a "war tax and such-like things" to be contrary to God's will, he and the elders of the community reversed this position later, decreeing on that occasion that such a tax differed in no essential way from ordinary taxes which all were agreed should be paid. The guilt, they said, for its misuse rested with the magistrate. Some of the brethren disagreed with this view, arguing: "There is little or no difference between slaying with our own hands, and strengthening and directing someone else when we give him our money [to slay] in our stead." A group that broke away from the Austerlitz brethren in 1531 and moved to Auspitz (Hustopeče) took this position. And it was the Auspitz brethren who became the "parent congregation" of the Hutterites.

In the *Account of Our Religion, Doctrine and Faith (Rechenschafft unserer Religion, Leer und Glaubens)*, which the intellectual leader of mid-century Hutteritism, Peter Riedemann, had composed in 1540-1541, we find a detailed exposition of his community's opposition to war taxation. When Christ told his followers to render unto Caesar the things that were Caesar's "he spoke not of taxation for the shedding of blood." Therefore, Riedemann continues, "where taxes are demanded for the special purpose of going to war, massacring and shedding blood, we give nothing. This we do neither out of malice nor obstinacy but in the fear of God, that we make not ourselves partakers of other men's sins." In contrast to his near-contemporary Socinus, Riedemann obviously regards all warfare as essentially aggressive, destructive rather than constructive in character, and different in its aims and methods from the enforcement of domestic order. He writes:

> We . . . desire to give the ruler willingly that which is ordained for his office, call it what one will—taxes, revenue, payment in kind, tribute, customs, toll or service—and to show our willing subjection therein, and to be ready to every good work. If, however, he goeth beyond this willfully, then he executeth not the office of the Lord, but his own office. For . . . the ruling power is a staff, stick, rod, and instrument of God's vengeance, through which God himself punisheth evildoers in anger. It is for this office that taxes and duties are appointed and not for wanton warfare and bloodshed. Therefore hath one no obligation to them for the same: yea, on the contrary, we are forbidden to give, not commanded, because we are not children of vengeance, and must no more yield our members to be weapons of unrighteousness, and serve no unrighteousness. Thus, it is always wrong that they turn to the extermination of nations. Now, whosoever payeth them taxes for this, helpeth them in their iniquity. . . .

The waging of war by the state he brands as "wanton wickedness." Neither Christ, nor St. Paul in his epistle to the Romans, had intended to justify support of this, while enjoining the payment of ordinary taxes for the upkeep of the magistrates.

> Then someone may say, "But they use it all wrongly in any case, so, from this point of view, one should give nothing." That they use all for evil—that is something for which they shall bear their own sentence. We, however, give it not for their wrong use, but for their appointed office. But because wars and the destruction of nations are more against their office than with it, nothing is ordained them for this purpose, and we can give nothing for this for the sake of the office, since it is not appointed. But everything wherein and whereby we can serve man for his betterment, we desire to do diligently. But whatsoever is against God, the conscience and our calling—there we want to obey God more than man.

And Riedemann's contemporary, the Hutterite locksmith and minister Claus Felbinger, expressed the matter this way in 1560: "The Lord has placed a sword in [the government's] hand, and its annual income in taxes, interest, duties, etc., that it may be able to execute its office and protect the just. . . . When, however, the government requires of us what is contrary to our faith and conscience—as swearing oaths and paying hangman's dues *and taxes for war* [my italics]—then we do not obey its command" (from translation by R. Friedmann in the *Mennonite Quarterly Review*, xxix, no. 2 [April 1955]). Refusal stemmed not from a spirit of pride but from "pure fear of God."

A group of Anabaptists at Kreuznach in the Palatinate whom a Hutterite missionary had converted to communitarianism in 1556 were required, before acceptance into the brotherhood, to sign a declaration which included the renunciation of payment of "blood money," i.e., war taxes, as well as recognition of weapon-making as a sin. (However, a century later, it should be added, a Hutterite settlement at Mannheim, which lasted from 1652 until 1684, agreed to pay a small annual tax for exemption from serving in the watch. But whereas the converts from Kreuznach had removed at once to Moravia, the Mannheim brethren, a mere dozen or so families, faced a hostile environment, alone and far removed from the parent settlements in Slovakia. This may explain the spirit of compromise they displayed in the matter.)

The Turkish threat had appeared again in Moravia at the end of the 1570's, and with it demands from the authorities for extraordinary taxation for the purpose of resisting the enemy. Thus, the Hutterites were now faced with putting their principles into practice; for it seems as if over the previous decades they had experienced little trouble in regard to this issue. In 1579-1580 on their refusing payment of a special war levy, cattle, sheep, horses, and other property were seized from the *Brüderhöfe* to meet this demand. In 1584 and again in 1589 when similar demands were made, the same procedure ensued on refusal. The brethren joyfully accepted the spoiling of their goods. For had not Paul the apostle said in his epistle to the Hebrews [10: 34] that for this they would receive in heaven "a better and an enduring substance"? Therefore it was preferable to suffer in this way "rather than do what would be a stain, spot, and burden to our consciences."

From 1596 on, special war taxation became an annual affair: war with the Turks had begun again three years earlier. In 1595, in expectation of the testing time which awaited them, the elders of the community had resolved:

> If something is taken away from us by force, for instance, taxation by the authorities, one should not resist them with improper words. Or if the soldiers take something away from us or press hard upon us with wicked words, then nobody should be caught in talking back to them which might cause them to do harm to the *Gemein* [community]. In this every earnest Christian should be very careful.

The elders told the governor (*Landeshauptmann*) of Moravia, Fridrich of Žerotín, that they conscientiously objected both to making contributions of money to the war against the Turks and to allowing their horses and wagons to be used for military purposes, because such aid would signify a willing participation on their part "in the shedding of blood." A little later they wrote to the Emperor, Rudolf II, in further explanation of their stand. Fear of God, they told him, had motivated their disobedience. Žerotín, moreover, was one of the Hutterites' warmest friends among the Moravian nobility: yet they had preferred to risk his displeasure and the possibility of expulsion from his lands rather than compromise on this issue.

The Hutterites manifested an equally uncompromising spirit in regard to war work. We have seen that whereas they had no scruples concerning their obligation to perform whatever *corvées* might be required of them if these were unconnected with war, they were not prepared to act as teamsters with the army, even at the risk of antagonizing a powerful protector. An even more heroic witness had been shown in 1539 after some ninety members had been arrested by order of Ferdinand I and sent as galley slaves to the Mediterranean fleet. There they refused orders to row—and despite floggings they persisted in this refusal, explaining that their disobedience resulted from the warlike character of such labor. For the fleet, they said, was organized to fight "against the Turks and other enemies [and] for use in plundering and war; . . . therefore they were as little willing at sea as they were on land to commit wrong or to sin against God in heaven."

In the same way Hutterites forbade their members to manufacture weapons of war. Riedemann has a section on this in his *Rechenschafft*, entitled "Concerning the Making of Swords." Pointing to Christ's commandment to beat swords into ploughshares and to eschew revenge, he goes on:

> Now, since Christians must not use and practice such vengeance, neither can they make the weapons by which such vengeance and destruction may be practiced by others. . . . Therefore we make neither swords, spears, muskets nor any such weapons. What, however, is made for the benefit and daily use of man, such as bread knives, axes, hoes and the like, we both can and do make. Even if one were to say, "But one could therewith harm and slay others," still they are not made for the purpose of slaying and harming, so there is naught to prevent our making them. If they should ever be used to harm another, we do not share the harmer's guilt, so let him bear the judgment himself.

This policy was consistently carried out by the communities throughout the subsequent decades. We find Hutterite craftsmen famous throughout Moravia and even beyond its frontiers for their axes, pruning-shears, bread-knives, and such instruments, the primary purpose of which was for domestic use. But they refused absolutely to have anything to do with the manufacture of guns, swords, pikes, daggers, etc.

Hutterite intransigence on the war question contrasts with the accommodating spirit shown in the matter by the Mennonites. The *Doopsgezinden*, as we have seen, bent over backward to prove their loyalty to their nation's cause by not merely paying every tax demanded of them, even when imposed for direct support of war, but also by undertaking auxiliary war service of a noncombatant character, and even by voluntarily contributing money for defense. In addition, their attitude toward manufacturing instruments of war was at times somewhat ambiguous. Moreover, even the more otherworldly "Prussian" Mennonites saw nothing wrong in selling provisions to the military as, for instance, the elder of the Chełmno congregation, Stephan Funk, did in 1703 in respect to Charles XII of Sweden's armies while they laid siege to Toruń. (Perhaps, though, as the Swedish king

240

had invaded the country, Funk may have regarded his conduct as an exemplification of Christ's injunction to feed one's enemies.)

The reason for this difference is not far to seek. In the case of the *Doopsgezinden*, obviously their progressive integration into Dutch society and the spread of patriotic sentiment among them account for their positive reaction to the wartime demands of the state. True, other evangelical Anabaptist and Mennonite groups who retained an attitude of strict nonconformity to the world much longer than their Dutch brethren were to do nevertheless accepted war taxation and noncombatant assistance to war as compatible with their nonresistant philosophy. None of them, however, lived in such isolation—whether physical or spiritual—as the Hutterite communities did. Dwelling in the midst of a linguistically and ethnically alien population and shut off from their Czech neighbors by their communal way of living in addition, the Hutterites could more easily insulate themselves from their surroundings. They experienced no patriotic urges; they felt no intimate ties with the people and region. The cohesiveness of the *Brüderhöfe*, their members' overwhelming sense of group solidarity, the knittedness of their lives, explain the boldness with which they presented their witness to the world.

Outsiders, even the Hutterites' enemies, testified to the high moral standards of these simple German peasants and to the consistency with which they lived out their religion. Writing in 1603, the Jesuit father Christoph Andreas Fischer admitted at least the "external holiness" of their lives, especially when one contrasted them with most contemporaries. "They call each other brothers and sisters; they use no weapons of defense. They are temperate in eating and drinking, they use no vain display of clothes. . . . They do not go to law before judicial courts, but bear everything patiently, as they say in the Holy Spirit." Such grudging admiration did not prevent the expulsion of the Hutterites from Moravia in 1622, a consequence of the Protestant defeat at the Battle of the White Mountain two years earlier. It was not, in fact, surprising that the Hutterites now had to go: all those unwilling to accept Catholicism were forced into exile, including proud noble families like the Žerotíns.

For the next 140 years the Hutterite brotherhood became centered in Habsburg-ruled Slovakia. Even though a limited measure of religious freedom continued to exist in this area and the noble landowners welcomed religious dissidents who brought them economic profit, the Hutterites, like other Protestants, were subjected to increasing pressure from the Jesuits and the other forces of the Counter-Reforma-

241

tion. To compound their difficulties, they also suffered not infrequently from the depredations of Turkish raiders based on the occupied central and southern parts of the Hungarian kingdom: in many *Brüderhöfe* men, women, and children were slaughtered or carried off into slavery. Their chronicles for this period continually lament the misfortunes which befell the brethren from the various soldieries—by no means only Turkish—who rampaged at intervals through the land.

The Turkish menace disappeared at the end of the seventeenth century: religious intolerance remained. It reached a climax in the reign of Maria Theresa (1740-1780). Prompted by her Jesuit advisers, the queen and her officials, by confiscating Hutterite devotional books, by suppressing their services of worship, by seizing their children and educating them in the Catholic faith, and by the forcible conversion of all but the most determined adults, succeeded by the 1760's in making the further existence of independent communities impossible. In Slovakia the sect was altogether suppressed, though after their forcible conversion to Catholicism its members were permitted for several generations to continue their communal way of life. (They were henceforward known as the *Habaner*, a nickname given them by the Slovak peasants.) In Transylvania, however, where a solitary *Brüderhof* had existed since 1621, the Hutterites remained intact. There the accession to the Hutterite faith in 1756 of a group of Lutheran migrants from Carinthia had instilled new life into the dwindling sect. But it felt insecure now under Habsburg rule; so in 1767 the whole group fled across the mountainous frontier into Wallachia, moving on three years later to Ukraine, where a Russian nobleman, Count Rumiantsev, had offered them a haven on his estate at Vishenka.

Once established in the Russian empire, the Hutterites eventually succeeded in making contact again with the *Habaner*, who continued to be attached to their old faith. In 1784, after Maria Theresa's son, Emperor Joseph II, had issued a patent granting limited religious toleration to his subjects (1781), three families who had belonged to the former *Brüderhof* at Subotiště were arrested at the border and imprisoned for attempting to reach the brethren in Russia. A Slovak scholar, Štefan Kazimír, has shown (in his article, "K otázke emigrácie habánov zo Slovenska do Ruska v druhej polovici 18 stor.," *Historické Štúdie* [Bratislava], vol. III [1957], pp. 368-74) that other *Habaner* families, as a result of their renewed contact with the main body of Hutterites early in Joseph II's reign, and of the somewhat less constricted atmosphere in his dominions, would have emigrated to Russia if the Habsburg authorities had not taken steps to prevent them from doing so.

Despite a modest revival of the *Brüderhöfe* in the middle of the seventeenth century under the able leadership of the miller Andreas Ehrenpreis, who proved a worthy successor to Hutter, Riedemann, and Walbot in the preceding century, the period from 1622 onward had been one of decline in most respects: size, economic development, cultural level, and spiritual vitality. This need not surprise us in view of the successive blows dealt the Hutterite brotherhood either by its rulers or by invaders from outside. During the Thirty Years' War the communities continued to refuse payment of war taxes "as our forefathers had also refused to do" (to quote the words of their *Klein-Geschichtsbuch*). As of old, various items of property were confiscated, and to this the brethren meekly submitted in consonance with their belief in nonresistance.

In 1633, however, an incident had occurred which shook the brotherhood to its foundations: at Sobotiště members of the *Brüderhof* offered violent resistance when servants of a local nobleman, Ferenc Nagy-Michaly, attempted to requisition some of their horses. True, it was not a very serious affair. The men of the community had seized the nearest lethal instrument to hand, whether it were ax, pitchfork, or stick, and driven Nagy-Michaly's people off. No one was killed or even seriously injured: a bruised limb or two and some cuts was all the damage that was done. The outbreak of violence took place at a time when the farm manager had just died and the elder of the community was laid up in bed, and there was no one present with sufficient authority to control the situation. It happened, moreover, when nerves were already strained as a result of the incidence of sporadic acts of violence at the community's expense: now these nerves had simply snapped. Although there are indications that in areas where the brethren had recently suffered assault a few members had gone around armed at least with nonlethal weapons, this does not really appear to have portended a wholesale abandonment of nonviolence even among those who participated in the *mêlée*. Yet the leaders of the brotherhood were profoundly shocked. For one thing, it threatened to have serious repercussions, since a member of the nobility was involved: several brethren who had taken part in the fray had been arrested and were threatened with deportation for forced labor at a fortress on the Turkish frontier. Moreover, even though Nagy-Michaly was eventually placated after the community had paid a large fine in compensation for the injuries done to his servants, the moral

243

stain remained. For the first time in the history of the brotherhood, violence had been used. Only a stern warning, thought the leaders, would bring home the gravity of this to all members.

At a "great assembly" of church leaders, held at Levar on 28 November of the same year, an ordinance was passed dealing with the subject of nonresistance. Its author was almost certainly Andreas Ehrenpreis. The conduct of the Sobotiště brethren was inexcusable, it stated. Not only did it constitute a sin against God who had bidden us accept despoilment without resisting, it also counted as a crime "in the eyes of the authorities." By this deed, now, "we . . . are labeled as impudent and refractory people, even proud scoundrels, by the big lords of the country." There was a danger that these nobles might "bring tribulation and ruin to the *Gemein,* even to our widows and orphans."

> We therefore command you by the power which the Lord has given us . . . that henceforth no brother shall protect himself with violence from such robbery, iniquity, and pressure. . . . And if someone should object to this (so to speak in an economic spirit): are we then to permit any violent taking away of the possessions of our *Gemein?* To this we answer according to the teachings of Christ: yes. For it is more blessed to us and also of greater profit than if we would resist with violence, and thus would spoil our conscience. We would bring ourselves into such danger with the authorities, and besides would have to pay so much hush-money, that it can hardly be imagined. . . . Also we will not suffer it any longer that people [i.e., brethren] go their way with hoes, pick-irons and such abominable big sticks. . . . Nowadays nobody wants to guard the cattle without having an ax with him. Long ago such practices were not allowed in the *Gemein,* for a cowherd has a better control of the cattle with a stick than with an ax. And if someone carried an ax with him for self-protection, then it will avail him to detriment as much as to profit. There is also some rumor that some brethren (mainly those on lonely farms) own and use guns. This should not be, for what profit is a gun to the brother? It has never been permitted in the *Gemein* (in the past), and shall also not be permitted in the future.

The brethren who, "in their eagerness to preserve the property of the *Gemein,*" had recently acted with violence, "rashly out of human weakness," were called upon to repent. Those who should transgress this ordinance in future, whether by open violence or by "cursing and slandering and [anything] which could provoke anger," were threatened with the ban and, if they remained obdurate, with consequent loss of eternal salvation. "We do not want to have communion with them."

The ordinance, unlike the—usually rather milder—decrees which were being passed contemporaneously on nonresistance by Dutch and German Mennonites, seems to have had its effect. At any rate, we do not hear again of any violent outbreaks of this kind among the Hutterites in the period prior to their settlement in Russia.

On the Rumiantsev estates the Hutterites enjoyed freedom from military service as one of the conditions of their settlement contract. When in 1787 a special war tax was imposed by Catherine II, the Hutterites, while they rejected a direct payment, finally agreed to a proposal of the count's agent that the community should give the count a fixed annual sum, out of which the latter would forward the monies owing to the government in the way of special taxation. The Hutterites knew that if the contribution demanded by the government did not reach its coffers somehow they faced the possibility of expulsion from the country. On the other hand, the count did not relish the idea of losing such excellent tenants and was anxious to find some way out of the dilemma. A new contract was drawn up immediately incorporating the proposal agreed upon. The arrangement, it would seem, was to some extent a face-saving device: the brethren could not have failed to be aware that included in the new impost was the war tax, the payment of which they had declared to be contrary to their consciences. It is difficult to imagine sixteenth-century Hutterites agreeing to a solution of this sort. Perhaps their descendants were made of weaker stuff than they were or, more likely, the tragic experiences of the two preceding centuries led the Hutterites at this juncture to value the advantages of a secure resting-place for their continued existence as a people above the merits accruing to each individual from a rigid adherence to the letter of the religious discipline.

Nine years later, when a new Rumiantsev owner took over the estate at Vishenka, he proceeded to double the amount of the yearly tribute. This brought home to the Hutterites the precariousness of their situation. They stalled at first—but finally paid up. "The community," wrote their chronicler, "had reservations about contributing such money, because it was known now that it had been raised by the young count instead of the recruitment, and they could not give aid to war in good conscience. After many discussions it was finally agreed to pay the required sum, but only for a short time . . . until our matter should be decided upon by the Emperor." The Emperor Paul, who had just succeeded to his mother's throne, continued, as she had done, to look with favor on groups like the Hutterites and Mennonites. His *Gnadenbrief* of September 1800, issued to the former and promising them and their descendants, among other things, freedom of worship and exemption from all military duties on payment of a general land tax to the state, parallelled the guarantees given simultaneously to the Mennonite community in Ukraine. These privileges were confirmed by Alexander I on his accession the next year. In 1802 the Hutterites left Vishenka to settle on nearby crown lands. For government purposes, henceforward Hutterites and Mennonites were classed together. Their experiences during the nineteenth century in respect to military service will be dealt with in a later chapter.

In the German lands unconditional pacifism was not confined in the sixteenth, seventeenth and eighteenth centuries to the strictly "Anabaptist" Mennonites and Hutterites. Individualistic Spiritualists and radical Pietists from time to time rejected all war (as did the small German Quaker Society of Friends discussed later in this book): to some extent their views on war reflected Mennonite influence and example, though other sources are apparent too, e.g., Socinianism, Quakerism, as well as direct study of the New Testament and burgeoning internationalist ideas.

The Spiritualists, who formed one branch of the Radical Reformation, represented an approach to religion rather different from that of the Anabaptists, whom they resembled in certain respects. The "spiritual reformers" (Rufus M. Jones's term) held "inspiration by the Holy Spirit above the word of the Scriptures." On the whole they did not seek to set up a new ecclesiastical organization, though a sect sometimes emerged as a result of their teachings. Many of them were mystics who sought direct contact with Godhead; this led some of them to break completely with the established church. They did not desire, particularly, a restoration of the apostolic brotherhood, for truth, they believed, did not reside in any institution. If the idea of Christian discipleship left them cold, the concept of a church discipline appeared abhorrent. They were individualists who listened to the voice within as their supreme guide.

Although some spiritual reformers expressed opposition to war in general terms (pacificism of this sort was not uncommon in the sixteenth and seventeenth centuries), they did not usually share the Anabaptists' faith in nonresistance. The Silesian nobleman Caspar von Schwenckfeld, for instance, supported the office of the sword, even though most of his followers eventually, at least by the 1730's when the sect left Germany to seek a home in Quaker Pennsylvania, came to accept nonresistance and follow Mennonite practice on the question of military service and public office. Another Silesian, the influential mystic Jakob Boehme, spoke out against war and praised peace as the proper condition of mankind on earth. "When He gave you the sword of the Spirit," he wrote, "did He command you to fight and make war, or to instigate kings and princes to put on the sword and kill?" Yet Boehme does not appear to have urged Christians not to participate in military duties as the evangelical Anabaptists and Mennonites did, and he approved of just wars.

In the seventeenth century, however, we find several mystical writers bearing an unconditional testimony against war. This development may have been a product of the cruelties and devastation of the Thirty Years' War, though the widespread antiwar feeling these generated did not usually take such a radical form. Paul Felgenhauer, a German Lutheran from Bohemia (though an unorthodox one) who as a young man had been forced to leave his native land after the Battle of the White Mountain, compiled in 1648, the year in which peace returned to the Germanies, a volume entitled *Perspicillum Bellicum* (*Perspect of War*). Among a number of works on mystical and chiliastic themes —understandably, he believed the calamities of his time portended the imminent end of the world—this was the only one Felgenhauer devoted to the problem of war. In it he defended a Mennonitelike nonresistance as the only way open for a true follower of Christ. The concept of defensive war he regarded as a ruse devised by Satan to cloud the understanding of Christians who were forbidden to fight under any circumstances. Even though the law of nature permitted homicide in self-defense, the law of Christ demanded the renunciation of lethal weapons. Those who bore arms, as soldiers did, were in mortal sin, and their prayers were ineffectual.

Two other pacifist mystics of the period of the Thirty Years' War deserve mention here: Anneken Hoogwand from Crefeld and Christian Hohburg, who lived part of his life in Hamburg. Little is known of Hoogwand's career: her books appeared in the 1640's and 1650's. Although she granted the magistracy a recognized place even in a Christian community, war she branded as a sin whatever the pretext for which it was waged. One armed conflict led to another, and a ruler who embarked on war acted in this case like a pagan. Hohburg, a university-trained theologian and author of a number of tracts on religious subjects, remained throughout his life a seeker after truth, exchanging his Lutheran pulpit for a Reformed church living and finally ending as preacher of a dissident Mennonite congregation. "War stems from the devil," Hohburg proclaimed, "the victor is a murderer and the vanquished is destroyed (*verdammt*) body and soul." Christ had replaced the old dispensation, allowing war and revenge, with a message of nonresistance. Therefore, said Hohburg, "the Christian's law is suffering"; his weapons "not muskets, but Bible and prayer to God." Wars of defense were forbidden: "to strike back is to take the offensive." The only way to put an end to war was by loving enemies, by reconciliation. Like Hoogwand, Hohburg approved the existence of a Christian magistracy—provided, however, that officeholders obeyed their Master's injunction not to resist evil. Although he continued to concern himself with the problem of war right up to his death in 1675, his pacifist position had already been clearly formulated in the 1640's, i.e., at a time when he was still affiliated to the Lutheran church.

Toward the end of the seventeenth and during the eighteenth centuries pacifist sentiment was strong among the radical Pietists of Germany. Their pietism may have induced a generally critical spirit in regard to the Lutheran and Calvinist establishments and a sensitivity in regard to war, which was not felt in orthodox Protestantism at that time. Pietism, too, to some extent marked an attempt to return to the New Testament roots of Christianity and to replace dogma by a living faith based on the Scriptures. More directly influential in shaping their nonresistant pacifism, however, was the practice of neighboring groups like the Dompelaars, i.e., immersionist Mennonites (the Mennonites ordinarily baptized by pouring) who from around the mid-seventeenth century had small congregations first at Hamburg-Altona —where Hohburg had been preacher—and then at Crefeld, or like the Quakers who were also to be found in the Rhineland and northwest Germany.

The scholar Gottfried Arnold, whose monumental work on church history (*Unparteyische Kirchen- und Ketzer-Historie*, 2 vols. in 4 parts, Frankfurt-am-Main, 1700-1715) gave, almost for the first time, a full and fair treatment of Christian sectarianism from the early church down to his own period, showed sympathy both for radical Pietiest ideas and for pacifism, although he retained his affiliation to the Lutheran church until his death in 1714. In an early work on the life of the apostolic church, *Die erste Liebe der Gemeinen Jesu Christi, das ist, Wahre Abbildung der ersten Christen, nach ihrem lebendigen Glauben und heiligen Leben* . . . of 1696 (I have consulted the enlarged edition in 2 vols. of 1712, also published in Frankfurt-am-Main), he developed the medieval sectarian theme of Christianity's having fallen as a result of the Emperor Constantine's conversion and of his subsequent establishment of Christianity as the state religion. Henceforward, the thesis ran, only the persecuted sects kept evangelical truth alive and free from the corruptions of official religion. One section of the book (vol. II, book v, chapter 5) is devoted to the views of the pre-Constantinian church on war ("Was sie von dem Kriege und Soldaten-Leben gehalten"). A sound scholar in all his writings, Arnold bases his account here on the works of the early church fathers and other contemporary documents. He stresses the strongly antiwar sentiment existing in the church throughout the first three centuries: war and soldiering, he shows, were frowned on, while the pacifist's was the typical stance. "The apostolic Christians," he wrote, "triumphed through their blood, and not by weapons. . . . Their view was that, whereas under the law of Moses, it is true, war had been allowed, in the Gospel, on the other hand, it was never permitted."

Early in the seventeenth century dissatisfaction with established Protestantism grew so strong among radical Pietists that whole groups, as well as certain individuals, took the decision to break completely with the churches in which they had been reared. One of those who did this was the evangelist Hochmann von Hochenau, who had been greatly indebted in his religious development to Gottfried Arnold. He also maintained contacts with Mennonites. In 1711 Hochenau publicly expressed the view that Christians should not take part in war; but his position was less radical than the Mennonites', for he did not call upon truly pious Christians to resign from office, too. Magistracy, he felt (as the Mennonites did), was a necessity in this world; it had the duty to protect the righteous and to punish evildoers with the sword. At the same time, homicide remained a sinful act. Others in Hochenau's circle (e.g., Johann Konrad Dippel, Johann Lobach) also spoke out against war. In 1708 a group of Hochenau's disciples (though Hochenau did not himself accede to them) under the leadership of a miller, Alexander Mack, Sr., baptized each other by immersion in the river Eder, near Schwarzenau in the little county of Wittgenstein. This act marked the genesis of a new sect whose members, all of them simple farmers and craftsmen, eventually became known, after their immigration to the New World between 1719 and 1736, as German Baptist Brethren or Dunkers. From the beginning the Dunkers accepted the full Mennonite position on war and magistracy, thus diverging a little from that of their first mentor, the aristocratic Hochenau.

I have discussed the Dunkers' nonresistance in my book on *Pacifism in the United States*. I would refer the interested reader to its pages for further information on this subject as well as on the experiences of the transatlantic Mennonite migrants. There were also other small German Separatist groups which, having broken away from established Protestantism in the course of the eighteenth and early nineteenth centuries, eventually emigrated to the United States; they too are dealt with in my book. The so-called Inspirationists, for instance, before their departure, suffered severely as a result of their refusal either to render military service or to conform to the state church. The sources are meager, but they indicate that these were not the only Separatists who experienced a similar fate.

My book on American pacifism (chapter 7) also discusses the somewhat "ambiguous witness" for peace of the early American Moravians (the first party arrived in the New World in 1735). The founder of the sect, Nicholaus Ludwig von Zinzendorf, was a Saxon aristocrat who early in his life had come under strong Pietist influence. The arrival on his estates of German-speaking refugees from Moravia, among whom the traditions of the *Unitas Fratrum* (or Czech Brethren) still lived despite that body's suppression throughout the Czech lands after the Protestant defeat at the White Mountain in 1620, inspired Zinzendorf to try to effect a religious renewal in the moribund Lutheranism of his day. At first, at any rate, he displayed no desire to renounce his membership of his ancestral church. As happened with John Wesley later, separation was forced on Zinzendorf largely against his will. He eventually, in 1737, obtained episcopal consecration in the church of the *Unitas Fratrum* and, with Herrnhut as his center, he ruled what had now become a separate denomination until his death in 1760. By this date the Moravian Church had spread to most of Protestant Germany. Members were also found in the British Isles, Scandinavia, Netherlands, and Russia, as well as in several colonies of British North America and scattered throughout the globe in many missionary fields.

The new church's creed was essentially a "religion of the heart," intensely emotional and opposed to the increasing rationalism of contemporary thought. Despite the exalted lineage of its founder, the Moravian Brethren were drawn mainly from the lower ranks of society (although, as so often before, the tendency grew for members to acquire middle-class status). And in the New World, the Brethren had organized themselves for a time on communal principles, as several other immigrant sects did when faced with the conditions of life on the frontier.

The Moravians during the eighteenth century were granted exemption from military service by most states in which they were settled. Frederick II of Prussia gave it in 1742; in 1749 a British act of parliament (22 Geo. II c. 30, sec. IV) did the same for all British dominions. Where the law did not provide this, the Moravians usually bought their way out of service by paying a fine or hiring a substitute. Nevertheless, even in the eighteenth century there were Moravian soldiers fighting in the continental armies; in America Moravians bore arms, too, in the French and Indian War (1755-1763) and in the American Revolution. Some of their mission stations were armed.

Since Moravians requested legal exemption from military service on religious grounds, most outsiders regarded them as unconditional pacifists. As one English peer remarked in the course of debate in the House of Lords on the 1749 bill mentioned above: "As to the exemption from bearing arms, as long as they are to pay in lieu thereof, I am for dispensing with them in this point also; which, I suppose, ariseth from a scrupulosity, which once actuated the Anabaptists of Switzerland" (from *Reasons and Objections for and against the Privileges granted to the Protestants known by the Name of Unitas Fratrum: or, United Brethren, in the British Dominions, as they are inserted in the Months of April and May of the Universal Magazine*, London, 1750). Many persons in Britain and America compared them to Quakers—but not Benjamin Franklin, for instance, who visited their settlement at Bethlehem, Pennsylvania, in 1756 and was amazed to find the brethren armed and the town "in so good a posture of defence" with "the principal buildings . . . defended by a stockade."

Clearly Moravian noncombatancy derived primarily from a desire to live separated from the world rather than from a principled non-resistance, even if some Moravians in the New World especially, like Bishop John Ettwein, who directed the Pennsylvania communities during the American Revolution, took up an essentially pacifist stand.

Zinzendorf's own views on war were not entirely consistent. He disapproved of military service whether undertaken voluntarily or as a result of compulsion. He exerted all his influence with legislators and rulers to gain complete exemption for his people, although he did not condemn paying a fine in lieu of personal service or even, if no other way out remained, hiring a substitute. In 1737 he wrote: "Nos Frères ne consentiront jamais ni de gré ni de force à aller tuer les gens dans des pays où ils ne recherchent que le salut des âmes, parce que si les paroles de Notre Sauveur adressés à ses disciples n'ont pas ce sens, ils n'en ont aucun." This sounds like a statement of unconditional pacifism. Yet on other occasions Zinzendorf expressed himself rather differently. Wars, like plagues and famines, he regarded as part of God's inscrutable design for mankind. "And were we to say," he wrote once, "that the Saviour has forbidden Christians, i.e., all Europeans, to wage war, we would be talking nonsense." He refused to believe either that Christian rulers (he was himself, by virtue of his extensive landed property, a magistrate) might not wage "a just war" to repel invaders of their territory or that a soldier who killed in battle necessarily en-

251

dangered his eternal salvation. There were pious men serving in Europe's armies: he did not wish to deny them the Christian name. There were even members of the Moravian brotherhood in the ranks and they conducted themselves as model soldiers: he uttered no word of reproof beyond remarking that it were best if the Brethren kept away from army life and devoted themselves, instead, entirely to the Lord's service.

Some writers have tried to prove a connection between eighteenth-century Moravian noncombatancy and the pacifism of the fifteenth-century Czech Brethren from whom the Moravians claimed a remote spiritual descent. Although some recollection of the Czech Brethren's antiwar stand may be detected in the writings of men like John Ettwein, I consider it unlikely that this played an important role in the genesis of Moravian noncombatancy. For one thing, pacifism was abandoned by the Unity of Czech Brethren around 1500, and in the remaining century and a quarter before their church's suppression in the 1620's the Brethren had done their best to remove all memory of its early antimilitarist stand. Again, the links connecting the exiles from Moravia, who found a refuge of Zinzendorf's Herrnhut a century later, with the Czech Unity were extremely tenuous: this makes it even more unlikely that the noncombatancy of the renewed *Unitas Fratrum* sprang from this "hidden seed."

Although, as we have seen, the pacifism of Zinzendorf and his followers was but partial, it probably reflected to some extent the influence of more thoroughgoing nonresistants like the Mennonites. A Hutterite brother from Slovakia, for instance, visited Herrnhut in 1727. Whereas direct contacts between German Mennonites and Zinzendorf are not proven for the early period, there is no reason to suppose that the count was unacquainted with their beliefs as well as those of the radical Pietist circles described above.

The last Moravians formally to give up their legal right to exemption from military duties seem to have been those of North Carolina, who made this renunciation in 1832. For a long time their peace witness had shown no signs of vitality: in fact, in America the sect had virtually ceased to be anything more than formally noncombatant since the American Revolution. Here Moravian communities became increasingly integrated with the surrounding society: their feeling of apartness diminished. The story is the same on the European continent (for the British Isles, so far as I am aware, we have no evidence of Moravians claiming exemption from militia service under the 1749 act). During the first quarter of the nineteenth century, Moravian military exemption either lapsed, or was given up voluntarily by the brethren themselves, or was abolished by governmental action. In Prussia, for instance, the War of Liberation against Napoleon I acted as a catalyst in accelerating the process. Young Moravians, like their co-religionists during the American Revolution, had rushed to the colors, anxious to serve along with their fellow citizens in the ranks of the national army against the foreign invaders. There was no stopping them—not that their elders, anyhow, exerted much energy in attempting this, for in many instances they too were carried away by patriotic enthusiasm.

Patriotic enthusiasm (as we shall see in a later chapter) was also displayed at this juncture in some sections of the Mennonite brotherhood, although more restrainedly. The majority of German Mennonites, especially in the West Prussian community and its offshoots, remained attached to traditional positions, that is, to nonconformity to the world, including the principle of nonresistance and its corollaries —refusal of office and conscientious objection to military service. Change had appeared first in the more integrated congregations of north-west Germany and the lower Rhineland, which, in addition, were exposed to the influence of the *Doopsgezinden* in the Netherlands with their liberal theology and their military conformity. The "democratic revolution" that swept Europe and colonial America toward the end of the eighteenth century demanded the equality of all citizens of the state. Groups like Mennonites or Moravians, who in many areas had not previously enjoyed full equality before the law, gained it now. But abolition of privilege constituted a second slogan of the democratic revolution. Therefore, since Mennonites usually enjoyed exemption from military service, along with other "freedoms" from the norms of social behavior, as a result of *privilegia* granted under the *ancien régime*, these came under attack now as vestiges of a bygone era. Liberals demanded their annulment: monarchs no longer felt impelled to defend them against popular agitation. Moreover, among the Mennonites themselves, as had happened with the Moravians, new, "democratic" ideas—nationalism, liberalism, etc.—began to find acceptance, especially among the younger generation. In a democratic age, conscription, "the nation in arms," the *levée-en-masse*, appeared to many of them to express a valid principle, whereas nonresistance began to seem as old-fashioned as the theology which had originally given birth to it. Or, at least, young men from Mennonite homes wished somehow to reconcile noncombatancy with the demands made by the modern state on its citizens.

In the third quarter of the nineteenth century Mennonite exemption from military service in its traditional form was abolished in Germany,

Austria, Russia, and Switzerland. Although it still remained possible for members of the sect to choose some form of alternative service—auxiliary army duties in the case of Germany, Austria, and Switzerland, and civilian work in Russia—in Central Europe, at any rate, the trend toward accepting full military service grew until in the interwar period nonresistance was abandoned altogether by the Mennonites of Germany and almost everywhere else in this area. For Mennonite nonresistance, the democratic revolution functioned as the executioner's ax.

SEVEN. *The British Quakers*
(SECOND HALF OF
THE SEVENTEENTH CENTURY)

ENGLAND during the two middle decades of the seventeenth century had been swept first by civil war and then by political revolution. It was the scene, too, of a great religious upheaval. Often religious extremism went hand in hand with political radicalism. From the camp of the Puritans who brought about the overthrow of the established Anglican church came the parliamentary leaders who executed England's anointed king. And among the left wing of the parliamentary forces were some who urged the adoption of full democracy, giving every man in the country a vote; a few even went so far as to advocate a form of agrarian communism.

The Quaker movement emerged around the middle of the century, after the conclusion of the civil war and at the outset of the new Commonwealth régime. Older historians viewed early Quakerism as essentially mystic, a kind of third way within the Christian church, lying between Protestantism and Roman Catholicism. This was the thesis elaborated with eloquence and learning by the late Rufus M. Jones, who sought the origins of Quakerism primarily in the mystical trends developed on the European continent during the previous century and a half. It was these "spiritual reformers" who were the true ancestors of the British Society of Friends (as the Quaker movement eventually became known). This view of Quaker origins has recently been revised as the result of studies by such church historians as the English Congregationalist Geoffrey F. Nuttall and the American Quaker Hugh Barbour. Although some continental influence cannot be altogether excluded, these writers have shown conclusively that the beginnings of Quakerism must be placed squarely within the framework of English Puritanism. Quakerism is an indigenous growth. "We may, if we like," Frederick B. Tolles has written, "call it the 'left wing' of the [Puritan] movement, but we cannot regard it as a separate or alien phenomenon." Quakerism—as much as its spiritual parent, Puritanism—sought to manifest the Holy Spirit by pursuing righteousness and godliness in man's dealings with his fellow men. A realization of early Quakerism's affinity with, rather than contrast to, Puritanism is indeed essential to an understanding of the conditions under which its peace testimony crystallized in the course of the 1650's.

The name "Quaker" appears to have arisen first in 1650 when it was applied by Justice Bennett "in scorn" to the founder of the sect, George Fox, and his associates because of certain physical manifestations they displayed such as trembling under the influence of the Spirit. Fox, the Leicestershire shoemaker and a man of deep religious insight and of charismatic religious power, had been active since about 1647 in propagating the need for a revived Christianity. What he preached was simple but of immense attraction for many earnest souls who at that period of spiritual unrest had in vain sought satisfaction for their religious needs within orthodox Puritanism. Under Fox's leading they were able to experience, as it were, a rebirth of the Holy Spirit within their hearts. According to Fox, this Inward Light, Christ's spirit moving within men, was essential to illuminate God's parallel revelation in Scripture. Armed with the Spirit and the Book a Christian had no need for outward sacraments or a visible priesthood. This was Fox's message to the world, for it was the world he and early Friends sought to conquer. Fox's aim, like that of the founders of so many other sects, was not to set up a new religious denomination; his endeavor was to turn men everywhere to follow the principles and practices of pure Christianity.

The first disciples he gathered—"Children of the Light" they called themselves at the beginning—came from the Midlands and North of England. They were drawn in many instances from small congregations of seekers and separatists. There were the "shattered" Baptists of Nottinghamshire, for instance, as whose leader Fox appears by the year 1649. In late 1651 the message was spread into neighboring Yorkshire; in the middle of the following year it was taken over into Westmorland, from where it was brought into the adjacent counties. The gathering of the Westmorland Seekers into the Quaker fold undertaken by Fox and his fellow apostles has led later generations to regard 1652 as a symbolic beginning date for the Society of Friends, for henceforward, after the accession of this considerable group of religious enthusiasts, the movement forged ahead rapidly. In 1654 Quakerism was brought to the south of England, which was evangelized largely by sturdy peasants from the North country. It soon took root, too, in the mountain valleys of Wales as well as in the even harsher environment of Scotland and across the water in wild and war-torn Ireland. In 1656 it was carried across the Atlantic, where a rich mission field opened up both on the North American mainland from the Carolinas to Maine and, for a time, in the Caribbean islands. About the same date Quaker emissaries began to win adherents among the Protestant Dutch and north Germans, though the seed fell here on comparatively barren soil (even less rewarding were Quaker efforts at this period to transplant their message to Catholic Europe and to the Muslim world). By 1660, according to Braithwaite's calculations, there were in England some thirty to forty thousand Quakers in a total population of around five millions.

True, this number fell far short of the mass conversion to the movement which Fox and his Friends had envisaged at the outset. But it testifies to the dynamism and attractive force of Quakerism in the first decade of its existence. It must be remembered, too, that during this period converts to Quakerism had been subjected to harsh, if sporadic, persecution by local authorities throughout Great Britain, which had only been partly ameliorated by the more friendly attitude at times of Oliver Cromwell and the central government. Fox's *Journal* and the journals of contemporary Friends tell a tale of constant harassment: prison, whippings (under a law against vagrants!), fines, mob violence. By such acts as interrupting church services or going naked as a sign, Quakers may have sometimes provoked harsh treatment. At other times such treatment resulted from Quaker peculiarities like their refusal to doff their hats as a sign of respect to the authorities or their unwillingness (displayed earlier, we have seen, by some medieval sectaries or by the Anabaptists and Mennonites) to swear a judicial oath. Usually persecution stemmed from general intolerance toward a group which seemed to be challenging the foundations of church and state alike.

Among the factors causing a clash with authority, pacifism does not figure until near the end of Quakerism's first decade. Indeed, the Quaker peace testimony seems to have crystallized only slowly in the course of that decade. The exact nature of this evolution is not in every respect clear; among writers who have studied early Quakerism there are considerable differences of view concerning the attitude of Friends at this period toward peace and war.

Equally unclear is the relationship between early Quaker antimilitarism and other contemporary manifestations of pacifism in England. We know that among General Baptists in the 1650's there were some who had scruples concerning war; though such persons were very few in number, of course, in comparison with those who had fought enthusiastically on the parliamentary side. Such feelings were almost certainly derived from earlier contacts with Mennonites on the continent; they demonstrate the continuance of an antiwar tradition within one branch of English Baptism (see earlier). The pacifistic Family of Love mentioned in a previous chapter remained in existence in England until the end of the seventeenth century. And that rather eccentric mystical group—the Muggletonians—which first appears during the Commonwealth era, was, along with its chief figure Lodowick Muggleton, also opposed to war and capital punishment. Yet Muggleton himself was something of a relativist, for we find him instructing a follower who had settled in Antigua that "in those strange islands, amongst the heathen," where conditions were so different from those prevailing at home, he might bear arms, if required to do so, "for the defence and preservation of the temporal life, and the estates of the people, against the heathen and any other enemies that seek to invade that island. . . . As the old proverb saith, 'If you will live at Rome, you must do as Rome doth' " (quoted in Alexander Gordon, *Ancient and Modern Muggletonians*, Liverpool, 1870). After the Restoration a lively theological polemic was to ensue between Muggletonians and Quakers. Another small group emerging in the 1650's, which advocated a more uncompromising nonviolence than the Muggletonians', were the Tryonites gathered round Gloucestershire-born Thomas Tryon, who eventually became a well-to-do London merchant. Their views have been described as forming "a curious compound of astrology, dreams, teetotalism and vegetarianism" (C. E. Whiting). Tryon later reproved the Quakers for failing to adopt vegetarianism. His own pacifism seems to have derived from contact quite early in his career with the ideas of the Anabaptists. Finally, we may mention the leader of the communistic Diggers, Gerrard Winstanley, who, together with several of his followers, almost certainly became a Quaker before his death (this has been proved by the recent researches of an American scholar, Richard T. Vann). He came very near to pacifism in some of his tracts published in 1650 or soon thereafter. He described war there as "a plague among mankind" and a root cause of social inequality, and he condemned the use of armed violence to achieve a new social order. "We abhor fighting for freedom," he wrote. "Freedom gotten by the sword is an established bondage to some part or other of the creation. . . . Victory that is gotten by the sword is a victory that slaves get one over another." The way of Christian love, he concluded, is the only path to bring about change. Whether, however, any of these groups influenced Fox and his Friends in their attitude toward war is difficult to establish.

The whole problem of the beginnings of Quaker pacifism is indeed very obscure. Therefore, we shall have to devote some space to examining its ramifications.

Fox appears fairly early to have reached a position where he personally repudiated the use of violent means, of "carnal weapons." While rejecting violence for himself, he did not at first require his followers to do likewise. Among those to whom he preached in the early years were soldiers: we do not find him admonishing them to abandon their profession. Some soldiers were convinced; only rarely did they then resign from the army because of scruples concerning the bearing of arms. Nowhere do we find evidence that their continued service encountered opposition or censure from either Fox or any of the other "Publishers of Truth" (as the first Quaker missionaries called themselves). Yet as early as the autumn of 1650 Fox had himself stepped forward as the protagonist of a vocational pacifism that gradually expanded into a tenet of the Society of Friends.

At that date Fox was just beginning the first of his many imprisonments; he had been sentenced to six months in jail by the Derby magistrates. While in the house of correction he was approached by Cromwell's commissioners, then engaged in raising additional militia in preparation for the expected attempt by young Charles Stuart to regain his father's throne, a venture that ended disastrously at Worcester in the following year. Evidently the commissioners and the soldiers they had raised fancied the idea of appointing a stouthearted young man like Fox to be a captain of militia. To this proposal Fox answered with a clear no. As he related afterward in his *Journal*:

> I told them I lived in the virtue of that life and power that took away the occasion of all wars: and I knew from whence all wars did rise, from the lust, according to James his doctrine. And still they courted me to accept of their offer, and thought I did but compliment with them, but I told them I was come into the covenant of peace, which was before wars and strifes was; and they said they offered it in love and kindness to me, because of my virtue, and suchlike; and I told them if that were their love and kindness I trampled it under my feet.

Later Fox was to boast proudly: "The postures of war I never learned."

Indeed, within a few weeks of that first encounter with the military Fox was again presented with the need to make a decision whether or not to participate in the warfare of the world. This time the authorities did not offer him a commission but attempted to "press" him "for a soldier." The substance of his response was the same as earlier. "I told them," he wrote, "that I was brought off from outward wars." Concerning soldiering he repeated: "I was dead to it . . . where envy and hatred are, there is confusion."

In these utterances, which may be considered the first tentative, embryonic statements of the Quaker peace testimony, Fox made no attempt to derive any elaborate defense of his noncombatancy from Biblical texts. Instead he appealed to "the covenant of peace," the spirit of Christ which leads men out from the way of violence and warfare. He did not try, either, to buttress his case with any rational arguments concerning the consequences of war or its renunciation. As Howard Brinton has remarked, his stand in the matter was primarily one of intuition; this stand, indeed, has been typical of Quaker pacifism at its best. As the Inward Light grew in intensity within a man, so the implications of the covenant of peace would open out. This seems to have been the way the Quaker peace testimony unfolded during the 1650's.

Fox, in his epistles, tracts, and occasional declarations to the authorities over these years, in which he repeated and elaborated the thoughts he had first put forward in that autumn of 1650, made clear that for him the use of the sword was no longer admissible. "Friends," he wrote in or around 1652, "that which is set up by the sword, is held up by the sword, and that which is set up by spiritual weapons is held up by spiritual weapons, and not by carnal weapons. The peace-maker hath the kingdom, and is in it." He vigorously denied the rumors frequently spread around that Quakers were disturbers of the peace, fomenters of civil war. Such stories were lies: "for dwelling in the word, it takes away the occasion of wars, . . . and brings to the beginning, before wars were." This statement comes from a tract Fox published in 1654. In March of the following year we find him assuring the Lord Protector of his peaceable intent toward the government and his abhorrence of all plotting. "I, who am of the world called George Fox, do deny the carrying or drawing of any carnal sword against any," he told Cromwell. "My weapons are not carnal but spiritual, and my kingdom is not of this world. Therefore with the carnal weapon I do not fight, but am from those things dead." In an epistle of 1656 he contrasted the old covenant, under which the Jews employed "the outward sword" against their enemies as well as against wrongdoers within their own community, and the new dispensation introduced by Christ, "who comes to save men's lives, yet slays and kills with the spirit, which is the word of his mouth." Love of enemies and not their slaughter was what Christ required of his disciples. True, Fox went on, Christians have been waging war and killing for over a millennium and a half. "But [those] who come to Christ, they come to reign (in spirit) over all these fighters with carnal weapons, that are got up, since the days of the apostles." Girded only with the truth, they will conquer without carnal weapons. Fox dwells continually on the fact that once a man allows the Inward Light fully to shine he can no longer wield a weapon for whatever cause. "For all dwelling in the Light, that comes from Jesus," he told Friends in 1657, "it leads out of wars, leads out of strife, leads out of the occasion of wars, and leads out of the earth up to God." Those Christians who still clung to the instruments of war were "all out of the royal spirit, . . . and out of the royal seed, which saith, Love enemies." Therefore, not only for himself but also for all Quakers—"we are of the royal seed, elect and precious, before the world began," he writes—the way of war and violence was inadmissible.

That was the conclusion he had reached by the year 1659 when he penned the last two sentences cited above. What had begun as a very personal renunciation of weaponry on his part had blossomed into a repudiation of war and violence incumbent on all who belonged to "the royal priesthood." Let us end this brief survey of the evolution of Fox's thinking on war during Quakerism's first decade by quoting from two of his epistles written in 1659:

> All Friends every where, who are dead to all carnal weapons, and have beaten them to pieces, stand in that, which takes away the occasion of wars, in the power, which saves men's lives, and destroys none . . . to bear and carry carnal weapons to fight with, the men of peace (which live in that, which takes away the occasion of wars) they cannot act in such things, under the several powers.

> Friends, live in the seed of God, that destroys the devil, who is the author and cause of wars and strifes, and bringing of men and people into the earth, where the war, strife and pride is; here the outward sword-men have not learned yet to beat their swords into plough-shares and pruning-hooks . . . But he that killeth with the sword, must perish with the sword. So, there was a time the Jews were to fight with outward weapons, with sword and spear; but there is a time, when nations shall not learn war any more, but shall come to that, which shall take away the occasion of wars, which was in the beginning, before the wars were. And Friends, take heed of blending yourselves with the outward powers of the earth.

But what of early Quakers other than Fox? Some writers have spoken of a lack of consistency, of a continued ambivalence throughout this whole period in the early Quaker attitude toward war. "Pacifism was not a characteristic of the early Quakers; it was forced upon them by the hostility of the outside world," writes Alan Cole, for instance. Cole and others have pointed, in the first place, to the fact that Quaker converts in the Commonwealth army did not in the vast majority of cases resign on account of any scruples concerning fighting (though there were indeed some who did so, like the soldier convinced by Fox while the latter was in Derby jail, who after the battle of Worcester "laid down his arms and saw to the end of fighting"). Quite the contrary, the Quaker soldiers were turned out of the forces because of the army authorities' desire to rid themselves of an unruly element of whose reliability they felt they could not be certain. Moreover, the Quakers' discharge led to strong protest from the Quaker leaders, including Fox himself: a circumstance which is hard to reconcile with any fixed pacifist principles on the part of Friends as a whole. Second, many Quakers at first, although they became increasingly dissatisfied with the military régime which had supplanted parliamentary rule, still showed marked sympathy with, indeed strong support for, the political and military objectives of the Good Old Cause. "The Quakers," Cole writes, "shared the radical Puritan conviction that [its army] had once been an instrument for the establishment of righteousness on earth. While that army continued to exist, Friends never completely abandoned the hope that it might resume its old role as a 'battle-ax in the hand of the Lord.' " Only after hope in a political and military victory of the Saints had to be given up did Quakers adopt pacifism as a fixed principle of their faith. This moment, it is argued, came only toward the end of 1659, perhaps even not before 1660. Thereafter it was not unnatural for Friends to project their pacifism backwards into the 1650's. However, the Quaker peace testimony, according to this revisionist view, was in fact the outcome not of a gradual growth, a slow crystallization, as Quaker historians from Besse in the mid-eighteenth century onward have usually maintained, but of a comparatively rapid political disillusionment, a disillusionment that went much deeper with Friends than was the case with the other radical Puritan groups, since Friends had been more uncompromising in their pursuit of the Kingdom of the Saints. In other words, as the sociologist David Martin has put it, Quaker pacifism is "post-revolutionary."

Let us look first at the problem of the Quaker soldiers of the Commonwealth army. (There were of course a few conversions among veterans of the royalist side but consideration of them is not relevant to the present discussion.) It is indeed evident that Fox and his fellow Publishers of Truth did not feel it incumbent upon themselves to condemn the profession of soldiering in general terms or to urge Quaker converts to lay down their weapons. Did this mean, then, that they approved the use of weapons in certain circumstances?

In 1655, for instance, we find that stalwart, Edward Burrough, issuing *An Invitation to All the Poor Desolate Soldiers to Repent, and make their Peace with the Lord*. His words were addressed to the lower ranks of Cromwell's army of occupation in Ireland. The men were warned against succumbing to the various temptations to which army service exposed them and which threatened their eternal salvation: whoredom, swearing, drunkenness, etc. Let them turn instead to the Light and repent their sins. The Light would teach them to act righteously in their capacity as soldiers of the Commonwealth: "to do violence to no man, but to be terrors and reprovers, and correctors of all violence, and of such who live in it." It would teach them to use their swords "in justice" against "every one that doth evil" and as an instrument for preserving peace. Burrough evidently regarded the occupation of Ireland by English troops as a just "visitation" by God on a "rebellious nation." When in the autumn of 1657 General Monk began a purge of Quakers in the army of occupation which he commanded in Scotland, and Henry Cromwell as Deputy of Ireland took similar measures in that country against those officers and men suspected of being Quakers, Burrough was prompt in protest. It was an act of injustice, he told Oliver Cromwell, committed against men who were his loyal servants and the Commonwealth's. "This thing the Lord is grieved with, and with thee because of it. For thou didst not obtain this victory of peace and freedom by thy own sword . . . this will make thy army less prosperous, and more unblessed, when such who fear the Lord, and against whom thou canst not justly charge evil, are cast out, and despised." Fox, too, rallied to the support of Quakers dismissed from the army "for truth's sake." And in the "Testimony of some of the soldiers that were turned out of the army who owned themselves to be Quakers," dated 20 October 1657, we may note that the eight signatories make no mention of any objections in principle to fighting.

Yet, on the other hand, we do hear of a Cornet Ward who, while stationed in Aberdeen two years earlier, declared that, if his growing sympathies with Quakerism ever led him to throw in his lot completely with Friends, "he purposed not to make use of any carnal sword, but was resolved for that thing to lay down his tabernacle of clay." The former leader of those militant democrats the Levellers, John Lilburne, acknowledged before his death in 1657 his gradual conversion to Quaker noncombatancy. Another witness to incipient antiwar feelings among soldier converts to Quakerism is found in the words of an army officer, Major Richardson, who wrote slightingly: "I fear that these people's principles will not allow them to fight if we stand in need, though it does to receive pay." And even among the dismissed soldiers, although their discharge had almost certainly been unconnected with any antimilitarist activities and although their protest may be considered as implying a demand for reinstatement in the army, there were glimmerings of a recognition that adoption of Quakerism might entail the renunciation of the way of war altogether. Take, for instance, the eight-page pamphlet entitled *To the Generals, and Captains, Officers, and Soldiers of this present Army; the Just and Equal Appeal, and the State of the Innocent Cause of us, who have been turned out of your Army for the Exercise of Our Consciences, who are now persecuted amongst our Brethren, under the Name of Quakers.* The authors stress their faithfulness to the Commonwealth and they recount in detail their trials in battle for the Good Old Cause against bishops, lords, and king and for liberty of conscience. "We were never otherwise minded, than to have stood in defence for the [British] nations against their enemies." Evil-minded men had brought about their expulsion from the army.

> Yet hath God turned it to our great good, and we are more confirmed and strengthened in the life and power of God, and brought to a kingdom that is not of this world, and have peace and rest in him over all the troubles and distractions and dangers which is befallen you, through your own apostacy, and we rest contented in the habitation of peace, suffering patiently under all with our poor brethren, till the Lord arise and plead our cause against all our enemies; and our kingdom, and victory, and weapons are not from below, but from Heaven, and out of wars and strife, are we come to the rest for our souls, that is in God over all the troubles and distractions that comes upon men, and our government is established, and our kingdom cannot be touched, for they are not subject to change; yet nevertheless, we as once fellow members, and fellow soldiers with you, in a good cause, and upon good engagements, wish well towards you in the Lord.

The sentiments expressed here somewhat confusedly are in fact not too far removed from the position Fox had reached in the course of the decade. He, too, we have seen, had come by now "out of wars and strife"—though the soldiers had needed the rough jolt of their dismissal to perceive that this might be the path they, as Quakers, were called upon to tread. And Fox also (this fact should not be forgotten)

264

wished the soldiers of the Commonwealth well "in a good cause and upon good engagements." For him they might still be an instrument for furthering the Lord's work, if they remained faithful to their mission. Thus alongside his personal noncombatancy he could nourish an extreme belligerency that stemmed from the messianic role he, like many other supporters of the parliamentary cause, assigned to Puritan England. In a pamphlet he addressed in 1659 *To the Council of Officers of the Army, and the Heads of the Nation, and for the Inferior Officers and Soldiers to read* he admonished the army authorities that, had they been faithful, they would already have brought Spain and the Papacy to the dust and destroyed the Inquisition and all its works. They would have swept on and rooted out the idolatry of Mohammedanism. "And," he concludes, "if ever you soldiers and true officers come again into the power of God which hath been lost, never set up your standard until you come to Rome, and let it be atop of Rome, then there let your standard stand." Fox had indeed voiced similar sentiments half a decade earlier in correspondence with Oliver Cromwell. And we find his co-worker, Edward Burrough, expressing them even forcibly in the same year. In a "A Warning to the Officers and Soldiers of the English Army" stationed in Dunkirk Burrough exhorts them to revenge the blood of those innocent Protestants slaughtered by the Papacy and Spain. This was the Lord's work, he told them; in doing it they need have no fear of death's sting. "You will be blessed and prosper, till you have set up your standard at the gates of Rome."

We may summarize Quaker views on war as they stood at the outset of 1659 (a crucial year, as it proved, in the development of the movement) roughly as follows: Fox and a number of other Friends had arrived at a position where they renounced the use of weapons for themselves. (William Dewsbury's conversion to pacifism appears indeed to have predated Fox's, for as early as 1645, according to his own account, Dewsbury had put his "carnal sword" into its scabbard and left the parliamentary army, feeling "that the kingdom of Christ was within, and the enemies was within, and my weapons against them must be spiritual, the power of God.") Yet at the same time noncombatancy was not yet a fixed tenet of the emerging Society of Friends, unlike the refusal of oaths or "hat-honour" or unwillingness to pay tithes, which had very soon become virtually obligatory on those professing to be Friends. There were many Quakers—some of them veterans who had only recently and, as we have seen, reluctantly, terminated their army careers—who had by no means abandoned belief in a righteous use of arms to further the cause of the Lord. However, among the dismissed veterans and their sympathizers were those, too, who were now led as a result of their disillusioning experience with the Commonwealth régime to doubt the righteousness of the carnal sword; Fox's utterances on the subject may have helped to awaken such doubts and hesitations. Nevertheless, even Fox still gave a qualified sanction to the use of force to further righteousness and the Good Old Cause of religious liberty, whether exercised by men who had attached themselves to Friends or by those outside the fold, provided that they had not personally repudiated the carnal sword. Moreover, the régime's failure to act decisively and aggressively to uphold the principles it professed was for Fox a matter of condemnation. Not peace but a sword was what he and other leading Quakers (e.g., Edward Burrough) demanded of those who had not abandoned earthly weapons.

Around the middle of 1659 the possibility opened up of inaugurating a new and less corrupt régime than the military government which had ruled England since 1653—or so it seemed at least to the ardent radicals on the Puritan left and to devoted republicans. Hopes of this kind were shared by most Quakers, including Fox and his nearest associates. This soon led to a crisis among Friends that nearly resulted in the abandonment of their emergent peace testimony (possibly for good?) and in their backing the military establishment of a government of the Saints.

In May of that year the Protectorate of Oliver Cromwell's son Richard had been overthrown and the rule of the Rump Parliament restored. This event generated much excitement among religious radicals. There was a feeling that great events were afoot, that a new and holier régime was about to replace the existing government. In the summer the leader of the Puritan left in Parliament, Sir Henry Vane, approached Friends with a view to engaging their collaboration in a thorough political reorganization of the country, offering them at the same time a number of posts in local administration.

Early Friends were drawn largely from the lower ranks of society and from the spiritually disinherited. They were mostly yeoman farmers or farm laborers, rural or town craftsmen, servants or housewives. A few gentry and well-to-do merchants joined the movement, but not many (nor did many recruits come, either, from the urban proletariat). Its adherents, in fact, were just the kind of people who shared the social and political aims of the Puritan left. The temptation now to share, too, in the endeavor to bring the left to power was obviously great.

In Bristol seven Quakers were nominated "Commissioners of Militia" and a dozen or so more were appointed to this office in London, Westminster, and elsewhere. When a Royalist uprising broke out in Cheshire, Friend Anthony Pearson was instrumental in raising militia to help put it down. This was in fact the same Pearson who, in July 1654 in a personal interview with Oliver Cromwell, had told the Protector: "Now the controversy should be no more between man and man in wars and fightings without, for the seed was redeemed out of all earthly things and that nature whence wars arise (which are from the lust and for the lust)." We know of at least one Quaker, John Hodgson, who actually re-enlisted in the army between June and November. It seemed as if among Quakers, as among Dutch and German Anabaptists in the period of the Münster uprising, militant millenarianism might now replace the peaceful pursuit of the Kingdom.

Not all Friends, however, approved such support of military means. A leading Publisher of Truth, Francis Howgill, denounced Pearson's stand as "wicked." Eventually Fox himself came out strongly against cooperation in government if this also entailed collaboration in carrying out military measures. Yet for a time, it seems, he hesitated; the sources at this point, however, are unclear and the whole crisis of 1659 is one of the most obscure episodes in Quaker history. At any rate, at first Fox appears to have looked with considerable favor on the government's overtures. But soon he began to have misgivings and hesitations. How far might Friends go in supporting the military aspects of the holy endeavor? To this question he could for some time give no clear answer. A Quaker wrote to him concerning Bristol Friends that they were "in some little strait about their acting as Commissioners [of Militia]. . . . I can neither persuade them to it nor dissuade them from it: I desire to have a word from thee." But no clear word came, only confused utterance. Beginning in late July and lasting ten weeks, a "time of darkness" had enveloped Fox, a period of deep depression, of agony of mind when he was unable to advise his followers in any clear way concerning the difficult decisions which then faced them. Writers like James F. Maclear, who has made a detailed study of this Quaker crisis, argue persuasively that Fox's mental condition stemmed directly from his own inner struggle. He feared an imminent Stuart restoration and was sympathetic with the aims and ideals of the Puritan political left; yet at the same time he dreaded the consequences of Quaker involvement now in the magistracy and the workings of the carnal sword, even if it were possible that the projected rule of the Saints would result in the eventual conversion of that sword into a ploughshare.

In October Fox emerged from his state of depression. The darkness was dissipated by a clear understanding henceforward on his part that Friends should remain free from entanglement with the politics of the sword. Growing disillusionment with the régime, which now, like its predecessor, appeared to be set mainly to further its own ends and an unlikely instrument, therefore, for furthering either social justice or the rule of the Saints, was probably a factor in swinging Fox and his Friends away from millenarian politics to political neutrality and to a reaffirmation of their peace testimony in even more decisive terms than earlier. But the path by which he reached his conclusion will probably never be exactly known. At any rate, however found, it set Quakers on the road leading them from radically social Puritanism to respectable nonconformity (Maclear's phrase).

"Fighters are not of Christ's Kingdom, but are without Christ's Kingdom": this was Fox's final judgment. "Men of peace (which live in that which takes away the occasion of wars)," such as Friends claimed to be, could not participate actively in administration if this meant they had "to bear and carry carnal weapons to fight with." When in January 1660 Francis Gawler wrote to Fox from Cardiff on behalf of several of his fellow Quakers who had recently been offered army commissions and evidently felt inclined to accept, to ask the leader's advice, he received a peremptory "no." "It was contrary to our principles, for our weapons are spiritual and not carnal," Fox commented.

The restoration of the monarchy and the return of Charles II to reclaim his throne in the following May finally put an end to all thought of militant action on the part of the Quakers—apart from one or two mavericks who continued for a few years to hanker after an armed dénouement. An age of severe persecution was soon to open up in place of the once expected reign of the Saints. In May 1660 we find even an ardent upholder of the parliamentary side like Edward Burrough, whose earlier adherence to Quaker noncombatancy appears somewhat dubious and who still continued to defend the righteousness of the Good Old Cause and to laud its stand against oppression, writing: "We are now better informed than once we were, for though we do now more than ever oppose oppression and seek after reformation, yet we do it not now in that way of outward warring and fighting with carnal weapons, and swords" (from *A Visitation and Presentation of Love unto the King and those call'd Royalists*). The definite crystallization of Friends' peace testimony came in January 1661 after the unsuccessful uprising of the Fifth Monarchy Men in London.

This abortive attempt to restore the rule of the Saints created panic in the capital and at court. Quakers, who in the Restoration era were generally regarded as potential disturbers of the peace, as they had also been under the Commonwealth, immediately became suspect; many Friends were thrown into prison. Therefore Fox, assisted by another leading Quaker, Richard Hubberthorn, immediately drafted a statement denying Quakers' complicity in any form of conspiratorial action and setting forth at the same time their essential peaceableness. The document, which was presented to King Charles II on 21 January as an official exposition of the Quaker position, was significantly entitled *A Declaration from the Harmless and Innocent People of God called Quakers, against all Sedition, Plotters and Fighters in the World: for removing the Ground of Jealousy and Suspicion from Magistrates and People concerning Wars and Fightings.*

The Quakers' principle and practice, states the Declaration, were "to seek peace and ensue it." They had renounced war, and the use of carnal weapons since these reflected man's selfish passions and were contrary to the way Christ had pointed out to mankind. "This is our testimony to the whole world." It flowed not from the exigencies of the present situation but from the adoption of a firm and unchangeable principle, for:

> The Spirit of Christ, by which we are guided, is not changeable, so as once to command us from a thing as evil, and again to move us to it, and we certainly know and do testify to the world, that the Spirit of Christ, which leads us into all truth, will never move us to fight and war against any man with outward weapons, neither for the Kingdom of Christ nor for the kingdoms of this world.

The authors of the Declaration pointed (perhaps a little ingenuously) to Friends' record in the past as proof of their loyal demeanor toward the powers that be. Rather than resist authority "we have been counted as sheep for the slaughter, persecuted and despised, beaten, stoned, wounded, stocked, whipped, imprisoned." In brief, they were truly a "harmless people, who lift not up a hand against them, with arms and weapons."

The appeal in this document, as in other works by Fox and the early Quakers, is to the spirit of Christ as revealed in both the New Testament and the heart of man, and not to any set texts from the Bible. It is an appeal to the spirit and not to the law. War is condemned because it is a sin against the Light and not on account of any economic or moralistic arguments. (It has been pointed out, too, that condemnation of killing because every man, even an enemy, has something of God within him, an idea frequently developed in modern Quaker pacifism, is not to be found either in Fox or among his Quaker contemporaries.) As the often-quoted words of James Naylor spoken on his deathbed in 1660 expressed it, Friends strove to create within themselves "a spirit . . . that delights to do no evil nor to enjoy its own to the end."

> Its hope [so Naylor goes on] is to outlive all wrath and contention, and to weary out all exaltation and cruelty, or whatever is of a nature contrary to itself. It sees to the end of all temptations: As it bears no evil in itself, so it conceives none in thought to any other: If it be betrayed, it bears it; for its ground and spring is the mercies and forgiveness of God. Its crown is meekness, its life is everlasting love unfeigned, and [it] taketh its kingdom with entreaty and not with contention, and keeps it by lowliness of mind. In God alone it can rejoice, though none else regard it or can own its life. It is conceived in sorrow and brought forth without any to pity it; nor doth it murmur at grief and oppression. It never rejoiceth but through sufferings; for with the world's joy it is murdered.

Quakers indeed now felt themselves to be engaged in a spiritual war which precluded the use of "outward arms" (Fox's term). This was the Lamb's War, the weapons of whose warriors were "love and patience by which they overcome." "The royal army," writes William Smith of Besthorpe (Notts.) of his fellow Quakers in *The Banner of Love* (1661, reprinted in his *Balm from Gilead*, 1675), "have put up their swords and would have all men saved." For them "the bloody or Lion's war" was ended. Even as late as 1697 we find a Quaker like John Crook (in his tract entitled *The Way to a Lasting Peace*) still hopeful concerning the outcome of their struggle. With the victory of the Lamb, "times will be settled," he writes, "in good earnest; and there will be no doubt of a firm, lasting and perpetual peace; for the Lion and the Lamb shall lie down together." By the end of the century, indeed, Quaker expectations of winning the world were waning, but two or three decades earlier optimism was still widespread among Friends. The title of a brief tract by Thomas Taylor which he published in 1667 (reprinted in his collected works *Truth's Innocency and Simplicity Shining*, 1697) breathes this somewhat naive spirit; he calls it *A Warning to the Nations, to lay aside All Prejudice and Enmity, the Ground of Strife and Wars; and to come and embrace the Light of Christ Jesus, that they may see themselves, and come to be saved and healed, and united in the Love of God.* In it he foretells the ending of the governments of this earth along with their armies, and the establishment of a warless world under God. "His Peaceable Kingdom . . . He hath begun to set up in his trembling people," the Quakers. Taylor called upon the nations to abandon their arms and convert them into ploughshares. Thus among Quakers a pacifist apocalypticism survived for some years the discarding of any sympathy with its more militant varieties.

The brief persecution of Quakers in 1661 was a portent of worse things to come. Excluded like other dissenters from office, they suffered even more severely than the latter—perhaps because of their more uncompromising stand—from the combined efforts of church and state to enforce religious uniformity on the country. Except for a brief lull between 1672 and 1675, this period of persecution lasted from 1662 until toward the end of the 1680's, when first Catholic James II's Declaration of Indulgence in 1687 and then the Act of Toleration of 1689 brought relief to religious nonconformity. When persecution was at its height, Quaker meetinghouses had been closed and sometimes even physically dismantled; members were fined and imprisoned, some were whipped and tortured, and a few even transported across the Atlantic. Friends continued to protest their loyalty to the state and ready obedience to all laws that were not against conscience. Time and again they stated their abhorrence of sedition and plots and reaffirmed their unwillingness on principle to use physical violence for whatever cause. "I say I am a peaceable man": thus William Mead, a former soldier and now co-prisoner with William Penn in the famous trial of 1670. "Time was, when I had freedom to use a carnal sword, and then I thought I feared no man; but now I fear the living God, and dare not make use thereof nor hurt any man." But all these protestations on the part of Friends did not succeed in averting the successive blows that were directed against their new Society.

Yet the Society of Friends emerged at the end of the ordeal strengthened in organization, a disciplined body with a network of local meetings spread throughout large parts of Great Britain as well as overseas. This was indeed gain. At the same time, as a result of the fierce pressure generated by persecution over nearly three decades, something of the wide sweep of the early Quaker vision had been lost. In place of a movement that sought to win a world for Christ there had emerged a sect, godly, sober, conscientious, yet cut off—partly by circumstances, increasingly by its own choice—from the world around it by a series of peculiar "testimonies," which once Quakers had hoped to make the principles of all mankind.

In regard to Friends' attitude to war and violence the paramountcy of the Spirit, which underlay their early peace testimony, gave way slowly before other motives for renouncing the sword, though the incompatibility of war with the Christian spirit never ceased to play a dominant role (at least until the evangelical movement with its emphasis on the letter took possession of large sections of the Society during the nineteenth century). In particular, two motivations for pacifism came now to have an increasing part in Quaker thinking: the idea of noncombatancy as the outcome of a quasi-legal New Dispensation, which Christ had promulgated and whose ordainments were to be found inscribed in the books of the New Testament; and, second, the argument from humanitarian or even economic considerations. Neither motivation was new in the history of Christian pacifism. The legalistic view had, as we have seen, been held by the Anabaptists and Mennonites, and the pragmatic case against war was pleaded with eloquence and energy by Erasmus and other Christian humanists, though they did not reach a position of absolute pacifism.

Among Friends as early as 1661 we find Peter Hardcastle (incidentally, one of the few soldier-converts to Quakerism to leave the Commonwealth army on account of a principled opposition to war) adopting a legalistic view of the peace testimony. In his brief pamphlet *The Quaker's Plea* where he refers to the conversion to pacifism of former army veterans who had since become Friends, he writes that they had come to believe: "That it is not lawful (in the administration of the gospel) to fight . . . or go to war with carnal weapons in any wise." This standpoint is much more clearly expressed in the works of the great Quaker apologist Robert Barclay, whose writings on peace date to the late 1670's. In his *Apology for the True Christian Divinity*, first published in Latin in 1676 and then in 1678 in an English version, he devotes Sections XIII-XV of Proposition XV to providing arguments in support of the thesis which he regards as a tenet binding on all members of the Society of Friends: "It is not lawful for Christians to resist evil, or to fight or war in any case." Trained in theology and educated in both Catholic and Calvinist environments, Barclay possessed an able pen and a subtle mind. He deals effectively with the opponents of pacifism, whether they based their case on the record of the Old Testament—which, said Barclay, had been superseded by Christ's fresh revelation—or on selected texts of the New Testament, which might seem to speak against a pacifist interpretation. He also cites the example of the early Christian church as further evidence in favor of the Quaker view of war. At the same time he is prepared to allow a conditional justification of war in the case of Christians unable to rise to the full demands of their religion—those "yet in the mixture," he calls them—and of non-Christians. For such as these (unlike Anabaptists and Mennonites Barclay, we may note, was not prepared to deny sword-bearing magistrates "altogether the name of Christians"), "we shall not say that war undertaken upon a just occasion is altogether unlawful." But for those who strove to follow Christ's precepts exactly, the sword was totally forbidden.

In Barclay's writings we continue to find, however, alongside the legalistic approach an appreciation of the wellsprings from which flows the spirit of peace. This emerges best in the tract he published in London in 1677: *Universal Love considered, and established upon Its Right Foundation.* Such love, he writes, "necessarily supposeth and includes love to enemies." "He that will beat, kill, and every way he can destroy his enemy, does but foolishly contradict himself if he pretend to love him." And such love is an essential component of "True Christianity." To an opponent who had charged the Quakers by their failure to approve defensive wars with a willingness to deliver the Christian world over to the Turks and the heathen, Barclay exclaims: "How men can love their enemies, and yet kill and destroy them is more than I can reach; but if it were so, such as rather suffer than do it do surely more love them, and to do so is no injury to ourselves nor neighbours, when done out of conscience towards God" (from *Robert Barclay's Apology for the True Christian Divinity Vindicated from John Brown's Examination and Pretended Confutation Thereof*, 1679).

Barclay introduces a new note into Quaker writing on peace when he pleads the material ill consequences as a major factor in repudiating war. A sense of sin and the guidance of the Holy Spirit, and not a consideration of consequences, had hitherto been uniformly at the center of Quaker pacifism. Barclay was quite prepared to address Europe's statesmen in favor of peace: a stand that would have been entirely alien, for instance, to the spirit of Anabaptist-Mennonite nonresistance or even in the thinking of the beginning period in Quakerism. In February 1678 we find him delivering in Latin *An Epistle of Love and Friendly Advice, to the Ambassadors of the Several Princes of Europe, met at Nimeguen to consult the Peace of Christendom, so far as they are concerned. Wherein the True Cause of the Present War is discovered, and the Right Remedy and Means for a Firm and Settled Peace is proposed* (published in English in 1679). To speak truth to power: this was to become a settled tradition within the Society of Friends. In Barclay's view and that of Quakerism subsequently, the terrestrial order was not irredeemable; it could become something more than a cockpit for bloody struggles between evildoers and scarcely less wicked and sanguinary powers into whose unworthy hands God had entrusted the sword of authority. The horrors of war, like the other evils of society, were a proper object of Christian concern. International politics were subject to morality; Christian values were applicable here as in public life at home.

In an eloquent passage of the *Epistle* Barclay addressed to the representatives of the European powers who had assembled at Nijmegen in 1678, he has given rein to his humanitarian pacifism:

Upon every slender pretext [he laments concerning the rulers of contemporary Christendom] such as their own small discontents, or that they judge the present peace they have with their neighbours cannot suit with their grandeur and worldly glory, they sheath their swords in one another's bowels; ruin, waste, and destroy whole countries; expose to the greatest misery many thousand families; make thousands of widows and ten thousands of orphans; cause the banks to overflow with the blood of those for whom the Lord Jesus shed his precious blood; and spend and destroy many of the good creatures of God. And all this while they pretend to be followers of the lamb-like Jesus, who came not to destroy men's lives but to save them, . . . not to kill, murder, and destroy men; not to hire poor men to run upon and murder one another, merely to satisfy the lust and ambition of great men; they being often times ignorant of the ground of the quarrel, and not having the least occasion of evil or prejudice against those their fellow Christians whom they thus kill; amongst whom not one of a thousand perhaps ever saw one another before.

Even more representative of Friends' growing interest in the practical implications of an antiwar stand than Barclay's writings—of their desire to ameliorate, if they could, the existing international anarchy—are the works of two other Quakers whose life-spans run over into the first quarter of the eighteenth century, William Penn and John Bellers.

Penn is, after Fox, certainly the best known of the two first generations of Quakers. Whereas Fox was a son of the people, Penn's father was an admiral who sent him first to Oxford and then on a round of foreign travel. His conversion in 1667 to the persecuted and despised Quakers did not, however, mean a complete break with his aristocratic and courtly background. His friendship with King James II was even, after the Glorious Revolution, to bring down on his head suspicions of Jacobitism and crypto-Stuart sympathies. Yet his acceptance of Quakerism was unconditional. A well-known story handed down in Quaker oral tradition but almost certainly authentic makes young Penn, soon after his decision to throw in his lot with Friends but while he was still hesitating to abandon the clothes and customs of the world, ask George Fox if he must cease wearing a sword. "Wear it as long as thou canst," Fox replied. When they next met, Penn was without his sword. "I have taken thy advice," Penn tells Fox, "I wore it as long as I could."

Penn's writings, as Margaret Hirst has pointed out, are filled with denunciation of war's unchristian character and of the pursuit of war by "apostate Christians" who outdo even the Turks in ferocity and bloodthirstiness. One might think from their behavior, he comments sarcastically, that Christ had taught not that the peacemakers or the meek are blessed but that "Blessed are the contentious, backbiters, talebearers, fighters, and makers of war." He repeats his belief that "love and persuasion" have "more force than weapons of war." Although in practical enterprises such as the founding and directing of the "Holy Experiment" in Pennsylvania, he was forced by circumstances to compromise on what he perhaps considered inessential forms (he has been severely criticized for this by writers like the contemporary Mennonite historian, Guy F. Hershberger), he nevertheless consistently maintained not merely a personal belief in the Quaker peace testimony but a weaponless state in his Quaker-ruled American province. "Not fighting, but suffering" was how he defined the quintessence of Quaker pacifism. Friends had the task of instructing mankind in a better method of resolving its differences than the way of arms; "somebody must begin it," he remarks (an idea, we may add, that is found earlier in the writings of Isaac Penington).

But Penn, too, used utilitarian arguments against war. He believed that peace was a better policy than war quite apart from the scruples of an informed Christian conscience. Thus he wrote: "Christianity set aside, if the costs and fruits of war were well considered, peace, with its inconveniences, is generally preferable." The nations in his day needed peace urgently, a speedy cessation of the senseless and fruitless series of wars which had occurred since the break-up of medieval Europe. Like Barclay, he was appalled by the readiness with which rulers plunged into war for trifles, leaving a legacy of destruction and death: ravaged countrysides, ruined cities, numberless dead as well as countless widows and orphans. "Our present condition in Europe," he concluded, "needs an olive branch, the doctrine of peace, as much as ever."

Considerations such as these led Penn to propound a plan whereby the peace of Europe might be established on firm foundations. He did not envisage a universal conversion to pacifism, a general abandonment of defensive as well as offensive armament. This seemed too utopian in seventeenth-century Europe. His design for peace, which he published in 1693 in the form of *An Essay towards the Present and Future Peace of Europe by the Establishment of an European Dyet, Parliament, or Estates*, was modelled to some extent on the earlier *grand dessein* of Henry IV of France's minister Sully. Penn wished to see the inclusion within the European confederation of such peripheral states as Turkey or Russia. Only in this way could it act as an instrument for preserving both peace and justice and as an effective organ of international government. Arbitration would replace war as the regular method of settling disputes and of adjudicating rival claims. Penn seems to have considered the provision of military sanctions as a last resort, necessary in case any member state refused to submit its case to arbitration by the diet of Europe. His plan, we see, was conceived not as an exposition of Quaker pacifism, but as a practical scheme which might be adopted at once by Europe's rulers, Its object was primarily humanitarian: to save lives which would otherwise be lost if Europe continued, as hitherto, to be rent by ceaseless warfare.

The same motive animated the other peace-planner within the seventeenth-century Society of Friends, John Bellers. Bellers was to acquire posthumous renown from his project, propounded in 1695, for erecting a "College of Industry" on cooperative lines: this led him to be regarded as a forerunner by modern socialists such as Robert Owen, Karl Marx, and Eduard Bernstein. Among Bellers's numerous philanthropic concerns the promotion of peace took a prominent place. In 1710 he published a tract whose lengthy title provides at the same time a brief summary of the contents: *Some Reasons for an European State, proposed to the Powers of Europe by an Universal Guarantee, and an Annual Congress, Senate, Dyet, or Parliament, to settle any Disputes about the Bounds and Rights of Princes and States hereafter.* . . . In his proposals Bellers drew not only on Sully but also on Penn. But he was more specific than Penn in his elaboration of the economic argument against war. "The vast treasure" expended in recent wars Bellers sets out in statistical form. According to his calculations the French monarchy, for instance, had lost on war a total of over £560,000,000 since the year 1688. And in addition to the material losses there was the "deluge of Christian blood" poured out in these struggles. No more than had Penn, did Bellers contemplate a federated Europe which would enforce its decisions on recalcitrant states merely by moral pressure. There was to be a pooling of armaments, but not their total abolition—at any rate Bellers does not conceive this to be a possibility within the immediate future.

With Penn and Bellers there enters a new element in Quaker thinking on peace that was to become particularly important in the nineteenth and twentieth centuries. Quakers of this school of thought regard the peace testimony as not solely concerned with personal morality or the ethos of the sect; they feel that their Society, while still guarding as far as possible a strict renunciation of all war on the part of its members, should broaden the outreach of its testimony for peace and attempt to lessen the incidence of war in the international arena. Gradualist in approach and optimistic in regard to the political order in general, the proponents of this view broke conclusively, though probably unconsciously, with an Anabaptist-like residue of "nonconformity to the world" present in early Quaker writing alongside apocalyptic yearnings for the earthly rule of the Saints.

Gradualism and optimism are revealed, too, in the seventeenth-century Quaker attitude toward the magistracy. At the beginning (long before Barclay, indeed) Quakers had envisaged the possibility of a Christian magistracy. They did not follow here in the footsteps of their Anabaptist-Mennonite forerunners in denying a place to the ruler within the Christian community. And, as we have seen in our discussion of the events of 1659, they were ready themselves to accept office in certain circumstances. For instance, at a general meeting of Friends held at Balby in Yorkshire in 1656 a resolution—the fourteenth—was accepted: "That if any be called to serve the Commonwealth in public service, which is for the public welfare and good, that with cheerfulness it be undertaken, and in faithfulness discharged with God, that therein patterns and examples in the thing that is righteous ye may be to those that are without." After the Restoration, of course, Quakers were excluded from the magistracy by law, and even after the Glorious Revolution and the coming of toleration their refusal to take the oath precluded them *de facto* from holding office. A more detached attitude developed among Friends. Passive obedience to authority, except in those matters against conscience, was now stressed in place of active participation in government. Yet across the Atlantic wherever Friends were admitted to office, whether in Pennsylvania, Rhode Island, or elsewhere for brief periods, they served willingly even in the most responsible places of command.

How did Fox and seventeenth-century Friends view the magistrate's office and the function of the state? Did they differentiate between permissible police duties and the—for Friends—inadmissible war-making powers with which all existing governments were endowed? This distinction was certainly to be made by Quakers later, but in regard to the two earliest generations there is indeed, and especially at first, a certain ambiguity, a lack of precision in defining the limits within which a weaponless people, such as Friends came to feel themselves, could consistently act. Let us now look rather more closely at what Quakers of this period had to say on this subject.

In his letter to Oliver Cromwell of 1654 cited above, Fox expounds his view of the purposes of government. Those like himself, who had renounced violence and "all the works of darkness," including war, did not need the control of "the magistrate's sword." They formed in other words a community patterned after that of Christ and his disciples. But within the world as at present constituted government was indispensable. Here it had a positive role to play. It should be, as St. Paul had taught, both "a terror to the evil-doers which acts contrary to the light of the Lord Jesus Christ" and at the same time "a praise to them that do well." "The magistrate bears not the sword in vain," wrote Fox, paraphrasing once again the words of St. Paul (Romans, 13). Five years later we find him repeating much the same thought when he writes in one of his epistles of "the sword of justice, which is to keep the peace, and is a terror to the evil-doers, and to keep down the transgressors, and for the praise to them that do well." "This is owned in its place," he says; at the same time, however, he reminds his readers of Christ's words: "all they that take the sword shall perish with the sword."

William Smith of Besthorpe is even more specific than Fox concerning what he considers the essentially repressive aspects of government. In an eight-page tract which also appeared in 1659 (*A Right Dividing or A True Discerning shewing the Use of the Sword, and how and where it is in its place, and what it is to be laid upon*) Smith lists as the main aims of the magistracy: "To suppress violence, to punish the evildoers, and to rule those that are unruly, disobedient, and disorderly." Such functions of those who wield power he describes as "manly"; they answer "the end for which the sword is put in their hands." In addition to protection from wrongdoers society also had the right to demand social justice from the magistrates. From his further argument it is clear, however, that Smith associates the sword-bearing magistrate with the profession of soldiering, and this in turn he considers incompatible with the Quakers' principles. "They are out of the place of a soldier, neither do know a soldier's place, which is under the state of a man, violently to kill and destroy each other." The Quakers' task was "to bring people to God and to Christ." With Smith, then, and perhaps with Fox too at this period, the maintenance of public order merges with the waging of war in a just cause; they are both proper functions of the magistracy (indeed at that time the two activities were not so clearly distinguishable as today) and are comprehended within God's plan for mankind. Yet Quakers as an elect people were exempt from participating in such work; moreover, they had an obligation to stand aside bearing witness to a higher righteousness than the world's.

This point of view is exemplified in a treatise written in 1661 by Isaac Penington, who even after his conversion to Quakerism in 1658 had retained much of his earlier sympathy for the Good Old Cause. The tract is entitled *Somewhat spoken to a Weighty Question, concerning the Magistrate's Protection of the Innocent, . . .*; in it the author included, too, "a brief account of what the people called Quakers desire, in reference to the civil government." He assumes, throughout, a separation of Quakers from the magistracy; Friends form a people apart whose function it is to follow "a gospel spirit" in their relations with their fellow men, whereby they "are taken off from fighting and cannot use a weapon destructive to any creature." Penington never goes so far as explicitly to deny that a Christian may exercise the magistrate's office. Yet in effect his position contemplates the withdrawal of Quakers from the political arena. Somewhat in the style of Origen in his defense of the early church's pacifism against Celsus' accusations of lack of patriotism, Penington saw Quakers' service to the state in acting within it as an island of godliness. The state, he believed, would recognize the advantage of having within its borders "a peaceable and a righteous generation (whom the Lord hath made and preserved so) breathing to the Lord for peace, good and prosperity to the nation and the magistrates thereof, and to stretch forth his arm to be a defence about them." True, a nation which renounced war, he believed, might rely on the Lord for protection. But Quakers did not aim at removing the sword out of the hands of present-day governments. Their pacifism, as he remarks in the course of his argument, constituted a long-range program, an ideal toward which mankind might strive.

> I speak not this against any magistrates or peoples defending themselves against foreign invasions, or making use of the sword to suppress the violent and evil-doers within their borders (for this the present state of things doth require, and a great blessing will attend the sword where it is borne uprightly to that end, and its use will be honourable; and while there is need of a sword, the Lord will not suffer that government or those governors to want fitting instruments, under them, for the managing thereof, who wait on him in his fear to have the edge of it rightly directed).

Thus the end of the 1650's, the time when pacifism became a definite feature of Quaker ideology, saw a subtle, though probably unremarked, shift in Friends' attitude toward the magistracy. It was not that the magistrate's office was, as it were, disfellowshipped, relegated to the sphere of the pseudo-Christians and the non-Christians, as with Anabaptists and Mennonites. For Friends the Christian magistracy remained a possibility. Yet writers like Penington obviously now approximated in practice, if not in theory, the Anabaptist-Mennonite tradition, for they had little doubt that the peace principles of Friends precluded them from participating in government as then constituted. Political disillusionment followed by exclusion from politics was largely responsible for this development. In this way discussion of the political implications of Quaker pacifism, of its limitations in regard to the domestic scene and its obligations in regard to international order, was cut short virtually before it got under way. Yet discussion was only postponed rather than permanently checked. Toward the end of the century William Penn, who believed that the magistrate's office was "both lawful and useful" (as he expressed it in his letter to King Jan III of Poland) and who by his founding of Pennsylvania opened up to his fellow Quakers a wide range of political activities, was one of those who began to seriously explore the political dimensions of the Quaker peace testimony. Since then Friends—or at least some of the most sensitive spirits among them—have not ceased to be alternately baffled and elated by this quest.

We have dealt hitherto with the theoretical aspects of Quaker pacifism as Friends adopted noncombatancy as part of the recognized program of their Society. A refusal to bear arms then became the expected position of those who wished to remain in good standing within it. We cannot point to any specific date when conscientious objection to military service became a requirement for membership (though it is of course implicit in the Declaration of January 1661). But from the record it is clear that by 1660 Friends understood that this position was incumbent on them. Barclay, for instance, when he published his *Apology* in 1676, takes it entirely for granted. "We have suffered much in our country," he writes, "because we neither could ourselves bear arms, nor send others in our place." In the previous year we see the Morning Meeting in London, which then constituted an important executive organ of the whole Society, advising Friends that "in the several counties they that find arms, etc. [for the militia] be tenderly admonished about it, according to the ancient testimony of Christ Jesus." Although there do not appear to have been any official directions in this period for disfellowshipping those who would not abide by the Society's testimony against bearing arms, or who did not at least manifest a penitent spirit for having deviated from it, disownment on this score was obviously practiced from early on. We read, for instance, of several west-country Friends being disowned for complicity in the Monmouth rebellion against James II in 1685, and a handful of Irish Quakers, who took up arms during the troublous period of 1689-1690 ending with James II's defeat at the Battle of the Boyne, were dealt with in similar fashion. (However, it is worth noting, neither William Edmundson nor his fellow Quakers saw anything incompatible with their pacifist principles in calling in the aid of "a guard of . . . soldiers" from the English garrison in Dublin to protect the Protestant settlers in their area from the depredations of Irish marauders and bandits: they evidently equated this step with a request for police protection.) There were, it is true, a few Quakers who did not hold to the Society's peace testimony and yet escaped censuring and eventual disownment (e.g., William Penn's private secretary and later his representative in Pennsylvania, James Logan). But this was only possible because they were fortunate both in not being faced with an actual military requisition and in being discreet enough to keep their opinions to themselves.

In Great Britain the earliest Quaker conscientious objectors are to be found among sailor converts in the Commonwealth Navy. As early as October 1656 a master gunner on the *Mermaid* handed in his resignation on account of scruples concerning the shedding of blood, which he had acquired through his contact with Friends. His captain, obviously puzzled by this unusual behavior, reported to the Admiralty commissioners as follows:

> He have [sic] not acted these two months but have altogether confined himself to his cabin, and have given out to our master-carpenter that no power shall command him to fire a gun as that from thence blood might be spilt, his tenets obliging him thereunto; the which myself with others do find to come nearest to those which are called Quakers, for his carriage towards me and others is without any outward respect, and from a spirit of delusion, as to the denying of ordinances and visible authority. . . . I earnestly desire that he may have his will as that I may discharge him with all speed.

Three seventeenth-century navy objectors have left accounts of their experiences and their tribulations before gaining final release from the navy's clutches. First in chronological sequence comes Thomas Lurting, "the fighting sailor turned peaceable Christian" (as he entitled the account he wrote in his old age).

Since the age of fourteen when he was pressed to fight for the parliamentary forces in Ireland, Lurting had become inured to the life of a fighting man. He had been in action later against the Dutch and the Spaniards: this time as a sailor on a man-of-war. His first contacts with Quakerism came around the middle of the 1650's when, now a boatswain's mate and a man therefore of some standing on his ship, he assisted in the manhandling of several of the crew who, after having turned Quaker, had refused to remove their hats in greeting the captain and appeared on other points of their behavior to display a lack of respect for authority. But soon scorn on Lurting's part turned to admiration; he became convinced of the "truth." At first he and his fellow Quaker seamen seem to have felt no scruples in taking part in battle. When their ship received orders to attack a fort at Barcelona, Lurting relates, "we called Quakers fought with as much courage as any, seeing then no farther." But suddenly in the midst of the *mêlée* Lurting, as he prepared to fire the guns, comprehends in a moment of revelation—so at least it appeared to him later—that bloodshed is contrary to the religious principles he now professes. "He that hath all men's hearts in his hand," he writes, "can turn them at his pleasure; yea, in a minute's time so far changed my heart, that in a minute before, I setting my whole strength and rigour to kill and destroy men's lives, and in a minute after I could not kill or destroy a man, if it were to gain the world." The thought struck him like a thunderbolt as he watched the shot from his cannon fall among the enemy: *How if I had killed a man.*" His mates seeing his confusion asked him if he were hurt. "I answered, *No: but under some scruple of conscience on the account of fighting,* altho' I had not heard that the Quakers refused to fight." After consultations between Lurting and the other Quaker sailors, they all decided that fighting was indeed against their religion. At first only Lurting felt strongly enough to determine on resistance to further orders to participate in battle, the others contenting themselves with the resolve to cease from fighting once they had returned home. Yet Lurting finally succeeded in persuading them to take their stand now, even though this made them liable to the death penalty. However, apart from one false alarm when the Quaker group stuck to their resolution, their ship fortunately was not involved in any further engagements with the enemy—as a result of the Lord's protection, in Lurting's view.

After the first decade we are not likely to find Quakers among the professional sailors of England's fleet. But right up into the eighteenth century many Friends served in the merchant navy. They were thereby frequently in danger, in peacetime as in war, of impressment into the fighting fleet; indeed any young Quaker resident in the coastal areas of the country was subject to the attentions of the press-gangs which roamed the ports in search of conscripts for the King's navy, as we may learn from the experience related in his *Journal* for the year 1694 of nineteen-year-old Thomas Chalkley, later to become an eminent minister of his Society on both sides of the Atlantic. Chalkley, however, was more fortunate than some, since the morning after being seized near his home in Southwark and taken aboard a man-of-war he was released by the captain's order. "What shall we do with this fellow? He swears he will not fight," the ship's lieutenant had enquired perplexedly. "No, no, he will neither swear nor fight," interjected the captain, who seems to have had some knowledge of Quaker principles.

We may now return once more to Lurting's narrative for material to illustrate our discussion of the Quaker and the press-gang. After leaving the navy Lurting had continued to earn his living as a sailor. "About the time of King Charles the Second's coming into England," he writes, "for the space of two or three years, I met with many sorts of exercises, being forced or press'd divers times; the which the Lord brought me through." In 1662 the press-gang yet again seized on him as their victim, and he found himself on board a man-of-war at Harwich. The captain was sympathetic—it seems that Lurting's story was not unknown to some on board—and proved willing to allow Lurting to perform noncombatant duties in lieu of actual fighting. In response Lurting displayed that uncompromising rejection of alternative service, even where such service appears to have a humanitarian purpose, which was typical of early Quaker conscientious objection (a stance indeed that has survived into the twentieth century when in the two World Wars the absolutist position was to draw many of its supporters from the ranks of the Quakers).

To Lurting's assertion of his pacifist beliefs the captain had replied: Very well. But he could assist him, since as he had heard, he had had command before over men, in giving orders and he might help, too, in handling the ropes.

> *This is not killing of men, to hale a rope.* I answered, *But I will not do that. Then,* said he, *thou shalt be with the coopers, to hand beer for them, there is great occasion for it.* I answered, *But I will not do that. Then,* said he again, *I have an employment for thee, which will be a great piece of charity, and a saving of men's lives, thou shalt be with the doctor, and when a man comes down, that hath lost a leg or an arm, to hold the man, while the doctor cuts it off; this is not killing men, but saving men's lives.* I answered, *But I will not do that; for it's an assistance.* Then he said, *I will send thee ashore to prison.* I answered, *I am in thy hand, thou may'st do with me what thou pleasest.*

While still confined aboard ship, Lurting remained stubbornly opposed to anything that smacked of complicity with war-making, even refusing to accept ship's rations unless he were allowed to pay for it first. "I cannot do the King's work," he stated, "therefore cannot eat the King's victuals."

The captain in fact did not commit Lurting to prison but allowed him to go on shore, where he obtained employment unloading corn into a lighter. Again the press-gang came upon him and hauled him off on board another man-of-war. There the following dialogue took place:

> CAPTAIN: Thou art no Quaker; for here thou bringst corn, and of it is made bread, and by the strength of that bread, we kill the Dutch; and therefore, no Quaker: Or art thou not as accessory to their death, as we?
>
> LURTING: I am a man that have, and can feed my enemies; and well may I, you, who pretend to be my friends.
>
> CAPTAIN: Turn him away, he is a Quaker.

Ingenuously perhaps, but effectively, Lurting had placed his finger here on the essential difference between activities which, while they might indirectly and incidentally contribute to the prosecution of war, were aimed primarily at peaceful ends, and those whose main objective was inextricably interwoven with the military machine, even if superficially they might seem to express a humanitarian concern. This distinction forms an essential part of the Quaker rationale for conscientious objection.

Lurting's conversion to pacifism appears to have been the result of an inner experience and not to have been connected directly with the Quaker sailors on his ship. On the other hand, merchant seaman Edward Coxere, our second memoirist, who had joined Quakers during a short leave in his home town of Dover in 1661, accepted Quaker pacifism—by this date, as we have seen, a fixed tenet of the sect—along with other aspects of his new faith. Yet this did not come without difficulty. The problem, as he confided to his new brethren, "lay on me as a very great burden, because it struck at my very life" as a sailor. In times of war like the present, even though in the merchant marine, he would be obliged to fight. Of the Dover Quakers whom he consulted concerning his dilemma he writes:

> They, being very mild, used but few words, I being a stranger to them, but wished me to be faithful to what the Lord did make known to me, and words to that purpose, so did not encourage me to fight, but left me to the working of the power of the Lord in my own heart, which was more prevalent than words in the condition I then was in.

What ensued after Coxere returned to his ship must be told in his own style.

> Oh the exercise I had in this very matter of fighting. . . . Fearing we should meet with an enemy to fight with, I did not dare let it be known in the ship, neither to the master nor men, but thought to myself, if the Lord ordered it that we should get well home, I would trust the Lord and not the arm of flesh, nor guns, in which was my confidence before . . . I being now in this very great strait, leaning on the ship's side by Richard Knowlleman [Knowlman], who had been a gunner of a man-of-war, and left his employ on the account of fighting [in 1657], and was counted a Quaker, yet (it seemed) would fight in a merchantman. I asked him that, if we should have occasion to fight, what must be done. His answer was that we must fire at the mast. The Lord at that time let me see that piece of deceit: that, if so, it was but a cheat [to] deceive them we were with . . . we had the men to deal with and not the mast. This would not serve, but my desire was to be true to God and man and not deceive my soul.

However, as in Lurting's case, fortune—or the Lord—favored Coxere, and his ship returned home again without an encounter with the enemy. His troubles were not ended yet, though, for no captain wished now to employ him. "The name of a Quaker and not fighting shut me quite out of esteem with them." One ship's master told him frankly: "He could not answer to his merchants or owners to carry me in the ship unless I would fight." After a lengthy spell of unemployment Coxere succeeded, however, in finding a Quaker shipowner, and his difficulties ceased.

Our third naval memoirist is a simple Yorkshire fisherman, Richard Seller, who dictated his story to a friend. It was eventually published by Besse in the second volume of his *Sufferings* (pp. 112-120). Seller was pressed for the Royal Navy in 1665, during the second Anglo-Dutch War of 1665-1667. Like Lurting a few years earlier, on board ship Seller refused to work and, less fortunate in his captain than Lurting had been, was subjected for his obstinacy to severe ill-treatment, although some of the crew, impressed by his steadfastness, became kindly disposed toward him. Seller was sentenced by court-martial to be hanged —and then, at the last moment, reprieved. Soon his ship, the *Royal Prince*, became involved in a series of actions against the Dutch. Seller in the emergency was ready to look after the wounded and "to look out for fire-ships." On one occasion one of the officers came up to him. "He asked me," Seller relates, " 'How came I to be so bloody?' Then I told him, 'It was with carrying down wounded men.' So he took me in his arms and kissed me; and that was the same lieutenant that persecuted me so with irons at the first." Seller's courageous carrying-out of his noncombatant duties, which seem to have been voluntarily undertaken and not imposed as an alternative to combatancy, evidently won him the friendship of the commander as well. On the fleet's return to its base Seller was released from further service and given a certificate to protect him from the press-gang: "to keep [him] clear at home, and also in [his] fishing," as the commander assured him.

The activities of the press-gang were to prove extremely troublesome to all the Quaker communities in coastal areas. Indeed, especially in wartime, no seafaring Friend was secure from the attempts of the authorities to force him into the fighting marine. Take, for instance, the following minute from the records of the Quaker meeting at Aberdeen for 1672:

> The meeting finding that the magistrates of the town have put Alexander Somerville, mariner, our Friend, in prison though he has given in a bill to the Council . . . for his liberation, that they have in plain terms denied to liberate him unless he give bond as the rest of the seamen have done and this having not only an appearance but plainly implying an engagement [to] answer them and list himself for the war, Friends thought fit to advise him not to give any engagement either by word or writ lest otherwise it might mar his peace and reflect on truth.

In 1678 we find the Meeting for Sufferings, which had been set up only a couple of years earlier, lamenting "the often sufferings of Friends by being imprest in the King's ships of war." It appointed Daniel Lobdy of Deal to act officially on Friends' behalf for the speedy release of such persons. He was requested "upon hearing or having account of any Friend or Friends prest into the King's ships to make application to the captains or other officers on board for their discharge." His expenses were to be reimbursed him by the respective meetings to which the pressed men belonged. Lobdy is found active in this service for some years ahead.

When we turn to consider Quaker conscientious objection to service in the armed forces on land we are struck at once by the exiguousness of the sources in this area. For one thing we lack such racy, graphic, if somewhat naive, accounts of their experiences in defying authority as Lurting, Coxere, and Seller provide for the navy. The volunteer system was in force both for the new standing army and for such additional troops as war or its threat might demand, so that conscription

applied only to the militia, or "trained bands" as that body was sometimes called. Service in the militia was only for short periods and,
therefore, any confrontation with authority on the part of an objector
was likely to be brief and much less dramatic than in the case of the
navy. Under the Commonwealth, writes Margaret Hirst, "those who
refused to train [in the militia] were to be fined £20, and the obstinate
imprisoned." The militia acts of Charles II's reign set the general pattern followed in subsequent legislation down to the middle of the nineteenth century. They punished a refusal to serve if called upon, or to
find a substitute, by a fine and subsequent distraint on the goods of the
delinquent if he failed to pay the fine. No distinction was made at first
between those who refused to comply on account of a conscientious
objection to fighting and those who did so from some other motive.

In the seventeenth century objection to military service does not
appear to have figured as a major cause of Quaker "sufferings." Sufferings on account of the nonpayment of tithes, for instance, figure much
more frequently than militia sufferings in the Quaker records. The
burden was not too onerous (it was often much more severe in the
American colonies or in the Caribbean islands) and only sporadically
and irregularly imposed. "References to Quakers being disciplined for
not maintaining this testimony are very infrequent," writes Arnold
Lloyd on the basis of a careful study of both printed and archival
sources. This was due not to a lack of discipline on the part of the Society but to the comparative ease with which the demands of the
militia could be met—as well, of course, as to the firm adherence to
their peace testimony of the post-Restoration generations of Quakers.

For difficulties there were indeed in regard to militia service. In the
first place, Friends enforced a rigorous absolutism in regard to their
members. Not only was the provision of a substitute sternly forbidden
—for was not this tantamount to shedding blood in one's own person?
But the payment of a fine was not allowed either. The payer thereof
was likely to find himself being dealt with by his meeting just as if he
had agreed to serve personally or find a substitute. Friends felt
strongly in this period that willingness to accept any obligation as an
alternative to doing what they considered right constituted an inadmissible compromise with the truth. Sometimes distraint of goods
might entail only an inconsiderable material loss. Often, however, and
especially when the distraining officers were hostile or avaricious,
much more might be taken than the usually low fines warranted.
Moreover, since many Quakers came from the poorer sections of the
population, even small sums might impose a considerable burden on
them. There were some members who did not even possess sufficient

worldly possessions on which a distress might be levied: young apprentices, for instance, or day laborers, the kind of men indeed who
would be most likely to receive a summons to muster with their local
militia. For such the penalty was imprisonment.

"The earliest known instances," writes Hirst of Quaker objectors to
military service, "are found in records for fines and distraints in kind
at Colchester in 1659, but it is almost certain that these were not isolated examples." In that year one John Furly had goods to the value of
£3.5.0 taken from him "for refusing to send an horse and man, when
summoned to serve in the county militia," while his fellow Colchester
Quaker Arthur Condon lost a coat valued at 20 shillings for refusal to
pay "a demand of 4 *s.* towards the charge of the trained-bands." Besse,
from whom these facts are derived, also reports for the previous year
a case in Maryland across the Atlantic where a Quaker, Richard
Keene, suffered distraint of goods for his refusal to train "as a soldier."
(Incidentally, the example of Keene and of such sailor objectors as
Thomas Lurting would appear to cast doubt on the thesis propounded
by writers like Alan Cole of a lack of widespread pacifist principle
among Friends until after the crisis of mid-1659.)

From the Restoration onwards militia "sufferings" became a regular
feature in Quaker experience. For instance, Besse records for Kent
under the year 1661: "In October this year, John Hogbin was imprisoned several months for not serving among the trained-bands, when
summoned. Nathaniel Owen of Sevenoaks was also fined and sent to
prison for refusing to bear arms; for which cause also William Brown,
Nicholas Homwood, and John Sladen were confined to prison at
Canterbury." (As a result of Hogbin's spending nineteen weeks in
Dover Castle his "trading was spoilt to his great damage.")

Fines and subsequent distress were, of course, the more usual
penalties for the Quakers' military delinquency. Whether in Wales or
East Anglia, the Midlands or the North country, the southern or the
western counties, the story is the same. In 1675 we find Bristol Quakers
reporting that the value of the goods distrained by the city marshals
much exceeded the amount of the fines imposed on members who refused to appear in arms. Complaints of this kind were very frequent
and clearly well founded. In the country Quaker farmers often had
their livestock seized for payment of their militia fines. Even women
were sometimes liable to penalties connected with refusal of militia
obligations: Besse, for example, noting the imprisonment at Winchester
for fifteen days of a group of Hampshire Friends in 1660 "for refusing
to pay toward the charge of the county militia," includes the name of
an Elizabeth Streater. There were indeed two separate counts in con-

nection with the militia under which Quakers could be prosecuted: a refusal to bear arms personally or by substitute and an objection to paying a rate toward the militia's upkeep (which was required of property-owners and thus explains the inclusion of a woman as a militia sufferer). In December 1678—once again at Bristol—Richard Snead, on "being summoned before the justices for refusing to bear arms," was required to take the oath of allegiance and "for refusing to swear was sent to prison." But this combination of charges appears to have been rare.

The city of London and the neighboring counties of Sussex and Kent were the areas where Friends suffered most severely from fines and imprisonments on account of the militia, for these were places exposed to a continuous possibility of invasion from the continent. "The [manuscript] minute-books of Kent Quarterly Meetings," writes Margaret Hirst, "show only fourteen years in the period 1660 to 1702 in which there is no record of fine or imprisonment for this cause. Kent Friends," she goes on, "were evidently men of small means, for the liabilities laid upon them are curious fractions of the normal claims. They are brought before the courts for 'refusing to send out three parts of an arms,' 'not finding arms for the quarter part of a musket,' 'not contributing to the quarter part of the charge of finding a musket 30 days at 2 *s.* a day,' and, strangest of all, for 'not sending in half a man to muster with a month's pay.'" London Friends, as the Meeting for Sufferings recorded (1690), also "suffered much for refusing." Many of those in the City whose property was now distrained to cover their militia fines were well-to-do tradesmen and merchants: Besse, for instance, notes under the year 1679 that "two clocks and two watches worth £11.5.0" were taken on this account from the well-known Quaker clockmaker, Daniel Quare.

In March 1679 the Meeting for Sufferings decided to regard the penalties Friends incurred through refusal to comply with militia requisitions—whether "by distresses of their goods or otherwise"—as "a suffering for the Lord and His truth" along with the hitherto more severe and more frequent punishment meted out to Friends for their ecclesiastical nonconformity, which were already officially reckoned as such by the Society. Now monthly meetings throughout the country were requested both to keep an exact record of their members' militia sufferings and to report these in due course to the Meeting for Sufferings.

On the whole post-Restoration Friends stood loyally by their peace testimony. True, we meet with Quakers like Thomas Ayrey, of whom it is reported that he "could suffer nothing for truth," for he not only agreed to take an oath but "when like to suffer for truth's testimony against fighting and bearing arms, he consented to take arms." Much more typical of the early Quaker spirit, however, was the faithfulness displayed, for instance, by the Quaker missionary Thomas Moore, who in 1652 travelled, along with a companion, John Philly, up and down the Austrian Habsburg dominions. Arrested by the authorities, the two men were thrown into jail as heretics and subjected to harsh tortures. On one occasion, Moore relates (his account is to be found in Besse's *Sufferings*), "the jailer did try me many ways, for he would have me learn to shoot, and hath tied match about my fingers, and hath struck to make me hold the musket, but I was like a fool. And they made themselves sport with me, and several times would put pistols in my hands, and bid me shoot." Or take the case of Richard Robinson from Wensleydale in Yorkshire, one of the First Publishers of Truth, who steadfastly refused either to bear arms himself or to find a man for the militia. "Never after his convincement," it was said of him, "would [he] pay anything directly or indirectly, but suffered for the same by fines and distresses, frequently encouraging other Friends to stand faithful."

A separate, though numerically small, category of military objectors consisted of serving soldiers who were converted to Quakerism in the course of their period of enlistment. We have had a good deal to say concerning their naval counterparts, whom we already found around the middle of the 1650's. At that date, although there were indeed Quaker soldiers in the army, most of them, we have seen, were more anxious to remain in the ranks than to get out of service. After the Restoration and the firm adoption of pacifism by the Society the situation changed. Henceforward the Quaker-inclined army objector became a permanent feature. His sufferings were usually more painful and more prolonged than those of the militia objector who was already a member of a Quaker meeting (though in the very rare instances where an actual Friend was pressed to serve in the army while it was on war-footing he was likely to meet with a parallel severity). In 1670, for instance, we read of one Christopher Hilary who, while serving in Ireland, came as a result of Quaker influence to be "convinced of the unlawfulness of wars and fightings under the gospel," and was sentenced first to ride a "wooden horse" and then to a short spell of imprisonment. Naturally, when Friends learned of such cases as Hilary's they exerted their utmost to obtain the objector's release from the army. They seem usually to have succeeded in their aim.

Whereas, in Great Britain at least, the twentieth-century conscientious objector, whether Quaker or not, has been required to submit a detailed statement of his motives for refusing military service and, in addition, has had to submit to often close questioning concerning his beliefs, a record of all of which is usually available, such materials are very rarely at the disposal of the historian of seventeenth-century Quakerism. Occasionally the sources lift the veil ever so slightly as when, for instance, a Quaker militia objector (the date is 1667) explains his refusal to muster not as an act of "contempt of the king or any of his officers" but as one of "obedience to the Lord, who had showed him mercy, and had called him from carnal weapons to love enemies according to Christ's doctrine, and not to take up arms against them." But this really does not tell us much that we did not know already concerning the nature of the Quaker objection to war.

A few years ago, however, Henry J. Cadbury uncovered in the Quaker archives preserved at Friends House, London, an account of a hearing, held in 1679 before the court at the Guildhall, of a London Friend who had been summoned to appear on account of his refusal to bear arms in the militia. This account Professor Cadbury subsequently published verbatim in the journal of the American Fellowship of Reconciliation (*Reconciliation*, 1 May 1960). It provides indeed fuller insight into the motivations of early Quaker conscientious objection than any other source known to me. The Quaker objector was Philip Ford, a substantial citizen and since 1669 William Penn's factotum (over whose subsequent career, however, a shadow was cast by his unscrupulous exploitation of his master's lack of business acumen, for the sake of private gain).

Ford, on being asked by the court why he had failed to muster, replied at once: "Before the first summons came I received a summons from the Prince of Peace to march under his banner, which is love, who came not to destroy men's lives but to save them. And being enlisted under this banner I dare not desert my colours to march under the banner . . . of the kings of the earth." The court then proceeded to probe him in regard to the payment of taxes, a question (as we shall see below) which was always to cause Friends much heart-searching. Ford indeed readily admitted to paying taxes, even with the knowledge that the money might be used by the king to construct warships or to buy guns and powder. He admitted, too, to having contributed his share toward the upkeep of the city watch, even though this body was armed and might, therefore, be responsible for shedding blood. "I make a distinction," he stated, "betwixt the military power and the civil. The military power's command is, Go, fire, kill and destroy. The civil power's command is, Go, keep the peace." The primary objective of a soldier must be, at the officer's command, to kill as many of the enemy as possible. True, Ford went on, Christ has commanded us to obey the magistrate in all things that are not against conscience. But he also tells us to love our enemies; he adjures us to refuse to do anything against conscience and instead meekly to endure the consequences of our disobedience. Christ's injunction to render Caesar the tribute due him cannot possibly (as the court had tried to argue) include the rendering of military service. "Your command to your followers is to kill your enemies. So that I choose rather to obey the captain of my salvation than you, whatever he may suffer you to inflict upon me for so doing." Meanwhile the court had shifted its ground and had begun to question Ford concerning the attitude of the early church to war. "Did not the Christians in former ages assist the Emperors in their wars?" "Yes they did," was Ford's prompt answer, "and please to peruse Tertullian. There you may find the product of their enterprises when their faith in God began to fail them, and they took to carnal weapons, there the apostasy entered, and the Pope got over most called Christians."

For the conclusion of Ford's case we may turn to Besse's *Sufferings*. Volume II contains the sparse comment: "Philip Ford . . . for a fine of £4.13s. 4d [imposed by order of the Guildhall court] had his goods taken away to the value of £24.2s." Although undoubtedly Ford's defense was more skillful and was supported by more learning than the average unschooled Quaker was capable of, his arguments reflect fairly accurately the sentiments of the Society at that time.

From Ford's testimony we see that demands for actual military service or its equivalent were not the only requisitions connected with war with which Friends had to deal. One of the most serious problems in this respect was the arming of Quaker-owned vessels. In the seventeenth century the merchant navy usually carried guns for use against the pirates who still roamed the seas or against the corsairs ready to carry their unhappy victims off to slavery until—or unless—their people at home were able to ransom them at a high price. Indeed the fate of captive Friends in Algiers forms a moving chapter in Quaker history. In wartime every ship became virtually a man-of-war; there were enemy privateers preying upon the shipping of the opposite side. Unarmed vessels were often refused the right to sail in the convoys which were organized to give ships greater protection by travelling together; sometimes unarmed vessels were even forbidden to sail at all.

No wonder, then, that among the growing number of Quaker shipowners there were some who yielded to the temptation to install guns on their vessels. For one thing, without them non-Quaker merchants would be wary of consigning their goods to so risky a means of transport as an unarmed ship then was. Again, although Quaker mariners were plentiful in those days, it was still not easy to find a crew all of whom were Friends or sympathetic to the Quaker viewpoint. And non-Quaker sailors, like non-Quaker merchants, were apprehensive of the risks involved in relying on the nonviolent approach. Chiefly, of course, Quaker owners armed because they were fearful of the losses they might incur by the seizure of ship and cargo by pirate, privateer, or enemy warship. True, Quaker annals record miraculous escapes from perils of this kind, yet Friends would not have wished to deny the dangers of their policy. They followed it because they believed it was right, and despite whatever sufferings and material loss might be involved.

From a passage in Edward Coxere's narrative we can sense something of the sacrifice which strict loyalty to their Society's peace testimony could entail for the Quaker ship-owning community and of the subtle ways in which the influence of their environment could undermine this loyalty:

William Ward [Coxere writes], being convinced [around 1662], had then a new ship built without guns, and used in the Straits, and made very prosperous voyages, and grew very eminent and in favour with the merchants, which at last proved to his hurt, his mind being lifted up therewith, so that that ship without guns did no longer suit his mind, but must be left, and [he] had another ship built, and put eighteen guns into her; so that here that spirit entered again that could kill and destroy enemies, and the other shut out, which was of a suffering nature, rather than to kill a man in his sins and wickedness could rather lose outward substance, which is the true love to enemies.

The Society indeed became worried by reports of backsliding by members. Injunctions sent down from the Meeting for Sufferings to remind straying members "that our weapons are not carnal but spiritual" do not always seem to have had the desired effect. In 1693 the matter came up at Yearly Meeting, when "a complaint" was "made about some shipmasters (who profess the truth, and are esteemed Quakers) carrying guns in their ships, contrary to their former principles and practice." Friends were especially disturbed since such conduct, they believed, would give occasion for "more severe hardships and sufferings to be inflicted on such Friends as are pressed into ships of war, who, for conscience sake, cannot fight, nor destroy men's lives." The Yearly Meeting, therefore, recommended to the subordinate meetings to which such deviants from Friends' peaceable principles belonged that they deal with them "in God's wisdom and tender love."

Thus the epistle; but in its minute on the subject Yearly Meeting had used rather stronger language urging that dealing be done "in love and plainness." Yearly Meeting hoped that in this way their consciences would be stirred up and awakened so "that they may seriously consider how they injure their own souls in so doing, and what occasion they give to make the truth and Friends to suffer by their declension." They would then realize that real security was not "in that which is altogether insecure and dangerous," i.e., worldly weapons, and that "their faith and confidence" can rest only "in the arm and power of God."

Yearly Meeting's endeavors appear to have had some effect. We learn (from the second part of an article by Maberly Phillips in *Archaeologia Aeliana*, 2nd series, vol. xvi [1894]) of the efforts that very winter of a Northumberland monthly meeting, North Shields, to reclaim a straying brother, one Lawrence Haslam, a sea captain. He was "tenderly admonished" by the meeting for "having guns in his ship" and asked to consider the evil consequences of this un-Quakerly behavior. Presumably Friends used the arguments furnished by the recent epistle from Yearly Meeting to convince him of the error of his ways. In any case Haslam, though not altogether graciously or seemingly with any really deep conviction, was eventually persuaded "for the satisfaction of Friends" to disarm his vessel. "He hath sold his guns and is to deliver them very shortly," concludes his monthly meeting's report of the affair. About the same date, that is, early in February 1694, Lancashire Quarterly Meeting, for instance, was making a special point of inquiring "how Friends stand faithful against carrying of guns in ships etc." (from extracts from the minute book of Marsden Preparative Meeting, published in the *Journal of the Friends' Historical Society* for 1931). The meeting at the same time advised "that Friends in their several monthly meetings do enquire into these things and advise against them."

Nevertheless, for all Friends' efforts the armed Quaker merchant-man remained a problem for the Society for more than a century to come. That the Yearly Meeting's recommendations of 1693 had to be repeated in 1709 is symptomatic of the deepseated character of this *malaise*. "Tender love," and even "plainness" of speech, were obviously ineffective in some cases. Disownment might follow for those who did not yield to persuasion. "It was only in 1744, however," as Braithwaite remarks, "that the Yearly Meeting directed disownment in the special case of Friends concerned in privateering or as owners of ships going with Letters of Marque." Radical measures were obviously harder to apply in regard to these kinds of deviation from the peace testimony, where the issue was neither so palpable nor so clearcut, than in the case of acceptance of actual military or naval duties.

Such borderline issues were indeed as numerous then as they are today in regard to twentieth-century pacifism. There was the question of watching, for instance, which had been brought up against Philip Ford in his hearing at the London Guildhall in 1679. Had Ford by any chance read the epistle which George Fox sent four years earlier from Swarthmore Hall to the small group of Friends on the island of Nevis in the West Indies? Or was it—as is really more probable—that the sentiments which Fox expresses there on the subject of watching were generally held in the British Society of Friends at that time? In this epistle Fox, writing in answer to inquiries from Nevis Quakers some of whom "scruple concerning watching, or sending forth watch-men," even though unarmed, gave a categorical affirmative in the mat-ter. Provided Friends were not required actually to carry arms, Fox clearly approved their participation in the watch, regarding it as a ful-filment of the duty incumbent on them to obey the magistrate in all things lawful. Indeed it was part of their civic responsibility to per-form such tasks gladly. They might do so in good conscience, in his opinion. To assist the authorities in suppressing crime, in resisting rob-bers, arsonists, ravishers, murderers was their bounden duty. "You cannot but discover such things to the magistrates, who are to punish such things . . . and if [they do] it not, [they bear] the sword in vain." "You know," Fox goes on, "that masters of ships, and Friends, have their watches all night long, and they watch to preserve the ship, and to prevent any enemy or hurts that might come to the ship by pas-sengers or otherwise."

Another question which has troubled many Friends and other pacifists both before and after Fox's time has been the proper response to be made to the state's demands for noncombatant service connected with the prosecution of war or with preparation for war. Quakers usu-ally rejected such work if it were offered as an alternative to full mili-tary service. Where this was not the issue their position was less clear. We hear, for instance, in 1660 of an active Friend who was engaged by the Commissioners of the Navy "to refit one of the King's frigates." Again toward the end of the century, in 1690, Quaker carpenters are recorded at work in the naval shipyard at Chatham. They do not ap-pear to have balked at constructing men-of-war; but when, on alarm of a French invasion, they were ordered to drill, they refused and were subsequently dismissed "without their wages" "because they could not bear arms." This appears to be a rather constricted interpretation of conscience, yet it was probably not untypical of many Friends at that time, including Fox and his nearest associates in the leadership.

Once more it was Quaker settlers in the West Indies—this time a group of young Quakers from the meeting on the small island of Antigua—who challenged such a narrowly conceived witness for peace. Perhaps it was the difficulties posed by the hostile Caribbean environment that made them more sensitive to the implications of their Quaker pacifism. At any rate, whatever its deeper source, their stand met with scant sympathy either from their elders in the Antigua meeting or from the Meeting for Sufferings in London, to whom the matter was referred for a decision.

In 1708 (though this date properly belongs to the time-span covered by the next chapter, it seems appropriate to deal with the incident here) disagreement had arisen among Antigua Friends concerning the attitude they should adopt toward the recent concessions made by the island authorities in regard to service in the militia. The authorities were now prepared to exempt Quakers from bearing arms on condition that they perform noncombatant duties: "building of watch-houses, clearing common roads, making bridges, digging ponds" as well as running messages in case of an alarm of invasion. Against the advice of older members, who considered that such concessions by the authorities should be welcomed by Friends as a genuine attempt to satisfy conscience, young Antigua Friends had come to feel that rendering such services was in effect indistinguishable from performing full combatant service. At best, they argued, it was "but doing a lawful thing upon an unlawful account and bottom." "We are very willing to dig ponds, repair highways, and build bridges, or such convenient things when they are done for the general service of the island and other people at work therein with us, and not to balance those things which for conscience' sake we cannot do."

This would seem to be a good exposition of the classic Quaker position as it had emerged at the end of Quakerism's first decade. Yet, strangely enough, its protagonists met with a sharp rebuff from London. In 1709 the Meeting for Sufferings sent a reply to Antigua, on which figure the signatures of George Whitehead, who had led the Society since Fox's death in 1691 and Fox's son-in-law, Thomas Lower. True, they could quote utterances of Fox himself, who had approved Friends' "planting potatoes for them that watched and builded the forts" in exchange for exemption from armed service as being "innocent things [that] might be safely done." Perhaps, too, they felt that prudence required a more yielding attitude from Friends who, as in remote Antigua, were isolated from their fellow Quakers and set down in a fiercely hostile environment. In this situation it might be unwise to give the impression of being, as Meeting for Sufferings expressed it, "a self-willed and stubborn people." Yet London Friends seem to have gone much further in arguing the case for alternative service than the situation demanded. "As for digging ditches and trenches and making walls," they write, "they are of like use with doors, locks, bolts, and pales, to keep out bloody wicked and destructive men and beasts; and to give warning and to awake our neighbours by messengers or otherwise to prevent their being destroyed, robbed, or burnt, doubtless is as we would desire should in the like nature be done and performed to us." Such arguments indeed, if consistently used, would have undermined the kind of peace witness Friends presented when they refused to pay their militia fines; they even seem to cast some doubt, though obviously this was not their authors' intention, on the validity of the Quaker variety of pacifism in general.

On the whole, however, British Quakers during this period were extremely scrupulous in avoiding any appearance of supporting military activities. They refused, for instance, to pay "Trophy Money" and suffered distraints and imprisonment for this refusal. Barclay in his *Apology* lists these sufferings, along with those incurred for unwillingness to bear arms: Friends, he writes, would not "give money for the buying of drums, standards, and other military attire." In the same passage of his *Apology* he draws attention to another aspect of Friends' peace witness. "We have suffered much," he says, "because we could not hold our doors, windows, and shops close, for conscience' sake, upon such days as fasts and prayers were appointed, for to desire a blessing upon, and success for the arms of the kingdom or commonwealth under which we live, neither give thanks for the victories acquired by the effusion of much blood." Of course there was sometimes backsliding here as in regard to other aspects of the peace testimony. In 1690 and 1691, at the time of "public fasts" held in connection with the Irish campaign, a Somerset Friend, John Whiting, reports that he had to remonstrate with some of his Quaker tradesmen neighbors before they were ready to face the risk of unpopularity and even accusations of disloyalty, which opening their shops on such occasions often brought down on the heads of Friends. Conformity to Quaker principles, however, usually prevailed over a not unnatural desire to avoid unpleasantnesses of this kind.

In the seventeenth century many Friends were unwilling to accept election to the office of constable, even though refusal brought a fine— and nonpayment of fine, which we have seen was Friends' usual practice in such matters, brought the penalty of distraint of goods. This action was not due to any objection to the inherent character of the constable's office; it stemmed from the fact that among the duties of a constable were some connected with the militia and the administration of the Test oath. A Quaker constable was not *per se* liable to be disciplined by the Society; one, however, who in the course of his duties got involved in these duties would almost invariably find himself being dealt with by his meeting for acting "contrary to the principle of truth which Friends own" (to quote the words used in one such instance).

Finally, we must tackle the problem of the seventeenth-century Quaker attitude to war taxes. The exact position taken by Friends is not altogether easy to determine; the evidence appears to be contradictory at times. Concerning the general obligation incumbent upon Friends, as upon other law-abiding citizens, to pay dutifully and without grumbling whatever taxes the established government saw fit to raise there was no doubt in Friends' minds. Beginning with George Fox in the 1650's Friends stressed this incessantly. "As for the rulers . . . for peace's sake and the advantage of truth, give them their tribute," Fox told his followers. Or take this official statement from London Yearly Meeting's epistle in 1693: "Because we are subjects of Christ's Kingdom, which is not of this world, we cannot fight; yet, being subjects of Caesar's kingdom, we pay our taxes, tribute, etc., according to the example of Christ and his holy apostles, relating to Christ's Kingdom and Caesar's; wherein we are careful not to offend."

Yet, as we have seen, when called upon to perform military service Friends refused on principle, and with the backing of the whole Society, to pay a monetary equivalent (the fine) in lieu of service. Perhaps, nevertheless, this was considered not so much a tax as a requisition of a different category. Such a view, however, is less easy to maintain in the case of Trophy Money, which Friends also unitedly refused to pay and which was clearly a contribution in much the same class as a tax.

Did Friends in this period, then, refuse to pay war taxes? Did they, in other words, add the proviso to their general approval of tax-paying, that the purposes for which the tax was raised (insofar as they could be determined) should not be against conscience? This does not appear to have been the case. We know from the account book kept by Fox's stepdaughter, Sarah Fell, for the Swarthmore Hall household that Fox and his family paid the poll tax, imposed in 1667 during the second Anglo-Dutch War and again in 1678 during the war against France, in the full knowledge that the money would be used for the prosecution of the war. These assessments were clearly not taxes "in the mixture," as Friends were to describe those taxes in which only a part, and then usually only an undefined part, went for warlike ends and which they have customarily paid. Fox at this time took the opportunity to advise Friends how they should react to the government's demands. "To the earthly we give the earthly," he told them, "that is, to Caesar we give unto him his things, and to God we give unto Him His things." If Friends refused to comply, then the government might justifiably ask: "How can we defend you against foreign enemies and protect everyone in their estates and keep down thieves and murderers, that one man should not take away another's estate from him?" Fox, it should be noted, obviously made no distinction, at least in this instance, between a government's police duties and its military defense policy. The aim of both, in his opinion, was "the punishment of evildoers," and in these activities the authorities deserved Friends' support in all ways short of actual fighting; otherwise, he felt, the Society would scarcely be in a position to make good its claims on government for respect of conscience where this was due.

It was not, then, for Friends to question the purposes to which the authorities might put the tribute they had levied. This clearly was Fox's view; and it remained the official attitude of the Society after his death (we find it expressed, for instance, in a minute of the London "Morning Meeting" dated 2 July 1695).

A classic exposition of the early Quaker attitude to taxation for war is to be found in the eminent minister Thomas Story's *Journal*. In 1697, at the time of Peter the Great's visit to London, Story, along with another Friend, paid a visit to the young Tsar and in answer to the latter's inquiry: "Of what use can you [Quakers] be in any kingdom or government, seeing you will not fight?," Story has this, *inter alia*, to say:

> Though we are prohibited arms and fighting in person, as inconsistent we think with the rules of the gospel of Christ, yet we can and do by His example readily and cheerfully pay unto every government, in every form, where we happen to be subjects, such sums and assessments as are required of us by the respective laws under which we live. . . . We, by so great an example, do freely pay our taxes to Caesar, who of right hath the direction and application of them, to the various ends of government, to peace or to war, as it pleaseth him or as need may be, according to the constitution or laws of his kingdom; and in which we, as subjects,

have no direction or share: for it is Caesar's part to rule in justice and in truth; but ours to be subject, and mind our own business, and not to meddle with his.

Story's words may be good scriptural exegesis, but they are a long way from the radical stand on the tax issue which makes its appearance within the Society's ranks, especially in some sections across the Atlantic, from the eighteenth century onwards.

A few paragraphs must be devoted in conclusion to the experiences of those small Quaker communities which early Friends succeeded in planting somewhat insecurely on the European continent. The early missionaries had little or no success outside Holland, northern and central Germany, and the German-inhabited autonomous city of Danzig in the kingdom of Poland. And even here Quaker meetings were small and comparatively shortlived. Almost all were to disappear in the course of the eighteenth century. In Holland membership was drawn mainly from dissatisfied members of radical religious sects like the Mennonites, Collegiants, and Labadists, among whom the idea of nonresistance was already a familiar concept. In north Germany there were Schwenkfelders as well as Mennonites who joined Friends, while at Danzig discontented Lutherans, as well as some Mennonites, became members of the Quaker group there.

Quakers on the continent at once encountered difficulties in respect to the customary demands for military service, demands that fell most heavily in urban areas, where Friends chiefly lived. Continental Quakers were not usually prepared, any more than were British Friends, to pay a monetary equivalent in lieu of actual service in arms for the city or state militia. Thus the *modus vivendi* in respect to military service worked out eventually, as we have seen, between Dutch and German Mennonites, and the state was not open to Friends. Quaker stubbornness even became a matter of reproach eventually from the side of the Dutch Mennonites, who feared that obstinacy on this issue might jeopardize the privileges their own ancestors had won from the authorities. "In Groningen," states William I. Hull, "the Mennonites, who purchased their exemption from persecution by yielding to military demands for war loans and [noncombatant] service, denounced the Friends for sticking to their peace principles and thereby endangering all toleration."

As in Britain, in Holland too, fines followed failure to muster, with distraint of goods or imprisonment for refusal to pay the fine. There were some young Quakers who agreed to bear arms, but most did not. As early as 1660 or thereabouts we hear of a Quaker called Jakob

Jacobs from the town of Hoorn having large quantities of his household effects seized on account of his nonpayment of a militia fine.

At the beginning, though, the Dutch authorities were fairly tolerant toward Quaker scruples against fighting; they were already accustomed to religious conscientious objection from the example of the Mennonites. We may illustrate this tolerance by citing the words of the magistrates of Amsterdam, which became the center of Dutch Quakerism, after they had permitted a Quaker, Pieter Hendricks, to acquire citizenship in their town despite his declared unwillingness either to take an oath or to shoulder a musket in its defense. "As they were sensible," they declared, "that bearing arms and swearing were also matters contrary to his religious persuasion, they should not be put upon him."

After the long-drawn-out struggle to defeat Louis XIV's attempt to smash Holland's independence had commenced in 1672, the Dutch became less kindly disposed toward Quaker pacifism. The official imposition of civil disabilities, unofficial harassment on the part of their fellow citizens, and prison sentences became the not infrequent lot of Quaker objectors. We read, for instance, in the course of these wars of a certain Jakob Klaasz from Aalsmeer, near Haarlem, suffering, along with his brother, several spells of imprisonment, one for as long as nine months, for refusing to bear arms or pay commutation money. In 1672 Jan Derx, a Groningen Quaker, was sent to jail for refusing to take his turn of watching on the walls during a siege of the city by the French; he thereafter suffered severe civic disabilities and endured much unpopularity among his fellow citizens for the stand he had taken on this occasion.

The Dutch Quakers were more thoroughgoing than British Friends insofar as they seem to have balked at contributing to war loans (which Mennonites felt no scruples in supporting). Their uncompromising witness against war appears to have constituted a major factor in the dwindling away of the Dutch Society of Friends in the course of the eighteenth century, both indirectly through promoting the emigration of men of military age to the New World, and to Pennsylvania in particular, as well as more directly by effectively discouraging conversion to the Quaker faith. "Demands for military training and service, and war taxes both upon themselves individually and upon their meeting houses, bore heavily on Quakers in Holland," writes Hull. No wonder, then, that during the eighteenth century Amsterdam Quakers branded the growing practice of military conscription as an "evil pit."

In Germany, where a Yearly Meeting was set up in 1683, four years after a similar body had come into existence for Holland, the situation was equally bleak. In many places, as in Danzig or in Emden in East Friesland, the authorities were in general hostile. Here the Quakers' noncombatancy merely added an additional count in the charge against them. London Yearly Meeting's epistle for 1697 mentions persecution endured by Danzig Quakers, *inter alia*, "for not bearing arms." Those in Friedrichstadt were in trouble with the authorities in 1700 for the failure of their members who owned shops to close them on days which had been officially designated as fast-days in connection with the current war. Information concerning early continental Quakerism is sparse and patchy. The few glimpses we get of German Friends' struggle to maintain their Society's traditional testimony against war reveal much the same story as in Holland. Pacifism, though by no means the only cause of Quakerism's failure to take root in Central Europe, was certainly one of the contributing factors.

The close of the seventeenth century marks the end of an epoch in Quaker history, at least if we do not pin it down too exactly to the year 1700. Fox had died in 1691; Barclay, though a much younger man, had predeceased him by a year. A number of other leaders died around this time. Penn survived until 1718, though he was incapacitated by a severe stroke during the last six years of his life. Braithwaite has divided the history of seventeenth-century Quakerism into two periods: first, the heroic age from Fox's first missionary efforts toward the end of the 1640's until the restoration of the monarchy around the middle of 1660, and then "the second period of Quakerism," which continued until some indefinable point during the first quarter of the eighteenth century. By then toleration for dissenters had been won, though not yet full civic rights or equality with the established church. Around 1680 Quakers in England numbered somewhere approaching fifty thousand out of a total population of five and a half millions. However, emigration to Pennsylvania during the last two decades of the century, which was undertaken either for economic motives or to gain a more congenial environment for the spread of Quakerism, served to drain off from the British Society some of its most energetic and active elements. By 1700 Quakers had long ceased to be an army of the Saints striving by spiritual weapons to win the whole world for their faith. They were no longer even a persecuted minority resisting by every means except arms the bitter blows rained down on them by state, church, and society alike. They had put aside the weapons of the Lamb's War and had assumed instead the meek stance becoming the members of a tolerated sect. They were certainly pious, but growing in many cases ever richer—in part because of their godliness. Substantial London merchants and bankers as well as men of education and culture had begun to carry most weight in the counsels of the Society. Gone were the days when God-filled ploughboys from the North country or ecstatic Midlands craftsmen or preaching apprentices set the tone for Quaker religion. A quietness had settled down on the Society, so that it was not always possible to detect whether Friends meditated or merely slumbered. Tradition had taken the place of inspiration. The confines within which a Quaker moved were closely defined, for in his outward behavior he was subject to a strict discipline. The birthright Friend had made his appearance; though formal membership was not established until 1737. Pacifism now became a characteristic of the Quaker culture, the culture of a sect apart. Almost all missionary zeal, almost all desire to proselytize on behalf of peace, was lost and was not indeed to revive again for more than a century.

EIGHT. *The British Quakers*
(EIGHTEENTH CENTURY)

MARGARET HIRST has called the chapter she devotes to the Quaker peace testimony during the first half of the eighteenth century "Days of Tradition." This epithet would indeed apply with almost as much aptness to its history during the remainder of the century. From time to time Friends set forth what they liked to call "our ancient and honourable testimony against bearing arms" but there was little that was fresh or discerning in such statements. Couched in somewhat stiff and formal language, these documents emphasized the duty incumbent on Friends to follow in the well-tried paths of their forefathers. In their apologies for pacifism Quakers increasingly stressed the place of scriptural texts; the atmosphere became more legalistic than in the previous century.

"Friends of this period lacked the gift which makes words strike home with an inescapable power," Rufus Jones has written of the eighteenth-century exponents of the Quaker peace testimony. Sometimes a cloying note enters in, as in the case of the adulatory addresses presented by the Society first to King George I after the defeat of the '15 and then to his son George II after the defeat of the '45.

In 1715 London Yearly Meeting had rejoiced at the defeat of a "black conspiracy": perhaps Friends recalled the sympathy entertained earlier for the House of Stuart by such leading Quakers as Robert Barclay or William Penn and wished to make quite clear once again their abhorrence of all designs to overthrow the established government. In 1746 their "humble address" expressed thankfulness to the Almighty for deliverance in bringing about the pretender's overthrow. "We beheld with grief and detestation," Friends declared, "an ungrateful and deluded people combined against thy person and government, wickedly attempting to subject a free people to the miseries of a Popish and arbitrary plot." Prosperous Quakers were indeed as alarmed as the rest of the business community when Bonnie Prince Charlie led his wild highland Scots as far as Derby; for Quakers, too, William, Duke of Cumberland ("Butcher" Cumberland) had appeared for a while as the God-sent savior of Protestant England. Certainly during the crisis Quakers, with a few exceptions who were disapproved of by the Society, had remained loyal to their pacifist principles. They had refused their collaboration in the "associations and voluntary subscriptions toward assisting in the great charge occasioned by this present rebelling," trusting, as they wrote, that their conduct would be "attributed to no other cause than a conscientious adherence to our Christian belief and persuasion." They had refrained from bearing arms. But in Cumberland and in Lancashire, both of which counties were threatened directly by the Young Pretender's invasion, many Friends paid Trophy Money, "it being a critical conjuncture in the county at that time," as Cumberland Friends explained in a rather feeble attempt to extenuate their action. (They also pleaded that the collection of the Trophy Money was so "mixt with other taxes" that they "could not well separate" it; yet, as Margaret Hirst remarks, this does not appear to have been their main reason for paying). In addition, patriotic zeal inspired a group of well-to-do Friends around Darlington (Co. Durham) to present the Duke of Cumberland's soldiers with "ten thousand woollen waistcoats to keep them warm." In gratitude for these "Friendly Waistcoats" a soldier composed a series of verses in which he promised to

> Exert my utmost art, my utmost might
> And fight for those whose creed forbids to fight.

In London, Devonshire House Monthly Meeting gave their meeting-house over for use as billets for government troops. And we even find a Friend from Clifton, near Carlisle, acting as an unofficial intelligence agent for the Duke of Cumberland, conduct for which he received no rebuke, but seemingly rather approval, from his fellow Quakers.

The events of '45 brought to the surface for the first time since the Commonwealth era the question of whether the "fighting Quaker" could find a place within the Society of Friends. Of course, the terms of reference for the debate were now quite different from what they had been around ninety years earlier: the Society since 1660 had firmly committed itself as a body to a refusal to bear arms. This was now the traditional, the time-honored position. Henceforward those who challenged it by word or in conduct were likely to be regarded by their fellow Quakers as mavericks who cast doubt thereby on the fundamental principles of the Society. An open acceptance of military service, since it constituted a flagrant contravention of Quaker discipline, was dealt with by the meeting and the delinquent either brought to a penitent frame of mind or ultimately expelled from the Society of Friends. The Quaker discipline would also be invoked in regard to such warlike actions as the arming of vessels; concerning certain other activities, which were in greater or less degree connected with the waging of war, no unanimous opinion existed among Friends whether they were permissible or not. These matters will be covered in greater detail below. First, however, I would like to deal with the attempt made at this time at theoretical defense of Quaker nonpacifism.

In the course of 1746 a small book of sixty-two pages had appeared in London under the title *The Nature and Duty of Self-Defence: Addressed to the People called Quakers*. It was published without an author's name—understandably, since its anonymity hid the person of a London Quaker merchant, Richard Finch. Finch dedicates his booklet to the Duke of Cumberland, for him an "illustrious hero." His main argument against the Quaker position on war is twofold: that the gospels never abolished man's natural right to self-defense and that armed defense against external aggression is of like nature to government's indubitable right to resist the rebel or the domestic lawbreaker. However, Finch condemns unjust wars and is still enough of a Quaker to support a conscientious objection to participation in them (though he does qualify this by adding a proviso that arms may rightly be borne subsequently in case of invasion, "notwithstanding the first false step").

Reaction to the booklet was immediate on the part of Friends. In the course of the following months no fewer than three tracts were published in reply. The first to enter the fray was "Irenicus"—or rather, Joseph Besse (soon to bring out his well-known volumes on Quaker *Sufferings*), who chose this appropriate pseudonym for editing Isaac Penington's 1661 tract on peace and the magistracy, *Somewhat spoken to a Weighty Question*. Besse's edition bore the title *The Doctrine of the People called Quakers, in relation to bearing arms and fighting; extracted from the Works of a Learned and Approved Writer of that Persuasion* (London, 1746). Christ's followers were called sheep and lambs by their master, wrote Besse in his preface. "To imagine an army of sheep encountering the wolves, or two armies of lambs worrying and destroying one another, would be an absurdity in nature." Besse seems also to have been responsible for a 67-page brochure which appeared in the following year with the title *An Enquiry into the Validity of a Late Discourse, intituled "The Nature and Duty of Self-Defence"* and under the pseudonym "Philanthropus." It is far better, Besse writes here in reply to Finch's plea for man's innate right to self-defense, if men wish to be good Christians, that they suffer patiently and without resistance rather than participate in the wickedness of war.

The third attempt to defend Quaker pacifism against Friend Finch's attacks was again anonymous (its author remains unknown). It appeared as *A Modest Plea in behalf of the People call'd Quakers*. The

writer was prepared to grant that the magistrate's sword might rightly
be wielded against external invaders by men who fell short of the nonresistant position. In such a case the Almighty would bless their arms
if used "in a good cause," especially if they protected the rights of
those who scrupled to bear arms themselves. "Our arguments are
urged only in behalf of those who are brought in themselves to the
knowledge of this inward and peaceable principle, and refusing to
fight with carnal weapons, have surrendered cheerfully their all into
the hands and protection of the Almighty." The anonymous author
stressed, as Quakers had done in the previous century, that their Society's peace testimony was not based "merely on the literal authority
of the precepts of our Saviour." It arose from the operation of the
divine spirit in men; "from the operation of a principle in the mind,
which men of the greatest understanding . . . believed to be divine" is
how the author, clearly influenced by the rationalism of his century,
expressed this idea.

The final outcome of the controversy is interesting. Nearly a decade
later Finch, whose broadside against pacifism had started the whole
affair, published a long recantation. His *Second Thoughts concerning
War, wherein that great subject is candidly considered, and set in a
new light, in answer to, and by the author of a late pamphlet, intitled
"The Nature and Duty of Self Defence, addressed to the People called
Quakers"* appeared in Nottingham in 1755. In it he vigorously denied
that the retraction of his previous views was in any way a result of
pressure from his coreligionists. Like Penington and other early Quakers, to whom Finch is obviously indebted for his reconversion to pacifism, he grants the place of war in a sub-Christian—or rather sub-
Quaker—world order. Yet a higher way exists for those who feel called
to walk exactly in Christ's footsteps. "The destruction of . . . people in
war . . . by the hands of such as believe themselves redeemed from all
war" would then be little short of "downright murder." His previous
departure from the Quaker peace principles on which he had been
reared he attributes to a period of unbelief, to which he had succumbed around the time he wrote his first pamphlet. Having again
returned to the faith of his fathers he felt it incumbent on him
voluntarily to give the society "that satisfaction which is due from her
members, who have flagrantly and publicly deviated from a fundamental doctrine."

Not all Quaker peace dissidents returned to the ancestral pattern as
Finch had done. As we have noted in the previous chapter, those
Friends who could not accept the peace testimony usually remained
silent on the issue and so escaped censure by their meetings—unless

they were also tempted to accept service in the militia, if called upon for duty, or to place armaments on vessels they owned or captained. But we find a Richard Finch around mid-century matched around the end of the century by a Samuel Hoare, who "looked upon [war] in the present state of society as a necessary evil." "It is the duty of a man to defend his country" was the opinion of this wealthy Quaker banker. In America pacifism at the time of the Revolution caused a minor schism within the Society, but there was no counterpart of the nonpacifist "Free Quakers" among Friends in the British Isles, who were not faced at any time during the century with dilemmas of the same magnitude as those the Revolution posed for American Quakers.

Throughout the century the peace testimony, despite the lukewarmness of the witness on occasion and the backsliding of a few members, retained something of its earlier vitality among British Friends. It proved itself in encounters with highwaymen and privateers. It was exemplified, in particular, in the conduct of the small community of Irish Quakers during the rebellion of 1798 (they had indeed already been tested earlier during the troubles of 1689-1690). Though under suspicion from both the Irish "rebels" and the troops of the English establishment, with very few exceptions Friends stood by their non-belligerency, impartially helping those in need on either side. Before the outbreak of the rebellion, as tension rose, Quaker meetings had advised members to destroy their sporting guns "to prevent," to quote the words of the Yearly Meeting in Dublin, "their being made use of to the destruction of any of our fellow creatures, and more fully and clearly to support our peaceable and Christian testimony in these perilous times." Those who refused to do so were usually disowned by the Society. In the midst of bloodshed and atrocities Friends experienced what seemed to them a wonderful preservation from harm. A Friend from West Meath wrote of his tribulations at the hands of the rebel troops: "All those in this quarter who professed principles of peace were marvelously spared from extreme suffering. . . . Through divine aid, and that alone, was I enabled to refuse to take up arms, or to take their oaths, or join them, assigning as a reason that I could not fight nor swear *for* or against them. They threatened, they pondered, they debated, marvelled, and ultimately liberated me." The story of Irish Friends in 1798, as published in 1825 in book form by Dr. Thomas Hancock ("Hancock on Peace," as his little work was popularly known), was to be much used in the nineteenth century by the Anglo-American peace movement as an illustration of the effectiveness of pacifism in a situation of violence.

Although eighteenth-century Friends preferred a quiet witness in regard to their peace principles as in other aspects of their faith, they had not altogether lost their desire to spread their views outside the Society. We see this, for example, in the behavior of William Hornould as he was returning from a pastoral visit to Holland in 1706: after he and his fellow passengers had narrowly escaped attack from French privateers, he had felt called "to open something of the principles of truth to them that we held." In the course of argument some agreed that the Quaker principle of love and non-injury would be fine if all consented to it, "for then there would be no fear of privateers." But would such a time ever come? "I told them," Hornould relates, "I did not question it at all, but that the Lord would bring such a day and time over the world, according to the testimony of holy Scripture . . . and so in this testimony I left them." A dozen years later in 1718, we find Thomas Story, whose interview with Peter the Great was mentioned in the previous chapter, expounding the Quaker peace testimony to another of the world's great ones, this time an English aristocrat, the Earl of Carlisle. If the English became Quakers, said the earl, the whole country would soon be overrun by the Spaniards and its inhabitants annihilated or reduced to slavery. "The Kingdom of Christ," Story answered, "is not of this world, neither is it national, but spiritual." In other words, Quakers insofar as they strove to follow the Christian way could not look to consequences, to the effect their action would have on national policies; they should be concerned solely, as Story states, with "conscience towards God, and obedience to . . . the Prince of Peace, . . . Christ Jesus." At a lower social level than the one on which Story sometimes moved, we find a country Quaker woman minister like Abiah Darby active in propagating Quaker pacifism in her area. The entry in her diary for 20 May 1760, for instance, reads as follows: "Sent many books relating to wars and fighting to Monmouth to be dispersed."

Quaker "diplomacy" was also active during this century. In the period immediately prior to the outbreak of the American Revolution, leading members of London Yearly Meeting like Dr. John Fothergill or David Barclay were active in efforts to avert the approaching conflict through exerting influence on sympathetic members of parliament and the administration. They were in touch, too, with Benjamin Franklin; indeed, English Quakers were more favorably inclined toward the American cause than many weighty Philadelphia Friends, whose position in some instances was not far removed from that of the Tory loyalists. In March 1775 London Meeting for Sufferings in an address to King George III spoke out openly for conciliation with the American colonists and the straining of every nerve to reach an accommodation agreeable to both sides. "We presume not to justify the excesses committed, nor to inquire into the causes which may have produced them; but, influenced by the principles of that religion which proclaims 'Peace on earth and goodwill to men,' we heartily beseech thee to stay the sword." British Friends, of course, no more approved of the final resort to arms to win independence from Britain than did most of their American *confrères*. During the American Revolution the English Society, in addition to sending relief to American Friends who were suffering as a result of the hostilities, concentrated its efforts on guarding a strict noncombatancy on the part of its members and warning them against "dealing in those things which tend to promote the terrible calamity of war," especially where such activities were undertaken for the sake of personal gain or to avoid personal discomfort or loss.

This emphasis on the prohibitory, the negative aspects of Quaker pacifism was indeed more representative of the eighteenth-century peace testimony than the examples of positive witness in word or action that we have cited above. The remainder of this chapter will be devoted, for the most part, to a discussion of Friends' reactions to the various military demands imposed on them either by government order or as a result of the pressure of their social environment.

The queries concerning Friends' faithfulness to the various testimonies of the Society which, starting in 1682, London Yearly Meeting delivered to its subordinate meetings to answer, do not contain a reference to the peace testimony until 1742. In that year an enquiry concerning "bearing arms" was appended to the existing eighth query, which dealt with the then much more pressing problem of tithes. Two years later an admonition was tacked on against "paying Trophy Money." In 1758, in the course of the Seven Years' War, the peace testimony was given a separate query of its own and its scope was broadened. The query now ran: "Do you bear a faithful testimony against bearing arms and paying Trophy Money or being in any manner concern'd in privateers, letters of marque or in dealing in prize goods as such?" In 1761 a phrase was added specifically enquiring whether any Friends had been involved in the militia, and in 1777 the term "armed vessels" was included in the list of prohibited activities. Thus in 1791 the peace query had come to read as follows: "Are Friends faithful in our testimony against bearing arms, and being in any manner concerned in the militia, in privateers, letters of marque or armed vessels, or dealing in prize goods?" This wording remained unchanged until 1833.

The evolution of the form of the Society's peace query is not without significance for the general state of Quaker pacifism during this period. Richard E. Stagg, on the basis of a thorough examination of the development of the queries and general advices of London Yearly Meeting between 1682 and 1860 (published in the *Journal of the Friends' Historical Society*, vol. 49, 1959-1961), remarks of the eighteenth century: "There was an increasing tendency for Friends to believe that, provided they complied with the queries in a legalistic sense, they were doing sufficient and that it was not necessary to see that they were complying with them in spirit." In his view, this explains why each successive addition to the query probes deeper to discover if Quakers were not in fact concerned in some manner in these illicit activities.

One of the problems which bothered Friends throughout this period (as well as in the previous and the following centuries) was the hiring of substitutes, which, as we have seen, was legally admissible and thus allowed an easy way out of militia service. The question became particularly troublesome in the course of the Seven Years' War, though possibly this impression is due to the lack of extant evidence for other times. At any rate, in 1760 the Yearly Meeting was clearly perturbed by this question, warning meetings everywhere to be watchful to prevent members from hiring substitutes. "We are sorrowfully affected to find," states the Yearly Meeting's "advice" for this year, "that some Friends in a few counties have failed in the maintenance of our Christian testimony against wars and fighting, by joining with others to hire substitutes," thus betraying the witness to peace borne by "our ancients" often at the cost of "cruel sufferings." And this warning recurs in the Yearly Meeting minutes two years later when a new militia bill was enacted.

We shall not wonder at this alarm after reading the minutes of a small rural Monthly Meeting, Felsted in Essex, for this very year 1762. (They have been published in the *Journal of the Friends' Historical Society*, vol. xxii [1925] under the title "A Militia-Substitutes Club"). On 4 May the meeting received the startling report that one of its young members, John Wallis, Junior, had "entered into a club to hire substitutes for such members of the club as should happen to be drawn to serve in the militia." Wallis's colleagues in the club were obviously not Quakers but young men who were disinclined, not through conscientious scruples but from less laudable reasons, to opt out of this not particularly onerous, yet tiresome, service. In fact, the whole matter "came to the knowledge of Friends" only because the lot on this occasion had fallen on a Quaker. The meeting hastened to recommend that "in order to prevent the like in others the same Friends [who were appointed to visit young Wallis and remonstrate with him on the unseemliness of his conduct] are desired to take an opportunity as soon as possible of advising and cautioning every particular member of our Meeting liable to be drawn for a militia man, from having the least hand in any practice so very opposite to our Christian testimony." The incident was closed not long afterward when, early in June, Wallis gave an assurance that he had in fact acted in ignorance, "not knowing it was contrary to our principles." If he had realized this, he added, "he should not have done it."

Equally regrettable from the strict Quaker point of view, and an even greater temptation to the unwary young Friend on account of its outwardly less objectionable character, was the payment of commutation money in lieu of mustering personally with the militia, which was also permitted by law to all who had sufficient funds. From time to time the minutes of monthly meetings record deviations from Friends' principles on this account as well as in regard to finding substitutes. There are warnings, too, against paying any rate levied for the upkeep of the militia; to comply with this appeared to Friends as much a contravention of their peace testimony as was payment of commutation money. In 1762, for instance, London Yearly Meeting issued a strongly worded "advice" on the subject: "It is our sense and judgement, that we cannot consistent with our well known principles actively pay the rate or assessment, which by virtue of the [new Militia] Act may be imposed upon such counties as shall not raise the militia, because such money is required expressly for, and in lieu of such militia." To Quakers in local office, who might be required to assist in raising such monies in their capacity as churchwardens, overseers of the poor or constables, the Yearly Meeting recommended that they should "with meekness and prudence . . . inform the Deputy Lieutenants and acting Justices within their districts, that they cannot be active" in this matter and should ask to be relieved of office if need be. Friends were advised further "that they cautiously guard against paying the said rates under some other name, or mixed with some other rate," a procedure which Yearly Meeting pointed out was in fact contrary to the law, since this directed that "such rates shall be made and collected separately." There were in fact attempts on occasion to levy the militia rate mixed in with the poor rate, to paying which Quakers had no objection. The warning of 1762 had to be repeated as late as 1801.

Rufus Jones in his account of the *Later Periods of Quakerism* has described eighteenth-century British governments' policy toward Quaker conscientious objection as one of "great lenity." Attempts were even made soon after mid-century to meet Quaker scruples concerning the bearing of arms, by actually writing into the militia legislation itself a clause exempting them from personal service. This was done, for instance, in the new Militia Act of 1762, which remained on the statute books for twenty-four years. According to the act, when a Quaker on whom the lot had fallen failed either to appear for service himself or to find a substitute, either the Deputy Lieutenants or their subordinate officers were instructed to levy a distress on his movable property to cover the expense of hiring a substitute. If the goods distrained came to more than the price of a substitute, the excess should be returned to the Quaker, who was also given the right to appeal if he thought the amount of distraint was excessive. However much the Yearly Meeting might appreciate the motives behind this legislation, its provisions could in no way satisfy Quaker scruples, which at that time would have accepted nothing less than unconditional exemption from military duties. The change in regard to Friends' obligations, therefore, amounted finally to an alteration in the letter rather in the substance of the law.

The main hardship endured by objectors stemmed at first from the fines imposed for refusal to muster in person or by proxy, which, on account of the Quakers' principle of noncooperation in the matter, were raised by distresses on the goods of the delinquent—and then, after 1762, from the direct distraint envisaged by the act of that year. The value of goods seized amounted on an average to about £3,000 per annum, a sum considerably in excess of the total amount of fines, had these been paid.

In addition, as before the poorer members of the Quaker community—apprentices, servants, laborers, etc.—suffered occasional imprisonment when they did not possess sufficient property on which a distraint could be made. The usual sentence was to a term of three months, which was served in the county jail. There had been for some time a difference of opinion among lawyers whether Quakers might legally be subjected to imprisonment. A King's Counsel to whom the Meeting for Sufferings applied in 1759 for an opinion in the matter answered in the negative. "I apprehend," he told Friends, "that the legislature, out of tenderness toward the Quakers' religious principles or scruples, who hold it unlawful to bear arms or fight in war, did not intend to make them liable to personal punishment." But imprisonings of impecunious young Friends who had the misfortune to be drawn for service in the militia ballot continued despite more learned legal opinion on the Quakers' side. The matter was finally tested during the American Revolution. When in 1776 Bernard Harrison, a servant in the household of the weighty Friend David Barclay, was chosen for the militia and was threatened with jail since he had nothing "save his clothes" on which a distress could be made, his master took the matter up with the highest authorities and finally received judgment from Lord Thurlow, the Attorney General. Thurlow's opinion ran as follows: "A Quaker cannot be legally committed by virtue of the Act [of 1762], and consequently that if the Commitment pursues the case, he may be discharged by Habeas Corpus." In his efforts to obtain his servant's release Barclay had received the full backing of the Meeting for Sufferings: Friends always stood up for their rights as freeborn Englishmen. They now circulated Thurlow's opinion among the subordinate quarterly and monthly meetings so that these might be prepared when next a similar case arose. In 1787 an attempt was made to persevere in conscripting a young Friend without means, Thomas French of Sibford, after a new ballot in his district had failed to uncover anyone else both fit and eligible to serve. The then Attorney General, Lloyd Kenyon, to whom Friends appealed, ruled that such a procedure was contrary to the spirit of the existing legislation.

In 1786, however, a new militia act was passed giving the authorities the right, if they so wished, to jail for three months a Quaker lacking goods on which to distrain, if in the judgment of the Deputy Lieutenants he was able to pay a sum of £10 in lieu of service. "The power was thus permissive and not obligatory," comments Margaret Hirst. "It was little used until war hardened the temper of the authorities." But from 1793 onward, throughout the long period of war first against Revolutionary and then against Napoleonic France, we find each year some dozen or so young men from the Society in prison (usually with three-month sentences) for failure to find a militia substitute.

In outlying possessions of the British Crown like the Channel Island of Guernsey, the lot of the Quaker militia objector, especially in wartime, might be harder than on the mainland, where Friends' principles had long been known. Quakerism had spread to Guernsey only around 1775 when a watchmaker's apprentice, Thomas André Naftel, was converted by reading Penn's *No Cross, No Crown*, which he had found discarded in an attic of his parents' house. At first he was the only Quaker on the island. Yet as his younger brother Nicholas (himself to become Guernsey's second Quaker) relates: "His religious opinions soon made him bear his testimony against wars and fightings, he being of age to serve in the militia, there being a strict law to that effect. Expecting to be sent to prison for noncompliance at one time he put his night-cap in his pocket as he started for the Court." At this period, however, neither the Naftel brothers nor others on the island who came gradually into the Quaker fold were penalized on account of their conscientious objection to the militia, even though at the beginning they were not yet affiliated formally to the mainland Society. But things changed somewhat with the coming of war toward the end of the century; the islands were threatened with the possibility of invasion by the forces of Napoleon, and all able-bodied male inhabitants were required to appear under arms. We hear now of at least one Guernsey Quaker being imprisoned around the turn of the century, Thomas Gallienne, who was incarcerated in Castle Cornet where, it is reported, he received some rough treatment, being "wheeled in a cart up and down the Castle . . . yard with a gun strapped in front of him before a company of soldiers."

Most difficult of all, of course, was the fate of the soldier objector. As in the post-Restoration period, in the eighteenth century too, there were a few professional soldiers who imbibed Quaker scruples against war and thereupon downed arms. There were even soldier objectors who reached a pacifist position on their own. (In my history of pacifism in the United States I have told the story of one such enlisted man, Thomas Watson, who was sent across the Atlantic to fight the Americans in the Revolutionary War.) And there seem also to have been several young Friends who joined the army for one reason or another and later, in the course of their service, returned to their ancestral noncombatancy.

Richard Finch, in his antipacifist tract *The Nature and Duty of Self-Defence* mentioned earlier in this chapter, at one point refers to four soldiers stationed at Bristol who, having become Quakers, "refused to wear the King's clothes, receive his pay, or bear arms." At the moment of writing, 1746, he reports their having been taken up to London "to be tried, as I suppose, by a courtmartial, where, if this charge appears to be matter of conviction and sincerity, they will doubtless meet with the same favour the rest of their Friends enjoy." Finch unfortunately does not mention either the ultimate fate of the four men or their names. But in view of evidence from other sources, it seems likely that they were reprieved in the way he supposed, despite the fact that the country was then involved in the War of Austrian Succession.

We know both the name and subsequent career of a soldier objector from this very time from an entry (p. 410) in the volume of "Extracts from Register Books surrendered to the Register-General, Somerset House," which is deposited in the Library of the Society of Friends, London. Of this Joseph Harwood, who had joined the British army around the age of twenty-one, the entry reports:

> He was . . . convinced of our principles when a soldier, and laid down his arms about the year 1747, was tried and convicted by

the martial law, but was pardoned by King George the 2nd and joined our Society. Soon after which he was called to the ministry and travelled thro' Ireland twice and through Scotland, and in several parts of the nation. Tho' his testimony was not large it was sound and tended to the edification of Friends and others; being of a very innocent life and conversation, he lived and died in true unity with Friends.

We learn more details concerning Harwood from information supplied by the well-known early nineteenth-century Quaker minister, Stephen Grellet. According to Grellet's account Harwood's doubts concerning war were awakened while he was on active service not long before the battle of Fontenoy (1745). Then, while sick in hospital, Harwood had been placed in a bed next to a wounded soldier who had been reared in the Society of Friends. This companion spoke with regret of his departure from its principles and so impressed Harwood that after his recovery and return to military duties he determined to lay down his arms. To the amazement of officers and troops he proceeded to carry out his resolve, whereupon two other soldiers, whose similar feelings had not been known to Harwood before, stepped forward and did the same. The objectors were returned to England for trial by courtmartial. Sentenced to be shot, they were later reprieved by special command of the King, who expressed his unwillingness "that any man should be put to death for conscience sake" during his reign. It seems improbable that Harwood and his companions were not the same men mentioned in Finch's pamphlet, although there is a discrepancy in the two accounts whether three or four persons were involved.

The last case of conscientious objection in the British army which I would like to cite here is that of one James Hastie who in 1782, toward the end of the American Revolution, was serving as a corporal with the troops stationed in Ireland. He was regarded by his superior officers as a model soldier. Spiritually restless, Hastie sought satisfaction first by attending Methodist services; then he tried the Friends, at whose meetings he became a regular attender. His experiences are related in the diary of a young woman Friend, Mary Shackleton of Ballitore.

He began now to see he must lay down his arms, and thought of doing it at the parade, but the reasoning part prevailed; and presently the account came that the French were landed at Bantry, and orders to march thither. The thought of taking away a man's life was distressing to James, but it was made known to him that the account was false, and he resolved that they should not have to say of him that he was a coward. On their way they were countermanded.

The company returned to its base at Waterford and Hastie continued to attend the Quaker meeting there.

He now resolved [Mary Shackleton goes on] upon his sacrifice and instead of going to parade, stayed in his barrack room. The sergeant came to see what was the reason, and said he must acquaint the colonel. James said he would have him do so. The colonel ordered him to the guard-house, and had him tried by a court-martial, they said he was mad . . . they sent him away to the black hole, denied him pen and ink, and to see his friends, but had him again and sentenced him to receive two hundred lashes which was executed with a whip of small cords, laid on with the strength of a man, and a fresh man every twenty five strokes. But he was enabled to rejoice in his sufferings. The soldiers brought him his clothes, washed his back with milk and water, applied dock leaves to it, and wept over him. He bid them not to weep for him, but for themselves. The soldiers' wives came to him with jugs of tea, and bread and butter, but though he accepted their kindness he refused their refreshment. . . . He was closely confined to camp, and the colonel told him he would release him, order him to his duty, and upon his refusal try him again, and have him shot; this James fully expected. At length the colonel told him he would have [had] him put to death before, only for his former regard for him.

Finally Waterford Friends, assisted by a donation from the wealthy Quaker Gurneys of Norwich, were able to put down £50 for Hastie's discharge from service. "And honest James, by his trade as a weaver, has been enabled to pay it off," thus Mary Shackleton concludes her account.

Friends, as well as rejoicing at the steadfastness to principle of followers like Hastie, were distressed by the periodic failure of some members to realize the full implications of their peace testimony. Quakers who consented to serve in the militia or collaborated in some way with its machinery were, as we have seen from the previous chapter, by no means the only offenders to be disciplined. We must now turn to discussion of deviant behavior among eighteenth-century Quakers in regard to such matters as the arming of vessels as well as commercial, financial, or industrial activities connected with war, etc.

In no area of its peace witness did the Society of Friends encounter more difficulty in maintaining consistent behavior than in regard to the arming of merchant vessels owned or captained by Quakers. The specific warnings issued in 1693 and 1709 against this practice, to which in 1730 was added a general statement concerning the objectionable character of any Quaker complicity in warlike affairs, certainly had some effect in discouraging Friends inclined to sanction the arming of their ships (especially in the years immediately following promulgation). Nevertheless it still continued to be done. During the eighteenth century there were even Quakers who, during periods of war, became involved in privateering and accepted "letters of marque" licensing the outfitting and employment of armed vessels for the harrying of the enemy's merchant fleet. In 1744, in the middle of the War of Austrian Succession, London Yearly Meeting issued a strongly-worded condemnation of such behavior: "a flagrant and lamentable departure from our peaceable principle . . . which . . . may be attended with injustice, barbarity and bloodshed." Quarterly and monthly meetings were instructed to deal with such offenders "speedily." This advice had to be repeated in the course of the next round in the protracted Anglo-French conflict of the eighteenth century. In Yearly Meeting's epistle for 1757 we find the following passage:

> It having been weightily under the consideration of this meeting to discourage all under our profession from that great inconsistency of being concerned in privateers, letters of marque, or ships armed in a warlike manner, we think it necessary very earnestly to recommend to all Quarterly and Monthly Meetings, to keep a watchful eye over their members in this important branch of our Christian testimony; and where any inclination towards such practices appears, that timely admonition and suitable counsel be given in the spirit of love and meekness.

Again, during the American Revolution we find a similar "admonition" in Yearly Meeting's epistle of 1779.

It was naturally the coastal meetings which caused the most trouble, for it was their members who engaged most frequently in the ship-owning and seafaring professions and were therefore specially open to temptation in these matters. Thus throughout the whole century, and on into the nineteenth century, Yorkshire meetings, like the Whitby and Scarborough Monthly Meeting, constantly have to report a "sorrowful defection" among their members. Sometimes this even led to the closing of a meeting, as happened at Robin Hood's Bay in the North Riding, which had been started in 1690. When members found that they would not be permitted to serve in ships carrying guns, most of them—sailors almost to a man—left, so that the meeting was unable to carry on. Elsewhere, of course, loyalty to the Society often prevailed eventually over business advantage or the very natural desire to avoid the difficulties which strict adherence to Quaker pacifism entailed in those days for all who made a living on the sea; in such cases the offenders declared to their meeting their sorrow at their "transgression," promising amendment for the future and expressing their willingness to "trust in the Lord, the great Jehovah, in whom is everlasting strength, to defend and preserve us all if we abide faithful" (to quote the words of Joseph Linskill, a prominent Quaker shipowner from Whitby). The story is much the same all along the coast from Cornwall to County Durham: sometimes Friends' "dealings" with an offending member reach a successful conclusion, at other times the delinquent departs from the Society unwilling to adapt his behavior to the norm then required of all Quakers. For disownment inevitably followed on a steady refusal to reform. At Scarborough in 1781 it was reported that even the clerk of the meeting, Samuel Clemesha, was among those who had become involved in these matters; he was requested to get rid of the shares he held in armed vessels. And at neighboring Whitby, a port of some importance in the eighteenth century, sympathy with the disowned ran so high around this time that many members, including the clerk of the Preparative Meeting, refused to cooperate in their expulsion and continued for a time to treat them as full-fledged participants in all the affairs of the meeting.

Sometimes Friends became unwittingly entangled in naval warfare, like those in Cornwall who in peacetime had invested money in outfitting a "packet employed by the General Post Office" only to find, during the American Revolution, that it had been "equipped in a warlike manner for defence"; it captured several French vessels as prizes before these Friends were able to withdraw participation in the enterprise. In the same conflict another Friend discovered that a vessel of which he was part-owner had, without his knowledge or consent, taken out a letter of marque and seized a Dutch ship, from which he was allotted £2,000 in prize money. The retention of prize money, along with the purchase of prize goods, had been specifically condemned in the Yearly Meeting's epistle of 1779. "Whoever amongst us," it reminded Friends, "so confederate with the captors, afford evident tokens that they either prefer the gain of a corrupt interest to the convictions of divine light in their own consciences, or that they are become insensible of them." In both the instances cited in this paragraph the Friends in question exerted their utmost, after the war was over, to locate the original owners and return the money they had received from their share of the prizes.

If the Society demanded from its members as part of their peace witness the disarming of any vessels with which they were associated either as owner or shareholder, captain or crew, it expected, too, that Quakers would have no hand in the workings of the press-gang. We have already seen Friends in the role of the press-gang's victims; both during the eighteenth century and earlier, resistance to impressment for the Royal Navy figured as a not unimportant item in Quaker "sufferings." But sometimes Friends were placed in a position where they were legally required to collaborate in pressing men for the navy; this could happen in the case of ship-owners. For instance, in 1735 when Thomas Chalkley, now settled as a prosperous merchant in the New World, was conveying a cargo from Philadelphia to London on one of his own ships, the vessel was boarded by a press-gang as it neared the shores of England. It was, he writes in his *Journal*, a period of "very great pressing for seamen"; the press-gang were in fact in search of some sailors—non-Quakers—whom Chalkley had added to the crew at Barbados. These men had quickly hidden from the danger that they apprehended would now threaten them, certainly with Chalkley's connivance. (Must he not have called to mind now his own plight when as a nineteen-year-old he had himself been seized by the press-gang and only narrowly escaped impressment?) At first Chalkley tried to prevaricate. But the lieutenant in charge of the press-gang interposed:

> It was vain to talk so much, but if I would say I had no more hands on board he would be satisfied (he having a belief that I would speak the truth, though he never saw me before). . . . But I made him no answer, not daring to tell a lie. "Now I know that there is men on board," said he. So he commanded his men to search the ship to her keel. So they stripped, and made a narrow search and sweated and fretted, but could not find them . . . so I carried my people safe up to London.

At the end of the century the Navy Act of 1795 posed a serious dilemma for all Quaker shipowners, for one of its provisions required the proprietors of merchant vessels to supply a quota of their sailors for the Royal Navy. The Meeting for Sufferings protested to the House of Commons that this clause imposed an impossible burden on Quaker owners, for Friends could in no circumstances provide "men for the purpose of war."

Quakers concerned with the sea were tested perhaps more than other sections of the Society in regard to their witness for peace, since a choice was more often demanded of them between private interest and the demands of the peace testimony. But a whole range of commercial and industrial activities could present Friends engaged in them with the same kind of dilemma. Through unwariness or desire for gain or from some other motive they might easily succumb. The sources do not easily reveal the full extent of the complicity of some Quakers in this sort of activity for, whereas it was difficult to conceal the fact that a vessel owned or captained by a Friend or manned by a Quaker crew carried armaments on its decks (just as it was plain to all when a Quaker mustered with the militia or consented to serve when pressed for the navy), a veil could be discreetly hung over some of the warlike interests of Quaker merchants, bankers, and industrialists.

Take, for instance, the role of John Hanbury, well-to-do merchant and a bulwark of the London Meeting for Sufferings around mid-century, in promoting the Ohio Company, whose very un-Quakerly activities did much to exacerbate the conflict between England and France in the Ohio River Valley. Only the recent archival researches (as yet unpublished) of Guy F. Hershberger have uncovered the full extent of his complicity in the imperialist diplomacy of his country and in military policy. And, to cite another and somewhat similar case, it was the publication over 150 years later of the letter-book of the London Quaker merchant, Robert Plumstead [in the *English Historical Review*, vol. xxxi (January 1916)], that first brought to light the waverings which he manifested in regard to entering the trade in arms during the Seven Years' War, a period when this business had become both patriotic and lucrative—though still un-Quakerly. It is clear that Plumstead entertained some scruples concerning the shipment of arms and ammunition across the Atlantic for use in the struggle against the French in the New World—or, at least, as to deriving profit from this trade. After the outbreak of war in 1756 he writes: "Ventured the dozen of sword blades in the cask and got Captain Warton to take the gun in his cabin." A little later, however, we find him telling another correspondent that he would not agree to transport arms; for this was against Quaker principles which forbade contributing to war and the shedding of blood or drawing profit from transactions of this kind. On the other hand, he could not condemn the participation in the arms trade of those who did not share his scruples. On another occasion he did indeed ship arms to America himself, but refused to charge for carriage, seemingly on the grounds that, while as a Quaker he could not make money from such trade, he did not wish to put obstacles in the way of any who believed in war.

Then there is the case of Thomas Cumming, Dr. Samuel Johnson's friend. Cumming had told the latter at the time of the '45 that "he would not fight, but . . . would drive an ammunition cart." Later

Friend Cumming, while engaged in business in London, devised a plan to extend British possessions on the west coast of Africa by acquiring the French trading settlements in this area, which were of prime importance for the trade in "gum-senega" and other valuable articles. This plan was actually carried out by the British government in 1758, though its new acquisitions were returned to France at the peace treaty in 1763. While it is true that Cumming, though a close adherent, may not have been an actual member of the Society at this date, there were certainly some "sensible Quakers" among the London merchant community who gave an equally flexible interpretation to their Society's peace testimony.

The Society as a whole, it must again be said, condemned the kind of double-thinking engaged in by Quakers like Hanbury or Plumstead. Its policy had always been the one plainly expressed in its advice of 1790: "If any be concerned in fabricating or selling instruments of war, let them be treated with in love; and if by this unreclaimed, let them be further dealt with as those whom we cannot own." It would be a shameful thing, and a reproach to the Society, for Friends "to refuse an active compliance with warlike measures and, at the same time, not to hesitate to enrich ourselves by the commerce and other circumstances dependent on war" (this "caution" comes from Yearly Meeting's epistle of 1798). We find private Friends, too, at great pains to dissociate themselves from every kind of activity that might be regarded as connected with war; John Gurney (1749-1809), the Norwich banker, for instance, wrote a letter to his local newspaper disclaiming responsibility for the fact that his nephew had allowed a subscription list for the outfitting of privateers to be deposited in the family bank and censuring the young man for his conduct.

It was probably easier for those selling instruments of war to conceal their activities from their fellow members, if they so wished, than for those who fabricated them to do so. Of course, there is no reason to believe that most Quaker merchants and industrialists did not desire to abide loyally by the requirements of their Society's discipline or, indeed, did not share wholeheartedly in the pacifist scruples of their Friends. Take the case of the Quaker Darbys, whose story has been related by Arthur Raistrick in his *Dynasty of Iron Founders : The Darbys and Coalbrookdale* (London, 1953). At first, Abraham Darby I, who died in 1717, consistently refused to have anything to do with the manufacture of armaments. But in 1739, after a reorganization of the firm in the previous year which made another Quaker family, the Goldneys, temporarily the dominant partners, a change occurred. From then until 1748—that is, throughout the whole period of the War of Austrian Succession—the Coalbrookdale works engaged in making guns. The Goldneys were less consistent Friends than the Darbys, for not only were they manufacturing guns at Coalbrookdale but, in their capacity as large-scale transatlantic merchants, they had been arming some of their vessels despite the official Quaker prohibition of this practice. Toward the end of the 1740's Abraham Darby II, who had remained as manager of the works, regained control and put a stop to the manufacturing of arms. Darby was active in the Society as a minister as well as clerk of his monthly meeting and, though he had not actually severed his connection with the family business during the period of Goldney control (an example of how difficult it sometimes was for the consistent Quaker pacifist, if he was engaged in trade or business, to keep entirely clear from involvement in warlike activities), he was obviously uneasy at the firm's policy. During the Seven Years' War the Coalbrookdale Works turned down a government order for cannon and later, during the American Revolution and the struggle against Revolutionary and Napoleonic France, it refused to accept any contracts for armaments. "The Darbys of Coalbrookdale," Hugh Barbour has written, "gave up cannon-making on pacifist grounds and thus lost pre-eminence in the iron industry but won fame by making the first iron bridge."

Whether there were more Goldneys than Darbys among Quaker manufacturers active in heavy industry in this period is hard to say. It is true that in England many eighteenth-century Friends (as Dr. Thomas Hancock remarked of Irish Quakers in that century) "were living with little more than an outward or formal profession of the principle against war, . . . they submitted to the opinion of their Friends, and followed traditionally the maxims of their education." They were not always willing to live out the implications of their Society's peace testimony in matters pertaining to their business interests and their everyday life. Yet at the same time it must not be forgotten that those members who caused no offense in Quaker eyes have remained mostly unrecorded; the names of offenders against the discipline, on the other hand, are to be found in the records of dealings and disownments preserved to this day.

Toward the end of the century, a *cause célèbre* occurred when a leading Friend and prominent citizen of Birmingham, Samuel Galton (grandfather of the famous eugenist, Francis Galton), was finally disowned after his case had been before Friends for four full years. The Galton family business, an old Quaker firm, had been engaged in the manufacture of guns since the first half of the century. In peacetime, of course, guns were largely used for sport: this might give Quaker

323

manufacturers an excuse for making them with a good conscience. But the activities of Farmer & Galton, as the business came to be known, were by no means limited to sporting rifles. Apart from some involvement in the slave-trade the firm was accepting large contracts for armaments from the government. Friends seem to have been very slow in this instance in taking action, and it was not until 1792 that a Birmingham Quaker raised the matter by impugning the propriety of the local meeting's acceptance of a donation from Samuel Galton and his father for the extension of the meeting house. "For us," he wrote, "to receive part of the thousands that have probably been accumulated by a forty years' commerce in these articles and apply it to the use of Friends is, I think, a matter that requires . . . very serious consideration." Eventually the meeting initiated disciplinary action against Galton, who displayed not a little indignation at this treatment. He told Friends: "My grandfather—afterwards my uncle, then my father and uncle—and lastly my father and myself have been engaged in this manufactory for a period of 70 years, without having received any animadversion on the part of the Society." He cited cases of other Quaker armament manufacturers who had been left untouched. Moreover, he showed no inclination to bow to the Society's opinion and abandon his part in making munitions of war. "The manufacture of arms implies no approbation of offensive war," for which he expressed "the most decided abhorrence." Yet he made it clear that he did not share the pacifist views of the Society. The application of arms "to the purposes of defensive war, to the support of the civil power, to the prevention of war, and to the preservation of peace" met with his entire approval. "If I should be disowned," he concluded, "I shall not think that I have abandoned the Society, but that the Society have withdrawn themselves from their ancient tolerant spirit and practice." The efforts of Friends to bring about Galton's submission and thus avoid the loss of so valuable a member were to no avail. Although disownment eventually came in August 1796, Galton's attachment to the Society in which he had been reared was such that he and his wife continued to attend the Friends' meeting until their death, and they lie buried in the Quaker cemetery belonging to their meeting.

Investment in war loans was another inconsistency to which Friends with money were liable. An advice from Yearly Meeting in 1790 specifically warned against such loans. But, so far as I am aware, no disciplinary action was taken against those who indulged in this practice. A four-page leaflet addressed by "Pacificus" *To the Society of the People called Quakers* (and attributed to one John Payne) was published in May 1793 chiding Friends over this issue. "It is true," its author remarks, "if a member of your society enlists as a soldier, you immediately reject communion with him: but if he only lends money to Government, for the avowed purpose of enlisting soldiers, you object not to him, but admit him to eldership, and even the ministry."

Quaker tradesmen, as in the previous century, were not always found willing to suffer the consequences of a failure to shut up shop during a public fast in case of a national defeat (as members of the Society at large were not always ready to risk the violence of the mob which might result from not illuminating their windows during a public thanksgiving for victory). It was not pleasant to have windows smashed, goods damaged, and property wrecked. From time to time Yearly Meeting felt bound to admonish Friends to bear as faithful a witness in this respect as in other aspects of their peace testimony. A good example of official action of this kind is the *Tender Advice and Caution to Friends, respecting their putting out Lights on those call'd Rejoicing Nights, and the not opening their Shops, on Days appointed by Human Authority for Publick Fasts, Feasts and Thanksgivings,* issued by the Morning Meeting on 10 March 1760. The advice recalled the witness of their ancestors, who had realized "that as they could not join with others in shedding the blood of their fellow creatures, neither could they be one with them in rejoicing for the advantages obtained by such bloodshed: As they could not fight with the fighters, neither could they triumph with the conquerors."

Concerning the payment of war taxes the Society was no more able in the eighteenth century than in the seventeenth to reach an entirely satisfactory stance. The payment of a tax in lieu of militia service or for the upkeep of the militia was, we have seen, generally regarded as inadmissible: Friends regarded this as indistinguishable from actually serving, even where the tax, as was sometimes the case, might be "mixed in" with the poor rate. When in 1795 a navy rate and in the following year a cavalry rate for the upkeep of the horses and their riders in that branch of the army were imposed by act of Parliament, the official Quaker position required members to refuse payment of these rates or of any fines imposed for nonpayment. In 1796 the Yearly Meeting reported distraints to the value of about £1,000 in connection with "the late assessment for manning the Navy," along with backsliding on the part of some members who had complied with the government's demands. Thus London Yearly Meeting's stand in this period does indeed appear more radical than the one taken up earlier by George Fox and Friends of his day in regard to the very similar poll tax and other imposts (see chapter 7). Yet in 1799, when a special tax was levied for the carrying on of the war—as "an aid and contribution for the prosecution of the war," as stated frankly in the act—there does not appear to have been any official ruling to guide Friends. Some paid, though with an "uneasy" conscience; others refused and suffered distraint of goods. "When an income tax was substituted," Margaret Hirst remarks, "they felt a relief which was probably not shared by their fellow citizens." For almost all Quakers felt able to pay a general tax of this kind.

An exception to the rule was provided by a Herefordshire merchant, reformer, and philanthropist, Nathaniel Morgan from Ross-on-Wye, who in 1799, along with his father who was also a Friend, refused to pay income tax because of its connection with financing the current hostilities. Father and son, according to the latter's account as given to the Duke of Gloucester during his visit to Ross in 1822,

> had refused it on its first coming out, and withstood it 16 years, except when peace was declared [i.e., 1801-1802] and . . . . our goods were sold by auction to pay it. . . . [The duke] asking me if we got anything by that, meaning, was anything refunded by the Society for such suffering, I immediately replied, "Yes, peace of mind, which was worth all." I told him I believed there was not 6 in the kingdom as had done so and that I myself had brought the subject many times before Yearly Meeting in London, and could never be once well seconded or supported; . . . few saw it from the same point of view. I told him we [i.e., he and his father] had written the Commissioners [of the Income Tax] saying we would suffer loss of goods, fine, or imprisonment rather than pay it, it being specifically for war, and that if for any other purpose we would most willingly pay it, it being the most just mode of raising money, as had been adopted.

At the Yearly Meeting of 1813 Morgan told the assembled Friends with indignation: "We have shrunk from that glorious cause [the Quaker peace testimony] and joined with the nations in blood, by assenting to the payment of a tax, specially levied for war." And afterwards, disgusted by his Friends' failure to accept his stand, he had confided to his diary: "I fear my fellow professors are led by paltry interest and fear of offending the high people of this day."

Pacifist radicalism of the sort propounded by the Morgans was alien to the spirit of the Society of their day. It would have found an echo, though, a half-century earlier across the Atlantic among country Friends of the caliber of John Woolman or John Churchman, who had preached to their brethren the same kind of noncooperation in regard to the paying of taxes in wartime. Like the Morgans, these American Quakers had argued that, where it was known that a considerable portion of the money raised was to be devoted to war, Friends should refuse payment even in the case of taxes "in the mixture." Thoroughgoing tax objection, however, was never adopted as the official policy of the Society on either side of the Atlantic. In America at certain times it had gained a number of adherents; as we have seen from the Morgans' case, in England, despite a somewhat more challenging stand now in comparison with George Fox's day, this policy was stillborn.

Before concluding this chapter we must say something about continental Quakerism. Our account will in fact be confined to Friends in France, for the meetings established in the seventeenth century in Germany and Holland all withered and died in the course of the eighteenth, while revived Quakerism in Germany dates only from the very end of that century. In contrast to groups elsewhere on the European continent which grew out of the missionary activities of British Friends, French Quakers had an indigenous origin. They sprang from a small circle of *inspirés* centered since about 1735 in the district of La Vaunage in Languedoc, who in turn derived from the Protestant Camisards active in the Cévennes at the beginning of the century. (The family of the American Quaker Anthony Benezet, who was of French origin, were connected with the *inspirés*.) In 1784 the La Vaunage group had been joined by a young nobleman, Jean de Marcillac, who seven years earlier had resigned from the army to become a medical doctor after he read Barclay's *Apology* and became convinced of the unlawfulness of war for a Christian. It was chiefly the dynamic Marcillac by whose intermediacy in the following year the *inspirés* came into contact with English Friends, and it was Marcillac and his English Quaker friends who were mainly responsible for transforming the group's previously rather inchoate pacifistic tendencies into a Quaker renunciation of all war.

After the outbreak of the Revolution, military conscription, which had not been effectively enforced before, now threatened French Quakers of military age (the group had meanwhile affiliated with Friends *en bloc*). On 10 February 1791 they petitioned the legislature for exemption; the document is entitled *Pétition respecteuse des Amis de la Société chrétienne, appelés Quakers, prononcée à l'Assemblée Nationale le jeudi 10 février 1791*. The petition was placed before the National Assembly by Marcillac and two American Quakers, William and Benjamin Rotch from Nantucket, representing a temporary settlement at Dunkirk of American Quakers, who on settling there in 1785 had been promised by the prerevolutionary government "an entire exemption from military requisitions of every kind" as well as the free exercise of their religion. The three men were well received

327

by the deputies, despite their remaining hatted throughout after the custom of their British and American *confrères*. Quaker principles indeed were well known to prominent members of the Assembly like the Girondin leader, J. P. Brissot de Warville, who had visited Quaker communities in the United States and whom Marcillac had diplomatically canvassed before presenting the petition.

The document began by drawing the deputies' attention to the fact that "plusieurs villes et villages du Languedoc renferment nombre de familles attachées à ce Christianisme primitif," the same faith held by Quakers across the waters who, like the early Christians, objected to shedding human blood and therefore to serving in any army. In Pennsylvania they had actually put their nonviolent principles into practice. In the United Kingdom and in the United States, the petition went on, the government had exempted Friends from military service, regarding them as lovers of their country and upholders of a strict morality, although forbidden to kill by their exact adherence to Christ's teachings. Surely France, the petitioners concluded, now become the seat of Liberty and the protagonist of religious liberty, would grant French Quakers the same right of conscience as has been given their coreligionists in Britain and America.

The duty of replying to the petition fell to the Assembly's president, the famous Mirabeau. As we might expect in a country where the legend of the "good Quaker" had remained a lively tradition among liberal thinkers since Voltaire's day, its representative spoke now with courtesy and understanding of Quaker principles. The new France too, said Mirabeau, desired peace among the nations; perhaps one day it would also become "une heureuse Pennsylvania." Concerning Quaker pacifism he did indeed express some reservations:

> Vous dites encore qu'un article de votre religion vous défend de prendre les armes, et de tuer, sous quelque prétexte que ce soit. C'est sans doute un beau principe philosophique . . . mais prenez garde que la défense de soi-même et de ses semblables ne soit aussi un devoir religieux. Vous auriez donc succombé sous les tyrans! Puisque nous avons conquis la Liberté pour vous et pour nous, pourquoi refuseriez-vous de la conserver?

He went on to ask whether the Quakers of Pennsylvania, if they had seen their wives and children and parents actually threatened with death at the hands of savages instead of remaining some distance removed from the wild Indians, would not have resorted to violence to ward them off. "Et les stupides tyrans, les conquérans féroces ne sont-ils pas aussi les sauvages?" Weakness breeds war; "une résistance générale feroit la paix universelle."

Despite the efforts of Marcillac to canvass support among leading politicians like Brissot de Warville and Lafayette, the petition remained without effect. The next year, when Marcillac with the support of British Friends proposed to establish a Quaker industrial school at Chambord, he asked for exemption from military service (along with oath-taking) for all pupils who had adhered to Quakerism for a period of at least a year and were accepted by Friends. In their comments on the project the local authorities objected to this clause, giving it as one of the reasons for rejecting the project as a whole; to grant exemption of this kind, they said, was contrary to the well-being of the republic. This attitude was typical of the reaction of the French government to Quaker conscientious objection.

In the 1790's, however, the revolutionary authorities, as in the case of the Mennonites (see chapter 11), did not force Quakers to serve against their will. The situation, however, changed for the worse with the coming of the Napoleonic era. It then became very difficult to escape service unless one had sufficient means to buy a substitute and no scruples against a practice of this kind. Whereas, when the war period was over, English Friends were inclined to be severe toward the young men who had accepted military service, French Friends, with a better understanding of the pressures to which these men had been subjected, were more sympathetic. "Not one of our members has to blush for having done violence to any," they wrote—by which presumably they meant that their conscripts, though in the army, had succeeded in avoiding actually having to kill.

Henry van Etten has printed from the Archives Nationales a "Réclamation des Quakers du Gard contre le service militaire," which was presented to Louis XVIII immediately after his first restoration. It is dated from Congénies (the center of the Quaker community), 7 August 1814. This plea to the new régime makes use of arguments similar to those employed in the petition of 1791; appeal is made now, however, to the Constitutional Charter as guarantor of religious freedom instead of to the Rights of Man. "Rien," the Quakers argue, "ne pourrait donc plus gêner nos consciences et porter une plus grande atteinte à la liberté dont le Roi veut faire jouir tous ses sujets que si nous étions contraints de contribuer de nos personnes ou de nos fortunes aux recrutements forcés de l'armée." They hope that the king will not try to force them to serve against their conscience as had been done under the recent reign of Napoleon.

The official to whose task it fell to comment on the petition paid tribute to the high moral level and the patriarchal simplicity of the little Quaker group. Yet, like Mirabeau earlier, he was puzzled by their unwillingness to serve their country in arms. "Si les Quakers ne veulent servir la patrie . . . je ne vois pas à quel titre ils ont droit à sa protection." Unlike the Mennonites, Quakers were unwilling, at least in principle, to accept noncombatant duties or to make a monetary contribution in lieu of military service: this made it harder for the government to find an agreed solution. In fact, no official recognition was granted to Quaker objectors.

In the early 1820's the group numbered around two hundred members. In the course of the following decades it became even smaller; by the early twentieth century only one or two members remained. In the Franco-Prussian War of 1870, Margaret Hirst relates, "one member, Jean Bénézet, underwent severe trials for his refusal to train as a National Guard." French Friends felt that perhaps they had failed to give "sufficient publicity" to their peace principles during the months of war. As earlier in Holland and Germany, in post-Napoleonic France, too, many young Quakers had been emigrating in order to escape the burden of compulsory military service. Under the Third Republic this burden became even more onerous. The weight of military conscription was one of the factors which helped to crush the tiny French Society of Friends.

NINE. *The British Quakers*
(NINETEENTH CENTURY)

IF tradition was the mark of eighteenth-century Quakerism, innovation crept into the British Society of Friends during the nineteenth century, although Friends still strove to maintain their traditional witness intact in regard to many issues, including the peace testimony. Early in the nineteenth century it was the evangelical movement and the philanthropic impulse that infused the somewhat moribund Society with new energy. In North America evangelicalism proved a major factor leading to the fragmentation of the Society; in the British Isles separation did not take place, apart from a few minor schisms. On both continents, toward the end of the eighteenth century, social reform became increasingly one of the major outlets for Friends' energies and an accurate reflection of their religious outlook. In the last decades of the nineteenth century and early in the twentieth many British Quakers came under the influence of the new liberal trends in theology that were affecting the other Protestant denominations, too. Many of the features which had characterized the Society as a sect apart, such as their peculiar dress and their peculiarities of speech, had already been almost entirely abandoned. The discipline had been relaxed, the ban on "marrying out" abolished. A decline in membership during the nineteenth century, to which this ban had been a major contributory factor, was stemmed before the end of that century. A new Society, with a more extended horizon and a broader spiritual vision, was in the making. At the same time something of the old-time Quaker solidity was lost in the transformation.

The early decades of the nineteenth century saw little change in the nature of the Quaker peace witness. The old forms of expression continued; the problems facing Friends in this area remained much the same. The year 1800 is scarcely more a landmark in the history of the Quaker peace testimony than it is in the annals of the country as a whole.

The evangelical reformer Thomas Clarkson, in the three-volume account of contemporary Quakerism which he published in 1806 under the title *A Portraiture of Quakerism*—a work, incidentally, of considerable insight, accuracy, and understanding—described the Quaker attitude to military requisitions in the following words taken from the third volume:

331

They believe it unlawful for Christians to engage in the profession of arms, or indeed to bear arms, under any circumstance of hostility whatever. Hence there is no such character as that of a Quaker-soldier. A Quaker is always able to avoid the regular army, because the circumstance of entering into it is generally a matter of choice. But where he has no such choice, as is the case in the militia, he either submits, if he has property, to distraint upon it; or, if he has not, to prison.

This account would indeed be equally applicable to any previous period in the Society's history from 1660 on.

The reorganization of the militia in 1802 and 1803, years of acute fear of French invasion, had, despite official recognition of the right of a duly certified Quaker to exemption from personal service, in actual fact left the Quaker objector in more or less the same position as before, since he was unable to accept commutation by a monetary payment. Fines and subsequent distraint for nonpayment continued to be imposed regularly on Quaker objectors.

In 1806-1807 the new Secretary for War and Colonies, William Windham, remodelled the militia so as to make service in it act as a preparation for army service. Now the number of Quaker objectors in prison climbed steeply from the previous average figure of two or three annually. Light is shed on the fate of propertyless objectors, after this reorganization was carried through, in a document transcribed in the fourth volume of the manuscript "Book of Cases" preserved in the Library of the Society of Friends, London. It is entitled "Abstract of the Returns made to an Inquiry instituted by the Meeting for Sufferings by Minute of the 1st of 9th month 1809 respecting Cases of Imprisonment, or of Exemption from Imprisonment, under the Local Militia Acts." From it we learn that the fines imposed at this date usually ranged between £5 and £10, though very occasionally they might be as low as £1 or as high as £30. We hear of one case where distraint was made on the goods of the father of a propertyless objector. The Abstract, which does not claim to be complete, records twenty-four cases of imprisonment over the period of a year; in addition twenty persons were reported to have been "exempted" as a result of the "discretionary power vested in the Deputy Lieutenants"; an unspecified number of "suspended" sentences were also given. The length of imprisonment varied between fourteen days and one month. As might be expected, the imprisoned men were mostly in their twenties and their occupations, where noted, show that they came from the poorer sections of the population. Husbandman, journeyman, weaver or shoemaker, servant to a husbandman, laboring tiler, apprentice, shopman: these are the designations found in the Abstract. Although most of those listed were actual members of the Society of Friends, six nonmembers—presumably attenders at Quaker meetings—were listed, of whom two were reported as receiving exemption and four as serving a prison sentence.

In one case, that of James Pollard, a twenty-year-old Sussex shopman, "the magistrate is said to have signed the warrant of commitment [to Horsham Gaol] very reluctantly." In some instances the treatment received in prison was good. At Horsham, for instance, Pollard was given "a bedroom to himself on the debtors' side." In Gloucestershire Quaker prisoners received similar treatment, the magistrates of that county having ruled several years back that in jail Quakers were to be considered on a footing with debtors. Of the nine Quakers imprisoned in the Carlisle Gaol it was reported: "All or at least eight of these young men were accommodated with rooms more comfortable than the common prison. Some difficulty occurred about the gaol fees, and one of them viz. James Miller was detained [after the expiry of his sentence] on this account; but on application to the magistrates, he, with some others, was released without paying any fees." At Carlisle, "although the magistrates were generally disposed to favour Friends," they were unwilling to grant any exemptions from imprisonment, which seem to have been quite common elsewhere. Of the Quaker lodged in the County Gaol at Hertford the Abstract reports that he was "very kindly treated." On the other hand, there were cases, too, of harsher treatment. Whereas at Dorchester a Quaker who was "committed as a common prisoner" was later given "comfortable accommodation" by a Friend's intervention with the sheriff, in Surrey Quaker prisoners were "placed with the 4th class of men felons." In the Wakefield House of Correction they were forced to wear "the prison dress . . . and their Friends not suffered to carry them any provisions; but upon application to the Deputy Lieutenants both these restrictions were taken off."

Among those who narrowly escaped jailing in this period was young Joseph Sturge (see below), then aged eighteen, who was drawn for the militia in 1813. "But for the fact of having a small farm with a flock of sheep upon it," he related later, "he should have gone to prison, as a testimony against any appeal to arms." But this form of Quaker witness was drawing to a close. After the conclusion of the Napoleonic wars, throughout which Friends by means of the "Parliamentary Committee" of the Meeting for Sufferings had continued to keep a watchful eye on all projected legislation concerned with military affairs, only

333

infrequently do we find cases of young Quakers imprisoned for refusal of militia service. By the Militia Act of 1852 their imprisonment became illegal. Distraint on the goods of militia objectors continued until 1860, when compulsory militia service was suspended indefinitely. From then until 1916 Britain was free of conscription. In fact, toward the end of the militia era the demand for personal service had been relaxed, though a rate continued to be levied for the upkeep of the by now semivoluntary militia. This, of course, Friends refused to pay.

In 1845, when the ballot was still enforced, we hear of the organization of "Anti-Militia Clubs." In January of that year a Quaker from Newcastle wrote to the *British Friend* that he had been asked to join such a club, the membership of which was drawn from Friends and others "who conscientiously refuse to fight, or hire others to fight for them." Each member had pledged himself to refuse to pay his militia fine if the ballot fell on him, and instead to allow his goods to be distrained. "After this, the 'Anti-Militia Club' steps in, and shares his loss,—the members thus bearing each other's burdens." The writer, could himself see no "impropriety" in a Quaker's joining such a club, but he would be interested, he wrote, in hearing the views of other Friends on the matter and in discovering if similar clubs existed elsewhere. Two replies were published in the next issue, both disapproving such behavior. A Birmingham Friend felt that it signified a regrettable lack of preparedness to suffer joyfully the consequences of doing right. Another Friend, from Saffron Walden, reported the existence of a rather different type of anti-militia club (similar, in fact, to the one in the eighteenth century), where members pooled their monetary resources to pay the fine or find a substitute for any member who was required to serve. In Newcastle, this Friend comments, "the members are men possessed of goods; in [Saffron Walden] the members generally are young men possessing only money." In neither case, in his view, could Friends join in, for such bodies displayed "no truly decided principle against war, no genuine suffering for truth's sake." These anti-militia clubs appear to have been of non-Quaker origin and to have sprung from the antimilitarist movement of the 1840's (of which more will be said in the next chapter). That some Quakers participated in such bodies is very probable, even though they were disapproved of by many Friends and were, indeed, in basic contradiction to the Quaker principle, still generally accepted in that period, of refusing all alternatives to military requisitions.

The year 1860, when the Militia Ballot Act finally became inoperative, saw the end of the two-century-long period of militia "sufferings." Only in the Channel Islands did compulsory militia service continue in force. Here, however, Quakers were now officially exempt from any such requirements. In 1886 two nonmembers, the sons of a Jerseyman, Edward Voisin, had objected on religious grounds to serving and were put in jail. This set the editor of the London *Friend* wondering whether Quakers might accept a privileged status, while others suffered for following the same principles as the Society held. Was it not perhaps the duty of Quakers to protest more strongly against the system of conscription instead of carefully guarding their exempt position within its framework? At that time these were largely theoretical problems for the Society in Britain. Although Australia and New Zealand introduced compulsory military service for boys in 1909-1910 and thereafter some Quaker youths, mostly the children of British immigrants, were put in jail for noncompliance, it was not until the outbreak of World War I that Friends once again faced military conscription at home and the various issues connected with it.

Britain's abandonment of compulsion for the militia still left the possibility of Quaker converts among soldiers in the regular army raised by voluntary enlistment. Such cases, naturally, were of rare occurrence, but we do hear of them occasionally. Several instances, concerning the details of which we have quite full information, occurred at the Chatham barracks around 1840. Here three serving soldiers in succession were attracted to Friends through contact with the meeting in nearby Rochester and came to accept the Society's peace testimony. One of these men, Henry Newton, was bought out of the army, but the other two were given prison sentences of three months and twelve months, respectively, for refusal any further to bear arms. In both instances the sentences were served in the Millbank Penitentiary.

The first of these two cases, in point of time, was that of twenty-one-year-old William Dyne, a drummer in the marines, who had enlisted at the age of twelve. While stationed at Chatham he had come to know Friends through acting as reader to a blind Quaker, Benjamin Bishop; the Bible and the journals of early Friends were what Bishop required him to read. Dyne's interest thus aroused, he paid a visit to the local Quaker meeting, which he then attended for the period of about a year before reaching his decision to refuse to carry a sword, the cause of his court-martial. (In the Quaker meeting house he had carefully left his sword in the anteroom each time before entering!) At Dyne's court-martial a barrister member of the Rochester meeting had helped him with his defense. Dyne admitted disobedience to military orders.

> I am well aware [he went on] that, in thus refusing any longer to perform the part of a soldier, I am guilty of a breach of discipline,

and am liable to the punishment which may be imposed by law in such a case. But my conduct proceeds not from a spirit of insubordination, or wilful disobedience; it is simply the result of a conscientious conviction that all war is inconsistent with the gospel of our Lord and Saviour Jesus Christ, and a direct violation of His precepts. . . . I am a servant of the Prince of Peace, and I can be a soldier no longer. . . . I was taken into the service when only twelve years of age, and when, consequently, I was too young to form a judgement on this subject, or properly to understand the nature of the engagement into which I was required to enter; and no opportunity has ever since been given me to determine for myself how I would act.

After his release from jail and his subsequent discharge from the army which resulted from the purchase price's being paid without his knowledge, Dyne had joined Friends. He was active for the Society thereafter both as a keen temperance advocate and as a worker for peace (in which connection he was among those chosen to do relief work in France after the war of 1870).

The other army convert made by Rochester Friends around this time, who like Dyne also suffered imprisonment, was William Batkin, a nineteen-year-old infantryman belonging to the "Buffs" regiment. Again it seems to have been blind Benjamin Bishop who was mainly instrumental in a soldier's conversion to pacifism. Bishop wrote to a friend concerning Batkin: "I lent him Barclay's Apology, but not without first feeling my way clear to do so, for I have not forgotten all I had to wade through on the laying down of the arms of Henry Newton and William Dyne." Indeed by this date Rochester Friends, although they did not attempt actively to proselytize on behalf of either pacifism or Quakerism, were beginning to be in bad odor with the military establishment on account of their contacts with some of the soldiers. Threatening to have Batkin given "a good flogging" after he had refused to go on guard duty, his colonel told him: "These people that made you do this will not come and receive any of your punishment."

The quiet influence for peace exercised by the Friends of Rochester meeting was typical of mid-nineteenth-century British Quakerism. Most meetings did not have a similar opportunity of placing their peace testimony before serving soldiers. But meetings everywhere, in the belief that the practice of their principles was the best form of recommending their views to those outside the Society, continued to be watchful to see that their members' conduct in regard to the activities of war, as in other areas of behavior, matched the principles they professed. As Yearly Meeting's epistle of 1804 had declared: "Friends, it is an awful thing to stand forth to the nation as the advocates of inviolable peace; and our testimony loses its efficacy in proportion to the want of consistency in any."

The old temptation to which Quaker shipowners had long been prone, of furnishing their vessels with guns, was now fading. We do find as late as 1828 two Scarborough Quakers being disowned for arming their vessels after one of them had been captured by pirates. In 1833, however, the reference to "letters of marque" finally disappeared from the queries: it was by this date an anachronism. It had always been easy, especially in time of war, for Quakers to slip into some activity which, while technically noncombatant, was yet of assistance to the country's military effort. In 1810, for instance, Yearly Meeting warned members against "in any manner aiding and assisting in the conveyance of soldiers, their baggage, arms, ammunition and other military stores." The problem took many forms. In March 1851 a writer in the *British Friend* enquired whether a Quaker manufacturer might supply clothing or other nonlethal materials to the army without contravening his Society's peace testimony. The editor's answer, based on the opinion of the Clerk of Yearly Meeting given a few years earlier, was unequivocal: "The supplying of such articles was clearly a violation of our testimony." During the winter of 1854-1855, while the Crimean War was raging, a well-known Quaker firm, C. & J. Clark of Street, which specialized in the manufacture of leather, came under criticism within the Society for supplying sheepskin coats for the troops' use in the hard Crimean winter. In explanation of their action Clark's replied that they had agreed to fill the order only after it had been pointed out to them that their firm alone held supplies of the necessary skins sufficient for the emergency and that, in addition, they had arranged for the profits from the sale to be used for building a new schoolhouse in their village. One Friend wrote in to the *British Friend* accusing the firm indirectly of bearing responsibility for the slaughter of the enemy, but this feeling does not appear to have been shared by the Society in general, for the matter was allowed to rest.

Quakers were expected to eschew the use of arms for the protection of themselves, their families, or their property. Apart from encounters with the occasional highwayman or robber, Friends in the British Isles were not tested in this regard to the same degree as were some of their brethren on the American frontier. In the nineteenth century public security throughout Britain distinctly improved over the rather more unsettled conditions of previous centuries. Concerning the propriety of Quakers' appealing for police protection in case of danger or unrest there appear to have been differences of view for, with a weakly developed police apparatus, the military were usually called out to quell any serious disturbance. This had happened, for instance, when in 1739 Dublin Quakers applied to the Lord Lieutenant for assistance for their Friends at Timahoe, Co. Kildare, who had been subjected to mob violence. On the other hand, during the Irish Rebellion of 1798, when the small Quaker communities were threatened with danger on all sides, we find a leading Friend like Joseph Haughton of Ferns telling the English commander that he hoped he would never "trust to or apply for military protection." And this appears to have been the attitude prevalent at that time among Irish Friends.

A related problem was that of collaboration with, and participation in, the administration of the police. We have seen that in the eighteenth century Quakers took their turn in serving as constables, and they continued to do so until the voluntary system was replaced during the second quarter of the nineteenth century by a paid service. They had of course refused to carry out such duties if they ran contrary to their religious beliefs, as sometimes occurred in connection with the mustering of the militia or the administration of oaths. During the unsettled years just prior to 1848, when fears of a Chartist uprising were rife, discussion arose among Friends whether they might allow themselves to be enrolled as special constables in view of the possibility that this service might entail the use of arms in an emergency. Most Friends felt that the office was of public benefit and that Friends should not withdraw cooperation unless faced with an order that actually conflicted with their conscience; a few, however, refused to serve when required to do so and were fined. A few years earlier, in 1839, Joseph Sturge had felt it to be his duty to refuse to pay his local Birmingham poor-rate, since a considerable portion went toward the upkeep of the newly established police force, which was at first supplied with arms. When a little later the arms were withdrawn Sturge renewed his payment of the rate.

The decline and eventual abandonment of compulsory service in the militia brought to an end, too, the disowning of Quakers for accepting such service or for failing to bear the full consequences of refusal. Occasionally a Friend whose convincement had taken place after long service in the armed forces had to struggle with the problem of whether to accept or reject the continuance of his army or navy pension. But this was a matter for personal decision according to conscience; to the best of my knowledge it never became a subject for disciplinary action.

In the course of the first half of the nineteenth century the character of the Quaker peace testimony underwent considerable change. The somewhat negative emphasis of the previous period, which saw the essence of this testimony in a refusal to bear arms and a careful avoidance of any action contributing to the waging of war, gave way before a more positive approach. This change was reflected, for instance, in the altered wording of the Society's official "query" dealing with the peace testimony. In 1860 the old style of enumerating the various forbidden activities, from arms-bearing to dealing in prize goods, was replaced by a simple question: "Are Friends faithful in maintaining our Christian testimony against all war?" Slightly revised in 1875, this query remained current until after the First World War. The content of this Christian testimony against war had gradually filled out into a many-sided witness for peace, which brought Quakers once more out of the quiet of their sectarian retreat into the bustle of political affairs and the whirl of social development.

The new evangelical trend, which was coming increasingly to dominate the British Society's religious thinking, affected its peace testimony as it did all other aspects of Quakerism. Clarkson, writing in 1806, noted: "The Quakers ground the illicitness of war on several passages which are to be found in the New Testament." This Biblical literalism comes out, too, in the unhappy Hannah Barnard affair when, largely due to the insistence of leading Friends of London Yearly Meeting, this visiting American Quaker was eventually disowned by her home meeting after her return to the United States, *inter alia*, on account of her denial of divine sanction for the Jewish wars chronicled in the Old Testament. This happened in 1802. (At the same time a group of Irish Friends led by Abraham Shackleton, whose doubts concerning the literal inspiration of the Old Testament had influenced Hannah Barnard were likewise disowned.) We see the letter of Scripture—"the plain precepts of our Divine Lord and Lawgiver"—rather than the spirit of Christ taking precedence, for example, in the passage devoted to the peace testimony in London Yearly Meeting's epistle of 1804. The evangelical party among British Friends later enjoyed the support and devotion of the talented Joseph John Gurney, brother of the famous Elizabeth Fry and one of the most prominent representatives of Quakerism in his day. His *Essay on War and on Its Lawfulness under the Christian Dispensation*, which was first published as a pamphlet in 1833 (it had originally formed part of his *Observations on the Religious Peculiarities of the Society of Friends*, 1824), was influential in disseminating the evangelical argument against war among

Quakers as well as outside the Society, for the pamphlet enjoyed a wide circulation and went through several editions on both sides of the Atlantic.

However, the most cogent exposition of the peace testimony to emerge from the nineteenth-century British Society of Friends was produced by Jonathan Dymond, a man who by no means shared all of Gurney's evangelicalism. True, this evangelical impulse was responsible for much of the growing concern within the Society for such issues as antislavery or temperance. But the reinvigorated Quaker peace testimony owed more to the humanitarian ideas of the Enlightenment with their vision of a warless world and an international community of nations, concepts which had their forerunners in the works of such men as Penn and Bellers. Drawing on this source of inspiration, though at the same time not losing sight of the New Testament basis of Quaker pacifism, Dymond in his brief life-span produced several works which would provide Friends—surprisingly enough, really for the first time in the history of the Society—with a clear and detailed presentation of, and a reasoned apologia for, their long-held peace testimony.

Dymond died in 1828 at the age of 31. His major work, the two volumes of *Essays on the Principles of Morality*, appeared posthumously in the following year. He had spent his life in his native town of Exeter where he ran a linen-draper's business: studious and earnest, the young Quaker was little known during his lifetime outside the ranks of his Society. But he was active in the new peace movement which had grown up after 1815 (see next chapter), and he became a leading figure in the Exeter branch of the Peace Society. After his death his writings on peace, which he had set within the framework of a wider discussion of moral philosophy, became standard texts for both the British and American peace movements. References to "Dymond on Peace" abound in the literature of the nineteenth-century peace societies on both sides of the Atlantic.

Dymond divides his discussion of war into four major headings: the causes of war, the consequences of war, the relation of war to Christian morality, and the practical implications of an adoption of pacifism. His arguments are clearly put forward and his style lucid. His pages are never overburdened, as is so often the case with similar works of that period, with citations or Biblical texts. He appeals to reason and practical morality as frequently as to passages in the Scriptures. His is a kind of reasonable Christianity, "a law of benevolence" which supplements the natural law implanted in the hearts of man. The pacifist principles he derived from reason and the New Testament were applicable as much to relations between states as to individual relations.

All this is indeed a far cry from the stand of the early Quakers, but it held great attraction for Dymond's contemporaries and successors. No wonder, then, that his writings on peace were constantly reprinted in Britain and America either *in toto* or in excerpts or abridgments.

Dymond's analysis of the causes of conflict anticipates much that was to be written on the subject in the twentieth century, although to some extent it already formed the commonplace of the case against war. He castigates the traditional unquestioning acceptance of war. As with the slave trade for many centuries, familiarity with war had made men indifferent to its miseries and cruelty. "They whom the idea of a single corpse would thrill with terror, contemplate that of heaps of human carcasses mangled by human hands, with indifference." But it is in national prestige—"national irritability," he calls it—that he detects the major source of modern wars, in the nations' touchiness at any supposed affront to national honor. Governments were also prone to use war for the pursuit of glory—an illusion. They were often swayed by sinister "interest," either public, as when they sought to maintain an equally illusory balance of power, or private, when the upper classes who controlled governments strove to find outlets for their sons in the trade of war. "If nations fought only when they could not be at peace," he concludes, "there would be very little fighting in the world," i.e., virtually all international disputes are subject to a solution by arbitration.

The consequences of war seemed to Dymond to be almost all of a negative character. There was the loss of life, and the excessive taxation. There was the "moral depravity," the degradation of character in all who were involved, whether as soldiers or as civilians. There was the "diminution of civil liberty." "If no other motive induced a people jealously to scrutinize the grounds of war, this might be sufficient." For the unlimited obedience demanded from the soldier, an obedience that was indeed essential for war's successful prosecution, signified a cessation of moral judgment and responsibility. "Such a resignation of our moral agency is not . . . tolerated in any one other circumstance of human life." This military "bondage," comparable in Dymond's view to slavery, makes bad citizens and has a deleterious influence, moreover, on a country's free institutions. Dymond also denounced the evil role of war propaganda aimed at blackening the enemy's character. "Pamphlets, placards, newspapers, caricatures—every agent is in requisition to irritate us into malignity."

Concerning the proper Christian attitude to war, Dymond as a Quaker finds no difficulty in inferring pacifism from the Sermon on the Mount and from other passages in the Gospels. True, such injunctions as "Resist not evil" are not to be interpreted absolutely literally. "But what then? To show that their meaning is not literal, is not to show that they do not forbid war." It is the spirit behind such utterances that must provide the key to their understanding. Even if Christ did not specifically ban war or the soldier's profession he forbade "the passions which lead to war." "The sum, the tendency of the whole revelation is in our favour." An evangelical Quaker, like Dymond's contemporary Joseph John Gurney, might have trouble in squaring the belligerence of the Old Testament with the pacifism he deduced from the New. Not so Dymond, who feels that the new dispensation introduced by Christ has entirely superseded what went before.

Dymond's main concern in regard to the practical application of what he designates as "the pacific principles of the New Testament" is to show that these do in fact have a bearing on the conduct of political states. Dymond was not a complete nonresistant. "It is the duty of the civil magistrate," he wrote, "to repress the violence of one man towards another, and by consequence it is the duty of the individual, when the civil power cannot operate, to endeavour to repress it himself." But both the magistrate and the individual citizen, if they were Christians, were bound by the same limitation to "the right of self-defence": they were forbidden to shed blood and enjoined to confine themselves to noninjurious coercion in dealing with wrongdoers. In external relations, too, governors were bound by the rules of Christian morality; Dymond found no justification for the time-honored view held generally among both Protestants and Catholics that statecraft was exempt from some of the precepts binding individual Christians. If taking life in self-defense were wrong for the latter, then it was equally wrong for states to indulge in the collective slaughter of war.

But could not a case be made out for the justifiability of wars of defense? Dymond did not deny that a war of defense was possible in theory. In practice, however, he believed no distinction between defensive and aggressive war might usefully be drawn (an argument much used in twentieth-century antimilitarist writing). What might well begin as a defensive struggle would, in his view, inevitably end up by becoming a welter of destruction, slaughter, and hatred, which clearly Christians should refrain from sanctioning. The "just war," then, was an illusion.

If the army of defence obtains success, it soon becomes an army of aggression. Having repelled the invader, it begins to punish him. If a war has once begun, it is vain to think of distinctions of aggression and defence. Moralists may *talk* of distinctions, but

342

soldiers will *make* none; and none can be made; it is without the limits of possibility.

But even in theory Dymond remains extremely sceptical concerning the likelihood of a war of defense. Whatever the claims put forward by belligerent governments, in actual fact almost all wars have been fought for motives other than pure self-defense. And he writes:

> If we had a right to kill a man in self-defence, very few wars would be shown to be lawful. Of the wars which are prosecuted, some are simply wars of aggression; some are for the maintenance of a balance of power; some are in assertion of technical rights; and some, undoubtedly, to repel invasion. The last are perhaps the fewest; and of these only it can be said that they bear any analogy whatever to the case which is supposed; and even in these, the analogy is seldom complete. It has rarely indeed happened that wars have been undertaken simply for the preservation of life, and that no other alternative has remained to a people, than to kill, or to be killed. And let it be remembered, that *unless this alternative alone remains*, the case of individual self-defence is irrelevant.

To one question ancillary to that of war, capital punishment, Dymond devotes considerable attention. We have seen that, like most Quakers before him, he did not deny the Christian character of the magistrate's office. Moreover, in this respect in disagreement with early Friends, he held that nonviolent coercion and not the sword should constitute the arm of government. The object of punishment, in his view, was threefold: reformation of the evildoer, deterrence of crime, and restitution for wrong done. The death penalty, apart from contravening the Christian ban on killing, very effectively prevented some of these major aims of penology. It thwarted reformation by destroying the criminal; it seldom acted as an object lesson to potential criminals. In addition, it demoralized those who administered it, and, since it was "absolutely irrevocable," an error in judgment could lead to the taking of an entirely innocent life. Finally, argued Dymond, the problem was really entirely separate from that of war. "The question of capital-punishment," he wrote to a fellow Quaker in April 1827, "does not alter the duty of Christians to promote the spirit which their religion enjoins. I do not know that the Peace Society ever denied the lawfulness of the punishment of death; though individuals do it, and I do it." In the United States a decade after Dymond's death (though

not in Great Britain), just this very question, however, was to become
a major factor in dividing the peace movement.

Three comments may be made in connection with Dymond's exposition of pacifism. In the first place, he presumes for the most part that
wars are fought by professional armies. He urges indeed that Christians have an obligation to refuse "mildly and temperately, yet firmly,"
all demands to submit to compulsory military service. "Refusal to obey
is the final duty of Christians." It would be quite wrong, he argues, to
place responsibility for any unchristian act one might have to commit
during war on the shoulders of the rulers of the state. The responsibility fell on each individual. But this point, we have seen, represented
a somewhat academic question for him, though it was not an entirely
theoretical one for a Quaker in the first half of the nineteenth century.
Dymond's general argument, however, is pursued on the assumption
that soldiers are usually regulars; as such, they are serving in the
forces in order to earn a living or make a career and are unconcerned
with, indeed often largely ignorant of, the causes of the quarrels in
which they fight. Second, selfdefense for him seems to mean bodily
defense, the prevention of actual physical annihilation. Though his
youth was spent in the aftermath of the French Revolution he tends to
underplay the ideological element in contemporary warfare. He has
little to say concerning a war for the maintenance of liberty or free institutions or for national independence. His arguments are directed
primarily against wars of prestige or ambition or against those waged
to uphold the balance of power or to gain material advantages.

Last, we may note that Dymond nowhere proposes any concrete
techniques of nonviolent resistance to aggression. (This development
in pacifist thought was to come really only in the twentieth century as
a result of the experiments conducted by Gandhi.) He does not discuss
the limits of noninjurious force. The seventeenth-century Quaker
Thomas Lurting wrote: "It is better to strike a [mild] blow than to
cleave a man's head or cut off an arm." Dymond ignores the question
of how much force a pacifist may legitimately use. By denying that a
defensive war was at all a likely occurrence he attempts to remove the
need for nonviolent techniques against external aggression. Besides,
his argument for pacifism, for all its utilitarian coloring that distinguishes it from many earlier and less elaborate statements of the
Quaker peace testimony, is still one deduced from premises rather
than based on consequences. War is forbidden Christians, *therefore*
it is wrong and can as little form part of public as of private morality.
We may believe God will protect us if we follow his commands: this
remains the core of what Dymond had to say. True, he does remark

344

that "even in reference only to the present state of existence . . . we shall find, that the testimony of experience is, that forbearance is most conducive to our interests." Yet the examples he cites to buttress this statement are rather meager: Friends' experience with the Indians in Pennsylvania and elsewhere in America, that old stock in trade of Quaker pamphleteers, and their more recent fate in the Ireland of 1798 (for describing which Dymond drew plentifully on the recently published account by his fellow Quaker and colleague in the Peace Society, Thomas Hancock).

In 1826 Dymond had written to a friend: "I am inclined to hope that (after the approaching day is passed when slavery shall be abolished) the attention and labours of Friends will be more conspicuously and publicly directed than they have hitherto been to the question of war —an evil before which, in my estimation, slavery sinks into insignificance. . . . I doubt not that now is the time for anti-slavery exertion. The time *will* come for anti-war exertion." Indeed, just as Friends had long been collaborating with non-Quakers (particularly reform-minded evangelicals within the Church of England and in the non-conformist denominations) in the movement to eliminate slavery, so now they were beginning to work alongside non-Quakers in the new movement for peace which had been started at the conclusion of the Napoleonic struggle. The original impulse which set this movement going derived from a Quaker source. On 7 June 1814 William Allen, a Friend active in the ministry and in various philanthropic enterprises, served as host to "a meeting to consider of a new Society to spread tracts, etc., against war" (as he noted in his journal). And he and another Friend, the Welsh ironmaster Joseph Tregelles Price, were among those most responsible for carrying this plan into effect. Their efforts were crowned by the establishment in 1816 of the London Peace Society, in which any who were willing to pledge themselves to work against all war might become members.

The Peace Society, which will be discussed in the next chapter, was not a Quaker body; its supporters, among whom were some who were not absolute pacifists (although its official platform was based on an absolutist stand) were drawn from nearly all Protestant denominations. But many Friends joined it. In 1832 we find a non-Quaker member of the Peace Society noting in a short *Address to the Members of the Society of Friends on their Aversion to War and Their Support of the Peace Society* a certain slackening of Quaker interest. He urged Friends to give greater support to the Peace Society than they had been doing, especially on the financial side. On the whole, however, Quaker work for peace increased with every decade, and for most of the nineteenth century part of Friends' effort was channelled through the medium of the Peace Society.

The Society of Friends around mid-century contained ardent peace propagandists like Edmund Fry (a relative of the famous Elizabeth) and Charles Gilpin. A bound volume of Fry's leaflets, which was issued in 1855 during the Crimean War, under the title *Peace Principles Scripturally Maintained,* contains sixteen items with such names as "What saith the Scriptures"; "War in relation to Liberty"; "Peace—at what a Price?"; "The Gun or the Gospel"; "Are Peace Principles practicable?"; "What would the Peace Party do?"; "What would England have done?"; "The Present Crisis"; "The Ultimate Issue." And they were also obtainable in assorted packets of eighty at eightpence per packet. The Quaker bookseller and publisher Charles Gilpin, who in 1857 was elected Liberal M.P. for Northampton, a seat he held until his death in 1874, was a close colleague of Fry's. Gilpin's firm was responsible for publishing during the middle decades of the century a whole series of popular pacifist, anti-imperialist and radically antimilitarist tracts. Typical of his titles were such productions as *How can a Christian Fight? Or what is a Soldier?* or *Sketches from the History of Pennsylvania, &c. intended for the Information of that numerous Class of Christians who denounce War in General as a Great Evil; but who consider defensive War as allowable and unavoidable* (London, 1845).

Sometimes a local Quaker meeting might set up its own organization to sponsor peace work outside the Society of Friends. In 1842, for instance, Leeds Friends founded a Peace Association for this purpose. Numbers remained small for some years as a result, according to a local newspaper, of the "high tone and the Hebrew severity with which their meetings are conducted." At first membership of the association's executive committee had been confined to members of the Quaker meeting. But in 1851 the composition was broadened to include non-Friends, and soon activities and public interest in the work of the association expanded too. "In the next ten years," writes Wilfred Allott in his study *Leeds Quaker Meeting* published by the Thoresby Society in 1966, "the Association created an informed public opinion in Leeds on war and foreign policy." It did this by distributing tracts and leaflets on peace and international problems, by holding public meetings, by organizing protests against the various continental and colonial wars in which Great Britain became involved in the course of the 1850's as well as against the continued conscription for the militia. "It is a great contrast [to earlier periods of Quaker history] to see these nineteenth-century Friends collecting and sifting information, marshalling facts, bringing their consequences home to the citizens of Leeds, and challenging statesmen in and out of Parliament to explain and justify the action they had taken."

Quaker peace action of this kind contrasts, too, with the attitude of large sections of American Quakerism of this period; in the United States many meetings frowned on collaboration of their members with the organized non-Quaker peace movement. Such conduct they considered as "creaturely" activity, which might endanger the purity of their Society's witness to the world. The coldness or indifference, and sometimes even downright hostility, with which the new peace societies of the United States were greeted by the Society of Friends has been a matter for surprise to historians of the American peace movement like Merle E. Curti. British Friends rarely displayed this attitude, perhaps because of their greater integration by now with their environment and of a less withdrawn stance on their part.

In 1838 the American peace movement was split when William Lloyd Garrison and some of his friends broke away to found a New England Non-Resistance Society, which placed the slogan "no-government" in the center of its program. Denying that a consistent pacifist could collaborate actively in the affairs of government, the Garrisonites for a few years carried on a vigorous campaign in favor of their views. The close Anglo-American connection of that time, which embraced the peace movement along with other political and philanthropic concerns, soon led to the spread of the idea of nonresistance across the Atlantic. During the 1840's both Garrison himself and his even more *outré* assistant, Henry Clarke Wright, visited the British Isles, where they propagated their views among political radicals and religious pacifists. Yet nonresistance never really found a foothold in Britain. Most Quakers were cool to the idea. In March 1845, for instance, the *British Friend,* reviewing H. C. Wright's recently published book *Six Months at Graeffenberg* in which he expounds the nonresistant philosophy, set down the differences between it and the Quaker type of pacifism. True, both doctrines renounced war and bloodshed. But Friends, the writer pointed out, did not share the nonresistants' desire to renounce allegiance to all human governments. They did not object to suing at law or to the institution of the police or to the imprisonment of wrongdoers. They usually voted at elections. In other words, they approved those nonlethal aspects of civil government which were of benefit to the country. "We would say, then, to our author, and to Americans generally—Beware of extremes." In the next issue, a North country Quaker, Elizabeth Pease of Darlington, wrote in support of the nonresistant position, but hers was a lonely voice. It is true that there were others within the Society of Friends, who sympathized to a greater or lesser degree with the nonresistants' position (e.g., Edmund Fry or Charles Gilpin); but they were in a decided minority. Friends, on the whole, continued to take a positive stand toward government and its tasks.

The problem of the police, of the maintenance of domestic order within the state, continued from time to time throughout the century to exercise the minds of Friends. If international war were wrong from the Christian viewpoint primarily because it involved bloodshed, might not a Quaker have, after all, to condemn the exercise of police power if it were found sometimes to necessitate the use of injurious force? Or did war offend rather on account of its objective of widespread human destruction than because it involved the taking of life? Should one distinguish between war, a culpable activity, and police action, a praiseworthy function, above all because of the motives in each case?

As during the nineteenth century Quakers became eligible for the magistracy and for government office and to sit in Parliament, these questions became increasingly relevant. In an essay published at York, in 1860 under the title *Is War Lawful for the Christian?* James Backhouse, Junior, attempted to grapple with the problem. While he answers the question posed in his title with a decided negative, he agrees at the same time not only that the magistrate's office is given sanction in the New Testament, but that "persons are at times justified, by their official position, in doing some things which otherwise would be unjustifiable." Nevertheless, he goes on, this concession by no means implies that armies and navies are merely an extension of the police system, because their functions are entirely different. "An army is a body of men scientifically trained for the *express purpose of destroying*. . . . The police force under magisterial authority is trained to maintain order *as far as possible without the shedding of blood*. Those weapons which most endanger the destruction of life are, as a rule, withheld." The magistrate acts within the framework of the law and takes life only after every precaution has been exercised to ascertain the guilt of the accused. Even where he has to undertake the suppression of a riot, he does everything to reduce bloodshed to a minimum. On the other hand, in war the exact opposite holds: neither is there any superior authority at whose behest a war-making power acts nor is there any limit to the killing and devastation it seeks to carry out.

"War is substantially international duelling," declared London Yearly Meeting in "An Appeal to Our Fellow-Christians on War" issued in 1878. A statement of this kind, as well as arguments of the sort used by Backhouse, could win the assent of the still small but growing number of Friends active in civic life who were sympathetic to, but did not fully share, their Society's traditional pacifism. Some Friends, such as Dymond, believed it was possible to exercise authority, even within the framework of present-day society, with the use merely of noninjurious forms of coercion. Many Quakers, on the other hand, continued to accept pacifism as a mainly personal witness, while feeling that men in public office, including perhaps any Friends who felt able to serve in the magistracy, might sometimes be justified in wielding the sword of authority. A typical expression of this viewpoint may be found in Caroline E. Stephen's very popular exposition of Friends' beliefs, *Quaker Strongholds*, first published in 1890 and many times reprinted since that date. "Would any one say that at the time of the Indian Mutiny the Governor-General of India ought not to have permitted the use of arms for the protection of the women and children?" she asks, though at the same time she surmises that "no true Friend" would have been prepared to take on an office of this nature. "No nation which had from the beginning of its history been thoroughly Christian could, I suppose, have found itself in the position which we occupied in India in 1857." Yet a nation running its affairs according to Christian principles was still a long way off. Meanwhile, she concludes, "our place still is mainly to leaven, not to govern, the world."

Yet more and more Friends were to be found ready to govern as well as to leaven. Old Quaker attitudes compounded of necessity and principle, which were set against any participation in public life or in the political system, died hard. Some British Friends, like some American Friends too, were opposed even to the exercise of the franchise— at least if they could not vote for a candidate sharing Quaker principles. In 1818, for instance, we find that stalwart Quaker tax objector, Nathaniel Morgan of Ross (see chapter 8), when pressed by a fellow member of the Society of Friends to vote for a military man who was standing for the local county seat, replying: "No Quaker could in his conscience vote for a man of blood." An even more categorical stand was displayed by John Grubb, a Quaker businessman from Stoke Newington, who wrote in 1832: "I do not think it quite consistent to choose a person to represent me in Parliament who I know would violate my religious principles—first he would take an oath to qualify himself—he would in some cases vote for war, and he would in some shape vote for the payment of the clergy—these are three instances wherein my representative would undoubtedly violate my religious principles—how then could I consistently or conscientiously vote for him as my representative?" (from the *Extracts* from his letters to Joseph Grubb privately printed by Janet F. Carroll and Olive C. Goodbody, Dublin, 1966). At the same time, John Grubb was much worried when in that year (for the first occasion in the century) a Quaker, Joseph Pease, whose election should have set his fears at rest concerning the conduct of at least one representative in the legislature, had stood for parliament, as candidate for Co. Durham. Grubb was alarmed by the thought of the increasing worldliness and the rapid assimilation of the Society to the world around it that he expected to ensue on Friends' entry into politics.

The reservations of men like Morgan or Grubb, however, could not stem the tide. The participation of Friends in the politics of Victorian England was considerable when viewed against the background of their history and the small size of their Society. Besides a number of lesser figures, the Society of Friends produced two outstanding personalities in the political life of the century: Joseph Sturge and John Bright.

Of the two Sturge was the lesser talent but perhaps the more consistent Friend. Throughout his life he adhered strictly to Quaker peace principles (several examples of his loyalty are cited earlier), and he was an active participant in the work of both the London Peace Society and the League of Universal Brotherhood (see next chapter) as well as in the peace work of his own Society of Friends. In politics he made his mark in the free-trade and franchise-reform movements. In the early 1840's he had organized the radical Complete Suffrage Union, which strove to achieve peacefully and by purely political pressure what the Chartist left wing hoped to bring about by a violent upheaval. For this prosperous corn-merchant free trade, by removing the barriers to international exchange of the world's products, and political democracy, by providing a safety valve for the expression of popular discontents, were essential prerequisites for the creation of peace.

Sturge had never entered Parliament. For Bright, on the other hand, the House of Commons and the electoral hustings were the scenes of his greatest triumphs—and defeats. But like Sturge, as well as Cobden and many liberals of that day, Bright identified free trade and political democracy with the crusade for peace. And he placed all his great powers as an orator at the disposal of these causes.

Bright once said concerning his opposition to the Crimean War: "I do not know why I differed from other people so much, but sometimes I have thought it happened from the education I had received in the religious sect with which I am connected." Indeed, his relationship with the Society of Friends far exceeded merely an upbringing in it and a formal connection continued into adult life. Throughout his whole career he remained warmly attached to the Society; he strove, it is clear, to make his political conduct to some extent a reflection of Quaker ideals. The cartoonists who loved to show Bright in Quaker garb (this in fact he had discarded not long after embarking on a political career) caught something of the spirit with which his political activities were transfused. Yet, for all his pacifistic utterances and his political opposition to concrete wars, there remains some ambiguity concerning the degree to which he subscribed to his Society's peace testimony. Herman Ausubel, for instance, has called it "demonstrably false" to describe Bright as "a rigid pacifist." "Though a Quaker," he says, "Bright was not a pacifist; but he did not believe in entering on a war lightly." Margaret Hirst, on the other hand, held that Bright nurtured a very personal belief in Quaker pacifism, while pleading in the political arena only nonreligious, utilitarian arguments against specific wars. "He always argued the question," she writes, "on a Blue-book basis." On this basis, but on this basis alone, he might be prepared to concede the possibility of a war being justified.

Let us, therefore, take a closer look at Bright's views on war and peace to see if we can find a satisfactory resolution of this problem.

Bright's antimilitarism was interwoven with the remainder of his political philosophy. In his view, the promoters of war were to be found among the landed aristocracy and the supporters of the *ancien régime*, among the bondholders and the title-seekers who were the only ones to profit from war: in other words, wars stemmed from the machinations of those groups in whom Bright saw the major opponents of his political program. In his view the working class, in whom Bright despite his *laissez-faire* opposition to factory legislation and his family cotton business entertained a lively interest, always lost through war. For "the working men find the main portion of the blood which is shed, and on them fall the poverty and misery which are occasioned by the increase of taxes and damage to industry." War, then, was produced by the political policies of the English ruling class and of the rulers of other nations. The series of imperialist ventures indulged in by Britain's political establishment, in Bright's view, merited the uttermost condemnation; "needless and terrible slaughter" was how he described them. He resigned from Gladstone's cabinet in July 1882 in protest against the bombardment of Alexandria by British forces (though, it must be admitted, he had failed a year earlier to take this step when fighting with the Boers broke out in South Africa).

The same sinister interests which furthered Britain's imperialist expansion were responsible for its inflated military expenditure and for proposals to intervene on the European continent. He fought furiously against the Russophobia which swept large sections of the populace around mid-century. He opposed all attempts to back by force of arms the insurgent nationalities of Eastern Europe—whether the Magyars against the Habsburg power or the Poles against the Russian Tsar. He rejected any notion of the British people's acting as "knight-errants in the cause of freedom to other nations." His principle in foreign policy he summed up in the words: "Nonintervention in every case where her [Britain's] interests were not directly and obviously assailed." The country could best help the oppressed by setting its own house in order (there was plenty to be done here at home, Bright never wearied telling people) and by acting as an example to the world how a free and Christian nation prospered by abiding by the principles it professed.

War brutalized those who engaged in it, increased the taxation weighing on the nation, blighted trade and industry, threatened parliamentary institutions, and hindered progress toward political reform. In fact, as Bright wrote to a friend in 1883, "war is rarely, perhaps never, worth what it costs." In his opposition to the Crimean War and to Britain's colonial wars he never departs from a purely pragmatic reasoning. His broadsides are always directed at what he considers his country's excessive, aggressive expenditure on armaments; he never pleads for total or unilateral disarmament, for ninety-nine out of a hundred persons were in favor of some sort of military defense.

I have not opposed any war on the ground that all war is unlawful and immoral. I have never expressed such an opinion. I have discussed these questions of war, Chinese, Crimean, Afghan, Zulu, Egyptian, on grounds common to and admitted by all thoughtful men, and have condemned them with arguments which I believe have never been answered. I will not discuss the abstract question. I shall be content when we reach the point at which all Christian men will condemn war when it is unnecessary, unjust, and leading to no useful or good result. We are far from that point now, but we make some way towards it.

In all disputes Bright believed there existed, only given the will on each side, a way out short of a military confrontation, which would prove more beneficial to all concerned than a resort to arms. But, where such good-will was lacking, might it not happen that war would be justified on the part of one of the contestants, unless this party were dedicated to nonresistance? Yes, Bright answers. And there appear to have been at least four occasions during his lifetime when he thought a resort to arms justified.

The Unionists in the American Civil War, the Christians of Turkey in 1876, the British at the time of the Indian Mutiny and the radicals of Upper and Lower Canada in the rebellion of 1838 were all forced to take to arms, in Bright's opinion, because no other honorable alternative was open to them, for in no case had they totally renounced war on principle. The Canadian affair of 1838 Bright once described as a "wholesome insurrection" productive of good results in furthering liberty. He thought the struggle in Turkey unavoidable since the Turkish government was clearly unwilling to accept any sort of arbitration. The action of the British in India in 1857 he regarded as simply an extension of the principle of police action to maintain domestic order within the state. "Does our friend Southhall," he wrote concerning a fellow Quaker who had criticized his attitude, "think our Government should rest quiet and allow every Englishman in India to be murdered? I don't think so." As for the American Civil War, Bright could not see how the Lincoln administration could have avoided war except at the price of a complete surrender to the Southern viewpoint. "I want no end of the war, and no compromise, and no reunion till the Negro is made free beyond all chance of failure," he wrote in August 1863. And he became one of the most eloquent advocates in Britain of the Unionist cause.

Yet if we say that Bright considered that governments, as at present constituted and in the present state of public opinion, might in certain circumstances have to wield the sword to maintain good order, or to defend the community from an outside threat, or to promote essential liberties, we are not saying more than could be said, too, of the first generation of Quaker pacifists after 1660. He was clearly not a non-resistant in either the Anabaptist or the Garrisonian sense. "I have never advocated the extreme peace principle, the non-resistance principle in public or in private," he once told Joseph Sturge. "I don't know whether I would logically maintain it." In regard to the Lincoln administration's conduct during the American Civil War he had expressed the view at the time that "no man who is not *absolutely* a non-resistant *in every sense*" (my italics) could challenge its rightness in taking up the sword.

It should be noted (this point has not to my knowledge been made before) that the four instances noted above, where Bright justified armed action in contemporary conflicts, might all be—indeed, at the time were—subsumed under a heading other than that of war. This is clearest in the case of the Indian Mutiny. But in regard to the Civil War many pacifists in the North argued that it represented merely a police action on a greatly magnified scale and that support for the Unionist cause by no means signified abandonment of opposition to all war—international war, that is to say. The armed struggles of the Christians in Turkey in 1876 or of the Canadian radicals of 1838 were likewise domestic affairs, due to malfunctioning of the established political systems, rather than war as ordinarily conceived. These exceptions to Bright's condemnation of war may not in fact disprove his opposition to all forms of *international* war.

Bright avoided any clear and public avowal of the precise stand he occupied in regard to the Quaker peace testimony as then held by the Society of which he was a member. Perhaps he never fully made up his mind. For him it was indeed an "abstract principle." "It will be time enough to discuss that question when we have abandoned everything that can be called unjust and unnecessary in the way of war." All war between nations was a crime; he could not see how it could be squared with the teachings of the New Testament. "In a short sentence it may be summed up to be the combination and concentration of all the horrors, crimes, and sufferings of which human nature is capable." True, in the present state of human affairs there were, he believed, certain rare contingencies when the exercise of even injurious force was necessary: to prevent physical annihilation, for instance, or to win the bare minimum of freedom needed for development of the human spirit. Yet this, in Bright's view, scarcely constituted war if we define war as armed conflict between organized states. And if it were true, too, that no politician, in the present condition of the world, could ask governments to leave their peoples totally without means of defense against external attack, "the moral law" still applied to men organized in states and nations as much as to individuals; international war signified the kind of international anarchy that was the exact opposite of a moral order.

J. Travis Mills in his study of *John Bright and the Quakers* has said that "if any one volume deserves the name of John Bright's text-book on the subject of War and Peace it is Dymond's *Principles of Morality*. Bright frequently commended it, [and] quoted it." To the 1889 edition of Dymond's essay entitled *War* he contributed a few pages of "Introductory Words" that form perhaps the most explicit expression of his personal approach to pacifism. Travis Mills is right to point out that Bright always "felt free to exercise his independent judgment, and did not accept each and every one of Dymond's dicta." It seems to me that Bright accepted, virtually in full, Dymond's critique of war as an "unlawful" means of settling international disputes but that he dissented from him, and from most Friends of his own time, in taking a broader and a more positive attitude towards physical coercion in the internal affairs of states.

It must be remembered, too, that an open avowal of Quaker pacifism, even as a purely personal creed, would have destroyed Bright's chances of making an effective impact in politics. As his friend and political colleague Cobden wrote on the eve of the Crimean War: "The enemy takes good care to turn us all into Quakers, because the Non-Resistance principle puts us out of court as practical politicians of the present day. Our opponents insist on it that we wish to totally disarm . . . they say we actually invite [the enemy] to come and invade us." (But "in the 1830's," writes Donald Read, "there is some evidence that Cobden may have been a complete non-resister.") Even convinced pacifists of the time thought it "more prudent" in certain political circumstances (the words are those of John Clarkson, one of the stalwarts of the early days of the Peace Society) not to discuss the question of defensive war, in view of the misunderstandings such discussion might arouse among the populace. Of course prudence is not always a virtue —even in a Quaker. But if a Quaker aspires to work for peace through political action, as Bright did, the attainment of his aim might well be jeopardized by a too-rigid insistence on the letter of the Society's peace testimony. This argument, it is true, might be reversed in favor of Quaker abstention from active politics altogether. But once the acceptability of Quaker participation in parliamentary affairs is granted, it certainly possesses cogency. And Bright, so far as we can tell, never saw any inconsistency in principle between his political career and his membership of the Society of Friends.

If Bright occasionally clashed with fellow Quakers on practical issues of war and peace, like the Indian Mutiny, he was at one with his coreligionists in a whole series of international episodes from the 1840's until his death in 1889. At times—for instance, during the Crimean War—he seemed to be almost a spokesman of the Society of Friends as well as for the wider "peace party" within the country.

Quakers' interest in international affairs as an area of concern in connection with their peace testimony was something new in the history of the Society of Friends. Throughout the first half of the century, Margaret Hirst has pointed out, except in regard to the antislavery cause to which British Friends gave wholehearted and official allegiance, " 'study to be quiet' was the advice pressed upon young and impetuous members," who sought to identify Quakerism with one or another political reform movement. This advice held, too, in regard to the cause of peace. Yet slowly the Society was beginning to relate its peace testimony to the exigencies of international politics. Gradually it ceased to seem enough for Quakers simply to restate the New Testament imperative against violent resistance and to reaffirm their conscientious objection to bearing arms and their trust in the protection of divine providence. Friends began to show increasing concern to uncover the roots of war and violence in the political and social order and to find means of resolving the actual conflicts arising between states. The writings of Jonathan Dymond had displayed such a concern; the official utterances of the Society and its actions during periods of international crisis, as well as those of Friends acting individually, moved in the course of the nineteenth century in this direction.

At the end of the Napoleonic Wars, when the Holy Alliance was set up under Tsar Alexander I's patronage, British Friends had tended to accept at their face value its promoters' assertions that they aimed to establish international peace and harmony. This naive trust in the good-will especially of the Tsar was shattered by the latter's support in the early 1820's of intervention against liberal movements everywhere throughout Europe. William Allen, a co-founder of the London Peace Society and an active Friend, wrote in dismay to the Tsar in April 1823: "It is said that the Emperor of Russia, who had so publicly patronized the Societies in America and England for the promotion of universal peace, had now become the secret and open abettor of war."

Relations with Russia remained throughout the century a matter of some concern to British Friends, largely because in influential sections of British public and government opinion Russia was then regarded as a natural enemy of Great Britain, with whom Britain was likely to become involved in conflict. The political interests of the two countries in this period did indeed clash, first in the Near East and later in Central Asia. War between the two countries threatened around 1840 and again in 1877-1878 and 1885-1887. And in 1854 friction led to actual fighting. It was during the Crimean War that we find the first example of Quaker "diplomacy's" being exercised in an attempt to avert the threat of war through the mediacy of the Society.

Usually, as for example during the dispute between Great Britain and the United States over the Oregon boundary in 1846 or in relation to the numerous colonial and imperialist wars indulged in by the British government in Asia or Africa, nineteenth-century Friends did not go much beyond a verbal declaration of their opposition to their country's resort to arms—"sorrow and distress at the bloodshed"—or, as in the Oregon boundary dispute, a call to each side to submit the dispute to arbitration. In some cases a deputation was formed to place Friends' views before the government. In January 1846, for instance, when they talked with the Prime Minister, Sir Robert Peel, Peel had asked Friends to intervene with their American brethren in favor of a peaceful solution. However when, early in 1854, a military clash with Russia appeared inevitable, Friends attempted something much more dramatic.

The idea of sending a Quaker delegation to put the case for peace before the Tsar had originated with Joseph Sturge. It was hoped that Friends' earlier and, on the whole, amicable contacts with Nicholas I's brother, Alexander I, would help to open the way now to obtaining a personal interview with the Tsar. On 17 January 1854 the Meeting for Sufferings approved the idea of a delegation of this kind in the following minute:

> This Meeting has been introduced into much religious concern in contemplating the apparent probability of war between some of the nations of Europe. Deeply impressed with the enormous amount of evil that invariably attends the prosecution of war, and with the utter inconsistency of all war with the spirit of Christianity and the precepts of its divine Founder as set forth in the New Testament this meeting has concluded, under a strong sense of religious duty, to present an address to Nicholas, Emperor of Russia, on this momentous question; and it also concludes to appoint Joseph Sturge, Robert Charleton, and Henry Pease to be the bearers of this address, and if the opportunity for so doing be afforded, to present the same in person. In committing this service to our dear brethren, we crave for them, in the prosecution of it, the help and guidance of that wisdom which is from above; and we commend them, as well as the cause entrusted to them, to the blessing of Almighty God.

After its arrival in St. Petersburg the delegation was successful in seeing both the Tsar and his foreign minister, Nesselrode. Neither in the address which they brought with them, nor in conversation with the Tsar and his officials, did the delegates enter into any political discussions or try to sort out the rights and wrongs of the conflict. This was probably wise, in any case; it was certainly in line with the Quaker approach, at that date, to international problems. Instead, the three delegates pleaded with the Tsar to show "his magnanimity in the exercise of forbearance" as the conduct proper to a Christian who "is persuaded of the justice of his own cause." They emphasized that the Quaker objection to war stemmed not from political considerations but from religious conviction held over a period of several centuries. But, without attempting to assess blame, they did dwell on "the unspeakable horrors of war, with all its attendant moral evil, and physical suffering."

Although the Tsar and his entourage received what the Quakers had to say in a spirit of good-will—and the Tsar himself appears to have been considerably moved after Sturge had spoken of the inevitable misery which a European war would bring to countless innocent people—the delegation was of course unable to stop the approaching conflict. War between Great Britain and Russia broke out in March.

At home the delegation, and Quakers in general, were denounced in the press and in Parliament as mischiefmakers, as unpatriotic, and a storm of abuse was unleashed during the ensuing months. Friends' opposition to the conflict remained unabated. To the religious arguments against war in general, to which the Society confined itself in its official pronouncements, prominent Quakers like Bright inside Parliament and Sturge outside, acting as leaders of the "peace party's" anti-war campaign, added denunciations of the war as unnecessary and immoral. An American peace worker, who from the vantage point of the United States was able to stand above the battle, told Bright: "You Quakers and those who act with you are the real heroes of the war."

On 8 December 1854 Quakers issued a strongly worded leaflet entitled *A Christian Appeal from the Society of Friends to Their Fellow-Countrymen on the Present War*. Its central theme was summed up in the sentence: "That which is morally or religiously wrong cannot be politically right." Some fifty thousand copies of the *Appeal* were published, and it circulated widely throughout the country. Among those who criticized its contents was the Magyar patriot, Lajos Kossuth, whose country had been resubjected to Habsburg rule as a result of Tsar Nicholas I's intervention in 1849. A couple of decades earlier, as shown in Marek Wajsblum's article "Quakers and Poland, 1661-1919" (*The Polish Review* [New York], vol. xi, no. 2 [Spring 1966]), there had been considerable sympathy among young reform-minded Friends for the Polish cause, but on the whole members of the Society were opposed to all thought of intervention on behalf of subject nationalities on the European continent. In his answer to Friends' *Appeal*, which Kossuth published in the *Sunday Times* on 15 January 1855, he accused them of "pleading peace at any price," the inevitable consequence, in Kossuth's view, of a belief in the wrongness of all war. Pacifism, he wrote, was a "false doctrine" without grounds in the Scriptures. The Quakers should not forget that it was Cromwell's sword that had given England the political and religious freedom essential for the development of their sect. Certainly, war was terrible but it was sometimes a necessary remedy for evil. Let Quakers show Christian charity to the oppressed peoples of Europe. "Make despots yield to justice and right, without having them compelled by the force of arms, and you shall be blessed. But, since you cannot do this, preach not impunible [*sic*] security to tyrants, by decrying necessary wars."

Whatever might have been argued in favor of the necessity of the Crimean War to achieve liberation for the oppressed (both Magyars and Poles, be it noted, were in fact bitterly disappointed at its outcome), the same plea could scarcely be urged for the Boer War, which ended in 1902 with a British victory and the incorporation of the Transvaal Republic into the Empire. Yet there were Friends who supported this war, the first war of any importance in which Great Britain had become involved since the conclusion of the conflict in the Crimea. Such persons were mainly wealthy members who now gave their political allegiance to the Unionist cause (most Quakers still remained loyal to the Liberal Party). Many of them were not particularly active in the affairs of the Society; most of them did not consider themselves pacifists. But, we should note, it was not entirely a question of pacifism. For instance Sir Edward Fry, the international lawyer and a Quaker, who was to be appointed Great Britain's representative at the Second Hague Conference of 1907, considered (according to the *Memoir* published by his daughter Agnes in 1921) that the Boer War was "unjustifiable and ought not to have been fought," although at the same time he felt unable fully to accept the Society's peace testimony. On the other hand, a stout defender of British policies in South Africa was to be found in a convinced Quaker pacifist like old John Bellows, compiler of a once-famous French dictionary and a lifelong participant in the religious and philanthropic concerns of the Society.

The Bellows affair for a brief while became quite a *cause célèbre* in Quaker circles. In November 1899 Bellows had confided to a friend. "But while I dare not kill, I am an Englishman" (from the posthumously published volume *John Bellows: Letters and Memoir*, London, 1904). For the British government and for all those—in fact, the majority of his fellow countrymen—for whom "war is not, *per se*, a sin," Bellows saw no honorable alternative now except war. In the following year he published a brief exposition of his views, which he entitled *The Truth about the Transvaal War and the Truth about War*. It soon went into a second edition. The pamphlet placed responsibility for the war exclusively on the shoulders of President Kruger and the Transvaal government. Britain, according to Bellows, had done all in her power to avoid war and to remove any cause for it that might have stemmed from mistakes in the past. For Bellows, the British government was indeed carrying out a civilizing role in the area. This view, he held, in no way invalidated the case for pacifism on purely religious grounds. But, he went on:

> I have no right whatever to condemn England, or any other nation, for defending itself with arms, because I dare not [on account of a religious objection] myself fight, nor dare I condemn the soldier because he does not see what is to me perfectly clear. On the contrary, in acting up to his own convictions he may be a much better man than I am, and I may derive help from the spirit in which I see him striving to live.

For his standpoint now Bellows claimed—not without some justification—the authority of Isaac Penington.

Concerning the "truth about war" there was indeed little difference of opinion between Bellows and his fellow Quaker pacifists. However, there was an ocean of difference in their respective assessments of the "truth about the Transvaal War." In *Some Comments on John Bellows's Apology for the War in South Africa* (1900) two Friends of the younger generation, Fred Sessions and Edward Grubb, expressed the distress which Bellows's views had caused to many in the Society. "It is a hard lot for us," Sessions wrote, "when we discover a serious hindrance from within our own ranks." In his view Bellows had seriously compromised the Quaker peace testimony and brought embarrassment to the Society, putting it into a false position *vis-à-vis* the general public. "His pamphlet . . . is intended solely and simply . . . to be an apology for one of the most reckless, needless, and cruel wars of the century." Indeed he blushed for Bellows's "professed Quakerism." Bellows's arguments would serve only to bolster the pro-war party and press, which were of course jubilant at getting "Quaker" support. Grubb was more restrained than was Sessions in the expression of the dismay which he too shared; he granted that Bellows was doing what he honestly and sincerely thought was right. The trouble was that in its political exposition the pamphlet was "mainly an *ex parte* statement." Its author, in Grubb's view, had not troubled to examine the Boer case with either thoroughness or impartiality. In discussing the genesis of the war no mention was made, for instance, of the notorious Jameson Raid of 1895, an essential link in the chain which led up to the conflict. Thus, Grubb concluded, "we find little trace of a judicial mind in the pamphlet."

Bellows hastened to answer his critics; besides Sessions's and

Grubb's, other Quaker voices had been raised in protest. His *Reply* was published in November 1900 as a Supplement to the *British Friend*, which had printed adverse comment in previous issues. Bellows ended the discussion on a conciliatory note. The points on which he and his critics differed were, he said, "in their nature but fleeting and momentary"; "the things in which we unite are weighty and lasting." This was indeed true. But the whole controversy, though soon forgotten, revealed one of the major difficulties facing the growing number of Quaker pacifists in the twentieth century, who were anxious to give their peace witness political relevance. This new outlook opened up possibilities for honest disagreement that an uncomplicated assertion—"all war is unchristian"—avoided. The Yearly Meeting of 1900, the year of the Bellows affair, had declared: "We fail to see how any war can be waged in the spirit of Jesus Christ." In December the Society had officially protested to the government against the burning by British troops of Boer farmsteads. All this could be easily comprehended within the older pacifist formulae. But situations of conflict might arise where it would be less easy than in the case of the Boer War, where Bellows's view remained an isolated one, for active Friends to reach agreement either on the causes of crisis, or on the responsibility of the parties involved, or on the practical steps to be taken to resolve a conflict as it actually developed.

On the eve of World War I British Friends stood almost united behind their peace testimony, although there might be differing views concerning its practical implementation. Britain's volunteer system had removed the old threat of militia conscription. Occasionally a Quaker might join a volunteer rifle club or even the Territorials and, with the abandonment of the previous rigid disciplinary system, such a step might no longer meet with disownment. But it was certainly frowned on by most members of the Society. Usually it was followed by the young man's resignation from the Society. That there were at the beginning of the twentieth century some Friends who were not pacifists, and that such members were more numerous than they had been in previous centuries, is clear. That there was a growing feeling that the question of individual participation in war should be left to the conscience of each member to decide for himself is equally apparent. In World War I 33.6 percent of Friends of military age enlisted in the armed forces (though the figures are incomplete). This number appears surprisingly high when viewed against the Society's past stand and its continued acceptance of the peace testimony as part of its official platform. Yet it must be remembered that many, though by no means all, of these "fighting Quakers" held merely nominal membership, for many birthright Friends retained their affiliation long after they had drifted away from the Society.

Alongside a marked "politicization" of the traditional peace testimony during the nineteenth century, a second area of witness appeared in this period for the first time. Quaker war relief caught the world's attention in the aftermath of the "Great War." Its origins, however, stretch back to the second half of the eighteenth century; apparently the first instance of Friends' bringing help to victims of war who were not members of their own Society had occurred in 1775 during the siege of Boston by Washington's army, when Philadelphia Friends sent supplies to the civilian inhabitants of the beleaguered city. British Friends were active in war relief on a number of occasions in the course of the nineteenth century. In the early 1820's they helped Greeks who had fled from the massacres perpetrated by their Turkish rulers, and later, in 1876 and again in 1912, they organized assistance for the noncombatant population of war-torn Bulgaria and Macedonia. After the Crimean War in Finland, and during the Boer War in South Africa, help went to the victims of British arms. But the best-known and most extensive example of Quaker war relief before 1914 took place in France after the Franco-Prussian War of 1870 in the areas devastated during the fighting. London Meeting for Sufferings then organized a "Friends' War Victims Relief Fund" and dispatched about forty workers to France as well as a large quantity of supplies: seeds, agricultural implements, cattle, household equipment, food, medicine, fuel, etc. It was in connection with this work that Friends adopted the red and black star which was later to become a symbol of Quaker relief in action. One of the Quaker workers, Robert Spence Watson, wrote later:

> I wish I could tell you how I loathe this war. It is too horrible. The misery which it brings with it is altogether incredible. I begin now to dream of it all night, for it has become a terrible reality. Bad I always thought it, but I never dreamed it could be so bad. I am glad I have seen what I have; it is a great lesson, and I wish all the editors in England could just see Bazaine's army; we should hear less of the glory of war for some years to come.

This is no place to describe in detail the war relief activities of nineteenth-century Friends, activities that formed only a part of their philanthropic "empire." The point I wish to make here is that war relief was now coming to be a significant mode of expression of Friends' traditional peace testimony; in the first place, because in this way Friends felt they could find a positive outlet for what in the past had frequently been—outwardly at least—a negative testimony against war, and second because such action might serve, on however small a scale, to witness more effectively to the reconciling power of love that had always underlain this testimony.

British Friends, as the nineteenth century wore on, strove increasingly to move forward into new areas of peace witness. The tiny Quaker groups on the continent, on the other hand, had perforce to confine themselves to a rearguard action against the swelling might of militarism. Universal military service was everywhere the rule; conscientious objection at best was given the barest recognition.

After a visit in 1867 to the German Quaker communities at Pyrmont and Minden, two prominent British Friends reported concerning their young men: "Their best alternative, as they approach manhood, [is] to emigrate to Great Britain or the United States" (from *Narrative of the Visit of Isaac Robson and Thomas Harvey to the South of Russia, &c.*). In 1800 the Prussian authorities had freed the Minden group from the obligation of personal military service. Those called up for service, however, were to have a distress levied on their goods in exchange for this privilege. Moreover, they were forbidden to proselytize or to marry outside their Society; the exemption indeed was confined to members of the six families, who then formed the Quaker community there and to their descendants. In December 1813, during the War of Liberation when patriotic feelings ran high, the Prussian cabinet exempted Quakers, along with Mennonites, from service in the army, again on condition that they make a contribution to the royal treasury. Friends appear to have complied. But difficulties soon arose, since exemption continued to be confined to the families of the original members. When two brothers, Christian and Ernst Peitsmeyer, farm lads who were members, but not birthright members, of the Society, were called up for military service in 1818 and 1822 respectively, they suffered severe ill-treatment for their refusal to become soldiers. This was repeated after each annual summons to the army, until finally the intervention of London Friends with the Prussian king put an end to their sufferings. British Quakers also succeeded in obtaining the release of an attender at the Minden meeting, Heinrich Schmidt, who had been called up for service in 1825. Not being actually a member of the Society, he was in an even less enviable position than the Peitsmeyer brothers had been. Concerning the fate of these men John Grubb reported in a letter dated 18 June 1826:

There was an account given to the Yearly Meeting of three young men who have suffered much in the King of Prussia's dominions for their conscientious scruples against bearing arms. They were confined, their property confiscated, and two of them . . . sentenced to what they call the punishment of the laths—a horrid torture indeed. Their clothes are taken off and a very thin covering given them instead. They are then shut up in a kind of closet, where they have nothing to stand or rest upon in any way, but the edges of laths shod with iron, about the thickness of the back of a knife, and placed about two inches asunder. The torture must be extreme. They are fed on bread and water . . . I understand it generally proves fatal in about eight or ten days. These young men were released in about three days. It did not appear, I think, that the king knew of it, though it was according to law, till they had been in some time, when he ordered them to be released.

On some occasions, writes Margaret Hirst, "the authorities tried to avoid conflict with the conscientious objector by dismissing him on various pretexts, generally that of health." This policy, combined with the emigration of young men to escape service and the small number of new recruits to the Society—only twenty-three persons, for instance, are recorded as joining between 1814 and 1840—explains the fact that so few conscientious objectors were in fact prosecuted. The greatest difficulties were encountered by objectors who, though not themselves members of the Society, had been led through their contacts with Quakerism to refuse military service. In 1855, for instance, a case occurred where a former theological student, Anton Finke, was imprisoned on this account. After he had been dispatched to a regiment his conduct was described by the military chaplain as follows:

Finke is here, Bible under arm. . . . Finke, indeed at once declared that [his job assignment] had military purposes and thus he could not work at it. This would be against his conscience. . . . He remained steadfast in refusing all work that had any kind of military purpose. He did the same, too, on Thursday when he was sent for labour in the punishment section. He even refused to work in the kitchen of the punishment section, in which he scented a military purpose too. Yesterday I again had a long talk with him in the Citadel. He was friendly, modest, but unyielding. . . . He has been since Thursday in the Citadel where he occupies himself with Bible reading. . . . The severity of the law must be carried out; otherwise anyone who has no inclination to serve can appeal to Quaker principles. . . . I told him he should not strive for self-elected martyrdom. He laughed, his eyes lighting up as he did so.

The two German meetings, Minden and Pyrmont, had both to be discontinued before the outbreak of World War I on account of declining numbers. Even though continental Friends, whether French, German, or Scandinavian, proved, in their much more trying situation, readier than British Friends usually were to find a compromise solution on the conscription issue which would be acceptable to the authorities, compulsory military service proved a burden which eventually crushed their tender growth. The German meetings, for instance, disowned members who accepted even noncombatant service in the army. Thus, loyal adherence to the Quaker peace testimony on Friends' part led not only to removal by emigration of promising young members; it also discouraged many who felt unable to accept—or to accept the consequences of—the profession of pacifist principles in so unfavorable an environment.

This factor also accounts in large part for the snail's pace at which the new Quaker groups in Norway and Denmark progressed during this period. Quakerism had spread to Scandinavia only in the nineteenth century. The Norwegian group dated back to the conclusion of war in 1815, while the first Danish Friends arose around 1866. In neither country was there provision for conscientious objection; thus here, too, emigration or repeated imprisonment were the only choices open to young Friends of military age. Whole families departed overseas on this account, often to the American Midwest, and especially to Iowa, where Quaker meetings of largely Scandinavian origin still exist today. In the early twentieth century, in both Norway and Denmark, the authorities expressed willingness to exempt Friends from combatant service. But again this alternative did not prove acceptable to them; they felt unable either to undertake work that was not of a civilian character and under nonmilitary control or to stand in a privileged position compared to non-Quaker objectors who were refused the same treatment.

Consideration of Quaker decline on the European continent during the nineteenth century might induce pessimism; indeed, a new, though still very modest, upsurge of continental Quakerism did not take place until after World War I. In contrast, the state of the Society in Britain by the beginning of the twentieth century showed a marked improvement over its position a century earlier. True, there had been an almost catastrophic decline in membership, but this had eventually been stemmed. A body small in numbers but spiritually in process of renewal and growth, the British Society of Friends could look with hope toward the future.

Above all, their country was free of the incubus of military conscription that oppressed the European continent like a nightmare. Bodies like the National Service League were indeed agitating for the introduction of some form of compulsory military service but for the time being, and as long, at least, as the Liberals were in power, it did not appear likely that Great Britain would abandon the system of voluntary recruitment. Friends, and indeed the whole peace movement, felt growing alarm at the diplomatic rivalries of the great powers and their ever fiercer competition in armaments. In 1909, for instance, the Meeting for Sufferings had declared in face of an increase in the naval estimates: "We regard any such increase at this juncture as calculated to bring about similar increases on the part of other nations, with whom we are now manifestly being drawn into more friendly relations." Friends deplored the intensified international tension which resulted from military preparedness. Nevertheless, on the whole they shared the optimism of many of their fellow countrymen in believing that the drive toward war might be stopped in time to prevent a catastrophe and that the nations could then be induced to turn their energies toward the firm establishment of peace. Barely a year before the guns of August sounded, London Yearly Meeting had stated in its epistle of 1913: "With thankfulness we note an advance in the Peace Movement. We are probably nearer to a complete understanding with Germany than has been the case for many years. The forces that make for arbitration and international good-will are gaining in strength and confidence." The events of the summer of 1914 shattered such hopes. Quakers in Britain were now to be confronted with a new time of troubles when their traditional peace testimony would be tested in the crucible of modern war, to a degree seldom experienced before.

TEN. *Non-Quaker Pacifism in*
Nineteenth-Century Britain

"THE soul of the peace movement is the Quaker sentiment against all war," thus wrote Cobden in 1853 adding: "Without the stubborn zeal of Friends, there would be no Peace Society and no Peace Conference" (letter printed by John Morley in his *Life of Richard Cobden*, vol. II, 1881). Before 1660, as we have seen, pacifist sentiments were sporadically held first by Anabaptists and associated groups and then by a few individuals on the Puritan left. But for over a century and a half after the Quaker peace testimony had crystallized, pacifism within the British Isles had been confined almost exclusively to the Society of Friends and its close sympathizers. Yet there were a few isolated forerunners of the non-Quaker pacifism which was to find organizational expression in the peace movement after 1815. To them we must devote brief attention before passing on to discuss the pacifist wing of the nineteenth-century British peace movement and the new forms of sectarian pacifism, which sprang up in the course of that century.

The first of these forerunners in point of time is the pioneer Methodist, John Nelson, a Yorkshireman by birth and a stonemason by trade. He heard John Wesley preach in 1739 and was at once fired with the idea of becoming an apostle of the renewed Christianity which Wesley and his colleagues were bringing to the masses long ignored by the predominantly upper-class church establishment. Himself a man of the people, Nelson knew how to bring his message effectively to the poorest and the least educated sections of the population. With Wesley's backing he became one of the most energetic preachers of the burgeoning Methodist movement. Early in May 1744 Nelson, then aged thirty-seven, was suddenly seized and pressed into the army, at the instigation of the opponents of Methodism in his home district of Bristol. In this way they had hoped to be rid of the importunate young preacher. However, they were to be disappointed. To the surprise of all, Nelson steadfastly refused to accept the King's shilling and, as reason for his unusual behavior, he told the officers: "I shall not fight; for I cannot bow my knee before the Lord to pray for a man, and get up and kill him when I have done. For I know God both hears me speak and sees me act, and I should expect the portion of the hypocrite, if my actions contradicted my prayers." After some days in jail, where he occupied his time with rebuking swearers, singing hymns, and preaching to his fellow prisoners, Nelson was taken out to parade with the troops while a gun was forced into his hands by a reluctant corporal.

> I asked [Nelson relates] why they girt me with these warlike habiliments, for I am a man averse from war, and shall not fight but under the Prince of Peace, the captain of my salvation; and the weapons he gives me are not carnal like these. Well, said they, but you must bear these, till you can get your discharge. As you put them on me, I answered, I will bear them as a cross, and use them as far as I can without defiling my conscience, for that I will not do for any man on earth.

Throughout the time he was held as a soldier Nelson reports that he was treated "civilly." On exercises the sympathetic corporal, who was already proving susceptible to his preaching, had carried his gun; on marches in which Nelson was obliged to participate, he received many offers from his fellow soldiers to do the same service for him. Nelson's attitude throughout was one of passive obedience. When required to stand sentry at night, he did so—though presumably with the intention not to shoot. The soldier's red coat he accepted only after he had been forcibly clad in it. The officers, he writes,

> said, they would make me wear it, and all the other clothing belonging to a soldier. I answered, you may array me as a man of war, but I shall never fight. They asked me, What is your reason? And my answer was, I cannot see anything in this world worth fighting for. I want neither its riches nor honours, but the honour that cometh of God only. I regard neither its smiles nor frowns; and have no business but to get well out of it.

John Wesley, though he was to speak out against war on occasion, was no pacifist. But he loyally supported Nelson in his trials—indeed, he considered Nelson's impressment an act of injustice and the result of malice directed against his movement by its enemies—and was instrumental in getting his discharge through hiring a substitute; Nelson himself obviously did not have the means to pay for it. His release from the army came at the end of July. On parting, the major said of Nelson: "I wish I had a regiment of such men as he is in all respects (save that one, his refusing to fight). I would not care what enemy I had to meet or where my lot was cast." Later the conversation between Nelson and the major developed as follows: "Well, said the major, if you are so scrupulous about fighting, what must we do? I answered, it is your trade, and if you had a better, it might be better for you. But somebody, he replied, must fight. I said, if all men lived by faith in the Son of God, wars would be at an end. That is true, he answered, if it was so, we should learn war no more."

From what sources did Nelson draw inspiration for his stand as a conscientious objector? It is clear that his rather otherworldly objection comprises more than a merely vocational pacifism, more than a desire to be free from the army in order to do the Lord's work. True, this motive is there but it is not the primary one. Yet apart from his reading of the New Testament (surely inspiration enough), his own account gives no indication of any outside influence which might have directed him to reject military duty. It is possible that he may have had contacts with neighboring Quakers; knowledge of their refusal of military service could then have acted as a stimulant to his own thinking on the subject. But this, of course, is only a conjecture.

It is a far cry from the simple and self-taught Methodist lay preacher John Nelson to a learned, if unorthodox, churchman like the nonjuror William Law, who appears in the course of the Seven Years' War as a fervent proponent of Christian pacifism. Law knew the Quakers well since he had devoted much energy to refuting their theological views! Perhaps Quaker peace principles may have been one of the factors impelling Law toward an antiwar position, since the nonresistance which the nonjurors upheld in regard to rightful rulers had, for all its Tory coloring, a certain outward resemblance to Quaker pacifism. In addition Law, whose famous devotional book, *A Serious Call to a Devout and Holy Life* (1729), has become a classic of mysticism, was profoundly influenced by the writings of the early sixteenth-century Silesian mystic, Jakob Boehme, who had urged a renunciation of the sword on the part of truly spiritual Christians.

In *An Humble, Earnest, and Affectionate Address to the Clergy,* which he published in London in 1761, Law included a passionate denunciation of war which, if it did not specifically discuss personal renunciation of military service, is hard to square with anything but a thoroughgoing pacifist position. He stresses, in particular, the idea of a loving God who could not from his very nature desire harm to any of his creatures. Christ on the cross, the Lamb of God, the meek savior, is the model for Christians to follow. Yet the history of Christianity is a record of constant war, Christ's followers becoming the practitioners of "every murdering art of war." While the material devastation of war is terrible, the spiritual harm flowing from it and the accompanying sin are much worse. If indeed it be true that Christian kingdoms today can be preserved only by means of armed defense, then in Law's view this only proves the total fall of Christendom

369

and the end of its universalism. Such a plea "stands upon no better a foundation of righteousness and goodness, than when one murdering knave kills another, that would have killed him." To discover whether Christianity permits the practice of war, we must look at it not in its fallen condition but in its pristine state of purity. In fact, the presence of war among Christians is one of the clearest signs of Christianity's decay. "But the Christendom which I mean, that neither wants, nor allows of war is only that where Christ is king, and his holy spirit the only governor of the wills, affections, and designs of all that belong to it." The need to maintain armaments for national defense Law brands as "the dragon's monster, that is equally brought forth by all and every part of fallen Christendom," by Protestants as well as by Catholics.

It is not really until near the end of the century that we find outside the Society of Friends a growing, though still very small, number of voices raised against all war. John Scott of Islington in 1796, while the struggle against revolutionary France was being waged, published a brief tract entitled *War inconsistent with the Doctrine and Example of Jesus Christ. In a Letter to a Friend. Recommended to the Perusal of the Professors of Christianity*; he was later to become a leading supporter of the London Peace Society. His pamphlet was several times reprinted by the Peace Society as part of its publishing program, as well as by the American peace movement. Scott's little work certainly deserved this attention, for he argues the religious case against war most effectively.

His arguments are directed primarily toward wars for defense since, as he says, aggression is usually condemned even by the military minded. It is almost impossible, however, "to decide where the aggression begins, or how one nation possesses a right to call in question what to another nation seems an equal right of theirs," and even where a satisfactory definition of aggression may be arrived at, war as a remedy almost invariably exceeds in evil the original offense. And for Christians there is, above all, "the plain, direct, and unequivocal commands of Christ and his apostles" to dissuade them from participation in war. If it be urged that many good Christians had in fact wielded the sword, "they did it," Scott answers, "as patriots, not as Christians —as lovers of their country, but not as the followers of Christ." War in all its forms is contrary to the spirit of the Gospels; Christians must trust to God to protect them if they follow his commandments; as proof that such protection has been given, Scott cites the history of the Quakers and the Moravians. "I have hope," he concludes, "that if we could but exchange sentiments, I should find thousands and millions who think with me."

Two years after Scott composed his plea for Christian pacifism an Anglican clergyman, a Welshman named J. Bradley Rhŷs, brought out a similar work—to my knowledge the first occasion on which a minister of the established church came forward openly in favor of pacifism, apart, that is, from the nonjuror Law. Originally entitled *An Answer to Some Passages in a Letter from the Bishop of Rochester to the Clergy, (dated May 1st, 1798,) upon the Lawfulness of Defensive War. By a Clergyman of the Church of England* (London, 1798), the little tract had appeared in a second edition before the year was out. This time it bore the title *The Lawfulness of Defensive War upon Christian Principles impartially considered by a Clergyman of the Church of England*. What had impelled Rhŷs to take up his pen on behalf of "that *still small voice* that . . . pleads for non-resistance" was Bishop Samuel Horsley's assertion, in a letter to the clergy of his diocese of Rochester, that Christian support of a "defensive war" like England's present struggle against Napoleon was justified, even though war in the abstract must be regarded as a sin when judged by Christian standards. Rhŷs accused the bishop of inconsistency in urging the correctness of behavior condemned by the master whom he served. "As to the distinction pretended between our own *private* enemies and those of the *public*, it is mere trifling, a distinction without a difference": war was in fact "murder," which the Christian clergy had a special duty to oppose in every guise, and death should be preferred to breaking the commandments of Christ. Rhŷs's pamphlet is indeed as outspoken as Scott's in its denunciation of war. Like Scott, its author attempts to rebut the various arguments commonly urged in favor of war. It was true, for instance, that God "for reasons known only to Infinite Wisdom" had permitted the Jews to fight under the Mosaic dispensation. But how could this fact be relevant to Christians who were subject to a new dispensation? Certainly Christian men had been serving in the armed forces since early days. But, the author explains, "the question is not, what Christians have done?—but, what they ought to have done?" if they had obeyed their master. "This opinion, that war is unlawful to Christians, is not either a new or singular opinion": it was one preached by Christ and practised by the early church. True, patriotism was fine, was natural in a human being; "but the love of which the whole world is the object" must lead a Christian to renounce war, indeed not only war but also capital punishment, for both manifest a "usurped power over human life which no mortal can justly assume."

371

To soldiers—"brave, but mistaken men, who are engaged in what is termed the service of their country"—the author directs a special plea, should a copy of his pamphlet by any chance come into their hands. (But "they must pardon me, if I cannot regard them as Christians," he interpolates.) Let them leave the military service and devote their energies to the propagation of peace; "there would they find a more ample field for the exertion of their fortitude and courage." In any case, the time had come for some individuals to withdraw totally from association with the prosecution of war and with killing. And the church should lead the way. "Admit that it is lawful for Christians, at the command of the magistrate, to serve in war, and what will follow? Will it not follow, that if this be lawful at the command of the magistrate of one country, it must be equally so at the command of the magistrate of another—of every country?" Thus finally, at the very end of his pamphlet, the author turns to face that major obstacle in the way of Anglican pacifism: the thirty-ninth article. He was bold enough to call it "evidently false"; "this truly antichristian tenet" was, in his view, "a dangerous and destructive error," "the very mark of Antichrist." And it was deeply to be regretted that candidates for the priesthood in the Church of England should be required to subscribe to the doctrines contained within that article.

The same kind of pragmatic, rational arguments against war and a similar humanitarianism obviously reflecting the spirit of the Enlightenment, enunciated both by John Scott and the Anglican clergyman, are also displayed to some extent in a slightly longer work first appearing in 1804 with the title *Christianity a System of Peace. In Two Letters*. The tract was to be several times reprinted before 1914. (I have used the London Peace Society's centenary edition of 1911 reprinting the second edition published at Stockport in 1813.) The initials "T. P." on the title-page hide the identity of the Reverend Thomas Parsons, a Baptist minister in Bath. Of his pamphlet a leading early nineteenth-century Quaker, Joseph Crosfield, wrote: "Perhaps before the *Solemn Review* [*of the Custom of War* by the American pacifist Noah Worcester, first published in Boston in 1814] came out there was nothing presented to the public so replete with sound argument, and in so mild, so polite, and so appropriate a style" (*The Herald of Peace*, June 1820). Like Scott before him, Parsons considered "the distinction between offensive and defensive war" to be "less solid than verbal." His object was to help strengthen the convictions of that growing number of people who had begun to feel that war "in any shape, or upon any ground," was incompatible with "the placid genius of the gospel." "The precepts of the gospel," Parsons argued, "enjoin the cultivation of benevolent principles, and amiable tempers . . . and restrain and forbid anger, wrath, revenge, and every hostile passion." Thus how could war ever be justified from the pages of the New Testament, even if these did not, as pacifism's opponents pointed out, contain any injunction expressly forbidding the waging of a defensive war? Indeed, the gospels did not explicitly condemn aggression, either. It was their spirit that testified against war. Parsons's work is commendably free from the legalism, the Biblical literalism, which mars many early pacifist writings.

At one point he tackles a question which was to occupy the thoughts of the nineteenth-century peace movement: Was there a difference in kind between killing in war and taking a life in self-defense? Could one withdraw his cooperation from every type of interstate warfare, yet retain his right to use injurious force against a personal assailant. Parsons acknowledges some distinction here. Whereas in the international sphere there is no impartial tribunal or universal law to which appeal may be made, he implies that domestically the existence of a generally acknowledged government and legal system justifies the exercise of some degree of force by the authorities, for its purpose is the enforcement of law. Besides, war between nations is rarely, if ever, a matter of unprovoked attack by one side on the other. In the case of an unpremeditated assault on one's person, on the other hand, there is little time for thought of anything but to ward off the blow "by a violent effort." By this means "perhaps the assailant [is] disabled from attempting to repeat it; should he fall in the struggle, I will not condemn the defender." Yet Parsons is obviously not quite happy at this concession to the right of self-defense. He wonders if it is in fact reconcilable with Gospel principles, though entirely understandable in such trying circumstances. "It is," he writes, "one of those actions which leave some doubt, some uncertainty, and some dissatisfaction upon the mind." He suggests that fleeing from the danger before it reaches us is a reaction quite as natural as the violent warding off of a blow. At any rate, if we may judge from the Gospels' general trend, "and from particular and appropriate passages" in the New Testament, uncompromising nonresistance appears the truly Christian course. Yet Parsons still remained hesitant concerning what was the correct conduct.

> Strict morality requires the calling for assistance, flight, disarming the ruffian, or submitting to his requisition, though unjust, before the last dreadful expedient be resorted to. Religion, in my opinion, forbids the last, but whether I judge right, or otherwise, the instances of such extreme urgency are so rare, and when they

occur, are so little susceptible of the intervention of principle, and so much determined by passions, at the time perhaps ungovernable, that they cannot nor ought to be considered as forming a basis capable of supporting the right of defensive war.

Parsons's pamphlet had originated in defense of a fellow pacifist among the Bath clergy, an Anglican minister, the Reverend Richard Warner, Rector of Chelwood and Great Chatfield and a distinguished Somerset antiquary, who on 25 May 1804 had spoken out against war from the pulpit of his church. "The fortitude and integrity of the preacher, who dared to avow a doctrine so little accommodated to the prevalent opinion of the age" had greatly impressed his Baptist colleague, so that, when pamphlets began to appear at once in condemnation of Warner's action, Parsons was inspired to set out his own views on the subject in corroboration of Warner.

Warner published his address under the title *War inconsistent with Christianity*. It was certainly a bold gesture to have preached in "the twelfth of the present war" in favor of a thoroughgoing pacifism. As his text Warner had taken Christ's words to St. Peter: "Put up again thy sword into his place: for all they that take the sword shall perish with the sword" (Matt. 26:52). True, these words should not be understood quite literally, Warner agreed. But "stripped of its oriental dress the declaration of Christ may fairly be taken as a direct and unequivocal reprehension of hostile violence, both in individuals and states." War he branded as "the greatest curse with which a nation can be afflicted," for its immorality and destruction of life, its savagery and its irreligion made it a misfortune to which no other social evil was comparable. Therefore had Christ forbidden his followers to fight, telling them to love even their enemies. It was no use arguing that these injunctions bound only subjects and not rulers, individuals and not states. There was only one moral law applicable to all. According to that law even defensive war was impermissible.

What had made Warner's sermon particularly challenging was the ceremonial attendance at his church on the day he preached of two companies of the Bath Volunteers accompanied by their officers, though in fact the rector had written the text before he discovered that they would be coming. Both the circumstances and the tenor of his address excited considerable indignation. People were angry, Warner reports, "because I have denounced war *in general* as being inconsistent with Christianity; and have made no distinction between *offensive* and *defensive* hostilities, between warfare of *aggression* and *repulsion*." The omission, he goes on to explain, was due to the fact that the New

Testament ("the only authority appealed to in my sermon") makes no mention of such a distinction, prohibiting instead every kind of injurious action. He saw no reason to alter his opinion, despite the unpopularity and abuse his sermon had earned him, unless his opponents were able to prove to his satisfaction that defensive wars did not infringe the precepts of the Gospels. For him it was not enough to argue, as the author of a *Remonstrance* against his sermon had done, that "without a defensive war we should have now left neither laws, constitution, nor religion." Warner asked instead for New Testament references. But another opponent accused him, above all, of imprudence in recommending nonresistance "at the moment of expected invasion."

Warner's plea for pacifism had been spoken "in the cause of evangelical truth." Another evangelical pacifist who appears around this time as a precursor of the small minority of evangelical Christians supporting the nineteenth-century pacifist movement is Thomas Clarkson, best known for his work in the antislavery cause. In the *Portraiture of Quakerism* which he published in 1806 he discusses not only the peace testimony of Friends but also primitive Christianity's attitude to war, as well as his own stand in relation to this question. Sections II-IV of chapter III (vol. III) represent, in fact, a first version of the short monograph he would publish a decade later on war and the early Christians (see below).

Clarkson was anxious at this juncture to show that to oppose war of every sort was as valid a position for Christians who were not Quakers as for members of the Society of Friends. "I would ask, what are Quakers but men; and might not all, if they would suffer themselves to be cast in the same mould as the Quakers, come out of it of the same form and character?" True, war would continue "while statesmen pursue the wisdom or policy of the world." But to argue that war was inevitable was "either to utter a libel against Christianity, or to confess that we have not yet arrived at the stature of real Christians." For Clarkson, most modern wars had resulted from the illusion of national prestige or from unwillingness to negotiate on matters considered to touch essential national interests, from hate propaganda or the building up of armaments or "the balance of power." If aggression were not the objective of both sides from the beginning, it became so "in the course of the dispute" (one of several arguments which would be repeated a little later by the Quaker Dymond). On the commonly held view that a Christian country which disarmed unilaterally would be speedily overwhelmed by its neighbors, Clarkson comments: "This argument is neither more nor less than that of the pagan Celsus, who said in the second century, that if the rest of the Roman empire were Christians, it would be overrun by the barbarians."

Apart from pleading the protection which an unarmed nation might expect "from the Moral Governor of the world," Clarkson also argues the case for unilateral disarmament on pragmatic grounds. In the first place, states usually armed because other states were arming too; the example of one country's throwing away its weapons would be followed by others and eventually perhaps by all, since they would see at least the material advantages in avoiding war's expense and destruction. A disarmed state, in addition, would take great pains to avoid provoking its neighbors either in its declarations or its actions. It would always be ready to negotiate, it would be just in its relations with the rest of the world, and it would thus gain the world's respect. Clarkson looked to the creation of a world state as the ultimate outcome of a practical implementation of "the doctrine of universal benevolence to man."

> Let us then cherish the fond hope that human animosities are not to be eternal, and that man is not always to be made a tiger to man. Let us hope that the government of some one nation (and when we consider the vast power of the British empire, the nature of its constitution and religion, and the general humanity of its inhabitants, none would be better qualified than our own) will set the example of the total dereliction of war.

The passionate optimism displayed by Clarkson in this passage presaged the atmosphere in which nineteenth-century pacifists would move. It suffused many of the utterances of the Peace Society, which was founded in London in 1816 and which soon became a rallying point both for Quaker pacifists and for pacifists in other denominations. Until the Peace Society came into existence, pacifists outside the Society of Friends had remained isolated, their efforts uncoordinated. They were oppressed by the overwhelming weight of opinion ranged against them. The years of war, when Britain was engaged in a prolonged and exhausting struggle against Napoleonic France, scarcely formed an auspicious environment for the propagation of pacifism. That here and there there were men and women who shared Quaker views on war without being associated with the Society of Friends is shown by the account given above. Further evidence is to be found in the published version of the Reverend Richard Warner's antiwar sermon of 1804. After its delivery, Warner reports, he received a letter from a small group of Anglican laymen in Newcastle-upon-Tyne, who met weekly in the vestry of their church "for the purposes of religious and moral instruction and mutual edification." The members of this group had perused Warner's sermon with approval; the views he expressed there coincided with their own. And they had thereupon passed a resolution: "It is evident, that the apostles and disciples of Christ well understood that the weapons of their warfare were not carnal, but spiritual." Christians should never employ the sword. The group observed with regret that so few Christian ministers were prepared to take this stand. Since churchmen who did so were frequently driven to despair at the thought of their lonely witness for peace, Warner's discourse, the group hoped, would circulate widely in its printed version among the educated and influential sections of the Anglican community and instill courage to persist into those who had already renounced all war.

The first clear call to form an organization on a pacifist basis seems to have come from the Reverend David Bogue, D.D., head of the Gosport Missionary Society. Again the connection between pacifism and the evangelical movement emerges. In October 1813 Bogue had delivered a discourse, *On Universal Peace*, in which he came out squarely in favor of unilateral disarmament as the only truly Christian policy. In his arguments he depended to a large extent on Clarkson; for his inspiration he acknowledged his debt to the historical witness of the Quakers. If, as he held, "the religion of the New Testament is a religion of peace," then all those who thought this to be true should rally together, should gather their strength so as to dissipate the disadvantages of isolation under which they had suffered hitherto. "To collect the force of all these into one centre . . . is a thing of high importance. This effect an association will produce; and as we live in an age of societies to combine individual efforts for public benefit, why should not one be formed for promoting peace among the nations of the earth?" With such a society in existence, he predicted with typical optimism that in ten years' time it would be almost impossible to draw the British people into war. Until recently, apart from groups like the Quakers, there had been few who professed a thoroughgoing pacifism. But "of late it has been embraced by considerable numbers among every sect."

And so, with the ending of the long war with France and with the statesmen of Europe turning their eyes toward the establishment of peace, the organized peace movement makes its appearance on the political scene. In Great Britain, as elsewhere, it formed part of a wider reform impulse which was already under way: prison reform and Sunday Schools, Bible societies and antislavery, and the numerous other reform causes, if sometimes they merely provided a salve to uneasy consciences, also witnessed to the growth of a genuine humanitarianism. The movement for the renunciation of war represents yet another, and by no means the least important, manifestation of this spirit.

The Society for the Promotion of Permanent and Universal Peace, or London Peace Society, as it was usually known, came into being on 14 June 1816. Membership was on a nondenominational basis, though Quaker influence was strong. We have seen in the previous chapter that the first practical steps to set up such a society were taken at a meeting held on 6 June 1814 at the house of a London Quaker merchant and philanthropist, William Allen. And Quakers remained prominent both in the Society's executive committee and in the work of the local branches. Yet the Society was able to enlist, too, the support of Anglicans (e.g., the brothers John and Thomas Clarkson, the former of whom became the Society's treasurer) as well as of Methodists and Congregationalists, Baptists and Unitarians, etc.: both clergy and laymen participated in the Society's activities. Only the Roman Catholics held aloof; the growth of a pacifist minority within this church is a twentieth-century phenomenon. The London Peace Society was not in fact the first peace society to be set up; this honor falls to New York, where in August 1815 a peace society was founded by a prosperous Presbyterian merchant, David Low Dodge. And on 28 December 1815 a Unitarian minister, Noah Worcester, established the Massachusetts Peace Society with headquarters in Boston. All three organizations appear to have come into existence without knowledge of the others' efforts. Thus in English-speaking lands, at least, the promotion of peace was in the air.

In its first *Address* to the public, dated 9 January 1817, the London Society had stated emphatically its pacifist stand: "The Society for the Promotion of Permanent and Universal Peace, in announcing themselves to the world, think it their duty to state most distinctly, that they are principled against *all war, upon any pretence.*" In its "Rules," published in the *First Annual Report . . . for 1817*, clause VIII reiterated this position: "No person shall be eligible as a member of the Committee, whose principles, on the subject of War, are not in strict accordance with those on which the Society is founded." However, though this rule remained unchanged for the next century, it may be noted that by itself it did not exclude from ordinary membership those peace workers who could not accept the full pacifist position. On this subject more will be said a little later.

The main objective which the Society set itself in the early years was the printing and diffusion of antiwar literature: pamphlets, leaflets, and from 1819 onward a monthly journal, *The Herald of Peace*. These publications were designed "to show, that War is inconsistent with the spirit of Christianity, and the true interests of mankind; and to point out the means best calculated to maintain permanent and universal peace, upon the basis of Christian principles." In its first year the Society distributed thirty-two thousand copies of its tracts; from 1824 publications were distributed free to the poor. The Society retained a tremendous faith in the power of the written word. During this period it did not attempt to act in any way as a political pressure group; it sought rather to spread the idea of peace as widely as possible, to influence public opinion against war, and to try to combat the age-old prejudices, still existing in the popular mind, against the possibility of establishing permanent peace. The Society remained a predominantly middle-class group. It succeeded in winning very few supporters either among the aristocracy and landed gentry or among the urban and rural poor. Evangelical clergymen of the established church, nonconformist ministers, Quaker merchants and businessmen, philanthropically minded industrialists and professional men, middle-class ladies with an interest in charity, earnest artisans and a sprinkling of self-taught workers: these were the kinds of people the Peace Society attracted into its ranks. Yet we must stress that within most of these social groups the adherents of peace were a tiny minority, a select few ignored by the vast majority of the population. Indeed lack of notice, rather than any unfavorable or downright hostile reactions, was the biggest obstacle in the way of the Society's spreading its view or of increasing its extremely modest numbers.

While the Society's London headquarters concentrated at first on its publications program, the main burden of work was carried by the auxiliary societies. By 1819 branches had been set up in ten towns; thereafter the number of these auxiliary societies slowly expanded, the practice being that wherever forty members could be mustered, there a new society would be brought into existence. Auxiliary societies organized meetings in their towns and in the surrounding villages; they presented copies of the *Herald of Peace* to their local libraries; their members wrote to the local press on the subject of peace; they tried also to promote the sale of the Society's tracts and to find subscribers to its journal. "The effect of all this," Beales writes, "was, of course, imperceptible for many years, apart from the small increase in actual membership. Publicity in the press, also, was on the smallest local scale."

Until the 1860's the most vigorous of the Peace Society's local branches was the Birmingham auxiliary, set up by the Quaker Joseph

Sturge in December 1827 when membership in the city reached a figure of forty-one. Whereas in Birmingham Quaker participation was a major factor in making this a flourishing group, in Wales, where the Peace Society put down roots early on, it was nonconformist bodies such as the Baptists, Congregationalists, and Methodists which provided the backbone of the nineteenth-century peace movement. Many of the movement's stalwarts, like Samuel Roberts, Henry Richard, and the two Quakers Joseph Tregelles Price and Evan Rees, were Welsh-speaking. And one of the very first auxiliaries to be set up, with strong Quaker support, was the Swansea and Neath Peace Society founded in 1817.

Exactly how much impact the Society's propaganda made, it is difficult to say. That by this means converts to pacifism were gathered and workers for peace gained, is undoubtedly true. Among its numerous publications one of the most effective was Thomas Clarkson's study of the early Christian attitude to war. This appeared in the second half of 1816 as the Society's Tract No. III, under the title *An Essay on the Doctrines and Practice of the Early Christians, as they relate to War. Addressed to those, who profess to have a Regard for the Christian Name.* Here the author elaborates in rather more detail the outline of the subject he had sketched in his *Portraiture of Quakerism* a decade earlier. The essay was clearly designed for popular consumption. Its twenty-eight pages contain no footnotes or references to sources, though it is obvious that Clarkson had consulted the works of the church fathers, whose views on war he sought to elucidate. But although lacking in the apparatus of modern scholarship, his findings were to be confirmed by the researches of twentieth-century scholars like Adolf Harnack and C. J. Cadoux. Clarkson stressed that war had found wide acceptance within the Christian church only toward the end of the third and in the early fourth centuries. The earlier objection of Christians to participation in military service was, he showed, the result not merely of repugnance to taking an oath involving idolatry, but of a sustained abhorrence of bloodshed.

> While the lamp of Christianity burnt pure and bright, not only the Fathers of the Church held it unlawful for Christians to bear arms, but those, who came within the pale of it, abstained from the use of them, and this to the certain loss of their lives; and . . . it was not till Christianity became corrupted, that its followers became soldiers. This is a most awful fact for those who profess the Christian religion, but who sanction war, at the present day. The

consideration of it ought to make them tremble as to the grounds of their opinions on this subject.

In conclusion, Clarkson asked his readers to ponder why there was so great a difference on the subject of war between the modern churches and primitive Christianity, the epoch in church history nearest to that of Christ's own time. He asked them to consider seriously whether arbitration rather than the sword should not once again become the sole method open to a Christian people of settling disputes.

As early as 1817 we find the Peace Society claiming conversions to pacifism as a result of the reading of its tracts. Even a few military men had now gone over to pacifism. A little later, the learned author of an anonymous booklet entitled *Peace and War: An Essay in Two Parts* (London, 1823), which he had composed after an invitation to become a member of the Peace Society aroused him to examine in detail the relationship of Christianity to war, inquired pointedly: "With what consistency can the *converted* Christian hold a place and commission for war, and receive the wages of war, in full opposition to the principles of his faith; for they are all for peace, and his office is for war." These words, addressed to officers of the army and navy, made it clear that in the writer's view resignation was the only appropriate response for one who had awakened to the full implications of Christian belief.

Within two years a much publicized case of this kind occurred when in January 1825 Captain Thomas Thrush, a naval officer on half pay, had resigned from the service. He did this after coming to the conclusion, to which undoubtedly Clarkson and the publications of the Peace Society, along with his private reading of the Scriptures, had contributed, that war was incompatible with the Christian faith. Thrush then proceeded to give publicity to his gesture by printing the *Letter* which he had addressed to the king in explanation of his views. His epistle is restrained and couched in the most respectful tones. "I believe," Thrush remarked later, "that it required more courage to write that letter than to fight a battle"; he became thereafter an "outcast from military society." But if he was now ostracized by many of his former associates, he was welcomed into its ranks by the supporters of the peace movement. In 1826 in its *Tenth Annual Report* the Peace Society commented on Thrush's resignation: "Such a sacrifice of honour and emolument at the shrine of duty is too rare an occurrence not to draw attention to the principle that could produce so unusual an effect. The impression it makes will, it is hoped, produce new advocates of the principles of this society."

Though the Peace Society was indeed to continue to gain adherents every now and again from among military men, it is worth noting that, unlike the Society of Friends, it does not appear, for all its staunchly pacifist principles, to have produced any conscientious objectors, although liability for militia service remained, as we have seen, a possibility until after mid-century. (Or at least I have not succeeded in discovering any.) The reason for this is not altogether clear. It is true that even in the case of Friends the increasingly moribund militia system signified a steadily decreasing demand for service and therefore correspondingly fewer militia objectors. But this cannot provide the full explanation. It is not improbable that in the rare cases when a young member of the Peace Society was drawn for the militia, he would not share the Quakers' objection to paying the fine which was a possible alternative to personal service. And the middle-class composition of the Peace Society made it scarcely likely that he would not possess enough funds to cover the minute sum involved. Again, supporters of the peace movement were, more often than not, middle-aged or elderly and therefore not liable in any case for service in the militia. The Society's propagandists, however, emphasized regularly the duty incumbent on Christians "to refuse to bear arms." Take, for example, the privately printed discourse by one of the Society's keen supporters, the Reverend John Jefferson of Stoke Newington, *The Unlawfulness of War* (London, 1832), where the preacher urges his hearers to refuse service should general conscription ever be enforced. "Let your refusal be . . . based on scriptural principles, firmly but meekly made, and temperately but clearly explained." At this period, at any rate, there was no ambiguity as to what the Society's official stand was in regard to conscientious objection to service in war.

Yet the promoters of the Peace Society did not wish to banish altogether from their midst the sincere peace worker who still felt that in certain circumstances a war of defense might be justified. On 24 February 1818 the executive committee had entered the following resolution (cited in Schou) in their Committee Book: "The Committee are of the judgement that the fundamental principle of the Society that all war is inconsistent with Christianity can not be conceded." They required that the committees of the auxiliary societies be composed of persons subscribing to unconditional pacifism. Yet almost from the beginning they opened ordinary membership of these auxiliaries to non-pacifists who would undertake to work along with them to eliminate war from the international scene, provided of course that they were also good Christians. (The Society rejected the collaboration of non-believers even when they shared its full pacifist platform!)

Some uncertainty remained, however, as to what policy the Society should pursue. The *Herald of Peace* in October 1821 published a leading article, "On the Establishment of Peace Societies admitting the Right of Defensive War." In it the author attacked the idea that the Society should water down its platform in order to increase membership. Let those peace men who believed in defensive war set up their own separate peace societies; absolute pacifists would welcome such efforts. "They may rest assured that, while we cannot consistently abandon nor conceal our peculiar views upon the subject, we shall never cease to cultivate towards them, as fellow-labourers in the same cause, a spirit of affectionate regard." No such initiative was in fact undertaken: for many decades the London Peace Society remained the sole organ of the British peace movement. The compromise eventually worked out whereby the direction of the Society was vested in the absolute pacifists, whereas auxiliary membership at the local level was open to all who wished to labor in the cause of peace, seems to have worked. At least, the organization was spared the protracted internal debates and final schism which rent the American peace movement. There, the Massachusetts (later American) Peace Society at first had taken no official stand in the matter of defensive wars and thereby provoked strong opposition on the part of the absolutists, many of whom felt this failure of their Society to commit itself officially on so vital a question to be a grave dereliction of duty.

In his *Thoughts on War, addressed to People of All Classes* (Sheffield, 1834) the Welsh pacifist, Samuel Roberts, explained the situation in the London Peace Society as it had established itself by that date. "Let it be understood," he wrote, "that no person, becoming a member of an auxiliary Society, pledges himself to any particular sentiments upon the subject. In the parent society unanimity is necessary, else they could not be agreed on the contents of the publications which they issue; but *here* all that is required is a desire to promote peace by every practicable means." The Peace Society, he went on, had been dubbed "a Quakers' Society," but its promoters had never wished this. They welcomed all who opposed war on Christian grounds. And if the Church of England were to take the lead in contributing members, this would only be cause for rejoicing to them. Indeed, before Roberts, others in the Peace Society had realized the disadvantage of the Quaker label's being attached to their activities. Newcomers to the movement, it was found, were apprehensive that they would have to swallow the full Quaker position if they joined the Peace Society. Its leaders did their best to dispel this notion.

At the same time, they insisted, at least for many decades, on keeping a firm control to see that the pacifist line was maintained in all contacts with the general public. For instance, an entry in the Committee Book for 6 March 1835 runs: "No person be eligible to give public lectures under the sanction of this Society, however otherwise qualified, unless he goes to the full length of the Committee on the subject of defensive war." There was anyhow a fairly general feeling among pacifist members that in fact a genuinely defensive war was an impossibility. All wars, if not from the very outset, then at least in the course of the conflict, took on an aggressive character. In a letter to William Ladd, editor of the New York *Harbinger of Peace* (printed in its issue of November 1828) an English Quaker member, Dr. Thomas Hancock, expressed this view as follows: "If it were left to the wise and good to determine what should be truly a defensive war, my opinion is, that our cause would be safe, and, as the world is constituted, no such war could occur in a nation desirous of maintaining peace." It should be noted that the continental peace societies, which the Britishers helped to bring into being and with which they remained in fairly close touch, never took a pacifist stand at all, preserving the right of governments to defend their soil by arms.

For the first decade and a half of its existence the London Peace Society seemed to make little headway after the original brief upsurge was over. It concentrated its efforts on arguing the moral case against war. This presumed that in a Christian country national policy should be regulated in accordance with the religious principles it avowed. Around 1818-1819 attacks had appeared in the press alleging that, if the ideas of the Society were carried into practice, nothing would stand in the way of Christian lands' being overwhelmed by Turks, Algerian pirates, and savages. In fact, the Society did not urge immediate unilateral disarmament as a practical policy so much as the slow dissemination of pacifist sentiment among the populace. In this period the Society was primarily an educational body. Caution was its motto. What a sympathizer wrote in some *Observations on the Subject of War by Pacificator* (Ipswich, 1817), "Let no one, in a zeal for the cause, outstep the bounds of prudence, and thereby frustrate the object he may wish to advance," was typical of the spirit in which these early peace advocates advanced their views.

The Peace Society, along with the Quakers, had welcomed the Vienna Settlement as an attempt to create an international order. Even the Holy Alliance seemed to the Society's supporters to foreshadow a

Christian Europe in which arbitration would replace war as the accepted method of resolving disputes between states. Their naive trust began rapidly to wane, however, as the reactionary policies of powers like Austria and Russia became inescapably plain. The Peace Society expressed its disapproval of the armed intervention practiced by these powers in the 1820's. Nonintervention in the affairs of another people, whether by Great Britain or by foreign countries, formed a part of the Society's platform from the beginning. At the same time its leaders had scant sympathy with the rising tide of nationalism in Europe, which sought to win independence by armed uprisings; this attitude remained broadly true of the Society for the whole period prior to World War I. Typical of this way of thinking was the *Herald of Peace*'s reaction to the Polish insurrection against Russia in 1830-1831: "The result has taught the useful but dear-bought lesson, that the battlefield is not to be relied on for the redress of wrongs, or as an equitable arbiter of differences." Whereas the Society gave verbal assent to the libertarian goals of the nationalists, it failed to put foward any positive suggestions how such goals might be achieved by nonviolent means. This the American radical nonresistants were to attempt to do, however imperfectly; contemporary British pacifists seemed scarcely aware that such an attempt was needed if their peace program were to have practical relevance. They remained content to draw somewhat complacently the moral that the defeat of the nationalists, when this occurred, proved the failure of the way of arms.

By 1825 the leaders of the Peace Society had become conscious of the inadequacy of a simple appeal to morality and Christian principle if it was not supplemented by a more positive program in the sphere of international relations. But, as Beales points out, "it was not until the religious pacifists of 1815 had been reinforced by free-trade internationalists that their programme became thoroughly practical." He distinguishes five major proposals as forming the keystone of the peace program of the ensuing period: "arbitration, arbitration treaties and clauses in treaties, an International Authority or Tribunal or Congress, the codification of International Law, and [simultaneous and proportional] disarmament." Although at various times the main emphasis was placed on one or another aspect, these five demands remained interlinked as essential prerequisites for the banishment of war from the intercourse of civilized nations. In striving for this goal, only one question divided internationalists, of whom Richard Cobden may be regarded as a typical representative, from religious pacifists *stricto sensu:* the sanctions issue. The pacifists remained adamant in rejecting the employment of military sanctions to back the power of the proposed international authority and to enforce the rule of international law. Yet, it must be stressed, the Peace Society did not oppose the rule of law within the domestic community. It did not share the anarchist proclivities of the American radical nonresistants, for instance. As an undated leaflet, *The Peace Society and Its Aims*, which was issued during Henry Richard's secretaryship, expressed it: "It believes in the *Policeman*, but not in the *Soldier*."

The transformation of the Peace Society from a body the primary purpose of which was to disseminate Christian pacifist sentiment as broadly as possible, to an organization which strove to implement clearly defined political objectives, took place only gradually. The process was not completed until the early 1840's. By this period the Society had a small but vocal lobby in the House of Commons: radical members like Joseph Hume were supporters of the Peace Society (though not necessarily absolute pacifists). They were prepared to act as its representatives in Parliament, as Cobden and Bright were prepared to do on occasion too. The Society now expended its energies and its funds not merely, as in the early days, on producing antiwar literature but in campaigning for its proposals in the constituencies and in memorializing Parliament in favor of international arbitration and "a just and courteous foreign policy" or against such colonial ventures as the Opium War against China in 1839-1842. At times of international crisis, as for example in 1845-1846 when relations between Great Britain and the United States were strained almost to breaking-point over the disputed Oregon boundary, the Peace Society worked with like-minded persons inside Parliament and outside it, as well as with the peace forces in the opposing country, where these existed, to urge arbitration and a policy of conciliation on the governments concerned.

In its first phase the Peace Society had acted as a moral agent. It had endeavored more to change men's hearts than to alter government policy. As a testimonial to the slow leavening of opinion that could result over the years from this kind of effort we may cite the following somewhat florid passage written by an Anglican missionary in Calcutta, the Reverend James Long (from Philip Berry, *A Review of the Mexican War on Christian Principles: and an Essay on the Means of Preventing War*, Columbia, South Carolina, 1849):

> I have seen the benefits conferred by the Peace Society, both at home and abroad; and I regard it as eminently calculated to promote the glory of God and the good of men. I rejoice to have an opportunity of co-operating, as a clergyman of the English

386

church, in the designs of so noble and excellent a Society. I have laboured among the Hindoos for eight years, a large number of whom have renounced idolatry, and are fully acquainted with English literature; but *their greatest objection to the reception of Christianity is the warlike spirit manifested by those who profess it*. They read the history of England, and then tell us, "You say that Jesus Christ taught his disciples to love their enemies; but we find that you English Christians have been engaged for hundreds of years in killing the French, and other nations! Your history abounds with scenes of blood, which are approved of by your best and even your religious writers, while your clergy offer thanks to God, as if he were a God of blood, like our Kale, when you gain a battle." They say, moreover, that since England put her foot in India, a century ago, there has been nothing but war; and I am sorry to say I cannot contradict them. This objection to the reception of Christianity is the most difficult to answer of any I have to deal with. I have for twelve years been advocating the principles of this Society; and as long as I have breath and strength, I will continue to advocate them.

Whereas the militarism of orthodox Christianity proved a stumbling block in the conversion of "Hindoos," the uncompromising religious pacifism of the Peace Society's platform had restricted the Society's appeal in Christian England. By the 1840's, as we have seen, the Society's leaders were attempting to extend its program and more effectively to enlist the support of sympathetic nonpacifists. With arbitration as its slogan, the Society now initiated a series of international peace congresses as a means of rallying all the peace forces in Britain and abroad. The first of these gatherings, the original suggestion for which had emanated actually from the American Peace Society, was held in London at Freemasons' Hall in June 1843. The subject of its sessions was not the compatibility of war with Christianity but how to abolish "the custom of war, in the proper sense of the term, as existing between independent nations." The "high ground" officially maintained by the Peace Society of condemning all war predominated among participants. But the small French delegation and a minority of the British and Americans were unwilling to go further than a condemnation of aggressive war and wished to avoid discussion of religious principle by confining debate solely to the ways and means of eradicating war from the civilized community of nations. An attempt made by two zealous nonresistants to amend the rules of the convention so as explicitly to condemn defensive, along with offensive, war failed to win a majority of votes. "Most of the speakers contended that the term 'war' was sufficient to express all that was needful." The convention busied itself mainly with elaborating the factual case against war and preparations for war and with the practical measures needed to implement international arbitration. Delegates agreed in condemning the militarist bias in education to be found in all countries and they deplored the manufacture of warlike toys for children.

The convention did not make a great impact at the time. The press either ignored its proceedings or waxed sarcastic at its expense. The *Times*, for instance, in an attempt to ridicule the convention's main proposal of substituting arbitration for war as the means of resolving international disputes, enquired disdainfully: "And how do our readers suppose that it is all to be brought about? By uniting into a society some half-dozen Whig members of Parliament, a score or two of Quakers, a few hundred less prominent Englishmen, and a scattering of not very influential foreigners." On the other hand, the staunchly pacifist Newcastle *Peace Advocate and Correspondent* felt that in rejecting the motion condemning defensive war the delegates had so watered down their principles as seriously to jeopardize their witness. The editor advised that at any future congress membership should be confined to those who took the absolutist stand. "No lower ground of union, we feel convinced, will prove sufficient for the great and holy object of such an association."

Understandably, advice of this kind did not appeal to the promoters of the convention. Three more Universal Peace Congresses, as they were known, came to be held: in Brussels in September 1848, in Paris in August 1849, and in London during the Great Exhibition of 1851. But at these meetings the nonpacifist delegates from the continent were present in much larger numbers than in 1843, and the pure pacifist note which had sounded in many of the declarations at the London convention was now muted, though not entirely absent from the discussion. The two moving spirits behind the congresses held between 1848 and 1851 were nonetheless both convinced Christian pacifists: the American blacksmith turned peace propagandist, Elihu Burritt, and a Welsh Congregational minister, Henry Richard, who in 1848 had become secretary of the London Peace Society, a post he was to keep until his retirement in 1885.

Beales has called Richard "the greatest pacifist in England during the nineteenth century." Indeed, the tribute is deserved. Although the Peace Society had earlier possessed an energetic organizer in its "Home Secretary," the Reverend James Hargreaves, he did not equal

Richard either in the range of his activities (Richard, for instance, sat in Parliament as the independent liberal member for Merthyr Tydfil from 1868 until his death twenty years later) or in the impact he made on the peace movement. Richard never concealed his pacifist convictions. His uncompromising rejection of "defensive war" as unworthy of both the individual Christian and the Christian nation—the pamphlet which he published under this title in 1846 he reprinted several times subsequently—did not, however, prevent his advocating close collaboration in the common cause between all shades of peace opinion. "The Peace Society," he wrote, "welcomes to its membership all friends of Peace, whether they accept the abstract view of Christian duty on the subject or not." "The society," he maintained, "has been established to create a public opinion against the War System, and to urge the adoption of rational and Christian methods for settling international disputes. To effect this, it advocates no *visionary schemes.*"

Richard, like Cobden and other liberal free-traders or like many of his fellow pacifists such as Burritt, had little sympathy, despite his Welsh origin, with the contemporary movements for national liberation on the continent. To his way of thinking the fragmentation of large political units into small nation-states was fraught with danger for peace. National animosities would be sharpened; free trade, which Richard, along with almost the whole British peace movement, regarded as an essential factor in creating a warless world, would be hampered. Therefore, when in 1863 a nationalist uprising against the Russians took place in Poland, he displayed much more sympathy for the Russian than for the insurgents' cause. Yet Richard was a staunch anti-imperialist who opposed the numerous colonial wars in which his country engaged and regarded the growth of the British Empire with a somewhat jaundiced eye. That these two stands were not altogether compatible does not appear to have struck him.

The outbreak of the American Civil War in 1861 presented Richard and the London Peace Society with a dilemma of another kind. His opposite number, the Reverend George C. Beckwith, secretary of the American Peace Society, had at once committed that organization to unqualified support of the Unionist war effort, arguing that it was not a question of war, even of civil war, but of police action against contumacious rebels. And most of his supporters clearly agreed with him; only a handful protested against the contortions of his logic. Even the radical nonresistants were carried by their abomination of slavery into wild enthusiasm for the Northern cause, an enthusiasm scarcely modified by adherence in some cases to a very personal pacifism. All this

389

shocked Richard profoundly. He felt it to be a betrayal of the common cause for which he and his friends in the American peace movement had been working in harmony for many years.

Beckwith's thesis he branded as an "evasion . . . so utterly weak and preposterous, and so flagrantly at variance with the doctrines taught in the American Peace Society's own publications, that we cannot bring ourselves to believe that such strong and clear-minded men . . . can possibly have practiced such delusion upon their own judgment and conscience by so pitiful a sophism." Whereas the Americans accused Richard of being prepared to sacrifice the freedom of the slave to the maintenance of peace with the South, the Englishman charged the American Peace Society with abandoning the peace cause without having the courage to say so plainly. For Richard there could be no doubt that the struggle now being waged was war. And, he went on, "we must say candidly that we are not prepared to buy the freedom of the slaves at so tremendous a cost." He was as opposed to the institution of slavery as anyone. But war was not the Christian method of abolishing it: fighting was a worse evil even than slavery. Moreover, Richard did not view the war so much as a struggle to free the slave as an expression of the national pride of the North. He admitted the South's right to secede and believed the British government was acting correctly when it recognized the Confederate States as a belligerent. Strict British neutrality and a negotiated peace were the policies he urged—to the profound annoyance of the American Peace Society. Relations between the London Peace Society and its American counterpart continued to be extremely cool for many years after the conclusion of hostilities.

The Civil War dealt the American Peace Society a severe blow. For all Beckwith's explanations, the sight of the peace men become ardent supporters of war discredited their cause in the eyes of outsiders and undermined confidence within the ranks of the peace movement itself. In England, a half-decade earlier, the Crimean War had marked the turning of the tide against the London Peace Society. The Society, under Richard's direction, had opposed the war both from pacifist principle and on the grounds, too, that it was unnecessary from a political point of view. But its antiwar campaign made little headway in the then state of public opinion, and the government was even more immune to its influence.

Beginning in the late 1860's a truly international peace movement— "the second great Peace crusade," Beales has called it—slowly emerged, first in Western Europe and then spreading to the central and eastern parts of the continent and even overseas. In the United

390

States, of course, its roots were as old and as deep as in Great Britain. This movement did not develop the religious opposition to war. It did not urge conscientious objection or call for unilateral disarmament. Whereas some of its supporting societies put forward federalist schemes or advocated republicanism and entertained vaguely working-class sympathies, they all centered their programs on arbitration, the development of international law, and phased disarmament. The London Peace Society, while retaining as its official creed the unconditional pacifism of its early years, subordinated this to the three aims just mentioned. But the Society was no longer the only body representing the peace cause in Great Britain. William Randal Cremer's Arbitration League, which dated back to the beginning of the 1870's and Hodgson Pratt's International Arbitration and Peace Association, founded in 1880, now each claimed part of the allegiance of the peace movement. Whereas Cremer worked amicably alongside the Peace Society, friction of a personal nature prevented Richard and Pratt from developing any close collaboration. W. Evans Darby, who in 1888, three years after Richard's retirement, became secretary of the Peace Society, remaining in his post till 1915, was a convinced Christian pacifist. Under his guidance the Society opposed the Boer War and participated, too, in the radical opposition to the power diplomacy of the pre-1914 period. But the Society itself had long ceased to be a vital center for the pacifist impulse in Britain. In World War I it played no perceptible role in the antiwar movement; it had spent its force decades earlier.

The eminently respectable Victorians who made up the membership of the Peace Society worked devotedly for the cause. They were prepared to risk unpopularity as well as ridicule, and sometimes abuse, by continuing to insist that war was incompatible with the Christian Gospel and in pleading the claim of pacifism as part of the great movement for the "evangelisation of mankind." All this was to their credit. And they eventually came to perceive the need for a more elaborate political program than their previous mere reiteration of the Gospel imperative against violence. There was indeed a growing feeling among them that, as an anonymous peace pamphleteer expressed it, "War may enrich an oligarchy, but peace is the welfare of the many" (from "Ampho," *War and Capital Punishment opposed to Christianity*, London, 1846). Yet, even later in the century, when practical proposals like international arbitration took first place in their platform, they rarely developed an adequate social and economic critique of war. How conservative their appeal often was may be illustrated by the by no means untypical argument used by one of the Society's sym-

391

pathizers (the Reverend George Wilson M'Cree, *War incompatible with Christianity*, London 1845): a national policy of noninjury, he wrote, "would place the throne of our Queen on an immovable basis." And what, above all, the Peace Society lacked among its members was the zeal of the crusader, the prophetic impulse, the ability to issue a clarion call against the behemoth, war.

Yet, at least during the middle decades of the century, there were a few men and women in the pacifist movement who could assume this role, whose voices rang out against war with the same uncompromising tone as the early Quakers had used in their onslaught on the church and state establishments. Such a one, for instance, was George Pilkington, "late captain, Corps of Royal Engineers," an earnest evangelical Christian who, after retiring from the army to a civilian career as an engineer, became caught up first in the antislavery and then in the peace movement. Adopting a more severe nonresistance than even the Quakers held, Captain Pilkington in the spring of 1834 began the first of a series of tours up and down the British Isles, lecturing on pacifism—on "the Horrors of War and the Blessings of Peace"—wherever he could find listeners. Quaker meetings opened their doors to him; sympathetic dissenting ministers allowed him to use their churches; and even Anglican parsons gave him a respectful hearing. At the end of three years Pilkington was able to gather up nearly two hundred testimonies from ministers to the effect that "all war, whether offensive or defensive, is Anti-Christian." The Independents (Congregationalists) led with eighty-eight contributions, followed by the Baptists with fifty and the Methodists with forty-one (if we include lay preachers). Even the Countess of Huntingdon's Connexion provided four and the "Scotch Secession Church" two, while six Church of England clergymen registered their support.

"The attendance . . . was numerous and respectable, and deeply attentive," was a not untypical comment. An Independent minister wrote enthusiastically: "Mr. Pilkington addressed a crowded congregation at Gloucester; he was listened to with profound attention; his remarks appeared to make a deep impression on all classes. Many left the place where the lecture had been delivered, declaring themselves to be convinced of the truth of the principle which he advocated" (26 June 1834). Several retired army officers were converted and as a result gave up their pensions as the wages of sin. After hearing Captain Pilkington speak on the subject of war, that radical Quaker pacifist Nathaniel Morgan of Ross was moved to confide in his diary: "Oh Lord My God, what are Monthly Meetings, Quarterly or Yearly Meetings, what is plainness of speech, behaviour or apparel, what are the observance of Sundays, Good Fridays, Christmas Days, christenings, baptisms or things called sacraments, compared with preventing the sorrow, fastings, dying, wounds and agonies of thousands who fall on the field of battle and millions pining and starving from their dire effects." Pilkington's message was simple. After contrasting the character of war with the precepts of the New Testament, he urged his fellow Christians to maintain a total abstinence from violence; he preached the total inviolability of human life. Politely declining an invitation from the directors of the London Peace Society to become a paid agent and lecturer on their behalf, Pilkington explained: "I find that the essential difference between my work and the duty required of your Agent, is, that he would be confined to a protest against war only, whilst I cry aloud unto the House of Israel, to cast away all dependence whatsoever on the arm of the flesh."

The kind of radical nonresistance preached by Pilkington, which opposed the policeman as much as the soldier, was not shared by most of the Peace Society's supporters—or, as we have seen, by many Quakers either. But in the United States around this time nonresistance was more strongly represented; William Lloyd Garrison had succeeded in giving it organizational form when he founded the New England Non-Resistance Society in 1838. In North America radical nonresistance, while it was militantly abolitionist, rarely went hand in hand with political radicalism or working-class sympathies, although some American nonresistants were connected with the communitarian movement. In Great Britain, on the other hand, while not all nonresistants were political radicals (Captain Pilkington, for example, did not concern himself with political issues), the nonresistance movement, although extremely tenuous, displayed a more acute social consciousness than its more vigorous, although still numerically slender, American counterpart. We must now take a look at this variety of militant antimilitarism, so different in quality and background from the decorous, bourgeois pacifism of the London Peace Society or the cloistered reserve of the by now middle-class Society of Friends.

The militants were impatient with the slow dissemination of pacifist sentiment by means of the printed word or by public meetings, which the Peace Society favored. They wanted to transmit a more radical message by more immediate means than those used by the peace moderates; they hoped to spread antimilitarism not merely among the educated but among the new working class in the country's industrial centers. They even toyed with the idea of agitating among the armed forces.

A forerunner of this trend in the movement is to be found in the activities of an obscure self-taught artisan, George Hale, described in the report of his trial in mid-September 1824 as "the ex-shoemaker." Hale had been arrested for circulating copies of his pamphlet, *The Two Opinions*, among the soldiers of the Woolwich garrison. The indictment accused him of "intending to incite them to acts of insubordination" by inducing them "to throw down their arms." Indeed, Hale's message was one of simple Christian nonresistance. Unless they obeyed God and disobeyed the command to fight, he had told the troops, they would risk eternal damnation, "for all they that take the sword shall perish with the sword." While the garrison chaplain expressed the view that Hale "was more fit for Bedlam than Maidstone Gaol," the presiding magistrate attempted sarcasm, according to the newspaper report exclaiming: "A pretty doctrine truly; you must not fight, even if the Prussians, Russians, or French were to invade the country, but trust only to faith in God; if a Frenchman was close behind you with his bayonet, and you trusted only to *faith*, you would find it a *fundamental* error (laughter)."

Hale might be dismissed as a harmless eccentric. The nonresistants who were active some two decades later presented a more formidable challenge—at least potentially. Their activities had stemmed from a prolonged visit to the British Isles, starting in late 1842, of the American Henry Clarke Wright. Wright came as the emissary of Garrison's New England Non-Resistance Society, and his purpose was to promote "the heaven-born cause of nonresistance" (Garrison's phrase), first among the British and then on the less amenable European continent. Wright was a man of tremendous dynamism, an indefatigable propagandist ready to argue his case wherever he might be: at public meetings or in private conversation, in the street or on the train or on the coach. He was filled with a sense of mission; he never doubted the rightness of his cause; his opponents, not altogether injustly, called him a fanatic. The doctrine he sought to spread during his European visit combined a Quaker-like pacifism with an un-Quakerly negation of civil government. "No-government" and nonresistance were the slogans of the movement. Garrison and his friends, after postulating the incompatibility of war with the spirit of Christ, went on to propound a form of Christian community. Their political ideology, however, differed from that of the Anabaptist-Mennonite tradition, since the American nonresistants did not share Anabaptist pessimism and hoped, by means of widespread conversion to their creed, for the eventual elimination of the state from the Christian world.

Armed with this "disorganizing" doctrine Wright arrived in Great Britain at a time when industrial unrest was ripe and Chartist agitation was at its height. The atmosphere seemed propitious for initiating a more vigorous attack—albeit a nonviolent one—on the military establishment than had been attempted hitherto by the peace movement. "Teetotalism is onward" (by which of course was meant the total renunciation not of drink but of violence), so Wright had written at the end of November 1842 from Dublin, his first stopping place, where he was, as he wrote, "doing what I can to diffuse the sweet spirit and principles of Peace among all I meet." Moving on to visit England and Scotland, Wright succeeded in the course of 1843 in setting up a number of "anti-war societies." "H. C. Wright," reported the Newcastle *Peace Advocate and Correspondent* in May, "prefers the name 'Anti-War Society' to 'Peace Society,' as being both more expressive of the real nature and interest of the association, and more aggressive in its character." It was certainly no chance that such societies sprang up in the new industrial areas. We hear of their foundation in Midland towns like Preston, Rochdale, Stockport, Warrington as well as in Glasgow. Members were required to take the following pledge: "We, the undersigned, are of the deliberate opinion, that *it is a sin for a man to take away the life of man; and that all wars and fightings are contrary to the spirit and precepts of Christianity, the prosperity of nations, and the true interests of mankind*; and are, therefore, determined to use every Christian means for the prevention of war, and the promotion of peace all over the world."

Wright also succeeded in interesting certain influential figures on the periphery of the radical movement in nonresistance. The Quaker Joseph Sturge, for instance, who was then engaged in the work of the Complete Suffrage Union, was one of these, as were also the antislavery propagandists George Thompson and John Scoble. But there were none who gave themselves so completely to Wright's cause as the Gateshead pamphleteer and peace advocate, Joseph Barker. In a letter to Wright he has expressed the quintessence of the nonresistance faith in its most "ultra" form.

I believe [he wrote] that there is no middle way between war in its wildest horrors, and absolute and uniform non-resistance of evil. I see no difference in principle between a policeman and a soldier, between a lawsuit and a war, between a lawyer and a military engineer. . . . The constable is one end of the system, the king is the other end, and the house of commons, the house of lords, the ministers of the crown, the army and navy, the tax-gatherers, the custom-house officers, the militia, and the army and navy contractors, are the middle. The constable's staff, in my eye, is but a blunt sword, and the soldier's sword is but a sharp staff; and if a man's head be cloven, it is of no matter whether it be done with a sharp sword or a blunt one, a wooden one or a steel one. I believe no one can successfully defend the principles of peace, who does not advocate non-resistance of evil in all cases, and under all circumstances. I believe that the advocates of war may always confound or conquer the advocates of peace, if the advocates of peace plead for the propriety of Christians taking part in the work of compulsory government, or prosecuting men for debts or crimes.

"Magistrates are soldiers also, as well as masters and commanders of soldiers," Barker states in a brief catechism on nonresistance which he composed. The only law which a Christian could recognize was the New Testament. "If they want bad ones, let them make them themselves." Human government was essentially military government. True, he concedes, "civil government as it exists in *England* is a great blessing, compared with human government in some other forms; but compared with the government of *Christ*, civil government is a plague and a curse." In place of government Barker wished to see "voluntary co-operation" implemented in all spheres of social life.

Nonresistants like Wright and his American colleagues, or like the Englishman Barker, opposed all talk of political reform as an illusion. "I believe," the latter wrote, "that government can only be reformed by being annihilated." But annihilation could only be brought about through "the transformation of men's souls by the spirit and doctrine of Jesus Christ." Although in some respects the nonresistants may be considered precursors of the nonviolent wing of the modern anarchist movement, and although the working-class discontent of the hungry '40's seemed to provide a not unfavorable setting for their growth in England, they nonetheless shared to a large extent the individualist spirit of contemporary middle-class radicalism. Barker at this time gave lectures on the evils of socialism; he even opposed the collection of the poor rate as an unjustified exertion of force on the part of the state. If the antiwar societies that Wright had set in motion undoubtedly drew some support from the working class, for all their bold attacks on the army and navy establishments and their fervent protests against the militia or against increased expenditure on the regular armed forces, they showed that the tone at least was given by middle-class radicals. The nonresistants' interest in promoting free trade as a factor for peace is only one example of this tendency.

In fact, the only prominent convert to nonresistance among working-class Chartists was Thomas Cooper, who in 1846 printed in pamphlet form his *Two Orations against Taking Away Human Life, under any Circumstances; and in Explanation, and Defence, of the Misrepresented Doctrine of Non-Resistance*. Cooper had not long before emerged from jail, an incarceration resulting from his activities as a "physical force" Chartist. Dedicating his booklet "to the working classes . . . with every sentiment of devotion to their truest interests that can possibly be felt, by one whose heartfelt pride it is to be, one of their order," Cooper struck a militantly proletarian note throughout its pages. He attacked war and standing armies and militias as a curse on "the unenfranchised toilers," "the manufacturing masses," who paid their cost in life and material prosperity. In prison, he writes, he had after long reflection finally "come . . . to the conclusion—the clear and conscientious conclusion—that all wars and fightings [were] wrong—that all taking of human life [was] wrong—even the taking of human life in self-defence." Killing a human being, even "the most desperate human ruffian in the world," was a crime against morality, for every human being was potentially capable of "moral transformation." (Yet as a freethinker, Cooper could not employ a refinement of this argument frequently used by contemporary Christian pacifists: that killing "a bad man" was wrong in all circumstances, since this act would forthwith consign to hell a soul that could still be redeemed if its owner were granted an extended span of life.) For Cooper human brotherhood, which was the goal of the working-class movement, could be achieved only through a thoroughgoing nonresistance. And it was as the only ethically acceptable method of resisting injustice and achieving the overthrow of "our depraved and immoral social and political system" that he now urged the adoption of "moral-resistance." Unlike the bourgeois nonresistants, Cooper did not base his objection to physical force on the Christian religion. He accepted the Christian *ethic*, nonetheless, while giving it a proletarian slant. St. Paul he calls "the working-man missionary"; the early Christians "belonged to our order—to the spurned and degraded and ill-treated working-class." Christ was "the Great Teacher" who, along with the other great religious philosophers from Confucius onward, had denounced the spirit of revenge and retaliation.

Part of Cooper's message found a ready response among Chartist supporters. There was a strong internationalist element on the Chartist left; in addition, "moral force" Chartists like William Lovett had already renounced the use of violence for the achievement of their political aims. So long as the workingman was deprived of the vote, the whole movement was united in opposing aggressive war, combating upperclass militarism, and protesting against the by now decaying militia system. Yet the full nonresistant position as outlined in Cooper's pamphlet found little echo among Chartists or workers. "Many of my own political party," he had to admit, found his views "peculiar and strange." Feargus O'Connor even went so far as to describe them as "beastly, slavish, unmanly, cowardly, debasing, un-christian, and un-chartist." Usually the response was more restrained but no less negative.

A working-class element, however, may be detected in a new pacifist organization which came into being in 1846, the same year that Cooper published his *Two Orations*. The League of Human Brotherhood, though it had no formal connection with political Chartism, succeeded in attracting a number of earnest artisans in addition to middle-class support. Its founder was another American "peace missionary," the learned though self-educated blacksmith Elihu Burritt, who arrived in England in May 1846 on a special journey of reconciliation. The tension between Great Britain and the United States over the Oregon boundary, which had originally prompted his visit, relaxed around this time and the two governments succeeded in reaching a solution to the crisis without war. Burritt, with his boundless energy ready to be expended on the cause of reform, turned at once to another project which he had been considering for some time: the creation of an international organization dedicated to the promotion of absolute pacifism. Burritt, unlike H. C. Wright, was never an unconditional nonresistant of the Garrisonian variety, but in recent years he had become increasingly disgusted with the direction the cautious Beckwith had been giving to the American Peace Society. He had every intention, therefore, in seeing that his new league to promote human brotherhood should stand on an indisputably pacifist platform.

In July Burritt set out on a tour of England, hoping *en route* to discover sufficient support to justify the establishment of a society of this kind. "We had conceived," he writes, "that in travelling from village to village through England, we might find many by the wayside and fireside especially among the poorer classes, who would be willing to subscribe their names to the pledge and principles of such an organisation." On reaching the village of Pershore near Worcester he decided to go ahead with his project; he therefore sketched out a pledge which he offered for signature that very evening to the villagers gathered to hear him speak. Nineteen members of his audience took the pledge. From this humble origin there sprang an organization which was to gather members from some half-dozen countries. The League's

English branch which, along with the American, was the most flour-
ishing section of Burritt's movement, gained adherents rapidly. Joseph
Sturge gave it support, as did the then secretary of the London Peace
Society, the Reverend John Jefferson, and the well-known radical
politician, James Silk Buckingham. His chief helpers in the work Burritt found in those two stalwart Quaker peace publicists, Charles
Gilpin and Edmund Fry, the latter of whom acted as secretary of the
English branch. The League had its own press organ, the monthly
Bond of Brotherhood, which Burritt edited from London and distrib-
uted not only in England but in the United States and even on the
European continent. In 1857 circulation had reached a figure of four
thousand but thereafter it declined as the work of the League began
to lose its original impetus.

The Pershore pledge which Burritt had composed for the League—
a "teetotal peace pledge" was how he described it—is worth quoting
in full, since it represents the first attempt to write a pledge of conscientious objection into the statutes of a peace society and may be
considered, therefore, a forerunner in Britain of such a body as the
popular Peace Pledge Union of the 1930's. Burritt's pledge ran as
follows:

> Believing all war to be inconsistent with the spirit of Christianity,
> and destructive to the best interests of mankind, I do hereby
> pledge myself never to enlist or enter into any army or navy, or
> to yield any voluntary support or sanction to the preparation for
> or prosecution of any war, by whomsoever, for whatsoever pro-
> posed, declared, or waged. And I do hereby associate myself with
> all persons, of whatever country, condition, or colour, who have
> signed, or shall hereafter sign this pledge, in a "League of Uni-
> versal Brotherhood"; whose object shall be to employ all legiti-
> mate and moral means for the abolition of all war, and all spirit,
> and all the manifestation of war, throughout the world; for the
> abolition of all restrictions upon international correspondence and
> friendly intercourse, and of whatever else tends to make enemies
> of nations, or prevents their fusion into one peaceful brotherhood;
> for the abolition of all institutions and customs which do not rec-
> ognize the image of God and a human brother in every man of
> whatever clime, colour or condition of humanity.

The high hopes entertained by Burritt and his colleagues of creating
a great international antiwar movement were, however, not to be
realized (yet the wording of the Pershore pledge, though framed for

399

use in a Christian milieu, could have gained assent not only from Westerners who did not subscribe to Christian belief but from persons reared in a quite different religio-cultural tradition).

On the European continent the spirit of *Realpolitik* was rising, and in the United States the sectional conflict grew increasingly acute. In Great Britain where some twenty-five thousand signatures to the League's pledge had been gathered by 1850, a slackening of interest was apparent in the early '50's. It was the Crimean War which dealt the British League the final blow.

Perhaps the main obstacle to the League's continued progress lay in the fact that many, perhaps most, of the peace pledgers had signed on merely nominally. Only a small minority of those taking the pledge did anything further to promote their antimilitarist stand. Tens of thousands of paper signatures were no substitute for a really effective instrument for exerting pressure on public opinion and governments, and such an instrument the League of Human Brotherhood never really succeeded in becoming. On the other hand, the League was able to demonstrate the potential strength of an antiwar organization which based itself mainly, as at least the British branch of the League did, on workers, artisans, and farmers. It pointed the way, however hesitantly and with whatever differences in basic ideology, to the working-class internationalism of the twentieth century.

In 1857 the League's British branch fused with the London Peace Society. In fact, it at once lost its identity; the older Society was more bourgeois, less militant, and by this time less assertively pacifist than the League of Human Brotherhood. Burritt's idea, however, was not entirely extinguished. It provided the inspiration, for instance, for the activities toward the end of the century of a tireless Quaker woman, Priscilla H. Peckover of Wisbech in Cambridgeshire. The local peace associations which she helped to set up, beginning in 1879 with a branch in her local town, derived from Burritt's experiment some thirty years earlier. The organization worked in close cooperation with the London Peace Society, but it had its own organ, a quarterly entitled *Peace and Goodwill* which Miss Peckover edited almost single-handed from 1882 until her death in 1931, and its own publishing program. On the eve of World War I the associations numbered some eight thousand members, including about a hundred Protestant clergy drawn from various denominations. The organization emphasized the stand of the conscientious objector, although it seems likely that not all who associated themselves with its work were complete pacifists. And the scope of its activities, of course, was minute in comparison with what Burritt had projected for his international pacifist league.

We have seen that, whereas rationalist sentiment against war was to be discovered among both middle-class radicals and working-class Chartists and socialists, a nonreligious, ethical pacifist like Thomas Cooper was an exceptional phenomenon in the nineteenth century. Even radical nonresistants almost invariably based their antimilitarism on the New Testament imperative; some were good evangelical Christians of unimpeachable theological orthodoxy. The Quakers remained an important element in the British peace movement. In addition, in the course of the century several new denominations arose with a radical objection to war. Small in numbers and in several cases practicing a strict abstention from the affairs of the world, these new religious bodies played little or no active role in the wider nineteenth-century peace movement. But something must be said here on their antiwar stand.

The most significant of these sects were the Plymouth Brethren. The Brethren had crystallized as an independent denomination in the course of the 1820's and '30's. "The Scriptural basis for their objection to the practice of war," writes Harold H. Rowdon in his recent study of their origins, "seems to have been the Sermon on the Mount with its prohibition of resistance to evil which they understood to apply literally and universally."

Literalism indeed was the hallmark of their theology. Considering themselves to be separated from the world and as communities to whom alone salvation would be granted, the Brethren refrained from participation in politics—or indeed in such secular activities (as they considered them) as the peace movement or other reform causes. Few of them exercised the franchise. They were a "peculiar" people, whose path led them away from the political arena.

The Brethren were eventually to become a predominantly lower-middle-class sect. At the beginning, however, the leaders who shaped its ideology were mostly from the upper ranks of society. Among them there were Oxford dons and Anglican clergy, evangelical aristocrats and landed gentry, and a sprinkling of army and navy officers. On conversion, officers resigned from the service, at least in the early period. One of them, Percy Francis Hall, who came from a county family (his father was Dean of Durham), composed an apologia for his action and published it under the title *Discipleship: or, Reasons for resigning His Naval Rank and Pay* (London, [1848]). His resignation he justified on two main counts: first, true Christians could take no active part in the workings of any worldly authority and, second, Christ had forbidden his followers to shed blood, urging them instead to love their enemies, an injunction that Hall (and the Brethren as a whole) saw as central

401

to the whole New Testament teaching. He explained the need he felt to make his views public, by pointing to the sharp cleavage between them and those of his family and professional background:

> In taking a step which, if warranted by the word of God, must cast discredit upon the service and discipleship of many now living, for whom I do feel the truest respect and affection as children of God, as well as place me in the more invidious position of sitting in judgment upon the almost universally accredited standard of Christian practice, I feel myself imperatively called upon to give to the Church of Christ, with meekness and fear, a reason why I should take upon myself a place of such moral distinction and authority. God knoweth it is not in pride, nor is it to please men.

Another member of the Brethren, a contemporary of Hall's, has left a personal account of his pacifist views, which dates from the time of the Crimean War. Charles Brenton came from the same social background as Hall. His father, Sir Jahleel Brenton, Bart., was a distinguished naval officer who had won the esteem of commanders like Nelson and the Earl of St. Vincent. The son had received a first-rate classical education; he was fluent, too, in Hebrew and was an accomplished Biblical scholar who might have attained high office in the Anglican hierarchy if he had not, around 1832, abandoned his Church of England orders for a layman's role among the Brethren. In a fragment of autobiography he, like Hall, depicts the contrast between his social environment and the pacifism of the sect which he had adopted as his own:

> Let it not be forgotten that from my birth upwards all my associations and impressions were in favour not only of the lawfulness but of the glory of war. All the scenes of my childhood were crowded with memorials of the past, or tokens of the present connection of my family with the profession of arms. I was, so to speak, born and cradled in the midst of them. Epaulettes and cocked hats, the grapeshot that pierced my father's hipbone, the sword voted to him out of the Patriotic Fund of *those* days, rich with blue steel and unwrought gold, my mother fainting at the news of my father's wounds—these are among the earliest visions of my infancy. The very playthings of our nursery were blocks, marlinespikes, or models of brigs and frigates with jacks and ensigns and appropriate rigging. War seemed the most normal condition of man, and peace a rare and vapid exception. . . . In after years the warlike associations of my life multiplied instead of de-

creasing. If I was the son and grandson of admirals, my wife was the daughter and granddaughter of admirals. . . . And at this day I am in mourning for a beloved brother-in-law, the only colonel killed at the battle of the Alma and who in many respects resembled my father. . . . Where, then, it will be asked, did you get these strange, Quakerlike, unwarlike, un-English notions?

Brenton himself chose to attribute his pacifism to the evangelical piety of his father's household. At home, he says, while of course he never learned of pacifism, he was taught to respect "the inspiration and consequent authority of Scripture." Though there were probably other influences as well, such as that of the Quakers or the publications of the London Peace Society, which he might unconsciously have played down in his account, the attribution may not be altogether incorrect. It is certainly true that the attitude of the Plymouth Brethren to war, like that of all nineteenth-century evangelical pacifists, was largely shaped by their appeal to the letter of the New Testament and the example of the early church. Theirs was a legalistic pacifism, like Menno's in the sixteenth century, and like the Mennonites they quickly succumbed to schism. However, neither the "Open" nor the "Exclusive" Brethren have disowned members who bore arms.

Whereas evangelical pacifists like the Clarksons or George Pilkington, and even Quakers in Britain by this period, were drawn by their objection to war actively to enlist the cooperation of all fellow Christians who could be persuaded to join them in total rejection of war and violence, the peace witness of the Plymouth Brethren was inward looking. They repudiated collaboration in any joint pacifist effort. Even the comparatively broadminded and tolerant Brenton wrote: "I am [not a] member . . . of any . . . 'Peace Society,' save that one true Peace Society, the Church of God, but I believe war to be unjustifiable." The Church of God, in other words the Brethren, remained an extremely small remnant.

The other newly formed peace sects of the nineteenth century were equally restricted in numbers. There was, for instance, the Christadelphian Church, whose origins date back to around mid-century. Its founder was British, Dr. John Thomas, who succeeded in gathering followers on both sides of the Atlantic. From the church's early days an objection to bearing arms was among its tenets: a testimony which members upheld in the New World during the difficult years of the American Civil War. In Great Britain in the second half of the nineteenth century the Christadelphians more than once protested against the possible reintroduction of some form of compulsory military serv-

403

ice. They stressed their neutrality in the conflicts of this world, which should, they thought, be of concern only to nominal Christians and, therefore, must be left to such persons to wage. In September 1876 one of their leaders declared: "Fighting is incompatible with New Testament saintship, and with that character for meekness, forbearance and love for which believers are to be distinguished." Yet, unlike the Plymouth Brethren who based their pacifism on the belief that Christ had forbidden the shedding of human blood, the Christadelphians' noncombatancy was conditional. They believed that wars were an essential ingredient of life in this sinful world, a necessary means for affecting God's judgments at a certain level of existence. Moreover, Dr. Thomas and the sect's leaders, while rejecting any possibility of establishing universal peace on this earth (the goal of the contemporary peace movement), also dropped hints of millennial warrings in the future in the name of an avenging Savior, when Christ would call his followers to help destroy the wicked. As Dr. Thomas stated in November 1876: "This is your hour. Our time is not quite yet. We look for our summons to 'the war of the great day of YAHWEH ELOHIM' (Apoc. 16:14), at any time. We shall then put on our harness for the work of punishing the wicked in all the earth." Whereas the Plymouth Brethren bring to mind the first Mennonites, the Christadelphians reflect the thought world of the earlier chiliastic Melchiorites. However, paucity of numbers seemed to preclude the possibility of a Christadelphian Münster.

Yet another new addition to Britain's pacifist churches were the Disciples of Christ, who had however originated in the United States (though, it is true, their founder, Alexander Campbell, was born in Ulster). The denomination came into being in the late 1820's, soon finding adherents on the western frontier as well as in the eastern and southern states. Campbell himself and some of the early leaders were opposed to war. Their pacifism formed part of their "restitutionalism," of their desire to recreate a community of believers modeled strictly on the pattern of the early church. By the time of the Civil War, when they already numbered around two hundred thousand with members on both sides of the fighting line, the American Disciples had largely abandoned their pacifistic views; only a minority in either camp opposed their government's war effort. In Great Britain, where the denomination had spread under the name "Churches of Christ," pacifism appears to have maintained itself much longer. At the time of the American Civil War, a prominent British Disciple, David King, declared: "The British brethren are united in proclaiming that the only weapons which a Christian can use without offence to the Lord are those which are not carnal. They cannot see the possibility of Christian love flowing forth with the deadly strife of the battle-field, . . . the work of slaughter cannot be ours. If the world-power must do this work those who serve the world, and not the servants of the Lord Christ, must engage in it." Jesus' followers in the early church had proclaimed: "We are Christians and cannot fight," and this stand remained the right one for later generations. "I am confident that I express the mind of the brethren in this country," King concluded.

The British Disciples, like the Christadelphians, were a very small group. By the early twentieth century, though the general feeling in the church remained hostile to the bearing of arms, the decision whether to serve or not had become one for the individual to determine according to his own conscience. (It is interesting, incidentally, to speculate if Lloyd George's upbringing in the Churches of Christ may not have been one of the factors influencing his opposition to the Boer War.)

When wartime conscription was introduced in 1916, we find among the community of conscientious objectors, besides Quakers and religious pacifists from the larger nonpacifist denominations—and pacifists of various ethical, rationalist, and humanitarian coloring, as well as nonpacifist socialist or anarchist antimilitarists—a fair number of men who belonged to minute churches which each took a collective stand against participation in war. Some resembled the politically aloof Christadelphians in foreseeing the ultimate possibility of serving under Christ's banner in an apocalyptic conflict to come. Such, for instance, were the Seventh-Day Adventists who held for the time being to a rigidly noncombatant interpretation of the Mosaic commandment "Thou shall not kill," or the International Bible Students (today known as Jehovah's Witnesses), or various Pentecostal groups: all these were fairly recent imports from the United States. Others were more like the sedate Churches (i.e., Disciples) of Christ in positing an exact Christian discipleship including nonresistance to evil, without at the same time demanding too fargoing a separation from society. Still others followed the pattern presented by the Plymouth Brethren with their strict otherworldliness and their belief in salvation as the sole prerogative of their own church. But all these bodies had developed in a period when Great Britain maintained the voluntary system of recruitment, in an era only toward whose end did the country begin to emerge from its previous diplomatic isolation. For most of this time war had not impinged very closely on the life of the average Englishman. And peace and war, too, were not among the primary concerns of the groups just mentioned.

Richard Cobden, speaking in the House of Commons in 1849, had referred to British pacifists as "that *influential* body of Christians who repudiate war in any case, whether offensive or defensive" (my italics). He was not drawing attention so much to withdrawn groups like the Plymouth Brethren, or even to the Quakers *per se*, as to that new source of pacifist opinion diffused now among other nonpacifist churches in addition to the Society of Friends and crystallizing to a large extent around the London Peace Society. Eventually, by the early twentieth century, almost every denomination in Britain possessed its small pacifist minority. Even the Salvation Army, for instance, produced a nonresistant high-ranking officer, A. S. Booth-Clibborn (a Quaker, we should add, by birth and early conviction, whose evangelical faith had subsequently led him out of the Society of Friends). Booth-Clibborn, until eventually silenced by "General" William Booth himself, passionately denounced Christian participation in battle, and during the Boer War he had urged young Christians not to fight. Not all twentieth-century religious pacifists, however, have shared Booth-Clibborn's intense Bible-centeredness, for the Social Gospel and the politico-economic case against war were to become as much a hallmark of religious pacifism in Great Britain as of their American *confrères'* credo.

Although Cobden probably exaggerated the degree of political influence exerted by absolute pacifists in the England of his day, pacifism was ultimately to gain greater strength and renewed relevance during the years of the First World War and in the decades which followed the peace settlement of 1919. Henceforward the pacifist movement, combining religious and nonreligious elements in a sometimes uneasy alliance, was to remain a not insignificant factor on the British intellectual scene. Although the post-1914 story forms a virtually new chapter in the history of British pacifism, expansion could not have taken place without the painstaking and often unrewarding work carried out in the nineteenth century by the movement's forerunners, both the moderates and the radicals.

ELEVEN. *The Later German Mennonites*

(FROM THE DEMOCRATIC REVOLUTION
TO THE FIRST WORLD WAR)

In the nineteenth and early twentieth centuries pacifism put down deep roots in Great Britain and the United States. Its condition, admittedly, was not always flourishing: it experienced renewal and decline. It continued nevertheless in organized form, attracting recruits in each generation as it appeared. Although in the first half of the nineteenth century American Quakers tended to stand aloof, at least in Britain they were particularly active in pacifist and near-pacifist organizations. But members of other denominations participated too. At the beginning of the twentieth century there was a strong pacifistic streak in the British labor movement. On the European continent, on the other hand, socialist antimilitarists, who as Marxists mostly espoused either the class war or as reformists of one kind or another a citizen army, sharply differentiated themselves from the protagonists of the peace movement *stricto sensu*, rejecting it for its predominantly bourgeois membership and outlook. Moreover, supporters of the continental peace movement, with very few exceptions, never accepted "integral" pacifism in the Anglo-American sense. For them, pacifism included all efforts to achieve international peace and understanding: the conscientious objector stand was virtually unknown among them. By 1914 the few tiny Quaker meetings on the continent had almost all disappeared. Apart from several obscure religious sects and the disciples of Tolstoy, the pacifist position was represented there only by the German-speaking Mennonites. But by 1914 German Mennonites had largely discarded their traditional nonresistance in Central Europe, still retaining it, however, in their Russian diaspora, though even there in none too dynamic a condition.

Two factors, one internal and the other external, were chiefly responsible for the decline of nonresistance among German Mennonites during the nineteenth century: their growing acculturation to a society which accepted war and militarism as normal, and the introduction throughout the continent of universal army service as a result both of military considerations and of egalitarian, "democratic" ideas about the role of the citizen in the state. We might also consider the failure to reformulate a sixteenth-century article of faith so that it could continue to have meaning and applicability within the context of a new age as a third important factor in this process.

The introduction of universal military service in Prussia-Germany and in Russia—the main areas under consideration in this chapter— took place in the late 1860's and early 1870's. These years, therefore, form a watershed in the history of German Mennonite nonresistance.

The small Mennonite communities in Switzerland, France, and Austria also faced the menace of modern "democratic" conscription during the nineteenth century. Popular rule in the cantons of the Swiss Confederation dated back indeed many centuries; the Revolution of 1789-1794 in France in many respects marked the climax of the democratic movement of the late eighteenth century; and even Habsburg autocracy had finally to give way before the *Zeitgeist*, the monarch assenting to the introduction of constitutional government in 1860.

The Swiss Mennonites, as a result of nearly three centuries of persecution and legal discrimination on the part of the state and of consequent emigration of members to escape these conditions, were greatly reduced in numbers by the beginning of the nineteenth century. They still lived almost exclusively in the canton of Bern. Unlike their *confrères* in Alsace-Lorraine or in the Germanies, they did not receive a guarantee of exemption from military service from the government of Bern until 1815; the position of Mennonite conscientious objectors up to that date was uncertain, and they continued to suffer sporadic harassment, although in the more tolerant canton of Basel they had been allowed since 1805 "to discharge their military duty in the (noncombatant) transportation corps." In 1815, after the Swiss Confederation regained its independence from Napoleonic domination, Bern permitted its Mennonite conscripts, if they felt scruples about buying a substitute, to choose the alternative of paying a special military tax. A few years later a Reformed clergyman grumbled: "Thus, one sees strong and healthy young men of families with means who are protected from military service." Despite jealousy and envy aroused in some quarters, the Mennonite exemption was renewed once again when a new military law was passed by the cantonal assembly in 1835. During the debates a senator remarked: "If we wished to compel the Anabaptists to do military service, we would make them martyrs of their faith. For not a single Anabaptist will allow himself to be forced to take up arms." In 1850 the regulation of military conscription was transferred from the cantonal to the federal level, and no special provision was now included for Mennonite objectors. Exemption, however, continued to be given along the old lines until 1874, when a new federal constitution eliminated all privileges of this kind: henceforward, service in the Confederation's army became compulsory for Swiss Mennonites, as for all able-bodied male citizens. As a special concession, however, they were permitted to do their term of service in the army medical corps. In return for having to submit to military conscription, Mennonites at last received the same political rights as the rest of the population.

The Mennonite community had opposed this change in their military obligation, petitioning the legislators in vain for retention of their right to opt out of army service altogether. Acceptance of military uniform and army discipline offended the susceptibilities of many Swiss Mennonites who not only objected to becoming part of the machinery of war but balked, too, at the degree to which their young men would now be exposed to worldly values. "Many stories are told," wrote Delbert Gratz in the early 1950's after interviewing a number of elderly Bernese Mennonites, "how the young men sought to evade military service. One cut off his trigger finger. Another sent a cripple in his place, who was naturally discharged. This was later discovered and punishment meted out to the evader." A few families emigrated to the United States; others crossed the border into Alsace where, by retaining their Swiss citizenship, they could avoid liability for military service at the price of a money payment to their home government (see chapter 6). But most Swiss Mennonites remained. The church perforce acquiesced in the situation, and eventually many of its young men accepted full military service, some even becoming officers. No measures were taken against those who did so: the peace witness paled and the question of nonresistance retreated into the background of the church's interests, even though Swiss Mennonites have remained officially "nonresistant" down to the present.

The Mennonites and Amish for whom by the nineteenth century Alsace and Lorraine had been home for a century or more could not, of course, obtain freedom from conscription by showing Swiss citizenship papers. They were liable to the law of the land (after the Franco-Prussian War of 1870 most of the area where Mennonites lived came once again under German rule). Under the *ancien régime*, as we have seen, a *modus vivendi* had been worked out with the state on this issue. But the French Revolution, with its slogan of *égalité*, threatened to sweep away all privilege based upon unequal rights, including the special Mennonite exemption from military service. In December 1790 male citizens had been required to register for the National Guard; although "Anabaptists" were exempted from this order, the situation became serious again in 1792 with the outbreak of war. Local officials, anxious to obtain as many recruits as possible, strongly opposed the idea of freeing Mennonites from their duty to defend the fatherland. One wrote in November 1792: "Leur principe de ne pas porter les armes est dangereux." He pointed to the possibility that, if the sect got its way, the military strength of this frontier province would be depleted. He accused them of "mauvaise volonté et . . . haine de la Révolution," concluding his report sententiously: "Enfin, dans les dangers de la patrie, tous citoiens autres que les fonctionnaires publics doivent faire personnellement leur service." The Mennonites naturally protested against attacks such as this. In a petition of 3 August 1793 which they presented to the legislators in Paris, they affirmed their devotion to the state while stating at the same time their loyalty to their traditional nonresistance: "Ils sont soumis aux Lois; ils reconnaissent la Constitution; ils supportent les charges publiques avec exactitude et sans murmure; ils fournissent leur contingent à cause des principes de leur religion. . . ." Their plea was favorably received. Whereas in 1791 the National Assembly, still dominated by moderates, had rejected the French Quakers' plea for unconditional exemption, now two years later the Jacobin-controlled Committee of Public Safety of the National Convention was more generous to the country's Mennonite community. It gave it virtually what it asked for.

In a decree of August 1793 carrying the signatures not only of Robespierre himself but also of Barère, Carnot, Saint-Just, etc., the Committee declared:

> Nous avons vu des coeurs simples en eux, et nous avons pensé qu'un bon gouvernement devait employer toutes les vertus à l'utilité commune. C'est pourquoi nous vous invitons d'user envers les anabaptistes de la même douceur qui fait leur caractère, d'empêcher qu'on ne les persécute, et de leur accorder le service qu'ils demanderont dans les armées, tel que celui de pionniers et celui de charrois, on même de permettre qu'ils acquittent ce service en argent.

Which alternative the Mennonite conscripts actually chose—to work as pioneers and teamsters with the Revolutionary army or to pay an annual military tax—is not clear, though the latter is the more likely. After Napoleon became emperor in 1804, official exemption was withdrawn and Mennonites who could not afford a substitute were forced into the imperial armies; yet in practice their noncombatant status still seems to have been respected and they were usually assigned to service in the transportation corps. A tradition preserved among the Mennonites of the Vosges told of a Mennonite soldier serving during the

Napoleonic wars in Germany who, in the midst of battle, called out in his local German dialect, "Don't shoot me, don't kill me, for my religion prevents me from resisting," and was recognized by an opposing soldier from West Prussia as a Mennonite and spared. The pressing of their young men into the armed forces had come as a severe blow to the congregations of Alsace and Lorraine after their favorable treatment by the Revolutionary administration. In 1809 a Mennonite delegation had travelled up from Alsace in an attempt to persuade the emperor to restore their old exemption, but he told them harshly: "No one, on account of religion, may refuse service in our army."

At the Restoration, the military obligation of Mennonites in Alsace and Lorraine (and in the neighboring principality of Montbéliard which had become part of France in 1793) remained unchanged, except that the long period of war was at last ended. Only by hiring a substitute could their conscripts escape service. During the next half-century young men, and whole families, crossed the Atlantic to escape this burden, settling particularly in midwestern states like Indiana, Illinois, and Iowa where there were already Mennonite communities and where, too, there was plenty of good land to spare. To some extent economic considerations also played a role in this migration. After 1870 those Mennonites who were incorporated in the new German Empire —in fact the vast majority—could take advantage, if they wished, of the noncombatant army service provided by the imperial legislation (see below). A few congregations remained in France and rapidly became French in language as well as in political allegiance. Here universal military conscription now offered no loophole for conscientious objectors. But nonresistance was on the wane, anyhow, in Alsatian Mennonitism. By around the end of the century it had disappeared altogether on both sides of the new frontier.

The small Mennonite community in eastern Galicia lost its old privileged position in 1868 when universal military service was introduced in Austria-Hungary, a year after the *Ausgleich* (Compromise) had created a dual monarchy out of the Habsburg realm. After its leaders had petitioned Vienna, the government agreed that Mennonite conscripts be employed in the army medical corps. Here too, as in Alsace and Lorraine, many eventually ceased to observe their church's traditional teaching on nonresistance, still officially upheld, and felt no scruples of conscience in accepting full military service: they received no censure for this from their congregations. Many Galician Mennonites, however, continued to be nonresistant and to ask for noncombatant status up to and during the First World War and on into the

411

interwar period when this area became part of the new Polish state, whose government also respected Mennonite objections to bearing arms.

The Mennonites of Switzerland, Alsace-Lorraine, and Galicia formed only a very small section of the brotherhood of European Mennonites; they numbered altogether about a couple of thousand members (no accurate statistics exist for this). Around the middle of the nineteenth century, according to Wilhelm Mannhardt, out of a total of some ninety thousand Mennonites in Europe, the Dutch *Doopsgezinden* accounted for thirty-nine thousand, the "Russian" congregations for thirty thousand, the West and East Prussian for twelve thousand five hundred, and the west and south German for six thousand five hundred. In addition, there were at this date some one hundred twenty thousand Mennonites in the United States and Canada. Since the *Doopsgezinden* had discarded nonresistance at the end of the previous century, in Europe the maintenance of the traditional Mennonite peace testimony depended, therefore, on the stance taken by the brethren in Germany proper and in the Russian diaspora. We must turn our attention now to these two areas.

"In southern Germany," writes Ernst Crous, "the principle of nonresistance disappeared early in the nineteenth century." The same is even truer of the congregations in the lower Rhineland and the northwest part of the country, where Mennonites by this time formed a predominantly urban element, in contrast to the still largely rural communities of the south and east. In the north-west, too, the influence of the nonpacifist *Doopsgezinden* was strong and the whole area constituted, as it were, a single province of the church. It would be impossible, however, to give any exact dates in this whole process. Not only did objection to military service survive longer in some congregations in a given area than in others; even in those congregations where practical consensus in abandoning the principle had been reached, there might always be a few individuals who continued to observe this traditional tenet. Such diversity of conduct was possible so long as universal military training had not been enacted, for until then the alternative of hiring a substitute, however repugnant formerly to the strict Mennonite conscience, usually remained open for any who possessed sufficient means, even in those places where a more acceptable alternative, such as a military fine, no longer existed. But with the creation of the German *Reich* in 1870 this door was finally closed; in some areas of the country it had already shut. Thereafter, though Mennonite conscripts could still opt for noncombatant service in the army, military training was unavoidable unless, as very occasionally happened, a young man was prepared to face repeated terms of imprisonment. The militarization of Mennonite youth inevitably followed.

At the beginning of the nineteenth century the south and west German brethren still stood unitedly behind a nonresistant witness. In 1803 a conference of southern church leaders held at Ibersheim in the Palatinate went on record to this effect, reiterating their intention of disfellowshipping any member who bore arms until such time as he expressed regret at his behavior; two years later another conference at Ibersheim forbade at least those who held administrative posts in the church to take public office. Yet, for all the confident tone of these resolutions, the old testimony against war and magistracy was already weakening among the younger generation. We find elders complaining of this: some of the young people, they say, can only with difficulty be restrained from taking up arms when their contemporaries are being called to the colors. And, after the creation of the Confederation of the Rhine by Napoleon in 1806, the old privileged exemptions were withdrawn: the same situation soon prevailed, too, in regard to the congregations west of the Rhine and those of the North Sea coast when their areas were incorporated directly into the French Empire, All able-bodied males, on reaching the age of twenty-one, now became liable for service in the imperial armies regardless of religious affiliation, unless their parents were able to find sufficient funds to hire a substitute.

In the grand duchies of Hesse and Baden and in the kingdoms of Württemberg and Bavaria, the final defeat of Napoleon in 1815 and the partial restoration of the old order did not lead to a return of the Mennonites' exemption. Whereas at first each congregation had felt itself under an obligation to provide substitute money if a family was too poor to do so on its own, this system eventually broke down. "Some families who had no sons of military age refused to bear the expenses of others. Thus the young men who were subject to military duty, if they had no money, had to choose between accepting military service and emigration."

In the lower Rhineland and Westphalia, which had fallen to Prussia as a result of the Vienna settlement of 1815, Mennonites were accepting military service in increasing numbers even though, according to W. Mannhardt writing early in the 1860's, they still remained in the minority (a view that might be contested, however). But the significant point is that, even though no official decision was ever taken to reject nonresistance and conscientious objection, members were no longer being disciplined for their break with the traditional Mennonite pattern of behavior. In most congregations a consensus of opinion upheld at least the right to a free choice on this issue. Some members,

413

indeed, continued to object to military service. For the traditionalists, the existing arrangement of hiring substitutes was not merely distasteful but financially onerous. After appealing to King Frederick William III for relief, they were granted exemption on payment of a 3 percent income tax. In exchange for this privilege, however, they were deprived, like their "West Prussian" brethren (see below), of the right to purchase non-Mennonite land without special permission and also made ineligible for government office. On the other hand, those Mennonites who accepted military service (*die wehrpflichtigen Mennoniten*) now became eligible for office along with the rest of the citizenry.

East Friesland, which contained several important Mennonite congregations, became part of the new kingdom of Hanover in 1815. During a brief return to Prussian rule (1813-1815) Mennonites had protested against attempts to conscript their young men into the army transportation corps, citing as a precedent the freedom from bearing arms which they had enjoyed before Prussia ceded the area to Napoleon in 1806. A delegation visited the king while he was at Frankfurt-am-Main and extracted from him a promise of exemption, in exchange for an undefined "proportional equivalent" in money to be paid over to the army authorities. To the Mennonites' chagrin the latter exacted a much larger sum from them than they had expected. This experience seems to have dampened the already declining interest of the East Friesland Mennonites in nonresistance. At any rate, after the province had passed under Hanoverian rule and the hiring of a replacement once more became the only method of escaping direct military service, the Mennonites of Emden in 1816 rejected a government proposal that the cost of buying substitutes for its young conscripts should be a collective responsibility, pleading as their excuse the heavy burden of poor-relief already resting on a comparatively small congregation. Next year, the government offered to exempt Mennonites in East Friesland if their congregation agreed to put foward the money in each case: the price demanded was one hundred thalers per conscript. "The Emden congregation refused this offer, whereas [the neighboring] Norden congregation collected a sum for the purpose." In 1831 the Hanoverian authorities were informed that nonresistance had ceased to be an official tenet of the church, and by the time East Friesland returned once again to Prussia in 1867, nonresistance among the Mennonites of this area was virtually extinct.

The doctrine retained more strength at Hamburg-Altona and in the congregations of Schleswig-Holstein. The most plausible explanation of this difference between not so far-distant communities lies in the degree of influence exercised by the Dutch *Doopsgezinden*: East Friesland, just next door to the Netherlands, was even more suscepti- ble to the latter's "liberal" views, whether on theology or military service, than were the Hamburgers and the Schleswig-Holsteiners. Even though among the latter too, the rising German nationalism stirred the Mennonite communities, it did so less vigorously than in the north-west of the country.

At Hamburg in 1818 the congregation found itself involved in legal difficulties when a Mennonite, disowned for accepting a militia lieutenancy, filed a suit against it in an effort to gain reinstatement in membership. Despite a court order in the lieutenant's favor, the con- gregation successfully resisted pressure by the authorities of the free city. But the position of the conscientious objector became more diffi- cult during the next few decades. The municipality in practice en- forced militia service on all without distinction, so that the old Men- nonite privilege of exemption in effect lapsed. At first the congregation opposed the practice of hiring a substitute, regarding it as being as objectionable in principle as the direct bearing of arms. But eventually they were forced to compromise and sanction this as the sole alterna- tive to emigration or imprisonment.

Until 1864 Schleswig and Holstein were united to the Danish crown by a personal union. Mennonite exemption from military service in the two duchies rested on privileges granted several centuries earlier. And so long as Danish rule lasted, the position remained unchanged despite mounting pressure from the community at large, which considered such things to be anachronistic, and despite efforts to enforce legisla- tion putting an end to the Mennonites' exceptional legal status in the matter. The church continued to disfellowship members who con- sented to bear arms and to petition the government in favor of retain- ing legislative provision for conscientious objection. Rural and small- town congregations like the one at Friedrichstadt took the strict view, at least in theory—"Hiring a substitute is tantamount to personal serv- ice (*Stellvertretung ist Dienst*)"—though it became increasingly difficult for their conscripts to live up to this maxim in practice.

The Springtime of the Peoples aroused the hopes of Germany's liberal nationalists that 1848 would see the restoration of German unity. Their expectations became fixed upon the proceedings of the all- German parliament at Frankfurt-am-Main. Two Mennonites held seats in the parliament: Isaak Brons of Emden, a prosperous businessman and deacon of his church, who was appointed commissioner for marine affairs (*Reichskommissar in Marinesachen*) in the provisional government (he was a keen enthusiast for a German fighting fleet), and Hermann von Beckerath of Crefeld, who also held a ministerial portfolio, that of finance.

In July the provisional German administration of Schleswig-Holstein had specifically exempted Mennonites from military service. But the next month, when several deputies at Frankfurt spoke in favor of including a similar clause in those sections of the new *Reich* constitution which dealt with universal military service, they were unsuccessful. The most vigorous opposition to their proposal came from no other than the Mennonite von Beckerath! He said:

> I do not deny that the proposals [for exemption] issue from a well-intentioned human point of view; but, Gentlemen, they are based on political concepts which no longer exist. It must be remembered that since no universal military service existed in Prussia at the time when the Mennonites received the right to withdraw from military service and as a compensation had to accept certain restrictions on their citizenship rights, the Mennonite privilege did not constitute an infraction of the right of other citizens. But when in 1808 in Prussia every able-bodied man was obligated to military service the Mennonite exemption constituted an abnormality, and now that a free state is to be established whose strength rests upon the equality of its citizens in rights and duties, such a special privilege becomes utterly untenable. . . . Mennonites in Rhenish Prussia with few exceptions render military service without question, and refusal of military service is in no sense considered as an integral part of Mennonite doctrine. It is certain that in other parts of Germany the heightened appreciation of the state will result in the performance there [by Mennonites] of this first duty of the citizen. But even if here and there this should not be the case, and individual conscientious objectors might arise, this would be a condition which it would be impossible to take into account in the establishment of the basic constitutional provisions. . . . I declare that it is contrary to the welfare of the Fatherland to provide for any exception in the fulfilment of citizenship duties, no matter on what ground.

However, von Beckerath's views aroused an immediate reaction among the conservative congregations in the eastern provinces of Prussia, the so-called Old Prussian or West Prussian Mennonites. On 14 September their leaders drew up a sharply worded protest which they dispatched to the legislators at Frankfurt. They contested von Beckerath's statement implying that almost all German Mennonites had abandoned nonresistance. Quite the contrary, they said, the West

Prussian congregations were united in their willingness to suffer civil disabilities if in this way they could retain their military exemption. "For most of our members, it is still today the object of their dearest conviction not to take any part in military service. A conviction which has become an innermost truth is not to be changed like a piece of clothing."

The liberal nationalist cause collapsed in 1849, the Frankfurt parliament being dissolved in June of that year. The end of the revolution did not signify the disappearance of the threat to the existence of special Mennonite military exemption, which was posed by the principle enunciated by von Beckerath: namely, that the duties of citizenship in a modern state precluded the acceptance of a privileged position in relation to the rest of the community. By mid-century, as we have seen, this view had won wide acceptance among the Mennonites of west and south Germany, even though von Beckerath in his speech quoted above seems to have given a slightly exaggerated picture of its incidence. In these areas no serious agitation was undertaken outside of Schleswig-Holstein to secure the right of conscientious objection. As in the Netherlands half a century earlier, here too the Mennonite peace testimony vanished as a result not so much of external pressure as of internal decay.

After the revolutionary events were over, the Prussian administration had assured the more traditionalist Mennonite communities in West and East Prussia of the continued application of their *Gnadenprivilegium* of 1780. Yet their anxiety on this score was not put at rest. And understandably, for not only did they feel less secure concerning the younger generation's allegiance to nonresistance but they also sensed that the will to sweep away their military exemption, exhibited by both state and society, had merely subsided temporarily and that it had not by any means disappeared for good.

Before we discuss the storm which blew up for the Mennonites of West Prussia in the late 1860's, we must retrace our steps and examine the record of their struggle to maintain exemption from military obligation since the end of the eighteenth century where we broke off in chapter 6.

King Frederick William II had been succeeded in 1797 by his son Frederick William III. Although the deceased monarch was not in fact able to do much for the Mennonites, he had been benevolently disposed toward them. This could not be said of the new ruler, who did not particularly relish the idea of noncombatant subjects. In 1801 he authorized the issue of a decree restricting the applicability of the *Gnadenprivilegium* of 1780 strictly to the lands then owned by Mennonites and still held by their descendants. In an effort to entice some of their young folk to do military service, he freed them from the obligation to take an oath on entering service. Restriction of land purchase led at once to a massive exodus of Mennonites. They looked now to Russia as the promised land, since their brethren settled there for over a decade enjoyed complete exemption from military service and almost unlimited possibilities of carving out good farms from the virgin territories of Ukraine. Thus, the Prussian government was forced to retreat a little in an effort to stop the loss of still more Mennonites. In 1803 it extended the advantages of the *Gnadenprivilegium* to all lands held by Mennonites in 1780, even when the present owner was not descended from the original Mennonite proprietor. Although the extent of Mennonite-owned land still remained frozen, this concession succeeded in appeasing at least part of their community which might otherwise have emigrated. The position remained unchanged until the dismantling of Mennonite military privilege at the end of the 1860's.

During the troubled period of the Napoleonic Wars the Mennonites made a series of free-will gifts to the monarch and his administration. As had been the case with similar gifts made by their Dutch cousins to the Netherlands government in the sixteenth and seventeenth centuries, the money was understood by both parties as a contribution to the war effort. Thus, in 1806 West Prussian Mennonites presented thirty thousand thalers to the king while he and his family were passing through the East Prussian town of Ortelsburg (Szczytno) after the disastrous defeats at Jena and Auerstadt. Four years later, a further sum of ten thousand thalers was donated to help the government, which was then experiencing difficulties in making up the *Contributionsgeld* owing to the continent's French master. And in the years of the Prussian War of Liberation from Napoleonic domination, 1813 and 1814, the Mennonite farming communities collected huge quantities of foodstuffs—butter, cheese, fruit, vegetables, meal, and meat—for use by the troops. They gave money, too, and clothing and footware.

All this of course did not necessarily signify a decline in their allegiance to nonresistance. It could be brought into line, without much difficulty, with the traditional, rather narrow concept of *Wehrlosigkeit*, which eschewed mainly a personal participation in war. It also expressed the Mennonites' warm gratitude to their government for continuing to allow them, even in those difficult times, to be "defenseless" as their forefathers had been. They might have reason to complain about certain restrictive conditions, but their position was still a privileged one when measured with the lot of their fellow Prussians who were not of Mennonite persuasion or with the fate experienced in the past by their coreligionists in other lands. But their action also reflected the rising patriotic sentiment which had made its appearance, at last, even among the rural Mennonites of West Prussia. This factor, though natural, was slightly ominous: it portended difficulties in the future for those who strove to keep the brotherhood on the path of nonresistance.

However, at this period near-unanimity on the subject prevailed. Only a few hotheads among the youth had to be disowned when they transgressed the discipline and joined the armed forces: some later returned to the church and were received back after expressing due regret at their un-Mennonite conduct.

Early in 1813, a potentially dangerous situation for the whole community was only narrowly averted. In the country's hour of peril the Prussian Estates ordered the creation of a special territorial reserve (*Landwehr*): at first it was ruled that no exemptions were to be permitted, the *Gnadenprivilegium* being held to be inapplicable to service in this new body. Finally, however, the military commander General Yorck, after the Mennonites had opened negotiations with him, agreed to a compromise whereby the Mennonite community "in the provinces of Lithuania, East and West Prussia" was required, as a collective obligation, to deliver within four weeks five hundred good horses for use by the cavalry as well as the considerable sum of twenty-five thousand thalers as a "contribution to the costs of the present formation of the *Landwehr*."

A few months later, despite their meeting their obligations under this agreement, the Mennonites were faced nonetheless with further demands from the military. With most able-bodied young men called up for combatant service in the army, there was an acute shortage of labor in such auxiliary branches as the transportation corps. Enlistment of Mennonites for this kind of work appeared a perfect solution for the army's difficulties. The military authorities could see no objection to compulsorily enrolling Mennonites; they would not be required to carry arms, their main duty being to help transport baggage and to care for the horses, nor would they be subject to military discipline, their status being that of paid civilian laborers. The congregations, however, saw the matter otherwise. Their objection to every variety of personal "military service" had been recognized by the government, they protested. True, they were ready to support the state "which respects and tolerates us"—but only in so far as conscience allowed. The commanding officer at Grudziądz, where a number of young Mennonites rounded up for such service were being held, agreed to delay further proceedings until Mennonites received an answer to their petition to the government. This, when it came, rather surprisingly coincided fully with the Mennonite position. It confirmed that the transportation corps formed an integral part of the army, and it ordered the release of all Mennonites who had been conscripted for service in the corps. In gratitude for this display of good-will, the Mennonites shortly afterward decided to make a voluntary contribution of two thousand thalers and six thousand ells of linen.

One cannot repress the thought that the authorities may have designed the whole proceedings as a form of pressure to extract just such a "free-will" offering from the "grateful" sect. This impression is strengthened by the fact that on two further occasions—in the summer of 1813 with the calling into being of another special emergency force, the *Landsturm*, and from the autumn of 1814 to the summer of 1815, when universal compulsory service was temporarily enforced in Prussia—the same play was enacted. First, the Mennonites were told that their privilege of exemption did not apply under the new military conscription and then, after their protest had been lodged with the government, the latter graciously relented and the Mennonite community, whether "voluntarily" or by order, made yet another considerable contribution to the military treasury. In Danzig Mennonites carried out fire-extinguishing duties during a siege of the city in 1813, while in Elbing they agreed to pay substitutes to take their places in the city watch.

Writing from Paris in June 1814, the Prussian Chancellor, von Hardenberg, had expressed his hope that the West Prussian Mennonite communities might eventually be weaned away from nonresistance, now that the conditions that originally gave birth to that doctrine had passed away. But, he added, "it is self-evident that this must proceed from their own teachers, since the intervention of the temporal power, as experience has sufficiently shown, would only harden them in it still further." To do this would be extremely foolish, since "the keeping of a settlement [like the Mennonites'] which is distinguished by affluence and civic virtues cannot be anything but an advantage for the state."

After peace returned to Europe in 1815, the Mennonites of West Prussia, too, enjoyed a long period of quiet in respect to their peace testimony. For over half a century their *Gnadenprivilegium* continued in force. A separate *Gnadenprivilegium* which had been granted by Frederick II in 1765 to the Mennonites of the not-far-distant Netzebruch was withdrawn, however, in 1831, whereupon they chose emigration to Russia rather than pay an additional tax of 5 percent for military exemption, which was the only alternative offered. The withdrawal was to prove an ominous precedent for the future.

At the conclusion of the War of Liberation the disownment of members who had participated either as volunteers or as conscripts caused a brief brush between the West Prussian Mennonites and the law. The courts, however, upheld the congregations' right to consider any who contravened Mennonite discipline on this point as having automatically severed their connection with the church by the act of serving with arms, and to refuse readmission thereafter to those who had been so excluded. The congregation at Königsberg well expressed the church's standpoint in a brief of July 1817:

> Their religious and creedal teachings have remained unaltered in their original purity, . . . it is an essential article of their belief not to engage in military service. And any Mennonite who acts contrary to these fundamental principles ceases at that moment to be a Mennonite. He himself cuts himself off voluntarily from the congregation, so that here there can be no talk of exclusion from the side of the congregation.

In addition, Mennonites disowned members who, even if they did not themselves personally bear arms, agreed to hire others to do so rather than surrender property purchased from non-Mennonites, to which the *Gnadenprivilegium* did not apply. (We may note, from the other side, that occasionally permission was given to accept new members from other denominations and that they received the privilege of military exemption, even though normally Mennonite proselytization continued to be disallowed by law.)

The prospect for an indefinite prolongation of the Mennonites' exemption from military obligation grew less promising as each decade passed. We have seen that it was challenged in 1848 by a prominent member of the Mennonite brotherhood and that among the congregations in the west of Germany nonresistance during this period was being discarded altogether. In the 1850's and early 1860's the "Mennonite question" was discussed several times during the debates of the Prussian Diet. There were calls to put an end to their privileged position, and petitions were presented, too, to this effect. Increasingly nervous now concerning the future, the leaders of the West Prussian congregations did all they could to avert what appeared, at least to some of them, to be the inevitable. And a few lost heart and decided to emigrate. One group left in 1853 to take up territory on the Volga. This so-called Trakt settlement had received a promise from the Russian government of complete *Wehrfreiheit* for twenty years and the possibility thereafter of paying commutation money in lieu of personal service.

Several West Prussian Mennonite authors engaged in attempts to rally their wavering coreligionists behind the traditional doctrine of nonresistance. One of these was Peter Froese, elder of the congregation at Orlofferfelde, which sponsored the publication in 1850 of his tract entitled *Loving Admonition to Mennonite Fellow Believers in regard to the Article of Faith concerning Nonresistance* (*Liebreiche Erinnerung an die mennonitischen Glaubens-Gennosen in Hinsicht des Glaubens-Artikels von der Wehrlosigkeit*, published at Tiegerweide bei Tiegenhof). The author admitted that "in our present politically disturbed time" some members of the church had come to feel that nonresistance was incompatible with the duties of a citizen. "Military service," they said, "is a necessity which we too must fulfil." Froese himself was far from wishing to deny that military power remained necessary "for maintenance of order and quiet" in the state. This was traditional Mennonite teaching. In fact Froese's whole exposition went along familiar lines, his chief object being to prove that acceptance of army service ran contrary to his church's understanding of the Christian message. Occasionally the pamphlet reveals the influence of the contemporary peace movement: for example, when Froese expatiates on the horrors of the battlefield or argues that war shows merely which side is stronger and not which is right. But, on the whole, it displays little intellectual vitality and illustrates what Ernst Crous has designated as "the petrification" of nineteenth-century German Mennonitism (until it was reinvigorated through the influence of trends like pietism or rationalism which, however, showed scant sympathy for nonresistance).

A more ambitious attempt to present the case for nonresistance came in 1863 with the publication of Dr. Wilhelm Mannhardt's historical presentation of the *Military Exemption of the Old Prussian Mennonites* (*Die Wehrfreiheit der altpreussischen Mennoniten*). The book appeared "im Selbstverlage der Altpreussischen Mennonitengemeinde," i.e., privately printed by the Old Prussian Mennonite community. The author belonged to the Danzig Mennonite church which his father, Jakob Mannhardt, had served as pastor for many decades. In 1863 Wilhelm Mannhardt held the post of *Privatdozent* at the University of Berlin, where he taught folklore and philology; he was perhaps the best-educated man among the West Prussian Mennonites. The West Prussian community, therefore, decided to appeal to Mannhardt to compose a defense of their church's position from a historical and legal position after its leaders had been warned by a prominent government official that their privileged position really could not last much longer. In his book, which contained two hundred two pages of text and ninety-one pages of supplementary documents drawn from the Prussian state archives as well as from congregational records, he strove to show that Mennonites had been staunchly and consistently nonresistant since their inception (for Dutch and west German Mennonites who had abandoned nonresistance were arguing that this doctrine was of comparatively late growth). He also sought to prove that forcing them now to do army service would signify a forcing of religious conscience incompatible with enlightened statesmanship.

The volume was printed in three thousand copies and distributed widely. Whether Wilhelm Mannhardt himself still held fully nonresistant views at this time is not clear; at any rate, in print he warmly upheld the right of his coreligionists to conscientious objection to being conscripted and he warned the authorities that, if they tampered with this right, they might expect these hard-working citizens to choose emigration rather than submit to force. Later developments seem to indicate, however, that Mannhardt overestimated the strength with which the Mennonites of West Prussia still cleaved to the old ways in this respect. Yet this interpretation may be mistaken for, without Mannhardt's able presentation of his coreligionists' case, the Prussian government might never have granted the qualified exemption which its Mennonites were to continue to enjoy even after the eventual abrogation of their old *Gnadenprivilegium,* and it was probably only this concession which stemmed a mass emigration.

Prussia's defeat of Austria in the "Seven Weeks' War" of 1866 led the next year to the creation, under Prussian dominance, of a North German Confederation. In the new Confederation all able-bodied males were to become subject to military conscription: a paragraph confirming the continued exemption of Mennonites was struck out by the legislators, and in November 1867 a law was passed formally ending the Mennonites' privileged position in regard to military service. This measure caused consternation among the "Old Prussians." The hour of trial seemed to have struck. Whereas a few members secretly rejoiced that they would henceforward be able to serve their country with arms without incurring the ecclesiastical penalties which such behavior had entailed hitherto, many more spoke openly of emigration to some other and more hospitable land. Over the winter of 1867-1868 a number of gatherings were held in which church leaders and rank and file consulted together on what should be done to avert the catastrophe about to overwhelm their community.

When a delegation of five elders visited Berlin, however, the king and his ministers assured them that provision would be made for the scruples of the conscientious. "I trust," the king had remarked, "that some way may be found, without any violation of your religious belief, to enable you to continue living here in conformity with your creed." But the delegates discovered that in any case their young men were still to be required to do army service along with other conscripts, only they would not have to carry weapons and would be assigned to non-combatant branches of the army. These proposals were incorporated in a special Royal Cabinet Order of 3 March 1868, "whereby," it was laid down, "such members of old Mennonite families as did not voluntarily express their readiness to do military duty under arms, would be allowed to fulfil the obligation to serve, by acting as attendants in military hospitals, or as clerks, etc., in the office of the district commander of the *Landwehr*, or as stewards, artisans, or drivers." "Such Mennonites as . . . were destined for service under the district commander would be exempt from training in the use of arms."

Whereas hitherto the overwhelming majority of the church had been opposed to acceptance of full military service, which the government seemed to contemplate forcing on them, now division arose concerning the point at which a line should be drawn between what was acceptable and what unacceptable. Roughly three positions emerged at this juncture, though many felt entirely disorientated, having been brought up from childhood to regard their immunity from military conscription as an unchangeable element in their environment. First, there were those members who considered any form of army service to be incompatible with a truly Mennonite witness. They therefore rejected the compromise offered by the recent Cabinet Order and urged the whole community to emigrate rather than to submit on such terms. Although small in actual numbers, this group included several church leaders who enjoyed a high moral standing in the West Prussian Mennonite community. Next came a middle party which advised submission to the Cabinet Order on the principle of rendering unto Caesar such things as were his, and among Caesar's prerogatives they included the right to demand service of his subjects. But even Caesar held no unlimited right to the allegiance of Christians. Therefore, they argued, the church, while permitting members to answer their call-up and take noncombatant service in the national army, ought at the same time to discipline any young Mennonite who accepted full military service, even as a conscript, and disfellowship him if he persisted in bearing arms. Third, a growing number within the brotherhood— among them, we may note, was now Dr. Wilhelm Mannhardt—wished to leave the choice between combatant or noncombatant service entirely to the conscience of each individual. His decision should enjoy the respect of the church, and they opposed any attempt to make a dogma of conscientious objection. Among those who supported this position were all those of course who, while still desiring to continue their affiliation with the church, no longer adhered to nonresistance and were therefore quite willing to undertake combatant service if called upon to do so. (The congregation of Prussian "Lithuania," we may note, had divided on this issue in 1855, a considerable section withdrawing because they did not feel bound to observe non-resistance.)

The division of opinion ran deep and the danger of a schism loomed ahead. Assemblies of the West Prussian brotherhood held in 1868 and 1869 reached no definitive ruling: indeed, they avoided one in order to prevent the occurrence of a split. Some members pinned their hopes at first on gaining official sanction for a postponement of the enforcement of the conscription law on Mennonites "for a period of twenty years"; others called for appointment by the government of special commissioners to negotiate a new agreement on the matter with the Mennonites. Concerning the first proposition the government had answered simply that it was out of the question since the law had already come into force, while the second proposal, said the government, was impractical. The most it would concede—"with the view of avoiding any pressure on the conscience of those members of the Mennonite communities, who, notwithstanding the favors extended to them in the Royal Order, still objected to army service, and also with the object of giving them an opportunity, by means of emigration, of avoiding a conflict between their duties as subjects, and their religious convictions"—was to postpone for two years the call-up of any who decided after all not to serve, thus facilitating their emigration during this period of grace. This regulation, issued in November 1868, was signed by Chancellor Bismarck and the minister of war, von Roon.

In fact, the number of those who finally decided on emigration amounted to far less than had originally been expected. In every congregation the majority elected to remain, and in many there were no members emigrating at all. Only at Heubuden, under the influence of Elder Gerhard Penner, who led the opposition to the Cabinet Order, a substantial minority followed him and left for the United States in the late 1870's. Elder Johann Andreas of the Elbing-Ellerwald congregation, who tried at first to have all who complied with the Cabinet Order excluded from the common communion, even if they took merely noncombatant service, found himself in opposition to the majority of his congregation and was forced to resign. He departed later for the United States along with a few other members. Fürstenwerder, the congregation to which Johann Wiebe, another leading opponent of any form of army service, belonged, almost unanimously voted to accept the Cabinet Order. Wiebe, therefore, gave up his office; he soon afterwards emigrated to Russia.

Qualified acceptance of the new situation, along however with unwillingness to open the doors to any who chose to reject nonresistance altogether, was illustrated in the stand adopted by the preacher of the combined congregation of Montau-Gruppe (near Chełmno), Elder Peter Bartel. Bartel, like most of the other church leaders, would have preferred to see the government allow their young men to perform some kind of alternative service under civilian auspices, yet he did not feel its restriction to noncombatant duties in the army to be reason enough for emigration. Therefore, he wrote, "I saw no other way out except perforce to bend to the Cabinet Order." After the Cabinet Order had come into force, Bartel insisted that in his congregation all male candidates for baptism pledge themselves to serve only in a noncombatant capacity within the framework of the Cabinet Order, and he refused the rite to any who failed to give this pledge. Bartel then proceeded to draw up a "Congregational Order (*Gemeinde-Ordnung*)," incorporating in it a clause which justified such action. "We wish," he wrote there, "to preserve our souls so that they should not be spotted with innocent blood." And members were given until New Year's Day 1871 to sign: those who had not done so, he decreed, might no longer consider themselves members of the congregation. A minority of ninety-five refused to append their signature, withdrawing to set up a separate congregation in the neighborhood. It was only many decades later, and after Bartel's death, that the two congregations came together once more.

The influential Danzig congregation had come out from the beginning in favor of a "liberal" attitude: each individual, while submitting to the new law of the land, should decide according to his conscience whether to accept noncombatant or combatant duties. And the gradual spread of this viewpoint until it came to be generally accepted in all the West Prussian congregations, was due in part to the influence of the minister of the Danzig congregation, Jakob Mannhardt, father of the author of the *Wehrfreiheit der altpreussischen Mennoniten*. Mannhardt had been reared in the laxer atmosphere of west German Mennonitism. He was a university-trained man: when he had enrolled at the University of Tübingen, he became the first German Mennonite formally to study theology. He was also quite an accomplished journalist, and the *Mennonitische Blätter* which he started up in 1854 was "the oldest periodical of the German Mennonites." It helped greatly to reinvigorate the somewhat drooping intellectual life of the church—

and of course it served, too, to win support in the brotherhood, and especially among the West Prussian congregations where the paper chiefly circulated, for the kind of policies for which its editor stood. In Jakob Mannhardt's mind there was no doubt where the church's duty lay. "If we do not wish to be untrue to our confession," he had told his congregation in September 1868, "we shall demonstrate that we place personal devotion at the service of our suffering brethren who are under arms higher than the dead gold and silver which we have paid hitherto to the state for our military exemption."

Preacher Mannhardt was able to enlist the even more eloquent pen of his son to plead with the brethren in favor of accepting the *fait accompli*, whatever reservations any might still nurse in respect to certain details of the Cabinet Order. Completely reversing the views he had expressed only a few years earlier, Wilhelm Mannhardt now argued, in a series of seven articles published in his father's journal between December 1868 and January 1870, that neither Christ himself nor any "general moral laws" had forbidden men to participate in war. "Thus," he went on, "we can regard the old principle [of Mennonite nonresistance] as not being an essential item of our confession of faith." Although he hoped his church would continue to act as a "pioneer of freedom between the peoples," this role, in his view, did not require it to hang on to outmoded pacifist dogmas of this kind. Where the early Mennonites had gone wrong was in their attempt to set up on earth a community of the perfect: it was just this ideal which had led them to refuse to share with their fellow citizens the obligation of military service (*die sittliche Pflicht der Nothwehr*) and thus eventually to make Mennonitism incompatible with the concept of citizenship in a modern democratic state. In Germany the West Prussian Mennonites, at least, had hitherto remained an antiquated, semi-feudal, privileged "corporation." This had not helped to preserve the faith in its old freshness. There were, he wrote, Mennonites today, who were no longer nonresistants, and yet they were shielded from sharing the burdens carried by their peers—to which indeed they felt no conscientious scruples—simply by the fact of having been born into the Mennonite brotherhood.

Dr. Mannhardt drew a distinction between *Wehrfreiheit*, i.e., total exemption from national service, which he considered to be harmful under the existing circumstances, and *Militärfreiheit*, i.e., exemption from combatant duties only—and only for those who were genuinely nonresistant in their beliefs. *Militärfreiheit* was what the Royal Cabinet Order of 1868 had given: Dr. Mannhardt wholeheartedly approved its conditions. Once his church came to accept the novel situation which it had created, the old isolation (so carefully nurtured, we may interpose, by generation after generation of Mennonites) would disappear. All that could only be of benefit, he considered. Mennonites henceforward might take advantage of the full citizenship with which they were now to be endowed; they would become part of the wider Protestant movement; they would enter unreservedly into the life of state and society and become co-builders in the new Germany that was coming into existence.

Whereas the old-school Mennonites cherished a personal devotion to the monarch who gave them the right to worship in their own way and freedom from the obligation of bearing arms, the liberal Mannhardt saw a rosy future for his coreligionists in the enjoyment of the fruits of political liberty in a modern state. He accused the "conservative" leaders who opposed acceptance of the Cabinet Order of forming an ecclesiastical "hierarchy," and he spoke of "the spiritual censorship" which they hoped still to maintain over the minds and consciences of their congregations. Only full freedom of conscience in the brotherhood would answer the needs of the time, he concluded.

Dr. Mannhardt's support for an open policy in regard to the choice of service made by Mennonite conscripts did much to swing opinion within the congregations behind this view. After all, was he not the man to whom they had turned to defend their "defenselessness" when it had still seemed possible to preserve it intact? But his arguments would scarcely have convinced if a majority of the brotherhood had not been ready for his message: they were already beginning to reach out, like the Mennonites of west Germany, for fuller participation in the life of the state.

Nonetheless, as a Mennonite historian (H. G. Mannhardt) has written, later generations would find it difficult to picture "what a sensation it was when, for the first time, young Mennonites appeared in church in the uniform of a Prussian soldier." At first each congregation decided for itself whether to accept as members those young men who did combatant service. Only Heubuden, under the influence of its Elder Penner, continued for a time to regard performance of any army service whatsoever as incompatible with the Mennonite faith. Naturally such a position was frowned on by the Prussian authorities: increasing numbers within the West Prussian brotherhood rejected it, too, as an infringement of the rights of individual conscience. And even at Heubuden, as we have seen, Elder Penner was eventually repudiated by the majority in his own congregation. Wisely from their point of view, "liberal" church leaders like the two Mannhardts made no attempt to force the pace, confining themselves to publicizing their point of view and admonishing the brethren to preserve "the band of love and fellowship" despite the sharp division of opinion on the issue.

The outbreak of the Franco-Prussian War in July 1870 caused a wave of patriotism to spread throughout the Prussian lands. Old Prussian Mennonites, especially the younger generation, succumbed to it, in many cases, along with the rest of the population. This patriotic enthusiasm helped to ease the painful transition between their former *Wehrfreiheit* and the new situation created by the Cabinet Order of 1868. Some young men from the brotherhood chose to serve their country under arms, a few even volunteering for such service, and in most cases they received no admonishment from their elders. On 2 October, a month after the French defeat at Sedan, the Danzig congregation (this was the congregation over which Jakob Mannhardt presided) passed unanimously the following resolution:

> Although we acknowledge, as our fathers did, that every war is a great evil and the outcome of sin and regard it as our special calling to present the love and the peace of the gospel of Jesus Christ through our constitution and through all expressions of our community life, yet it seems to us very difficult to perceive in the utterances of the holy Scripture the unconditional inadmissibility of the military obligation resting on every [male] citizen. Therefore we refrain now from passing a binding and obligatory regulation concerning participation in military service, and, amending our existing confession on this point [i.e., where it forbade any form of army service], we unite in leaving each one of our brethren free to decide in his conscience before God in what manner and to what degree it is permissible for him to submit to the government's demands. At the same time, however, we declare that we regard it as most suited to the character of our community when our members participate in military service only as drivers, attendants in military hospitals, clerks, or artisans.

The Danzig congregation, which contained the largest agglomeration of urban Mennonites, led the way here: the country brethren, sooner or later, followed them.

On the conclusion of hostilities the preacher Mannhardt composed an editorial entitled "Peace!," which appeared in the March 1871 issue of his *Mennonitische Blätter*. Patriotic emotion suffused its author, who barely found time at the beginning for a line or two of thankfulness that the bloodshed was over and peace returned. Our fatherland is united, he goes on, thanks to the heroic German soldiers who fought and died. They fought "to defend the German Rhine against wanton and rapacious attack. A terrible judgment has been meted out to the frivolous French." And he rejoiced, above all, at the return of his Mennonite brothers in Alsace and Lorraine "from foreign rule to their homeland (*aus der Fremde in das Vaterhaus*)."

Jakob Mannhardt's was by no means an isolated voice among the West Prussian Mennonites. Even if ecstasy did not reach such heights as it did among some Mennonites in west Germany (e.g., the sermon by Jakob Ellenberger, Jr., to his congregation at Eichstock, Bavaria, printed in the Danzig *Mennonitische Blätter*, November 1872), the same enthusiasm at the uniting of Germans in the new *Reich*, the same glowing pride in being German, is expressed here too. The Lord of Hosts had given Prussia victory!

Gradually, concern for nonresistance, even in the watered-down form still possible after 1868, drained away in the West Prussian brotherhood. In the early 1870's the *Mennonitische Blätter* occasionally printed articles in its defense. But as the controversy over noncombatant service died down, and as its intransigent opponents emigrated singly or in groups, these slowly disappeared.

The establishment of a united Germany led to the extension of the terms of the Royal Cabinet Order of 1868 to the rest of the new *Reich*. In the west and south of the country there were by now few young Mennonites anxious to take advantage of the possibility of noncombatant service thus opened to them. In the north-west, as we have seen, nonresistance was already a thing of the past. "The [Mennonite] catechisms of the Palatinate and Hesse . . . of 1861, and of Baden . . . of 1865 had already tacitly dropped the principle." Even the Amish of central Germany, who were in the process of finally amalgamating with their Mennonite brethren, at a conference held in 1867 had decided to leave the matter of army service open: "How each congregation and each young man will indeed preserve our ancient Mennonite nonresistance, in order to satisfy his own conscience and the demands of the authorities, we leave to the judgment of each one." "This," comments Ernst Crous, "was the formula later often repeated to save the principle and at the same time abandon it."

In her pioneering history of Mennonitism (first published at Norden in 1884 as *Ursprung, Entwickelung und Schiksale der Taufgesinnten oder Mennoniten in kurzen Zügen übersichtlich dargestellt*), Anna Brons, a devoted member of the Emden congregation and wife of the liberal nationalist politician Isaak Brons, discussed briefly in the ninth chapter of her book the attitude then held by the church in regard to war. Among Mennonites, *das Vaterland*, she wrote, was now considered worthy to be defended. She praised the Christian heroism of the

Mennonite soldiers who fought and fell in the Franco-Prussian War. "A war of defense, such as Germany waged in the War of Liberation [1813-1814] and in 1870-1871, no one [among us] would have the effrontery to condemn." Of course, she was not thinking primarily of the West Prussian Mennonites but of those in the north-west of the Empire, the section of German Mennonitism in which she had spent her life. Among the former, nonresistance still remained a possible alternative to the acceptance of war as waged by the nation-state, as it did too, though to a very much less extent, among a few congregations in south Germany. (The American Mennonite *Herald of Peace* of 1 July 1895 even reported the case of a brother Troehnert, who had just been sentenced to a year's imprisonment for refusing induction into the German army; but by that date such rigorism must have been quite exceptional.)

"It is an honor to wear the king's uniform," wrote a respected leader of south German Mennonitism, Christian Neff, in 1908. During the half-decade remaining before the outbreak of World War I, about half the Mennonite conscripts were serving under arms even from the area where nonresistance maintained some kind of standing. Out of a total of fifty-nine Mennonites from all parts of the country in the army in 1913, only twenty-one had chosen to do this in a noncombatant branch. "Among the Mennonites killed during World War I there were three times as many officers as among the other denominations" (E. Crous). In the Danzig congregation about half of those called up into the armed forces served as officers or noncommissioned officers. Yet there was a small minority of Mennonites, even in 1914-1918, who still chose to make use of the noncombatant option offered since 1868. In the interwar years, however, nonresistance disappeared altogether in German Mennonitism, even in its more traditionalist West Prussian branch (whose congregations had been divided by the Treaty of Versailles between the Free City of Danzig, the restored Polish state, and Germany). After Hitler's accession to power in 1934, the official organization of German Mennonitism—the "Vereinigung der Mennonitengememeinde im Deutschen Reich"—formally renounced nonresistance on behalf of its members, and when conscription was reintroduced in Germany Mennonites made no attempt to reclaim their old right to noncombatant army status. The former *Wehrlosen* were now eager to defend the fatherland. Nazi ideology proved attractive to the younger generation of Mennonites, especially those who lived in the east either under Polish rule or in the territory of the Free City. However, the church, though strongly nationalist, did not succumb as a whole to Nazi indoctrination. Of nonresistance or conscientious objection, however, there was no talk until after the downfall of the Hitlerite regime.

During the interview which the delegates of the West Prussian Mennonites had had with the Prussian Crown Prince in February 1868, one of them, Peter Bartel, had remarked that the brethren were ready to emigrate rather than be forced to enter the army. "Emigrate—and where to, then?" the crown prince interjected. "To the southern provinces of Russia, Your Highness," said another delegate, Johann Wiebe. To which the Crown Prince responded: "Ay, then leave the way open to your children to return, since in Russia what has happened here is going to happen shortly and then you'll be sorry!" The Crown Prince had guessed correctly, for within a couple of years a bill to enforce universal military service was under way in Russia.

The "Russian" Mennonites' *Wehrfreiheit*, their exemption from military obligation, had been solemnly guaranteed "for ever" by Catherine II and by her successors. From small beginnings in Catherine's reign the Mennonite colonies which dotted the steppes of Ukraine had slowly expanded. The original settlements at Chortitza and Molotschna in the course of the decades gave birth to a number of daughter settlements, and by the end of the century these were to be found not only in Ukraine, Crimea, Transcaucasia, Congress Poland, Volhynia, and several other provinces of European Russia, but in central Asiatic Russia as well. Hard work and good farming methods brought prosperity. But this prosperity unfortunately had not been evenly distributed throughout the brotherhood. By the mid-nineteenth century, whereas on the one hand about two-thirds of the Russian Mennonites formed "a landless proletariat," on the other vast landed estates were being piled up by a handful of their coreligionists. Although something was done thereafter by communal action to remedy the land shortage within the existing colonies or to found new colonies, social tensions between the landed and the landless continued to trouble the Mennonite community up until the Revolution. Economic differentiation found expression, too, in religious life: a schismatic group arose in 1860 under Pietist and Baptist influence and formed its own separate *Brüdergemeinde* (later to be known as the Mennonite Brethren Church). Membership of the *Brüdergemeinde* was drawn chiefly from the poorer strata in the various settlements: the well-to-do at first tried to suppress the new development, attempting even to enlist the state authorities on their side.

In fact, the Mennonites in Russia formed, as it were, "a state within a state," enjoying wide-ranging political and cultural autonomy in rela-

432

tion to the Russian administration. Their communities incorporated
the kind of close interconnection of church and state against which
their ancestors had reacted in the sixteenth century, thereby becoming
pioneers in the separation of these two institutions. Moreover, their
elected officials like the mayor were legally endowed with governmental authority and could impose sentences of fines, prison, flogging,
and forced labor. Even if their powers in this respect were very limited and their jurisdiction restricted to petty offenders, the principle
might seem to conflict with the traditional Mennonite view of nonresistance, which rejected the coercive aspects of police and government. However, since more serious crimes came under the purview of
the state courts and no powers were exercised over non-Mennonites,
the community undoubtedly came to regard the position as merely
extending congregational discipline in a way that remained consistent
with the tenet of nonresistance. Yet a feeling of unease continued in
respect to this situation. At the beginning of the *Brüdergemeinde*, for
instance, "in the white heat of consistent, radical zeal, some even went
so far as not to ask for the return of stolen goods, and even not to seek
the aid of the police" (Krahn).

The Russian Mennonites, growing rich—at least some of them—
under the protection of the Autocrat and isolated from their environment by their communal self-sufficiency, continued to feel secure both
in regard to their exemption from military service and to the maintenance of their German language and culture. Yet in nineteenth-
century Russia the winds of change were blowing. Great Russian
nationalism had powerful adherents in official circles: these resented
the influence, and sometimes even the mere presence, of non-Russian
peoples within the empire. Militarism and the pursuit of *Realpolitik*
led army leaders and ambitious politicians to urge the need for universal conscription in order to keep abreast with other powers, like
France or Prussia, which were reorganizing their military system so
as to create a nation in arms.

The announcement in 1870 that a bill to enforce universal military
service was to be introduced seems, indeed, to have taken the Russian
Mennonite community by surprise, despite the recent experience of
their West Prussian brethren (with whom they shared not only a common ancestry but the same traditional culture). At first the leaders,
trusting in the benevolence of the monarch, expected that by direct
appeal to him they would be successful in maintaining their privileged
status in regard to army service, though they were prepared, if necessary, to pay a tax in exchange for this as their brethren in Germany
had done in the old days. Therefore, during the next five years we find

a series of Mennonite delegations being sent to St. Petersburg for negotiations with high Tsarist officials. Sometimes the delegates represented individual colonies or groups of colonies; at other times they spoke in the name of the whole Mennonite community.

Hopes of speedy success in their mission were soon dampened. In February 1871 the government announced that, while Mennonites were not to be required to bear arms, they would have to serve in the army along with other conscripts. They would be assigned to hospital or similar noncombatant duties. The idea of a money payment in exchange for a guarantee of collective exemption, which the Mennonites had suggested, the government declared to be unacceptable. How could Mennonites object to humanitarian service whose object lay in saving life, asked officials impatiently. Their irritation was increased by the fact that few of the delegates could speak Russian, and even fewer could speak it well.

The Mennonites tried to explain that, whereas they had always been ready to care for wounded soldiers as individuals and outside the military framework—as the record of their settlements in the Crimean War showed—they objected to doing this under army auspices, since they believed that thereby they became accessory to the killing of fellow human beings. In addition, they expressed fears concerning the profane influence of army life on their boys should they be forced to serve (officials, on the other hand, thought such training would do them a world of good). A friendly Moravian pastor, Theodor Hans, who was resident in St. Petersburg, now offered to act as a kind of unofficial mediator between the government and the Mennonites and to represent their interests in the absence of a delegation in the capital. In May 1872 Hans informed them of a recommendation just made to the Council of State by the Military Service Commission. "Those Mennonites who will be called to military service," it declared, "will only be used behind the front in hospitals or similar establishments (not munition factories), and are to be exempted from the bearing of arms. This ruling, however, does not apply to such Mennonites who join the sect after the appearance of this ruling or such as enter the Russian realm as immigrants after its appearance." At the same time that Pastor Hans transmitted the proposed ruling to the Mennonites, he informed them that the government regarded it as a big concession from its side and an earnest of its willingness to respect their scruples concerning arms-bearing.

Meanwhile, back in the Mennonite settlements unease had given place to alarm as it became clear that some form of service would probably be required of them. Agitation for emigration grew among those unwilling to compromise on this issue: it found an able leader in Cornelius Jansen, a prosperous grain merchant from Berdyansk. During 1872 Jansen wrote and published at his own expense several pamphlets arguing the incompatibility with Mennonite principles of any kind of army service; though published in Danzig and not in Russia, they circulated freely throughout the Mennonite settlements. Even though Jansen was expelled from the country early in 1873 as an unfriendly alien (he was born in West Prussia and was the nephew of the rigorously nonresistant elder, Gerhard Penner of Heubuden, in whose household he had been reared), the movement for emigration continued to gain strength. In that same spring a delegation, consisting of twelve members and including two Hutterites, journeyed across the Atlantic to explore the possibility of settlement in the United States and Canada. The governments of both countries welcomed the idea of gaining such pious, sober, and hard-working immigrants, and did all they could to facilitate their coming. Although only the new dominion of Canada was prepared to give a legal guarantee of military exemption, there was no military conscription in effect in the United States, either, and there too the prospect of compulsory service appeared remote. Eventually, some eighteen thousand out of a total of forty-five thousand, over a third of the Russian Mennonites, left for North America, including all the Hutterites. The main body of immigrants left Russia in 1874, though the migration continued in decreasing intensity until the mid-1880's. Those who emigrated formed the more traditionally minded, the more culturally conservative, and the economically less well-to-do. Certainly the main impulse which led to emigration stemmed from religious conscience: the desire for land, however, also played a role, though a secondary one.

The migration might have taken on still larger proportions if the Russian government, seriously disturbed at the dimensions of the movement and the thought which this conjured up of losing most of its Mennonites, had not now decided on further concessions to the Mennonite standpoint. Whereas undoubtedly a section of the brotherhood, influenced perhaps by the example of the West Prussian community which had finally accepted noncombatant army service as defined in the Royal Cabinet Order of 1868, felt few scruples in regard to the noncombatant duties being offered by the Russian government, the vast majority rejected this position, though it was not yet clear how many of them went so far as to oppose any kind of alternative service run by the state.

On 1 January 1874 universal military service became law. Three months later, on 10 April, Pastor Hans wrote to the Mennonites: "I have just heard that His Majesty the Tsar [Alexander II] has decided to acquaint himself with your problem personally in the person of General Totleben [a Lutheran of German origin], with the hope that he can head off the projected emigration and keep you in his land. You know, dear brethren, . . . that His Majesty is kindly disposed toward you. Now you have the proof of action in your hands." The general set off soon after to visit the chief Mennonite settlement at Molotschna, where a committee of leaders was gathered to consult with him. The message Totleben brought from the Tsar was this: they would be permitted some form of service "entirely outside of the jurisdiction of the War Department." The Mennonite response was favorable. After the general's departure the assembled elders recorded their acceptance of "the principle of personal service in the name of the greater part of our brothers in the faith." They asked only "that it be made possible for us to situate our boys in places where we can have efficient supervision of them in closed groups, in order to give them the necessary spiritual care, and to maintain among them our church discipline, our articles of faith, and our church organization."

Agreement on principle had been reached. Therefore, on 14 May 1875 the Tsar issued a special ukase applying to all Mennonites who were members of the denomination and resident in Russia prior to the beginning of 1874 as well as to their descendants.

> The Mennonites are to be exempted from shouldering weapons, and are to do duty in the marine workshops, in fire protection, and in special mobile commands of the Forestry Service. . . . The length of service shall be identical to that of the military service law. The men in service shall be grouped separately in order to permit the practice of their church services according to their persuasion. After the completion of a term of service the men shall in case of war be called up only for the type of service indicated above.

Through Totleben's intermediacy Mennonite fears concerning the possible military implications of work in marine workshops were set at rest, the government agreeing, at the community's request, to assign all Mennonite conscripts to forestry service under the department of crown lands. The actual supervision of the camps was to reside with the Mennonites themselves. Such work was incontestably of a civilian character; it was of benefit to the whole community; moreover, arboriculture was an activity in which Russian Mennonites had made an important contribution from their first arrival in the almost treeless steppes of Ukraine nearly a century before.

436

Yet further lengthy negotiations were needed before the detailed arrangements were finally settled to the satisfaction of both sides. General Totleben, who meanwhile had been appointed governor general of the Odessa district, acted as honest broker between government and Mennonites. The latter wished to make absolutely sure that no connection existed between their service and the military. They wanted, too, to obtain a watertight guarantee that the running of the camps would remain a Mennonite responsibility. Negotiations were concluded by September 1880, and in the following year the first inductions took place, when two camps were opened with a complement of one hundred twenty-three young men.

The Forestry Service for Russian Mennonites lasted until its disbandment in 1918-1919 after the revolution. The work included afforestation, caring for nurseries and orchards, fighting pests and blight, etc. The conscripted men wore a special uniform and were under semimilitary discipline, while their leaders, sometimes elected and sometimes appointed, ranked as noncommissioned army officers. However, assignees were officially designated not as soldiers but "obligatory workers"; they ran the camps themselves under the supervision of directors who were appointed by the church and responsible to a special Mennonite Forestry Service council (in which the ministers had the largest say). The government, on the other hand, took care of the work projects and had a right of veto where the camp elected its leaders.

Maintenance of the Forestry Service placed a heavy burden on the church's resources. Whereas the government provided work tools and implements, medical care and pocket money, the Mennonite community paid the cost of upkeep of the barracks and of food and clothing for the men. At first it attempted to raise the money by voluntary subscription, but a mounting deficit forced it in the end to seek governmental approval for a tax on members of the church, graded according to the value of property held. Thus by 1914 "the large estate owners, though numbering only 1.9 per cent of the Mennonite population, contributed one third of the total . . . annually for the maintenance of the Forestry Service."

The term of service lasted four years. The numbers serving in any given year rose from about four hundred in 1881 to over one thousand in 1913. The Mennonites who remained in Russia accepted alternative service almost without a murmur. The only opposition now came from two small Mennonite subsects: the ultratraditionalist Apostolic Brethren (*Apostolische Brüdergemeinde*), whose conscripts, almost up to World War I, refused to go voluntarily to the forestry camps and had

437

to be removed there by force, and a chiliastic group which at the beginning of the 1880's, after the main body had finally accepted the Forestry Service, removed to Russian Turkestan, where universal conscription did not yet apply. But members of this group eventually conformed too, or emigrated: the only alternatives open to them once the same system of military service as prevailed in the rest of Russia came into force in this area, as well.

The Russian Mennonites' preference for emigration when faced with the prospect of having to do noncombatant duties within an army framework contrasts with the submission, admittedly somewhat reluctant, of the West Prussian Mennonites less than a decade earlier. Both communities were still largely rural; in addition they were close kith and kin, since most of the Russian Mennonites derived from families which had left West Prussia around the beginning of the century. But the West Prussian Mennonites had begun to assimilate with society more rapidly than had their "Russian" cousins, whom language and nationality, as well as location and religion, divided from the mainstream of Russian life. Many thousands of the latter, as we have seen, rejected even civilian alternative service as a compromise unworthy of the Mennonite profession. The majority, it is true, accepted the Forestry Service once they felt certain that it would remain under civilian control and that their young men could be preserved in Mennonite nonconformity to the world while undergoing their years of service. Such acceptance revealed a limited degree of acculturation but, except in the case of the wealthy Mennonite grandees who lived in the style of the neighboring gentry (one of them, for instance, was to be elected to the Duma on the conservative Octobrist ticket) or the well-to-do businessmen and industrialists of the community, this had scarcely gone very far before the outbreak of World War I. The Russian Mennonites remained a farming people, German in language and traditionalist in their culture.

In the First World War about fourteen thousand Mennonite men were called up. About half of them worked in the forestry camps, the other half being assigned to medical service, chiefly under the auspices of the "All-Russian Union of Zemstvos for Relief of Sick and Wounded Soldiers." This service was performed with the agreement of the church; the work, though carried out in close association with the army, was under civilian control. Indeed a handful of Mennonites had served in this way during the Russo-Japanese War of 1904-1905. Just as the Mennonite Forestry Service may be considered as in some respects a prototype of the Civilian Public Service (C.P.S.) instituted in the United States in World War II, this medical work paralleled to

438

some extent the work carried out in the two world wars by the Friends Ambulance Unit (F.A.U.) unofficially sponsored by British Quakers.

With Russian Mennonites there are indications that by 1914, at any rate, not all was well with their peace testimony. A Mennonite writer (Frank C. Peters) has pointed to the lack of initiative shown by the Mennonites when faced with the government's intention to enforce conscription: "Any advance in the attempt to offer some alternative service was made under pressure of government." The creative spark had already disappeared from their peace witness. This was even more true of the period which followed the inauguration of the Forestry Service in 1881. To the young men who, decade after decade, reported dutifully in camp for their term of alternative service, nonresistance as it was still being presented in the sermons they heard in church or in the articles they read in their church papers frequently meant little. For some Mennonites, indeed, nonresistance now appeared chiefly as one of the symbols of their German nationality rather than as a doctrine which was valid for the whole of mankind.

All this emerged into the open only after the revolution, for earlier the privileged status of Mennonite conscientious objectors shielded them from reality, while the continued exercise of congregational discipline, accompanied by threat of disownment for infringement of the Mennonite peace witness, prevented deviant behavior on this point, unless a dissident member was prepared to go so far as to break his ties with the church. Beginning in the late summer of 1917 the Mennonites, in view of the increasingly unsettled condition of the country, had slowly begun to dissolve the Forestry Service camps: the assignees returned home. "It was these demobilized boys who formed the nucleus of the ill-starred *Selbstschutz* [Self-defense]" (Sudermann), i.e., the improvised armed protection of Mennonite settlements in Ukraine and elsewhere organized during the troubled times from the end of 1918 to early 1920. These Mennonites took to arms only after great provocation, whole villages having been plundered and most of their inhabitants massacred by marauding bands (the followers of the anarchist chieftain Nestor Makhno gaining an especially bad name in this respect). Arms, ammunition, and training were provided mainly by the retreating Germans or by the "White" army of General Denikin. "The majority of the Mennonites of all settlements did not approve of any measure of self-defense, although they probably did not always clearly protest against its use," writes Krahn.

Although the Russian Mennonite peace testimony had been severely jolted by these experiences, even now nonresistance was not abandoned as a tenet of the faith as it was in the Netherlands and large

parts of Germany. In the early years of Soviet rule fairly generous
alternatives to military service were offered to religious pacifists,
Tolstoyans like Vladimir Chertkov taking the lead in defending their
interests: Mennonite conscientious objectors performed work under
civilian control, sometimes, as in Tsarist days, being employed in the
Forestry Service. There were still Mennonite objectors serving in this
way in the early 1930's. Even before this date some Mennonite conscripts, however, had accepted full military service (though there
were some, too, who chose prison if their application for exemption
was turned down). Evidently the congregational discipline in regard
to nonresistance fell into desuetude: it could scarcely have been upheld in view of the Soviet government's attitude. "Gradually young
men were forced to serve in the regular army." Fewer exemptions
were given, and "the alternative service camps resembled slave labor
camps in severity of treatment and difficulty of physical survival."

Yet general provision for conscientious objection was not formally
abolished until 1939—and then on the pretext that no applications for
exemption had been submitted from any quarter during the previous
two years. This was the heyday of Stalinism. That there have been a
few objectors to military service in the Soviet Union since that date is
certain; some may have been able to obtain assignment to noncombatant duties in the army, others may have been imprisoned or shot.
Little is known concerning their fate.

The 1930's and 1940's brought disaster to the Russian Mennonites.
Their settlements were dispersed and their inhabitants deported.
Thousands went into exile: many who remained suffered imprisonment and forced labor, and some were executed. But this tragic story
belongs outside the chronological framework of the present study.
Whether after the mid-1930's any Mennonites refused to serve with
arms in the Soviet forces is not known. However, Stalin destroyed their
communities, along with their cultural and religious life, not on account of their nonresistant views (however distasteful such opinions
might have been); he did it because he regarded Mennonites as
"kulaks" and an obstacle in his program of collectivization, and because their German ethnic origin appeared to him as a menace to the
security of the Russian state.

Since the death of Stalin a slight improvement has taken place in the
situation of the Russian Mennonites: at least the private celebration of
their cult has become possible once again. Following World War II,
which resulted in the expulsion of the West Prussian Mennonites from
the restored Polish state along with the rest of the German population,
a revival of interest in their nonresistant heritage has become appar-

440

ent among the German- and Dutch-speaking Mennonites of Western Europe, whose predecessors many generations ago had voluntarily given up their collective opposition to war. But a similar development does not at present appear likely among the Mennonites of the Soviet Union, despite the fact that there coercion from without more than interior conviction led to their abandoning pacifism only within the last half-century.

TWELVE. *Russian Sectarian Pacifism:*
The Tolstoyans

PACIFISM in Tsarist Russia extended beyond the enclosed community of the German-speaking Mennonites, for nonviolence and conscientious objection also formed part of the religious beliefs of several indigenous Russian sects, even if repudiation of war was not always strictly observed. In addition, toward the end of the nineteenth century the great Russian writer Leo (Lev) Tolstoy (1828-1910) spoke out in favor of an unconditional rejection of the state, and especially of its coercive aspects like war and capital punishment. Nonresistance to evil became the watchword of his disciples: these Tolstoyans were to be found not only in Russia, but in many other European lands as well as in North America. Tolstoyan ideas eventually took root even further afield; they were influential, for example, in shaping the philosophy of nonviolence propounded and practised by Mahatma Gandhi in India.

Religious dissent occurs in Russia as early as the fourteenth century, but most of the sects still existing at the outset of the twentieth century go back no farther than the seventeenth century, many being of fairly recent origin. The late medieval heresies have not survived. Like Western Protestantism, Russian sectarianism has been subject to fissiparous tendencies: the congregational organization common to most groups often led to division and still further subdivision. The typology of Russian sectarianism evolved so far by students of the subject leaves much to be desired. Older writers used such contrasting terms as "rationalist" or "mystical" sects; Soviet scholars like A. I. Klibanov speak of "pre-emancipation (*doreformennye*)" as against "post-emancipation (*poreformennye*)" sectarian movements. A more convenient classification perhaps would be their division into (1) denominations deriving from the great schism (*raskol*) within the Russian Orthodox Church of 1667, whose adherents are known collectively as Old Believers and are divided broadly into "priestly (*popovtsy*)" and "priestless (*bezpopovtsy*)" branches, (2) sects of independent, indigenous origin, and (3) sects introduced from abroad in the course of the nineteenth and twentieth centuries. We must remember, however, that some overlapping exists among these three categories.

Pacifism has been confined mainly, though not exclusively, to the second category. Several of the nativist sects, of which the Dukhobors and the Molokans are the most important, rejected violence on principle and included nonparticipation in war among the obligations of their members—at least in theory. Among the imported faiths which soon, however, put down roots among the Slav population of the empire, a small number of conscientious objectors emerged in recent times from among the Baptists, the Seventh-Day Adventists, and the Pentecostal sects. But in Russia these groups have not subscribed to any official peace witness, the vast majority of their members serving both the Tsarist and the Soviet state with arms when called upon to do so. Certain extreme priestless sects among the Old Believers approached a quasi-anarchist position and regarded the imposition of taxes and the enforcement of laws, the swearing of judicial oaths and the obligation of military service as incompatible with the Christian life. Such views were held, for instance, by the so-called prayerless (*nemolentsy*), a group founded by a former Don Cossack, Gabriel, in the second quarter of the nineteenth century and closely associated with the priestless Old Believers. Whether these opinions led to actual refusal of military service on the part of those who held them is not, however, certain. Finally, we may note that toward the end of the nineteenth century (and probably earlier, too, though the evidence here is not entirely clear) cases of Orthodox peasants refusing military service on account of religious scruples occur occasionally, though in most instances either Tolstoyan influences or contacts with Molokans or Dukhobors were responsible for a stand which ran directly contrary to the official teachings of the established Orthodox church.

If we disregard the Old Believers, the Molokans formed the most numerous and geographically the most widely distributed sectarian group in the empire. As with many other Russian nativist sects, the origins of the Molokans remain obscure. Their name seems to derive from their habit of drinking milk (*moloko*) during seasons of fast when this was forbidden by the Orthodox church. Most probably, they first emerged as the result of a schism which took place among the Dukhobors in the reign of Catherine II (see below) when one of their leading figures, Semen Uklein, feeling that the Dukhobors had strayed too far from a Bible-centered Christianity, broke away and started his own separate religious fellowship. Restitutionism—tempered, it is true, by a somewhat erratic interpretation of the Word with frequent eschatological undertones—remained the central feature of Molokan religion. To take human life was forbidden, at least without explicit instruction from the Almighty; for to do so, said a "Confession" of their faith composed in 1862, infringed both the Decalogue and the Sermon on the Mount.

Peasants, mostly free peasants, formed the majority of the sect, though artisans and small traders were represented in it, too. Many sources, including Orthodox writers hostile to sectarianism, testify to their refusal to bear arms. Exactly how Molokans reacted when called up for military service is not always easy to determine. They were eventually forbidden by law to hire substitutes among other denominations (their complaints on this point indicate that they would have liked to go on making use of this way out of military service if the authorities had not forbidden it). Before the introduction in Russia of universal military service in 1874 their young men, when drafted, probably went into hiding or deserted as soon as opportunity offered —or conformed. After 1874 we hear of their being assigned by the military authorities to noncombatant duties in the army, such as medical or transport work. Only once, in the year 1826, do we know of a widespread movement openly to refuse induction into the army: this was answered by sentences of flogging, hard labor in a penal battalion, and even incarceration in a lunatic asylum. Among the "Evangelical Christians," as those Molokans who came under strong Baptist influence in the latter part of the nineteenth century were known, opposition to bearing arms was officially withdrawn. Even among the remainder of Molokans the conscientious objector stand, though upheld in principle, seems to have fallen largely into desuetude around this time. It was revived again at the beginning of the twentieth century among certain members of one of the main branches of the sect (the *Skakuny* or Jumpers). Here the example of Dukhobor antimilitarism and the teachings of Tolstoy account for the radicalism of the stance now adopted: these men refused to serve in the army even in a noncombatant capacity. Like the Dukhobors, they eventually chose to emigrate, the outbreak of the Russo-Japanese War and the consequent tightening of the draft system acting as a stimulant to their decision. Between 1905 and 1908 some five thousand of the Jumpers left for the United States, where they settled in Los Angeles. In the New World, many Molokans, when conscripted, adopted an absolutist stand; this occurred in both world wars. However, in their homeland, where the Molokans were becoming increasingly middle-class and beginning to evolve slowly from a rural peasant sect into a bourgeois Protestant denomination, they relinquished their collective protest against war. In World War I the Molokans mostly bore arms; many became noncommissioned officers, and some took commissioned rank. We do not know how many held out for noncombatant service. But the number of those who refused to enter the army and appeared on this account before a military tribunal was exceedingly small in view of the fact that at that date there were several hundred thousand Molokans within the empire.

There were other Russian sects besides the Molokans and Dukhobors whose tenets forbade members to bear arms. But even in the case of the two larger bodies it is extremely difficult, at least until near the end of the nineteenth century, to trace actual incidence of conscientious objection or to extrapolate a coherent antiwar position for them from what we know concerning other pacifist sects elsewhere. Adherents of the smaller groups were recruited largely from illiterate peasants. They possessed, of course, no denominational press and no records of their own and rarely, if ever, published accounts of their faith. What we know of them is drawn from the works of outsiders, who were often hostile to the principles for which the sectarians stood. The accounts of such observers are often marked by superficiality and inaccuracy; in any case, the question of war does not figure prominently either among the interests of the observer or, seemingly, in the minds of the observed. We do know, however, that the Malevantsy, followers of the former Baptist, Kondratii Malevannyi, who foretold the coming end of the world and an approaching millennium, usually refused military service, as did those of the poet and mystic A. M. Dobrol'iubov. A Quaker relief worker in 1921 reports meeting members of a religious sect who called themselves Quakers. They possessed no formal organization or membership and conducted their religious services in a style resembling that of the Anglo-American Society of Friends. "They carried their disbelief in killing to such lengths," wrote Tom Copeman (in "The Strange Episode of the Russian 'Quakers,'" *The Friend* [London], 27 April 1945), "that they did not even kill lice but 'put them somewhere else.'" Their young men had suffered imprisonment under the Tsarist regime for refusal of military service. Who exactly these sectaries were and whether any genetic connection existed between them and Quakers in the West has never been established for certain. There were also cases of conscientious objection among members of such sects as the *Trezvenniki* and the New Israelites (*Novoizrail'tyane*) which arose around the turn of the last century, though refusal of military service does not appear to have been a fixed tenet.

Most information concerning sectarian pacifism in Russia may be gleaned from the example of the Dukhobors. The sensational nature of their antimilitarism at the end of the century, their connection with Tolstoy, and later developments within the sect after their resettlement in western Canada brought them to the attention of the general public both inside Russia and abroad. Definitive evidence of the existence of

445

the Dukhobors (or "Wrestlers for the Spirit") does not reach further back than the second half of the eighteenth century, despite a number of unsubstantiated theories deriving their origin from earlier religious movements such as the Balkan Bogomils or the English Quakers. When they emerge into the light of history, the Dukhobors form a peasant sect scattered over large areas of south-central and south Russia, especially in the provinces of Tambov and Yekaterinoslav. They were made up mainly of free peasants: Soviet scholars like Klibanov rightly see in such movements as those of the early Dukhobors and Molokans an expression of protest against the serf system, which was not abolished in Russia until 1861. Whereas the Molokans eventually evolved into a denomination with a literate upper stratum and an influential urban element, the Dukhobors until long after their departure for Canada in 1898-1899 remained a peasant sect with few literate members even in the leadership.

Both church and state had persecuted the Dukhobors at the beginning. But the accession of the more tolerant Alexander I in 1801 eased the situation at last: the young and liberal Tsar now permitted the Dukhobors to live in peace in compact settlements on the Molochnaya river, in the province of Taurida. Most Dukhobors transferred to Molochne Vody in the period between 1802 and 1816.

The Dukhobors' faith, as it crystallized around this time, was a universalist and undogmatic form of Christianity, rejecting outward forms and rites and a separate priesthood. The seed of God, they held, dwells within every man, as it dwelt supremely within the man Jesus: true believers, therefore, may be found outside the Christian fold. (According to Paul Miliukov, the indwelling God appears as one of the most frequent motifs in Russian sectarian thought.) Although the Dukhobors have continued to quote the Bible copiously to outsiders, they soon came to regard it as of secondary importance compared to the inspiration of the living word of God within each individual. A book, they said, even the Bible, may serve rather to kill than to quicken the spirit (this provided, as we have seen, the main bone of contention between Dukhobors and Molokans). Love and brotherhood they regarded as central tenets of their religion. Thus arms-bearing and military service were forbidden to adherents of the sect, at least in theory. Whereas they have denied any need for coercive government, at the same time Dukhobors have tended to place the affairs of their community in the hands of a semi-divine leader. Dukhobor faith and practice, from the outset, has been a strange blend of religious anarchism and theocratic autocracy. In addition, a proclivity to concealing their true beliefs, generated by long years of governmental persecution, has made it difficult for outsiders fully to comprehend their outlook.

A psalm composed by Ilarion Pobirokhin, who led the sect in the late eighteenth century, states that "war and the taking of human life and all forms of hate toward our fellow men are the most impermissible deeds for a servant of God." Under Tsar Paul (1796-1801) and probably earlier too, though no record of this has survived, Dukhobor conscripts refused to use weapons after being inducted, and cases occurred of soldiers converted to Dukhoborism refusing to serve any longer under arms. Punishment with hard labor failed to put an end to such refractoriness. One of the reasons impelling the authorities to grant permission in 1802 for the Dukhobors to settle as a group at Molochne Vody may have been the consideration that here, in a remote area, these sectaries would have little chance to subvert the Orthodox and law-abiding population. During their years at Molochne Vody the government, understandably, made little attempt to conscript Dukhobors directly for military service.

Relaxation of the harsh measures which the authorities had originally directed against the Dukhobors, and the unlimited power given by their community to a small ruling clique, led eventually to a degeneration of morale. The strictly Orthodox Nicholas I, who had succeeded his brother Alexander I in 1825, eventually used this decline in moral standards as an excuse to deport the Dukhobors en masse from Molochne Vody, now clearly within the settled belt, to the wild and inhospitable Caucasus. This region remained their home from 1841-1844, the years of their migration thither, up into the twentieth century.

In the settlements on the Molochnaya river, the Dukhobors had agreed to construct roads and to provide timber for the imperial army. They consented to hire substitutes if they were ever called upon for military service (an alternative of this kind remained open to them only until 1839). At the same time, converts to Dukhoborism among the non-Dukhobor peasantry or among serving soldiers continued to be subject to savage penalties, leading in some cases to the death of the person concerned. Meanwhile, after transference to the Caucasus, "military service," write Woodcock and Avakumović, "was no longer a problem, since the Dukhobors were doubly protected from it: their settlements were technically, according to the terms of their exile, penal colonies, and therefore exempt from conscription which was not in any case introduced into the Caucasus" at this time. After their removal to Transcaucasia, though the moral decline was stemmed—its dimensions, in any case, may have been inflated by Tsarist officials

447

for their own purposes—and increasing prosperity came to the Dukhobors under the able guidance of the community's woman leader Luker'ya Vasil'evna Kalmykova, the nonviolent impulse apparent at an earlier date began to wane. They sold the produce of their farms to supply the needs of the Russian army of occupation. During the Russo-Turkish War of 1877-1878 Kalmykova agreed to her followers' acting as teamsters for the army, though with some reluctance and only after the military authorities had exerted a considerable amount of blackmail by threatening to apply the recent military conscription law (of 1874) to the Dukhobor settlements. With their horses and wagons Dukhobors now helped to transport equipment, supplies, and ammunition for the siege of Kars across the border in Turkey. During Kalmykova's "reign," too, Dukhobors began to carry rifles and other lethal weapons to defend themselves and their homesteads: the area was certainly wild and infested with brigands and fierce mountain tribesmen. Armed bodyguards accompanied the sect's. leaders when they travelled from settlement to settlement. And we hear of one Dukhobor, Ivan Makhortov, serving in the Russian navy for twenty-eight years.

Dukhobors never officially abandoned a theoretical belief in nonviolence. Lacking the moral stamina to resist the demands of the authorities and undermined by the inconsistency of their own practice in this regard, they merely bowed to circumstances. When forced to accompany the army in 1877, the Dukhobor teamsters had been adjured by Kalmykova to refrain from using arms to kill, if they should be forced to carry them. In fact this dilemma did not present itself. But a decade later, in 1887, military conscription began to be enforced in earnest in Transcaucasia, including the Dukhobor settlements. The moment was a particularly difficult one for the Dukhobor community. Kalmykova had died at the end of the previous year; a disputed succession ensued when the candidate supported by the authorities failed to win election. The sect now divided into two rival parties. The successful candidate, supported by the majority, was a spirited young man of twenty-nine, Petr Vasil'evich Verigin, with whose accession to the leadership of the Large Party a new and indeed revolutionary chapter in Dukhobor history commences. From the very beginning his rule was marked by confrontation with the government, which continued to give its favor to the Small Party gathered around Kalmykova's brother and supported by former dignitaries of the sect. Shortly afterward, Verigin was arrested and sent into northern exile for a number of years. For the time being, even conscripts from the Large Party which followed Verigin obeyed their call-up notices and entered upon their term of military service. There were no conscientious objectors: there was no attempt, either, to obtain noncombatant status within the army, though some of the conscripts may have determined in their minds never actually to use the weapons issued them for the purpose of killing their fellow men. Their pacifism appeared to belong to past history.

Yet a Dukhobor spiritual awakening was at hand. Its direct instigator was Verigin himself—"Peter the Lordly," as he became known among his followers on account of his charismatic gifts. But Verigin, who for all his later authoritarianism and lapses into antinomianism had a genuinely religious side to his character, in fact drew his inspiration for reform largely from the social and ethical writings of Tolstoy, with whose works he first became acquainted only during his exile. His conversion to Tolstoyism began around 1893. During the next two years Verigin, in a series of written and oral instructions taken back to the Large Party by visiting emissaries from the Caucasian settlements, elaborated a bold program of moral reform, strongly tinged with asceticism. He bade his followers refrain from eating meat or drinking alcohol or smoking; he commanded the unmarried to remain celibate and married couples to refrain from sexual intercourse, at least for a time; he admonished the settlers to establish a communalist economy in their villages; and finally, in the summer of 1895, he ordered them henceforward to swear no oaths and to withdraw from all association with the waging of war.

Verigin concealed from his followers the fact that he was often copying, sometimes literally, from Tolstoy. And Tolstoy himself, when he became aware of Dukhobor practice of the theories he had been preaching for some years, did not at first realize that this, instead of reflecting, as he thought, the spontaneous and living presence of these ideas among the peasant masses, represented to a large extent merely a reflection of his own image. Nevertheless, it should be remembered that vegetarianism and the simple life, agrarian communism and pacifism were all deeply embedded in the *Weltanschauung* of the Dukhobors, though it needed a stimulus from outside to reactivate them. Pavel Opršal in his monograph on the Dukhobors has argued in favor of Verigin's sole initiative in bringing about the moral revival in "Duchoboria," asserting that the Dukhobor leader actually read Tolstoy's major writings on ethics after 1895. This does not appear to me convincing. For, if not directly from actual reading. Verigin's indirect acquaintance with these works through his companions in exile who belonged to the intelligentsia began earlier. The seed of the Tolstoyan gospel, however, undoubtedly fell on fertile soil. Clearly,

449

Dukhobor antimilitarism, for instance, did not begin in 1895. Without the sect's pacifist tradition it is doubtful if the prestige of the leader alone could have persuaded his followers to embark now on a head-on collision with the government. And without this tradition, Verigin could scarcely have maintained their antimilitarist stance for over three years thereafter in the face of the harsh measures dealt out to them by the authorities.

The "strategy of civil disobedience" which he now implemented showed the hand of a master. It was planned in two stages, with the ultimate object of making manifest the sect's total repudiation of a state which sanctioned armed violence, along with the violence itself. First of all, from Easter 1895, on Verigin's instructions Dukhobor soldiers began to hand in their rifles, uniformly stating their belief that war and Christianity were incompatible. One of these objectors, in conversation with an American Quaker a few years later, recalled as follows the kind of argument he used to explain his actions to the amazed officers: "The Lord Jesus commanded us not to fight, but to be kind and meek; to love equally all who live on the earth, as Christ the Saviour of our souls loved us all, and gave his body to be crucified for us sinners, and has manifested his love before all nations. He said, 'Resist not him that is evil.'" The military authorities became alarmed: such insubordination, they feared, might prove infectious and spread to other soldiers outside the sect. They decided, therefore, to make an example and so, after every effort had been made to browbeat the men into submission, sentences of from two to three years' hard labor in the notorious penal battalion were dealt out by court martial to those Dukhobors—about sixty in all—who persisted in their refusal to bear arms.

After this demonstration of the new antimilitarist trend in the Dukhobor community a second and even more startling step was taken —once again on Peter Verigin's orders. On the night of 28-29 June (which coincided with the celebration of St. Peter's day) the Caucasian Dukhobors gathered in their villages, bringing with them the arms which many families possessed whether for hunting or for even less pacifistic purposes. These they proceeded to heap in piles, and in the depth of the night they set fire to the piled-up weapons, accompanying this nonviolent *auto-da-fé* with the singing of Dukhobor psalms. Klibanov claims that, beforehand, some members were unaware of the exact purpose to which the arms would be put and were ready to use them if, as seemed possible, the rival Little Party attacked. The evidence on this point remains unclear. The authorities, though they really seem to have feared an outbreak of violence on the part of Verigin's supporters, did not succeed in intervening until the burning of the weapons had been completed, but they rewarded this act of defiance by deporting a part of Verigin's following to the unhealthy lowlands around Batum.

Thereafter, Dukhobor antimilitarism intensified. The events of July 1895 were reported in the foreign press, and at home Tolstoy and his associates came forward to espouse the cause of the Dukhobors, publishing a number of pamphlets and articles on the subject, most of which had to be printed abroad on account of the domestic censorship. In Great Britain and North America pacifist groups like the Quakers began to take an increasing interest in the fate of the Dukhobors. A prominent English Friend, John Bellows, in a letter to another Quaker (dated 23 April 1898 and printed in *John Bellows: Letters and Memoir* [1904], while finding the religious tenets of the Russian sect not very "enlightened" and its members usually "ignorant—some of them in the extreme of ignorance—for they have not had teaching," went on to praise them for their staunch witness for peace:

> Measured by their faithfulness to the one point that has been shown them—*the duty of loving all men*—they have attained a high degree of perfection. I say this because we are all apt to judge those who differ from us in important doctrines. We are narrower than the Father of all, and need broadening, to be just to those whom he has accepted, but who have not had our training.

Further contacts between the two groups would emphasize the wide gap that in fact yawned between the sober middle-class nonconformity of the contemporary Anglo-American Society of Friends and the ecstatic religion, anarchistic social philosophy, and pantheistic leanings of these Slav peasant sectaries.

Meanwhile, Dukhobor young men who had done their term of military service and had been placed on the reserve began to hand back their military papers declaring their unwillingness to commit "murder" any longer. They were arrested and imprisoned. The government then went over into the offensive, calling up a number of Dukhobor reservists for a further training period of twenty-five days and, when they refused to obey their call-up notices, arresting them, too. "Why do you not accept the military service?" officials asked the men. They replied: "We cannot kill nor use violence, according to the word of God, towards our brothers who are created in the image of the Lord." "But how is it you did not know this formerly?" the officials countered. The reply came quickly: "Formerly we also knew well the Lord's law, but did not profess it, living disorderly and giving way to drunkenness." Court-martials followed, with sentences of two years in jail. "At the expiration of this term," wrote one of the objectors, Vasilii Pozdnyakov, who had previously served as a noncommissioned officer (in his *Razskaz dukhobortsa*), "they wanted to send us back home so that we should accept our reserve papers; but when we would not accept, they exiled us to the district of Yakutsk for eighteen years." Here they and the other imprisoned objectors who were similarly banished on the expiry of their term in a penal battalion remained until the outbreak of the first Russian revolution of 1905 brought them release.

From his exile in Siberia Verigin wrote, on 1 November 1896, to the Empress Alexandra asking her to intervene with the government to allow his coreligionists to emigrate to England or America, unless it were prepared to grant them exemption from military service. "All state obligations in the form of taxes we would pay," he wrote, "only we cannot be soldiers." During the next two years arrangements for a mass emigration of Verigin's followers were undertaken in earnest. Tolstoy volunteered to complete an unfinished novel and donate the royalties to help cover the cost of emigration: *Resurrection* appeared in 1899. British and American Quakers provided funds too and, together with the Tolstoyans, played a major role in planning and organizing the emigration. Canada was finally chosen as the Dukhobors' new home. In December 1898 its government passed a special Order in Council applying the exemption from militia service already extended to the country's three peace churches—Quakers, Mennonites, and Brethren in Christ—to the Dukhobors as well. In fact, at this very time the first party of Dukhobors had left Batum on the *Lake Huron* bound for Halifax, where they arrived early in January 1899. The rest of Verigin's followers, with the exception of those sentenced to administrative exile, departed in the course of the next few months. The number of those emigrating amounted to almost seventy-five hundred, not quite half the total number of Dukhobors in Russia. The reason for urgency in carrying through the emigration emerges in a letter of a Canadian sympathizer, James Mavor, Professor of Political Economy at the University of Toronto. "The circumstance," he wrote on 24 October 1898, "that in a few months a number of their young men will fall to be drawn for military service, and the fear that the permission granted by the Czar to leave the country may be withdrawn, coupled with the dread of a return to active persecution, are the chief impulses which impel them to seek another country at all hazards of suffering from inadequate shelter in an inclement winter."

Those who remained permanently in Russia belonged either to the

Little Party, which had opposed Verigin's election as leader, or to the so-called Fleshers (*myasniki*) who, though they followed Verigin at first, had refused to accept the radical reforms he introduced in the mid-1890's. Neither the members of the Little Party nor the Fleshers, therefore, shared in the revival of the sect's peace testimony which Verigin had initiated in so striking a fashion. There were a few cases of Russian Dukhobors conscientiously objecting to military service in World War I as well as in the years immediately following the Bolshevik revolution. But this was obviously a minority position now within the sect, which, moreover, was in a state of disintegration due to the removal of its most spiritually alive elements represented by Verigin's followers.

In Canada the Dukhobors split into three separate and eventually competing factions: on the right, the Independents, who opposed Verigin's authoritarian ways and his communal system of agriculture (the "Yakutians" mostly joined this group when they came to Canada in 1905); on the left, the Sons of Freedom, who practiced nudity and even arson as a form of social protest in religious guise; in the center the majority party of Community Dukhobors following the leadership first of Verigin, who was allowed to leave Russia in 1902, and then of his successors. An offer by the Russian premier Stolypin in 1906 to grant the Dukhobors a new home in Siberia as well as exemption from military service failed to tempt Verigin and his followers back from Canada. There all three Dukhobor groups have adhered to pacifism, and their members declared themselves as conscientious objectors when conscription was enforced in Canada during the two World Wars.

Among those who became most concerned over the fate of the Dukhobors was, as we have seen, Leo Tolstoy. He and his followers regarded the imprisoned Dukhobor objectors as "Christian martyrs." They protested against their incarceration and against the sufferings they had to endure in the penal battalion, and they burned with a desire to share their fate, a fate which the Tsarist government wisely declined to impose upon them. Tolstoy, writes one of his biographers, E. J. Simmons, "felt humiliated in being a modern Christ without a cross to bear." In January 1897 we find Tolstoy declaring: "I by no means see why the government, persecuting those who refuse military service, does not turn its punishment upon me, recognizing in me an instigator. I am not too old for persecution, for any and all sorts of punishments, and my position is a defenseless one."

For the earliest expression of Tolstoy's adherence to a nonviolent way of life, we must go back almost two decades. His "conversion," the birth of "Tolstoyism," dates to the late 1870's. True, his new religious outlook had not formed suddenly in his mind; a long spiritual and mental evolution lay behind its emergence into the open then. The landowning aristocrat was not transformed overnight into the populist opponent of property, nor the successful novelist into the Puritan moralist, nor the former army officer into the exponent of unconditional nonresistance to evil. Even as an adolescent Tolstoy had been impressed when reading the Sermon on the Mount and, with Rousseau, he had enthused over the simple life unspoilt by civilization. His turbulent youth proved but a comparatively brief episode in a life marked by intense seriousness of purpose. In 1857, after witnessing a guillotining in Paris, he had experienced a profound revulsion against homicide, a feeling which probably went back earlier to the period of his military career, and this revulsion was deepened by the execution nine years later of a soldier in whose fate he had become interested. And the seeds of his later undogmatic religion and of his break with Orthodoxy may already be found in Tolstoy even in his mid-twenties. There is no space here, of course, for an intellectual and psychological biography of Tolstoy, even in brief. I shall have to concentrate almost exclusively on a discussion of his idea of nonviolence.

The composition of *A Confession* in 1879 marked both his final break with the church in which he had been reared and the first tentative expression of the concept of "nonresistance to evil," which was to play the central role in his system of social ethics. In this intensely moving spiritual autobiography Tolstoy wrote of his disillusionment with established Christianity for its support of "war and executions." During the recent Russo-Turkish War of 1877-1878 he had not yet broken entirely with the war tradition; during the course of the fighting he had been swept at moments with patriotic emotion. Yet at the same time he found it impossible to reconcile war and patriotism with the Christian faith which for some years now he had been seeking to renew within himself. As he relates in his *Confession*:

> At that time Russia was at war. And Russians, in the name of Christian love, began to kill their fellow men. It was impossible not to think about this, and not to see that killing is an evil repugnant to the first principles of any faith. Yet prayers were said in the churches for the success of our arms, and the teachers of the Faith acknowledged killing to be an act resulting from the Faith. . . . And I took note of all that is done by men who profess Christianity, and I was horrified.

Tolstoy emerged after the war was over as a thoroughgoing pacifist, equating war—and capital punishment, too—with "murder."

His new-found faith in nonviolence was strengthened by contacts around this time with the followers of a now forgotten apostle of humanist religion, Aleksandr Kapitonovich Malikov, founder of a short-lived sect of "deo-humanists (*bogocheloveki*)." The tutor of Tolstoy's sons, V. I. Alekseev, who was a disciple of Malikov, acted as the main link between the two. "In every man there is a divine principle": this was the central tenet of Malikov's teaching. Human divinity, for those who had perceived it and begun to transform their lives accordingly, precluded the use of injurious force against a fellow man under any circumstances. Evil could be conquered only by love: "love to one's neighbor—without division into good and bad." "I was a Tolstoyan when Tolstoy himself was not yet one," said Malikov later after he had returned to the Orthodox fold and abandoned his belief in absolute nonviolence.

Malikov had begun to put forward views of this kind around 1874, while still in his mid-thirties, and he found a ready response among the radical youth. It was the period of the famous "journey to the people (*khozhdenie v narod*)," when young persons from the intelligentsia went out in a crusade to spread the idea of agrarian socialism among the peasantry. These populists were mostly agnostics and atheists; yet despite his mystical—though nondogmatic—religious creed, Malikov, a peasant's son, felt close to them in their populist aims, and some of the *narodniki* joined his circle, including a leading figure in the early populist movement Nikolai Chaikovsky. In the following year Malikov and his friends, warned by the Tsarist police that they would be liable to prosecution if they proceeded with their intention of proselytizing among the countryfolk, decided to emigrate as a group to the United States and set up an income-pooling community on the Kansan prairies, where they hoped they would be free to live out their nonviolent principles. This experiment, like so many others before and after, proved a disillusionment to those who participated, and it broke up within two years. Some deo-humanists, like the founder Malikov, who returned to Russia, drifted away fairly soon from radicalism; others, like Chaikovsky, were to develop as political populists and eventually to join the Socialist Revolutionary Party when this was founded in 1902; still others preserved their faith in nonviolence and became Tolstoyans.

Unlike Tolstoy, however, Malikov did not concern himself particularly with the problem of war. Seemingly, he never committed any of his ideas to writing, despite the fact that he and his followers were almost all men of education; therefore it is not easy to determine precisely what he preached concerning nonviolence, just as it is difficult to locate exactly the sources from which he drew in shaping his views on this subject. Prugavin states that he condemned both war and revolutionary violence, and this position indeed appears to be implied in his whole philosophy of nonviolence.

But whereas Malikov derived his nonviolence from a mystical belief in the God within each man, Tolstoy saw nonviolence as an ethical imperative expressed in its purest form in the teachings of Christ. When Christ said "Resist not him that is evil," he meant these words literally. This was the conclusion at which Tolstoy had arrived by the end of the 1870's, after many years' heartsearching. The Sermon on the Mount, the Beatitudes, and the various Gospel admonitions which throughout the centuries the churches had sought to transform into mere counsels of perfection not to be taken at their face value by the ordinary believer, all these the real Christian must take seriously. There would be no salvation for mankind if they were disregarded, or their implications for society as well as the individual ignored. In the course of *An Examination of Dogmatic Theology*, which Tolstoy wrote in 1880, he first set forth these views in some detail. And they gained definitive form in *What I Believe*, first published—in Geneva, on account of the censorship at home—in 1888 but already finished in 1884.

The framework of Tolstoyan nonresistance was now complete; later additions would be of relatively minor significance, even if subsequent acquaintance with the work of others who had reached roughly the same conclusions as he had undoubtedly helped to reinforce his faith in nonresistance. He learned of the fifteenth-century Czech pacifist Chelčický from a young Prague professor, later president of the Czechoslovak Republic, T. G. Masaryk. Wendell P. Garrison, son of the American nonresistant William Lloyd Garrison, brought his father's work for peace and that of his associates in the New England Non-Resistance Society to Tolstoy's attention after he had read a translation of *What I Believe* and been struck by the similarity between the two views. Tolstoy, it is true, before his conversion knew vaguely of the Quakers' and Mennonites' rejection of participation in war, but he did not have any contacts with them yet. It was only later that he read some of their peace literature and entered into correspondence with members of these sects. Likewise, his personal acquaintance with indigenous Russian religious groups like the pacifistic Molokans or the Dukhobors postdated his first espousal of nonresistance. The story of his expanding awareness of the historic pacifist witness is told by

Tolstoy himself in the first chapter of *The Kingdom of God is Within You*. But until the mid-1880's, apart from the works of certain anti-militarist church fathers like Origen and Tertullian, and Tolstoy's contemporary Malikov, it was the New Testament which provided the major intellectual influence from outside on his emerging doctrine of nonresistance.

Tolstoy had always been fascinated, in particular, by the Sermon on the Mount. Its uncompromising demands evoked an answering chord in his psyche. "The Sermon on the Mount," he wrote concerning those years of spiritual turmoil, "always stood out for me as something special, and I read it more than anything else. Nowhere else did Christ speak with such authority—nowhere else does he give so many clear, intelligible moral rules directly appealing to the heart of every man." The principle of nonresistance and its corollaries—turning the other cheek, going the second mile, giving away cloak as well as coat, love of enemies and persecutors—implied readiness to suffer. But this was not to be done for its own sake: it represented a negative expression of a positive moral law, the Law of Love. When he understood all this, writes Tolstoy, "everything that had been confused, became intelligible; what had been contradictory, became harmonious, and, above all, what had appeared superfluous became essential. All merged into one whole. . . ."

The Gospels Tolstoy once described as "the teaching of welfare." For him they represented a universal message which mankind as a whole, whether belonging to the Christian faith or not, could neglect only at its peril. Thus, he often appears as a prophet of rapidly approaching doom—"repent ye, and believe the Gospel." But the Gospel message, with nonresistance to evil at its core, signified something more than mere teaching. It formed "an obligatory rule—a law to be fulfilled" at whatever cost. Tolstoy's Christianity transcended Christ, for he came to see in the Master's teaching the expression of a body of wisdom common to all the great teachers and prophets of mankind. And in every man, of whatsoever faith, God's light dwells, for all men are equally sons of God, endowed with "reason" or "conscience." If Christ had expressed this light, this reason, in its highest form, it simply meant that what he taught his followers was most exactly in consonance with the laws of the universe. Therefore, nonresistance to evil and the Law of Love, since they represent the essential meaning of the Gospels, need not—indeed should not—be confined to persons accepting the Christian tradition. All mankind must be led to renunciation of violence and war.

Tolstoy's is primarily a system of individual ethics; it is based upon the concept of personal responsibility for actions done. It postulates control of the passions as an essential condition. But its application embraces the whole of society. Indeed its practice demands the total transformation of society, a nonviolent revolution which would replace the law of violence presently prevailing by a new law of love. Tolstoy became a vegetarian to exemplify his belief in the sacredness of all sentient beings. Yet he valued human life above that of the animal kingdom. As he once remarked: "One feels more pity for a man and his sufferings than for the sufferings of a horse, and more pity for the sufferings of a horse than of a rat or a mouse, while one does not feel sorry for a mosquito. This feeling of sequence constitutes true wisdom." Since homicide and violence stemmed from the institution of property, the Law of Love demanded the renunciation of all rights to property, even collectively owned property, which might be retained only on a basis of use and with the understanding that violence never be employed in its defense. "Property has been [the] Achilles' heel for the Quakers," Tolstoy wrote. But, in his view, the greatest obstacle to the embodiment in social life of the Law of Love lay in the existence of the state. In a letter to a Hungarian admirer, Dr. Eugen Heinrich Schmitt, Tolstoy expressed this thesis in theoremlike form when he wrote: "Government is violence; Christianity is meekness, nonresistance, love. And, therefore, government cannot be Christian, and a man who wishes to be a Christian must not serve government." He must abstain from public office: he must refrain from swearing official oaths, using courts of law, or collaborating with the police in any way; he must refuse to pay taxes; above all, he must resist military service and war. Eventually, if men follow this path of political boycott and civil disobedience, governments everywhere will disintegrate by becoming superfluous. To secure mankind's happiness the state must be destroyed. *"Carthago delenda est,"* he concluded.

For Tolstoy, the state remained exclusively an instrument of violence and oppression: "armed men using force" (from *What then must we do?* [1886]). If the need for violence disappeared, then need for a state, he believed, vanished too. Every state was inevitably a slave state, kept in being solely by intimidation and fear and organized for the sole purpose of exploiting a subject population. His attitude obviously reflects to some extent the political condition of Russia under the Tsarist autocracy. Resistance, even nonviolent resistance, tended there to adopt a "maximalist" form. No more than the fifteenth-century Czech Brethren or the later Anabaptists and Mennonites could he conceive of government divorced from the exercise of armed force. A recent writer (William B. Edgerton) has argued: "Tolstoy's Christian anarchism . . . is not really the basic article of his faith, but only a questionable corollary. The essence of his message is his belief in Love as the fundamental law of the universe." We may agree that anarchism is not an inevitable corollary of Christian pacifism; yet it appears, at least to me, as an essential element in Tolstoyism.

Nonetheless, just as Tolstoy's nonresistance to evil expresses in negative form a positive principle of love, so his anarchism—indeed every theory of anarchism—reflects a positive idea. It posits the idea of society based on a maximum of consent; it urges the need to reorganize social life on the basis of voluntary cooperation and, in Tolstoy's words, to liberate "public opinion, whose action is impeded by violence" under a governmental regime. Unless people consent to submit, "they cannot be forced into submission"; even though they may be exterminated by a superior force, they will nevertheless succeed in maintaining their moral integrity. For Tolstoy (as for Gandhi later), this last was the preferable alternative, since the life of the individual was less precious than obedience to conscience and maintenance of the right ethical stance.

Tolstoy distinguished between, on the one hand, an "instinctive . . . spontaneous" love of country which, while it ought not to be regarded as a virtue—even in the case of oppressed nationalities like the Poles or the Jews—for it represented a manifestation of "egoism," was still pardonable, and, on the other, the patriotism exhibited by dominant nations like Russia, Germany, or Japan, indeed by all the so-called civilized and progressive peoples of his day. Such patriotism was not merely egoistical, it was built upon oppression of others, social injustice, envy, hatred, and war. It formed a survival "from an outlived past," a harmful and amoral anachronism which all persons of goodwill must discard as an obstacle to the brotherhood of man. Tolstoy spoke of "the gross fraud called patriotism and love of one's country" and lauded "rejection of fatherland" as "good and noble." "I cannot," he declared in *What I Believe*, "take part in all those affairs which are based on the diversity of nations, not in custom-houses and the collection of taxes, nor in the preparation of military stores and ammunition, nor in any activity for creating armaments, nor in military service, nor (still less) in war itself against other nations—and I cannot help other people to do so." Thus his antipatriotism was indissolubly linked with his antimilitarism.

During the Russo-Japanese War of 1904-1905 Tolstoy confided to his daughter Alexandra: "I cannot get rid of a feeling of grief when I hear that the Russians are getting beaten." Yet he realized that this feeling stemmed from human weakness, that it was an atavistic voice that spoke within him. In a long essay which he composed on the war in April and May 1904 ("Bethink Yourselves") he castigated impartially the Buddhist supporters of the Japanese, and the Orthodox Christian supporters of the Russian, war effort. Both proclaimed brotherly love and the sanctity of human life as basic principles of their religion and both had betrayed these principles. And he refused to be enticed into a discussion of war responsibility, while declaring at the same time that refusal of support for or service in the war was the only path open to a man who took his religion seriously.

War itself was the enemy: war resistance was the instrument which would liberate mankind from the scourge of war. Revolutionary violence was both useless and immoral, but war waged by states was "incomparably more cruel than the murders committed by anarchists," he had written in 1900 in an essay significantly entitled "Thou shall not kill." "If Alexander II and Humbert did not deserve death, still less did the thousands of Russians who perished at Plevna, or of Italians who perished in Abyssinia." Tolstoy put no faith in international arbitration—the panacea of the contemporary peace societies—as a method of abolishing armed conflict between men. To think that arbitration between states could achieve this was, he thought, a delusion, since it was the very existence of governments and state apparatuses that made domestic violence and international war inevitable. When in 1899 the first Hague Peace Conference took place, largely on the initiative of Tsar Nicholas II, Tolstoy was filled with contempt for those peace workers who imagined that this marked a step forward in the direction of a warless world. "The aim of the Conference," he wrote, "will be, not to establish peace, but to hide from men the sole means of escape from the miseries of war, which lies in the refusal by private individuals of all participation in the murders of war." He envisaged a time in the future when personal conscientious objection would reach such dimensions as to take on the character of a general strike against war, of a boycott of the army by masses of individual objectors.

He admitted that no specific proof-text could be found in the Gospels requiring the Christian to refuse military service. Instead, he pointed, very sensibly, to their whole tenor, which reflected a spirit of peace and unconditional nonviolence. As he wrote in *What I Believe:*

> We forget that Christ could not imagine people believing in his teaching of humility, love, and universal brotherhood, quietly and deliberately organizing the murder of their fellow men. Christ could not imagine that, and therefore could not forbid Christians to go to war, any more than a father, when giving his son instruc-

tions to live honestly, to wrong no one, and to give to others, could
bid him abstain from highway robbery.

Time and again he expresses astonishment at the failure of "the nominal church" to recognize that Christianity could never fulfil its mission
until it sincerely adhered to "the divine truth of the non-resistance
principle." "I am fully convinced," he wrote eleven years before his
final excommunication by the Holy Synod of the Russian Orthodox
Church in 1901, "that the churches are and have always been the worst
enemies of Christ's work. They have always led humanity not in the
way of Christ, but out of it."

We find Tolstoy alternately amazed and indignant at the fact that
men continued killing each other at their governments' behest when
it appeared so obvious to him that their true interests demanded that
they refuse to obey. Yet a Kantian absolute moral imperative rather
than a nice calculation of profit and loss determined the important
place Tolstoy gave to conscientious objection in his philosophy of life.
To a Japanese Christian who contemplated refusal of military service
he wrote in the last year of his life: "For such a man there is not and
cannot be any question of the consequences (no matter what they may
be) of his actions, or of what will happen to his body and his temporal,
physical life. . . . For such a man only one thing is important and necessary: to fulfil what is required of him by the spiritual essence that
dwells within him." He criticized the bourgeois peace societies of his
day for shutting their eyes to the fundamental importance of a personal witness against war, to "the question of the rightness or wrongness of taking part in military service," and for side-tracking the main
issue by concentrating on secondary problems. At the same time he
condemned the revolutionaries for their failure to realize that one
should not judge the value of a moral stand solely by its effect in bringing nearer a more just social order. For Tolstoy the modern system of
conscription symbolized the total corruption of contemporary Western
civilization (we may detect here a thinly veiled slavophilism which
emerges not infrequently in his thinking), and he regarded destruction of the system as an essential prerequisite for a peaceable world.
"Universal military service," he wrote in *The Kingdom of God is Within You*, "is the last stage of violence that governments need for the
maintenance of the whole [power] structure, and it is the extreme
limit to which submission on the part of their subjects can go. It is the
keystone of the arch holding up the edifice, and its removal would
bring down the whole building." Thus, even though the impact of any
isolated act of conscientious objection might appear to be nil, the total

effect of a witness of this kind, once it had got under way, would serve eventually to destroy the rule of violence and to inaugurate the new moral order of love.

Tolstoy remained strongly opposed to any idea of providing alternative service for genuine conscientious objectors to war, even if such service were placed under civilian control. Like the Quakers during their first two centuries, who considered that such a proposal constituted an infringement of human freedom since a penalty was being demanded for obeying conscience, Tolstoy was an absolutist on this point. He regarded acceptance of a scheme of alternative service as an emasculation of the antimilitarist witness. Conscientious objection would achieve its goal of subverting the war-making state only if objectors refused to have anything to do with the conscription system. Moreover, he doubted—not quite correctly as it turned out—if in fact governments could ever be persuaded to permit an effective alternative to service in the army since conscripts, he believed, would sooner or later begin in overwhelming numbers to opt for such service—and then there would be no soldiers left.

One aspect of Tolstoyan nonresistance which puzzled not only Tolstoy's opponents but some of his pacifist friends as well, was its total repudiation of force, even when used noninjuriously. In this respect, indeed, Tolstoy became increasingly uncompromising. In 1884, in *What I Believe*, he had made an exception concerning the employment of noninjurious "physical force" in respect to a child if it were essential "in order to save it from immediately impending danger." But this reservation he dropped later; henceforward, whereas persuasion was legitimate, only the unconditional repudiation of all forms of physical force appeared to him to be compatible with Christian discipleship, or with universal morality. He quoted the ethnologists to show that a truly nonviolent man would most likely remain unharmed even among primitive savages. It was, indeed, in regard to civilized barbarians that he appeared less convincing. In answer to the objection that some degree of force might on occasion be necessary, for instance in restraint of a murderer or lunatic, Tolstoy replied—not without a measure of sophistry, we may think—that no human being is competent to judge who is evil and who good, or who is sane and who mad. And how, he asked, might one know beforehand which was the greater moral evil—the preventive violence or the violence one sought to prevent? (For instance, to give an imaginary illustration of Tolstoy's argument, *objectively speaking* would it really have been morally preferable to kill an attempted murderer of a juvenile Hitler who would grow up to slaughter millions, though one could not know this at the time, than to observe strict nonresistance and allow the child to be killed?) Likewise, one could not know when a murder would take place until after it had actually happened: since every man was potentially responsive to the truth, even the most hardened criminal might finally relent and cease from evil. Moreover, since Christ's rule of non-resistance to evil formed an absolute moral law, it could admit of no exception. "Except by renouncing participation in evil and acknowledging the truth" no man might hope to be perfect.

Christian perfection, this was the ideal that Tolstoy sought from the beginning of his conversion and that so maddeningly eluded him. He seems to have feared that any attempt "to lower the demands of the ideal" would end disastrously: he could point with effect to the history of the Christian church as an example of what had happened when this was attempted and the principles of the Sermon on the Mount became mere counsels no longer binding on the faithful. He declared: "Only this ideal of complete, infinite perfection acts on men and moves them to action. Moderate perfection has no power to influence men's souls."

Yet, we may note, a moral dualism existed in Tolstoy's thought here as well as in the orthodox churchmen whom he criticized. This fact emerges most clearly from a perusal of the correspondence which took place in 1889-1890 between Tolstoy and two American pacifists, Adin Ballou, the founder of the Hopedale Community, and his associate, the local Unitarian minister, the Reverend Lewis Gilbert Wilson (Tolstoy's letters to them are to be found in the Soviet Jubilee edition of his works, vol. 64, no. 391, and vol. 65, nos. 26 and 100). It is worth examining more closely what Tolstoy had to say on this occasion.

Ballou, though a nonresistant, supported the use of noninjurious force against drunkards and the insane. Tolstoy, while expressing his respect in general for the American's advocacy of pacifist principles, nevertheless felt bound to register his disagreement on this point. "A true Christian," he wrote, "will always prefer to be killed by a madman rather than to deprive him of his liberty." A few paragraphs later, however, he interposes the following qualification that in effect made his own stand less radical than Ballou's: "the *application* of every doctrine is always a compromise, but the doctrine in theory cannot allow compromises; although we know we never can draw a mathematically straight line, we will never make another definition of a straight line [than] as the shortest distance between two points." And in answer to the doubts Ballou expressed concerning this view, he declared his belief that men could never achieve absolute perfection here on earth, that in fact all their actions represent a compromise of some kind. What he considered essential was never to lower the absolute standard according to which the degree of failure of these actions could be judged. It must remain uncontaminated by inevitable human weakness in order to act as the goal of human endeavor. "The great sin," he wrote, "is the compromise in theory, is the plan to lower the ideal of Christ in view to make it attainable. . . . I consider the admission of force (be it even benevolent) over a madman . . . to be such a theoretical compromise." Tolstoy was in fact arguing for what the twentieth-century Scottish theologian G.H.C. Macgregor has called "the relevance of an impossible ideal." He was grappling with the same problem that the medieval church had faced when it came up with the somewhat different solution of monasticism: the age-long tension between man's search for perfection and the fact of human sin or, in nontheological terms, irrationality. He was too much of a realist to believe that the old Mennonite ideal of the community "without spot or wrinkle" could actually be embodied in practice: at the same time he was too much of a visionary to be willing to renounce the effort to realize this "impossible ideal."

Not all his followers succeeded in matching the tempered realism of their master. "I am Tolstoy, but I am not a Tolstoyan": this reported saying of his shows Tolstoy's awareness of the dangers of too doctrinaire an approach to nonviolence such as he must have observed in some of his disciples. Among them were those, for instance, ready to carry the principle of nonresistance to evil to the point of allowing predatory urchins to strip them of their personal possessions or unscrupulous neighbors to run riot in competition for taking over their property. These excesses, one feels, could not have met with Tolstoy's approval.

In the course of the 1880's "Tolstoyism" had already begun to gain adherents inside Russia; by the next decade, as Tolstoy's writings on social and ethical problems became known abroad through translations, the doctrine spread to other countries too. Tolstoyan circles sprang up in England and the United States, Holland, and Austria-Hungary, and sympathizers were to be found in lands as far distant as Bulgaria and Japan (there, for instance, Toyohiko Kagawa, the well known Christian pacifist and socialist leader, while still a very young man came under Tolstoy's spell). Outside Russia, where until 1905 censorship prevented the publication of Tolstoy's more controversial works, a Tolstoyan press arose both in Russian, manned by Tolstoyan exiles, and in other languages, edited by non-Russian sympathizers. In some places his disciples established agricultural colonies, usually short-lived ventures, where men and women attempted to exemplify in practice the principles of community enunciated by their master. The

Tolstoyans formed a variegated group. In Russia itself "penitent" land-owners (Tolstoy himself was one of these, as were so many nineteenth-century Russian revolutionaries) figured prominently in the movement. Tolstoy's chief aid and the main exponent of "Christian anarchism" in Russia after his death, Vladimir Chertkov, had been an army officer until his conversion to Tolstoyism, and Tolstoy's semi-official biographer, Pavel Biriukov, was a naval officer until he, too, saw the light. There were several princes in the Tolstoyan circle, including D. A. Khilkov, who helped the Dukhobors in their emigration to Canada (he left the movement later and eventually met his death in 1915 fighting against the Central Powers). On the other hand, Tolstoyism appealed, too, to uneducated peasants; Soviet ideologists like to define Tolstoyism as an expression of the peasant's "patriarchal reaction" to the advance of capitalism into the countryside. Like the *narodniki*, Tolstoy himself, with his cult of manual work, tended to idealize the character and way of life of the peasant. But in Russia, and even more so abroad, Tolstoyans usually belonged to the intelligentsia.

Since nonresistance to evil figured among the most important tenets of the Tolstoyan faith, conscientious objection appeared, at least to those who had accepted this faith *in toto*, as an essential part of its practice. For instance, we find a leading Dutch disciple and former Reformed clergyman, Dr. Louis A. Bähler, in a lecture to a gathering of "modern theologians" expounding the thesis: "God is Love. . . . Refusal of military service is thus a duty of the religious man" (quoted from his pamphlet *Hoe uit een godsdienstig oogpunt te oordeelen over dienstweigering?*, Amsterdam, 1897). And, from the mid-1890's onward—and a decade earlier in Russia itself, with the appearance of the first Tolstoyan objector, Alexei Petrovich Zaliubovskii, toward the end of 1884—cases of conscientious objection occur on the part of young men whose impulse was religious but whose convictions derived from their acquaintance with Tolstoy's interpretation of Christian ethics. The state's procedure in dealing with these men differed in detail from country to country; the principle, however, remained the same—a sentence of imprisonment which might be repeated indefinitely unless the objector chose to emigrate or the army authorities chose conveniently to forget his existence.

In the Netherlands several of these objectors came from a Mennonite (*Doopsgezinden*) background, e.g., the bookseller J. K. van der Veer, on whose behalf Tolstoy early in January 1897 penned an essay entitled "The Beginning of the End," or Jan Terwey. More frequently, the objector sprang from a religious denomination without even the most tenuous connection with pacifism, or from a nonreligious milieu.

In every instance the Tolstoyan objector had already severed his connection with organized religion. In Hungary, in 1895, a Slovak army surgeon, Albert Škarvan, refused, a few weeks before the expiry of his term of military service, to serve any longer, after being convinced by reading Tolstoy that the practice of Christianity precluded any association with the machinery of waging war. Like many of those who underwent a spiritual awakening after encounter, often, as Edgerton has remarked, "a chance encounter with one of Tolstoy's prophetic works," Škarvan experienced this as a kind of self-realization. He wrote: "For me it was always as if I had really only been waiting for what this Tolstoy was to tell me." As the son of a peasant people, Škarvan had shared "since childhood" their "resistance to the authorities, to the judicature, to the army, to the state, to the landowning class and its way of life"; thus Tolstoy's doctrines, when he learnt of them, came as a confirmation of his own innermost but as yet barely revealed convictions rather than as a message from without. Eventually Škarvan, who was a talented writer, became, along with his fellow Slovak and Tolstoy's medical adviser during his last years, Dr. Dušan Makovický, one of the most devoted interpreters of Tolstoy's ideas in the Slav world. Yet objectors like Škarvan were mostly isolated witnesses; at any rate, out of Tolstoy's teachings no large-scale movement of war resistance, such as Tolstoy hoped for, arose in Western and Central Europe during the years preceding the outbreak of world war in 1914.

In Russia the pattern was similar but the penalty for dissent was usually more onerous. Tolstoy, who continued throughout the last three decades of his life to write, intervene, and agitate whenever possible on behalf of any of his fellow countrymen refusing to obey the summons to bear arms, has described official procedure in such cases, as it stood in the early 1890's, in the following passage taken from *The Kingdom of God is Within You:*

> First they apply all the methods of coercion that are employed in our times to "correct" the refuser and bring him to "a proper state of mind," and these methods are kept profoundly secret. . . . They usually begin by sending the man to the priests, and they—to their shame be it said—always admonish him. But since admonitions in Christ's name to renounce Christ are generally fruitless, he is then sent to the gendarmes, and they, usually finding nothing of a political nature to charge him with, send him back again, and then he is sent to learned men, to the doctors, and to an insane asylum.

During all these recommitments the refuser is deprived of liberty and has to endure all kinds of indignities and suffering, like a convicted criminal. . . . The doctors dismiss the refuser from the insane asylum, and then all sorts of cunning shifts are practiced to avoid releasing him (and run the risk of encouraging others to refuse as he had done) and at the same time not to leave him among the soldiers, lest they should learn from him that the levy for military service is not in accord with the law of God as they have been assured, but is contrary to it. . . . Either he is sent to some distant place, or he is provoked to insubordination and then tried for breach of discipline and sent to prison or to the disciplinary battalion [usually for three years] where he can be ill-treated in secret, or they declare him to be mad and lock him up in a lunatic asylum.

Tolstoy believed that the government feared these isolated objectors more than the violent revolutionaries. Against the latter it could defend itself by the traditional violent means. "But," he asked, "what are governments to do against these people who show the uselessness, superfluity, and harmfulness of all governments, and instead of contending with them merely show that they do not need them, that they get along without them, and therefore are unwilling to take part in them?" Moreover, most "Tolstoyan" objectors, in contrast to the pacifist sectarians who had been the only people in Russia before to object to military service, were "men of fair or higher education," whose scruples could not easily be dismissed as the product of ignorance, superstition, or religious fanaticism. Instead, wrote Tolstoy, they presented "very clear and simple reasons for their refusal, understandable and recognized as true by everybody."

Tolstoy overestimated the impact his followers made when they refused military service or other demands of the state such as paying taxes, swearing oaths, or taking part in the functioning of the administrative and legal machinery of government. However, as a movement of social protest by withdrawal, Tolstoyism survived World War I. In wartime Russia Tolstoyan objectors were sentenced to long periods of imprisonment. Though the revolutions of February and October 1917 brought them release, subsequently during the turmoil of the Civil War, in 1919 and 1920, many were shot by one side or the other for refusing to bear arms. After a few years of relative toleration by the Soviet government in the early 1920's, Tolstoyism once more came under a shadow. By the mid-1930's Stalinism had finally destroyed the movement. Elsewhere, too, it had virtually disintegrated by the time war again engulfed Europe and eventually the entire globe. In the post-1945 world Tolstoyism has played no direct role.

A movement so amorphous as Tolstoyism proved to be was unlikely to prove an effective agent for rallying the antiwar forces of the twentieth-century world. In any case, as W. B. Edgerton has remarked, "anarchism—even Christian anarchism—is incapable of serving as the organizing principle of society." In this century the number of those espousing pacifism and accepting the renunciation of service in war as part of their religious or ethical beliefs has greatly increased (though it is still very small in comparison with the supporters, however reluctant, of military methods of conflict resolution). Yet few among them have been prepared to follow Tolstoy to his final conclusion and repudiate not only the state in all its aspects but the use of even noninjurious forms of force. Thus, Tolstoyism eventually became a narrow sect, sufficient unto itself and standing aloof from the mainstream of pacifist thought.

The contribution, however, made by Tolstoy to the twentieth-century pacifist movement has been considerable. In the first place, we may note the seminal influence exercised by Tolstoy over Mohandas Karamchand Gandhi, the greatest apostle of nonviolence in modern times. Gandhi read *The Kingdom of God is Within You* almost immediately after its first publication. Although a variety of intellectual sources, both Western and Indian, including the Sermon on the Mount, lay at the back of Gandhi's practice of nonviolent resistance, of *Satyagraha* or "truth-force" as he preferred to call it, Gandhi himself acknowledged that one of his deepest debts was to Tolstoy. "Russia gave me in Tolstoy a teacher who furnished a reasoned basis for my nonviolence," he wrote many years later ("To American friends," in *Harijan*, 9 August 1942). And when in 1909 Tolstoy first learned of Gandhi's long-drawn-out, yet moderately successful, campaign of civil disobedience in South Africa in support of that country's Indian minority, which was subjected by its rulers to social and legal discrimination, he wrote to the Indian leader congratulating him for his contribution to the cause of nonviolence and welcoming his "passive resistance" as "of very great importance not only for Indians but for the whole of mankind." True, Gandhi differed from Tolstoy both in his much more positive attitude toward the state and the nation (though there are anarchist elements in the Gandhian philosophy of nonviolence, too) and in his belief in the need for active resistance to evil, albeit nonviolent resistance. Thus, whereas Gandhi, more than any other Indian statesman, may be regarded as the architect of Indian national independence and though his disciples and associates became the founding fathers of the contemporary Indian state, however remote its policies may now seem from the nonviolent principles of Gandhi himself, Tolstoy, on the other hand, remained a prophet in the wilderness and the voices of his followers died away seemingly without echo.

Consideration of Tolstoy's influence on Gandhi leads on to a second —and perhaps in the long run the most valuable—contribution made by Tolstoy to contemporary pacifism, which has already been touched upon above. Gandhi was a Hindu, reared within a cultural milieu that was independent of the Western intellectual tradition based on ancient Mediterranean civilization. True, he had come early in his life into contact with Western thought and mores and was, therefore, amenable to influences from this quarter. But if pacifism were ever to make headway in the twentieth-century world, it was not only essential that it should emerge from strict enclosure within the confines of Christian sectarianism and reach out to those who had rejected orthodox religion (this was already being attempted by a few Quakers of liberal persuasion and by some absolute pacifists in the Western peace movement); it had, too, to find a common language with the rest of mankind which, like Gandhi, did not belong in the Western tradition. It was the merit of Tolstoy that he perceived this and acted upon his perception. He believed that the nonviolent imperative and the duty of conscientious objection to war were implicit in all the higher religions of the world, even if the Law of Love from which the former derived had been "most clearly expressed" in the Christian religion. What is more, every individual, in his view, could comprehend this Law of Love by light of his reason, which Tolstoy equated with the conscience implanted by God in each human being. "If you consider it irrational to go to kill Turks or Germans, do not go . . . ," he advised. To a young Hessian who wrote to him in 1899 in connection with the draft, Tolstoy replied: "It is not only Christians but all just people who must refuse to become soldiers—that is, to be ready on another's command (for this is what a soldier's duty actually consists of) to kill all those one is ordered to kill." Certainly Tolstoy would have approved of what today is known as "selective objection," i.e., a refusal on conscientious grounds, whether religious or nonreligious, to fight in a given conflict without commitment, however, to reject participation in all wars. But of course he went further, pleading for a total renunciation of war (as well as of the state). Resistance of this kind, he argued, was "universal to all mankind" because it was rooted in an ethical principle which was "intelligible and common to all men, of whatever religion or nation, whether Catholic, Mohammedan, Buddhist, Confucian, whether Spaniards or Japanese"—to humanists and deists as much as to those who were professedly theists. He saw each act of conscientious objection as a drop of water which, once it oozes through a dam, begins to burst it asunder. Eventually, with the accumulation of countless such drops, the dam breaks. Then the time would have come when "of wars and armies, as these are now, there will remain only the recollection."

These were dreams. The six decades since Tolstoy's death have brought two world wars of unparalleled destructiveness, totalitarian regimes in some areas (including his own Russia) of undreamed-of oppressiveness, and the mounting threat in these latter years of a reversion to barbarism, if not of universal obliteration, should nuclear war ever be unleashed. Tolstoy's hopes that refusal of military service might eventually become so widespread that governments would find it impossible to undertake war, and would be forced thereby to relinquish their sway over their subjects' lives, have not been fulfilled. Mankind seems no nearer to renouncing violent resistance to evil than it was when he first appeared with his message to humanity. Nevertheless, certain elements of his doctrine—the universality of the Law of Love, for instance, or the belief in the power of a nonviolent alternative to the law of violence—have been given renewed relevance today precisely on account of the baneful developments in military technology, which are threatening the continued existence of civilized life on this planet. Tolstoy sought to reinvigorate, to reconstitute, and to extend the antimilitarism of Christ and the early Christian church. In attempting this he became, by the sheer force of his moral will, a major influence in bringing into being a new pacifism, more universal in its outreach than the sectarian Christian pacifism with which I have been mainly concerned and more conscious than previous religious pacifism had usually been of the extent to which war and violence were rooted in the social environment. As an organized movement and as a compact intellectual system, Tolstoyism disappeared. Its influence has remained, helping to produce a healthy fermentation of ideas in twentieth-century pacifism and an increased awareness of the need for individual moral responsibility in regard to social violence and war.

Conclusions

In the present volume, as well as in my two companion volumes, *Pacifism in the United States* before 1914 and *Twentieth-Century Pacifism*, I have attempted to isolate—with the least possible harm to the texture of a complex whole—one particular approach to peace and to trace its development from its first appearance at the outset of the Christian era up until the present. (Sociologists, I hope, will forgive me for stating my general conclusions at the end instead of the beginning of my researches.) The main problem, therefore, in defining the object of study has been to disengage the history of pacifism from the broader current of thought which A.J.P. Taylor has called "pacificism," i.e., from the history of mankind's efforts to devise a way of abolishing war or reducing its incidence to a minimum. Pacificism in this sense is much older than pacifism, and it is historically rooted also in traditions other than the Judaeo-Christian, which pacifism is not. Pacificism is relativist; pacifism is integral, absolutist. At the center of pacifist ideology is "the element of personal responsibility" (A.C.F. Beales) predicating an individual moral decision to withhold cooperation in the process of waging war. For instance, the absence of integral pacifism in the Chinese and Indian pasts, despite the presence of strong pacifistic trends, may perhaps be attributable to the absence in their religio-political traditions of that strong element of personal responsibility which is especially conspicuous in the Judaeo-Christian tradition.

"Conscientious objection," embodying this sense of personal responsibility, forms an essential part of pacifist ideology, even if we grant that it may feature sometimes as a submerged element rather than an explicitly articulated fact: for instance, in periods and with social groups where compulsory military service was not enforced rigorously or at all. Here we may have to extrapolate a position of individual war resistance from more generally framed support for nonviolence. (The antimilitarist witness of the early Christian church is a case in point.) However, this must be done with care; otherwise we may be attributing thought-patterns to persons or groups which in fact did not possess them.

Two areas of possible ambiguity appear at this point. First, as our narrative shows, the exact point where pacifist noncooperation in war and violence begins has varied enormously in the course of the cen-

471

turies and from group to group. On the one hand, it may involve complete dissociation from the environing society and state, which has been attempted by Hutterite communities since their inception in the sixteenth century, or, on the other, it may be limited solely to a refusal to commit homicide. In this case a pacifist will be prepared to accept conscription into the armed forces provided only that he is not required to use lethal weapons. In the second place, many different opinions have existed within the historic pacifist movement concerning exactly which forms of violence and coercion are unacceptable. Most pacifists, for instance, have not been vegetarians: however, the nonviolent philosophy of a Tolstoy or a Gandhi rejected the killing of animals as well as men. Some pacifists, especially those in the Anabaptist-Mennonite tradition, have repudiated the whole apparatus of government, along with war, as essentially violent in character and therefore incompatible with the realization of human brotherhood. Distinctions have been made between injurious and noninjurious coercion (see the debate between Tolstoy and Ballou). Even rejection of all war does not appear to be a normative factor in pacifism, since pacifists (as for example during the American Civil War) have sometimes distinguished here between international war and species of civil war which should be regarded properly not as war but as police action. Moreover, until the coming of modern Biblical criticism, Christian pacifists, including even the Quakers, granted the God-approved character of Old Testament wars which took place before Christ had replaced the law of revenge by a new and more loving dispensation.

If pacifism eludes watertight definition, its classification presents equally formidable problems. More work has been done on the typology of nonviolence (e.g., by the sociologist Gene Sharp) than on that of pacifism *stricto sensu*. For the latter I would like to suggest, tentatively, classification into the following types: (1) vocational, (2) soteriological, (3) eschatological, (4) separational, (5) integrational, (6) goal-directed.

(1) *Vocational pacifism*, in fact, scarcely fits within the definition of pacifism attempted above. Although for the vocationalists nonviolence is absolute in respect to an individual who has accepted it for his own way of life, they make no claim for its integral acceptance by others who have not chosen the same calling. For the rules of one calling are not incumbent on those who have adopted another, even if a less elevated one. We may describe, if we like, the members of certain Buddhist, Jain, and medieval Christian monastic orders as vocational pacifists, provided we bear in mind the reservations made just above. Perhaps a maverick pacifist like Dwight L. Moody in the nineteenth

472

century (see my *Pacifism in the U.S.*), or certain conscientious objectors in the twentieth century who have refused military service on the grounds of a higher calling to artistic or humanitarian work, may also be described most properly as vocational pacifists. The non-combatant position of the eighteenth-century Moravian Brethren in regard to military service (as a perusal of the relevant chapter in my *Pacifism in the U.S.* will show) was very close to that of vocational pacifism, even if at times and with certain Brethren it took on a more principled character; and the same may be said of those medieval nonviolent sectarians who belonged to the category of the "perfect." Yet in both these cases there seems to have been present something more than a merely vocational pacifism.

(2) *Soteriological pacifism* is found rather rarely. By this term I mean an objection to shedding human blood (and sometimes animals' as well) because it leads to ritual impurity and thus to the loss of personal salvation, at least until some form of purification is undergone. Vocationally this has been the standpoint of the priesthood in various primitive religions. The early Christian repugnance to homicide stemmed in part from a similar feeling which continued to linger after the official church had abandoned its opposition to soldiering. (Yet, I would stress, the antimilitarism of the early church resulted primarily from other factors.) Soteriological considerations are to be found at the roots of the early Cathar objection to war, though here, too, moral concepts developed and finally came to predominate. In its pristine form, however, the soteriological type is not easily comprehended within the normative pacifism outlined above.

(3) *Eschatological pacifism*, a kind of nonviolent interim-ethic, still lies in the border zone between a principled and a conditional pacifism but it merges more easily with pacifism proper than the first two categories, for what begins as an interim-ethic may eventually be transformed into a settled moral code if the expected "final things" do not take place. It is doubtful if we should count as pacifists either the chiliastic Taborite priests who preached peace in 1418-1419 but then called for a sword to extirpate the godless when it appeared that this would not happen without the intervention of human hands, or the pre-Munsterite enthusiasts who on the very eve of their "reign of terror" still urged their fellow "Covenanters" to put aside their weapons and wait peacefully for the Lord to do his work. But the fiercely apocalyptic Melchior Hofmann may have espoused a consistent non-resistance to evil despite the violent stance which his followers were to adopt as a result of his eschatological visions (though the sources are not at all clear at this point). In more recent times, the eschatolog-

ical pacifism of Plymouth Brethren, Seventh-Day Adventists, and Christadelphians—as well as of several less familiar Russian sects—contains in practice a larger element of nonviolence than of repressed apocalyptic warfare, though the Jehovah's Witnesses still stress battles to come and the final struggle at Armageddon.

(4) *Separational pacifism* represents the typical position of the sectarian pacifist and is best exemplified in the nonresistance doctrines held successively by Czech Brethren, Anabaptists—Swiss, German, Dutch, and Polish—and Mennonites. Tolstoy preached a more secularized version of nonresistance in the nineteenth century, as did William Lloyd Garrison and his New England nonresistant associates. The Hutterites have practiced it in its most rigidly sectarian and most consistent form, while many other small sects in Europe and North America have adhered to it with more or less exactitude. Some writers have tended to blur the distinction between vocational and separational pacifism—in my view quite unwarrantedly. Separational pacifists, while affirming both the impossibility of transforming the existing sociopolitical structure on a peaceable model and the need for its continuance until the end of time, simultaneously postulate the indispensability of all the redeemed separating from society as completely as possible so as to shape their lives according to a higher righteousness than the one accepted by the unredeemed. At the core of the nonresistance doctrine as historically exemplified especially in the Anabaptist-Mennonite tradition is the idea of discipleship, of full restitutionism, i.e., a more exact reproduction of the practice of the primitive Christian congregation than was ever contemplated in the piecemeal restitutionism of Protestant reformers like Luther or Zwingli. In the minds of the evangelical Anabaptists, and of their forerunners and successors, the New Testament is seen as law, with its center the Law of Love which has superseded the Mosaic Law and annulled the sway of all earthly legal codes over the consciences of believers. Separational pacifists have not sought to abolish war directly (an impossible task in their view, in any case) and have only rarely appealed to humanitarian sentiment in their critique of war. Yet in their eyes war stands condemned absolutely and the children of light should have nothing to do with this work of darkness. The principle of nonresistance to evil not only judges carnal warfare and finds it wholly wanting, but repudiates temporal society. It does not attempt, indeed, "to speak truth to power," because this would prove useless; power, that is, the sword-bearing magistracy, belongs to the realm of evil which, though conditionally justified, stands "outside the perfection of Christ." The

ethical dualism implied in this view is thus by no means identical with that embodied in vocational pacifism.

(5) *Integrational pacifism*, though a fairly late development in the history of pacifism, represents its most characteristic expression in the twentieth-century West. Emerging in embryonic form among sectarian pacifist groups like the Polish Socinians or the Anglo-American Quakers, it has expanded with the growth, since the early nineteenth century, of pacificistic sentiment in the Protestant denominations and of an institutional peace movement opposing war and violence primarily from humanitarian and rationalist, rather than strictly religious, motives. It has tended to replace legalism, a textually bound Law of Love, by the "Spirit of Christ" which forbids the use of "carnal weapons," eventually broadening out to include ethical approaches other than the Christian. This type of pacifism combines a pacifist ethic with participation in an existing—or possibly reformed—politicosocial system, without, however, positing the conversion of all to a monolithic religious ethic. It rejects not government itself but only its use of injurious force, seeking at the same time to integrate pacifism into the worldly order. Thus, "it will criticize some traits of the social system, but hardly reject it *in toto*" (Werner Stark).

Although the Society of Friends long remained a typical sect in Ernst Troeltsch's definition of this term, the Quaker peace testimony, once it had crystallized, became integrational—apart, that is, from occasional (and temporary) Quaker lapses into a separational stance. Quaker pacifism had emerged out of the political experience of the mid-seventeenth-century English Revolution: early Quakers in many instances never entirely shed their enthusiasm for the Good Old Cause. For all their disillusionment with the practical outcome of that Revolution, they continued to be optimistic concerning mankind's potentialities for good and to reject the deep-rooted pessimism concerning politics which we find in the Anabaptist-Mennonite *Weltanschauung*. In fact, the integrational type of pacifism is conceivable only in conditions of religious and political pluralism, which existed scarcely anywhere before the English Revolution. The thinking of Penn and Bellers on peace and war prefigured that of nineteenth- and twentieth-century Friends who have acted as a yeast within the wider peace movement. Quaker pacifists have usually sought to leaven the world rather than withdraw from it as the separational pacifists have done. The same may be said of such twentieth-century pacifist organizations as the British Peace Pledge Union or the various Fellowships of Reconciliation, even if here, as with many contemporary leftist political parties (for example, the Independent Labour Party in Great Britain or the nonpacifist Jewish *Bund* in interwar Poland), we may indeed easily detect a tendency to take up sectarian positions.

(6) *Goal-directed pacifism,* while closely linked with the integrational type, merges at the same time with the "nonintentional" application of nonviolence to conflict situations, i.e., with what may be described as "selective nonviolence." It posits as a moral principle the consistent employment of nonviolent techniques to achieve desired political or social goals on the grounds that, at least in the long run, these techniques are practically more effective than, and/or ethically superior to, violence. The idea of nonviolent resistance to wrong and nonviolent coercion to achieve the right (terminology varies here: Gandhi spoke compactly of *Satyagraha,* truth-force, which also has the advantage of stressing that the ethical component is essential) does not appear as a definite concept in the history of pacifism, except at a very embryonic stage, until the nineteenth century, although its practice "nonintentionally" dates back millennia. At first, pacifists had been of the separational type and had urged nonresistance and not nonviolent resistance; later, as in the case of the Quakers and the peace societies, they had developed the institutional approach to "the promotion of permanent and universal peace." But nonviolence is potentially a revolutionary weapon, since it seeks political or social change also outside existing mechanisms for reform and may involve civil disobedience under certain circumstances. Among its forerunners have been the Garrisonian nonresistants, who used nonviolent direct action in the cause of antislavery (only a handful of them were actually blacks), as well as Tolstoy, who hoped that the spread of conscientious objection would ultimately destroy both war and the war-making state; Mahatma Gandhi should be considered as both its greatest exponent and its greatest practitioner so far. National independence, civil rights, social change (or nonviolent revolution), and the prevention of war have been among its chief objectives in this century.

I have spoken above of conscientious objection as constituting a central component of pacifist ideology; it plays, indeed, an important role in all the types of pacifism enumerated, except perhaps the last. Before the sixteenth century, however, its incidence is hard to determine, and it becomes an insistent problem only with the arrival of universal conscription at the end of the eighteenth century. Despite the fact that many writers have attempted to depict pacifism as a negative creed, conscientious objection forms merely the reverse side of what is primarily positive: the Law of Love of the nonresistants, or "that life and power that [takes] away the occasion of all wars" (George Fox),

476

or Gandhian *Satyagraha*. And conscientious objection itself, although outwardly negative, epitomizes a positive factor, the individual pacifist's responsibility for his behavior in regard to the social phenomena of war and violence. It acts, as it were, as a symbol making the individual's position clear to others (sometimes of course it may also do very much more). It is primarily a moral stance deriving from religious or ethical motives, though since the nineteenth century pragmatic considerations have also been present sometimes.

The distinction commonly made in this century between alternativist and absolutist objectors is a valid one and has its roots in history. The Mennonites throughout their history have incarnated the alternativist approach, whereas the Quakers until almost the twentieth century required members to take an absolutist position if called upon to perform military service, disownment most frequently resulting from failure to follow this regulation. Such differences are of course rooted in differing historical environments and in differing *Weltanschauungen*. With separational pacifists like the Mennonites the office of the sword enjoyed conditional justification (and the same is true in the case of several of our other pacifist types); it enjoyed the right to demand from them the things that are Caesar's, taxes and *corvées* and auxiliary services, even when these were connected in some way with the waging of war. Guilt for bloodshed was not theirs but the ruler's. Naturally they refused to render direct military service: they refused, too, to perform noncombatant service in the army or to hire a substitute to take their place in the ranks, unless no other more acceptable way out offered itself. The foregoing narrative has shown the bewildering variety of alternatives accepted by Mennonites down the centuries in lieu of serving with weapons, payment of commutation money being the most usual form: the right to do this was granted Dutch Mennonites by William of Orange in 1575 in the first piece of legislation providing for conscientious objection to military service.

Anabaptist-Mennonite nonresistance was the product of a pre-democratic age: the Quaker peace testimony emerged immediately following a proto-democratic revolution. Friends not only fought valiantly in the Lamb's War; they also became among the most stubborn upholders of the freeborn Englishman's rights, whether at home or across the Atlantic. When a man's religion forbids him to bear arms, so they argued, the state infringes his liberties in requiring him to pay a "tax" or perform some alternative service in exchange for permission to follow conscience, since to follow conscience without impediment is a free man's inalienable right. The demand for unconditional exemption from military duties expressed by groups like the Quakers or the

477

Shakers was conditioned in part by the emphasis given to individual liberty in the English political tradition and in its offshoots overseas; the practice of absolutism, too, was eased in the British Isles and in North America by the comparatively light penalties normally imposed for refusal to conform, especially when compared to those suffered by absolutists on the European continent. Individualism helps to explain, too, the extreme sensitivity of the Quaker conscience at most times in avoiding any activity which could be regarded as contributing, even indirectly, to the waging of war. The readiness of George Fox and some early Friends to advise payment of war taxes (Quakers, except for an occasional tax radical, have ordinarily paid taxes "in the mixture") may be explained, perhaps, by a sediment of Anabaptist sentiment still present at the beginning of the Quaker peace testimony. On the other hand, the consistent refusal to contribute such taxes on the part of the Anabaptist Hutterites may stem from the radical character of their Christian discipleship and from the fact of their isolation in an alien society.

Once the original anti-Anabaptist fury had died down, the Mennonites, along with similar pacifist sects, were able to establish a *modus vivendi* with the governments of the *ancien régime*, at least in the Protestant countries of the continent or in areas like Catholic Poland where a measure of religious tolerance prevailed. This *ancien régime* was founded on privilege: the *privilegia* issued to the Mennonites, granting them, *inter alia*, the privilege of exchanging personal military service for a monetary payment, fitted perfectly into the existing political pattern. The sectaries were valuable to their rulers as economic assets. And the arrangement arrived at answered, too, the needs of the Mennonites' conscience: it allowed them to pursue the path of a separated but intense discipleship while at the same time giving due recognition to the God-ordained powers working "outside the perfection of Christ." The advent of egalitarian democracy altered all this; it swept away the Mennonites' *Wehrfreiheit* together with other remnants of a "feudal" order. Prussian Mennonites meekly accepted noncombatant duties in the army, but German Mennonitism as a whole was in a state of decay. When, in the 1870's, universal conscription was also introduced in Tsarist Russia, the Mennonites' threat to emigrate *en masse* (their centuries-old answer to persecution when it became unbearable) helped to obtain more acceptable conditions for those who eventually agreed to remain. Yet the crisis of the 1870's showed that in Russia, too, the Mennonite peace witness was watered down.

We may note that most eschatological pacifists, whose main attention is concentrated on judgment to come, have accepted noncombatant service (but the Jehovah's Witnesses have not). In recent times, that is, since the widespread introduction of universal military service, both separational and integrational pacifists, on the other hand, have asked for something more—either alternative civilian service or unconditional exemption (a minority position).

Finally, in this discussion an answer, if only a provisional one, must be attempted in regard to the following two questions: (1) What social situations have led to the genesis and growth of pacifist ideologies, and (2) what are the factors leading to the decay of pacifist groups? In both cases we are hindered by the fact that little serious work has been done hitherto to investigate the social structure of pacifist sects and organizations. What we possess, at best, are merely fragmentary data and the often unsupported generalizations of previous writers. With regard to the early church or the medieval sects, the sources on this aspect are never likely to yield very much: the same is true of some other areas of pacifist history.

(1) Pacifism cannot be traced in an unbroken succession of genetically connected groups back to its first emergence (so far as we know) in the early Roman Empire. The links are severed at three points in time: first in the fourth century when the acceptance of Christianity as the established religion of the Empire rapidly brought to an end the profession of pacifist sentiments in the church until such ideas reappeared almost a millennium later among heretical groups like the Cathars (though they may have had a distant link with the pacifistic Marcionite heresy of the second century A.D.) or the Waldenses; then in the early sixteenth century when evangelical Anabaptism emerged without having any genetic connection, it would seem, with late medieval sectarian pacifism; and finally in the mid-seventeenth century when Quakerism evolved a peace testimony which was influenced, in a remote way if at all, by earlier pacifist thought. But in our discussion we must take into consideration not only these four "ports of entry"—the apostolic church at the outset, the emergence of pacifistic Catharism and Waldensianism, the founding of the Swiss Brethren, and the crystallization of the Quaker peace testimony—but also the more important secondary formations, the Unity of Czech Brethren, the Dutch Mennonite community, the pacifist trend within the nineteenth-century peace movement, Tolstoyism, and Gandhian nonviolence.

All geneses of a pacifist ideology, whether primary or secondary, display certain features in common: (1) a background situation of acute social tension, and (2) the pre-existence of a pacificistic tradition which acts as a catalyst in crystallizing the new integrally pacifist ideology; its absence, as for example in prerevolutionary France, would make the generation of a new pacifist strain extremely improbable. In addition, (3) a new pacifist group usually, though not invariably (exceptions are the nineteenth-century peace movement and the Gandhian movement), possesses a quasi-proletarian complexion even if its intellectual leaders may be drawn largely from higher social strata including the nobility (the lowest social strata are almost always absent), and it usually is in part an expression of social protest. Nonviolence, as well as revolutionary violence, is often found among "the churches of the disinherited," to use H. Richard Niebuhr's well-known definition. Indeed pacifism could scarcely be generated afresh within a completely stable and static environment or inside a rigidly orthodox church. At the same time, to regard "proto-revolutionary," parallel-to-revolution, and "post-revolutionary" pacifism as basic categories in the aetiology of pacifism (as David A. Martin, for instance, has done) seems to me to be stating no more than the obvious, that pacifism as the product of a period of tension will probably occur before, during, and after revolution. Investigation of environmental tensions, pre-existing pacificistic traditions, and the social composition of membership, while by no means likely to explain everything, appears to be the most promising avenue of approach.

Thus, for example, the early Christian church sprang up in the unsettled social and political conditions of the eastern Mediterranean world in the first century A.D., its opposition to war and violence was rooted in the conditional pacifism of sects like the Jewish Essenes or the Gnostics, and it tended to rally the outcast from society to its cause (although by no means exclusively these). The Waldenses, the main exponents of pacifism in the High Middle Ages, expanded at first in the strife-torn north Italian cities, taking over pacifism as a result of contacts with the older Cathars, whose nonviolence may have developed for soteriological purposes and then been strengthened by the influence of a Christian restorationism. In the beginning they spread chiefly among urban artisans and, later, among peasants. In late medieval Bohemia the Chelčický Brethren and their immediate successors of the Unity of Brethren were the product of the political and social tensions generated by the Hussite Revolution and the Hussite Wars; their pacifist ideology clearly reflects its Waldensian origins; and the Czech Unity, for as long as the Old Brethren controlled its destinies and maintained pacifism as an obligatory tenet, remained a rural sect despising book-learning and the ways of town and castle.

The Swiss Brethren, with whom the evangelical trend in German Anabaptism began, arose in 1524-1525 on the eve of the Peasants' War in neighboring Germany and of sporadic outbreaks of rural unrest nearer home, while Menno Simons's renewal of Anabaptism commenced in 1536, a year after the *débâcle* at Münster. With both the Swiss Brethren and the early Mennonites (despite the one's being "pre-revolutionary" and the other "post-revolutionary"), an identical vision, the idea of restitution and of an exact discipleship such as the Magisterial Reformers had put forward too at the outset of the Protestant Reformation, provided the exterior intellectual influence which prompted them to an even more rigorous application than the Magisterial Reformers could countenance themselves. Whereas the latter retained the sword-bearing magistracy inside the Christian community along with infant baptism, the evangelical Anabaptists and the Mennonites discarded both as incompatible with the restoration of the congregation "without spot or wrinkle." Erasmian pacificism may also have played a role in the genesis of Anabaptist nonresistance: the ideology took shape in the circle of burgher humanists gathered around Conrad Grebel in Zürich. However, the backbone of early Anabaptism (Paul Peachey has shown) was formed by the artisan element. Peasants and handicraftsmen preserved the movement in Switzerland and Germany during the dark years of persecution; these social strata, as revealed by Vos and Mellink among others, were foremost, too, in sixteenth-century Dutch Anabaptism, or Mennonitism, as it became, though they lost importance later as the composition of the sect became more bourgeois.

The conditions giving rise to the pacifism of the Polish antitrinitarian Anabaptists are not easy to discern: the problem, in fact, merges imperceptibly with a wider one involving the origin of the whole radical ideology of the Polish Antitrinitarians. Antitrinitarian pacifism, as a secondary formation deriving from the primary Anabaptist root of nonresistance—and, at least in regard to its later Socinian variant, possibly from Renaissance pacificism too—can be located without difficulty in pacifism's family tree. But why should we find social radicalism, including pacifism, in a sect which attracted members of the landed nobility in considerable numbers? Moreover, why did such social radicalism arise in a country like Poland which remained free in this period from serious outbreaks of political or social disorder? Polish historians have so far failed to come up with any very convincing answers. We have noted in chapter 4 the presence of "plebeian" elements within the ranks of the antitrinitarian Minor Church, which gave it its direction until the landed nobility and their intellectual mentors, like Socinus, took over control. In fact, from the beginning these elements—a non-noble pastorate and largely artisan urban con-

481

gregations, together with a handful of "penitent" gentlemen anxious to renounce their noble status in exchange for a clear conscience—provided the mainstay of the Minor Church's antimilitarism and social radicalism (though not, however, of its theological radicalism). Where the noble element was strongest, as in the Grand Duchy of Lithuania, pacifism was almost nonexistent. The half-submerged social tensions of Polish urban life undoubtedly constituted a factor in producing pacifism and social radicalism, as did the clashing religio-political interests within the Polish Commonwealth. In addition, a wide measure of religious toleration and the political freedoms of a *Ständestaat* provided in Poland of the age of Reformation, as it had done in the Hussite kingdom of Bohemia during the previous century, an environment favorable to such social experimentation—the nobility's growing oppression of the peasantry in these two countries notwithstanding.

England in the third quarter of the seventeenth century, in contrast to Poland a century earlier, presents a clear picture of social fermentation. Whereas recently Richard T. Vann, while admitting that the evidence available is not easy to interpret, has argued "that in the beginnings of Quakerism the [lesser] gentry and wholesale traders were especially drawn to it" along with many yeomen, and that it was these strata, and not the *petite bourgeoisie*, which provided most of the leadership, hitherto "almost all writers dealing with the earliest period of Quakerism have emphasized the relative poverty of most of the early Friends." In any case, politically they represented elements gravitating toward the parliamentary left. The sources of their pacifism are scarcely easier to discover than the pattern of their social stratification: but it represents probably yet another attempt at New Testament restitutionism illuminated this time by the Holy Spirit of Puritan religion.

Neither the nonsectarian pacifism of the nineteenth and twentieth centuries nor Gandhian nonviolence constitutes a primary formation of pacifist ideology, though they possess certain independent features of importance. We have discussed their derivation in the course of this history of pacifism. Neither movement possessed quasi-proletarian origins or resulted at all directly from a situation of social tension. Whereas Gandhi and his followers were primarily nationalists, modern Western pacifists have for the most part continued to be recruited largely from the ranks of middle-class political radicalism or ethical socialism. (The British Campaign for Nuclear Disarmament [C.N.D.] in the late 1950's and early 1960's, for instance, has been aptly compared to that archetype of Victorian middle-class radicalism, the Anti-

Corn Law League of the early 1840's.) It would be unwise indeed to try to squeeze modern pacifism into categories designed primarily to explain the genesis of earlier phenomena. Indeed the urgency taken on by the problem of war in the course of the last century and a half has introduced a new dimension into the discussion.

Indigenous Russian pacifism, though also of comparatively recent vintage, fits more easily into the traditional pattern. Dukhobor ideology, for example, with a pre-existent model for pacifism in the somewhat nebulous ideas of the priestless wing of the Old Believers, gained adherents among the peasantry in the restless era preceding the abolition of serfdom in 1861 (as the closely related pacifistic Molokans did too). Tolstoy's doctrine of nonresistance to evil found its main support in the same kind of circles of the youthful intelligentsia as provided the mainstay of the revolutionary movement. Indeed, Tolstoyism has a "totalism" characteristic of Russian pre-revolutionary thought: however, the reason why an individual chose Tolstoyan nonviolence rather than the path of violent revolution is by no means clear. Tolstoyism provides perhaps the most effective model of what has been defined as "proto-revolutionary" pacifism. (We have seen in the text that certain alleged instances of proto-revolutionary pacifism prove on nearer acquaintance most likely either to be examples of an interim-ethic, as in the case of the Taborite chiliasts in 1418-1419, or to have been incorrectly extrapolated from the pacifism of a closely related movement, as in the case of the Dutch Anabaptist Melchiorites of the early 1530's.)

(2) The factors leading to the decay of a group's pacifism are no easier to locate than are those resulting in its genesis. But we may hazard the generalization in regard to sectarian pacifism that decay usually results from a fossilization of the pacifist ideology as well as of other aspects of the sectarian outlook accompanied, and in part caused by, acculturation of the group to the environing society. However, there have often been extraneous factors causing decay, too, separate, that is, from those generated by a fossilizing pacifist witness or by acculturation. The evolution from sect to denomination, i.e., from social alienation to social adjustment, has proved disastrous for pacifism in almost all cases, and we find the pacifist leadership of a newly formed denomination usually unable to impose its pacifism on the denomination (the Disciples of Christ in the United States are a good example of this phenomenon). Only exceptionally has external intervention on the part of state or society proved the decisive factor in eliminating pacifism. The Waldenses for instance, although severely hampered by persecution, managed somehow to survive for many cen-

turies before finally jettisoning their pacifism; the Unity of Czech Brethren and the Minor Church of the Polish Antitrinitarians, although eventually suppressed, had already abandoned their pacifist witness before this took place. Some pacifist sects like the Anabaptists even made a virtue of necessity and valued martyrdom and small numbers as marks of the true church. In lands embraced by the Anglo-American political tradition toleration of pacifism has continued uninterruptedly, punctuated only in wartime by more restrictive attitudes. Although the system of universal military conscription introduced in the nineteenth century on the European continent has proved indeed a severe handicap in the maintenance of pacifism in this area, only in the Soviet Union and temporarily in Germany under the Nazis have pacifist movements of any size suffered complete repression. We must seek within, therefore, for the roots of decay.

The history of Mennonites in the Netherlands and Germany provides perhaps the best case-study here (although unfortunately in this field no one has so far completed any social research in depth). Mennonites required formal adherence to nonresistance and conscientious objection from all members, and they excluded from their fellowship any who openly transgressed the congregational discipline on this point. However, formal adherence to these things came to be matched only occasionally by internal allegiance to them, so that when the discipline ceased to be enforced as a result of the process of acculturation's transforming the other worldly sect into a nonexclusive denomination, personal conviction failed to uphold the Mennonite peace testimony for much longer. It lacked inner strength; no dynamism remained to effect its renewal. The strata which originally composed a majority of the Mennonite community—the simple artisans and raw peasants who upheld its peace testimony during the martyr age—had been replaced (at first it was a matter of influence but finally became one of numbers) by prosperous and cultivated bourgeois and well-to-do farmers. Nonresistance remained a living faith longest among the obscure craftsmen who filled the extreme separatist congregations in the towns of the Netherlands or within the isolated rural congregations in Friesland, the Vistula delta, or the south Russian steppe. The various special *privilegia* granted the Mennonites, though sparing them hardship on account of their refusal to bear arms, contributed in the course of time to the fossilization of their pacifism by effectively preventing its adaptation to the needs of a new and more democratic age. When the Mennonites of Holland and Germany eventually broke out of their sectarian enclosure, they abandoned everything that was as-

484

sociated with their previous captivity—not only peculiar social customs and old fashioned theology, but their repudiation of war.

Another, almost classic illustration of the explanation of decay given above, though one less thoroughgoing in its scope, is to be found in the history of the Czech Brethren (see chapter 1). The effectiveness of city-bred scholars and men of rank in the 1490's in reshaping the sectarian and rural ideology of the "Old Brethren" in a spirit more in line with contemporary society could scarcely have occurred unless the old sociopolitical ideology had already become largely fossilized. The Polish Antitrinitarians present a more complex picture. Here sectarian nonresistance and a more lax sociopolitical position existed alongside each other from the beginning and continued to do so, at any rate in theory, until the dissolution of the Minor Church. The presence of an influential noble element strongly entrenched within the Church prevented the sectarian view from being enforced on the membership by disciplinary measures, although from time to time it was attempted unsuccessfully. Loyalty to a state which granted religious toleration and a wide measure of political freedom (except for the enserfed peasantry which mostly remained faithful to the Catholic religion) affected all strata represented in the Minor Church: not only the Antitrinitarian nobles but its spiritual leaders of plebeian origin, and even the numerous foreign immigrants who sought a refuge in Poland from persecution at home (the views of the radical pacifist Baron von Wolzogen provide an example of the strength of these feelings). In the case of Polish Antitrinitarianism it was not fossilization of the pacifist ideology, followed by its thoroughgoing rejection on behalf of the whole body by an acculturated section of the membership, that occurred, but rather its gradual adaptation, amounting, in fact, to a piecemeal but virtually complete deradicalization of the sociopolitical ideology dominant within the church hitherto. Faustus Socinus was responsible for providing the intellectual arguments to justify the transition from social radicalism to social conformity.

The Anglo-American Society of Friends presents the only example so far of a major pacifist group which has made the transition from sect to denomination without eventually discarding its pacifism in the process; but the Mennonites in North America may prove another instance of this (whereas the closely related Church of the Brethren appears to be moving slowly, but perhaps irreversibly, toward a total abandonment of pacifism). True, pacifism has been virtually dropped in certain sections of the Society of Friends (e.g., in some of the pastoral yearly meetings of central and western United States) but it still

485

remains firmly embedded in the thought and practice of the Quaker mainstream on both sides of the Atlantic. Indeed, the Society's "capacity for renaissance" in regard to its social testimonies is apparent throughout its history; deradicalization has never been complete.

Despite the fact that the Quaker peace testimony became institutionalized soon after its inception, with the penalty of disownment attached for infringement of the group discipline on this point, in principle the pacifism of Friends, as we have seen, was integrational rather than separational. Therefore it was easier for them to adapt their peace testimony so as to make it meaningful in a changed world, and thus both to prevent fossilization and at the same time to meet the challenge of acculturation. (William Penn, though perhaps not George Fox, would surely have experienced little difficulty in collaborating in the work of the twentieth-century peace movement, which is itself the product to some extent of earlier Quaker efforts—either directly, as in England, or indirectly, as in the United States.) But the process of adaptation did not happen of itself; it was fraught with obstacles. The Quaker objector to service in the militia, like other sectarian conscientious objectors, had been the conformist within his own religious community. In the "Holy Experiment" of Quaker Pennsylvania, pacifism, far from being a mark of social alienation, was professed—sometimes, it is true, in word more often than in deed—by the political establishment. Fossilization of so carefully nurtured a plant as the Quaker peace testimony became in the eighteenth and early nineteenth centuries might easily have ensued, and efforts to renew without disintegrating it might have come to nought.

In regard to such modern integrally pacifist organizations set up on a nonsectarian basis as the London Peace Society, New England Non-Resistance Society, League of Universal Brotherhood, Universal Peace Union, No-Conscription Fellowship (N.C.F.), Peace Pledge Union (P.P.U.), etc., it is hard to generalize concerning the reasons for their failure to maintain themselves. Sometimes the passing of a particular crisis which the organization was created to meet—for instance, conscription in Britain in World War I in the case of the N.C.F., or the struggle for national independence with the first generation of Gandhians in India—may account for a movement's disintegration. In some instances fossilization on the sectarian model, a process, as we have seen, present also in extreme doctrinaire political parties, may provide an explanation, as in the case of the Garrisonian Non-Resistance Society or Alfred H. Love's Universal Peace Union. Failure to adapt to changed political circumstances can be operative, too: this, for example, may help to elucidate the rapid expansion of the P.P.U.

486

immediately prior to World War II and its dwindling influence after 1945. Some integralist bodies like the London Peace Society or Elihu Burritt's League of Universal Brotherhood soon became wider in scope and broader in membership than their official platforms indicated, and thus their later history cannot be comprehended easily within the framework of pacifism *stricto sensu*.

In this concluding section I have attempted first to give a working definition of normative pacifism and a typology of pacifism as well as conscientious objection, and then to examine briefly the aetiology of pacifism and the factors leading to its decline. These are extremely complex problems. More work of a detailed nature needs to be done, and especially—the sources permitting—statistical study (an area into which I have not ventured), before answers can be assayed with any kind of assurance; thus what has been said above is clearly of a tentative and provisional character. The problem of war and violence, however, has become more pressing today than ever before, and consideration of the various ways proposed for achieving lasting harmony between men, pacifism included, will continue to occupy the attention of concerned persons. The present volume, together with its two sequels on the United States before 1914 and on the twentieth century, will be able to make, I hope, a modest contribution to this quest.

Appendix

In the century before 1914 sectarian pacifism in the central and western areas of the European continent was not confined to the small groups of Mennonites, Quakers, and Tolstoyans described in previous chapters. Several new denominations arose professing a strict Christian nonresistance, and their members clashed from time to time with the state which attempted to conscript them into the armed services. There were also a number of individuals unaffiliated with any church (a few of whom were professedly nonreligious) or belonging to religious bodies in which pacifist sentiment had not been voiced hitherto, who now came forward in total condemnation of war. Though they shared a belief in the nonviolent imperative, these groups and individuals were unconnected with each other either genetically or by contemporary contacts (though in some instances there was a tenuous link with Quakers or Mennonites or a vague Tolstoyan influence). It seems best, therefore, to reserve treatment of them for an appendix, since it is hard to weave a coherent narrative from what must necessarily appear disjointed and episodic.

Europe in the nineteenth century—as in the preceding century, though at a slower pace—produced an expanding number of moral protests against war, which did something to counteract the very much larger body of educated opinion in favor of militarism and of an uninhibited national egotism. Philosophers vied with political economists and sociologists in branding war as a crime against civilization and an offense against humanity; they drew up blueprints for a European society of nations and planned new moral orders to embrace all mankind. From 1815, peace advocates organized peace societies in most states on the continent; some of these societies were socially conservative and looked on universal peace as a final preservative of the old order, whereas others were politically radical and, from the mid-nineteenth century onward, sometimes advocated socialism as well.

By the beginning of the twentieth century antimilitarism was written into the programs of the newly formed continental socialist parties from France to the Balkans. However, the parliamentary socialists did not repudiate national defense, urging only that a citizen army be instituted in place of the existing military system dominated by a professional officer caste. This *armée nouvelle—la nation armée*—was to be organized on egalitarian lines; it would, claimed its advocates (like

489

Jean Jaurès, for instance), prove the most effective way of protecting the fatherland. Yet there were some left socialists and anarchists or anarchosyndicalists, who refused military service when conscripted and went to prison, and some who dodged being drafted by emigrating to countries like Great Britain or the United States, where compulsory military service was not then in force. In Holland, from the 1890's, the libertarian socialist leader, Domela Nieuwenhuis, advocated refusal of military service on the part of the working class as a practical method of war resistance, alongside working-class strikes against war and antimilitarist and revolutionary propaganda in the armed forces. In 1904 he was instrumental in setting up an International Anti-Militarist Union, which gained support among anarcho-socialist groups in western and southern Europe. It upheld members who decided to resist conscription by refusing to serve as soldiers. In 1907, at an international congress of anarchists held in Amsterdam, a resolution was passed calling on "all men aspiring to liberty" to support both "isolated or collective refusal of [military] service . . . and the military strike." But conscientious objection was coupled with a call to answer "any declaration of war by insurrection." George Woodcock, from whose history of anarchism (Cleveland and New York, 1962) I have quoted the words of the resolution, calls it "a bold-sounding but vague resolution." In fact, anarchist antimilitarism was even more ineffective than other varieties of antimilitarism in halting the drive toward war.

Although a few of these socialist or anarchist objectors may have been pacifists in the sense in which I have used the term in this book, the overwhelming majority were not (absolute pacifism was more widespread among socialists in the nonconscriptionist English-speaking lands). While reluctant to bear arms in defense of a capitalist state, these men favored the use of armed force to overthrow the rule of the bourgeoisie and maintain the revolutionary regime in power, so long as it might still be threatened with attack. And at this time the philosophical "pacifists," the moral opponents of war, the peace society enthusiasts, were likewise objectors to the war system rather than proponents of nonviolence. They all rejected the idea of individual moral responsibility in the matter of military service, feeling that under certain circumstances the state retained the right to use force to resist aggression from without and that the state, and not the individual citizen, bore the guilt if its use were illegitimate.

Even the early nineteenth-century German philosopher, Karl Christian Friedrich Krause, an admirer of Immanuel Kant's proposal for perpetual peace and perhaps the closest, from among the moral pacificists, to the integral pacifist position *stricto sensu,* was to some extent a "relativist" (as de Ligt has pointed out). While positing the attainment of eternal peace and the establishment of a universal and weaponless state (*der Menscheitbund*) as the chief aim of human endeavor, he was ready to endow more limited federal unions, whose task it would be to prepare the ground for a world commonwealth, with the right to employ military sanctions against refractory member-states. Nevertheless, Krause does advocate a kind of vocational pacifism; he approves the idea of personal conscientious objection on the part of those who share his views on peace. Let such men buy their way out of military service, if drafted, or go abroad—but, should all attempts to find a way out fail, then, he tells them, choose "rather to be scourged, or to be killed," than to serve, even in a righteous war. For war, even defensive war, Krause equated with murder. He praised the Quakers for their long testimony for peace and, stigmatizing military service as a form of human slavery, he condemned the states of his day for making cannon-fodder out of the youth.

Krause's philosophy (essentially a form of pantheism) found disciples in Germany as well as abroad. But the professor's antimilitarism—in addition to his strongly worded strictures on the growing power of the modern state (views which, understandably, hindered his academic career by antagonizing the governments controlling the German universities)—failed to make much impression on his fellow countrymen; it was soon forgotten by all but a few students of political thought. Even among the nonsectarian pacifist radicals in central Europe in the early years of the twentieth century, Tolstoy, rather than Krause, was the prophet of the new pacifism.

We do, however, find Krause's name mentioned with special respect and admiration by one of the first complete pacifists to object to military service on ethical and humanitarian rather than on strictly religious grounds. This man was Dr. Hermann Wetzel, a young philosopher living in Potsdam, the very heart of the new *Reich.* In 1905, on being called up for service, Wetzel had returned his papers to the military authorities with a note stating: "My moral-religious conviction unconditionally forbids me in any way to participate in military service (*Soldatendienst*)." He appealed for support of his position to the teachings of the great spiritual leaders of mankind from Lao-tse onward. The highest religious ethic condemned military service which the most exalted philosophies, too, considered to be "irreconcilable with the dignity of a reasonable being." In further support of his unusual behavior he soon afterwards proceeded to compile a sixty-four-page account of this historical peace witness, publishing it that same year in Potsdam at his own expense. The work is entitled *The Refusal of Army Service and the Condemnation of War and Military Conscription in the History of Mankind* (*Die Verweigerung des Heerdienstes und die Verurteilung des Krieges und der Wehrpflicht in der Geschichte der Menscheit*). The booklet, though long superseded, constitutes one of the very earliest attempts at presenting a systematic and scholarly history of the idea of nonviolence. The decision of the army authorities to postpone his call-up and place him, instead, on the reserve list was motivated ostensibly by his unfitness for active service. Perhaps a reading of Wetzel's little tract may have contributed to this decision; however, its most probable cause lay in the army's unwillingness to have on its hands a misfit such as he must have appeared to be. He had been ready to submit to medical examination; but he protested vigorously against his assignment to the reserve and reconfirmed his objection to even a passive connection with the machinery of war-making.

Tolstoy's influence is apparent in Wetzel's case. His booklet reflects his close acquaintance, too, with the antimilitarism of the early Christian church and with medieval sectarian pacifism and the Mennonite and Quaker peace testimonies. Wetzel knew quite a lot about Garrison and the New England nonresistants; he was well read in the works of Erasmus and other Renaissance advocates of peace as well as in the peace literature of the European Enlightenment. It was this pacificism of the Age of Reason, rather than Christian sectarianism, that seems to have provided inspiration for the militant war resistance proposed a half century before Wetzel by a scholarly French social radical, J. Boucher de Perthes, in the third volume of his *Hommes et choses* (Paris), which he published in 1851, that is, not long before Louis Napoleon's coup overthrew what remained of the revolutionary regime of 1848.

In a section of this work devoted to the subject of the "nation" the author, addressing the laboring masses, pleads with them to refuse to serve in the national armies. He urges them "ni pour or, ni pour argent, ni par promesses, ni par menaces, de ne toucher ni à ce fusil ni a sa baïonette."

> Là-dessus, on vous enverra les gendarmes; laissez venir les gendarmes. On vous mènera en prison; laissez-vous mener en prison. On vous conduira devant le juge; laissez-vous conduire devant le juge. On vous condamnera à joindre un régiment; allez joindre le régiment. Là, on voudra vous faire l'exercice, et pour faire l'exercice on vous représentera ce même fusil.

Remember now, de Perthes goes on, if you consent to shoot, you will be killing a fellow human being who has done you no harm and who, like yourself, has been forced to serve against his own wishes and better interests. "Ne touchez donc pas plus à ce fusil."

> Sur ce refus, on vous traitera d'insoumis, de réfractaire, de lâche, de sans-coeur; n'en touchez pas plus au fusil. On vous montrera l'étranger envahissant la patrie; laissez l'étranger envahir la patrie. On vous le montrera renversant le trône ou le fauteuil présidentiel; laissez-le renverser le trône et le fauteuil présidentiel. Tout cela ne vous regarde pas le moins du monde. Ne vous ai-je pas dit que vous n'avez pas de patrie, là où vous n'avez pas de pain!

Finally, de Perthes looks forward to the time when "tous les soldats de France, tous les soldats d'Europe, tous les soldats du monde" would throw down their arms at the feet of their officers and declare their determination to use them no longer.

In some ways de Perthes appears rather as a forerunner of the non-pacifist working-class antimilitarism of a Gustave Hervé early in the present century than of Gandhian nonviolence or of the various projects for a strike against war proposed by anarchopacifists like Bart de Ligt in the interwar years. Not religious scruples but rational considerations inspired de Perthes's antiwar protest, which of course remained purely a paper project. Although ideas similar to the Frenchman's were sometimes voiced contemporaneously by English Chartists and radicals as well as by the continental left, it was not for another half-century that the working-class movement gained sufficiently in strength and cohesion for a proposal like de Perthes's to have some appearance of reality. And even then the experience of August 1914 showed that nationalism still remained a much stronger force than proletarian solidarity.

The Bible, not the rational case against war, was at the source of the pacifism of several small sects which arose in Western Europe in the course of the nineteenth century. Three such sects are known to me, and I suspect that there may have been several more of whose existence I am unaware; they lived in obscurity, so that it is sometimes difficult to discover traces of their activities. The three to be dealt with briefly here are: the "New Lighters" (*Nieuwlichters*) in the Netherlands; the New Baptists (*Neutäufer*) in Switzerland, with their offshoot, the Nazarenes, in Austria-Hungary and the Balkans; and the Hinschistes in France.

The New Lighters came into existence at the end of the Napoleonic Wars when in 1816 sixteen men and women decided to form an income-pooling community at Zwijndrecht in Holland; the next year a second community was set up at Mijdrecht not far from Amsterdam. Among the new sect's founders were several well-to-do people, including a magistrate, as well as a prophetess named Maria Leer. Their central aim was to revive the apostolic communism practiced at the beginning of the Christian era. Within half a decade several hundreds had joined the two communities: a development which aroused alarm in the populace at large. Their venture in cooperation smacked of social radicalism (the New Lighters did indeed represent a very early example of the flourishing nineteenth-century communitarian movement); and the fact that members refused to contract civil marriages, regarding this ceremony as superfluous in the case of true spiritual union, brought accusations of immorality. Members were arrested and imprisoned, under the vagrancy laws! In regard to two other, and interrelated, issues, the New Lighters found themselves also in conflict with the authorities. First, they refused to comply with the law demanding the registration of births. The cause of their civil disobedience here reflected, however, a second and deeper conflict with the state: their objection to military service as a contradiction of the Christian religion. "The use of the sword," wrote one of them, "is not the mark of discipleship of Jesus but of the Beast. . . . The spirit of the sword's power is the man of sin's, the son of corruption's." They hoped, therefore, by refusing to divulge the required details, to shield their young men, when they grew up, from the reach of the conscription regulations.

This in fact proved a vain hope. Whereas in peacetime the New Lighters do not appear to have been troubled by demands for military service, things changed at the beginning of the 1830's with the outbreak of hostilities between the northern, Dutch Netherlands and the Belgian south. Their men of military age now became liable for active service in the National Guard, which was employed in suppressing the Belgian uprising. In vain did the communities petition King William I for exemption, explaining the grounds of their objection to shedding human blood. Those young men who were unfortunate enough to be ballotted for service were taken off from the communities, sometimes by force, to join their regiments. Here they refused voluntarily to don uniform or to handle arms. Rough treatment in the detention barracks, which included beatings, chaining, and threats of the firing squad, failed to melt their resolution not to serve, even though one man is reported to have died as a result of experiences of this kind. Fortunately,

494

a well-wisher in the person of a Leiden professor named Tydeman succeeded in intervening with the king and obtaining a royal order to employ these communitarian conscripts only in such noncombatant branches of the army as the commissariat, the kitchen, and the hospital services.

By the 1840's the sect had begun to decline. As in the case of so many other communities, internal dissension rent the experiment. Some members returned to the outside world; several groups departed for the New World where they mostly settled among the Mormons. The New Lighters eventually disappeared altogether. During his period of tribulation in the army ranks one of their conscientious objectors said: "God should show through him how much more powerful He was than those who transgressed His holy laws." The spirit shown here is that of the sixteenth-century Anabaptist martyrs. Though the sources from which the New Lighters derived their pacifism are not clear—apart, that is, from the direct inspiration of the New Testament—there may possibly have been some influence of the *Doopsgezinden*, who only abandoned their nonresistant witness at the end of the eighteenth century.

Mennonite influence, however, is quite clear in the case of another new sect, the Evangelical Baptists or *Neutäufer*, whose first congregations emerged in Switzerland in the first half of the 1830's under the leadership of a former Reformed minister, Samuel Heinrich Frölich. If Frölich accepted adult baptism from the British Baptists, he took the idea of nonresistance from the Swiss Mennonites (to whom, in turn, he brought a revivalist message). In addition, some members of the Emmental Mennonite congregation, feeling that their own church had become spiritually dry, joined Frölich's movement, which also attracted dissatisfied elements in the Reformed church. At first the new denomination encountered heavy opposition from the established church; for a time it was hindered in its work by legal discrimination, too. However, it slowly expanded, sending out offshoots into the neighboring lands of Central Europe, and from around mid-century emigrants transplanted the church to the United States, where it became known as the Apostolic Christian Church. In the Habsburg Empire and the Balkans its adherents were called Nazarenes. Since their inception these Nazarenes have borne a steady witness to their pacifist beliefs despite the heavy burden of long-term military conscription.

In Switzerland, Evangelical Baptists of military age at first met with considerable hardship, too. They were not covered by the exemption granted the Mennonites in 1815, which permitted them to pay commutation money; instead, they were faced with the alternatives of either hiring a substitute, which was expensive and difficult to square with their consciences, or of suffering imprisonment. Although after mid-century the army relaxed somewhat its earlier harshness in dealing with New Baptist conscripts who could not afford the cost of a substitute, a term of imprisonment still remained their usual lot. Repeated efforts to persuade the authorities to grant them the same privileges as the Mennonites failed, until in 1874 the introduction of universal military service in the Swiss Confederation put Mennonites and New Baptists on the same footing. Henceforward, both were required to undergo army service in a noncombatant capacity.

However, the conciliatory stand of the New Baptists, which sanctioned (at least where a more satisfactory alternative did not exist) the purchase of a substitute or the performance of noncombatant duties in the army in exchange for the privilege of not having to bear arms, did not shield its young men who refused military service from harsh persecution on this account in the other countries of Central Europe to which the sect had spread. In Alsace, it is true, from 1882 onward its conscripts were usually permitted to opt for the noncombatant branches of the army to which Mennonites had been assigned by the Prussian Cabinet Order of 1868. This concession came only after an intervention with Kaiser William I on behalf of an imprisoned objector made by the commanding officer of the man's regiment. The officer wrote: "If . . . in one way or another the members of this sect may be permitted service without arms, the command of this battalion, in view of his personality and his worthy conduct, can recommend him to the highest grace of his imperial majesty." In Austria, on the other hand, where no Mennonite communities existed to provide a historic precedent for exemption for religious objectors, the Nazarenes fared badly. Visiting Vienna just after the conclusion of the Austro-Prussian War of 1866, two English Quakers, Isaac Robson and Thomas Harvey, reported as follows on the basis of information received from the Nazarene congregation in that city:

Their testimony against war has been faithfully borne. One Peter Zimbrigh, a tailor, was in prison on this account in Vienna previous to the late war. Through the indulgence of the governor of the prison, he was occasionally allowed to go out and spend an evening with his friends, who endeavored to strengthen his faith. When the war broke out, he was sent to the army, and ordered to fight. His sword and musket were tied to his body; and at last at the battle of Könniggrätz (Sadowa), his officer ordered him to be

496

shot. While almost in the act of pronouncing sentence, a cannon ball killed the officer. Zimbrigh (we understood) was still in prison. . . . He offered, when first conscripted, to act as a servant, but this was refused, though we understand hospital and other work was sometimes accepted in lieu of direct military service.

In fact, most Nazarene objectors continued to receive lengthy prison sentences.

The Emperor Francis Joseph, whose court shoemaker was a Nazarene and the brother of the sect's pastor in Vienna, acknowledged the sincerity of the Nazarenes' refusal to bear arms; yet, as he informed the Nazarene shoemaker when during the 1880's the latter pleaded for alleviation of his conscripted coreligionists' fate, he considered that they must prove themselves true Nazarenes by enduring at least two years in jail. Then, but only then, would they be offered some alternative, noncombatant way of doing their military service. Probably the emperor was apprehensive—quite unnecessarily, I may add—that, if the Nazarenes' path were made too easy, army discipline would be undermined. The sect did, it is true, make converts even in the frontier regiments, among the *Grenzer*, who were brought up from early childhood for the career of a soldier. For 1869, for instance, we may read the testimony of one Adam Leitenberger, a Lutheran *Grenzer* turned Nazarene nonresistant. When asked what would become of the soldier's profession if all decided to act as he had done, Leitenberger answered simply: "For myself I cannot any longer remain a soldier. . . . I cannot continue to bear weapons to kill, since it is love that I owe my fellow men." Yet the number of serving soldiers who became Nazarenes was in fact very small.

The further east we move the harsher becomes the treatment meted out to Nazarene objectors. Pre-Trianon Hungary contained the largest settlements of Nazarenes; here the sect included not only Magyars but also members of the ethnic minorities, especially Serbs and Rumanians. The Hungarian Nazarenes may have numbered as many as thirty thousand members, perhaps even more. Their difficulties over military service were compounded by the fact that for long the government did not officially recognize them as a separate religious denomination. The pattern of imprisonment that prevailed in the Austrian half of the Empire was repeated in Hungary, but the Hungarian sentences were heavier. In particular, converts to the sect were treated more harshly than were birthright members, who might eventually be given some alternative, such as work in the army medical corps, which proved acceptable to their consciences. The Nazarenes repeatedly petitioned the government both at Budapest and in Vienna, for alleviation, but in vain.

Across the southern frontiers of Hungary, in the small Balkan state of Serbia, congregations of Nazarenes were also to be found. As in Hungary, the Serbian Nazarenes were almost exclusively a peasant sect. They remind us of the Russian Dukhobors in their steady resistance to authority, in their peasant stubbornness in defense of their religious beliefs. (Tolstoy and his disciples, we may note, were to be active in the Nazarenes' defense, as they were on behalf of the Dukhobors.) A Western traveller who visited Belgrade in 1877 reported that there were a number of Nazarenes imprisoned in the fortress there for refusal to do military service. They had been sentenced to twenty years' hard labor (from which, however, they were in fact released by the Serbian ruler four years later). He describes meeting them during his inspection of the fortress "heavily chained among a thousand convicts—fine, tall, strong fellows, simply bearing this punishment without one word of complaint or the slightest token of retraction." Another visitor described these prisoners of conscience as "reserved and exceedingly meek." "They would rather die than carry arms," they told him, for this, they believed, would gain them eternal life. Their neighbors considered the Nazarenes "peculiar" folk but "very pious." However, despite the efforts of sympathetic outsiders like the English Quakers the authorities did not relent, and no alternative to service with arms was open to the Nazarenes of Serbia. In the twentieth century the situation of the Nazarenes of south-east Europe, whether in Yugoslavia, Hungary, or Rumania, did not improve substantially. In World War I some objectors in the Serb-inhabited southern frontier districts of the Hungarian kingdom were executed under the martial law imposed by the government. First in the interwar successor states of the Habsburg Empire and then under the post-World War II communist regimes Nazarene objectors have continued to undergo long terms of imprisonment, all efforts so far having failed to persuade their respective governments that the offer of an acceptable form of alternative service would not undermine national security.

The third sect we need to consider here, the *Hinschistes*, originated in France in the mid-1840's. Its founder was a middle-aged woman, Marguerite Coraly Hinsch, daughter of a German Protestant who had emigrated to France under the First Empire. Believing that she was the recipient of a prophetic call to reform the spiritual life of the church, she began to gather disciples, finding them mainly among the poorer classes of the population. Among the tenets of the new sect was a New Testament based pacifism. Both under the older French selective-service regulations and under the universal military service introduced in 1872-1873, young Hinschistes came into conflict with the law. After periods of imprisonment differing in length from case to case, they were usually, though not invariably, assigned to the army medical corps and freed from the obligation to do arms drill. A sympathetic Protestant lawyer, O. Kellerman, who acted as defending counsel at the trials of several Hinschiste objectors, wrote of their pacifist witness: "The example of these strictly evangelical Christians and their submission to the law of the Lord, will complete the action of the peace propaganda of economists and philanthropists."

These Hinschiste evangelicals remained a small group (they have survived in France, however, up to the present). The atmosphere of nineteenth- and early twentieth-century continental Europe was in-auspicious for the development of sects which not only opposed the Catholic and Protestant establishments but also challenged the rising militarism of the nation-state. We do hear occasionally of completely isolated religious objectors unaffiliated to any denomination which professed pacifism. To give just one example, the London Peace Society's organ, *The Herald of Peace*, in its issue of 1 December 1876, reported that a young Frenchman, after being called up, had refused to drill, asserting that war and killing were contrary to the spirit of the gospels. His lawyer at the court-martial pleaded that he be given the same treatment as conscripted Quakers, three of whom had recently been placed by the army authorities "as clerks in the offices or as wardsmen in the hospitals." In Scandinavia there were Baptists who refused military service and, in Holland, even a few Salvationists (probably under the influence of that ardent Salvation Army pacifist A. S. Booth-Clibborn; see chapter 10). These were mostly working-men or farmers' sons. Before the end of the nineteenth century the Seventh-Day Adventists, an apocalyptic group originating in the United States soon after mid-century, had already started up mis-sionary work in Europe. They usually objected to bearing arms in the wars of this world, as did also a more recent sect of American prove-nance, the International Bible Students (or Jehovah's Witnesses, as they eventually called themselves). Courts-martial and jail sentences, sometimes repeated until the expiry of the objector's term of service, resulted for these people; sometimes, however, by administrative means an objector might ultimately be assigned to noncombatant duties in the army. If we disregard the special privileges restricted to particular groups like the Mennonites in Russia or Germany, only in Norway from 1902 did official provision for exemption exist in the case of religious objectors; there they were not required to perform any kind of military or alternative service. The severity elsewhere is all the more difficult to comprehend, considering the fact that groups like the ones being considered here would almost all gladly have accepted noncombatant service in the army.

The protagonists of unconditional pacifism in late nineteenth-century continental Europe were confined almost exclusively either to the Mennonites of Russia and the more conservative of their brethren in the *Reich*, or to small sects like the Nazarenes, or to Tolstoyan intellectuals and isolated objectors in nonpacifist Protestant denominations. When the Frenchman O. Kellerman undertook to write an exposition arguing the incompatibility of military service and war of every kind with the requirements of the Christian religion (it was published in Paris in 1900 as *La guerre et la paix*), he had assumed the invariable hostility to pacifism of the Roman Catholic church. Indeed, since the fall of the Roman Empire there had been no recorded instance of Roman Catholics' supporting conscientious objection to war, at least on pacifist grounds, until the late nineteenth century; for Erasmian pacifism was by no means unconditional. Under Napoleon I, it is true, there was a simple and saintly "draft-dodger," Jean-Baptiste-Marie Vianney, the later *curé d'Ars*, who was canonized in 1925. In 1809 Vianney, then aged twenty-three, upon being called up for service in the Peninsular War had promptly deserted from his regiment and gone into hiding until he was able to emerge safely into the open again. Whether his refusal to commit homicide was based on an objection to all war, or whether it was a vocational pacifism akin to that of medieval monasticism, is unclear, however. Vianney, despite his lack of education, felt an overriding call to the priesthood: his training for this was interrupted by the draft and thus his behavior may have been governed primarily by his attachment to his exalted calling.

At any rate, to my knowledge, the first occasion on which a modern Roman Catholic writer spoke out in favor of pacifism had occurred only four years before the appearance of Kellerman's book. This writer was also a Frenchman, Jean de Triac, and he entitled his work *Guerre et Christianisme* (Paris, 1896). A decade and a half later another French Catholic layman, Grillot de Givry, published in his *Le Christ et la patrie* (Paris, 1911; I have used the 1924 edition) an even more passionate plea for the church's rejection of all forms of war. De Givry had been working at his book since 1899. Both authors condemned the traditional Catholic concept of the just war: "Les théologiens ont inventé les termes de *guerre juste* et de *guerre injuste*," wrote de Givry, for instance. He and de Triac, therefore, took a more radically pacifist stand than did those Roman Catholic antimilitarists later in the twentieth century, who retained the concept of the just war while considering all modern warfare incompatible with the requirements which this concept laid down. Neither work received the church's *imprimatur*; neither writer's views found acceptance among his co-religionists. True, there was no official condemnation; but this, in all likelihood, merely reflected the fact that the books remained largely unread.

De Triac does not broach the question of conscientious objection directly. Yet the Christian's obligation to refuse military service appears to me implicit in what he writes; he argues that homicide was forbidden not only in the Gospels but also by the Sixth Commandment. This prohibition was "absolute." "Nous . . . concluons," he writes, "que le bien consiste à conformer à la lettre du Décalogue et à l'Esprit de l'Évangile." He cites the total opposition to war expressed by church fathers like Origen and Tertullian, and he writes with approval of the radical peace witness of the Quakers. "Et qui donc a décidé, même pour nous, catholiques, que, sur ce point, la conscience faussée est celle de Quakers plutôt que celle . . . des partisans [catholiques] de la guerre?" Indeed, even if the church, "malgré le commandement de Dieu," proclaimed officially that homicide was justifiable in certain circumstances, this ruling ought not to have weight with Catholics; the church was merely the depository and transmitter of Christian doctrine with no right to alter God's commandments and admonitions. Although the establishment of a "Truce of God" by the medieval church might seem to give the stamp of ecclesiastical approval to wars of "legitimate defense," such an arrangement, in de Triac's view, constituted merely "une condescendance nécessaire à la barbarie du temps." All war, in short, was "meurtre en grand."

Whereas de Triac writes for the most part dispassionately, de Givry hammers out his work at white heat. He attacks not only war but patriotism; de Triac merely condemns war as a means of preserving independence and national identity and wishes to replace "la gloire militaire" and chauvinistic nationalism by readiness to arbitrate and the pursuit of international justice. According to de Givry, "pour le vrai chrétien, la patrie n'existait pas"; for him there was only "la nation chrétienne," and its members were dispersed throughout all lands. Ecclesiastical approval of war since Constantine's day he regarded as an "aberration," an act of treason to Christ. (Both de Givry and de Triac devote considerable attention to the views of Catholic archreactionaries like Joseph de Maistre.) Such movements as the Protestant Reformation or French Gallicanism, which had undermined the universalist concepts of the medieval church, marked further steps in paganizing Christianity. Patriotism had ousted the pacific spirit of Christ in the minds of Catholics as much as in those of their non-Catholic fellow citizens, and had made them forget their mission to be peacemakers. De Givry lambasted the Roman church for sanctioning the militarism of the modern nation-state instead of preaching anti-militarism as the early church had done and for leaving war resistance, which should have been the church's task, to anarchists and atheists (a point made by de Triac too). Catholics should invariably be conscientious objectors. "Le Christ a interdit de porter les armes." Therefore, de Givry went on, "un chrétien ne doit pas porter les armes; il ne doit pas verser le sang ni souiller sa main d'un homicide; il ne doit sous aucun prétexte frapper un chrétien, puisque tout chrétien est son frère, ni aucun homme, puisqu'il est tenu de donner aux ennemis du Christ l'example des vertus que ceux-ci n'ont pas." The church's failure to condemn war and to uphold the conscientious objector to military service was unpardonable.

De Givry's pacifism has a Quaker-like quality; it is centered on the Sermon on the Mount. We can detect, too, as with de Triac, the influence of Tolstoy's nonresistance. There are also repeated echoes of the socialist case against war, which was being developed in the press and publications of the contemporary French extreme left. For de Givry regards patriotism as largely a smoke-screen to conceal the sordid motives at the back of all wars. "L'armée est avant tout la protectrice du capital." And Catholics support militarism because the official church, which had once been a refuge for the poor and lowly, had become the church of the rich and powerful. De Givry does not put forward any program of nonviolent direct action against war, however; he confines himself to verbal protest.

"L'avenir appartient à l'antimilitarisme," he proclaimed. Yet, at the time, his book was completely ignored. No reviews appeared in the press; scarcely any copies were sold. The author had apparently expected this, for he begins it as follows:

J'écris ce livre pour les catholiques, avec la certitude qu'ils ne voudront ni lire ni le comprendre. Je l'écris, non pour prouver ou convaincre, non pour faire des prosélytes ou prétendre exercer une influence quelconque sur les événements futurs; mais uniquement pour laisser un témoignage de mon opinion. . . . Le sort de ce livre m'indiffère donc; et cependant je le crois gros de l'avenir. Je suis certain qu'il vient rigouresement à son heure.

And, in fact, after the holocaust of the First World War was over, and with the upsurge of antiwar feeling that ensued, de Givry's anti-militarist treatise was rescued from oblivion. In 1922, as the publishers were on the point of dispatching the still almost intact stack of copies to be made into pulp, the work was rediscovered by French antimili-tarists. The first edition soon sold out, and in 1924 a second edition appeared with a new preface and notes added by the author. Though full of historical erudition, *Le Christ et la patrie* is primarily a polemi-cal tract and not a work of scholarship—it is a protest against Catholic complicity in war and national egotism. With the growth of a small but vigorous Roman Catholic pacifist movement after the two World Wars, de Givry's pioneer effort has proved itself to be indeed a tract for the times.

Bibliographical Notes

A. GENERAL

No general history of pacifism has hitherto been published. The nearest approach to such a study comes from the pen of the Dutch anarchist Bart de Ligt: *Vrede als daad: Beginselen, geschiedenis en strijdmethoden van de direkte aktie tegen oorlog*, 2 vols. (Arnhem, 1931-1933). The second volume, somewhat confused in its arrangement but still valuable, remains untranslated, but an expanded version of the first volume appeared in French as *La paix créatrice: Histoire des principes et des tactiques de l'action directe contre la guerre*, 2 vols. (Paris, 1934). De Ligt's work represents a truly pioneering venture; I am happy to acknowledge the inspiration which the French edition gave me, when I read it thirty years ago, to study the subject further. The author concentrates mainly, as his title indicates, on tracing the antecedents of the idea of "direct action against war." Unfortunately, in places the narrative is marred by a tendency toward erratic historical interpretation and a rather doctrinaire approach. Another pioneering Dutch work on the history of peace, though long outdated, is G. F. Haspels, *De weerloosheid: Een hoofdstuk van levensleer* (Amsterdam, 1901). A recent volume by David A. Martin, *Pacifism: An Historical and Sociological Study* (London, 1965), while including many perceptive and interesting sociological insights, is based on extremely exiguous source materials for the period before the twentieth century. Moreover, Martin defines "pacifism" more broadly than appears to me to be warranted. The section entitled "The Violent *versus* the Non-Violent Sect" in volume II (*Sectarian Religion*, London, 1967) of Werner Stark's multi-volume work *The Sociology of Religion: A Study of Christendom* is stimulating but spoilt, as is the rest of the volume, by doubtful generalization and inadequate sources. A brief outline is offered by Geoffrey F. Nuttall in his *Christian Pacifism in History* (Oxford, 1958).

There are two monumental histories of the wider peace movement: Jacob ter Meulen, *Der Gedanke der internationalen Organisation in seiner Entwicklung* (The Hague, vol. I [1300-1800], 1917; vol. II, pt. 1 [1789-1870], 1929, pt. 2 [1867-1889], 1940) and Christian L. Lange and August Schou, *Histoire de l'Internationalisme* (Oslo, vol. I [by Lange, to 1648], 1919; vol. II [joint authorship, 1648-1815], 1954; vol. III [by Schou, 1815-1914], 1963). Both works focus primarily on the various projects for international peace conceived in the course of the centuries and on the peace societies which arose after 1815, but they also touch from time to time on pacifism *stricto sensu*. Sylvester John Hemleben, *Plans for World Peace through Six Centuries* (Chicago, 1943) is a useful compilation, which stops at 1918.

Two broad historical surveys of the attitude of Christianity (both the non-pacifist churches and the pacifist sects) toward war and peace are, Umphrey Lee, *The Historic Church and Modern Pacifism* (New York and Nashville, 1943), from a nonpacifist viewpoint, and Roland H. Bainton, *Christian Attitudes Toward War and Peace* (New York and Nashville, 1960), from a pacifist viewpoint. A long chapter on "Kirche und Kriegsdienst" in Peter Meinhold, *Römer 13: Obrigkeit, Widerstand, Revolution, Krieg* (Stuttgart, 1960) surveys the attitude of the Christian churches and sects to war and military service from New Testament times to the twentieth century. Blanche Wiesen Cook's *Bibliography on Peace Research in History* (Santa Barbara, 1969) is useful, particularly for the twentieth century.

There is not very much specifically on the history of pacificistic thought outside the Judaeo-Christian tradition. But see Leonard Tomkinson, *Studies in the Theory and Practice of Peace and War in Chinese History and Literature* (Shanghai, 1940).

B. The Early Church

My chapter on this subject has no claim to original research; it is compiled almost exclusively from secondary authorities. The standard work on the subject is by a pacifist Congregational minister, Cecil John Cadoux, *The Early Christian Attitude to War* (London, 1919; reprint, 1940). Although clearly a product of deep scholarship, it has sometimes been criticized for an unconscious bias toward the pacifist interpretation. Later, in a large volume entitled *The Early Church and the World* (Edinburgh, 1925), Cadoux included the materials he had used in his 1919 monograph and added some new data, arranging all this on a different pattern according to chronological periods and placing the church's attitude to war against a much wider background covering the whole early Christian *Weltanschauung*.

The older scholarly literature on early Christian antimilitarism, from Grotius in the seventeenth century up into the second decade of the twentieth century, is reviewed by Cadoux in his study of the *Early Christian Attitude to War* (pp. 6-13). I have not myself consulted any work published prior to 1905 (apart from Clarkson; see below). In the twentieth century, besides Cadoux, there is also a full-length study of the attitude of Christians of the early centuries to war by a Polish nonpacifist Roman Catholic, Leszek Winowski, *Stosunek chrześcijaństwa pierwszych wieków do wojny* (Lublin, 1947). The author argues that the early church, apart from a small minority of rigorists, never condemned war and military service *per se* but only from such secondary considerations as fear of contamination by paganism, etc. Strangely enough, Winowski does not appear to be aware of Cadoux's book. Further volumes by twentieth-century scholars devoted to the early church and war are: the pioneering study by the great German Protestant theologian Adolf Harnack, *Militia Christi: Die christliche Religion und die Soldatenstand in den ersten drei Jahrhunderten* (Tübingen, 1905); K.H.E. de Jong, *Dienstweigering bij de oude Christenen*

(Leiden, 1905), a brief essay in Dutch on early Christian conscientious objection; Albert Bayet, *Pacifisme et christianisme aux premiers siècles* (Paris, 1934), from the pen of a French rationalist who accuses the early church of fostering a dual morality in regard to war; Jean-Michel Hornus, *Evangile et Labarum* (Geneva, 1960), the work of a French Protestant theologian who has supplied it with an excellent bibliography.

Among books touching on the question of early Christian pacifism I should call attention to two studies, among many, of the New Testament attitude to war: G.H.C. Macgregor, *The New Testament Basis of Pacifism*, first published in 1936 (I have used the new and revised edition, London, 1953), and Jean Laserre's work, translated from the French, *War and the Gospel* (London, 1962). Both are written by pacifist Protestants. The non-pacifist Protestant theologian Hans Windisch has written an account of *Der messianische Krieg und das Urchristentum* (Tübingen, 1909) on the background of Jewish eschatological thought. He does not, however, go beyond the early second century A.D. Another useful volume, also by a Protestant, is Walther Bienert, *Krieg, Kriegsdienst und Kriegsdienstverweigerung nach der Botschaft des Neuen Testaments* (Stuttgart, 1952). Richard Klein's short monograph, *Tertullian und das römische Reich* (Heidelberg, 1968), contains an appendix, "Tertullians Stellung zum Kriegsdienst," in which he argues that "Tertullian was not a pacifist at any price." On the other hand, Michel Spanneut, unlike most other Roman Catholic scholars, admits in his study, *Tertullien et les premiers moralistes africains* (Paris, 1969) the uncompromising character of the antimilitarism and nonviolence of the four writers discussed: Tertullian, St. Cyprian, Arnobius, and Lactantius. The early portions of G. J. Heering's *The Fall of Christianity* (translated from the Dutch, London, 1930) are significant as a modern restatement of the centuries-old sectarian thesis that the establishment of a church-state alliance under Constantine and the resulting abandonment of Christian antimilitarism represented "the fall of Christianity." A Roman Catholic theologian, Bernard Schöpf, has recently made an interesting study of the early Christian attitude to the taking of life in general, *Das Tötungsrecht bei den frühchristlichen Schriftstellern bis zur Zeit Konstantins* (Regensburg, 1958). He covers not only war but capital punishment, personal self-defense, euthanasia, suicide, abortion, gladiatorial shows, etc.

I should also note the thesis propounded by the English scholar, S.G.F. Brandon, in such works as *Jesus and the Zealots: A Study of the Political Factor in Primitive Christianity* (Manchester, 1967) and *The Fall of Jerusalem and the Christian Church: A Study of the Effects of the Jewish Overthrow on Christianity* (1951; 2nd edn., London, 1957) that Jesus sympathized with, if he was not actually a member of, the Zealot movement which advocated armed opposition to Roman rule. He was one of "Israel's resistance fighters." "The concept of the pacific Jesus," Brandon argues, was mainly the work of St. Paul and the four Evangelists, who strove in this way to expunge the original and subversive message of Jesus. Their viewpoint gained the adherence of the rapidly increasing Gentile Christian communities. On the other hand, "Palestinian Christianity," centered in Jerusalem and dominated by Paul's opponents, "from its origins was closely associated with the nationalist aspirations of Israel." Although some Jewish Christians might not have taken up arms in the insurrection against the Romans of 66-70 A.D., in Brandon's view most did do so and suffered the consequences of defeat along with their orthodox Jewish compatriots. We may perhaps detect the *Zeitgeist* lurking behind Brandon's learned volumes.

Finally, I need to mention at least some of the scholarly literature on the early church and war which has appeared in this century either in periodicals or in the form of chapters in *Festschriften* or collected volumes. Roman Catholic theologians have contributed virtually as much here as Protestants. An early example is the 42-page study by E. Vacandard on "La question du service militaire chez les chrétiens des premiers siècles," in his *Etudes de critique et d'histoire religieuse* (2nd series, 3rd edn., Paris, 1914: first published in 1909). See also Edward A. Ryan, S.J., "The Rejection of Military Service by the Early Christians," *Theological Studies*, vol. XIII (1952), which views pacifist opinion within the early church as being tainted with heresy; Hans von Campenhausen, "Christians and Military Service in the Early Church," in *Tradition and Life in the Early Church* (London, 1968), a piece that was originally printed in *Offener Horizont: Festschrift für Karl Jaspers* (Munich, 1953). A particularly useful item is the bibliographical study by Jacques Fontaine, "Christians and Military Service in the Early Church," published in a series issued by the Paulist Press, *Concilium: Theology in the Age of Renewal*, vol. 7 (Glen Rock, New Jersey, 1965). Here Fontaine surveys the quite extensive literature produced over the previous three decades in various Western languages, including, e.g., Dutch and Norwegian. He notes the emotional tone of some of this literature, which has resulted from authors' pro- or anti-pacifist leanings.

An early contribution to Protestant periodical writing on the subject is Henri-F. Secrétan, "Le christianisme des premiers siècles et le service militaire," *Revue de théologie et de philosophie* (Lausanne), new series, vol II (1914), which supports the view that during the church's first three centuries military service was normally regarded as incompatible with the Christian's role. The eminent Quaker New Testament scholar, Henry J. Cadbury, has written on "The Basis of Early Christian Antimilitarism," *Journal of Biblical Literature* (New Haven, Conn.), vol. XXXVII (1918). Another excellent summary from the pacifist viewpoint is Roland H. Bainton, "The Early Church and War," *The Harvard Theological Review* (Cambridge, Mass.), vol. XXXIX, no. 3 (July 1946), reprinted in Rufus F. Jones, ed., *The Church, the Gospel and War* (New York, 1948) and largely incorporated later in Bainton's book on *Christian Attitudes Toward War and Peace* (1960), mentioned above. See also Heinrich Karpp, "Die Stellung der Alten Kirche zu Kriegsdienst und Krieg," *Evangelische Theologie* (Munich), vol. 17, no. 11 (Nov. 1957).

C. THE CZECH BRETHREN AND THEIR FORERUNNERS

Sources for the pacifism of the pre-Hussite sects in Europe are scattered among a number of publications. In fact, little may be gleaned from these beyond the fact that there existed a general repudiation of human bloodshed and war on the part of such medieval sectarian groups as avowed a belief in nonviolence. Though pacifism figures only very incidentally in it, the scholarly literature on medieval sectarianism is, of course, immense. I have perused only a very small portion, naturally, and from this I will mention below only a few titles. On the Cathars I found Arno Borst's authoritative study *Die Katharer* (Stuttgart, 1953) useful, and on the Waldenses Kurt-Victor Selge's two volumes, *Die ersten Waldenser* (Berlin, 1967). The second volume of Ignaz von Döllinger's extensive collection of sources, *Beiträge zur Sektengeschichte des Mittelalters*, 2 vols. (Munich, 1890) contains items here and there bearing on the pacifism of both the Cathars and the Waldenses, as does the recent compilation of documents in English translation, edited by Walter L. Wakefield and Arthur P. Evans, *Heresies of the High Middle Ages* (New York and London, 1969). There is a critical edition of the "Noble Lesson" by Antonino de Stefano: *La Noble Leçon des Vaudois de Piémont* (Paris, 1909). "The Twelve Conclusions of the Lollards" of 1395 have been printed by H. S. Cronin in the *English Historical Review* (London), vol. XXII, no. 2 (April 1907). In the *EHR* we also have S. Harrison Thomson's valuable study, "Pre-Hussite Heresy in Bohemia," vol. XLVIII, no. 1 (January 1933). A brief review of the transition from pre-Hussite heresy to Hussitism has been published in French by the eminent Czech church historian Amedeo Molnár: "La non-violence des Vaudois et des Hussites," *Cahiers de la Réconciliation* (Paris), no. 6 (June 1965).

Pacifism really comes into its own only with the emergence of Hussitism in Bohemia. Then the primary sources available become much more extensive, as does the scholarly literature on the subject. The Taborite and chiliast background to Chelčický's views on war and the state is ably presented in Howard Kaminsky, *A History of the Hussite Revolution* (Berkeley and Los Angeles, 1967); early Hussite attitudes to war were the subject of a special study by an earlier scholar, Karel Hoch, "Husité a válka," *Česká mysl* (Prague), vol. VIII (1907). Concerning Chelčický himself, apart from a few minor omissions the entire literature to that date is listed in Eduard Petrů's bibliography, *Soupis díla Petra Chelčického a literatury o něm* (Prague, 1957). The more important works on Chelčický, who should indeed rank as the first European pacifist of note, and the main editions of his treatises are given in the bibliography of my book, *The Political and Social Doctrines of the Czech Brethren in the Fifteenth and Early Sixteenth Centuries* (The Hague, 1957), an earlier version of which was submitted to the University of Oxford in 1954 as a D. Phil. thesis.

More up-to-date bibliographical data may be found in Petrů's edition of four shorter treatises by Chelčický, *Drobné spisy* (Prague, 1966). Unfor-

509

tunately, Chelčický's writings are not easily available in any Western European language. An exception is Howard Kaminsky, "Peter Chelčický: Treatises on Christianity and the Social Order," in *Studies in Medieval and Renaissance History*, ed. William M. Bowsky, vol. 1 (Lincoln, Nebraska, 1964), which, in addition to a long introduction by the editor, contains translations of "On the Triple Division of Society" and "On the Holy Church." "The Net of Faith" has been translated somewhat freely into German by Carl Vogl (Dachau, 1923). No full-length and scholarly monograph on Chelčický exists in any language. In German there is a somewhat prolix volume by Vogl, *Peter Cheltschizki, ein Prophet an der Wende der Zeiter* (Zürich and Leipzig, 1926); in Czech a short and popular book was recently published by Alois Míka, *Petr Chelčický* (Prague, 1963). Among Czech scholars who have contributed most to Chelčický studies is the outstanding authority on Hussitism of the interwar generation, František M. Bartoš. His findings are scattered over a dozen or more articles, often in almost inaccessible periodicals or newspapers. He has attempted to summarize some of these materials in his booklet, *Petr Chelčický-duchovné otec Jednoty bratrské* (Prague, 1958), but a major study on Chelčický never emerged from his pen. Until now the most scholarly treatment of Chelčický is to be found in the hundred pages which Rudolf Urbánek devoted to him in the third volume of his monumental—and never completed—history of the age of King George of Poděbrady, *Věk poděbradský* (Prague, 1930), a work which forms part 3 in the great composite history of the Czechs (likewise still incomplete and likely ever to remain so) published under the title *České dějiny*. In English Matthew Spinka published a concise account of the ideology, including pacifism, of "Peter Chelčický, the Spiritual Father of the *Unitas Fratrum*" in *Church History* (Chicago), vol. xii, no. 4 (Dec. 1943); this item I inadvertently omitted from the bibliography of my study of the Czech Brethren, which also treats Chelčický's pacifism in the course of a lengthy chapter at the beginning devoted to his ideas.

Two recent studies relevant to our subject, which postdate the publication of my book and could not therefore be listed there, are Erhard Peschke, "Peter Chelčický's Lehre von der Kirche und der weltlichen Macht," *Wissenschaftliche Zeitschrift der Universität Rostock*, vol. 5 (1955-1956) (Sonderheft) and Viktor Hájek, "Učení Petra Chelčického o užívání násilí a o válce," in the *Festschrift* for J. L. Hromádka, *O svrchovanost víry*, ed. J. B. Souček (Prague, 1959). Although I have intentionally omitted mention here of most of the titles relating to Chelčický listed in my book on the Czech Brethren, I would still like to refer to two works by the outstanding nineteenth-century Czech historian Jaroslav Goll, which contain important primary sources relating, *inter alia*, to Chelčický and his ideology: *Quellen und Untersuchungen zur Geschichte der Böhmischen Bruder*, 2 vols. (Prague, 1878-1882), especially volume ii, and the posthumously published collection of articles *Chelčický a Jednota v XV. století* (Prague, 1916).

Both of Goll's books are important also for the study of the Unity of

Czech Brethren. In regard to the sources for, and literature on, Unity pacifism I shall once again refer the reader to my monograph on the sect's politicosocial ideology, on which I have largely based my present account. Although the book was published a decade and a half ago, not much has appeared on the subject since, if we except Peschke's article, "Die Gegensatz zwischen der Kleinen und der Grossen Partei der Brüderunität," in *Wissenschaftliche Zeitschrift der Universität Rostock*, vol. 6 (1956-1957) (Gesellschafts- und Sprachwissenschaftliche Reihe, no. 1) and the standard history of the Unity by Rudolf Říčan, *Dějiny Jednoty bratrské* (Prague, 1957), the bibliography of which is the most comprehensive compiled so far on the Unity. Říčan's work does not entirely replace the older three-volume *Geschichte der Böhmischen Brüder* (Herrnhut, 1922-1931) by the Moravian Church historian J. Th. Müller. Its time coverage is not so comprehensive as Müller's, but it is more compact and of course takes into consideration nearly four decades of subsequent research. Müller's first volume, which goes down to 1528 and deals, therefore, with the period of interest to students of pacifism, is best read in the revised translation into Czech made by F. M. Bartoš, *Dějiny Jednoty bratrské* (Prague, 1923).

A few words need to be said concerning the main primary sources for the history of Unity pacifism. Many of these are still in manuscript. The "Akta Jednoty bratrské," a unique collection of Unity archives put together in the sixteenth century, are invaluable, especially volumes IV and V, which contain the records of the controversy between the Major and the Minor Parties. The writings of the Old Brethren have been edited from the manuscript "Akta" by Jaroslav Bidlo and printed in two volumes as *Akty Jednoty bratrské* (Brno, 1915-1923). The gradual adaptation of the old rigorism to the surrounding social ethos and the final codification of the new *Weltanschauung* may be followed in Anton Gindely's edition of the *Dekrety Jednoty bratrské* (Prague, 1965). The sociopolitical treatises of Brother Lukáš, the chief opponent of the pacifist-anarchist position among the Brethren, either still lie in manuscript (this remains the fate, too, of the writings of his adversaries of the Minor Party) or are to be found in probably unique copies in the Library of the National Museum in Prague.

In conclusion, I may mention that I have drawn my information concerning the somewhat ambiguous pacifist testimony of the Habrovany Brethren from two lengthy articles published by Czech historians in the interwar period: Otakar Odložilík, "Jednota bratří habrovanských," *Český časopis historický* (Prague), vol. XXIX (1923), and Jan Hanák, "Bratří a starší z Hory lilecké," *Časopis Matice moravské* (Brno), vols. LII-LIII (1928-1929). A pacifist witness was possibly held by yet another small Hussite sect of mid-fifteenth-century origin, the so-called Weeping Brethren, but the evidence on the point is contradictory, and I have not considered the group in my narrative. For further details, see my article "The Weeping Brethren of Bohemia," *The Iliff Review* (Denver), vol. XIII, no. 1 (Winter 1956). pp. 15-20.

511

D. THE ANABAPTISTS

The literature on sixteenth-century Anabaptism is vast, and growing. Although in historiography the rehabilitation of Anabaptism began only a little over a century ago, a steady flow of books and articles, most of them reasonably objective in approach, has appeared since that time, in place of the occasional item usually depicting Anabaptists as—at best—deluded fanatics, which had previously passed as historical writing. Here I am able to indicate, from among a large array of source collections, monographs, and scholarly articles, only those items which bear most directly on the subject of Anabaptist nonresistance. For further information on this literature, Hans Joachim Hillerbrand, *A Bibliography of Anabaptism 1520-1630* (Elkhart, Indiana, 1962) should be consulted. (A German-language edition of this bibliography was published simultaneously at Gütersloh.) Subsequent publications may be found in the annual lists given in *Mennonite Life* (North Newton, Kansas), usually in the April issue. The four-volume *Mennonite Encyclopedia* (Scottdale, Pa., 1955-1959) is another essential tool for all aspects of Anabaptist history; the *Mennonitisches Lexikon*, 4 vols. (Frankfurt-am-Main and Weierhof; later Karlsruhe, 1913-1967) is also useful, since it contains materials not included in the American encyclopedia. With the expansion of Anabaptist studies in the United States, the *Mennonite Quarterly Review* (Goshen, Ind., 1927 ff.), which I cite below as *MQR*, has been devoting increasing space to articles on this subject, many of them by non-Mennonite scholars, and Anabaptist nonresistance is frequently dealt with in them.

George H. Williams has written the standard work on the Radical Reformation (London, 1962). It is important in our context for its overall treatment of the left wing of the Reformation, and particularly valuable concerning its theological aspects. In his anthology of *Spiritual and Anabaptist Writers* (Philadelphia, 1957) the same author has printed in English translation, among a number of documents illustrative of the Radical Reformation, several pertaining to nonresistance: Conrad Grebel's letters to Müntzer (1524), the account of the trial and execution of Michael Sattler (1527), and Obbe Philips's "Confession" (ca. 1560). One of the most thought-provoking studies of sixteenth-century Anabaptism is by Franklin Hamlin Littell, *The Origins of Sectarian Protestantism* (New York, 1964; originally published in 1952 as *The Anabaptist View of the Church*); Littell's comments on nonresistance show considerable insight into the sociological implications of the doctrine. For the historical development of Anabaptism two handy popular accounts, though to some extent outdated, are R. J. Smithson, *The Anabaptists: Their Contribution to Our Protestant Heritage* (London, [1935]) and John Horsch, *Mennonites in Europe* (Scottdale, Pa., 2nd edn., 1950). The denominational bias of the author is marked in each instance; Horsch, an immigrant from Germany, was the first among Mennonites in America to study their European heritage seriously.

Up into the present century most writers on the history of Anabaptism had continued to ignore the most significant sources for the subject; they tended to rely mainly on the polemical works of the Anabaptists' enemies. There were only a few historians who did not take up a more or less hostile attitude to the sect. The doctrinal writings of the Anabaptists were generally neglected. Some of these have been reprinted in recent decades, and the sixteenth-century editions have been widely utilized by twentieth-century specialists. Moreover, a new and extremely revealing set of sources is in process of publication: the *Taüferakten*, i.e., the official records containing innumerable testimonies of Anabaptists under examination by the courts. The great series of *Quellen zur Geschichte der Taüfer* (Leipzig and Gütersloh, 1929 ff.) includes *Taüferakten* from Württemberg, Bavaria, Baden and the Palatinate, Alsace and Austria, as well as the writings of Balthasar Hubmaier, Hans Denck, the early Hutterites, and other south German Anabaptists. The emphasis so far has been on the first decade of Anabaptism. In addition, the fourth volume of the *Urkundliche Quellen zur Hessischen Reformationsgeschichte* is devoted to *Wiedertäuferakten 1527-1626*, ed. Günther Franz (Marburg, 1951), while Paul Wappler has printed documentary material relating to nonresistance in his study of *Die Täuferbewegung in Thüringen von 1526-1584* published in 1913 (however, I did not use Wappler at first hand). The Swiss, too, have their series of *Quellen zur Geschichte der Täufer in der Schweiz* (Zürich, 1952 ff.), though publication is proceeding very slowly in this case. Volumes II, V, VII, and X of the ten-volume *Bibliotheca Reformatoria Neerlandica*, eds. S. Cramer and F. Pijper (The Hague, 1903-1914) are devoted to Dutch Anabaptism. A new multi-volume series of *Documenta Anabaptisca Neerlandica* is in preparation. Materials on nonresistance are scattered throughout all these publications. Some volumes are well indexed; others are not, and therefore are difficult to use when one is investigating a specific theme. I have done no more than dip occasionally into these documentary collections in search of illustrative material. The various series mentioned above by no means exhaust the list of publications containing archival materials relevant to Anabaptism. I would like to mention only three further items, which are especially important for the development of nonresistance: Beatrice Jenny's scholarly edition of "Das Schleitheimer Täuferbekenntnis 1527," published in *Schaffhauser Beiträge zur vaterländischen Geschichte*, vol. 28 (Thayngen, 1951); Hans J. Hillerbrand, "An Early Anabaptist Treatise on the Christian and the State" [*Aufdeckung der babylonischen Hurn*], *MQR*, vol. XXII, no. 1 (January 1958); and Samuel Geiser, "An Ancient Anabaptist Witness for Nonresistance" ["Das Urteil von dem Schwert"], *MQR*, vol. XXV, no. 1 (January 1951).

I owe a large debt to the history of early Anabaptist nonresistance written by a young American historian, James Mentzer Stayer, "The Doctrine of the Sword in the First Decade of Anabaptism" (unpublished Ph.D. dissertation, Cornell University, 1964; University Microfilms 64-13, 819). Although I have occasionally dissented from his judgments, the existence of this thorough and scholarly account has made my task very much easier than it would otherwise have been. Stayer has published several articles extracted from his dissertation: e.g., "The Earliest Anabaptists and the Separatist-Pacifist Dilemma," *Brethren Life and Thought* (Oak Brook, Illinois), vol. x, no. 1 (Winter 1965); "Hans Hut's Doctrine of the Sword: An Attempted Solution," *MQR*, vol. xxxix, no. 3 (July 1965); "The Münsterite Rationalization of Bernhard Rothmann," *Journal of the History of Ideas* (New York), vol. xxviii, no. 2 (April-June 1967). Equally important is the more philosophically and theologically oriented study by an American Mennonite, Clarence Bauman, *Gewaltlosigkeit im Täufertum: Eine Untersuchung zur theologischen Ethik des oberdeutschen Täufertums der Reformationszeit* (Leiden, 1968). This is a long, detailed, and discursive work, with many digressions which sometimes take one far from the subject of nonviolence (*Gewaltlosigkeit*), but it is nevertheless extremely valuable. In his exposition of Anabaptist nonresistance Bauman has made extensive use of the protocols of the seven great *Religionsgespräche* or "disputations," held at intervals throughout the sixteenth century between representatives of the Anabaptists and theologians belonging to the magisterial Reformation churches. Contemporary printed protocols exist for Bern (1531), Zofingen (1532), Frankenthal (1571), Emden (1578), and Leeuwarden (1596); for Bern (1538) and Pfeddersheim (1557), however, there are only manuscript ones. I have not myself consulted any of these protocols directly.

There is a brief but penetrating essay by Harold S. Bender (to whose efforts we are principally indebted for the compilation of the *Mennonite Encyclopedia*), "The Pacifism of the Sixteenth Century Anabaptists," in *Church History*, vol. xxiv, no. 2 (June 1955), reprinted in *MQR*, vol. xxx, no. 1 (January 1956). "The Anabaptist Theology of Martyrdom" is studied by Ethelbert Stauffer in his article, translated by Robert Friedmann, in *MQR*, vol. xix, no. 3 (July 1945). It was originally published in German in 1933. Two other German scholars just prior to World War II— Ulrich Bergfried and Fritz Heyer—published expositions of Anabaptist nonresistance in works devoted to the general *Weltanschauung* of the Anabaptists; both authors treat the subject topically rather than chronologically and both tend to lump the peaceable and the violent together in one undifferentiated whole. Bergfried's volume is entitled *Verantwortung als theologisches Problem im Täufertum des 16. Jahrhunderts* (Wuppertal, 1938), and Heyer's *Der Kirchenbegriff der Schwärmer* (Leipzig, 1939). John Horsch's pamphlet, *The Principle of Nonresistance as held by the Mennonite Church: A Historical Survey* (Scottdale, Pa., 1951 edn.) originally published in 1927, which deals with the Mennonites' roots in sixteenth-century Anabaptism as well as with the subsequent centuries, is useful now mainly for the extensive translations it includes of some of the most important primary sources for Anabaptist nonresistance.

Nonresistance among the Swiss Brethren and their descendants is discussed in Ernst H. Correll, *Das schweizerische Täufermennonitentum: Ein soziologischer Bericht* (Tübingen, 1925). Its thematic method of treatment, however, makes it sometimes difficult to place events and opinions in the time sequence. Nonresistance is also dealt with by Robert Kreider in his unpublished Ph.D. dissertation, "The Relation of the Anabaptists to the Civil Authorities in Switzerland" (Chicago, 1953); the author is concerned mainly with the first two decades of Anabaptism. The findings of the dissertation are summarized in a chapter Kreider contributed to *The Recovery of the Anabaptist Vision*, ed. Guy F. Hershberger (Scottdale, Pa., 1957), under the title, "The Anabaptists and the State." H. S. Bender's biography, *Conrad Grebel c. 1498-1526: The Founder of the Swiss Brethren Sometimes Called Anabaptists* (Goshen, Ind., 1950) does not contain a great deal relating directly to nonresistance, but the book provides essential background for the genesis of this concept and for comprehension of the Swiss milieu in which it arose. The same may be said of the sociological study by Paul Peachey, *Die soziale Herkunft der Schweizer Täufer in der Reformationszeit* (Karlsruhe, 1954). Nonresistance is one of the topics dealt with in another two studies by the American Mennonite historian, John H. Yoder: *Täufertum und Reformation in der Schweiz: Die Gespräche zwischen Täufern und Reformatoren 1523-1538* (Karlsruhe, 1962) and *Täufertum und Reformation im Gespräch* (Zürich, 1968).

For the doctrine of the sword among Anabaptists in south Germany there is a slim but most scholarly volume by Hans J. Hillerbrand, *Die politische Ethik der Oberdeutschen Täufertums* (Leiden and Köln, 1962). Chapter III (4) deals specifically with "Die Frage des Kriegsdienstes." Hillerbrand, who covers to some extent the Anabaptists of Switzerland and central Germany as well, published a summary of his monograph in English in the *MQR*: "The Anabaptist View of the State," vol. xxxii, no. 2 (April 1958). There is quite a lot about sixteenth-century nonresistance, too, in Elsa Bernhofer-Pippert, *Täuferische Denkweisen und Lebensformen im Spiegel oberdeutscher Täuferverhöre* (Münster, 1967). Kreider has concentrated on Strasbourg in his article, "The Anabaptists and the Civil Authorities of Strasbourg, 1525-1555," *Church History*, vol. xxiv, no. 2 (June 1955), and Ruth Weiss on Hesse in her article, "Herkunft und Sozialanschauungen der Täufergemeinden in westlichen Hessen," *Archiv für Reformationsgeschichte* (Gütersloh), vol. 52, no. 2 (1961), in which she devotes a section to the Anabaptist attitude to the *Obrigkeit*. A Marxist historian, Gerhard Zschäbitz, has published a volume, *Zur mitteldeutschen Wiedertäuferbewegung nach dem Grossen Bauernkrieg* (Berlin, 1958); in chapter II (1) there is a little about nonresistance, but the discussion is vitiated by the author's failure to distinguish between Anabaptists and various other contemporary sectaries. John S. Oyer, in his *Lutheran Reformers against Anabaptists: Luther, Melanchton and Mencius and the Anabaptists of Central Germany* (The Hague, 1964) includes, *inter alia*, an account of the reformers' differences with the Anabaptists on war and the state.

Among early Anabaptists, Hubmaier was the most able exponent of a nonpacifist position. I have used Henry C. Vedder's translation of Hubmaier's treatise "On the Sword," which he included in his biography of this Anabaptist leader (New York and London, 1905). Hubmaier's *Schriften* have been reprinted in *Quellen z. Gesch. der Täufer*, vol. IX (1962), eds. Gunnar Westin and Torsten Bergsten. Among biographies of Hubmaier the following deal in greater or less detail with his doctrine of the sword: Johann Loserth, *Doctor Balthasar Hubmaier und die Anfänge der Wiedertaufe in Mähren* (Brünn [Brno], 1893); Carl Sachsse, *D. Balthasar Hubmaier als Theologe* (Berlin, 1914); Torsten Bergsten, *Balthasar Hubmaier: Seine Stellung zu Reformation und Täufertum 1521-1528* (Kassel, 1961). Robert Friedmann, in a discussion of the "Nicolsburg Articles" in *Church History*, vol. XXXVI, no. 4 (December 1967), inclines toward the opinion that Hubmaier's opponent in debate, Hans Hut, defended not nonresistance but chiliasm against him. For the view that Hut took a nonresistant position during this Nikolsburg *Gespräch* of 1527, see part I of Herbert Klassen, "The Life and Teachings of Hans Hut," *MQR*, vol. XXXIII, nos. 3 and 4 (July and October 1959).

Munsterite Anabaptism scarcely belongs—directly at any rate—to a history of pacifism. The serious historiography of the Münster episode really did not begin until the publication of C. A. Cornelius' never completed *Geschichte des Münsterischen Aufruhrs*, 2 vols. (Leipzig 1855-1860); before Cornelius, who based his work mainly on the documents, historians had relied primarily on contemporary chronicles which were almost always strongly biased against the Anabaptists. For literature on Münster I would refer readers to two recent works: the bibliographical essay by Robert Stupperich, *Das Münsterische Täufertum: Ergebnisse und Probleme der neuren Forschung* (Münster, 1958) and to Gerhard Brendler, *Das Täuferreich zu Münster 1534/35* (Berlin, 1966). In part II of his work Brendler gives a Marxist interpretation of the events of 1534-1535 and their immediate background; in part I he includes a valuable 60-page bibliographical survey from the sixteenth century to the present ("Die Beurteilung des Täuferreiches von Münster 1534/35 in der Historiographie").

The history of Dutch Anabaptism is surveyed in Cornelius Krahn, *Dutch Anabaptism: Origin, Spread, Life and Thought (1450-1600)*, (The Hague, 1968), and its theology in William Echard Keeney, *The Development of Dutch Anabaptist Thought and Practice from 1539-1564* (Niewkoop, 1968). Both volumes are useful for general background, but neither goes into much detail concerning nonresistance. Rather more information on this subject is to be found in a work by a Flemish historian, A.L.E. Verheyden, dealing with the southern Netherlands, *Anabaptism in Flanders, 1530-1650: A Century of Struggle* (Scottdale, Pa., 1961), though here, too, nonresistance remains only a minor theme.

For an understanding of the Dutch Anabaptists' doctrine of the sword before Menno Simons' conversion in 1536, the publication of three Dutch historians are particularly important: W. J. Kühler, K. Vos, and A. F. Mellink. Over 200 pages of Kühler's *Geschiedenis der nederlandsche Doops-gezinden in de zestiende eeuw* (Haarlem, 1932) deal with this early period. For Kühler, the overwhelming majority of Dutch Anabaptists, though not yet complete nonresistants in the style of the Schleitheim Confession, re-mained nevertheless "peaceable (*vreedzaam*)"; on the other hand, those deviants who supported revolutionary violence and became Münsterites were only a small minority of the whole brotherhood. Vos, who was Kühler's cousin and former pupil, opposed this point of view in a number of articles. The controversy between the two men, who in addition were both minis-ters in the *Doopsgezinden* church, became at times rather acrimonious. For Vos, early Anabaptists throughout the Netherlands represented an upsurge of revolutionary feeling among the socially oppressed and outcast; almost to a man, he claimed, they had adopted a violent stance, and they had continued like this until after mid-century. Vos put this view forward as early as 1917 in an article in the *Doopsgezinde Bijdragen* (Leiden): "Kleine bijdragen over de Doopersche beweging in Nederland tot het optreden van Menno Simons." To this challenge Kühler answered with a long study which he published in the same journal in 1919: "Het Nederlandsche Anabaptisme en de revolutionnaire woelingen der zestiende eeuw." A fur-ther round in the contest came a few years later when Vos published another article—"Revolutionnaire Hervorming"—in the Amsterdam *De Gids* (1920, pt. 4) and was promptly answered by Kühler ("Het Anabaptisme in Neder-land," *De Gids*, 1921, pt. 3). Vos died in 1926 before the publication of Kühler's *Geschiedenis* of sixteenth-century Dutch Anabaptism. However, his mantle seems to have fallen on a non-Mennonite historian of the younger generation, A. F. Mellink. Mellink, in his *De Wederdopers in de Noordelijke Nederlanden 1531-1544* (Groningen, 1954), elaborates Vos's thesis on the basis of detailed archival studies, and he devotes special attention to inves-tigating the socioeconomic conditions which formed a background to the rise of Dutch Anabaptism. For Mellink, Anabaptist acceptance of Munsterite doctrine was virtually total, while peaceableness, in his view, did not become a characteristic of Dutch Anabaptism until many years after Münster's fall. However, the Kühler thesis has also found protagonists in recent years: for example, Kühler's successor in his chair at the University of Amsterdam, N. van der Zijp, defended it in his synthesis of *Doopsgezinden* history (see Section F).

E. The Polish Antitrinitarians

In 1932 Stanisław Kot, the leading Reformation expert in interwar Poland and editor of the periodical *Reformacja w Polsce*, published in Warsaw his study of the sociopolitical ideology of the Polish Brethren. A revised and expanded version was later tranlated into English by the American Unitarian historian, Earl Morse Wilbur, and published as *Socinianism in Poland: The*

Social and Political Ideas of the Polish Antitrinitarians in the Sixteenth and Seventeenth Centuries (Boston, 1957). I am personally much indebted to Kot's magnificent exposition not merely in preparing this chapter, but also on account of the incentive which, some years ago, a reading of the original Polish edition gave me eventually to undertake a similar project in connection with the Czech Brethren of the fifteenth and early sixteenth centuries. In comparing Kot's text with several of the primary sources on which he based his account (my own researches for this chapter have been very modest in comparison with his), I am struck both by his accuracy and his perceptive interpretation. The problem of war, although occupying only part of his narrative, does figure prominently in its pages, and indeed this subject is intelligible only within the broader framework which he gives.

G. H. Williams's volume on the Radical Reformation, mentioned earlier, provides some valuable insights into the Anabaptist nonresistance of the early Polish Brethren; and E. M. Wilbur's magisterial study of *Socinianism and Its Antecedents* (Cambridge, Mass., 1945), which forms volume I of his two-volume history of Unitarianism, is also essential background reading, even though it contains merely a few pages on Antitrinitarian pacifism *stricto sensu*. The one item devoted solely to this subject is by Józef Walczewski, "Nauka arian polskich wobec zagadnienia wojny," *Studia i materiały z dziejów nauki polskiej*, vol. I (Warsaw, 1953). It is brief and not particularly helpful. An older essay by Stanisław Estreicher, "Pacyfizm w Polsce XVI stulecia," *Ruch prawniczy, ekonomiczny i socjologiczny* (Poznań), vol. XI, no. 1 (1931), surveys both Antitrinitarian pacifism and the ideas on peace and war of some of its leading opponents.

Among the studies touching on our theme which have appeared in Poland since Kot prepared the revised version of his book, I will mention only three: Wacław Urban, "Losy Braci Polskich od założenia Rakowa do wygnania z Polski," *Odrodzenie i Reformacja w Polsce* (Warsaw), vol. I (1956), interesting as an intelligent example of the postwar Marxist historiography of the Polish Reformation; Ludwik Chmaj, *Faust Socyn (1539-1604)* (Warsaw, 1963), a full-scale biography by a historian of the older generation; and Stanisław Tworek, *Zbór lubelski i jego rola w ruchu ariańskim w Polsce w XVI i XVII wieku* (Lublin, 1966), dealing with the social and intellectual currents in this important Antitrinitarian congregation which included leading radicals like Niemojewski and Czechowic among its members.

Stanisław Kot was responsible for bringing out a scholarly edition of one of the most valuable sources for the early Antitrinitarian attitude to war: Szymon Budny's *O urzędzie miecza używającym* (Warsaw, 1932), after he had uncovered in the Czartoryski Library in Cracow what is almost certainly the sole surviving copy of the book, which was originally published in 1583. There are numerous references to war and other social questions in Stanisław Szczotka, "Synody arjan polskich od założenia Rakowa do wygnania z kraju (1569-1662)," *Reformacja w Polsce* (Warsaw), vol. VII/

518

VIII (1935-1936). Socinus' Latin Raków lectures of 1601-1602 remained in manuscript until extracts from Smalcius' notes on them were published in *Per la storia degli eretici italiani del secolo XVI in Europa*, eds. D. Cantimori and E. Feist (Rome, 1937). After the last war two Polish scholars, Lech Szczucki and Janusz Tazbir, printed Smalcius' notes on the 1601 sessions in full: *Epitome colloqui Racoviae habiti anno 1601* (Warsaw, 1966). Szczucki and Tazbir have also been responsible for editing an anthology of early Antitrinitarian literature, *Literatura ariańska w Polsce XVI wieku* (Warsaw, 1959); it contains not only a complete translation into Polish of Grzegorz Paweł's "Adversus Iacobi Palaeologi de bello sententiam responsio" of 1572, but also the vital Colloquy XII of Marcin Czechowic's *Rozmowy christiańskie* of 1575. In 1959, too, Chmaj published in Warsaw a scholarly edition of Socinus' letters (*Listy*). The two volumes contain, in Polish translation, all known letters, both those written by Socinus and those written to him; war and civil government, however, figure only in the correspondence contained in volume II.

F. THE MENNONITES

If Menno Simons may rightly be called the first Mennonite, he was by no means the last Anabaptist. Anabaptism, with the exception of its communitarian Hutterite branch, eventually fused with Mennonitism into a single movement; the process, however, evades precise definition in terms of dating and chronology. Naturally, works on Mennonitism often include materials on Anabaptism; some of these have already been mentioned in section D (see especially its first two paragraphs) and will not be listed again here. Likewise, some of the titles discussed for the first time below also contain information on Anabaptism. No comprehensive history has been compiled of the nonresistant thought and practice of Mennonites in Europe.

Menno Simons wrote either in Dutch or in the *Oosterisch* Low German dialect; he left nothing in his native Frisian. I have used the collected edition of his works in English, edited by John Christian Wenger and translated by Leonard Verduin: *The Complete Writings of Menno Simons c. 1496-1561* (Scottdale, Pa., 1956). This is based on the Dutch collections of 1646 and, especially, of 1681; there has been, in fact, no modern scholarly edition of Menno's works as yet. From a number of biographies of Menno I have found two especially useful: K. Vos, *Menno Simons 1496-1561. Zijn leven en werken en zijne reformatorische denkbeelden* (Leiden, 1914) and Cornelius Krahn, *Menno Simons (1496-1561): Ein Beitrag zur Geschichte und Theologie der Taufgesinnten* (Karlsruhe, 1936). N. van der Zijpp printed a short study of "Menno en Munster" in *Stemmen uit de Doopsgezinde broederschap* (Assen), vol. II, no. 1 (January 1953). The Wismar resolutions have been printed a number of times, e.g., in Vos's biography of Menno and in the *Bibliotheca Reformatoria Neerlandica*, vol. VII (1910), and there is a German translation in J. ten Doornkaat Koolman, "Die

Wismarer Artikel 1554," *Mennonitische Geschichtsblätter* (Karlsruhe), vol.
22 (new series 17), 1965. Doornkaat Koolman is also the author of *Dirk
Philips: Vriend en medewerker van Menno Simons 1500-1568* (Haarlem,
1964). Though Philips did not write much about nonresistance or war, his
views supplement the more abundant evidence on these subjects contained
in Menno's works. An article by an American theologian, Ralph L. Moel-
lering—"Attitudes toward the Use of Force and Violence in Thomas Muent-
zer, Menno Simons, and Martin Luther: A Comparative Study with Reference to Prevalent Contemporary Positions," *Concordia Theological Monthly*
(St. Louis, Missouri), vol. xxxi, no. 7 (July 1960)—contains some interesting comments on Menno's outlook. The author, for instance, remarking on Menno's cheerful acceptance of the eternal torments of the damned,
asks if this should not be seen as a "compensation" for the sufferings inflicted on Anabaptists by their enemies.

A history of the Dutch Mennonite peace testimony, which would utilize
the extensive congregational archives still extant, is much needed; I felt
the lack of such a work in compiling my chapter. Johannes Dyserinck, "De
weerloosheid volgens de Doopsgezinden," *De Gids* (Amsterdam, 1890),
pt. 1, pp. 104-61, 303-42, is still useful and contains important information.
But his arrangement is rather chaotic and his data are not always accurate.
Karel Vos wrote a 15-page pamphlet, *De weerloosheid der Doopsgezinden*
(Amsterdam, [1924]). Apart from its extreme brevity, the work is marred
by overemphasis on the nonpacifist elements in sixteenth- and seventeenth-
century Mennonitism. The best account is that given by N. van der Zijpp,
De vroegere Doopsgezinden en de krijgsdienst (Wolvega, 1930). Once
again, the work is a sketch covering only 36 pages, though it is written
with intimate knowledge of the subject.

W. J. Kühler's classic history of the *Doopsgezinden* was unfortunately
never completed. The author's lively style and profound learning make
reading of the volumes which did appear a pleasure. For our subject the
sixteenth-century volume (mentioned above) contains important materials.
The same is true of his *Geschiedenis van de Doopsgezinden in Nederland,
1600-1735* (Haarlem), of which the first ten chapters were published in
1940. (Chapter 11 appeared posthumously in 1950, but this is not concerned
with nonresistance. The remaining eight chapters were never committed to
paper; one section, however, would have dealt with the Mennonite attitude
to the state.) Kühler's volumes form essential background reading for any
study of Dutch Mennonite history. For detailed and sometimes sharp criticism of Kühler's first volume by the American Mennonite historian John
Horsch, see his review article in the *MQR*, vol. vii, nos. 1 and 2 (January
and April 1933). Another work providing the same kind of essential background as Kühler's is the briefer but chronologically more comprehensive
history by van der Zijpp, *Geschiedenis der Doopsgezinden in Nederland*
(Arnhem, 1952); the sections on nonresistance are drawn in large part from
his earlier pamphlet. A list—though an incomplete one—of items written by

Doopsgezinden authors on peace and nonresistance will be found on pages 184 and 305 of the *Catalogus der werken over de Doopsgezinden en hunne geschiedenis aanwezig in de Bibliotheek der Vereenigde Gemeente te Amsterdam* (Amsterdam, 1919). There are useful articles on the nonresistance theory and practice of the sect in the periodical, *Doopsgezinde Bijdragen* (Amsterdam, Leeuwarden, and Leiden, 1861-1919): I have used many of these in my account. Some of the articles reprint archival sources or are based directly on such sources.

I have not made much use of histories of local congregations. On the whole, they do not appear to be particularly helpful in respect to our subject, and I will mention only one here: Vos's *De doopsgezinde gemeente te Rotterdam* (Rotterdam, 1907). The older volumes by S. Blaupot ten Cate on provincial Mennonite communities contain source materials on nonresistance: *Geschiedenis der Doopsgezinden in Friesland* (Leeuwarden, 1839); *Geschiedenis der Doopsgezinden in Groningen, Overijssel en Oost-Friesland,* 2 vols. (Leeuwarden and Groningen, 1842); *Geschiedenis der Doopsgezinden in Holland, Zeeland, Utrecht en Gelderland,* 2 vols. (Amsterdam, 1847).

Turning now to works covering limited time-spans or special aspects of nonresistance, we should mention first of all Tieleman Jansz van Braght's famous *The Bloody Theater or Martyr's Mirror of the Defenseless Christians* (as the title runs in the English translation published at Scottdale [Pennsylvania]; I used the fifth edition, 1951). First appearing in 1660 as *Het bloedig tooneel der Doops-gezinde . . .* in an edition of 1290 pages, it soon became known simply as the "Martyr's Mirror," both in the Dutch original and later when translated into German and English. The sixteenth-century Netherlands martyrs occupy most space in van Braght's account: his book, therefore, is valuable as a reflection of the *Weltanschauung* of rank-and-file Mennonites of that time. The problem of war and military service in sixteenth-century Dutch Mennonitism is dealt with directly in Jan Hendrik Wessel, *De leerstellige strijd tusschen Nederlandsche Gereformeerden en Doopsgezinden in de zestiende eeuw* (Assen, 1945), chap. XI: "De overheid." Information on the attitude of the stadholders of the House of Orange toward Mennonite conscientious objection in the sixteenth and seventeenth centuries is contained in Vos's pamphlet, *Orange en de Doopsgezinden* (n.p.p., 1909). I have dealt briefly with the Dutch Mennonite Pieter Cornelisz Plockhoy's pacifist colony in New Netherland in my *Pacifism in the U.S.* (see below, section G). See also Leland and Marvin Harder, *Plockhoy from Zurik-zee: The Study of a Dutch Reformer in Puritan England and Colonial America* (Newton, Kansas, 1952). The settlement had existed for barely a year (1663-1664) when a British admiral "destroyed the Quaking [*sic*] society of Plockhoy to a nail"; the settlers themselves, however, survived the destruction of their colony. A brief section on the pacifism of the Collegiants and their Mennonite sympathizers is to be found in Kühler's study *Het Socinianisme in Nederland* (Leiden, 1912); see pages 192-195. But for Collegiant pacifism C. B. Hylkema's two volumes on the

Reformateurs (Haarlem, 1900-1902) are essential. An excellent summary in English of these volumes has been made by Geoffrey F. Nuttall, "Early Quakerism in the Netherlands: Its Wider Context," *The Bulletin of Friends' Historical Association* (Philadelphia), vol. 44, no. 1 (Spring 1955), but one needs to read the original, as well as to consult some of the Collegiants' own writings, to get an adequate picture of their nonresistant views. For the story of the Collegiants' orphanage, see Fred. Kuiper, "Het weeshuis der doopsgezinde Collegianten 'De Oranje-Appel,' " *Jaarboek van het Genootschap Amstelodamum*, vol. xviii (1920). For the Mennonites of Balk, Friesland, see the article with this title by Carl F. Brüsewitz in the *MQR*, vol. xxx, no. 1 (January 1956). Among several contemporary items written by Dutch Mennonites in connection with the introduction of universal military service in 1898, I will mention only one: S. Cramer, "Hoe een van onze vroegere kenmerken is te niet gedaan," *Doopsgezinde Bijdragen* (1898). Its title—"How one of our earlier characteristics is cancelled"—well sums up the significance of this event for Mennonite history.

The Mennonites of Germany maintained nonresistance longer than the *Doopsgezinden*. Unfortunately no overall account exists of the development of the German Mennonite peace testimony. Most valuable is Wilhelm Mannhardt's *Die Wehrfreiheit der altpreussischen Mennoniten* (Marienburg, 1863) which deals principally with the West Prussian Mennonites, emphasizing particularly the historico-legal aspects of their military exemption. But this work is now over a century old. Emil Händiges, *Die Lehre der Mennoniten in Geschichte und Gegenwart*. (Eppstein and Ludwigshafen am Rhein, 1921) bases his chapter on nonresistance (14) largely on Mannhardt. Händiges has also published a short historical outline of Mennonite nonresistance, with special reference to Prussia in 1867-1868: "Historisches Memorandum zur Wehrlosigkeit der Mennoniten," *Der Bote und Christlicher Bundesbote* (Rosthern, Saskatchewan), 1950 (nos. 49-51), 1951 (nos. 1-3). Ernst Crous, "The Mennonites in Germany since the Thirty Years' War," *MQR*, vol. xxv, no. 4 (October 1951), is also useful.

Monographs dealing with particular sections of the German Mennonite community often contain information concerning the history of nonresistance and conscientious objection. I may mention *inter alia* the following: Delbert G. Gratz, *Bernese Anabaptists and Their American Descendants* (Goshen, Indiana, 1953) for the Swiss; Alfred Michelis, *Les Anabaptistes des Vosges* (Paris, 1860) and Ch. Mathiot, *Recherches historiques sur les Anabaptistes de l'ancienne principauté de Montbéliard, d'Alsace et des régions voisines* (Belfort, 1922) for the congregations in present-day France; Claus-Peter Classen, *Die Widertäufer im Herzogtum Württemberg und in benachbarten Herrschaften* (Stuttgart, 1965), and Erich Drumm, *Zur Geschichte der Mennoniten im Herzogtum Pfalz-Zweibrücken* (Zweibrücken, 1962) for south and central Germany; Robert Dollinger, *Geschichte der Mennoniten in Schleswig-Holstein, Hamburg und Lübeck* (Neumünster, 1930), an especially valuable study on account of the thoroughness of its archival research;

Peter Bachmann, *Mennoniten in Kleinpolen 1784-1934* (Lwów, 1934), for the small Galician settlement; Max Schön, *Das Mennonitenthum in Westpreussen* (Berlin, 1886), which may be used in conjunction with W. Mannhardt's earlier but more detailed account; Erich Randt, *Die Mennoniten in Ostpreussen und Litauen bis zum Jahre 1772* (Königsberg, 1912).

In respect to the West Prussian Mennonites, L. Stobbe's brochure on the congregation of Montau-Gruppe (Montau and Gruppe, 1918) contains documentary materials concerning its relations with the government over military demands in 1813-1814 and 1867-1868 ff., while H. G. Mannhardt's history of the Danzig congregation—*Die Danziger Mennonitengemeinde* (Danzig, 1919)—has also quite a lot to say on our topic. H. G. Mannhardt supplemented W. Mannhardt's book by carrying on the story of the Old Prussians' *Wehrfreiheit* from the point where he broke off down to the end of the 1860's: "Zur Entstehung und Geschichte der Königl. Kabinettsordre vom 3. März 1868, betreffend den Heeresdienst der Mennoniten," pp. 97-107 in *Des Christlichen Gemeinde-Kalenders belehrender und unterhaltender Teil für das Jahr 1919* (Kaiserslautern).

A salutary antidote to the somewhat nationalistic tone of much German Mennonite historiography, especially prior to 1945, is Kazimierz Mężyński's study, *O Menonitach w Polsce* (Gdańsk, 1961), originally published in *Rocznik Gdański* (Gdańsk), vol. xix/xx (1960-1961) and summarized in *Mennonitische Geschichtsblätter*, vol. 25 (new series 20), 1968. (Mężyński, however, seriously misinterprets the stand of Elder Peter Bartel of Montau-Gruppe after 1868, asserting that he refused baptism to any of his congregation who would not promise to enter military service; see my text.)

For the great crisis in West Prussian Mennonitism over universal military service, the *Mennonitische Blätter* (Danzig) is an important source. I have found the years 1868 and 1870-1871 particularly useful in compiling my account. Wilhelm Ewert's apologia for nonresistance, which was published in that paper in 1873, has been republished in the original German, but slightly abridged, in the *MQR*, vol. xi, no. 4 (October 1937), under the title, "A Defense of the Ancient Mennonite Principle of Non-Resistance by a Leading Prussian Elder in 1873." Peter Froese's earlier pamphlet of 1850 on the same theme was republished in 1926 at Newton, Kansas in a photographic reprint; I used this edition. Although long outdated, the Quaker Robert Barclay, Jr.'s book on *The Inner Life of the Religious Societies of the Commonwealth . . .* (London, 1876; I used the 1879 edition) contains—its title notwithstanding—some materials of interest concerning the nineteenth-century German Mennonites' attitude to military service.

A primary source for south German Mennonite nonresistance not long before its collapse has been published by Paul Schowalter, "Die Ibersheimer Beschlüsse von 1803 und 1805," *Mennonitische Geschichtsblätter*, vol. 20 (n.s. 15), 1963. The "Soldaten-Kommission der Konferenz süddeutscher Mennoniten" was responsible for the issue of a handbook for Mennonite conscripts in the imperial army ("Liebe Brüder in Soldatenrock"): *Warnun-*

gen und Winke für die Militärzeit (Kaiserslautern, 1908). It contains material on noncombatant status and seems to have been designed, in the first place, for those who chose this alternative.

Quite an abundant literature exists on the "Russian" Mennonites, although no general up-to-date scholarly history of their activities either under the Tsars or under the Soviets has appeared. Cornelius Krahn's article, "Some Social Attitudes of the Mennonites of Russia," *MQR*, vol. IX, no. 4 (October 1935), though brief, contains many valuable insights into the sociology of Russian Mennonitism. My account of the Forestry Service and its genesis is based mainly on Jacob Sudermann, "The Origin of Mennonite State Service in Russia, 1870-1880," *MQR*, vol. XVII, no. 1 (January 1943); though concerned primarily with the 1870's, the author outlines the history of the Forestry Service down to 1917. See also Krahn's "Public Service in Russia," *The Mennonite* (North Newton), vol. LVIII (1943), 8 and 22 June, 31 August, and 2 September, and Frank C. Peters, "Non-Combatant Service Then and Now," *Mennonite Life* (North Newton), vol. X, no. 1 (January 1955). I have also consulted the following for this subject: Abr. Görz, *Ein Beitrag zur Geschichte des Forstdienstes der Mennoniten in Russland* (Gross-Tokmak, 1907); P. M. Friesen, *Die alt-evengelische Mennonitische Brüderschaft in Russland (1789-1910) in Rahmen der mennonitischen Gesamtgeschichte* (Halbstadt, 1911), pt. I, chaps. XXXII, XXXIII; and monographs on the two main colonies—D. H. Epp, *Die Chortitzer Mennoniten* (Odessa, 1889), chap. v, and Franz Isaac, *Die Molotschnaer Mennoniten* (Halbstadt, 1908), chap. 3, sections 3 and 4. All four volumes contain many documents from the 1870's, either in full or in excerpts. The most recent scholarly contribution to the mass Mennonite emigration to North America in the 1870's and 1880's is by Gustav E. Reimer and G. R. Gaeddert, *Exiled by the Czar: Cornelius Jansen and the Great Mennonite Migration* (Newton, Kansas, 1956). Among works utilizing United States and Canadian archival sources are the articles published by Ernst Correll in the *MQR* (listed in my *Pacifism in the United States*) and Georg Leibbrandt, "The Emigration of the German Mennonites from Russia to the United States and Canada, 1873-1880," *MQR*, vol. VI, no. 4 (October 1932), and vol. VII, no. 1 (January 1933).

The Hutterites, who accompanied the Russian Mennonites to the New World, were excellent record-keepers; their chronicles, therefore, provide rich materials for the sect's history and doctrines. Of these chronicles, there are three major collections available in modern scholarly editions: *Die Geschichts-Bücher der Wiedertäufer in Oesterreich-Ungarn*, ed. Josef Beck (Vienna, 1883), a mosaic of shorter items arranged chronologically; *Geschicht-Buch der Hutterischen Brüder*, ed. Rudolf Wolkan (Macleod, Alta., and Vienna, 1923), known usually as "Das grosse Geschichtsbuch"; *Das Klein-Geschichtsbuch der Hutterischen Brüder*, ed. A.J.F. Zieglschmid (Philadelphia, 1947), written by elder Johannes Waldner between 1793 and 1802, to which the editor has appended documents drawn from the subsequent period together with a comprehensive bibliography of the Hutterite movement. Zieglschmid also published an orthographically exact replica of the manuscript "Grosse Geschichtsbuch," which was compiled by successive annalists between ca. 1565 and 1665: *Die älteste Chronik der Hutterischen Brüder* (Ithaca, N.Y., 1943). All these volumes contain some material on Hutterite nonresistant principles and practice. For the Hutterite view of war, as for every other aspect of their ideology, Peter Riedemann's *Rechenschafft* is essential. With every page studded with Biblical quotations or paraphrases, the treatise is marked by the clarity, cogency, and force with which the author sustains his arguments and by the graphic character imparted by the occasional example taken from daily life. Since there is a static quality about Hutterite doctrine, Riedemann's exposition holds for most of the subsequent history of the group. (His book was written in 1540-1541 but not published until 1565.) I have used the translation made by Kathleen E. Hasenberg: *Account of Our Religion, Doctrine and Faith* (London, 1950). The Hutterite ordinance of 1633 on nonresistance has been translated and published by the leading authority on the Hutterites, Robert Friedmann. It originally appeared in the *MQR*, vol. xxv, no. 2 (April 1951) and was reprinted in his *Hutterite Studies* (Goshen, Ind., 1961). Information on the history of Hutterite nonresistance is to be found, among other places, in Victor John Peters, "A History of the Hutterian Brethren 1528-1958" (Ph.D. dissertation, University of Göttingen, 1960). Peters is also the author of an excellent introduction to the twentieth-century *Brüderhofe* in the New World: *All Things Common: The Hutterian Way of Life* (Minneapolis, 1965). František Hrubý published in his study, "Die Wiedertäufer in Mähren," pt. 2, *Archiv für Reformationsgeschichte*, vol. xxx (1933), on pages 185-196, a general account of the taxes imposed on the Hutterites between 1570 and 1620.

Materials on Spiritualist and Pietist pacifism are scattered among a number of sources. For Hohburg, see Ernst Kochs, "Das Kriegsproblem in der spiritualischen Gesamtanschauung Christian Hohburgs," *Zeitschrift für Kirchengeschichte* (Gotha), vol. xlvi (n.s. ix), no. 2 (1928). Friedrich Nieper, *Die ersten deutschen Auswanderer von Krefeld nach Pennsylvanien* (Neukirchen, 1940), has a little on Anneken Hoogwand and Johann Lobach, while Heinz Renkewitz, *Hochmann von Hochenau (1670-1721): Quellenstudien zur Geschichte des Pietismus* (Breslau, 1935) touches upon Hochenan's views on peace and war. Quotations in English from Zinzendorf I have translated from Otto Uttendörfer, *Zinzendorfs christliches Lebensideal* (Gnadau, 1940). In addition to the materials cited in my book on pacifism in the United States, two other items in particular shed light on the eighteenth-century Moravian attitude to war and military service: an article by Glenn Weaver, "The Moravians during the French and Indian War," *Church History*, vol. xxiv, no. 3 (September 1955), and Kenneth Gardiner Hamilton's book on *John Ettwein and the Moravian Church during the Revolutionary Period* (Bethlehem, Pa., 1940). Although neither study deals directly with Moravians in Europe, each sheds light indirectly on the contemporary situation in the European congregations with regard to military service.

G. British Quakerism

The evolution of the Quaker peace testimony has been ably chronicled by Margaret E. Hirst, *The Quakers in Peace and War* (London, 1923). This is a most thorough study and is amply documented. The reader who knows her work will at once perceive the big debt I owe to its pages in my account of Quaker pacifism in the British Isles. Only in its discussion of the genesis of Quaker pacifism and in regard to the American chapters, and perhaps too in its rather idealized treatment of John Bright, is Hirst's book open to considerable revision for the period before 1914. Her survey can of course be augmented by more recently discovered materials, especially relating to the nineteenth century. But in broad outline it still stands intact. A brief, yet perceptive, introduction to the development of Quaker pacifism is given by Howard H. Brinton, *Sources of the Quaker Peace Testimony* (Wallingford, Pa., [1941]). The relevant volumes in the Rowntree Series of Quaker Histories contain material on the peace testimony as well as essential background: William C. Braithwaite, *The Beginnings of Quakerism* (1912), 2nd edn., ed. Henry J. Cadbury (Cambridge, 1955), and his *The Second Period of Quakerism* (1919), 2nd edn., ed. H. J. Cadbury (Cambridge, 1961); Rufus M. Jones, *The Later Periods of Quakerism*, 2 vols. (London, 1921). See also Arnold Lloyd, *Quaker Social History 1669-1738* (London, 1950), and Richard T. Vann, *The Social Development of English Quakerism 1655-1755* (Cambridge, Mass., 1969), though this last is not much concerned directly with the peace testimony. Much information on the peace testimony can be mined from articles in the *Journal of the Friends' Historical Society* (London). Many, but not all, of the articles I have used are mentioned below (cited as *JFHS*) or in the text. I also found useful the comments on the Quaker peace testimony in the essay by Thomas F. Green, "The Basis of Christian Pacifism," *The Friends' Quarterly* (London), vol. 6, no. 2 (April 1952). Among a considerable number of works of reference on Quaker history and bibliography one in particular deserves mention here: Joseph Smith, *A Descriptive Catalogue of Friends' Books*, 2 vols. (London, 1867). Current books and articles as well as research in progress are listed bi-annually in *Quaker History*, published in the United States.

The revisionist viewpoint in regard to the Quaker attitude to war during the 1650's is developed, in particular, by W. Alan Cole in his unpublished doctoral dissertation, "The Quakers and Politics, 1652-1660" (University of Cambridge, 1955), from which he has printed two articles: "The Peace Testimony in 1659: More Light on John Hodgson," *JFHS*, vol. 46, no. 2 (Autumn 1954) and "The Quakers and the English Revolution," *Past and Present* (London), no. 10 (November 1956). For the crisis of 1659, see also James F. Maclear, "Quakerism and the End of the Interregnum: A Chapter in the Domestication of Radical Puritanism," *Church History*, vol. XIX, no. 4 (December 1950); Frederick B. Tolles, *Quakers and the Atlantic Culture* (New York, 1960), chap. III: "Quakerism and Politics." Extremely valuable for the genesis of Quaker pacifism is the book by Hugh Barbour, *The Quakers in Puritan England* (New Haven and London, 1964). Geoffrey F. Nuttall, *The Holy Spirit in Puritan Faith and Experience* (Oxford, 1946) is useful for Quakerism's Puritan roots, though the peace testimony is touched upon only briefly. For the 1650's, see also Mabel Richmond Brailsford, *A Quaker from Cromwell's Army: James Nayler* (London, 1927) and George R. Burnet, *The Story of Quakerism in Scotland 1650-1850* (London, 1952). For pacifism or near-pacifism in England around the time Quakerism first arose, see Louise Fargo Brown, *The Political Activities of the Baptists and Fifth Monarchy Men in England during the Interregnum* (Washington, D.C., 1912) and David W. Petegorsky, *Left-Wing Democracy in the English Civil War: A Study of the Social Philosophy of Gerrard Winstanley* (London, 1940); also C. E. Whiting, *Studies in English Puritanism from the Restoration to the Revolution, 1660-1688* (London, 1931), chap. VI: "The Minor Sects."

The main sources for the evolution of the founder of Quakerism's views on peace include the *Journal of George Fox* and *A Collection of Many Select and Christian Epistles, Letters and Testimonies . . .* (London, 1698); *Gospel-Truth Demonstrated, in a Collection of Doctrinal Books . . .* (London, 1706). This last volume contains a collection of Fox's pamphlets and declarations, though by no means a complete one. The *Journal* was first published in 1694 in one volume, edited by Thomas Ellwood. There have been many subsequent editions, of which the most important are the Bicentenary edition, 2 vols. (London, 1891), the two-volume edition edited by Norman Penney (Cambridge, 1911), and the most recent scholarly edition by John L. Nickalls (Cambridge, 1952). See also H. J. Cadbury, "George Fox and Peace," *The Friend* (London), vol. 64 (1924), no. 28 (11 July), no. 29 (18 July).

For the views of early Quaker publicists on war and peace, see *inter alia* William Bayly, *A Briefe Declaration to all the World from the Innocent People of God, called Quakers. Of Our Principle and Belief concerning Plottings and Fightings with Carnal Weapons against Any People, Men, or Nations upon the Earth, to take away the Reproach or Any Jealousies out of the Minds of All People, concerning us in this particular, and to answer That Common Objection whether we would not fight if the Spirit moved us* (London, 1662); *A Collection of the Several Books and Writings given forth by That Faithful Servant of God and His People, George Fox, the Younger* (London, 1662); Edward Burrough, *The Memorable Works of a Son of Thunder and Consolation: . . .* (London, 1672); *Balm from Gilead. A Collection of the Living Divine Testimonies. Written by the faithful Servant of the Lord, William Smith* (London, 1675); *The Works of the Long-*

Mournful and Sorely-Distressed Isaac Penington . . . In Two Parts (London, 1681). For Robert Barclay's pacifism, see—apart from his own writings mentioned in the text—the recent study by D. Elton Trueblood (New York, 1968).

Modern reprints of William Penn's writings on peace include *No Cross, No Crown* (1669), ed. N. Penney (London, 1930); *The Peace of Europe: The Fruits of Solitude and Other Writings* (London: Everyman's Library edn., [1915]). Some of the items in *A Collection of the Works of William Penn*, 2 vols. (London, 1726) are relevant to his pacifism. The literature on Penn's relations with his "Holy Experiment" in Pennsylvania is large, as may be seen, for instance, from the footnotes to chap. 2 of my history of *Pacifism in the United States: From the Colonial Era to the First World War* (Princeton, 1968). One further item should be mentioned here: H. J. Cadbury, "Penn as a Pacifist," *Friends Intelligencer* (Philadelphia), vol. 101 (1944), no. 43 (21 Oct.). For Bellers on peace, see *John Bellers 1654-1725: Quaker, Economist and Social Reformer*, ed. A. Ruth Fry (London, 1935). An essential source for seventeenth- and early eighteenth-century Quaker conscientious objection is the two-volume compilation by Joseph Besse, *A Collection of the Sufferings of the People called Quakers, for the Testimony of a Good Conscience* (London, 1753), usually known simply as Besse's *Sufferings*. Insight into the motives leading to conscientious objection is provided in the autobiographical accounts left by two early navy objectors: *The Fighting Sailor turn'd Peaceable Christian: Manifested in the Convincement and Conversion of Thomas Lurting. With a Short Relation of Many Great Dangers, and Wonderful Deliverances, he met withal. First written for Private Satisfaction, and now published for General Service* (London, 1710) and *Adventures by Sea of Edward Coxere*, ed. E.H.W. Meyerstein (Oxford, 1945). See also "Friends and the Press-Gang," *JFHS*, vol. xxix (1932), p. 61.

Hirst's volume remains the best guide to the pacifism of eighteenth-century Friends. The *Journals* of at least three Quaker ministers of the early part of that century contain materials relevant to the peace testimony as it had by then developed in both the British Isles and the New World: William Edmundson (Dublin, 1715); Thomas Story (Newcastle-upon-Tyne, 1747); Thomas Chalkley (Philadelphia, 1754 edn.). For eighteenth-century Quaker conscientious objection I have used *inter alia*: "A Conscientious Objector in the Eighteenth Century," ed. Isabel Grubb, *JFHS*, vol. xxxiv (1937) and William J. Allinson, *Right in the Abstract* (Philadelphia, 1862) (where the army objector Joseph Horwood is erroneously called John Haywood). On Quaker pacifism in Guernsey I have consulted Edith Carey, "The Beginnings of Quakerism in Guernsey," *Report and Transactions 1918*, vol. 8 (1919), of the Guernsey Society of Natural Science and Local Research. The standard account, though long outdated, of the experiences of Irish Quakers during the Rebellion of 1798 is Thomas Hancock, *The Principles of Peace exemplified in the Conduct of the Society of Friends in Ireland during the Rebellion of the Year 1798* (London, 1825). See also William Rathbone, *A Narrative of Events, that have lately taken place in Ireland among the Society called Quakers; with Corresponding Documents, and Occasional Observations* (London, 1804), which formed a major primary source for Hancock's account.

Collections of documents put out by London Yearly Meeting often contain important declarations on the peace testimony. The Meeting's first discipline dates from 1738: "Christian & Brotherly Advices given forth from Time to Time by the Yearly Meetings in London alphabetically digested under Proper Heads." It was never published, but the Library of the Society of Friends, London, possesses a manuscript copy. Almost all this material, however, with later utterances added, was printed in *Extracts from the Minutes and Advices of the Yearly Meeting of Friends held in London, from Its First Institution* (London, 1783; 2nd edn., 1802). The *Epistles from the Yearly Meeting of Friends, held in London, to the Quarterly and Monthly Meetings in Great Britain, Ireland, and elsewhere; from 1681 to 1857, inclusive*, 2 vols. (London, 1858), is also important, though references to the peace testimony here are mainly of an exhortatory character. From 1858 the epistles are printed in the annual *Extracts from the Minutes and Proceedings of the Yearly Meeting of Friends, held in London . . .*, where one must also seek the minutes and advices from the early nineteenth century on.

"It is remarkable," writes Howard Brinton, "how little space in the vast sum of seventeenth, eighteenth, and nineteenth century Quaker literature is devoted to the exposition of peace principles." The first really thorough exposition of the Quaker peace testimony does not come until the third decade of the nineteenth century with the writings of Jonathan Dymond. In 1823 Dymond published *An Enquiry into the Accordancy of War with the Principles of Christianity, and an Examination of the Philosophical Reasoning by which it is defended: with Observations on Some of the Causes of War, and on Some of Its Effects*. I have used the second, "corrected and enlarged" edition (London, 1824). Dymond later revised his *Enquiry* and in 1829 presented his arguments, better arranged and with greater clarity, in the course of the two volumes of his *Essays on the Principles of Morality, and on the Private and Political Rights and Obligations of Mankind*. I have used the second edition (London, 1830). I have also consulted a short version of his pacifist exposition published by the London Peace Society as its Tract No. VII: *Observations on the Applicability of the Pacific Principles of the New Testament to the Conduct of States: and on the Limitations which Those Principles impose on the Rights of Self-defence* (2nd edn., London, 1825). See Charles William Dymond, *Memoir, Letters and Poems of Jonathan Dymond* (Bristol, 1911 edn.), pp. 152-160, for a list of editions of Dymond's antiwar writings. A number of Friends carried on Dymond's work of propagating Quaker pacifism by means of pamphlet and book. In most cases the pragmatic arguments against war stressed by

Dymond take an increasingly prominent place beside the religious case for pacifism. From among many such productions let me cite only three as representative examples of this trend: James Boorne, Jun., *On the Unlawfulness and Impolicy of War* (Newcastle-upon-Tyne, 1846); William Rowntree, *War and Christianity* (1861) (4th edn., London, 1900); William E. Wilson, *Christ and War* (London, 1913). For nineteenth-century Quaker thought and action in regard to peace and war the periodical press of the Society represents an important source, and especially the London *Friend* (1843 ff.) and the *British Friend* (Glasgow, etc., 1843-1913).

There is unfortunately no really up-to-date scholarly biography of Joseph Sturge; I have used Henry Richard, *Memoirs of Joseph Sturge* (London, 1864) and Stephen Hobhouse, *Joseph Sturge: His Life and Work* (London, 1919). On the other hand, there are a number of good studies on Bright, the most recent of which are: Herman Ausubel, *John Bright: Victorian Reformer* (New York, 1966); Donald Read, *Cobden and Bright: A Victorian Political Partnership* (London, 1967); and James L. Sturgis, *John Bright and the Empire* (London, 1969). They all have something to say on Bright's attitude to the peace movement and its problems. J. Travis Mills in his *John Bright and the Quakers*, 2 vols. (London, 1935), devotes chapters XVII and XVIII to this subject. On Quaker relations with Russia in the nineteenth century, see Richenda C. Scott, *Quakers in Russia* (London, 1964).

Conscientious objection was ceasing in the nineteenth century—for the time being—to be a vital issue for Friends. Their legal position in the first half of the century with respect to the militia is one of the subjects dealt with by Joseph Davis in *A Digest of Legislative Enactments, relating to the Society of Friends, commonly called Quakers, in England* (1st edn., Bristol, 1820; 2nd edn., London, 1849). My information concerning William Dyne's case is drawn from a small publication by the Friends' Tract Association: *The Changed Warfare* (2nd series, London, 1906). For William Batkin I have used the article in *JFHS*, vol. xix (1922), no. 1/2.

The changing Quaker attitude toward the state's demands for war taxes is a matter which still needs further clarification. A preliminary survey has been presented by Ernest R. Bromley, "Did Early Friends pay War Taxes?", *Friends Intelligencer*, vol. 105 (1948), no. 42 (16 October). For Nathaniel Morgan's radical tax objection, see two contributions to the *JFHS:* "Nathaniel Morgan and the Duke of Gloucester," vol. xv (1918), no. 4, and John S. Stephens, "Nathaniel Morgan of Ross," vol. xlvi (1954), no. 1. Another topic demanding more detailed investigation is the relationship between Quakers' growing economic prosperity and the pacifist thought and practice of members of the Society during the eighteenth and nineteenth centuries; among published work there is a little on this subject in I. Grubb, *Quakers and Industry before 1800* (London, 1930).

The Society of Friends' outgrowth in the New World is dealt with in detail, insofar as the Society's peace testimony is concerned, in my history of *Pacifism in the United States* mentioned above; the Quaker chapters have been reprinted separately as *Pioneers of the Peaceable Kingdom* (Princeton, 1970). One brief but valuable item on the colonial period inadvertently omitted in my history is Frederick B. Tolles, "Nonviolent Contact: The Quakers and the Indians," *Proceedings of the American Philosophical Society* (Philadelphia), vol. 107 (1963). For the West Indies, see Hirst. It is usually stated—on the whole correctly—that American Quakers in the nineteenth century were inactive in regard to the non-Quaker peace movement, in comparison to the British Society of Friends. That this was not always the case is shown by the Quaker-sponsored "Salem (Indiana) Peace Society Minutes" for 1819-1826, printed by Pamela J. Bennett in the *Indiana Magazine of History* (Bloomington), vol. LXIV, no. 4 (December 1968).

Sources for the history of Quaker pacifism on the European continent are very meager in comparison with those existing for British or American Quakerism. Indeed, the whole story of these communities is an obscure one. William I. Hull, "Dutch Quaker Peace-Makers," *Bulletin of Friends' Historical Association*, vol. 23 (1934, Spring and Autumn issues), throws some light on the conduct of Dutch Quakers in the seventeenth and eighteenth centuries. For French Friends we may consult Henry van Etten, *Chronique de la vie quaker française 1745-1945* (2nd edn., Paris, 1947) and for German Friends, Wilhelm Hubben, *Die Quäker in der deutschen Vergangenheit* (Leipzig, 1929). Hirst's volume also contains information on the pacifism of Quakers on the European continent.

H. NON-QUAKER PACIFISM IN
NINETEENTH-CENTURY BRITAIN

For the story of the Methodist lay preacher John Nelson's conscientious objection to military service I have consulted *The Case of John Nelson, Written by himself* (2nd edn., London [?], 1745). I used the fourth edition, "with large additions," of Richard Warner's *War inconsistent with Christianity: A Fast Sermon*, originally published in Bath in 1804. Two pamphlets protesting against this sermon were also printed in Bath in the same year: the Reverend Thomas Falconer's *A Letter to the Rev. Richard Warner* and Dr. William Falconer, M.D., *A Remonstrance, addressed to the Rev. Richard Warner, on the Subject of His Fast Sermon, May 27, 1804*. Both appeared anonymously. Warner himself returned to the subject of peace many years later in his *The Sermon on the Mount; in Five Discourses; Preached in Chelwood Church* (Bath and London, 1840), though he does not explicitly discuss war there. David Bogue's *On Universal Peace; being Extracts from a Discourse delivered in October 1813* was published by the London Peace Society in 1819. Bibliographical details about other precursors of the post-1815 peace movement are to be found in my text. I may mention one additional—and strongly worded—testimony to the irreconcilability of war and "the profession of arms" with the Christian religion, which dates from around the year of the Peace Society's foundation: it comes from the pen of an evangelical Anglican divine, the Reverend Legh Richmond (d. 1827) and is to be found on page 106 of his biography, *Domestic Portraiture; or the Successful Application of Religious Principle in the Education of a Family, exemplified in the Memoirs of the Deceased Children of the Rev. Legh Richmond* (London, 1833).

The history of the London Peace Society has not hitherto been adequately studied by historians. The narration embedded in A.C.F. Beales, *The History of Peace: A Short Account of the Organized Movements for International Peace* (London, 1931) is the most thorough so far. The third volume (1963) of the Norwegian Institute of Oslo's *Histoire de l'Internationalisme* by August Schou also contains much information concerning the British peace movement before 1914. But of course both Schou and Beales are concerned with a much broader topic. The Society's monthly organ, *The Herald of Peace*, which appeared from 1819 until the 1930's, is an invaluable source for the history of nineteenth-century pacifism, as are the Society's *Annual Reports* from 1817 on. Another peace journal, *The Peace Advocate and Correspondent*, published first in Newcastle-upon-Tyne and then in London from 1843 until the early 1850's, is also useful for our subject. The Quaker periodicals mentioned earlier contain reports on the general peace movement. For pacifism in Wales before 1914, see the early chapters of Goronwy J. Jones, *Wales and the Quest for Peace (from the Close of the Napoleonic Wars to the Outbreak of the Second World War)* (Cardiff, 1969). The development of the Peace Society in Wales is dealt with, too, by Richard Leonard Hugh, "The Theological Background of Nonconformist Social Influence in Wales, 1800-1850" (unpublished Ph.D. thesis, University of London, 1951), chap. IX (b). Also the outcome of a doctoral dissertation is James R. Andrews, "The Rationale of Nineteenth-Century Pacifism: Religious and Political Arguments in the Early British Peace Movement," *Quaker History*, vol. 57, no. 1 (Spring 1968).

The point to which thinking on peace had developed within the Society by the early 1840's may be seen in such productions as the extremely lengthy prize essay by H.T.J. Macnamara, *Peace, Permanent and Universal: Its Practicability, Value, and Consistency with Divine Revelation* (London, 1841) or *The Proceedings of the First General Peace Convention: held in London, June 22, 1843 and the Two Following Days* (London, 1843). Among several other items of this kind we may note the booklet by a Peace Society sympathizer, the radical politician and reformer James Silk Buckingham, *An Earnest Plea for the Reign of Temperance and Peace, as conducive to the Prosperity of Nations* (London, [1851]). The British peace movement around mid-century is discussed *inter alia* in Christina Phelps, *The Anglo-American Peace Movement in the Mid-Nineteenth Century* (New York, 1930). For expressions of absolute pacifism during the Crimean War see, for instance, the essay by the Reverend J. Jenkinson, *Does Chris-*

tianity sanction War? (London and Oakham, ca. 1855) and W. Stokes, *All War inconsistent with the Christian Religion and the Best Interests of Nations* (4th edn., London, 1855). Stokes was a Baptist minister, who had worked for a time as an agent of the Peace Society. The 1855 edition of his pamphlet, originally published in 1844, contains some "Practical Directions" for organizing the work of Christian pacifists "chiefly, and respectfully, addressed to young men." Stokes's piece, like Macnamara's mentioned above, was originally a prize essay. The same is also true of a long pamphlet by a nonconformist minister, the Reverend G. Barker: *The Expediency of Principle. An Attempt to show what is Erroneous or Defective in the Thirty-Seventh Article of the Church of England, in its Teaching on the Lawfulness of War, and what is the Christian's Duty under Such Circumstances* (London, 1862). The author urges the serving soldier "to abandon his profession; at all hazards." The great figure among British pacifists throughout most of the second half of the nineteenth century is of course Henry Richard, secretary of the London Peace Society from 1848 until 1885. I have used the following two—far from adequate—biographies, both published in London in the year of his death, 1888: Lewis Appleton, *Memoirs of Henry Richard, The Apostle of Peace* and Charles S. Miall, *Henry Richard, M.P.—A Biography.*

For representative expositions of early twentieth-century pacifism I may cite Walter Walsh, *The Moral Damage of War* (1902); James Barr, *Christianity and War* (1903); W. Evans Darby, *The Christ Method of Peace Making* [1908] and *A Catechism of Christian Non-Resistance* (1914). All four items were published in London. While they still place their pacifism on a religious background, they usually emphasize pragmatic arguments against war of a political or economic character.

An early illustration of the influence of evangelical Christianity in making pacifists out of pious military men is to be found in Horatio Bardwell, *Memoir of Rev. Gordon Hall, A.M., One of the First Missionaries of the Amer. Board of Comm. for For. Missions, at Bombay* (Andover, Mass., 1834), pp. 82-91, where an account is given of the conversion to pacifism and subsequent resignation from the army, around the year 1813, of two young British officers in India.

Sources for the activities of two ex-officer pacifist missionaries of the second quarter of the nineteenth century, Thomas Thrush and George Pilkington, are their own works, mainly of a semi-autobiographical character. For Thrush: *A Letter addressed to the King, by Thomas Thrush, on resigning His Commission as a Captain in the Royal Navy, on the Ground of the Unlawfulness of War* (2nd edn., London, 1825), his *Observations on the Causes and Evils of War: Its Unlawfulness; and the Means and Certainty of Its Extinction: In a Series of Letters addressed to a Friend* (York, 3 pts., 1825, 1826, 1827), published in 1828 in one volume as *The Apology of an Officer for Withdrawing from the Profession of Arms* (which I have not seen), and his *The Last Thoughts of a Naval Officer, on the Unlawfulness of War,*

&c. (London, 1841), put together at the age of eighty. These works are in part overlapping in content. See also his biography by a Unitarian minister, the Reverend C. Wellbeloved, *Memoir of Thomas Thrush, Esq., formerly an Officer of Rank in the Royal Navy: who resigned His Commission on the Ground of the Unreasonableness of War* (London, 1845).

For George Pilkington: *The Doctrine of Divine Providence; or, the Divine Guardianship over the Most Minute Concerns of Man, Illustrated and Defended, in Biographical Reminiscences* (London, 1836), his *Testimonies of Ministers of Various Denominations, showing the Unlawfulness of All Wars, Offensive or Defensive; . . .* (London, 1837), a privately printed work—now existing possibly in a unique copy, at the Haverford College Quaker Collection—which provides invaluable information concerning interdenominational pacifism at that date, and his *Travels through the United Kingdom in promoting the Cause of Peace on Earth and Good-will towards Men, (Being a Continuation of the Work entitled "The Doctrine of Particular Providence")* (London, 1839). I have used the second, enlarged, and revised edition of this last book, published in the same year as the first edition but under a slightly variant title. My account of the antimilitarist agitation carried on by George Hale among the troops of Woolwich garrison is drawn from the report given by the London *Morning Chronicle* (16 September 1824). I was unable to locate a copy of Hale's pamphlet, *The Two Opinions.* It is worth noting that the British Museum possesses a much later 4-page pamphlet by Hale entitled *War. Is it lawful under the Christian Dispensation? And what are the Best and Surest Means of putting, for ever, a Stop to Human Warfare? Addressed to Soldiers and Sailors who fear God* (London, [1858]).

The activities of the English nonresistants of the 1840's form an as yet unwritten chapter in the history of the British peace movement. The sources are extremely scattered, and it is difficult to obtain a coherent picture. Joseph Barker's nonresistant views are taken from the booklet jointly published with Henry C. Wright, *Non-Resistance. In Two Letters* [Newcastle-upon-Tyne, 1842]. See also *The Life of Joseph Barker. Written by Himself,* and edited by his nephew John Thomas Barker (London, 1880). Barker, whose pacifist and "no-government" ideas may have derived in part from the influence on him in his thirties of the Plymouth Brethren (see below), was a prolific pamphleteer on a wide range of political and religious topics; among his writings are a couple of short tracts, *All War Anti-Christian* and its sequel *Objections to Peace Principles Answered,* both published in Newcastle-upon-Tyne around 1840. I may also mention two anonymous pamphlets which I came upon, giving a glimpse into radical antimilitarist thought and activity in the mid-1840's: *Report of the Great Town's Meeting, to petition against the Proposed Increase of the Navy Estimates, and to protest against Standing Armies and Navies* (Birmingham and London, 1845) and *Proceedings at the Public Meeting of the Glasgow Anti-War Society, held in the City Hall, 23rd April, 1846* (Glasgow, 1846).

My volume on *Pacifism in the United States* goes into more detail concerning Elihu Burritt and his League of Universal Brotherhood than is possible in the present volume; it also contains a number of chapters on the activities and ideology of the American Peace Society and the New England Non-Resistance Society. These sections of my book have also been published separately as *Radical Pacifists in Antebellum America* (Princeton, 1968). On Burritt essential sources are Merle E. Curti, *The Learned Blacksmith: The Letters and Journals of Elihu Burritt* (New York, 1937), and the biography by Peter Tolis, *Elihu Burritt: Crusader for Brotherhood* (Hamden, Conn., 1968). For Priscilla H. Peckover and her Local Peace Associations, see the quarterly *Peace and Goodwill* (London and Wisbech, 1882-1931). Her brochure, *Incidents in the Rise and Progress of the Wisbech Local Peace Association* (2nd edn., London and Wisbech, 1925), is from its discursive style most unsatisfactory.

On the Plymouth Brethren the best study is the recent monograph by Harold H. Rowdon, *The Origins of the Brethren 1825-1850* (London, 1967). But only a brief appendix(2(IV))deals with their attitude to war. My account of Sir L. Charles L. Brenton's pacifism is drawn from what might seem at first sight an unlikely source: his preface to the second edition of the *Memoir of Vice Admiral Sir Jahleel Brenton, Baronet, K.C.B.* (London and Ryde, 1855). On p. xvi Brenton, quoting from a letter written in November 1846, uses the phrase "my *conscientious objection* to war under any circumstances" (my italics). Is this possibly the first use of that term? I might also mention as a curiosity Charles Brenton's memoir of his brother-in-law, *Alas, My Brother: A Letter to the Friends of Harry George Chester, Late Lieut.-Col. of the 23rd Royal Welsh Fusiliers, who fell at the Battle of the Alma, Sept. 20, 1854* (London and Ryde, [1854]). Colonel Chester was a hard-drinking professional army officer, a keen hunting, shooting, and fishing man and an orthodox Anglican. In the course of the narrative, written at the height of the Crimean War, Brenton several times hints at his own pacifist stand, finally remarking discreetly: "I had entertained thoughts of adding a few lines on the subject of war, and my views of the lawfulness or unlawfulness of it. But nothing is farther from my intention or desire at present than to engage in controversy. . . . And to engage in a keen strife of words about the evil of a strife of swords would argue anything but a pacific spirit." Christadelphian noncombatancy is touched on in Robert Roberts, *Dr. Thomas: His Life & Work* (Birmingham, 1st edn., 1884, and 3rd edn., eds. E. C. Walker and W. H. Boulton, 1954). An article by F. R. Shuttleworth, "War and Arms-Bearing" from the *Christadelphian* (September 1876), and other materials on the sect's attitude to war towards the end of the nineteenth century have been reprinted in the church's *Bulletin No. 11* (Dec. 1939). The Swarthmore College Peace Collection possesses a brief mimeographed document "Christadelphians—Denominational History covering a Period of Ninety Years" (n.d.), which includes some facts concerning the sect's early stand in favor of conscientious objection. However, although present-day sociologists of religion have shown an interest in the Christadelphians, their early history remains obscure. A. C. Watters, *History of British Churches of Christ* (Indianapolis, 1948), contains a little information on this denomination's antiwar stand before 1914. For American Christadelphians and Disciples of Christ, see my volume on *Pacifism in the United States.*

The Salvationist Arthur Sydney Booth-Clibborn's strongly antimilitarist tract, *Blood against Blood,* was published in London in 1907. On the end-page is placed an advertisement for a sequel "shortly to appear" under the title *Blood for Blood.* I have been unable to find any further trace of this publication and presume that in fact it never appeared in print. This is a pity. It promised *inter alia* to offer "practical suggestions drawn from an experience of thirty years upon the Continent as to how young Christians can obey Christ in presence of Conscription Laws, or anti-Christian vows and oaths": a topic of relevance to the neglected history of pre-1914 European antimilitarism.

For contemporary British pacifism, see my book, *Twentieth-Century Pacifism* (New York, 1970), which deals largely, though by no means exclusively, with Great Britain and the United States.

I. RUSSIAN SECTARIAN PACIFISM
AND TOLSTOY

A considerable literature on Russian sectarianism, largely in Russian, exists from prerevolutionary times, but apart from propagandist writings by the Tolstoyan champions of the Dukhobors most of these works are concerned only very incidentally with the sectarian view of war. Under the Soviets there have been few serious contributions to recent sectarian history if we exclude polemical pieces designed to unmask the "counter-revolutionary" activities of the sects or studies devoted to the *raskol.*

An exception to this is the work of A. I. Klibanov. For instance, in his *Istoriya religioznogo sektantstva v Rossii (60-e gody XIXv.—1917g.)* (Moscow, 1965) he devotes a lengthy chapter apiece to both the Dukhobors (chap. 3) and the Molokans (chap. 4), in which he discusses, *inter alia,* their pacifism and their conscientious objection. He deals exhaustively and often very effectively with the economic background, as might be expected. But Klibanov's view (p. 111) that the famous "burning of the weapons" in June 1895 was both "an antimilitarist demonstration" and a reactionary "disarming of the Dukhobors" on the part of Peter Verigin appears to me to be a prime example of the malformation produced when a fine scholar is encased in a tightly fitting Marxist straitjacket. Klibanov is also the author of another important work, *Religioznoe sektantstvo i sovremennost' (sotsiologicheskie i istoricheskie ocherki)* (Moscow, 1969), which is worth mentioning here even though its subject lies outside the time-span of the present volume. A whole section is devoted to the problem of conscientious objection among religious sectarians and Tolstoyans during the half-decade following the Russian Revolution ("Sektantstvo i stroitel'stvo vooruzhennykh sil sovet-skoi respubliki [1918-1921 gg.]," pp. 188-208). In this account Klibanov makes use of the Chertkov Papers as well as other archival sources and, like Lenin himself (probably under Vladimir D. Bonch-Brueyvich's influence), he is not altogether unsympathetic to the position of the Russian pacifist movement at this date; however, his narrative closes before the repression of the movement by the Soviet authorities began in earnest a few years later. It is to be hoped that a competent Western scholar, too, may be able to undertake a study of conscientious objection in the U.S.S.R. from 1917 to 1939 based on the archives listed by Klibanov. (In addition, see John B. Toews, "The Russian Mennonites and the Military Question [1921-1927]," *MQR*, vol. XLIII, no. 2 [April 1969].)

George Woodcock and Ivan Avakumović, *The Doukhobors* (Toronto and New York, 1969), has superseded all previous histories of this sect. The authors show a lively interest in its peace testimony both prior to, and after, the emigration to Canada in 1898-1899. A doctoral dissertation written by a Czech scholar in Dutch—Pavel Opršal, *De russische sekte der Doucho-boren 1886-1908* (Groningen, 1967)—is also valuable; and, among older accounts, I have found the American Quaker Joseph Elkinton's *The Doukho-bors: Their History in Russia, Their Migration to Canada* (Philadelphia, 1903) most useful here. See also my edition of "Vasya Pozdnyakov's Dukhobor Narrative," *The Slavonic and East European Review* (London), vol. XLIII, nos. 100 (Dec. 1964), pp. 152-176, and 101 (June 1965), pp. 400-414: another version of Pozdnyakov's narrative was published in Russian, "Pravda o dukhoborakh," *Ezhemyesyachnyi zhurnal literatury, nauki i obshchestvennoy zhizni* (St. Petersburg/Petrograd), nos. 6, 7, 8/9, 10 (June-October 1914), although I was not aware of this when I edited the anonymous English translation. Vladimir Bonch-Bruyevich, Lenin's friend (and the Dukhobors' too) edited Peter Verigin's letters: *Pis'ma dukhobor-cheskago rukovoditelya Petra Vasil'evicha Verigina* (Christchurch, Hants., 1901), with an important introduction of his own outlining the Dukhobor philosophy of life and the development of Verigin's religious beliefs. The experiences of Dukhobor conscientious objectors in the penal battalion were edited, largely in their own words, by V. and A. Chertkov, *Dukhobortsy v distsiplinarnom batal'one* (Christchurch, 1902), while Bonch-Bruyevich published Vasilii (Vasya) Pozdnyakov's account of his imprisonment and exile for refusing military service as *Razskaz dukhobortsa Vasi Pozdnyakova* (Christchurch, 1901).

For the personal beliefs and experiences of other Russian objectors to military service under the Tsarist regime, see the following accounts: E. I. Popov, *Zhizn' i smert' Evdokima Nikiticha Drozhzhina 1866-1894* (1895) (2nd edn., ed. V. Chertkov, Purleigh, Essex, 1898); *Pis'ma Petra Vasil'-evicha Ol'khovika* (London, 1897); *Chto Andrey Ivanovich Kudrin raz-skazal' Tolstomu* (Berlin, n.d.). Drozhzhin was a Tolstoyan village schoolmaster who eventually died as a result of prolonged ill-treatment in prison and penal battalion; Ol'khovik a peasant from a nonsectarian background who derived his pacifism directly from reading the Gospels (to the alarm of the military he quickly converted a fellow soldier to the same position); and Kudrin a convert from Molokanism to the Dobrolyubovtsy. A curiosity is the pamphlet by a political objector, the journalist N. F. Nasimovich-Chuzhak, *Kak i pochemu ya otkazaltsya sluzhit' tsaryu* (Moscow, 1928). The author, a member of the Bolshevik faction of the Russian Social-Democratic Party, in 1904 refused to serve in the army of "the worst enemy of the Russian people," the Tsar. Placed under arrest, he subsequently succeeded in escaping abroad. To my knowledge this is the only case of a principled political objection in pre-1917 Russia, and Nasimovich-Chuzhak himself seems to have entertained doubts later whether antimilitarism of this kind was appropriate to an orthodox Bolshevik. However, he adds, "I only know that I could not have behaved in any other way." (For Chuzhak's career, see the brief entry in the *Bolshaya sovetskaya entsiklopediya* [Moscow], 1934 edn., vol. 61, pp. 743-744.)

For the nonviolence of Malikov and his sect of "deo-humanists," which at first formed a more powerful influence on Tolstoy's emerging theory of "nonresistance to evil" than did strictly religious, sectarian pacifism, I found the following accounts most useful: A. Faresov, "Odin iz 'semi-desyatnikov,'" *Vestnik Evropy* (St. Petersburg), vol. 229, September 1904 (pp. 225-260); A. Prugavin, "Lev Tolstoy i 'bogocheloveki,'" *Russkoe bogatstvo* (St. Petersburg), August 1911 (pp. 146-165); V. G. Korolenko, "Istoriya moego sovremmenika," in *Sobranie sochinenii*, vol. VII (Moscow, 1955 [chapter on Malikov]). For adverse comment on Faresov's reliability, see the letter from Malikov's disciple, the populist leader N. V. Chaikovsky, in *Vestnik Evropy*, May 1905, pp. 447-448.

Biographies of Tolstoy covering the second half of his life must necessarily deal to some extent with his views on government and war, for "nonresistance to evil" became his major concern in this period. Key texts here are *What I Believe* (1884) and, especially, *The Kingdom of God is Within You* (1893), which are available in Aylmer Maude's translations (Oxford Centenary Edition, vols. 11 and 20). In addition, Tolstoy wrote a large number of occasional pieces expressing his nonresistant viewpoint, some of them being composed on behalf of imprisoned objectors to military service in Russia or abroad. A handy, though far from all-inclusive, collection of such essays is *Tolstoy's Writings on Civil Disobedience and Non-Violence* (New York, 1967). Virtually everything he wrote is included in the Soviet Jubilee Edition of Tolstoy's works, *Polnoe sobranie sochinenii* (90 vols., Moscow-Leningrad, 1928-1958); see also the separate volume of indexes *Ukazateli . . .* (Moscow, 1964). However, it seems that this monumental collection is not in fact quite complete, since only recently *The Atlantic* (Boston, Mass.) published in translation a hitherto unknown letter by Tolstoy of "Advice to a Draftee" (vol. 221, no. 2 [February 1968]). The later volumes of the third series of the Jubilee Edition, which contain Tolstoy's letters (*Pis'ma*), should prove a major source for the future historian of Tolstoyism; I have consulted them myself only very occasionally.

Studies of Tolstoy's nonresistant theory are numerous but not often particularly instructive; most rewarding is to consult Tolstoy's own writings on the subject. On Tolstoy's influence on Gandhi I should mention the following: Milan I. Markovitch, *Tolstoï et Gandhi* (Paris, 1928), a serious and scholarly study; Alexandre Kaplan, *Gandhi et Tolstoï* (*Les sources d'une filiation spirituelle*) (Paris, 1949); Kalidas Nag, *Tolstoy and Gandhi* (Patna, 1950); Pyarelal, *Mahatma Gandhi,* vol. I: *The Early Phase* (Ahmedabad, 1965), chap. XXII (pp. 627-708); Sarla Mittal, *Tolstoy: Social and Political Ideas* (Meerut, 1966), chap. XII. The Tolstoy-Gandhi correspondence of 1909-1910 is printed with full critical apparatus in A. Sergeenko, ed., "Perepiska Tolstogo s M. K. Gandhi," *Literaturnoe nasledstvo* (Moscow), vol. 37/38 (1939).

"The history of Tolstoyism as a world-wide movement still remains to be written," William B. Edgerton has remarked in his short but illuminating study of "The Artist turned Prophet: Leo Tolstoj after 1880," in *American Contributions to the Sixth International Congress of Slavists*, vol. II (Literary Contributions; ed. William E. Harkins), The Hague, 1968, pp. 61-85. Edgerton has also examined the well known Russian writer Nikolai Leskov's acceptance of Tolstoyan nonresistance in his article on "Leskov and Tolstoy: Two Literary Heretics," *The American Slavic and East European Review* (New York), vol. XII, no. 4 (December 1953), where he argues convincingly against "the usual interpretation . . . that Leskov strongly disagreed with Tolstoy's nonresistance and yet was attracted to him and the rest of his teachings in spite of this disagreement." "Leskov," according to Edgerton, "shares Tolstoy's great faith in the power of nonviolent means of resisting evil." Where he did not agree with Tolstoy was in his belief (similar to Gandhi's) that violent resistance to evil is preferable to a nonresistance based on indifference or cowardice. Important documentary materials relating to Tolstoyan efforts on behalf of the Dukhobors at the end of the nineteenth century are printed in French translation in J. W. Bienstock, ed., *Tolstoï et les Doukhobors* (Paris, 1902).

Many volumes have been devoted to Tolstoy's influence abroad but, apart from studies of the Gandhian connection, these have concentrated almost exclusively on his literary influence. An exception is Rudolf Jans, *Tolstoi in Nederland* (Bussum, 1952), which includes several chapters on the Dutch Christian anarchists who adopted Tolstoy's social and pacifist ideas. On the Slovak Tolstoyan objector Škarvan, see the chapter in Andrej Mráz, *Z ruskej literatúry a jej ohlasov u Slovákov* ([Bratislava], 1955), on "Albert Škarvan-slovenský tolstovec"; also Katarína Mičatková, "Literárna činnosť Tolstého stúpenca dr. Alberta Škarvana," and several more essays (in Slovak and Czech) by other authors in *Z ohlasov L. N. Tolstého na Slovensku*, in *Slovanské štúdie IV* (Bratislava, 1960). His stand made a big impression on Tolstoy and his disciples since it was virtually the first such case to occur outside Russia. Škarvan's own story is to be found in his book *Moy otkaz ot voennoy sluzhby: Zapiski voennago vracha* (Purleigh, Essex, 1898), which the author later twice revised in Slovak.

The period after 1914 does not come within the scope of the present volume. However, statistics concerning the incidence of conscientious objection in Russia in World War I quoted by F. M. Putintsev, *Politicheskaya rol' i taktika sekt* (Moscow, 1935), on pages 96-97, also throw light on the prewar situation of sectarian pacifism. Of the 837 objectors recorded there as appearing before military tribunals between the outbreak of war and 1 April 1917, Evangelical Christians provided 256, Baptists (and Stundists) 114, Seventh-Day Adventists 70, Molokans (and Spiritual Christians) 28, Malevantsy 27, Tolstoyans 18, Dukhobors 16, Sabbatarians 16, Dobrolyubovtsy 13, Free Christians 8, Judaizers 8, Jehovists (Ilin's followers) 7, "Quakers" 6, Moravians 1, while the religious affiliation of 249 was not known. The figures are obviously incomplete. But they do indicate that most conscientious objectors by this time came from nonpacifist denominations like the Baptists, Seventh-Day Adventists, or Evangelical Christians, which were either of non-Russian origin or had come strongly under the influence of Western Protestantism. Yet the moving spirit behind Russian pacifism—though the statistics just cited do not reveal this—continued to come from the Tolstoyans, despite the fact that they formed a much smaller group than the sectarian objectors.

J. Miscellaneous Nineteenth-Century Pacifist Sects on the European Continent

G. P. Marang's monograph on *De Zwijndrechtsche Nieuwlichters* (Dordrecht, 1909) contains a short section on the New Lighters' nonresistant principles and practice. The well known Dutch historian of socialism, H.P.G. Quack, devoted a lengthy article to this communitarian group in *De Gids* (Amsterdam, 1892, pt. III) ("De Zwijndrechtsche Broederschap: Godsdienstig communisme in de eerste helft onzer eeuw"); it is reprinted in P. J. Bouwman's collection of selected essays by Quack entitled *Uit het levenswerk van H.P.G. Quack* (Amsterdam, 1955, pp. 135-171). Again, only a few pages are devoted to the group's peace testimony. An account of the Mijdrecht community was printed in the London Peace Society's *Herald of Peace* (April 1847) as "The Christian Brotherhood in Holland," pp. 245-247. See also de Ligt's *La paix créatrice*, vol. II (pp. 391-393).

The most thorough and impartial treatment of the main body of Nazarenes in the nineteenth century is to be found in a lengthy article translated by G. Schwalm from the Magyar original by Lajos Z. Szeberényi, "Die Secte der Nazarener in Ungarn," *Jahrbücher für protestantische Theologie* (Braunschweig), vol. XVI (1890). See also two contributions published in the Mennonite periodical *Doopsgezinde Bijdragen* (Leiden): J. G. de Hoop Scheffer, "De Doopsgezinden der zestiende eeuw nu in Hongarije herboren"

(1891, pp. 67-92), and C. B. Hylkema, "De Nazareners" (1904, pp. 160-183). The two Dutch authors, like the Magyar, deal in some detail with conscientious objection among the Nazarenes. The sect's Swiss homeland is given greater attention than its central and south-east European diaspora in Herman Ruegger, Sr., *Apostolic Christian Church History*, vol. I (Chicago, 1949). This work is a confessional history, translated from the German; the first volume (the only one to appear so far) covers the European branches of the church, with brief sections dealing with nonresistance and military service. The two eyewitness accounts of imprisoned Nazarene objectors in Serbia are quoted, respectively, from an obscure London periodical, *The Messiah's Kingdom*, which in its March 1889 issue (vol. I, no. 3) printed a brief article entitled "The Nazarenes," and from a leaflet in the Swarthmore College Peace Collection entitled *Prisoners in Serbia* (Leominster, 1877).

O. Kellerman's *War and Peace: A Moral Study* (London, 1901; translated from the French) contains information concerning the antiwar stand of the *Hinschistes*. There are also materials on this subject, as well as on the Nazarenes and other religious objectors on the European continent, scattered throughout the issues of *Peace and Goodwill* (Wisbech). Nominally the organ of the Wisbech Peace Association, this periodical was in fact the product of the almost single-handed efforts, beginning in the early 1880's, of the English Quakeress and peace enthusiast, Priscilla H. Peckover. The *Herald of Peace* and the British Quaker papers also contain similar materials.

The pre-1914 peace movement in the Netherlands, including a number of cases of conscientious objection (*het antimilitarisme van de daad*) occurring during the previous quarter-century, is discussed briefly in the early pages of a work by a Roman Catholic antimilitarist, J. Giesen, *Nieuwe geschiedenis: Het antimilitarisme van de daad in Nederland* (Rotterdam, 1923). Some of these objectors were Tolstoyans or religious sectarians; others belonged to the anarchosocialist movement; still others objected on ethical or humanitarian grounds. See also the second, untranslated volume (1933) of Bart de Ligt's *Vrede als daad* for nonreligious objectors before, as well as after, 1914. In two articles in *Die Friedens-Warte* (Berlin), vol. XXIV (1924), the international jurist Hans Wehberg surveyed briefly the discussions of conscientious objection and of defensive war, which had taken place at peace congresses before 1914: "Das Problem der Kriegsdienstverweigerung auf den Weltfriedenskongressen der Vorkriegszeit" (no. 10/11, pp. 290-292), and "Der Verteidigungskrieg auf den Weltfriedenskongressen der Vorkriegszeit" (no. 12, pp. 330-333). The question of conscientious objection appeared only at congresses held in 1901, 1903, 1904, and 1907.

Bibliographical Postscript

THIS book was completed in the summer of 1970. Therefore, only materials published before 1970 have been used in its preparation and listed above. Some recent items of value, however, have come to my attention since.

J. C. Wenger has brought out a new edition of documents discussed in Chapter 2: *Conrad Grebel's Programmatic Letters of 1524* (Scottdale, Pa., 1970) and has included his own translations as well as the original German text. Two articles in the October 1970 issue of the *MQR* (vol. XLIV, no. 4) are useful. Karl-Heinz Kirchhoff in "Was there a Peaceful Anabaptist Congregation in Münster in 1534?" affirms the peaceable character of the city's Melchiorite congregation during the first weeks of its existence without confirming any knowledge of nonresistance among its members. J. M. Stayer in "Anabaptists and the Sword" summarizes the findings of his extensive research on the Anabaptist doctrine of the sword. Another contribution from Stayer is printed in the July 1971 issue of the *MQR* (vol. XLV, no. 3), "Melchior Hofmann and the Sword"; he argues that Hofmann preached "apoliticism" but not uncompromising nonresistance. The Institute of Philosophy and Sociology of the Polish Academy of Sciences recently issued a photostatic reprint of Stanisław Lubieniecki's *Historia reformationis Polonicae* (Warsaw, 1971), originally published in 1685; the volume occasionally touches on the attitude of the Anabaptist Antitrinitarians to war and the state.

Quaker pacifism continues to attract the attention of historians. Alfred W. Braithwaite, "Early Friends' Testimony against Carnal Weapons," *JFHS*, vol. 52, no. 2 (1969) [1970], deals with the post-Restoration period. The *Minute Book of the Men's Meeting of the Society of Friends in Bristol 1667-1686*, ed. Russell Mortimer, Bristol Record Society's Publications, vol. XXVI, 1971, contains occasional references to Friends' "sufferings" in connection with their refusal "to find a man for the militia."

The *Pennsylvania Magazine of History and Biography* (Philadelphia) has recently published two articles which, despite primary concern with the peace testimony of Pennsylvania Friends, throw some light also on that of their English brethren: Hermann Wellenreuther, "The Political Dilemma of the Quakers in Pennsylvania 1681-1748"

542

(vol. xciv, no. 2 [April 1970]) and Jack D. Marietta, "Conscience, the Quaker Community, and the French and Indian War" (vol. xcv, no. 1 [January 1971]). In his study, which is based on an unpublished Ph.D. thesis in German, Wellenreuther examines in detail the relationship between pacifism and politics as this was exemplified in the Holy Experiment. Marietta concentrates on the crisis of pacifism within Philadelphia Yearly Meeting during the Seven Years' War. He deals, too, with the ambiguous position taken up during the early years of the war by the prosperous Quaker merchants and professional men who dominated London Meeting for Sufferings. "English Friends," he concluded, "were less conscientious and patriotic than their American brethren"—than those, at least, outside the Pennsylvania Assembly who, under the leadership of John Woolman, had objected to paying taxes in support of war. Among "English . . . country Friends," however, these "conscientious Pennsylvanians" aroused much sympathy.

The state of the British Quaker community during Queen Victoria's reign has not been intensively studied hitherto. An important contribution is now made by a sociologist, Elizabeth Isichei, in *Victorian Quakers* (London, 1970). But she deals only briefly with Friends' opposition to war and their contribution to the contemporary peace movement. In the issue of *JFHS* just cited, Stephen Frick discusses (to quote his title) "The Quaker Deputation to Russia: January-February 1854." Friends failed to prevent Great Britain's entry into the Crimean War, but their deputation represents an important landmark in the story of Quaker efforts for peace. In the next issue of the *JFHS*, vol. 52, no. 3 (1970) [1971], Frick examines "the most successful pacifist propaganda effort of the Crimean War" in an article entitled "The *Christian Appeal* of 1855: Friends' Public Response to the Crimean War."

Mennonites in prerevolutionary Russia, we have seen, gave a different response to war and conscription from that of Quakers in modern Britain. Gerhard Lorenz, "The Beginning of Alternative Service during the Russo-Japanese War (1904-05)," *Mennonite Life*, vol. xxvi, no. 3 (July 1971), describes the work in military hospitals of Mennonite volunteers "who had completed their alternative Forestry Service."

Finally, mention should be made of John Rae's book (originally a doctoral thesis), *Conscience and Politics: The British Government and the Conscientious Objector to Military Service 1916-1919* (London, 1970); for even though it falls outside the chronological limits of my volume, it helps to illuminate British pacifism before 1914. Basing his account on government archives and private records, Rae centers primarily on "official treatment" of the conscientious objector, in contrast to earlier studies by John W. Graham (1922) and David Boulton

(1967), which are more sympathetic to the C.O. While Rae attempts to remain impartial between authorities and objectors and indeed succeeds in amassing a wealth of evidence on their relationship, some of the conclusions which he draws concerning the antiwar movement may well be contested.

Index

N.B. The Bibliographical Notes and Postscript are not included.